Microeconomics

Robert L. Sexton
Professor of Economics
Pepperdine University, Malibu, California

PRENTICE HALL
Englewood Cliffs, NJ 07632

Library of Congress Cataloging-in-Publication Data

Sexton, Robert L.
    Microeconomics / Robert L. Sexton.
        p.   cm.
    Includes bibliographical references and index.
    ISBN 0-13-103672-6
    1. Microeconomics   I. Title.
    HB171.5. S5448   1995
    338.5--dc20   94-43116
                                                  CIP

Production Editor: Pencil Point Studio: Suzanne Visco
In-house Project Manager: Alana Zdinak
Acquisitions Editor: Leah Jewell
Interior Design: Pencil Point Studio: Patricia Amirante
Cover Design: Pencil Point Studio: Patricia Amirante
Design Director: Patricia Woszcyk
Proofreader: Pencil Point Studio: Salvatore G. Allocco
Manufacturing Buyer: Marie McNamara
Assistant Editor: Teresa Cohan
Editorial Assistant: Elizabeth Becker

Technical Art: Pencil Point Studio: Particia Amirante, Mario Viera,
            and Elaine Kilcullen
Cover Photo: SuperStock

©1995 by Prentice Hall, Inc.
A Simon and Schuster Company
Englewood Cliffs, New Jersey 07632

Printed in the United States of America

10 9 8 7 6 5 4 3 2 1

ISBN   0-13-103672-6

Prentice-Hall International (UK) Limited, *London*
Prentice-Hall of Australia Pty. Limited, *Sydney*
Prentice-Hall Canada Inc., *Toronto*
Prentice-Hall Hispanoamericana, S.A., *Mexico*
Prentice-Hall of India Private Limited, *New Delhi*
Prentice-Hall of Japan, Inc., *Tokyo*
Simon & Schuster Asia Pte. Ltd., *Singapore*
Editoria Prentice-Hall do Brazil, Ltda., *Rio de Janeiro*

To Julie Beth,
Elizabeth, Katherine and Tom

About the author

Robert L. Sexton is currently Professor of Economics at Pepperdine University. Professor Sexton has also taught at the University of California at Los Angeles.

Professor Sexton's research ranges across many fields of economics—law and economics, labor economics, environmental economics, economic history, economic education, and public choice. He has written four textbooks and numerous articles in refereed journals such as the *American Economic Review, Southern Economic Journal, Economics Letters* and the *Journal of Urban Economics.* He has also written over 70 articles that have appeared in books, magazines and newspapers.

Professor Sexton received the Pepperdine Professor of the Year Award in 1991 and the Howard A. White Memorial Teaching Award in 1994. He is also a Harriet and Charles Luckman Distinguished Teaching Fellow.

Professor Sexton resides in Agoura Hills with his wife Julie, their three children, Elizabeth, Katherine and Tom, and their two Alaskan Malamutes, Chinook and Tuffy.

Contents

Part 2
Consumers, Producers and Competitive Output Determination   105

Chapter 8
The Costs of Production 197

Chapter 9
Competitive Price Determination 250

Part 3:
Imperfectly Competitive Markets   *293*

Part 4:
Factor Markets   401

Chapter 13
Factor Pricing and Labor Markets 402

Part 5:
Efficiency, Exchange and Intertemporal Issues 497

Preface

Recent decades have witnessed profound changes in economic analysis. Fifty years ago, the professional journals were as innocent of mathematics as modern principles texts, and most students of intermediate microeconomics would finish the course learning more about social and economic institutions than about the formulation and analysis of economic models. Today the same students would be more likely to end the session with partial derivatives glazing their eyeballs and hardly any notion of the actual working of any economic system, least of all the one they know best. As Martin Shubik has so aptly put it:

> The consumer with his indifference curves confronts the price system which functions smoothly for the individually operated profit-maximizing firm. The owner combines factors by setting marginal everything equal to marginal everything else. Supply and demand curves are obtained and for three quarters of a semester the God-given, institution-free, frictionless markets of upper-middle class Western, utilitarian man function in neo-Newtonian fashion.*

Not that anyone would wish to return to the "Good Old Days;" progress has blessed us, though the blessing be mixed.

This book is not intended to resist the tide of formalism for that would be misguided. Its purpose is rather to harness some energy from that tide to support an analysis of individual and market behavior whose institutional structure bears some resemblance to the world in which we live.

This book is intended for undergraduate courses in which the instructor wishes to provide a more intensive training in microeconomics theory than is customarily attempted in elementary courses. The text is complete in its coverage of topics such as: the principle-agent problem, asymetric information, moral hazard, intertemporal choice, public choice and so on. The text is essentially nonmathematical, but for those who use a more mathematical approach calculus is included in the footnotes.

To help students get a better feel for economic theory the text will feature many examples and applications of microeconomics and the study guide will include many hands on problems for students to solve. Some of these are intended to reinforce the student's comprehension of the analysis while others are intended to demonstrate the usefulness of theory in the real world.

ALTERNATIVE FORMATS

With such a full menu of topics, there are many ways to use this textbook in a one-quarter or one-semester course. Those on a tight schedule might select only the core chapters (1–3, and 5–13). A class stressing micro-macro interrelationship would want to include Chapter 4 ("Stocks and Flows in Supply and Demand"), Chapter 14 ("The Theory of Interest and Capital Markets") and Chapter 19 ("Asset Management and Intertemporal Income Allocation").

LEARNING TOOLS

* Applications

Each chapter will feature numerous solved problems and economic "stories" presented throughout the text. Some of these are intended to reinforce earlier concepts while others are intended to be thought provoking. I believe that problem solving stimulates students, creating active thoughtful readers.

* Graphs

I have take particular caution in constructing the graphs, realizing that they are of vital importance in microeconomics texts. Detailed captions accompany each graph. The use of color, shaded areas and bold lines all assist in making graphs appealing and easy to understand.

* End of Chapter Aids

Every chapter will end with a **Summary** listing the important concepts and a list of **Words and Concepts for Review**. There will also be a set of **Review Questions** at the end of the each chapter. **A Supplementary Reading List** will be included for outside assignments and for the curious reader. There will be two **appendices** at the end of the text. In a class with a serious time constraint, the appendices could easily be omitted. The material in the appendices present slightly more difficult theoretical material. The appendices will include the following topics: "Econometrics and Supply and Demand" and "Linear Programming".

SUPPLEMENTS

Study Guide

By James Marchand of Westminster College, the student *Study Guide* contains applications, chapter outlines, chapter summaries, list of key concepts, and word problems and multiple choice problems.

Instructor's Manual

Also by James Marchand, the *Instructor's Manual* contains chapter outlines, lists of learning objectives, answers to end-of-chapter text questions and a test bank with problems and multiple choice questions (with answers).

ACKNOWLEDGEMENTS

I am thankful to the many reviewers and colleagues who helped me in the preparation of this book. Scott Atkinson (University of Georgia), David Butz (University of Michigan), Ron Batchelder (Pepperdine University), Robert Clower (University of South Carolina), John Due (University of Illinois), Gary Galles (Pepperdine University), David E.R. Gay (University of Arkansas, Fayetteville), Philip E Graves (University of Colorado-Boulder), Simon Hakim (Temple University), Tom Hazlett (University of California, Davis), Stephen Jackstadt (University of Alaska-Anchorage), Dwight Lee (University of Georgia), Leonard Lardaro (University of Rhode Island), James Marchand (Westminster College), Tom Potiowsky (Portland State University) and Carol Horton Trembly (Oregon State University).

Part 1

INTRODUCTION

CHAPTERS

1. THE ROLE AND METHOD OF ECONOMIC ANALYSIS

2. THE NATURE AND GOALS OF DECISION UNITS

3. SUPPLY AND DEMAND

4. STOCK AND FLOWS IN SUPPLY AND DEMAND

Part 1, the introduction will cover such topics as methodology, goals and decision making by economic agents in the market system and supply and demand from both a flow and a stock/flow perspective. Chapter 1, "The Role and Method of Economic Analysis," provides an introduction to the scientific approach. Chapter 2, "The Nature and Goals of Decision Units," offers a novel treatment of the nature of economic decision units and the nature of markets. Chapter 3, "Supply and Demand," is a review chapter on the standard treatment of supply and demand analysis including elasticities and consumer surplus.

Chapter 4, "Stocks and Flows in Supply and Demand," serves as an important bridge to macroeconomics. This unique, but optional chapter allows the student to understand how microeconomic tools shed light on familiar macroeconomic problems such as the impact of changed stock demands on inventory holdings, hence on production and income.

Chapter One

THE ROLE
AND METHOD
OF ECONOMIC ANALYSIS

Questions to Think About

1. What is the purpose of economic analysis?

2. What are the important basic functions of every economic system?

3. Why do marginal benefits and costs play such an important role in microeconomic analysis?

4. How do scientific "stories" resemble those told by writers of fiction?

5. What is the difference between normative and positive science?

6. What is the difference between general and partial equilibrium analysis?

7. What is the difference between statics, comparative statics, and dynamic analysis?

8. Why do economists disagree on some issues but agree on others?

1.1 INTRODUCTION

*E*conomic analysis allows us to evaluate the consequences of alternative actions, thereby providing us with a basis for choosing intelligently among them. To business leaders, consumers, workers, union officials, and those responsible for governmental policy, economic analysis provides a framework for rational decision making. Given the goals of individuals and of society, economic principles may be used to evaluate various policies in terms of their efficiency (Are the benefits greater than the costs?) and equity (Are the benefits and the costs "fairly" distributed?).

Economic analysis also provides a basis for predicting the future consequences of current actions or policies. The application of economic analysis to current situations can improve estimates of future conditions. Business firms are always concerned with future trends in the prices of the goods they buy and sell. By studying price-determining forces in each industry and by using economic principles to analyze the facts of particular situations, businesses can often improve their predictions about future prices.

Prediction enables action to be taken to avoid undesirable outcomes. The knowledge of economic principles is particularly important in determining what actions the government should take to avoid unfavorable developments in the economy. Sometimes, the future is predicted to be much like the present, and action is required to make the future better. More commonly, the future is perceived to be different from the present, and action must be taken to alter future events.

Finally, economic analysis provides us with a basis for judging the performance of various segments of the economy and of the economic system as a whole. For example, if maximizing aggregate real income or wealth is accepted as a goal of the economic system, then unemployment should not be undesirably large. If at any time too many workers are unemployed, economists need to know the principles that govern the determination of employment levels to decide whether the unemployment is the result of an inherent weakness in the structure and functioning of the economy or of particular factors such as minimum-wage legislation, welfare programs that discourage people from accepting jobs even if they are able to find them, restrictive union policies, and immobility of workers because of ignorance or high mobility costs.

Economic analysis is not as confining as it might sound. In fact, economics can be applied to anything that human beings consider worthwhile. Many sources of enjoyment are often said to be "noneconomic:" love, sexual activity, religion. These activities or feelings, however, have a substantial economic dimension. Even love and sex have received scrutiny from economists. One product of love, the institution of the family, is an important economic decision-making unit. Sexual activity leads to the production of children, perhaps the most important "good" that humans desire. It's expensive, too—raising children to age 18 costs many tens of thousands of dollars, and this expenditure must be less than or equal to the anticipated value of a wanted child. As economic units, families produce, consume, and distribute goods among their members.

This discussion by no means exhausts the enormous list of possible uses of economic analysis. However, we must not expect the impossible. The operation of the economic system is much too complex to be characterized by a few simple laws; given the difficulties of developing economic theories that predict observed events with a high degree of accuracy, it is unlikely that we will ever be able to forecast and control economic activity perfectly. By and large, therefore, we must treat economic principles as aids in selecting data that require study. As J.M. Keynes once said:

> The object of our analysis is not to provide a machine, or method of blind manipulation, which will furnish an infallible answer, but to provide ourselves with an organized and orderly method of thinking out particular problems; and, after we have reached a provisional conclusion by isolating the complicating factors one by one, we then have to go back on ourselves and allow, as well as we can, for the probable interactions of the factors amongst themselves. This is the nature of economic thinking.[1]

1.2 SCARCITY AND CHOICE: THE ESSENCE OF THE ECONOMIC PROBLEM

If all goods—physical objects and services capable of satisfying human wants—were present in quantities in excess of the amounts that persons desire, as is air (but not clean air!) or sunshine in Arizona, for example, then economic institutions would be nonexistent. All wants would be satisfied without effort and without conflicts with other persons; increased use of a good by one person would not reduce the ability of other people to satisfy their wants. No organization would be needed to regulate the use of resources, and no control would be required over this phase of human behavior.

This does not, however, describe the world in which we live. As long as most goods are scarce relative to the demand for them, conflicts over their possession will occur, and institutions for controlling individual action will be necessary. In primitive societies, each person could satisfy his or her wants by obtaining the required goods directly from nature through individual effort, so economic institutions played a lesser role in human life. Compared with primitive societies, however, modern economic society is characterized by a high degree of interdependence. Each person performs a highly specialized task in the production system and, by the use of the income received for performing this task, purchases desired goods. For such a system to function, an elaborate mechanism of economic institutions is necessary to coordinate the choices of individuals. (See Problem 1–1.)

---

[1]J. M. Keynes, *General Theory of Employment, Interest and Money* (New York: Harcourt, Brace, 1936), p. 297.

1—1 True or False? The "rich and famous" do not have to deal with the problem of scarcity.

False. No matter how rich you are, you face scarcity (unless you truly have no desire for any more goods, including privacy, health, and additional time to enjoy everything). Not only are things scarce for everyone, but they are usually equally scarce in the sense that anyone must give up the same amounts of other goods to obtain more of a given good, regardless of income level. For example, a rich person and a not-so-rich person still pay the same price for a new Mercedes, say $70,000. Specifically, the cost is what they had to give up and they both have given up the ability to use that $70,000 to purchase other goods. A rich person may be more willing to give up an enormous amount of income to obtain what a less-wealthy person might consider to be a frivolous good (for example, a safe trip to the moon), but the cost of the good would be the same to either person. The amount of resources needed to produce a good does not depend on who buys it.

Everyone is influenced by scarcity and as a consequence all of us must make choices. Because each person has limited wealth, when a person purchases units of a particular good or service, that person reduces the ability to buy other things he or she would also like to have. You may recall from your principles course that this notion of the highest or best forgone opportunity resulting from a decision is called **opportunity cost**. (See Problem 1–2.)

1—2 Is the time that an activity takes an opportunity cost?

No. The cost is what that time could have been used for, not the time itself—time ticks by no matter how you use it. It is the value of time that is important. Thus, if you were thinking "time in Europe" is the cost of "time in Hawaii," that is a correct view of opportunity cost.

Scarcity will never be eradicated. Even religious or humanitarian individuals who give up most worldly goods, transferring their income to others less fortunate, are constrained by the limits imposed by scarcity; if greater resources were available, they could do still more for others.

1.3 BENEFITS AND COSTS

Economists proceed with their analysis of human behavior on the assumption that people try to maximize their own betterment. In trying to make themselves better off, people alter their behavior if the expected **marginal benefits** from doing so outweigh the expected **marginal costs**. The term **marginal** is applied to benefits and costs because we are interested in comparing the costs and benefits of incremental adjustments in behavior. The word *expected* is used because the consequences of current actions occur later and the world is uncertain in many important respects. The actual outcome of altered behavior will not always be known with certainty. As a matter of rationality, however, people are assumed to engage only in behavior that they think will make them better off. This fairly unrestrictive and realistic view of individuals seeking self-betterment can be used to analyze a variety of social phenomena.

Consider crime. Sociologists look at the impact of social conditions and the urban environment on criminal behavior, while psychologists tend to look at crime as "aberrant" or "deviant" behavior. Economists generally view crime as an economic activity. Why do criminals engage in their "occupation?" Presumably because the "job" is better than alternative forms of employment. In some cases, the criminal cannot get a legitimate job at an acceptable wage, so the cost of engaging in crime in terms of other income forgone may be quite low. If the expected marginal benefits from crime outweigh the expected marginal costs, the activity is pursued. However, the actual outcome on any given day—being "caught" in the present example—may make it look like the individual did not compare benefits with costs. Crime, of course, has other explanations—social institutions, group pressures, mental illness, and so on. For most policy purposes, however, we are not interested in what causes the level of crime to be what it is; rather, *the concern is with what causes the level of criminal activity to change.* Given people's attitudes toward crime (which vary according to religion, group pressure, psychic health, and so on), if the marginal benefits of crime rise (say, in the form of larger real "hauls") and the marginal costs fall (because of less likelihood of being caught or of being imprisoned if caught), then the economist would expect the level of crime to rise.

The ultimate presupposition of all social science is that individual conduct is capable of rational explanation and prediction on the basis of logic and past experience. In fact, almost all of economics can be reduced to individual-level incentive "stories."

1.4 THE MEANS TO SATISFY HUMAN WANTS

Material objects and services that are capable of satisfying human wants are called goods. Few **consumption goods**—commodities that directly satisfy personal wants—are available in nature in the form, place, and time that individuals desire. Instead, there are **factors of production**—that is, resources (also limited in supply) used to produce goods that will directly provide services that satisfy human wants.

The factors of production can be classified into three general groups:

1. Land
The factors of production found directly in nature—for example, the land used in wheat production, the coal in the veins of a mine, or a waterfall harnessed to generate electric power.

2. Labor

All human activity used in production. The nature of the labor service being rendered is controlled not only by the native capacity of human beings to work, but also by the skills they have acquired and the effort applied to a task. It is not possible or necessary to separate labor services into categories to reflect the contributions of each of these elements. It is useful, however, to distinguish entrepreneurial activity (the undertaking of risky business opportunities) from labor activity of a more routine kind, such as production, management, or sales.

3. Capital goods

All humanly produced material goods to be used in production, such as factory buildings, machinery, and trucks.

1.5 THE FUNCTIONS OF THE ECONOMIC SYSTEM

Every economic system performs certain basic functions:

1. Resource allocation (What?)

Most factors can be used to produce a wide variety of goods. Steel, for example, can be used to produce automobiles, washing machines, railroad cars, or paper clips. The services of a carpenter can be used to construct houses, shopping malls, or government buildings. Every economic system needs some method for determining the uses to which resources will be put—for selecting the goods to be produced and determining the level of output of each good.

2. Production methods (How?)

Most goods can be produced by a number of possible methods at any given time, so there must be some system for selecting the actual methods to be used. For example, is coal to be mined by hand labor or by machinery? Is a factory to use oil or coal for fuel? Selection must be made not only among particular techniques but also among various possible methods of organizing production. Should production of a commodity be centered in one locality or scattered throughout the country? Should production be concentrated in the hands of a few large producers or distributed among many small firms?

3. Distribution of output (For whom?)

If production were sufficient for each person to obtain as much of every product as he or she desired, then the outputs of the economy would not have to be shared among members of society. In fact, however, some products are scarce relative to the demand for them, so some method of allocating them must be devised.

These three functions are inevitably performed by every economic system, but the precise manner in which they are performed varies greatly from one economic system to another.

1.6 MAJOR DIVISIONS OF ECONOMIC ANALYSIS

If the world were simple enough or if human ingenuity were great enough, then all areas of scientific knowledge could be brought within reach of a single unified theory. But that is not the way it is. Apart from the separation of empirical science into three main divisions—physical, biological, and social—these divisions are further separated into specialized fields, possibly ad infinitum. The only unifying element in the entire scheme is scientists' acceptance of certain broad standards of scholarly conduct in the development, presentation, discussion, and evaluation of their individual work.

Economics is divided into overlapping segments according to **subject matter** (microeconomics, macroeconomics, industrial organization, public finance, welfare economics, development, trade, and so on), **analytical objective** (positive and explanatory or normative and prescriptive), **theoretical perspective** (partial or general equilibrium, static or dynamic analysis), and **mode of presentation** (literary or mathematical). A closer inspection of these segments is necessary to understand how the contents of this book relate to the broader field of economics.

1.7 MICROECONOMIC ANALYSIS

Microeconomic analysis is just what its name suggests: a study of the behavior of individual households and business firms and of the working of individual markets, considered either in isolation or in groups, its object being to provide a logical, coherent description of the structure and working of a market economy. Most microeconomists believe that microeconomics is the "bread-and-butter" item on any menu of economic theory. If you understand it, you have acquired a tool essential to all economic analysis. The rest of the economics menu is interesting—some of it is nutritious, and most of it is intellectually palatable—but a lot of it would amount to very little without microeconomics as its foundation.(See Problem 1–3.)

1–3 True or False? Microeconomics is relatively insignificant for macroeconomic topics.

False. Both microeconomics and macroeconomics are primarily interested in explaining things in the large. Microeconomics analyzes things in the small to better understand the large. The study of microeconomics has helped economists gain a greater understanding about many macro topics, including interest rates, economic growth, unemployment, and the price level.

1.8 POSITIVE AND NORMATIVE ECONOMICS (ANALYTICAL OBJECTIVE)

Most economists would identify themselves as scientists seeking truth about the way people behave. They make predictions about human behavior derived from **theories**, and then, ideally, they try to assess the empirical validity of these generalizations based on human experience. Their theories attempt to explain how people will actually behave rather than how they should behave. In the role of scientist, the economist tries to observe patterns of behavior objectively without reference to the appropriateness or inappropriateness of that behavior. This objective, value-free approach using the scientific method is often called **positive economics**. Positive theory deals with *what is* rather than *what ought to be.*

It is doubtful, however, that even the most objective economist is totally value-free in his or her analysis of economic events. Suppose an economist obtains a mass of evidence about an economic event, some of which is contradictory. The economist may well emphasize the evidence that supports policy conclusions more to his or her liking, putting less weight on other evidence that supports policies less acceptable to his or her values. This, alas, is human nature. Indeed, the very topics economists study are those reflecting values about what is important in life: Do we want more schools or fewer? Should a rich society have food or medical care provided at no charge to the individual receiving it? The chemist does not have to worry about whether society "wants" oxygen to unite with hydrogen to form water. Nonetheless, the good economist/scientist strives to be as fair and objective as possible in evaluating evidence and in stating conclusions based on the evidence.

Economists, of course, have opinions and make value judgments. When economists, or anyone else for that matter, express opinions about some economic policy, they are often stating how they think things should be. Such opinions about the desirability of various economic actions are called **normative economics**. For example, how equal should the income distribution be? Of course, if a change in tax policy makes incomes more equal, there will be positive questions that can be answered, such as will labor substitute between work and other activities. As objective scientists, however, we cannot say that such a policy is good or bad; rather, we can point to how people would rationally adjust their activities if a policy is implemented. (See Problem 1–4.)

1–4 True or False? Income is concentrated in the hands of a relatively few wealthy individuals. It is only fair that the government step in and make income and wealth more equal. Both of these statements are examples of normative economics.

False. The first statement is a *positive* statement because it describes what is observed and may be shown to be "correct" or "incorrect." Only the second statement is a *normative* statement because it implies that some action ought to be taken. One important difference is that most positive statements can be falsified (tested); normative statements cannot be tested because they are based on value judgments.

1.9 ECONOMICS AND SCIENCE: FACT OR FICTION?

Contrary to popular opinion, the bulk of all knowledge commonly regarded as scientific is expressed in terms of stories not unlike the stories told by writers of serious fiction—and this resemblance is not accidental. The novelist tries to persuade us that the story could almost be true; the scientist tries to persuade us that certain events fall into a certain meaningful pattern. In contrast to the novelist, the scientist does not (or is not supposed to) invent the underlying "facts" of the story. A scientist does, however, select certain facts from among many facts that could have been chosen, just as the novelist chooses from an infinite number of possible characters and situations only those *certain* to make the story most persuasive. In either case, the artist "invents" the story. Therefore, we should not be surprised to find *order* in economic or social theory any more than we are surprised to find order in a good novel. Scientists would not bother to write about "life" if they were not convinced that they had stories worth telling.

What makes a story "worth telling"? When we look for order in nature, we cannot suppose that the "facts" are sufficient for understanding observed events. The basic problem is that the facts of a complex world simply do not organize themselves. Understanding requires that a conceptual order be imposed on these "facts" to counteract the confusion that would otherwise result. For example, objects of different weights falling freely in the air do not travel at *precisely* the same rate (largely because of different wind resistance). Yet this piece of information is generally much less significant than the fact that falling bodies do travel at *almost* the same rate (which presumably would be identical in a vacuum). By focusing on the most significant fact—the similarity, not the difference—Galileo was able to impose order on the story of gravity.

When choosing a set of facts to weave into a story (a theory), a scientist views events not as they *actually appear* but as they *would appear* if certain outside complications were ignored. If Galileo had focused his attention on a falling feather and a falling brick, the persuasive story of how objects generally fall might never have been written. In the same way, to interpret the impact of rising housing prices, say as a result of an earthquake or a hurricane, economists must ignore the impact of increasing wealth, population, and other contributing factors. Failing to do so would obscure the central insight that people tend to buy less housing at higher prices. Without a story—a *theory of causation*—scientists could not sort out and understand the enormous complexity that occurs in the real world. (See Problem 1–5.)

1–5 There is a positive statistical correlation between ice cream sales and the crime rate. Why do you think this relationship occurs?

Some might think that the higher crime rates may be caused by a "sugar high" (the so-called Twinkie defense). A more plausible reason, however, is that crime rates peak in the summer because of weather, teenagers out of school and so on. It just happens that ice cream sales also peak during the summer months because of weather. One must always be careful not to confuse correlation with causation.

SCIENTIFIC EXPLANATION

Unlike fictional stories, scientific stories exhibit a cumulative character. That is, stories told by one scientist are seized upon by others, reworked, expanded, and passed on to other scientists with similar interests. During these ongoing efforts to tell a better story, scientists must share certain ground rules that govern the arrangement, analysis, and communication of ideas. Because each science discipline deals with different events and problems, each has certain procedures that are peculiar to it. Thus, the "experimental method" plays a crucial role in biology, physics, and chemistry where repeatable controlled experiments are possible; this experimental method has a lesser role in economics where individual events ("experiments") are generally neither controlled nor repeatable.[2] Nevertheless, the sciences are more like various breeds of cats or dogs than like different species. Though the different disciplines may vary in details of approach, all conform to a common logical structure and conceptual orientation.

1.10 ECONOMIC THEORY—THE STORY

Economic theories are statements or propositions about patterns of human behavior relating to the production, distribution, or consumption of goods and services. These patterns are expected to prevail under certain stated circumstances.

---

[2]For an example of experimental economics, see Don L. Coursey and Vernon L Smith, "Price Controls in a Posted Offer Market,: *American Economic Review* 73, no. 1 (March 1983): 218–21.

What makes a good scientific story, or "theory?" A theory should provide the reader with enough information to figure out what the storyteller is saying, that is, what is supposed to cause what. A theory should also give a sense of the story's importance and of how the story fits in with other stories the reader already knows. A good scientific story will also be phrased in a way that forces us to ask "if/then" questions. For example, along a given demand curve *if* the price of bread increases, *then* the quantity demanded of bread will fall.

People ask many things of their theories, most notably that they should explain and predict events well. Since we are primarily interested in prediction, we are obligated as economists to use all the information we can to tell a better predictive story. This means not just comparing predictions with the "facts" (as many facts could have been chosen, this can result in error) but also examining the realism of all the elements of a theory.

What are the elements of a good economic theory? At least three elements are common to most economic theories: (1) Theories proceed from certain explicit or implicit assumptions or conditions that are plausible with respect to the real world. (2) All theories have one or more testable hypotheses. (3) Nearly all theories in economics involve some form of functional relationship. In the interest of telling a good economic story, we are obligated to take a careful look at each of these ingredients.

ECONOMIC ASSUMPTIONS

Consider economic assumptions first. Predictions about human behavior vary with the conditions or environment in which people live. For example, if a given population is completely illiterate and unknowledgeable about certain economic circumstances, they may behave very differently than if they had complete, accurate information about those circumstances. For example, suppose a worker moved to a town where two jobs were available, one a dangerous 12-hour-a-day coal-mining job at a wage of $60 per day, and the other a pleasant, safe job in a factory at a wage of $120 for an 8-hour day. If we assume in our economic theory that all workers have perfect knowledge about employment opportunities, then we would predict that each would choose the high-paying, pleasant job. In fact, some new workers might enter a community ignorant of employment opportunities, taking the coal-mining jobs because they were unaware of the better factory jobs. If this actually were the prevailing practice, the theory would not be terribly useful in either explaining or predicting human behavior, because it proceeds from an assumption about knowledge of alternative job opportunities that is not valid.

You may recall from your principles course that all theories in economics make one assumption, usually expressed by the Latin expression *ceteris paribus*, which roughly means "let everything else be equal" or "hold everything else constant." In trying to assess the impact of one event on another, we must isolate the two events from other events that might also influence the event that the theory is trying to explain or predict. For example, one of the most important theories of economics is the law of demand.

According to the law of demand, the quantity demanded of a good or service varies inversely with its price, *ceteris paribus*. Why the *ceteris paribus* assumption? Because many things other than the price of the good influence how much consumers wish to buy. For example, if a person's income rises, he or she is likely to buy more of most goods; if an extensive advertising campaign is begun, sales will usually rise, and so on. To assess the impact of the change of the price of a good on the quantity demanded, we must hold constant all other factors (sometimes called **determinants**) that might also influence consumer willingness to purchase the good. No interesting aspect of human behavior is determined by only one factor; life is more complicated than that. How we isolate the effects of one variable to check the validity of a theory is a question of considerable philosophical and practical difficulty. This question is taken up in economic statistics and econometrics courses. For the present, bear in mind that it is important to think in terms of the *ceteris paribus* assumption, ignoring for the purpose of simplification other factors that influence the variables of interest.

HYPOTHESES

The heart of all theories is the hypothesis, the statement that predicts behavior in response to certain changed conditions. In the preceding statement of the law (actually theory) of demand, all the words in the first sentence before the expression *ceteris paribus* form the hypothesis. A hypothesis is the statement of how people will behave or react to a change in economic circumstances. As already indicated, the hypothesis is likely to be flawed, especially for purposes of prediction, by faulty assumptions. Once formulated, the hypothesis is tested by comparing what is predicted with what actually happened. However, note that this is a very iffy proposition, because the choice of "facts," although not as unconstrained as it is for the storytelling novelist, is somewhat arbitrary.

FUNCTIONAL RELATIONSHIPS

Economic theories generally involve functional relationships. They attempt to show how the magnitude of one thing (a variable) is influenced by one or more other things (variables). The law of demand, for example, hypothesizes that the quantity demanded is a function of price. In other words, the quantity demanded depends on price. The variable that depends on another variable or variables is called the **dependent variable**, while the variables that help determine the size of the dependent variable are called **independent variables**. Thus, in the law of demand, the quantity demanded can be called the dependent variable, because its magnitude depends on the independent variable, the price of the good.

As scientists, economists are concerned not only with formulating theories of behavior but also with observing whether the theories are useful. Theories are useful if they enable us to better understand or, ideally, predict human behavior. To see if we understand more or predict better as a result of a theory of behavior, we must engage in an "empirical analysis" of appropriate facts. This analysis enables us to determine that what happened (or what we expected to happen) could be explained (or predicted) by the theory.

One difficulty in telling a convincing scientific story is isolating the variables included in the theory from other influencing factors present in the real world. In other words, the *ceteris paribus* assumption is seldom realized completely. It is possible through techniques of statistical inference to overcome this sort of problem. For example, one commonly used technique, multiple-regression analysis, provides a means of at least partially separating the influence of factors external to the theory in an attempt to avoid violating the *ceteris paribus* assumption. A branch of economics called **econometrics** is concerned with combining statistical techniques with economic theory in order to tell more empirically convincing scientific stories. However, the reader must be very careful in accepting such stories, for a multitude of technical statistical problems underlie them.[3] Moreover, like any storyteller, the economist tends to use data that most strongly support his or her story and to analyze the data in ways that might seem suspicious at best to those wishing to tell a different story. In spite of these difficulties, econometric evidence has in many cases been strong enough to convince economists and policymakers that a theory has some merit. (See Problem 1–6.)

1–6 True or False? People vary so much that economic theory cannot possibly lead us to any meaningful conclusions about human behavior.

False. Group behavior is often more predictable than individual behavior. When the weather grows colder, more firewood will be sold. Some individuals may not buy firewood, but we can predict with great accuracy that a group of individuals will establish a pattern of buying more firewood. The same is true of gasoline in the summertime.

1.11 THEORETICAL PERSPECTIVE

General equilibrium analysis is often described as the part of microeconomic analysis that examines mutual interrelationships among the prices and outputs of all goods traded in the economic system. **Partial equilibrium** analysis is equilibrium analysis

---

[3]For an engaging, accessible discussion of econometric difficulties, see E. Leamer, "Let's Take the Con Out of Econometrics," *American Economic Review*, 73 (March 1983): 31–43.

that isolates and examines one or more individuals, firms, or markets while assuming that all other factors in the economy remain constant. **Partial equilibrium** analysis is most clearly reflected in modern textbook accounts of the supply-and-demand determination of the market price for a particular commodity. If you were estimating the demand for automobiles, for example, you would incorporate the prices of substitutes (such as public transportation), the prices of complements (tires, oil, gasoline), and income; but you would generally ignore the price effect of many unrelated goods (pillows, pencils, aspirin, and so on). Both general and partial equilibrium analyses are useful; the nature of the problem being considered dictates the type of analysis to employ. As is appropriate to its subject, this book mainly employs partial equilibrium analysis.

1.12 STATICS AND DYNAMICS

A clear distinction between *statics* and *dynamics* can be made through a mechanical illustration. Imagine a room in which a pendulum (consisting of a "bob" on a string) is suspended from a domed ceiling by a hook. We can ask several kinds of questions about the behavior of the pendulum. First, if the pendulum is pegged at a particular point and left undisturbed, what will be the ultimate position of its bob? Clearly, the bob will lie directly below the hook on which it is hung, at a distance given by the length of string that connects the bob with the hook. In this example of (informal) static analysis, our only concern is to describe the stationary equilibrium state of a physical system, which, if attained at some point in time, will be maintained indefinitely in the absence of external "shocks." The familiar textbook discussion of the determination of market equilibrium price in terms of the intersection of demand-and-supply curves provides an example of **static analysis** applied to an economic system.

Second, we can ask how the equilibrium position of the bob will be affected if the hook is withdrawn and screwed into another location in the ceiling. Clearly, this procedure will be followed by some erratic movements in the bob, but when it has once again come to rest, the new equilibrium position will differ from the old only by virtue of the change in the location of the hook. This illustrates what economists call **comparative statics**, the study of the variation in equilibrium positions corresponding to specified changes in underlying data. An economic example is provided by textbook discussions of the effects of changes in demand (shifts in demand curves) on the equilibrium price, if supply conditions remain unchanged.

Third, we can ask how the pendulum behaves over time, starting from some arbitrary date on which the position of the bob is given. That is, what happens as we move along the path of adjustment from one equilibrium to another? This question is much more complicated than the previous two. To answer it, we must engage in **dynamic analysis**; we must deal explicitly with a variable representing time in order to characterize the *motion* of variables with equilibrium values.

Serious dynamic analysis requires the use of some fairly complicated mathematical tools and is therefore not a suitable topic for elementary or intermediate microeconomic textbooks. Even in elementary discussions, however, it is desirable to indicate, at least qualitatively, how economic systems are likely to behave when they are out of equilibrium. Without such information, the very notion of equilibrium becomes almost meaningless. Knowing the equilibrium values is much less useful if movement between equilibria essentially takes *forever* than if movement between equilibria is rapid. Recall that instantaneous adjustment is implicitly assumed in principles accounts of supply and demand analysis. (See Problem 1–7.)

1–7 A structural engineer compares the stress on a bridge at average- and peak-use periods. Is this type of analysis static, comparative static, or dynamic?

Because the engineer is comparing two static equilibrium positions, comparative statics are used. Specifically, the implications of two alternative traffic volumes are being compared at two different time periods. However, if the issue was how the stress of the bridge changed with traffic flow, the analysis would then be dynamic—since the change in stress is altered overtime as the traffic volume changes.

1.13 LITERARY AND MATHEMATICAL ANALYSES

The current trend in economic analysis emphasizes mathematical modeling of theoretical ideas. The virtues of the mathematical approach are evident in long-established sciences, such as theoretical mechanics. However, the use of mathematics in unsettled research sciences such as economics may be a mixed blessing. Although mathematical analysis contributes greatly to clarity and precision of argument, it also encourages users to place more stress on logical form than may be desirable in areas in which many questions of subject matter and conceptual perspective have yet to be resolved.

Mathematical analysis cannot be carried out effectively without the frequent use of words; literary analysis cannot be carried out efficiently without the occasional use of symbols and graphs and at least the implicit use of mathematical frameworks. It has been suggested that literary analysis constitutes a form of "intellectual masochism"— that it is simply wrongheaded to insist on splitting fine hairs with a blunt instrument when sharper (mathematical) tools are readily available. The case for mathematical economics may be considerably weaker than the case for mathematical physics. The most active areas of modern physics rely, though, as much on literary as on mathematical modes of analysis.

However, many key concepts in economics can be more easily understood when calculus or even set-theoretic topological methods are employed. Consequently, mathematical footnotes appear throughout the text to clarify the discussion more precisely. In the body of the text itself, however, no advanced mathematics beyond the use of graphs appears.

1.14 WHY ECONOMISTS DIFFER

Although professional economists differ frequently on economic policy questions, they probably disagree less than the media would have us believe. Disagreement is common in most disciplines—seismologists trying to predict earthquakes differ, historians are often at odds over the authenticity of manuscripts, psychologists differ on proper ways to raise children, nutritionists debate the merits of large doses of vitamin C. Economists, when placed in a room with many other scientists, find much common ground. Part of the remaining differences relate to normative goals of society and to certain noneconomic consequences of economic policies.

Some economists, for example, are very concerned about individual freedom and liberty, thinking that any encroachment on individual decision making is, other things equal, bad. Persons with this philosophic bent are inclined to be skeptical of increased government involvement in the economy unless the objective evidence is overwhelming that the intervention will have profound, beneficial economic consequences. On the other hand, other economists are very concerned with what they consider an unfair or unfortunate distribution of income, wealth, and power, in a free-market economy and they view governmental intervention as desirable in righting injustices within the economy. To these persons, the threat to individual liberty is not sufficiently great to reject governmental intervention in the face of perceived economic injustice.

Aside from philosophic differences, economists may differ on any given policy question for a second reason. Specifically, they may disagree about the validity of a given economic theory relevant to a specific policy. What makes one story come to be accepted over others? Some economic storytellers do a recognizably better job of holding constant other variables as appropriate. Also, information tends to become better over time—either because we have longer time periods to analyze or because databases can be assembled to answer a specific question. Moreover, as statistical techniques for analyzing the available data are improving, some of these techniques are becoming more accepted than others. Finally, human behavior sometimes actually changes over time, and a theory that explained behavior fairly well in the past is replaced by another theory more relevant to current behavior. (See Problem 1–8.)

1—8 True or False? Although economists are often at odds with each other over some issues, there is still an amazing consensus among economists on certain specific issues.

True. Most economists agree on certain issues (rent control, import tariffs, export restrictions, price controls on natural gas, and the like). Indeed, economic analysis can predict certain phenomena with a high degree of success. For example, if Florida suffers a severe winter, and frost ruins the state's orange crop, then the price of oranges will rise, *ceteris paribus* (that is, holding all other things constant). Alternatively, higher (relative) gasoline prices will eventually lead to lower gasoline consumption through carpooling, increased use of mass transportation, the purchase of smaller cars, and less automobile travel.

1.15 A FINAL COMMENT

It might seem to some that a rather odd methodological stance has been taken here. The "modern" view is that scientists should select among the competing theories that one which *predicts* the best. However, very little in the way of scientific progress is actually made this way. Questions of realism of assumptions also cannot be decided in this manner. Theoretical models should be tested by any means possible, whether by direct tests of assumptions or indirect comparisons of the hypotheses flowing from various theories with observable behavior. Hidden assumptions are a major source of the mistrust and contempt that many people feel for economics and economists. As Nobel laureate Sir John Hicks once observed: "Pure economics has a remarkable way of producing rabbits out of a hat—apparently *a priori* propositions which apparently refer to reality. It is fascinating to try to discover how the rabbits got in, for those of us who do not believe in magic must be convinced that they got in somehow."[4] The trouble is that economists too often fail to communicate to others their own knowledge about "how the rabbits got in." I do not propose to make that mistake, at least consciously, in this book.

Scientific advances may stem, as Amelie Rorty notes, "from our ability to engage in continuous conversation (rhetoric), testing one another, discovering our hidden presuppositions, changing our minds because we have listened to the voices of our fellows. Lunatics also change their minds, but their minds change with the tides of the moon and not because they have listened, really listened, to their friends' questions and objections."[5]

---

[4]John R. Hicks, *Value and Capital*, 2nd ed. (Oxford, England: Oxford University Press, 1946), p. 23.
[5]Amelie Rorty, "Experiments in Philosophic Genre: Descartes' Meditations," *Critical Inquiry* (March 1983): p. 562.

SUMMARY

1. Economic analysis provides a basis for evaluating the consequences of alternative actions, judging the performance of the economy, predicting future events, and planning.

2. Resources are scarce, relative to the demand for them. These scarce resources are used to satisfy the wants of individuals.

3. Almost all of economics reduces to individual incentive stories. That is, individuals pursue an activity as long as they perceive the expected marginal benefits to be greater than the expected marginal costs.

4. Every economic system must make choices in three basic areas: resource allocation, production methods, and the distribution of output. Another way to express this is to say that all societies must decide What? How? and For whom?

5. Positive economics covers analysis of data and facts that are for the most part testable, but normative economics is not verifiable because it relies on value judgments.

6. Like other scientists, economists are involved in storytelling. Economists try to persuade, select their facts, and "invent" their stories. That is, economists are looking for a theory of causation (a story).

7. Stories are often seized by others, reworked, expanded, and passed on again. Thus, there must be consistent ground rules. All scientific disciplines conform to a common pattern in logic and concept.

8. General equilibrium theory emphasizes mutual interdependence and gives us insight into the overall performance of the economy. Partial equilibrium theory analyzes part of the system (one or more individuals, firms, or markets) in isolation, holding other things constant.

9. Static analysis refers to a state that will be maintained indefinitely if not disturbed by some external shock. The position that is maintained is called the equilibrium state.

10. Comparative statics is the comparison of equilibrium states after an external shock. Dynamic analysis observes the *motion* of variables once an equilibrium state has been altered.

11. Economists disagree on normative issues or on the validity of a particular economic theory (story). However, on many issues in economics, there is much common ground.

WORDS AND CONCEPTS FOR REVIEW

opportunity costs

consumption goods

subject matter

theoretical perspective

theories

normative economics

dependent variable

econometrics

partial equilibrium analysis

equilibrium state

dynamic analysis

marginal benefits and costs

factors of production

analytical objective

mode of presentation

positive economics

determinants

independent variable

general equilibrium analysis

static analysis

comparative statics

REVIEW QUESTIONS

1. What are economic principles? What is an economic model?

2. If the results anticipated from the use of an economic principle in a particular case do not occur, what are likely to be the sources of difficulty?

3. In what sense can empirical studies show that a principle is applicable in a particular case, yet never prove that a principle is universally applicable? (Hint: proof versus refutation)

4. "The generality of a theoretical model cannot be determined except in the relation to another theoretical model that is similar in structure, or in relation to a particular set of phenomena the model purports to describe." Give an example to illustrate this proposition.

5. It has been suggested that the only difference between macro- and microeconomics is that the former deals with larger numbers. Does this seem to you a suitable basis for the distinction? Discuss.

6. Classical hydrodynamics deals with the properties of "ideal fluids" that are entirely lacking such properties as viscosity and friction. No such fluid exists in practice; even air is highly "imperfect," as the possibility of heavier-than-air flight indicates. Evidently, classical hydrodynamics is highly unrealistic. Do you suppose that it is also useless? Discuss.

7. In economic analysis, an equilibrium position is often described as an "optimum." Do you see any danger in this association of ideas? Discuss.

8. Should economists make policy recommendations? What if two economists offer different recommendations? How do we decide which economist, if either, should be trusted?

9. Distinguish between partial and general equilibrium theory.

10. What aspects of the behavior of the pendulum of a grandfather clock would you mention if you were analyzing its static properties; that is, how would you describe the equilibrium position of the pendulum? Would a dynamic analysis of the behavior of the pendulum involve anything more in the way of general principles? Discuss.

11. Can a definition be right or wrong?

SUGGESTED READINGS

Blaug, Mark. *The Methodology of Economics: Or How Economists Explain.* Cambridge University Press, Cambridge, 1980.

Friedman, Milton. "The Methodology of Positive Economics," *In Essays in Positive Economics.* Chicago: University of Chicago Press, 1953, pp. 3-43.

Koopmans, Tjalling. *Three Essays on the State of Economic Science.* New York: McGraw-Hill, 1957.

McCloskey, Donald. *If You're So Smart.* Chicago: University of Chicago Press, 1990.

Pirsig, Robert. *Zen and the Art of Motorcycle Maintenance.* New York: Bantam Books, 1974.

Chapter Two

THE NATURE AND GOALS
OF DECISION UNITS

——————— *Questions to Think About* ———————

1. What is the meaning of a household, a factor owner, a firm, and an industry?

2. What is purposeful action?

3. What are the assumed objectives and constraints of typical households, factor owners, and firms?

4. What are the conflicts that may arise when owners and managers are different persons?

5. What are some possible firm objectives other than profit maximization?

2.1 INTRODUCTION

Before undertaking the task of explaining the price system and the allocation of resources, we must devote some attention to the basic decision-making units of the economic system, the goals they are presumed to follow, and the nature of their relationships with each other.

2.2 BASIC DECISION UNITS

There are three primary types of decision-making units or transactors. First, those that carry on consumption activities are known as **households** or consumers—persons, or more commonly families, who use funds from current or past income either to acquire goods and services to satisfy current personal wants, purchase assets to add to previously accumulated savings or reduce indebtedness. A second group consists of **factor owners**. Factor owners may supply labor, land, financial capital, or entrepreneurial services. These services yield income in the form of wages, rent, interest, and profit (residual net earnings).

The third group consists of **firms**. Firms consist of persons who undertake production activities. A firm may be a single individual, say a dentist, or an extensive organization with the legal status of a corporation.

For some purposes, it is useful to group firms into **industries**—firms that produce commodities that are technically similar to or close substitutes for one another. Thus, the retail grocery industry consists of firms operating retail grocery stores, the steel industry consists of steel-manufacturing companies, and so forth. Of course, in the real world, markets do not have sharp boundaries, and neither do industries. The products of one group of firms may shade off gradually into those of another, and brands at opposite ends of the quality scale may be poorer substitutes for one another than each is for some entirely different commodity. Sellers of low-priced cars may compete more directly with bus companies, for example, than with sellers of the most expensive cars. As a rule, however, the definition of an industry is relatively clear in practice. For example, various brands of refrigerators are substitutes for one another much more than they are substitutes for television sets. (See Problem 2–1.)

2–1 In what ways do households act as firms? Why is production not always carried on by households?

Households engage in substantial home production. Many functions performed in some households can be purchased in the market: child care, cleaning, meal preparation, vegetable and fruit production, car and home repairs, clothing manufacturing, and financial management. Many of these services, however, can be produced more cheaply by firms because specialization increases efficiency, and high set-up costs (such as the costs of worker training and tools and machinery) can be spread out over high production levels.

2.3 THE FUNCTIONS OF BUSINESS FIRMS

The business firm, considered as a contractual entity distinct from the individuals who own and manage it, performs several functions. First, it enters into a contractual relationship to purchase the services of productive factors (such as raw materials, buildings, and labor) and retains title to products produced by those inputs until they are disposed of in the market. To acquire factor services prior to selling its products, the firm must typically make monetary payments to factor owners which the firm's owners may obtain from their own funds, from previously accumulated profits, or by borrowing.

Second, the firm coordinates production activities. In a market economy, decisions must be made by firms about types and quantities of commodities to produce and offer for sale, about methods of production (and thus types and quantities of factors to be used), and frequently about marketing and pricing policies.

Third, the firm must speculate about future market conditions and make current decisions in light of these projections, despite uncertain knowledge about future conditions.

In a static society, management functions would involve only routine decisions, once a satisfactory program of products, factor combinations, outputs, and prices had been attained. In a changing and growing world, however, the firm's owners must constantly estimate future prospects and adjust their policies gradually in light of realized results. Decisions may stem from informed judgments about the future, but those in control can never be certain about the correctness of their forecasts.

As a consequence of the firm's role in undertaking production and making decisions in a dynamic economy, the firm's owners bear the risk of financial loss. Because the firm contracts to pay for factor services and makes most payments before the products, are sold, the owners bear the greatest chance of loss if operations are not successful. Even lenders have prior claim to any earnings before they are available to the firm. Of course, other factor owners run some risk of loss: Workers may not receive their full pay, and investors may not receive the "promised" returns on their investments. However, the greatest loss, like the greatest gain, falls to the firm's owners—the coordinating agents who direct the firm's development. (See Problem 2–2.)

2–2 True or False? For a firm to be profitable, it must be large.

False. Many smaller firms have witnessed phenomenal profits (and growth rates), especially in the computer industries. Small firms are just as likely to show a profit as large firms. Adapting well to change is what is critical; large firms may be no better able to anticipate, observe, and react to change than are small firms.

2.4 THE PERFORMANCE OF FUNCTIONS WITHIN THE FIRM

Decisions obviously must be made by human beings. Which person or group of persons within the firm actually performs its various functions? To answer this question, we must classify business firms into two groups: (1) those in which the owners and managers are the same persons, and (2) those in which the two groups are largely separate.

In the first case, regardless of the legal form of organization, the persons who own the business constitute the entrepreneurial group making the policy decisions, so they must perform the management functions and estimate future conditions. Because, as owners, the entrepreneurial group directly controls the disposition of earnings, it receives the profits if the firm is successful and bears the greatest loss if it fails. In sole proprietorships and partnerships, even the personal property of the owners may be taken to satisfy the firm's debts.

Matters are more complicated in the second case that in which owners and managers are separate groups. The typical corporation is owned by large numbers of relatively small stockholders who are not individually in a position to influence management and are not as a rule interested in doing so. Even the holders of relatively large blocks of stock are rarely interested in management policies, concerning themselves only with dividend payments and increases in the market value of their holdings. The typical part-owner of a large corporation performs no entrepreneurial functions beyond the purely nominal one of ownership, plus providing financial capital. Thus, the part-owner's position differs very little from that of a bondholder, except that the part owner faces a greater risk of loss. The stockholder does receive a share of the earnings, of course, provided that the persons in control decide to make dividend payments; profits, however, do not necessarily accrue directly to the stockholders. Most large corporations retain substantial shares of their net earnings, thereby raising the value of the firm and its stock.

The primary functions of large corporations are ultimately directed by the executive group—top management officials or business leaders. These persons typically own only a small percentage of the corporation's total stock, though these holdings may constitute a major part of individual managers' personal wealth and income. In some cases, the stock holdings of the management group are too small to give them a significant financial stake in its operations, except as these operations affect their salaries and bonuses. Technically, the executives are always responsible to the stockholders, but the influence stockholders exercise is often very limited in practice. The notion that managers may not always be acting in the shareholders' best interests gives rise to what is called the *principal-agent problem.* (See Problem 2–3.)

2–3 Do business firms have a social responsibility?

Some companies carry on educational enrichment programs for communities, take on projects in low-income areas (like improving inner-city school systems or assisting in urban housing projects), subsidize public television, or become involved in cleaning up the environment. Are such actions appropriate for firms?

The opponents of firms' engaging in social programs believe that executives are responsible for maximizing the returns to shareholders without violating laws or ethics. Indeed, it can be argued that increasing earnings (or seeking them whether they are realized or not) is *itself* an act of social responsibility: We want to convert *low*-value goods into *high*-value goods through production—and profit seekers attempt this. Moreover, opponents claim that executives have no right to spend the firm's money on social programs. Let the individual firm owners—stockholders or proprietors—spend as they wish on social concerns. On the other hand, some social problems such as air, water, and visual pollution may be caused by the firm. The firm might feel obliged to pick up the costs it has imposed on the community. Furthermore, many social programs might be considered to be consistent with long-run profit maximization. Such programs often create customer loyalty and respect, which bring in greater profits in the long run.

2.5 GOALS OF THE DECISION UNITS

It is conceivable that the space shuttle suffers traumatic shocks when it is shot into space; and who knows how a sports utility vehicle feels when it is launched off a bridge on a bungee cord for a television commercial? Even if objects had feelings, however, these feelings would be ignored by physical scientists, for scientists have devised models for describing and predicting physical behavior that are valid, regardless of such considerations. Social scientists might follow the same procedure; after all, from one point of view, human beings are just material objects. In practice, however, human beings do not follow simple patterns of behavior. They take **purposeful action** in response to opportunities to increase their material welfare or social prestige. So in formulating economic theories, economists generally have found it convenient to proceed partly by describing regularities in behavior (as in the physical sciences) and partly by assuming that individuals maximize welfare through goal-seeking behavior.

The assumption that individuals act purposefully does not in itself say anything about behavior. It implies merely that whatever individuals do is done with a purpose. To get any mileage out of the assumption, we must specify not only what is to be maximized but also the choices facing an individual.

A note of caution on theories: Making the assumption that every type of economic unit pursues similar goals can *not* be entirely satisfactory. If the assumption is too general, it will apply only to a limited number of cases. The best procedure, therefore, is to start with a very general assumption that is open to a variety of interpretations and later introduce more specific assumptions to deal with particular cases. The traditional assumption of economic analysis is that each decision unit seeks to maximize its own economic well-being, where "economic well-being" is assumed to be a function of the quantities of commodities produced, consumed, and traded. The application of this assumption to household consumers encounters relatively few difficulties. Its application to business firms poses certain problems, however, especially in cases where ownership and management are separated.

MAXIMIZATION OF HOUSEHOLD SATISFACTION

The maximization assumption relates quantities of various commodities to a hypothetical index of satisfaction called **utility**. Utility is assumed to increase when the quantity of any good consumed increases. In choosing among alternatives that involve the purchase and sale of commodities, the household is constrained—the value of its purchases cannot be greater than the value of money or whatever else is supplied to finance them. Market exchange is a peculiar two-way street in which traffic (demands for goods) is permitted to move in one direction only when a volume of traffic (supplies of goods) of equal money value simultaneously moves in the opposite direction.

The nature and implications of assumptions about utility maximization will be developed later. Here, we merely observe that these assumptions imply that households will seek to purchase units of a given good from the cheapest available source, with allowances made for differences in quality.

MAXIMIZATION OF FACTOR INCOME

Factor owners and holders of financial capital are assumed to make units of factor services available in such quantities and in such a manner as to maximize their net gain.

If, for example, workers are to maximize satisfaction from the provision of labor services, they must offer an amount of of labor hours such that the satisfaction associated with a marginal gain in income from an additional hour just offsets the dissatisfaction of the additional labor. Because the provision of labor hours (at least beyond a certain point) involves increasing disutility of work, eventually a point will be reached (short of the maximum number of hours the person could possibly work) at which the additional utility from income just balances the additional disutility from work, and the person will not rationally supply additional labor. Thus, it cannot be assumed that workers seek to maximize income but rather that they seek to maximize overall satisfaction from allocating their available time between work and leisure. Attainment of this adjustment is restricted by the fact that many workers have little discretion about the number of hours worked. Because standard work periods, say 8:00 A.M. to 5:00 P.M., are set for groups of workers it is not always possible for each person individually to strike an optimum balance between work and leisure. However, families may make some adjustments in this regard by working overtime or by sending teenagers or spouses out to work. The maximization assumption also requires that each worker supply his or her services to the business firm that offers the highest reward, taking into consideration not only money wages but other conditions of work such as prestige, job security , and the conditions of the workplace.

The maximization assumption requires that holders of loanable capital allocate it between liquid (monetary) holdings and various forms of loans and other uses. Because holding wealth in itself offers certain advantages, the quantity made available will not necessarily be the amount that will maximize dollar income, but rather the amount that will balance income gains from making funds available to business firms against liquidity advantages of keeping funds in monetary form. It is also assumed that money will be made available to those users who offer the maximum return, with due allowances for different degrees of risk. For owners of land and capital goods, maximization relates simply to money income received, net of any cost associated with maintaining assets intact.

MAXIMIZATION OF BUSINESS PROFITS

As applied to business firms, the maximization assumption requires that firms seek to maximize the net earnings of the enterprise. Examination of the application of **profit maximization** suggests that several modifications to the assumption are necessary.

1. Firms do not strictly maximize their profits in the short run.

If firms maximized profits by the day or the week, they might decide not to lubricate their machinery or to reduce the quality of their products to their customers. While these decisions might reduce costs in the short run, they certainly would hinder the firm's long-run position. Hence, we assume that a firm's objective is to maximize the value of their future profit stream in its choices.

2. Disutility Incurred in Gaining Additional Earnings

In small owner-managed businesses, higher earnings may require greater personal effort on the part of the owner-manager. If in order to gain additional earnings the owner must devote more time to business and less to leisure, the owner will then seek a balance in the trade off between additional money income on the one hand and gains from additional leisure on the other. It is important to note in this case that the individual is still maximizing profits as long as he or she is accounting properly for the opportunity cost of his or her time.

3. *Uncertainty and Profit Maximization*

By and large, businesses operate under conditions of considerable ignorance and uncertainty about prices, prospective sales, costs, and so forth. This being so, there is no objective way to determine whether a firm "really" seeks to maximize profit since different firms (and different managers of the same firm) may have very different ideas about what future circumstances will prevail and may therefore operate on very different assumptions about expected profits. One strategy may promise high potential gains with great uncertainty while another may promise moderate gains with little risk. In choosing among alternative business strategies, the firm must consider not only expectations of gain and the likelihood of their receipt but also the possible consequences for the firm if the policy it selects turns out to be wrong.

4. *Separation of Ownership and Management in Large Corporations*

The typical owner—the stockholder—has little direct voice in making business decisions. The typical executive may have interests that diverge more or less from those of the owners; he or she may strive for power or prestige within the business community in ways that either do not affect profits or affect them adversely. Executives can always rationalize actions taken in pursuit of personal rather than corporate goals on the ground that they are "in the long-run interest of the corporation," despite appearances to the contrary. One should not be too ready to accept this picture, for corporate officials tend to regard their corporation as a separate entity, distinct from the stockholders who own it, and to identify their own welfare with that of the corporation even though they may not themselves receive any portion of its net profits. Almost all executives tend to regard their firm's profits as the best measure of their own professional success. If executives fail to earn as high a rate of return as informed stockholders believe possible, the stockholders may revolt and seek a new set of executives. Failure to earn a normal rate of return can also endanger the continued existence of a firm, for if it fails for long enough, a firm will be forced into bankruptcy and reorganization. Finally, a satisfactory profit is essential for continued expansion of the firm. Profits provide funds for expansion and make it easier to acquire additional capital. The enterprise's growth not only increases executives' income but also enhances their prestige and power. (See Problem 2–4.)

2–4 How might small firms be more profitable than big firms?   What advantages do big firms have over small firms?

In small owner-operated firms, there is no conflict of interest between owners and managers.   Because a small firm is much less complex and bureaucratic than a big firm, it is easier to organize and adjust to changes in economic conditions.   In addition, small firms are just as likely to be lucky as big firms. Big firms, however, have greater financial resources, giving them a better access to economic forecasts, research & development groups and investment opportunities.   They also may be able to take advantage of a lower per unit production cost at high-output levels.

5. Conficts between Maximization of Profits and the Interests of Executives

When there are true conflicts of interest between owners and managers, the managers' interests will often prevail. Executives might, for example, oppose a projected expansion that would be profitable to the firm over a period of time but involve bringing in new stockholders who might gain control of the firm and eliminate the present management. In other instances, executives may sell current assets at a heavy loss to obtain funds to meet pressing obligations that, if ignored, would lead to immediate reorganization. Most drastically, management may be able to delay complete liquidation of an unprofitable business beyond the point at which it should be undertaken in the stockholders' interests.   Managers not only dislike seeing the firm to which they have long been attached disappear but also seek to avoid losing their positions.   Through undermaintenance of plant and equipment, depletion of inventories, failure to cover depreciation charges, and sale of assets, the firm may continue to operate until the owners' equity is completely dissipated, whereas earlier liquidation might preserve a substantial portion of the value of the firm

6. Vigor in the Pursuit of Goals

Many apparent qualifications to the profit-maximization assumption have to do not with the goal itself but with how vigorously it is pursued.   Particularly at junior levels, managers in large-scale businesses may be less energetic than those in individual enterprises.   Managers of a large business can easily become overcautious.   The desire to maintain the status quo—to protect the positions of present executives—may encourage managers to avoid changes that appear profitable for fear that expected gains will not materialize. Because profits seldom accrue directly to executives, the dynamic qualities of management frequently found in smaller enterprises may be stifled out of fear of "rocking the boat."   The large corporation's complex structure may itself discourage change. The goals of top, middle, and lower management often diverge, and top management may have difficulty getting enough information from lower echelons to ensure that their policies are carried out. (See Problem 2–5.)

2–5 Define *economic profits*. Can a firm maximize these profits? If so, is it best to maximize profits precisely?

Economic profits are defined as revenue minus all costs, where all costs include the opportunity cost of using specific resources owned by the firm. Whether a firm can or wants to maximize economic profits depends, of course, on how we define the term *maximizing economic profits*. One could argue that with incomplete information, firms do not know their demand and cost curves and hence cannot determine how either total revenue or total cost will vary as consumer and producer behavior and circumstances change. If long-run profit maximization is the goal, perhaps only the "fittest" firms will survive, although "fitness" is difficult to determine at any point in time. Profit-maximizing firms will, however, gradually accumulate financial assets, and non-profit-maximizing firms will be eventually eliminated. Also, maximizing profits precisely may have costs greater than benefits: Information is costly to acquire, so firms might try to do as well as they can subject to the constraints of uncertainty and lack of information.

2.6 ALTERNATIVES TO PROFIT MAXIMIZATION

If profit maximization is not to be regarded as the primary goal of business firms, what alternatives might seem reasonable? Several have been proposed.

1. Satisfactory Profits
Business firms may aim at a "satisfactory" rate of profit rather than a maximum figure. Top management may be more concerned with a steady growth in earnings than with higher but fluctuating earnings.

If a firm accepts "satisfactory" profits in the short run, this does not necessarily mean that the firm is failing to seek maximum returns over the long run. Management may, for example, believe that long-run profits will be greater if the firm avoids fully exploiting every temporary situation that might generate higher profits, but encourage new firms to develop. Emphasis on "satisfactory" profits, however, does affect the firm's decisions in the short run. If a firm is attempting to maximize short-run profits, an increase in demand will almost surely lead to a price increase, but if the firm is seeking only "satisfactory" profits, prices may be left unchanged.

2. Sales Maximization
Professor William Baumol has argued that maximization of *sales* rather than profits is the primary goal of the management of larger businesses, given a satisfactory rate of profit. Sales are a more readily observable measure of management success than profits, particularly given that most firms accept the doctrine that a firm's share of total

industry sales is of primary importance for its long-term success. Baumol also suggests that there is a closer correlation between executive salaries and gross sales than between salaries and net profits; thus, executives are more concerned about the former than the latter.

3. *Nonpecuniary Goals*

In both small, owner-managed enterprises and large corporations, the persons making decisions are often influenced by nonpecuniary motives, which may take precedence over profit maximization. If prestige is very important to executives, they may undertake policies that enhance their standing in the community or in the industry but do not contribute to profit maximization.

Closely related is the desire of some business leaders to control as large a business empire as possible. Although, in many cases profit maximization is the best path to expansion, in other cases it may not be. History offers many examples of business firms that undertook unprofitable expansions merely because their executives wished to exercise authority over more extensive empires. Such policies are more likely to be followed in large corporations, where executives do not directly benefit from higher profits, than in small enterprises; but they are not absent even in the latter.

Large firms sometimes follow policies that they believe best serve the interests of the community or nation as a whole, even though they do not contribute directly to profit maximization. Such firms may be reluctant to cut wages or lay off workers in a depression in the (possibly correct) belief that such action will aggravate the decline in economic activity. Or, for apparently humanitarian reasons, they may not fire unproductive employees, for example, those impaired by health or age-related difficulties.

Businesses operate within a complicated and restrictive framework of legal and social institutions. They rarely seek to maximize profits by taking illegal action, although criminal behavior is certainly not unknown. Furthermore, they are likely to avoid certain practices that, although legal, are contrary to accepted standards of business practice. Thus, for example, they may avoid price cutting if such practices are generally frowned upon by other firms.

4. *Preference Maximization*

The preceding remarks suggest that for a more satisfactory analysis, the profit-maximization assumption should be replaced by a more general assumption of "utility maximization," which could include various goals besides profit maximization. Such an assumption would seem particularly desirable in situations of ignorance and uncertainty; for in such cases, the profit-maximization rule is inadequate because executives are confronted by a group of possible outcomes with different degrees of probability rather than a single profit potential. Further progress in certain portions of economic analysis may require such an assumption. The complexity of economic analysis would be tremendously increased, however, if profit maximization were replaced by a broader goal such as utility maximization. (See Problem 2–7.)

2–7 It has been argued that the utility-maximization assumption is circular. For example in order to make himself happy (maximize his utility), Mark buys and consumes spinach. Therefore, consuming spinach makes Mark happy. Why might this assumption pose more difficulties for psychologists than for economists?

The economist focuses on the economic choices made by the typical household or firm. The psychologist studies what motivates an individual and how tastes are formed. The psychologist cares whether Mark buys spinach because it tastes good to him, because it is nutritional, or because he hates it and is irrational. The economist, however, cares only about how average or typical consumers respond to economic forces—for example, whether people on average buy more spinach when the price of spinach declines or when income rises. Thus, the utility-maximizing assumption allows the economist to make predictions about economic outcomes without taking up the task of the psychologist, explaining the preferences of each individual.

2.7 THE NATURE AND GOALS OF DECISION UNITS: THEORY AND PRACTICE

Clearly the "households" and "firms" of theoretical analysis, although modeled after flesh-and-blood consumers and hard-driving business executives, cannot be more than pale and imperfect reflections of real people. To avoid confusion, it may be helpful to think of theoretical households in terms of typical consumers rather than specific individuals. In effect, theory deals with statistical sterotypes, decision-making units that conform to the behavior of an "average" household. The models conform much less well to the behavior of any specific household or kind of household (for example, professional households, households with three children, "hard-hat" households, and so on). Thus, the usefulness of a theory of household behavior is not diminished by the contradictory behavior of a particular individual. The issue is seldom whether the theory applies to particular people but rather whether it describes average behavior with reasonable accuracy.

A similar set of observations applies to the concept of a "firm." No actual business firm could possibly be as simple as the firms considered in theory. Actual firms typically produce many different outputs, while theory generally deals with single-product firms. Actual businesses use inputs at earlier dates to produce at later (sometimes much later) dates, meanwhile holding large stocks of raw materials and goods in process; theoretical firms are usually regarded as instantaneous converters of raw materials into finished outputs. Actual firms stumble and fumble about rather than adjust their operations decisively to changing conditions. Theoretical firms are typically treated as if they not only knew exactly what they should do at any moment but also were able to jump immediately from one situation to another without any delay or cost.

As in the case of households, therefore, so with firms and factor owners: it is essential to view decision units as "average" or typical representations. It may happen that simplifications introduced into theoretical work ignore features of the real world that are crucial in describing actual behavior, in which case the theoretical analysis may be worthless. It may also happen, however, that these simplifications can also be benign—they may facilitate analysis and permit us to derive useful conclusions that might have been obscured by a more complex theory. It is no use doing purely theoretical work in an empirical science with one's head in the clouds; potential flaws in basic assumptions should be borne in mind at every stage. But neither is it sensible to scorn a theory for lack of realism before its implications for observed behavior have even been revealed.

As in video games, physics or skiing, so also in economics, one learns best by doing. We have said enough about economic theory and the economic system to set the stage for interested learners; it only remains to raise the curtain for the play to begin.

SUMMARY

1. A household is a group of one or a few people who provide business firms with labor, land, money capital, or entrepreneurship (in various combinations) in exchange for wages, rent, interest or profit.

2. A firm is a group of people who undertake and carry on production activities. A firm may consist of a single person or hundreds of thousands of people (stock holders, managers, and employees). A firm is a decision unit, while a plant is a technical production unit.

3. Markets do not always have well-defined boundaries.

4. The firm must acquire ownership of factors of production or their services, coordinate production activities, and make decisions in an environment of incomplete information and uncertainty.

5. Business firms can be usefully classified into two groups: those in which owners and managers are separate and those in which they are the same.

6. Individuals act purposefully—that is, people do things with a purpose.

7. Households seek to maximize utility (satisfaction).

8. Businesses seek to maximize profits subject to the constraints of technology.

9. The goal of profit maximization is the topic of some debate among economists. Instead of aiming for maximum profits, top management may choose to accept satisfactory levels of profit with stable growth rates, may seek to maximize sales as an alternative to profits, or may focus on prestige and other so-called nonpecuniary goals.

10. When studying the behavior of households and firms, it is best to think in terms of average or typical representations.

WORDS AND CONCEPTS FOR REVIEW

households	factor owners
firms	industries
factors	purposeful action
utility	profit maximization
economic profit	satisfactory profits
sales maximization	nonpecuniary goals
preference maximization	

REVIEW QUESTIONS

1. Imagine that three people become stranded on an island in the Pacific and that one of them claims all rights to the only source of water (a small spring), another claims possession of the only indigenous source of food (a grove of coconut trees), while the third takes possession of a canoe and becomes the sole source of protein (fish). Theorize about trading possibilities in this situation: Will trade take place? If so, will it occur randomly, or will definite trading posts be established? What factors will govern rates of exchange among commodities traded? How will rates of exchange be expressed—in terms of one commodity, in terms of an arbitrary unit of account such as dollars, or what? How often will individuals trade? Specifically, will there be any reason for them to trade in large lots rather than small? Under what conditions will production specialization lead to greater total output? (These are not simple questions. Some possible answers are suggested in later chapters, but you should try to work some of them out at this stage.)

2. What is the difference between a firm and an industry? Between a firm and a plant?

3. As the term *industry* is usually used, does potato farming constitute an industry? law practice? university teaching?

4. Would you regard firms producing toasters, refrigerators, and air conditioners as constituting separate industries, or is each an element of the electrical-appliance industry? Discuss.

5. What are some examples of firms that operate in more than one industry?

6. Indicate the major functions of business firms.

7. Indicate the principal characteristics of the two major types of business firms.

8. What is meant by maximizing?

9. Suppose that you operate a small restaurant. What may serve as a constraint on profit maximization?

10. What is the significance of uncertainty for the goal of profit maximization?

11. In a large-scale firm, is it more realistic to assume that top management is seeking to maximize the firm's profits, or the personal income of the management personnel? Why may the two goals in large measure not be conflicting? In what types of situations may they conflict?

12. Are large firms or small firms more likely to be influenced by nonpecuniary goals? Explain.

SUGGESTED READINGS

Alchian, Armen. *Economic Forces at Work.* Indianapolis: Liberty Press, 1977, pp. 1–35.

Alchian, Armen, and Harold Demsetz. "Production, Information Costs and Economic Organization," *American Economic Review,* 62 (December 1972), pp. 777–95.

Baumol, William. *Economic Theory and Operations Analysis,* 4th ed. Englewood Cliffs, N.J.: Prentice-Hall, 1977, Chapter 7.

Cyert, Richard M. and James G. March. *A Behavioral Theory of the Firm,* Englewood Cliffs, N.J.: Prentice-Hall, 1965, Chapter 7.

Machlup, Fritz. "Theories of the Firm: Marginalists, Behavioral, Managerial," *American Economic Review,* 57 (March 1967), pp. 1–33.

Scherer, Frederick M., and David Ross. *Industrial Market Structure and Economic Performance,* Boston: Houghton Mifflin, 1990, pp 38–54.

Simon, Herbert. "Rational Decision Making in Business Organizations," *American Economic Review,* 69 (September 1979), 493–513.

Williamson, Oliver E. "The Modern Corporation: Origins, Evolution, Attributes," *Journal of Economic Literature,* 19 (December 1981): 1537–1568.

Chapter Three

SUPPLY AND DEMAND

Questions to Think About
---

1. What is a market?

2. What are market imperfections?

3. What is the difference between absolute and relative prices?

4. What factors shift the demand curve?

5. What factors shift the supply curve?

6. What creates a shortage? a surplus?

7. How do shifts in the supply and demand curves affect the equilibrium price and quantity?

8. What is price elasticity of demand? How does the numerical value of the elasticity change along a linear demand curve?

9. How does price elasticity of demand relate to total expenditure?

10. What factors affect the price elasticity of demand?

11. What is income elasticity of demand?

12. What is cross elasticity of demand?

13. What is consumer surplus and in what sense does it measure social welfare?

3.1 INTRODUCTION

*L*ike scissors, which function by the interaction of two distinct blades, supply and demand interact to determine value (price) and quantities exchanged. Supply and demand, however, do not operate in a void. Prices and quantities exchanged of various outputs and inputs (such as land, labor, and capital) are also affected by the structure of markets—that is, the prevailing relationships among potential buyers and sellers. If, for example, the entire supply of a good is controlled by just one firm, the price and the output of that good is normally different than if it is provided by a large number of independent sellers. The number of buyers and the relationships prevailing among them likewise affect price and output, although independent competitive behavior is more pervasive on the demand side. The nature of the factor market affects factor prices and, thus, the costs of producing the products made with them and the distribution of income among factor owners.

3.2 THE CONCEPT OF A MARKET

In every advanced economy, a large portion of resources is devoted to market activities: wholesaling, retailing, advertising, banking, and transport, to name just a few. Most of us spend substantial amounts of our scarce labor resources traveling to work, banks, stores, and back again. One must be either very young or very dead to be ignorant of the general nature of markets and trade. However, it is not a simple task to define a market. How do we throw together all the different markets such as supermarkets, department stores, discount warehouses, drugstores, and restaurants? An incredible variety of exchange arrangements exist: organized securities markets, wholesale auction markets, foreign exchange markets, real estate markets, labor markets, and so forth. The problem of defining a market is further aggravated by goods being priced and traded in various ways at various locations by various kinds of buyers and sellers. In short, narrow definitions tend to be too specific while broad definitions tend to be too vague to be useful.

In the past, economists have dealt with this problem by ignoring it. They either leave the reader to decide what a "market" is or they define a market so broadly that the concept is of little value—for example "an area where supply and demand interact to determine price." Although such definitions are relatively harmless, they are also uninformative. In fact, one comes away from most theoretical models with such a vague idea of markets that one might almost suppose prices and quantities are determined by "ghostly forces" (supply and demand) rather than by people.

The reason it is so difficult to define a market is that there is no such animal as a market. The closest we can get to defining a **market** is as "an organized set of institutional arrangements (a set of rules or customs) for the negotiation of exchange between buyers and sellers." This excludes elementary barter (where nothing is "organized" about trading arrangements) and includes highly organized markets that have no particular physical location (such as markets for foreign exchange). At the heart of this definition is the presumption of an exact set of institutional arrangements governing trading.

So the best we can do is to say that a market consists of a group of buyers, sellers, and intermediaries in close enough contact to carry on exchange under stipulated rules or customs. For some goods, such as gravel, markets are numerous and more or less isolated. Because transportation costs are so high relative to selling prices that the good will not be shipped any substantial distance, buyers are in contact only with local producers. Price and output are thus determined in a number of small markets, and the total production of gravel is the sum of the amounts of output determined separately in each of the markets. In other industries, markets are nationwide. Automobile manufacturers, for example, sell to dealers throughout the country and determine (wholesale) price and output on the basis of considerations relating to the entire economy.

PERFECTION IN MARKET CONDITIONS

Price and output are determined not only by market relationships prevailing among buyers and sellers but also by other institutional factors that affect the behavior of both the buyer and the seller. The two major considerations are the extent of knowledge about market conditions and the mobility of factors such as labor and capital. Deviations from perfect knowledge or perfect mobility of factors are known as **imperfections.**

A market characterized by complete absence of imperfections, as well as by purely competitive market conditions (many buyers and sellers of homogeneous products), is described as **perfectly competitive**. In this type of market, all sellers and buyers have complete knowledge of market conditions, and frictions restraining the immediate adjustment of price and output are absent. Because producers have complete knowledge of costs and market conditions, they are able to maximize profits at all times. Because factor units are freely mobile, they will always move quickly to the most attractive employments.

The assumption of perfection is frequently useful to make a first approximation. Actually, all markets are characterized by substantial imperfections. There are two major types: imperfect knowledge and imperfect mobility.

IMPERFECT KNOWLEDGE

Factor owners and business firms rarely, if ever, possess all the information they need to attain their maximization goals. Workers may be uninformed about their employment alternatives. Persons about to establish new business enterprises have only limited knowledge of profit possibilities. Sellers have imperfect knowledge of potential sales and production costs. Information about income possibilities, sales, and costs depends on the institutions and feasible production technologies—the state of education, the state of market research and cost analysis techniques, the activity of government agencies in preparing and distributing information about job and profit possibilities, trends in national income, and so on. Because of imperfect knowledge, outputs of various goods differ from what they would otherwise be, and both resource allocation and income distribution are affected. Too many producers enter some lines of production, while others make unwarranted plant expansions or fail to make other changes that would be profitable. Prices may be set at levels that do not maximize profits, and production may exceed or fall short of the quantities that can be sold at profitable prices.

IMPERFECT MOBILITY OF FACTOR UNITS

In practice, numerous restrictions affect the **mobility of factors**—that is, the movement of factors of production from one use to another. Many specialized factors are not easily adaptable to changing conditions. Machinery constructed for one purpose is often unsuited for any other use. A railroad grade, including expensive bridges and tunnels, is ordinarily useless for any purpose except railroad operation. An apple orchard can produce only apples.

In some instances, it is possible, but not feasible, to transfer resources because of costs of transference. For example, in some older cities streetcar rails on abandoned lines are often left in the pavement because the costs of removing them are prohibitive. Because specialized resources are not adaptable, these resources will remain in a particular use long after they have ceased to yield the return which was necessary to bring them into operation.

Labor is likewise not entirely adaptable. Persons with job specific skills trained in certain lines of work cannot easily shift to employment requiring different skills. For example, the "human capital" embedded in economics professors may be ill-suited to producing television sets or football games. The geographical mobility of labor is seriously restricted by moving costs, family ties, and preferences for living in certain areas. Hence, workers are often reluctant to shift from present employers and occupations to other employment areas.

3.3 ABSOLUTE AND RELATIVE PRICES

In the past fifty years few goods have fallen in **absolute price**—that is, the money price one pays in dollars and cents. There have been a few well-known examples of falling absolute prices—the personal handheld calculator, the video recorder, the home computer, cellular telephones and so on—but the evidence suggests that, in money terms, *most* prices have risen.

The laws of supply and demand, however, are concerned with the price of one good measured in units of another good—the **relative price**. If the price of movies rises relative to all other goods, we would predict that the quantity of movies demanded would fall, if all other relevant factors are held constant.. Moviegoers would look for substitutes, like video rentals, bowling, the video arcade, or television, or they would just go to the movies less frequently. (See Problem 3–1.)

3–1 True or False? Compared with a childless couple, it is relatively cheaper for a couple with young children to dine out at an expensive restaurant than at an inexpensive restaurant. Therefore, the couple with young children would be more likely to dine at an expensive restaurant than the childless couple.

True. The key to this problem is relative prices. Add a $10 babysitting charge to the cost of an inexpensive meal and to an expensive meal:

Inexpensive		Expensive	
Babysitting	$10	Babysitting	$10
Meal for two	$10	Meal for two	$40
	——		——
	$20		$50

The babysitter cost raises the total price of the inexpensive meal by 100 percent but the total price of the expensive meal by only 25 percent. Thus, the price of an expensive meal (relative to an inexpensive meal) for couples with children is lower. So, for those with small children we would predict a greater *proportion* of dinners out to be at expensive restaurants. Note, however, that those with young children are also expected to go out less often because going out to either type of restaurant is *relatively* more expensive than staying home for them.

3.4 THE CONCEPT OF DEMAND

In a market economy, characterized by freedom of choice, consumer demand plays a major role in determining product prices and resource allocation. Firms will produce only those goods for which demand is expected to be sufficient to support prices that cover production costs, and the quantities produced will in turn influence the employment and earnings of factor units. To clarify these concepts and relationships, we begin with an account of the nature and determinants of demand.

The demand of an individual buyer for a product, known as *individual demand*, is a schedule of the number of units of the product the person would buy at various per unit prices during a particular time interval. A shopper enters a store to buy oranges for use during the coming week. Finding the price to be 60 cents a pound, she buys 4 pounds. Had the price been 70 cents for oranges of the same grade, she might have bought 3 pounds; had it been 80 cents, she might have bought none; at 50 cents, she might have bought 5 pounds. Her demand for oranges at the particular time is the schedule of the various amounts she would purchase at the different prices. This schedule is illustrated in the table adjoining Figure 3–1. Even though the shopper may not be aware of the amounts she would purchase at other prices this does not alter the fact that she would have bought other amounts had other prices prevailed. The schedule is simply a list of possibilities; at any time, only one of the prices prevails.

The data in the demand schedule can be plotted graphically, as shown in Figure 3–1. The data as given provide a series of points that, when connected by a continuous curve, constitute the demand curve. This procedure provides by interpolation estimates of quantities demanded at prices between those for which information is given. In graphs employed for price and output analysis, price is always plotted on the vertical axis, and quantity on the horizontal axis.

In the typical market, there are numerous buyers, each with his or her own individual demand schedule. The sum of these schedules, known as *market demand*, or more commonly, **demand**, is thus a schedule of total amounts that would be purchased in a given time by all buyers in a particular market at possible prices. The market demand for oranges for a certain week might appear as shown by the graph of the market demand schedule shown in Figure 3–2.

When a good is *homogeneous* in the sense that buyers have no preferences for particular brands and thus no preference for the product of any particular seller, the concept of market demand is precise; the individual demand schedules can be added without conceptual difficulty. When a product is *differentiated*, however, the concept of market demand, although still useful, becomes less precise. With differentiation, individual buyers have preferences for brands of particular producers; a buyer's schedule is not, for example, for "cola" but for a particular brand of cola. The amount that he or she is willing to buy depends on the brands available, and he or she may demand less of the good if the favorite variety cannot be obtained. Likewise, with product differentiation, the selling prices of different firms may not be identical; in one situation some brands may sell for $3, some for $4, and others for $2. Thus, there is no clear-cut market demand schedule of certain amounts being purchased at particular prices. Instead, the schedule must be regarded as showing the total amounts of particular brands that would be purchased at various possible levels of a pattern of prices, recognizing that the amounts individuals will buy are different for the various brands. Even with these qualifications, the concept of "market demand" has significance. It is useful to be able to speak of "an increase in the demand for automobiles," for example, even though what is meant by "demand" is a set of closely related demands for particular kinds of cars rather than the demand for a single homogeneous car.

The demand curve records the pounds of oranges a consumer desires at various prices in a given week holding all other factors fixed. Because the individual desires more oranges at lower prices, the demand curve slopes downward.

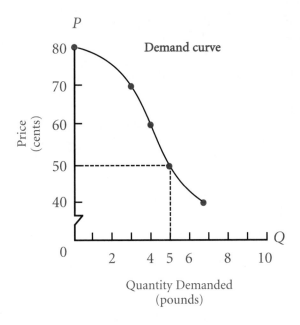

Market Demand Schedule of a Consumer for Oranges, Week of December 10–16

Price (cents/pounds)	Quantity Demanded (pounds)
80	0
70	3
60	4
50	5
40	7

The horizontal sum of the individual demand curves defines the market demand curve, the schedule of quantities of oranges desired by all consumers in the market at alternate prices *ceteris paribus.*

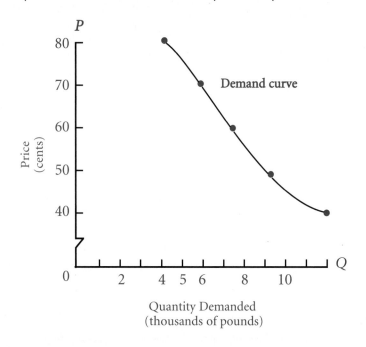

Quantity Demanded
(thousands of pounds)

Market Demand Schedule for Oranges in a Particular Market,
Week of December 10–16

Price (cents/pounds)	Quantity Demanded (pounds)
80	40,000
70	60,000
60	75,000
50	90,000
40	120,000

THE DEMAND FUNCTION

The concept of demand, as defined in the previous section, describes a functional relationship between two variables: the price of a product and the quantity of the product demanded. As a general rule, however, the demand for any given product depends on a host of other considerations besides price. Therefore, other influences should be taken into account by introducing additional independent variables into the demand function. These other variables include the prices of related goods, income, number of buyers (consumer population), tastes, expected future prices, and so on.

When we speak of demand, or the demand function, the price is the only independent variable, and all other influences are "shift" parameters (that is, variables that, if their values are altered, produce a shift on the graph of the demand function relating quantity to price). These shifters are called determinants because they determine the height of the demand curve.

DEMAND DETERMINANTS: THE SHIFTERS

Relaxing the *ceteris paribus* assumption, we can list five factors other than price that influence demand. As a memory device use PYNTE, the Old English spelling of pint— (P) the price of other goods (Y) Income (N) Number of buyers (T) Tastes and (E) Expectations of future relative prices.

1. The Price of Other Goods (P)

Empirical evidence suggests that in deciding how much to buy, consumers are not only influenced by the price of a good or service but also by the prices of other goods and services. For example, to some consumers butter and margarine, lobster and Alaskan king crab, or hamburgers and hot dogs are substitute goods. Generally speaking, the closer the substitutes, the greater the impact of a change in the price on the willingness of consumers to buy the substitute. A fall in the price of a substitute good will, other things equal, reduce demand for the good in question; conversely, an increase in the price of a substitute will increase demand for the good in question. For example, if the price of hot dogs rises, it is likely that some buyers will demand more of hamburgers, say, at the prevailing price. However, it is important to remember that a substitute good for one person may not be so for another person because tastes may differ (or may do so to a greater or lesser degree).

Economists believe that individuals are influenced not only by the prices of substitute goods but also by the prices of complementary goods. Complementary goods are things that "go together." A decrease in the prices of stereo equipment probably will lead to an increase in the demands for compact discs and tapes, because falling stereo prices should, other things equal, lead to greater sales of stereo equipment. Similarly, an increase in the price of motorcycles should lead to a decrease in the number of motorcycle helmets purchased; the two are especially close complements in states that have mandatory helmet laws.

One important caveat should be mentioned in discussions of substitutes and complements. The relationship between the price of one good and the demand for related goods (substitutes or complements) mentioned in the two previous paragraphs will depend on what caused the price initial change. That is, was the initial price change caused by a demand shifter or a supply shifter?

For example, if the price of motorcycles rises because of an effective advertising campaign by major motorcycle producers, then the increase in the price of motorcycles may be caused by a rightward demand shift. Assuming a positively sloped supply curve, this shift will lead to an increase in price and an increase in the quantity of motorcycles purchased. In addition, if more motorcycles are purchased, we would expect a greater demand for motorcycle helmets. So in this case, the increase in the price of motorcycles will lead to an increase in the demand for motorcycle helmets. Recall that in the previous paragraph we argued that a price increase will cause a decrease in the demand for the complement; that would be true if the initial price increase was caused by a supply shifter.

Substitute goods pose the same problem. Imagine that there are two types of gasoline, brand A and brand B. The makers of brand A announce a new additive purported to do less damage to the atmosphere. Those who are environmentally concerned and believe the announcement increase their demand for brand A. If the increase in demand for brand A causes a higher price, then consumers will buy more of brand A at a higher price and substitute away from brand B. Hence, if we expect to arrive at the same outcome presented in the standard textbook treatment on substitutes and complements, then we must always use the *ceteris paribus* assumption to hold all demand determinants (shifters) constant when investigating the prices of substitutes and complements.

2. The Income of the Consumer (Y)

Economists have observed that the consumption of goods and services is generally positively related to the income, (Y), available to consumers. (You may recall from macroeconomics that the letter I is used to denote investment.) Income and prices form a vital part of the theoretical model that explains consumer behavior.

Other things held equal, rising income usually leads to an increase in the demand for goods; these are called **normal** goods. Some goods, however, experience reduced demand as income rises; these are called **inferior** goods. Suppose most individuals prefer hamburger to beans but low income people usually buy beans because they are less expensive. As incomes rise, many persons may switch from buying beans to buying hamburger. Thus, the demand for beans may actually fall as incomes rise. Also, hamburger may be an inferior good in some countries, for as incomes rise still further, steak or chicken may be substituted for hamburger. Whether goods are normal or inferior, the point here is that income changes will typically shift demand—usually positively (normal goods) and sometimes negatively (inferior goods).

3. Number of People (N)

The demand for a good or service varies with the size of the potential consumer population. The demand for wheat, for example, rises as population increases, because the added population wants to consume some wheat-derived products, such as bread. Marketing experts, who closely follow the patterns of consumer behavior regarding a particular good or service, are usually concerned with the demographics of the product—the vital statistics or the size of the potential consuming population (and also economic and age characteristics). It is the number of people in the potential market such as moviegoers, college students, or the elderly that is targeted by "entrepreneurs." Baby food companies, for example, keep a close eye on birth rates.

4. Shifts in Taste (T)

The demand for a good or service may increase or decrease suddenly with changes in fashions or fads—these nonprice, non-income-related causes of changes in demand are said to be the result of "taste changes." For example, look at the recent popularity in country music. Clubs all over the country—and the world—are featuring country music and dancing to cash in on the increased demand. Taste changes may be triggered by advertising or promotion, by a news story, by the behavior of a popular public figure, and so on. One area in which taste changes are always very important is in apparel.

Tastes, or the intensity of consumers' preference for goods depend upon a wide variety of social, climatic, demographic, and economic factors about which we have little knowledge. In the actual process of decision making, moreover, habit plays an extremely important role, in part because habit buying saves time for the customer. Numerous studies have shown a wide variation in the care exercised in consumer decisions, particularly about consumer durables. Such decisions are also subject to deliberate outside influence in the form of advertising.

Changes in preferences naturally lead to shifts in demand. The power of economic theory, however, stems from the assumption (usually implicit) that tastes are stable, at least over substantial periods of time. If tastes are in fact stable, then only changing opportunities (relative prices and income) will alter an individual's behavior, and we are generally much more interested in changes in behavior than we are in the absolute levels of behavior.

Tastes do change, though. A person may well grow tired of one type of recreation or of peanut butter and try other types. Changes in occupation, number of dependents, state of health, and age tend to alter consumption preferences. The birth of a baby may cause a family to spend less on recreation and more on food and clothing. Illness increases the demand for medicine and lessens purchases of other goods. A cold winter increases the demand for fuel. Changes in customs and traditions also affect preferences; changing styles in clothing, for example, produce significant modifications in demand. In addition, successful advertising campaigns divert purchases from some products to others. Development of new products draws consumer preference away from other goods: Compact discs have replaced record albums, just as the jet airplane quickly eliminated consumers' preferences for "prop planes."

5. *Expectations about Future Prices (E)*

For individuals as well as for the market, the position of a demand curve during the current period is affected by expectations about prices in future periods. This influence is in a sense transitory because consumers will not buy indefinitely in anticipation of future higher prices, nor will they continue to postpone purchases of desired goods if expected price decreases fail to materialize. At any given time, though, expectations may be of substantial importance, and changes in them may produce major shifts in demand. If consumers expect future price increases, they may buy large quantities today in anticipation of the price increases and thus cause substantial increases in current demands. If decreases come to be expected, buyers may reduce current purchases drastically. For example, you might decide to wait to buy a home computer because price reductions on electronic goods now often lead to expectations of further price reductions in the future.

CHANGES IN DEMAND

Because *demand* is defined as a schedule of amounts that would be purchased at various prices, a **change in demand** occurs only if persons will buy larger or smaller quantities at particular prices as a result of a change in one or more of the shift parameters noted in the preceding paragraphs. An increase in demand is illustrated graphically in Figure 3–3. The change in demand is reflected in an entirely new demand curve (D_1 in Figure 3–3).

A change in demand must be distinguished from a **change in quantity demanded** resulting from a price change. The latter is illustrated by a movement along an existing curve. A change in the price of a good is not said to cause a change in the demand for the good, because demand is defined as the entire schedule of the quantities that would be purchased *at various possible prices*. The effects of some of the determinants that cause a change in demand (shifters) are highlighted in Figure 3–4.

FIGURE 3–3
ILLUSTRATION OF AN INCREASE IN DEMAND

When the price of a related good, income, the number of consumers, tastes, or expected future prices change, the demand curve shifts. An increase (decrease) in demand is illustrated by a rightward (leftward) shift in the demand curve. With an increase in demand the quantity demanded increases at every price.

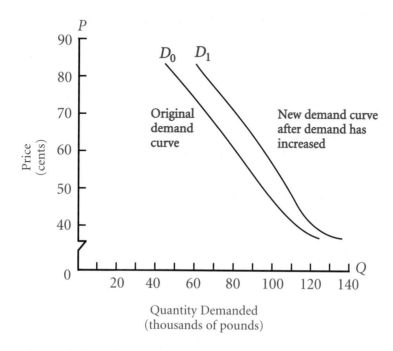

Increase in Demand

Price (cents/pounds)	Quantity Demanded (pounds)	Quantity Demanded after Change (pounds)
80	40,000	55,000
70	60,000	78,000
60	75,000	93,000
50	90,000	105,000
40	120,000	132,000

FIGURE 3–4
POSSIBLE DEMAND SHIFTERS

Recall that *PYNTE* is the acronym for the major shifters of the demand curve With regard to the price of related goods, we have made the standard textbook assumption that the price change has been initiated on the supply side.

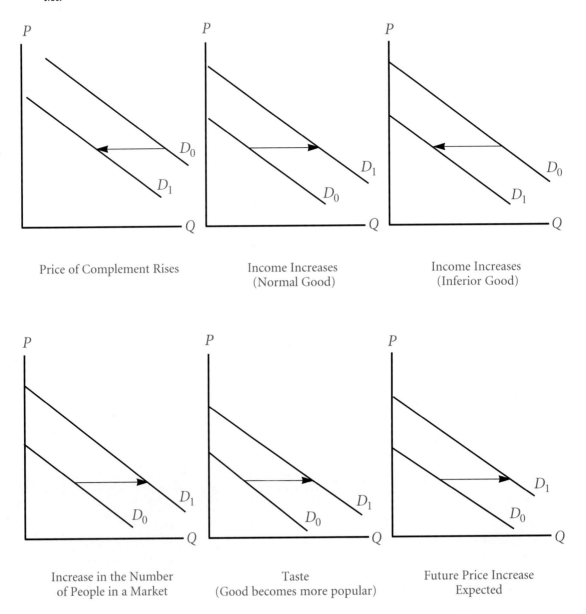

Price of Complement Rises

Income Increases
(Normal Good)

Income Increases
(Inferior Good)

Increase in the Number
of People in a Market

Taste
(Good becomes more popular)

Future Price Increase
Expected

At any time a certain demand schedule exists for each good, in the sense that if current price levels prevail, consumers wish to purchase certain quantities. It is difficult, however, to determine this schedule accurately. For most goods, total sales in particular markets with existing prices can be ascertained; many data are collected by various private and government agencies. The data, however, may not represent equilibrium quantities, in that consumers may not have completed their adjustments to the existing circumstances. Moreover, quantities that would be demanded at other prices can only be estimated with the aid of statistics for sales at various prices in the past.

The greatest care must be used in interpreting these statistics, because the changes in sales from one period to another are the result not only of price changes but also changes in other determinants of demand. Incomes, preferences, prices of other goods, and expectations are constantly changing. It is possible to isolate the effects of these other changes by various statistical techniques, but such techniques are by no means entirely accurate or reliable. It is particularly difficult to determine the effects on sales of changes in tastes that may occur during a period for which data are available. Thus, statistical estimates of demand schedules necessarily involve a substantial margin of error. Such work is nevertheless of great value in providing additional information about demand behavior.

3.5 SUPPLY

As with demand, economists consider several factors in determining supplier willingness to provide goods and services. One factor, again, is the per-unit price of the good. While behavior varies among individual suppliers, the **law of supply** states that other things equal, the *quantity supplied will vary directly with price.* The higher the price of the good, the greater the quantity supplied; the lower the price of the good, the smaller the quantity supplied.

Why do suppliers behave in this fashion? A detailed, rigorous answer will absorb much of our attention later in this book, but a brief response is that firms supplying goods and services have marginal costs that increase as output increases; hence, higher prices are necessary to coax additional output from profit-maximizing firms.

The law of (short-run) supply is illustrated in Figure 3–5. Again, oranges are the product, but now we are considering the amount of oranges that farmers, operating through grocers, are willing to provide to consumers during the week. Note that the supply curve is upward sloping from left to right; movements along this curve are called **changes in the quantity supplied.**

FIGURE 3—5
HYPOTHETICAL SUPPLY CURVE, ORANGES

The market supply curve for oranges depicts the relationship between price and the quantity of oranges offered for sale by all suppliers, *ceteris paribus*. The supply curve is positively sloped because grocers are willing to sell more oranges at higher prices. The dots indicate quantities of oranges that suppliers (grocers, acting as middlepersons) will provide at various prices: the line connecting the dots is a supply curve.

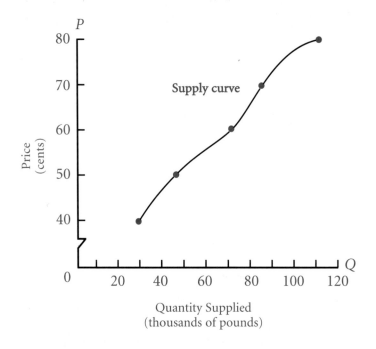

Quantity Supplied
(thousands of pounds)

Market Supply Curve for Oranges
in a particular Market, Week of December 10—16

Price (cents/pound)	Quantity Demanded (pounds)
80	110,000
70	90,000
60	75,000
50	50,000
40	30,000

Changes in supply shift the entire curve. An increase in supply shifts the curve to the right; a decrease shifts it to the left. Shifts in the supply curve occur for reasons unrelated to the price of the good—these include changes in the price of other goods, expectations of future prices, factor prices, technology, or taxes. If production costs rise because of a wage increase, then, other things constant, we would expect a decrease in supply. When this happens, the whole curve shifts to the left.

The market supply curve for a product represents the horizontal summation of the supply curves of individual suppliers, much the same as the market demand curve is the summation of the demand responses of many consumers.[1] In the case of supply, an increase in the number of suppliers leads to an increase in supply, denoted by a right-ward shift in the supply curve, while an exodus of suppliers leads to a decrease in supply, denoted by a leftward shift in the supply curve.

SUPPLY DETERMINANTS—THE SHIFTERS

Changes in the price of a product lead to changes in quantity supplied, just as changes in price lead to changes in quantity demanded. By contrast, a change in supply, whether an increase or a decrease, will occur for reasons unrelated to the price of the product itself, just as changes in demand are related to factors other than the price of the good. What are some of the factors leading to a change in supply (a shift in the entire price/quantity-supplied relationship)? The factors can be easily remembered by using the acronym SPENT.

1. Supplier Input Prices (S)
First, output suppliers' production decisions are influenced by the costs of inputs used in the production process. Other things equal, the supply of a good at any given price will decline if labor costs rise, meaning that the supply curve shifts to the left. Higher labor costs raise the cost of production, reducing the per-unit profit potential at existing output prices. Producers tend to respond by insisting on higher prices.

2. Price of Related Goods (P)
As with substitution effects of demanders, producers will want to produce relatively less of a good if the price of some other good that it could produce rises. If cotton prices rise sharply, less alfalfa or barley will be grown as farmers substitute the now more prof-itable production of cotton.

3. Expectations (E)
A third factor shifting supply is the expectations of suppliers. If producers expect prices to rise next year, they will supply less now; if they expect prices to fall next year, they will

---

[1]We will see in the next chapter that horizontal summation of "flow" curves is not generally true when inventories are included in the analysis.

supply more now. Suppose you have 100,000 barrels of oil sitting in your backyard. Will you sell them now if you expect a war in the Middle East to drive up oil prices next year? Indeed, such behavior tends to stabilize prices over time; that is, speculators perform a useful service.

4. *Number of Suppliers (N)*

The more firms that can supply the commodity, the greater the market supply at any given price. For example, an increase in the number of firms producing personal computers will increase the supply of personal computers, *ceteris paribus*.

5. *The Two T's: Technology and Taxes (T)*

Costs often decrease because of technological progress. Human creativity works to find new ways to produce goods and services using fewer inputs or less labor, natural resources or capital. We have all seen the relative and absolute prices of videocassette recorders, hand calculators, cellular telephones, and digital watches fall dramatically. These products represent technological breakthroughs that cause a supply increase, or a rightward shift in the supply curve.

Taxes, too, are a production cost to the firm. Taxes influence supply, and a tax increase on a good supplied will usually have the same impact on supply as an increase in labor or raw material costs. Increased taxes tend to reduce supply, and reduced taxes or subsidies tend to increase it. Thus, if governments want to alter the availability of a good or service as a matter of social policy, they can do so by changing the taxes on the good or service as well as using other means, such as outright prohibition of production of the good or subsidies to encourage production by lowering costs to the firm. Supply may also change because of changes in the legal and regulatory environment in which firms operate. Government regulations can influence the costs of production, leading to cost-induced supply changes analogous to supplier input price changes. For example, if new safety or antipollution requirements increase labor and capital costs, the increased cost will result, other things equal, in a decrease in supply. An increase in a government-imposed minimum wage may have a similar effect.

In addition, weather certainly plays a role in affecting the supply of certain commodities such as agricultural products. A drought or freezing temperatures will almost certainly cause the supply curves for many crops to shift to the left.

Figure 3–6 illustrates the effect of some of the determinants that cause a shift in the supply curve.

FIGURE 3—6
POSSIBLE SUPPLY SHIFTERS

Recall that SPENT (the acronym for supply shifters) and factors such as weather are the major supply curve shifters.

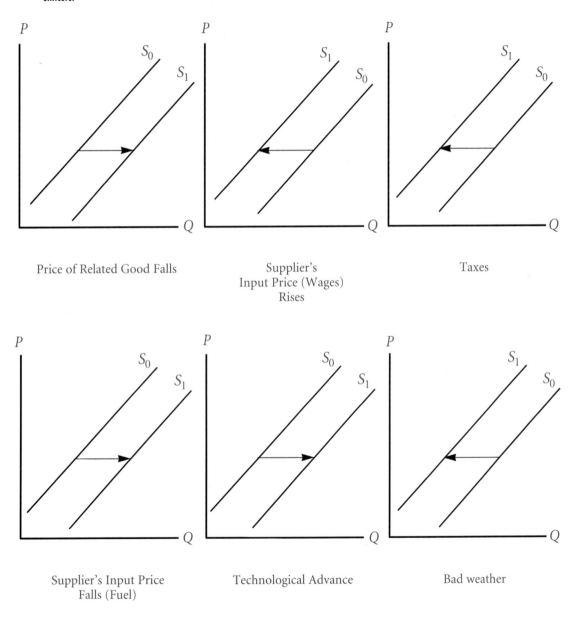

Price of Related Good Falls

Supplier's
Input Price (Wages)
Rises

Taxes

Supplier's Input Price
Falls (Fuel)

Technological Advance

Bad weather

3.6 EQUILIBRIUM PRICE AND QUANTITY

Enough has been said for now about demand and supply separately. How do they operate together to answer the first fundamental question of economics—namely, what do we produce and in what quantities?

The market solution to this basic question is classic in its simplicity: *Output tends to be at that price where quantity demanded equals the quantity supplied.* This level of output is called **the equilibrium quantity**, and the price associated with it is called **the equilibrium price**, because neither tends to change until something else—the price of related goods, income, expectations of future relative prices, tastes, technology, or factor prices—changes and leads to a new equilibrium. As long as these other factors remain unchanged, however, price and quantity tend to remain at their original equilibrium levels. (See, however, the stock/flow approach discussed in the next chapter for a more precise understanding of equilibrium conditions.)

The equilibrium market solution is easily depicted. Consider again the orange example. Figure 3–7 combines the demand curve for oranges (Figure 3–2) with the supply curve (Figure 3–5). At a price of 60 cents per pound, the community is willing to buy 75,000 pounds of oranges per week; local grocers are willing to supply 75,000 pounds at this price. The planned action of the demanders and the suppliers are "mutually compatible." At any other price, such is not the case. At 70 cents a pound, the quantity is 60,000 but the quantity supplied is 90,000. At that price a *surplus* exists—grocers are supplying more than they can sell and are accumulating the unsold oranges. To ease the predicament, grocers will cut their price to get rid of the unsold surplus. What if the grocers cut the price to 50 cents a pound? Not only will they get rid of any previously accumulated surplus, but they will also find the weekly quantity demanded of 90,000 pounds greater than the 50,000 pounds that they are willing to supply at this low price. So at 50 cents a pound a *shortage* exists. Only at 60 cents a pound does neither a shortage nor a surplus exist. Thus, this is the equilibrium price, one that will remain until the demand and/or supply curve is shifted by some factor other than the price of oranges. The grocers will, by trial and error, manipulate the price at which they sell oranges until they discover that at 60 cents per pound they can sell their product without unintended surpluses or shortages. (See Problem 3–2.)

Market equilibrium requires that quantity demanded equals quantity supplied. This occurs at the intersection of the demand and supply curves. In this example, equilibrium price is 60 cents and equilibrium quantity is 75,000 pounds. A price higher than 60 cents creates a surplus, and price will be driven down to reduce the surplus. Similarly, a price less than 60 cents will result in a shortage, and buyers will offer higher prices to eliminate the shortage.

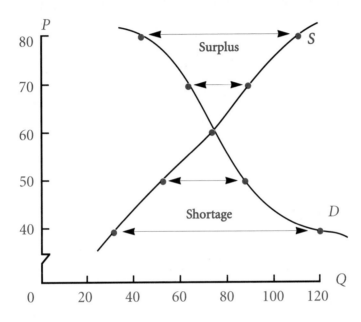

Market Demand and Supply Schedule for Oranges in a Particular Market (December 10—16)

Price (cents)	Quantity Demanded	Quantity Supplied
80	40,000	110,000
70	60,000	90,000
60	75,000	75,000
50	90,000	50,000
40	120,000	30,000

3–2 True or False? If effective price controls are imposed by the government at levels that are either above or below the equilibrium price, the quantity of goods bought (and sold) will be less than the equilibrium quantity.

True. If there is a price ceiling (that is, a legally established maximum price) set below the equilibrium price, quantity demanded will be greater than quantity supplied—there will be a shortage at that price. Because producers will only increase the quantity supplied at higher prices, *ceteris paribus*, only Q_1 will be bought and sold. Alternatively, if there is a price floor (that is, a legally established minimum price) set above the equilibrium price, quantity supplied will be greater than quantity demanded—there will be a surplus at that price. Because consumers will only increase their quantity demanded, *ceteris paribus*, at lower prices, only Q_1 will be bought and sold.

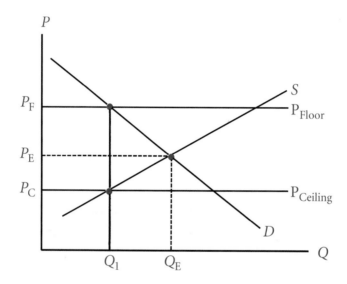

3.7 CHANGES IN EQUILIBRIUM PRICE AND QUANTITY

In reality prices and quantities do change fairly frequently. Why? *Because factors other than the price of the good itself are often altered,* leading to a change in demand (a shift in the demand curve) and/or a change in supply (shift in the supply curve).

Suppose incomes rise, and people, now more affluent, increase their demand for oranges. This means that at any given price, the quantity of oranges demanded will be greater than before. Thus, the demand curve shifts to the right (Figure 3–8). What is the impact of these shifts on equilibrium price and quantity? As indicated in the figure, both price and quantity increase. Let D_0 represent the original demand curve and D_1 the demand curve prevailing after the increase in income. The supply curve remains unchanged, for a rise in general income levels does not directly influence the grocer's ability or desire to supply more oranges. The new equilibrium price and quantity are higher; people are buying more oranges and paying more for them because of the increase in their demand. We can say that there has been "an increase in quantity supplied," as there has been a movement along a supply curve (as opposed to a shift in the curve) because of the shift in demand. We do *not* say that there has been an "increase in supply," because we reserve that expression for *shifts* in the supply curve.

In general, equilibrium quantities increase over time (except for inferior goods), while equilibrium *real* prices may be rising or falling. It is in fact common for both equilibrium price and equilibrium quantity to increase over time. This is not a refutation of the law of demand (which states that when prices rise, quantity demanded falls), because nonprice factors such as income and technology have worked to increase both demand and supply above earlier levels. In short, many factors have worked to shift both the demand curve and the supply curve to the right over time.

FIGURE 3–8
AN INCREASE IN DEMAND FOR ORANGES

At any given price, the amount of oranges that consumers want to purchase is greater than before; therefore, a change in one of the determinants (for example, income or number of consumers) has increased consumer demand. The demand curve shifts to the right (from D_0 to D_1) and increases the equilibrium price and quantity.

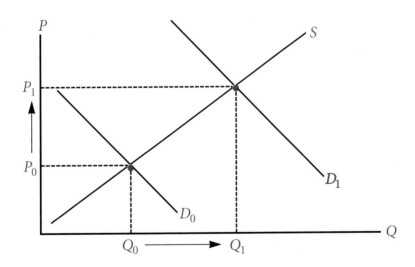

Similarly, shifts in supply curves reflecting changes in supply influence both price and quantity even if consumers have not changed in their basic willingness to buy the product at any given price. Take the calculator example. The sharp decrease in equilibrium price and large increase in equilibrium quantity during the late 1970s reflected primarily an increase in supply, as illustrated in Figure 3–9. If supply were to decrease, perhaps because of an expensive labor settlement, the reverse would hold: Equilibrium price would increase, but equilibrium quantity would fall. Again, we can say "quantity demanded has increased" and "supply has increased" in the case of Figure 3–9, but we *cannot* say "demand has increased" because that expression is reserved for shifts in the demand curve reflecting changes in demand factors unrelated to the price of the good. (Problems 3–3, 3–4, and 3–5 provide concrete examples of the effects of these shifts.)

FIGURE 3–9
IMPACT OF INCREASED SUPPLY

When the quantity supplied increases for every possible price, supply increases because of a change in a supply curve shifter such as technology or falling input prices. The rightward shift in supply reduces the equilibrium price but raises equilibrium quantity.

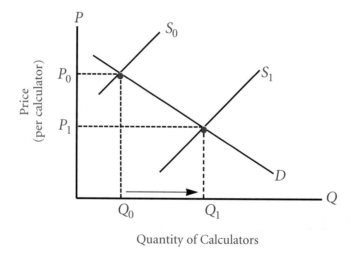

Quantity of Calculators

3–3 In ski resorts such as Sun Valley and Aspen, hotel prices are higher in March (in season) than in May (off season). Why is this the case? If the May hotel prices were changed in February, what problem would arise?

In the (likely) event that supply is not altered significantly, demand is chiefly responsible for the higher prices in the prime skiing months. If prices were maintained at the off-season rates all year long, excess demand would exist. It is this excess demand at the off-peak prices that causes prime-season rates to be higher.

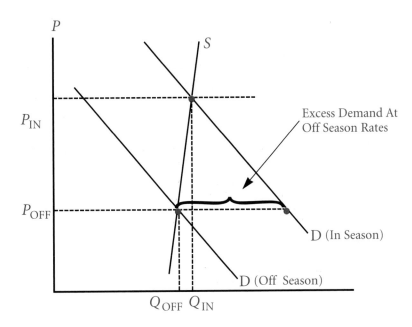

3—4 Why are strawberries more expensive in winter than in summer?

Assuming that consumers' tastes and income are fairly constant throughout the year, the answer lies on the supply side of the market. The supply of strawberries is lower when strawberries are out of season and more abundant when in season. Again, if prices do not adjust, we will be out of equilibrium. In this case there will be excess supply if prices are not lowered when strawberries come into season, and it is this excess supply that drives the price down.

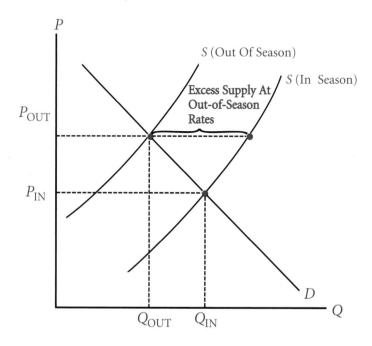

3–5 With improvements in telecommunications technology (for example, "hair-thin" fiber-optic cable), we have witnessed lower costs of production and lower prices for long-distance phone calls, *ceteris paribus*. Graph this phenomenon. What happened to the equilibrium price and quantity? What happens if there is a simultaneous increase in demand because of a rise in income?

With an increase in supply, the price of phone calls falls and the quantity demanded (and exchanged, in equilibrium) rises. If there is a simultaneous increase in demand, equilibrium quantity rises, but the impact on equilibrium price now becomes indeterminate—that is, we need to know the magnitude of the increase in demand to determine whether the price will rise or fall.

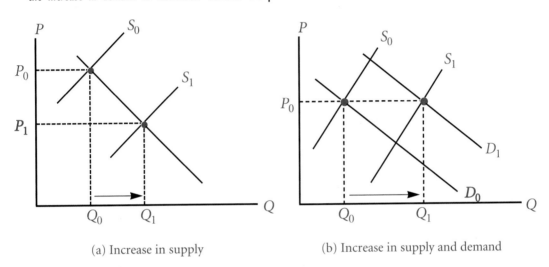

(a) Increase in supply   (b) Increase in supply and demand

The implications of equilibrium output for efficiency are critical. You may recall from your principles course that the demand curve represents a collection of maximum amounts that consumers are willing and able to pay while the supply curve represents a collection of minimum amounts that suppliers need to receive for various output levels (see Figure 3–10). For example, suppose a consumer is willing to pay $7 for the first unit, and a producer must receive at least $1 to induce the production of that unit. It is clear that there is a joint gain from producing that unit. This is also true for each unit of output less then the equilibrium output. Once the equilibrium output is reached, all the jointly beneficial opportunities for exchange between suppliers and demanders will have taken place. (See Problem 3–6.)

FIGURE 3–10
MUTUAL ADVANTAGEOUS EXCHANGE

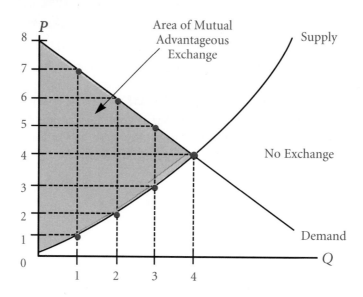

3–6 Show that a per-unit tax results in the same equilibrium level of output and net price received by sellers, whether the tax is levied on buyers or on sellers.

In the figure below, D_0 and S_0 are demand and supply curves without taxes. Q_0 and P_0 are the corresponding equilibrium quantity and price. D_1 is the demand curve when the tax is levied on consumers. For each unit of output, buyers are willing to pay the price they were paying before, minus the tax. The equilibrium quantity and the price received by the seller in this case are Q_1 and P_1. If the tax is levied on producers, the supply curve shifts to the left, to S_1. For every level of output, sellers require a price that exceeds the original price by the amount of the tax. In this case, the equilibrium quantity is also Q_1, equilibrium price is P_2, and the price received by sellers is P_1.

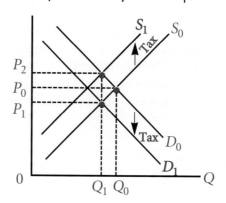

3.8 ELASTICITY OF DEMAND

The concept of elasticity characterizes the *relative* responsiveness of a given variable to a change in the value of another variable to which it is functionally related. By using relative changes (or percentages), the units of measurement (say, ounces versus pounds or quarts versus gallons) does not affect the numerical value of elasticity. With the demand curve relating the quantity demanded to its price, for example, elasticity refers to the relative percentage response of quantity demanded to a given percentage change in price. If one is relating demand to income, while price is treated as a given, elasticity refers to the percentage response of the quantity demanded at a given price to a percentage change in income. With a function relating the demand for one good to the price of another good, elasticity refers to the relative percentage change in the quantity demanded of one good at a given price to the percentage change in the price of another good. The terms *price elasticity of demand, income elasticity of demand,* and *cross-price elasticity of demand* are given to these three concepts, respectively. *Price elasticity of supply* will also be defined. Each will be considered in turn.

PRICE ELASTICITY OF DEMAND

A reduction in price (*ceteris paribus*) will result in an increase in the quantity demanded. **Price elasticity of demand** measures the magnitude of the proportional change in quantity demanded that results from a given proportional change in price. More specifically, price elasticity may be defined as the ratio of the percentage change in quantity demanded and the *percentage change* in price; thus, the numerical coefficient of elasticity is obtained by dividing the percentage change in quantity demanded ($\Delta Q_D / Q_D$) by the percentage change in price ($\Delta P / P$):

$$e_p = \frac{Q_0 - Q_1}{Q_0} \div \frac{P_0 - P_1}{P_0} \quad \text{or} \quad \frac{\Delta Q_D}{Q_D} \div \frac{\Delta P}{P} \quad \text{or} \quad \frac{\Delta Q_D}{\Delta P} \cdot \frac{P}{Q_D}$$

where Q_0 and P_0 represent the initial quantity and price, and Q_1 and P_1 represent values of the same variables after the change. It is conventional to omit the negative sign, which indicates the inverse relationship between price and quantity demanded.

When the changes in price and quantity are of significant magnitude, the exact meaning of the term *percentage change* requires clarification, and the terms *price* and *quantity* must be defined more precisely. The issue is this: Should the percentage change be figured on the basis of price and quantity before or after the change has occurred? For example, a price rise from $10 to $15 constitutes a 50 percent change if the original price ($10) is used in figuring the percentage, or a 33 1/3 percent change is the price after the change ($15) if used. For *small* changes this distinction is of little consequence, but for large changes it is not. The most common way of resolving this problem is to use the midpoints between the old and new figures for both price and quantity demanded. In this **arc elasticity of demand** formula the sums of the prices ($10 plus $15 in the example) and of the quantities before and after the change, respectively, may be used instead of the averages of these, because the result will be exactly the same. (A fraction is not altered by dividing both the numerator and the denominator by 2.) The formula thus becomes:

$$e_p = \frac{Q_0 - Q_1}{Q_0 + Q_1} \div \frac{P_0 - P_1}{P_0 \cdot P_1}$$

The elasticity of demand depends on the degree of substitutability between the good in question and other goods, the proportion of income spent on the good, and the amount of time that has elapsed since the initial price change. The closer or more numerous the substitutes the greater the numerical value of elasticity. For example, the elasticity of demand for a particular model of car will be more elastic than the demand for cars, because there are more and better substitutes for a particular model than for cars in general. The smaller the proportion of income spent on the good, the lower the elasticity. For example, a 50-percent increase in the price of salt will have a much smaller impact on consumers' behavior than, say, a 50-percent increase in the price of a new laptop computer. Finally, the more time that has elapsed since the initial price change, the greater the elasticity of demand. The primary reason is that it allows consumers more time to find suitable alternatives or to change consumption pattern (See Figure 3-11).

The elasticity of demand for a good also has implications for the total expenditures on a good as its price changes. To find total expenditures, we merely multiply the price of the good by the quantity demanded by that price. It is important to note that total revenue for producers is equal to total expenditures for consumers. When the demand is elastic (has a value greater than 1), total expenditures will rise as the price declines because the percent increase in the quantity demanded is greater than the percent reduction in price. If a price is cut in half and the quantity demanded more than doubles, total expenditures will rise. Alternatively, if demand is inelastic (less than 1), the total expenditures will be less at low prices than at high because a given price reduction will be accompanied by a proportionately smaller increase in quantity demanded. If the elasticity is 1, the relative changes in price and quantity are the same, and total expenditures will be the same, regardless of the price.

Demand schedules[2] can be separated into three classes based upon the numerical values of the price elasticity of demand; Numerical values of elasticity range from: 0 to ∞.

1. Elastic demand segments—those segment(s) with elasticity numerically greater than one (e > 1). In this case the price change is accompanied by a more-than-proportionate change in quantity demanded, and total expenditure is greater at lower prices than at

---

[2]An entire demand schedule would be rarely have the same elasticity throughout. (A rectangular hyperbola for example would have an elasticity of 1 throughout the range of the curve.) Remember that elasticity measures refer to particular points or regions on demand schedules, not the entire curve.

higher ones. In the limiting case of perfect elasticity, an increase in price causes the quantity demanded to fall to zero; at a certain price and at any lower figure the quantity demanded is infinite.[3] In Table 3–1 a typical elastic demand is illustrated, as well as a perfectly elastic schedule.

2. Inelastic demand segments—those segments(s) with elasticity less than one (e < 1). In this case the price change is accompanied by a less than proportionate change in quantity demanded, and total expenditure is greater at higher prices. The limiting case is a perfectly inelastic demand; the quantity demanded is the same, regardless of the price. A typical inelastic schedule and one of perfect inelasticity are illustrated in Table 3–2.

3. Demand segments of unitary elasticity—those with a numerical expression of elasticity of 1 (e = 1). In this case, lying between the previous two, the percentage change in quantity demanded is the same as the percentage change in price. For example, if price is cut in half, the quantity demanded doubles, and total expenditure is the same regardless of the price. The demand curve is a rectangular hyperbola in this case. (Graph the data in Table 3–3 to see what such a demand curve looks like.) It is unlikely that a demand schedule would possess exactly unitary elasticity over a substantial range; the case merely constitutes the dividing line between elastic and inelastic segments. Figure 3–12(c) shows a demand of unitary elasticity.

At any given price/quantity point on a graph of a demand curve, an inelastic demand appears as a steeper curve than an elastic demand. A perfectly inelastic demand appears as a vertical line, and a perfectly elastic demand as a horizontal line. A demand of unitary elasticity appears as a rectangular hyperbola. These are illustrated in Figure 3–12. Great care, however, must be taken in estimating elasticity from the slope of the curve, beyond the extreme limiting cases; when segments of curves appear on different portions of the graph, the relative slope tells little about elasticity. A straight-line demand curve with a constant slope changes elasticity continuously along its course, because the denominators of the fractions in the formula are continuously changing while the numerators remain unchanged. The top half of a linear demand schedule is elastic. The midpoint is unitary elastic and the bottom half is inelastic, regardless of the slope. For example in Figure 3–12, if you complete the demand where it intersects the price axis, it becomes clear that this graph represents the lower portion of the demand curve—the inelastic region. (See Problem 3–8.)

---

[3]Strictly speaking, the quantity demanded is not defined but is said to be infinite. Individual and total demand schedules cannot be perfectly elastic throughout their range; the fact that incomes are limited prevents persons from buying infinite amounts of any positively priced goods. The market demand schedules confronting individual sellers, however, may appear to be approximately horizontal, and thus, perfectly elastic from the standpoint of the sellers themselves.

TABLE 3—1
ELASTIC DEMAND

| Price ($) | Typical Elastic Demand | | Perfectly Elastic Demand | |
	Quantity Demanded	Total Expenditure	Quantity Demanded	Total Expenditure
$5	8	$40	0	0
4	12	$48	0	0
3	20	$60	0	0
2	35	$70	Infinite	Infinite
1	80	$80	Infinite	Infinite

TABLE 3—2
INELASTIC DEMAND

| Price ($) | Typical Inelastic Demand | | Perfectly Inelastic Demand | |
	Quantity Demanded	Total Expenditure	Quantity Demanded	Total Expenditure
$5	8	$40	8	$40
4	9	36	8	32
3	11	33	8	24
2	14	28	8	16
1	19	19	8	8

TABLE 3—3
DEMAND OF UNITARY ELASTICITY

Price ($)	Quantity Demanded	Total Expenditure
$5	8	40
4	10	40
3	13 1/3	40
2	20	40
1	40	40

FIGURE 3–11
DEMAND ELASTICITIES: SHORT RUN VERSUS LONG RUN

The more time that elapses since the initial price change, the greater the elasticity. Hence the short run demand curve is less elastic than the long run demand curve.

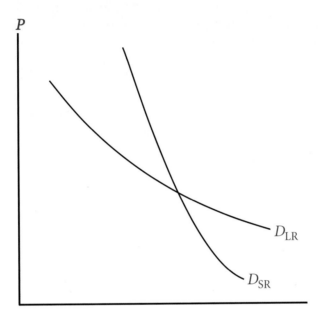

3–8 True or False? A poor harvest is always bad for farmers.

False. Without a simultaneous reduction in demand, a reduction in supply because of weather will mean higher prices. If demand for the product is inelastic over the pertinent portion of the demand curve, the farmers' total revenue will rise (by the area A minus C in the figure below). Clearly, if some farmers lose their entire crop, they are worse off; but *collectively*, farmers can profit from events that reduce crop size—and usually do because most agricultural demands are inelastic. (Remember: what is total revenue for producers is total outlay, or expenditures, for consumers.)

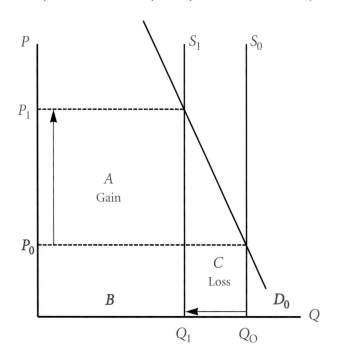

Because of shifts in supply and demand curves, researchers have a difficult task when trying to estimate empirically the price elasticity of demand for a particular commodity. Despite this difficulty, Table 3–4 presents some estimates for the price elasticity of demand for certain goods. As one you would expect, certain low-priced goods such as salt, matches, and toothpicks are very inelastic. Because these items compose an insignificant portion of most people's total expenditures, the quantity demanded is relatively insensitive to changes in price in the relevant region. On the other hand, air travel is one that is much more sensitive to price (elastic) because the available substitutes are much more plentiful. Table 3–4 shows that the price elasticity of demand for air travel as roughly 2.5; that means that a 1 percent increase in price will lead to a slightly less than 2.5 percent reduction in quantity demanded.

TABLE 3-4
PRICE ELASTICITIES OF DEMAND FOR SELECTED GOODS

Good	Short Run	Long Run
Salt	—	0.1
Air travel	0.1	2.4
Theater, opera	0.2	0.3
Gasoline	0.2	0.5
Medical care and hospitalization	0.3	0.9
Jewelry and watches	0.4	0.7
Physician services	0.6	—
Alcohol	0.9	3.6
Movies	0.9	3.7
China, glassware	1.5	2.6
Automobiles	—	1.5
Chevrolets	—	4.0

Source: H. S. Houthakker and Lester D. Taylor, *Consumer Demand in the United States: Analysis and Projections*, 2nd ed. (Cambridge, Mass.: Harvard University Press, 1970).

FIGURE 3–12
VARIOUS DEMAND ELASTICITIES

The price elasticity of demand measures the responsiveness of quantity demanded to a change in price. Part (a) shows that a minute change in price evokes an infinite response in quantity demanded: hence, demand is perfectly elastic. A fair response to price changes is exhibited by the relatively elastic demand curve in part (b), whereas rigid responses are captured by the relatively inelastic demand curve in part (d) and the perfectly inelastic demand curve in part (e). The case of constant, unitary elasticity is reflected in the demand curve in part (c).

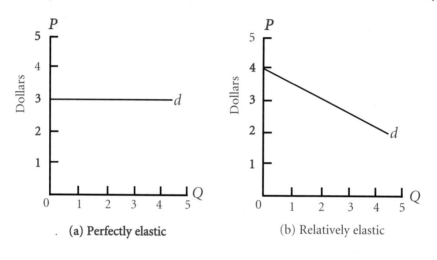

(a) Perfectly elastic   (b) Relatively elastic

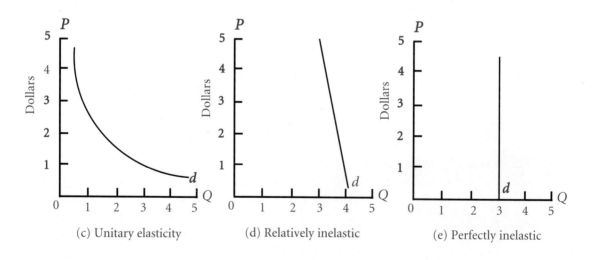

(c) Unitary elasticity   (d) Relatively inelastic   (e) Perfectly inelastic

INCOME ELASTICITY OF DEMAND

While the most widely employed demand relationship is that relating price and quantity demanded, the relationship between income changes and demand is also useful. Specifically, **income elasticity of demand** is a measure of the relationship between a relative change in income and the consequent relative change in demand, *ceteris paribus*. Expressed symbolically, the income elasticity of demand is given by the formula:

$$e_y = \frac{\dfrac{Q_0 - Q_1}{Q_0 - Q_1}}{\dfrac{Y_0 - Y_1}{Y_0 + Y_1}} = \frac{\dfrac{\Delta Q}{\overline{Q}}}{\dfrac{\Delta Y}{\overline{Y}}} = \frac{\Delta Q}{\Delta Y} \cdot \frac{\overline{Y}}{\overline{Q}}$$

Here the percentage change in quantity purchased at a given price is divided by the percentage change in income. This relationship could be positive or negative. For most goods, one would expect an increase in income to result in an increase in purchases, but the magnitude of the income elasticity may vary substantially. For example, if income were to rise by 10 percent and consumers increased purchases of good X by 15 percent, then the income elasticity, .15/.10, would be positive 1.5. In contrast to normal goods, the relationship for inferior goods is negative; as incomes rise, consumers will buy fewer units of these goods. A good such as hamburger may, of course, be a normal good over some range (switching, for example, from beans to hamburger as income rises) but inferior over some other range (e.g., switching from hamburger to steak or lobster at still higher incomes).

CROSS-ELASTICITY OF DEMAND

Another useful elasticity of demand measure relates the price of one commodity to the quantity demanded of another; the concept of **cross-elasticity of demand** describes the behavior of this functional relationship. As the price of coffee rises, what is the effect on the demand for tea at a given price of tea? Let's say the price of coffee (P_C) rises by 10 percent, and as a consequence, the quantity of tea (Q_T) purchased rises 20 percent. If this were the case, we would know that coffee and tea are substitutes because $e_{T,C}(\Delta Q_T/\Delta P_C \cdot P_C/Q_T)$ is positive, or more precisely, .20/.10 = +2. As long as the sign on the cross-price elasticity coefficient is positive, the goods are substitutes. If the coefficient is negative, then the two goods are complements (like hot dogs and hot-dog buns are to most individuals).

As before, *cross-elasticity of demand* may be defined as the relationship between a certain percentage change in the price of one commodity, P_Y, and the consequent percentage change in the demand for another good Q_X:

$$e_{X,Y} = \frac{\Delta Q_X/Q_X}{\Delta P_Y/P_Y} = \frac{\Delta Q_X}{\Delta P_Y} \cdot \frac{P_Y}{Q_X}$$

PRICE ELASTICITY OF SUPPLY

An increase in price, *ceteris paribus*, will typically result in an increase in quantity supplied. The **price elasticity of supply** measures the responsiveness of a change in price and the corresponding change in the quantity supplied. However, unlike the price elasticity of demand, which has a negative sign on the coefficient, the elasticity of supply will have a positive coefficient. This merely indicates that there is a positive relationship between price and the quantity supplied—that is, the supply curve is upward sloping. The larger the positive coefficient, the more responsive the quantity supplied is to a given price change. For example, a supply price elasticity of 5 would imply that a 1 percent increase in the price would induce a 5 percent increase in quantity supplied. The formula for the elasticity of supply is:

$$\frac{(\Delta Q_S/Q_S)}{(\Delta P/P)} = \frac{\Delta Q_S}{\Delta P} \cdot \frac{P}{Q_S}$$

The same problem that existed for the price elasticity of demand is also present with supply elasticities; that is, when changes in price and quantity are of significant magnitudes, the terms *price* and *quantity* need to be more clearly specified. The common approach to this problem is to use midpoints as we did in our earlier discussion of price elasticity of demand.

Time is usually critical in supply elasticities, because it is more costly for producers to bring forth and release resources in a shorter period of time. Hence, supply tends to be more elastic in the short-run than in the long-run— See Figure 3–13. (See Problem 3–9.)

FIGURE 3–13
SUPPLY ELASTICITIES: SHORT RUN VERSUS LONG RUN

Supply is less elastic in the short run than the long run because it is generally more costly for producers to bring forth and release resources in a shorter period of time.

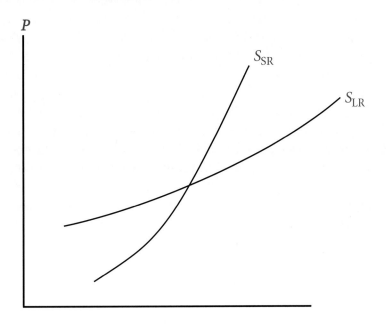

3–9 True or False? Consumers will pay a larger share of a tax if demand is less elastic than supply and a smaller share of the tax if demand is more elastic than supply, *ceteris paribus*.

True. It is the *relative* elasticity of supply and demand that is responsible for the distribution of the tax burden. If demand has a lower elasticity than supply in the relevant tax region, the largest portion of the tax is paid by the consumer. However, if demand is more elastic than supply in the relevant tax region, the largest portion of the tax is paid by the producer.

In the figures below we see that when a 40 cent tax is imposed, the supply curve shifts vertically by the amount of the tax. In the case where demand is less elastic than supply in the relevant region, almost the whole tax is passed on to the consumer, *ceteris paribus*. For example, in Figure (a) the consumer pays $1.30 per unit, 30 cents more than the consumer paid before the tax increase, and the producer receives 90 cents per unit which is 10 cents less than the producer received before the tax. In Figure (b) the demand is more elastic than the supply in the relevant region. Here we see that a greater burden of the same tax of 40 cents falls on the producer, *ceteris paribus*. That is, the producer is now responsible for 30 cents of the tax (75 percent of the burden) while the consumer only pays 10 cents.

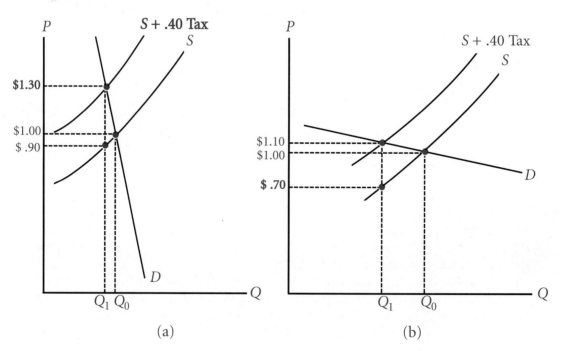

(a)   (b)

CONSUMER SURPLUS

Whenever prices and/or quantities change consumer welfare changes. Economists have developed a concept called **consumer surplus** which can be employed to measure these changes. Consumer surplus is useful in benefit/cost studies or in measuring welfare losses resulting from monopoly or other market imperfections.

The height of the demand curve at any quantity level can be interpreted as measuring the consumer's marginal willingness to pay for that increment in quantity. The greater the height of any particular demand curve, the greater the consumer's willingness to pay for a marginal unit of that good. It follows that the area under the demand curve up to some quantity level measures the total willingness to pay for all units up to that level, as seen in Figure 3–14.

However, what a consumer is required to pay for each unit of a good is usually less than what the consumer is willing to pay. For example, say the price of a box of disposable contact lenses is $40. If the consumer did not place value of at least $40 on those lenses, the contacts would not be purchased. On the other hand, if someone was willing to pay $200 for the contacts but was only required to pay the market price of $40, then he or she would receive a surplus of $160. This monetary difference between what the consumer is willing to pay and what the consumer is required to pay is called consumer surplus. This is depicted graphically in Figure 3–15 as the area under the demand curve and above the market price (area A). Areas A and B together represent total willingness to pay for quantity Q_0, while area B is the amount the consumer is required to pay for quantity Q_0 rather than go without. The difference is consumer surplus area A. (See Problem 3–10.)

Suppose, for example, the price of good X is $10, but the consumer is willing to pay $15 for the first unit, $12 for the second unit, and $9 for the third unit. How much consumer surplus will this individual receive? First, it is important to note the general fact that if the consumer is a buyer of several units of a good, the earlier units will have greater consumer surplus because the marginal willingness to pay declines as greater quantities are consumed in any period. This is demonstrated by the consumer's willingness to pay $15 and $12 respectively for the first two units. Thus, the consumer will receive $5 of consumer surplus for the first unit and $2 of consumer surplus for the second unit. The third unit would not be rationally purchased because the required price is greater than the consumer's willingness to pay.

To measure consumer surplus geometrically (in the simple case of linear demand) we just need to measure the area of a triangle (base times height). In Figure 3–16 we find that this is simply $10(\$60-\$40)/2 = \$100$ of consumer surplus, for a situation in which 10 units of some good are purchased at a price of $40 per unit with the given demand relation. (See Problem 3–11.)

FIGURE 3—14
DEMAND AND TOTAL WILLINGNESS TO PAY

An individual's demand curve shows the maximum amount the consumer is willing to pay for each unit of a commodity. The area under the demand curve represents the total willingness to pay for all units of the good and measures the dollar value of the benefits received by the consumer from the good.

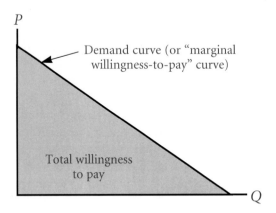

FIGURE 3—15
CONSUMER SURPLUS

A buyer receives consumer surplus when consumption benefits exceed expenditures on a commodity. The buyer is willing to spend the amount represented by the area A plus B for Q_0 units of the product. At the price P_0, however, the buyer pays only B amount and earns a consumer surplus equivalent to area A.

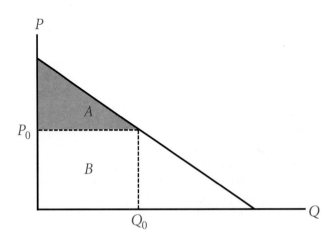

FIGURE 3–16
A CONSUMER SURPLUS CALCULATION

The dollar value of the consumer surplus (the shaded area) can be calculated by using the formula for the area of a right triangle, (base x height)/2. In this example, the base is 10 units, the height is $20, and therefore, the consumer surplus equals $100.

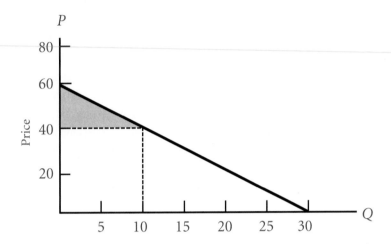

3–10 According to Adam Smith in 1776: "Nothing is more useful than water: but it will purchase scarce anything. . . . A diamond, on the contrary, has scarce any value in use; but a very great quantity of other goods may frequently be had in exchange for it." Use the concept of consumer surplus to evaluate the social value of water versus diamonds.

The classic water–diamond paradox demonstrates the inconsistency between market value and use value. Market value depends on supply and demand. Thus, the limited supply of diamonds generates a high per unit price (that is, *market* value) while an abundant supply of water results in a low per-unit price. The benefits to society of diamonds and water, however, are better represented by consumer surplus. The figure below shows that the consumer surplus for water (the shaded region in part b) far surpasses the consumer surplus for diamonds (the shaded region in part a). In other words, the value-in-use of water (consumers' total willingness to pay) is very large in comparison with what consumers have to pay. This is not the case with diamonds, where the amount of consumer surplus is very small.

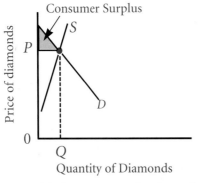

(a) Consumer surplus from diamonds

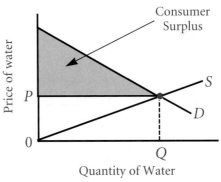

(b) Consumer surplus from water

3–11 Show how a technological advance affects equilibrium price, equilibrium quantity, and consumer surplus.

The figure below shows that technological change, that reduces per-unit production costs, *ceteris paribus*, will lower the price, increase the equilibrium quantity, and add area $P_0 BCP_1$ to consumer surplus.

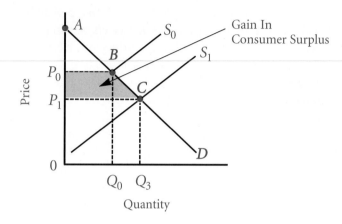

SUMMARY

1. Prices and outputs are affected by the structure of markets.

2. Market behavior depends on available information on market conditions.

3. Markets comprise buyers, sellers, and intermediaries that interact under a set of enforceable rules or customs.

4. Lack of knowledge and immobility of factors lead to imperfections in the perfectly competitive model.

5. Imperfect knowledge is pervasive and factors of production often do not move freely between production activities.

6. The important price to consider in microeconomics is the relative price—the exchange rate of one good in units of another good.

7. The law of demand states that there is an inverse or negative relationship between price and quantity demanded.

8. The law of supply states that there is a positive or direct relationship between price and quantity supplied.

9. Equilibrium price and quantity occur at the point of intersection of the supply and demand curves.

10. Shifts in supply and demand curves are caused by changes in something other than own-price—PYNTE and SPENT are acronyms for important curve shifters.

11. Price-elasticity of demand measures the ratio of the percentage that quantity demanded changes as a result of a given percentage change in price and is independent of the units chosen to measure either quantities or prices

12. There are three identifiable elasticity segments on a straight-line demand curve: elastic (e > 1), unit elastic (e = 1), and inelastic (e < 1).

13. Income elasticities proportionately relate demand to income while cross-price elasticities show the percentage change in the demand for one commodity resulting from a given percentage change in the price of another commodity.

14. The price elasticity of supply measures the responsiveness of a change in price and the corresponding change in quantity supplied.

15. Consumer surplus is the difference between what a consumer is willing to pay for an amount of some good and what a consumer is required to pay for that amount of the good.

WORDS AND CONCEPTS FOR REVIEW

markets	imperfections
perfectly competitive	mobility of factors
absolute and relative prices	demand
substitute goods	complementary goods
normal goods	inferior goods
quantity demanded	supply
quantity supplied	equilibrium price and quantity
surpluses and shortages	price ceiling
price floor	demand shifters

supply shifters

price elasticity of demand

arc elasticity of demand

income elasticity of demand

cross-price elasticity of demand

price elasticity of supply

total revenue

consumer surplus

REVIEW QUESTIONS

1. What is a "market"?

2. List some imperfections in market conditions.

3. Distinguish between an increase in demand and an increase in quantity demanded. Show each graphically.

4. Indicate several possible causes of a decrease in demand.

5. Why does the supply curve have a positive slope?

6. Name some variables that cause the supply curve to shift.

7. Indicate the general meaning of the concept of elasticity as it relates to demand schedules.

8. How are price elasticity, income elasticity, and cross-price elasticity of demand different?

9. What is the formula used to obtain a numerical coefficient of the price elasticity of demand?

10. Suppose that when a firm reduces price, its total revenue from the sale of the product increases. Will the coefficient of demand elasticity over this range be positive or negative? Will it exceed or be less than 1? Why?

11. You land in a strange country and are told, upon inquiring, that a beer costs 1,000 gubbles (the gubble being the local currency). Is this a "high" price? How could you find out if it was a high price? What does your answer say about the truth of our assertion that only relative prices matter in microeconomics?

SUGGESTED READINGS

Alchian, A. and W. Allen. *Exchange and Production: Competition Coordination and Control*, 3rd ed. Belmont, Cal.: Wadsworth, 1983, Chapters 2, 3, 4.

Hayek, F. A. von. "The Use of Knowledge in Society," *American Economic Review*, 35 (September 1945), 519–30.

Marshall, A. *Principles of Economics*, 8th ed. London: Macmillan, 1920, Book III: Chapters 1, 2, 3.

Chapter Four

STOCKS AND FLOWS
IN SUPPLY AND DEMAND*

Questions to Think About
---

1. What is the difference between a stock variable and a flow variable?

2. Why do households and firms hold inventories?

3. What is stock demand? Stock supply?

4. What is stock excess demand? Stock excess supply?

5. How do stock demand and supply affect flow demand and supply?

6. What conditions must be satisfied for market equilibrium?

7. How does stock and flow analysis aid our understanding of business cycles?

---

*This chapter presents optional material that is a bit more difficult. Those without a particular interest in micro-macroeconomics issues or durable goods may wish to omit this material.

4.1 INTRODUCTION

The discussion in Chapter 3 dealt exclusively with **flow variables**. A flow variable is one that has a time dimension, such as the quantity of wine purchased in Los Angeles in 1993. It is important to know not only how much wine was purchased but also over what duration: days, months, or years. After all, 40,000 cases over a day is clearly a larger amount than 40,000 cases over a year. A second kind of variable is a **stock variable**.[1] A stock variable has no time dimension. An example is inventories, for example, an inventory level of 1,000 cases of wine in a store. Many goods are a mix of both stock and flows. Automobiles and household appliances, for instance are stocks on hand, but at the same time they provide a service flow over many periods. In a pure stock economy, assets could be exchanged only for other assets—with no time dimension, nothing would be produced; in a pure flow economy, income (the flow return to the owner of a factor input) could only be consumed. Why? If you saved income, it would be a stock rather than a flow.

To ignore the distinction between stocks and flows would considerably hinder our understanding of business cycles. Explicit analysis of savings, investments, and growth processes is conceptually possible only in the context of a stock-flow model. The terms *supply* and *demand*, unless properly defined to include stock and flow analysis, may conceal as much as they reveal about *forces* governing market behavior.

The term *supply* can refer either to the quantity of a good in existence at any particular moment (stock) or to the rate or flow at which it is produced—quantity per day, per month, or per year. Similarly, the term *demand* refers either to the quantity of the good that individuals desire to possess at a particular moment (stock) or to the rate at which it is currently being consumed (flow).

In everyday discussion, one can usually infer from the context whether a speaker is referring to stock or flow aspects of any activity. If a strike is in progress in the automobile industry, for example, and car production is currently at a standstill, the term *supply* will normally refer to stocks already in the hands of dealers. Alternatively, if the industry is operating normally, stocks in existence at any time are typically small relative to, say, yearly output; in this case, the term *supply* will almost always refer to the annual rate of production. In economic analysis, however, there is no contextual basis for distinguishing between the two interpretations; we must either make the distinction explicit or risk serious confusion and misunderstanding. (See Problem 4–1.)

---

[1]See Sexton, Clower, Graves and Lee "Incorporating Inventories into Supply and Demand Analysis," *Atlantic Economic Journal*, Volume 20, Number 4, December 1992.

4–1   True or False?   The salary that one makes is a stock variable.

False. A salary is a flow variable; whether it is paid by the hour, the month, or the year, it is a *flow* of money income. On the other hand, all your assets considered at *one moment* of time would be a stock variable. Other stock variables might be the value of your car, of your house, of a company's inventories or assets, and so on.

4.2 STOCKS, FLOWS, AND EXCHANGE

If the activity of exchange involved nothing more than matching what is produced with what is consumed, then the distinction between stocks and flows would not matter much. In fact, stocks could be ignored altogether on the ground that they would have little impact on the ultimate equilibrium of supply and demand. However, the real world is not so simple. A contractual commitment, for example, might obligate one party to deliver certain goods to another party in exchange for a specific amount of money. In most cases, goods promised for delivery are already held as inventories. Production flows do not move directly from business firms to consumers but instead pass through an intermediate stage in which they are temporarily held as **inventories** (a stock). Also, goods delivered to consumers seldom flow directly into consumption; on the contrary, they are normally used to replenish household inventories (stocks) and probably are not consumed for days or even months after they are purchased. After all, if we had no household inventories (stocks), we would not have a use for refrigerators, or kitchen shelves. Wine producers, to cite another example, keep large stocks of wine on hand, while wine consumers often have inventories ranging from a few bottles to cellars containing hundreds or thousands of bottles.

It may appear that a great fuss is being made over a minor matter. Surely it cannot matter that much if household and business inventories are ignored and we then suppose that trade proceeds as if such inventories did not exist. If, however, we wish to provide a discussion of short-run **disequilibrium**, then it is unwise to ignore an aspect of the real world—inventory depletion or accretions—that is an important source of economic variability. To appreciate just what is involved, we only need to ponder a moment about the number of automobiles, new and used, or the quantity of money that are held by households and firms. Although some kinds of inventories truly are minor and can be safely ignored, no serious analysis of market behavior can afford to proceed on the assumption that all inventories are inconsequential. In the discussion that follows, therefore, the case in which inventories are important is the rule rather than the exception.

4.3 STOCK DEMAND AND SUPPLY

If an individual offers to *sell* units of a given commodity, this implies a willingness to deplete current inventory holdings. The individual is said to have **stock excess supply**; that is, this individual has excess stock or inventory of this good. Similarly, if an individual offers to *buy* units of a given commodity, this implies a willingness to add to present inventory holdings. The person who wants to "stock up" is said to have **stock excess demand**. (See Problem 4–2.)

4–2 True or False? Producers hold inventories of goods all the time; however, this is not the case with consumers.

False. While it is more common to think of producers holding inventories, consumers also maintain inventories of goods. Virtually all durable goods (which typically yield service flows) are held as inventories. Our clothes, VCRs, computers, and automobiles are all inventories of services.

Individuals may wish to hold inventories for various reasons: to provide a reserve against future predicaments, to serve as a hedge against inflation, or to avoid the high cost of frequent, small-lot transactions. In normal circumstances, only the last of these motives is important. Why? Because it costs nearly as much in terms of time and effort or other resources to buy or sell a small quantity as a large quantity. Thus, if an individual trades always in small lots, the total cost of trading a given quantity of goods during a given period of time will be vastly greater than if she trades infrequently in relatively large lots. To appreciate the importance of this consideration, we need only to reflect on observed behavior. Do you buy gum by the stick or by the pack? Do you cash small checks every day or larger ones every week? Do you purchase gasoline by the gallon or by the tank? Business firms are much more conscious than households of the costs that can be avoided by holding relatively large average inventories and buying and selling in relatively large lots. However, the factors governing holdings of inventories are essentially the same for households and for business firms. (See Problem 4–3.)

4–3 How does consumption affect the stock of a good, say, ice cream in your freezer?

If you continue to eat ice cream regularly without replenishing your inventories, the stock will fall. The only way to add to the stock is to put more ice cream into the freezer (increase market purchases) than you take out to consume.

Individual holdings of inventories depend on many factors—political, institutional, and technological—that lie outside the traditional scope of economic analysis. It can be shown, however, that an individual's willingness to hold stocks of any particular commodity will vary inversely with the good's market value (price), *ceteris paribus*. The higher the price of a commodity, the greater the amount of wealth that commodity represents. Anytime that wealth is used to replenish inventories, the opportunity to earn interest on that wealth or to consume other goods is forgone. Consequently, the cost is relatively greater for high-priced goods as compared with low-priced goods.

The **stock demand** for any given commodity is negatively sloped, as illustrated by the stock demand curve, D, in Figure 4–1. The curve is drawn on the assumption that the values of all variables relevant to stock demand other than market price are fixed. If any of these values change, the position of the stock demand curve will shift.

Unless all goods purchased are instantaneously consumed (as, perhaps, with a restaurant meal), when an individual offers to buy units of a given commodity, this implies a willingness to add to present inventory holdings. The desire to add to inventories under current market conditions implies there is a stock excess demand. (See Problem 4–4.)

FIGURE 4–1
STOCK DEMAND AND SUPPLY

The stock demand curve represents the quantity of a particular commodity that transactors are willing to hold as inventories at various prices, *ceteris paribus*. People want smaller holdings the greater the price. Thus, the stock demand curve slopes downward, as shown. The stock supply curve depicts the amount of the commodity available at a point-in-time. Stock supply cannot respond to price changes, in the market (or momentary) period.

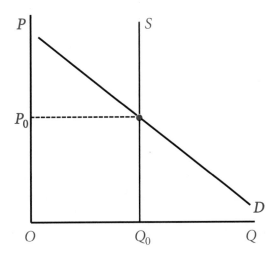

4–4 The following are some occurrences that would most likely cause your stock demand curve to shift. Will it shift to the left or the right?

* A new shopping center close to your home opens. (Left)
* A more fuel-efficient automobile lowers your transportation costs. (Left)
* You become a vegetarian and we are considering your stock demand curve for meat. (Left)
* A meteorologist predicts that a severe hurricane will hit your area in two days. (Right)
* Your stockbroker tells you that there is ample evidence "stock" prices will decline. Your stock demand for stocks might fall, *now*; you may sell now in anticipation of replenishing stocks at lower prices later. (Left)

The quantity of any good actually held by individuals at any given moment is a legacy from the past, as is the aggregate stock of the good available to the economy as a whole. Thus, at any moment of time, the aggregate stock is "frozen" and cannot be changed. Of course, an individual can increase his stock of a good right now by acquiring it in exchange from somebody else, but the economywide (aggregate) stock of that good is not affected. Although the *future* magnitude of a stock supply of a commodity can be altered by human action, its *current* level is simply a fact. This is illustrated in Figure 4–1, where the stock supply curve, S_0, is a vertical line to indicate that the quantity of the existing stocks does not respond to changes in the current market price.

Evidently, the quantity of a commodity demanded to be held at any moment will be equal to the quantity in existence only at one level of market price, namely, the level at which the stock demand curve intersects the stock supply curve (P_0 in Figure 4–1). At any other price, either stock demand will exceed stock supply (stock excess demand), or stock supply will exceed stock demand (stock excess supply). This difference between stock demand and supply implies that some individuals desire to alter their existing holdings. Consumers or firms may each have *either* stock excess demands or stock excess supplies, depending on whether they wish to build up or deplete their inventories at the current market price, *ceteris paribus*. Normally, for example, an increase in stock demand (stock excess demand at current prices) by consumers reduces firm inventories, transferring the stock excess demand to firms; the firms in turn typically respond by increasing production to eliminate their stock excess demands. (See Problem 4–5.)

4–5 In January of 1994, a devastating earthquake rumbled through the Los Angeles area causing serious structural damage, power outages, and tainted tap water. How would this event affect the stock demand for, say, bottled water?

In the aftermath of the earthquake, many residents of the Los Angeles area scrambled to increase their stock of uncontaminated water. Since drinking tap water was safe only if it was chlorinated and/or boiled for 5 minutes, there was a major run on bottled water. Hence there was an increase in the stock-demand for bottled water from D_0 to D_1 in the figure below, causing a stock excess demand, (Q_1-Q_0), to occur at the current market price, P_0.

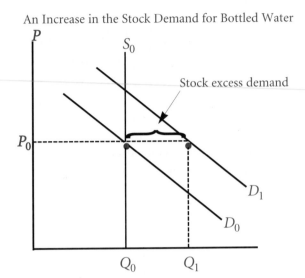

An Increase in the Stock Demand for Bottled Water

4.4 FLOW DEMAND AND SUPPLY

Individuals who wish to alter their holdings of current stocks of goods may do so by changing their present rate of consumption (or production) or by changing current market purchases (or sales). The stock of any good will vary over time only if the aggregate production of the good currently differs from the aggregate consumption; otherwise, trades among individuals would involve nothing more than a redistribution of the existing stock. Current levels of aggregate production and consumption thus play a crucial role in determining the rate of change of stock supplies of various commodities. This rate of change in turn directly influences prevailing levels of stock-excess demand. To complete the groundwork for demand-and-supply analysis of market behavior, we must deal with the determinants of aggregate production and consumption. To be sure, some consideration is given to timing lags in traditional accounts of supply and demand, but that consideration appears mainly in the distinctions between the "momentary," "short-run," and "long-run" periods. *Within* each of those periods, the impact of time is ignored by implicitly or explicitly assuming instantaneous equilibration. As students perceive the power of the "period simplifications" for certain problems (partial equilibrium problems), they often forget that these simplifications are abstractions from the impact of time in the real world. Unfortunately, for *other* problems, these simplifications hinder an understanding of adjustments in supply and demand in the real world.

Let us begin by noting that the quantity (flow) of any given good that individuals in the aggregate are willing to produce at any particular moment in time is upward sloping: The higher the price, the greater the quantity supplied. Similarly, suppose that the quantity (flow) of any given good that individuals in the aggregate are willing to consume at any particular moment in time is downward sloping: The higher the price, the lower the quantity demanded. So far, this is analogous to our supply-and-demand discussion in Chapter 3. These assumptions are illustrated in Figure 4–2; the flow demand curve, d, represents the relation between market price and desired consumption, and the flow supply curve, s, represents the relation between market price and desired production. In general, the position and form of the flow demand-and-supply curves depends on many factors in addition to current market price, including population, income, suppliers' input prices, technology, and other factors that are usually considered in supply-and-demand analysis. The desired rate of consumption will be equal to the desired rate of production only at one particular value of market price (p_0 in Figure 4–2). At any other price, either a flow-excess demand or flow-excess supply will occur.

FIGURE 4–2
FLOW DEMAND AND SUPPLY

The flow demand curve shows the quantity demanded for consumption of a particular product at alternate prices over a specific period of time—a day, a week, a year. The quantity supplied at various prices over a given period, the production flow supply curve, slopes upward because producers will want to produce greater amounts of a commodity in response to higher prices.

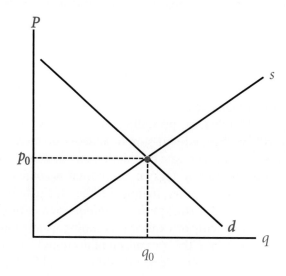

At this point, we might conjecture that the prevailing market price determines both the flow excess demand and the current rate of change in stock supply. This is not so. The rate of change of stock supply at any point in time depends not on desired but rather actual rates of production and consumption. That is, the market demand-and-supply curves are not the same as the flow demand-and-supply curves just discussed.

Only under conditions when there are no desired changes in stocks will the market curves correspond to the flow curves. Suppose, for example, that market price in Figure 4–2, having been constant at a level p_0 over an extended time interval, suddenly increases. It seems sensible to suppose that actual quantities produced and consumed will adjust instantaneously to desired levels as defined by the flow demand-and-supply curves. Such a supposition, however, surely does not accord with experience. In practice, people tend to do what they have been doing until they have fairly strong reasons for changing their behavior. Small changes in market price may cause some households to respond almost immediately, but many households will continue consuming commodities at much the same rate as before. Business firms are likely to be even more insensitive to small price changes because for them any change in production operations, however small, generally involves significant administrative and other overhead costs.

A typical aggregate response pattern of household consumption to variations in the market price of a commodity is illustrated in Figure 4–3. Figure 4–3(a) depicts a flow-demand curve. Assume that the market price starts at p_0 at time $t = 0$, rises to p_1 at time t = 1, and then drops back to p_0 at time $t = 2$. The series of points in the diagram represent observations of market price and quantity actually consumed at various moments of time. The quantity observations are represented in Figure 4–3(b) by the time series $q(t)$. In this illustration, the adjustment of actual to desired quantities, as indicated by $q(t)$, is anything but rapid. If such adjustments occurred almost instantaneously, the quantity time series would look more like the dotted curve, $q^*(t)$.

FIGURE 4–3
ADJUSTMENT OF ACTUAL DEMAND TO DESIRED FLOW DEMAND

The dotted line $q^*(t)$ represents an instantaneous adjustment to price and output. This is what is assumed in the standard comparative statistic framework of supply and demand. However, the typical response would be much less rapid as depicted by $q(t)$.

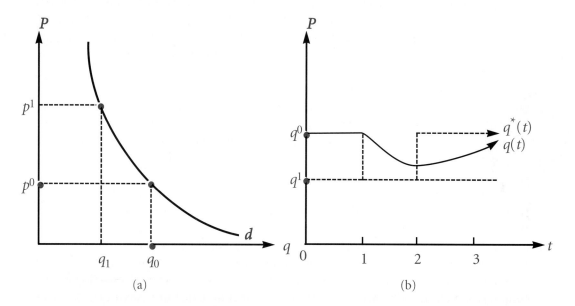

(a)   (b)

We now must consider flow demand and supply together with stock demand and supply to understand what occurs when exchanges take place in actual markets. This follows from the fact that increases in *market* demand stem from either a desire to consume more or a desire to add to stocks. There is no obvious way to know which motive is at work. Similarly, increased supplies to the market may come from either increased production or the attempt by suppliers to reduce stocks on hand. (See Problem 4–6.)

4–6 Can *actual* stocks be different from the *desired* stock? If so, explain.

Yes, for a *particular* price. However, price tends to move in the market if desired stock holdings differ from actual stock holdings. If, for example, people collectively (buyers and sellers) have more than they want of a good, efforts to get rid of the excess stocks will lower price. At this lower price, production will be lower and consumption will be higher. Hence, *flow* behavior is affected by excess stock demands or supplies.

4.5 MARKET SUPPLY AND DEMAND

Again, it is important to emphasize that decisions about rates of production and consumption and desired holdings of inventories are separate from decisions about quantities demanded for purchase or offered for sale. *The principles that govern market exchange are related to, but not derivable from, the principles that control production and consumption.* That is, supply is more than merely the sum of individual-firm supply curves (marginal cost of production schedules); demand is more than merely the sum of individual consumption demands. It remains to establish the relation between stock demands and supplies, flow demands and supplies, and market offers to buy and sell.

It is customary to define *market demand* as a relation that indicates, for each possible market price, the quantity of a commodity that individuals in the aggregate are willing to purchase during a given time period. Similarly, it is customary to define *market supply* as a function that indicates for each possible level of market price the quantity of a commodity that individuals in the aggregate are willing to sell. An initial difficulty with these concepts is that they do not permit us to distinguish between purchases for use (flow) and purchases to hold (stock), or between production for sale (flow) and production for stockpiling (stock). To state the same difficulty in another way, we can hardly suppose that the quantity of a commodity that individuals are willing to purchase depends only on market price; it must also depend on current stocks held by prospective buyers. Similarly, we can hardly suppose that quantity offered for sale depends only on market price; it must also depend on current stocks held by prospective sellers. The conventional definitions of market demand and supply are flawed by their failure to recognize explicitly these facts. The emphasis in traditional texts is always on the rather special case where inventory depletions or accretions are ignored.

This difficulty is remedied most conveniently by supposing that market demand, measured as a flow, is an increasing function of stock excess demand of both households and firms whose desired stocks currently exceed actual holdings. For example, if consumers want to increase their stocks, then they must increase the inflow by purchasing in the market more than they plan for current personal consumption. This implies that the market demand for any commodity is a function of its current market price and of stocks currently held by prospective purchasers of the commodity. Hence, the determinants of demand are now PYNTES, with the S in the acronym denoting stocks. Similarly, we suppose that market supply, measured as a flow, is an increasing function of stock excess supply of all transactors whose actual stocks currently exceed desired holdings. That is, if businesses perceive that they are holding excessive stock in inventories—stock excess supply—they may offer more for sale to increase their market outflow. This implies that the market supply of any commodity is a function of its current market price and of stocks currently held by prospective sellers of the commodity. Now the determinants of supply become SPENTS, with the second S in the acronym denoting stock.

These relations are illustrated in Figure 4–4 by the market supply curve, s(SPENTS) and market demand curve, d(PYNTES). (See Problems 4–7 and 4–8.)

FIGURE 4–4
MARKET DEMAND AND SUPPLY

The market demand curve measured as a flow depends on current stocks held by buyers. Deviation of desired stocks from actual stocks will shift the market flow demand curve. Stock holdings of a commodity are also a market supply curve shifter. At price p_1, quantity supplied exceeds quantity demanded creating excess flow supply. Excess flow demand exists at p_2. Buyers will offer higher prices until the price reaches p_0.

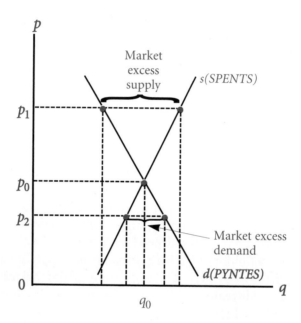

4–7 Imagine you owned a redwood hot tub. In terms of stocks and flows, what would you call the water already in the hot tub? How about the water that entered the hot tub through the garden hose? Or the water that drained out through a leak in the bottom of your hot tub? Finally, how would you change the stock of water in the hot tub?

The water already in the hot tub is a stock, and the water flowing in (garden hose) and flowing out (leak) are both flow variables. Even if the leak were to become larger and more water were entering the hot tub via the garden hose than leaving through the leak, the stock of water in the hot tub would increase. Remember this little equation.

Stocks will ↓ if inflows > outflows

Stocks will ↑ if inflows < outflows

4–8 Because of its convenience, Julie uses the ATM cash machine on campus at least once a week. Recently, the manager decided to remove the ATM machine because it was too costly to maintain. Is Julie's flow demand for money affected, her stock demand for each, or both? Explain.

Because banking is more costly for Julie now that transactions are less convenient, her stock demand for cash will rise and her flow demand will temporarily rise as she adds to her new desired stock level.

4.6 MARKET EQUILIBRIUM

If we take the word *equilibrium* to mean an "absence of motion," a market is in equilibrium if, and only if, market price and quantity traded do not change over time. This definition merely permits us to recognize an equilibrium situation when we see one; it does not allow us to say what conditions must be met if market price and quantity are to be *stationary* over time, much less to describe how such an equilibrium might be attained. To say anything about these matters, we must introduce explicit assumptions about the forces governing the determination of market price and quantities at each moment of time.

In describing the behavior of market price, we assume (following Chapter 3) that in an unfettered market, the price tends to rise whenever market demand exceeds market supply and to fall whenever market supply exceeds market demand. This is illustrated in Figure 4–4.

Because market price tends to rise when a commodity is in excess demand and to decline when it is in excess supply, it is only natural to suppose that market price will be stationary over time if market demand is equal to market supply. But this is not correct. This may be seen most easily by supposing that price at time t=0 is at p_0 in Figure 4–4; that is, at the level where the market demand-and-supply curves intersect. At the initial instant, no force will be acting to drive market price either up or down. However, if current production at price p_0 exceeds current consumption at the same price (and there is no reason why this should not be so), aggregate stocks will increase, which means that the market demand-and-supply curves (whose positions depend on stocks as well as flows) will shift over time. Indeed, only if both producers and consumers each hold exactly their respective desired stocks of inventories will production and consumption coincide with no stock changes. Thus, the "equilibrium" defined by the intersection of the market demand and supply curves at time $t = 0$ will be strictly transitory in this case, for market demand will shortly cease to equal market supply.

Therefore, for market equilibrium to occur at any given date:

1. stock excess demand and stock excess supply must equal zero; and
2. market (flow)-excess demand and market (flow)-excess supply must equal zero. (If the first condition holds, another way to express the second condition is: Actual production flows must equal actual consumption flows.)

It should be emphasized before we proceed further that market a equilibrium does *not* imply an absence of motion or change. *Individual* holdings of commodity stocks vary more or less continuously over time. For example, a typical household may replenish its inventories of consumer goods at the end of each week and then run down its holdings during the course of the week to meet daily requirements. Business holdings of inventories constantly fluctuate in much the same manner and for much the same reasons. In the midst of all these changes, however, *average* holdings of inventories and *average* levels of production, consumption, and trade are constant from period to period as long as equilibrium prevails.

4.7 MARKET DISEQUILIBRIUM

The statement of conditions for market equilibrium does little to advance our understanding of market behavior and, in particular, of the impact of market behavior on business fluctuations. To gain additional insight into this problem, we must deal directly with disequilibrium states and attempt to describe salient features of the adjustment process through which the market ultimately approaches a state of equilibrium. For this purpose, we shall examine both the stock-and-flow demand-and-supply curves shown in Figures 4–5.

Suppose that market price and existing stocks are initially at levels P_0 and S_0, consistent with market equilibrium when stock demand is represented by the curve D_0 and flow demand and supply are represented by the curves d_0 and s_0. Suppose, also, that actual levels of production and consumption always adjust immediately to desired levels as indicated by prevailing market (flow) demand-and-supply conditions. (In other words, disregard the time it takes for consumers to increase consumption of a good whose price falls or for firms to increase production of a good whose price rises). What will happen to market price and to quantities produced, consumed, and held if at some instant of time, $t = 0$, the stock demand curve shifts to the left in Figure 4–5(a), say from D_0 to D_1 (perhaps in response to an improvement in transportation facilities that encourages households to shop more frequently and hold smaller average inventories)?

The shift in stock demand will almost immediately increase inventories held by business firms, for households will work off their excess stocks ($Q_0 - Q_1$) by delaying their next shopping trip until their initial inventories have been reduced to conform with their revised shopping schedules (d_0 falls in the market to d_1). Hence, there will be a temporary dip in business sales and a consequent accumulation of undesired inventories in the hands of retailers (seen in Figure 4–5(b) as the excess supply at P_0 with the initial supply curve and the new demand curve). The increase in business inventories will temporarily increase overall business costs, for business firms will now incur higher in interest expenses on enlarged holdings of inventories. The effect of this increase in costs will be to shift the market (flow) supply curve to the right, say from s_0 to s_1. This shift indicates that at each possible market price, producers may wish to temporarily supply somewhat larger quantities per unit of time to rid themselves of excess inventories.[2]

Because market demand has decreased (due to consumer stock-excess supply) and because market supply has increased (because of firm stock-excess supply), market price will fall. Although production will fall at this lower price, the costs of changing production plans will make many firms reluctant to alter their normal production operations to meet what appears to them (correctly) as a temporary drop in sales. Thus, the response market to the initial decline in stock demand will consist partly of a reduction in price (tending to reduce existing stocks) and partly of a reduction in quantity produced (reducing existing stocks even more quickly). As soon as surplus inventories are eliminated, production, consumption, and market price will tend to return to their initial equilibrium levels. That is, d_1 will return to d_0 as purchases in the market again correspond to flow demands for consumption (rather than to changes in desired stock holdings); similarly, s_1 will return to s_0 as offers to sell in the market again correspond to flow production supplies (rather than to changes in desired stock holdings). The only permanent effect of the original decline in stock demand will be a reduction in aggregate inventories (from S_0 to S_1 in Figure 4–5(a)), unless this reduction in aggregate inventories permanently alters the positions of the flow demand-and-supply curves—which is not likely for reasons that will become clear in later chapters. (See Problem 4–9.)

---

[2]There is another response that the firm might make, in combination with the response of increasing the supply to the market. The firms may also reduce *production* flows at the original price, P_0. Such a response may seem inconsistent with profit maximization, because the marginal cost curve has not shifted and, recalling economic principles, $P = MC$ is the condition for profit maximization. But that profit maximization condition presumes that production and sales are equivalent, which is not the case here, as firms are unable to sell current production. The response of adjusting production *before* market prices adjust may be of particular importance in the macroeconomics setting. However, we shall ignore changes in production flows as an *initial* response to inventory buildup: we shall soon see that production flows will fall, in any event, as market price begin its (rapid) fall.

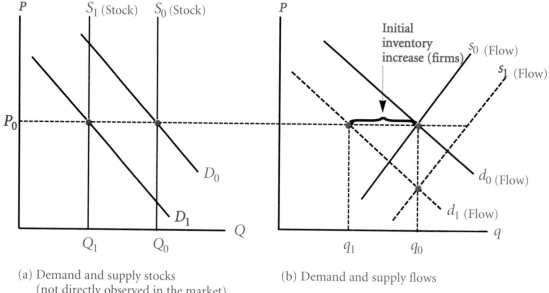

FIGURE 4–5
ADJUSTMENT TO CHANGE IN STOCK DEMAND

(a) Demand and supply stocks
(not directly observed in the market)

(b) Demand and supply flows

1) Households shop more frequently and hold smaller average inventories in the future; that is, the stock demand curve shifts left from D_0 to D_1 in Figure 4–5(a).

2) Households immediately start to work off their excess supply of stock (delay their next shopping trip). This shifts the *market* flow demand curve to the left from d_0 to d_1 in Figure 4–5(b).

3) Business sales fall while families consume their excess inventories in this manner; sales temporarily decline from q_0 to q_1 in Figure 4–5(b).

4) Business costs rise because of higher inventory costs; hence, firms are willing to supply more at each possible market price to rid themselves of excess inventories, and so s_0 shifts rightward to s_1 in Figure 4–5(b).

5) As a consequence of the preceding shifts, at p_0 there is substantial excess flow supply that leads to a temporary fall in price and the amount that is optimally produced (recall $P = MC$ at a profit maximum). Price may not actually fall all the way to the intersection of s_1 and d_1, but it will adjust in that direction.

6) Stocks of inventories fall from S_0 to S_1 as consumption (which is higher at lower prices) and production (which is lower at lower prices) combine to work off the initial, excess inventories.

4–9 When newscasters forewarned Floridians of the potential danger of Hurricane Andrew, how do you think those newscasts affected the stock-and-flow demand and supply for food?

A potentially severe hurricane raises the risk that holding normal inventories of food will be inadequate if the hurricane hits, because the future flow supplies of food may be cut off for a period of time. The newscasts would temporarily raise the stock-and-flow demand for food. After the danger of the hurricane passes, stock demand would return to its original level.

4.8 STOCKS, FLOWS, AND THE BUSINESS CYCLE

Consider now the impact of disequilibrium on the business cycle. Suppose consumers wish (perhaps because of increased uncertainty about the future) to increase their stock holdings of money. To do this, they must either attempt to sell stocks of other goods or assets or reduce their flow consumption. But to whom can they sell their stock? In the aggregate, they cannot eliminate the excess stock supply at the going price. Alternatively, and perhaps more plausibly, the consumers reduce their flow demands for goods until their stocks of these goods (in terms of money) have fallen by as much as they wished to increase initially their stocks of money. Depending on the size of the increase in the stock demand for money, a considerable period of reduced flow purchases may follow.

In either case, firms will see, at original flow supply (and production) levels, steadily increasing inventory levels of either producer goods or consumer goods. These unintended business inventory buildups lead to excess-stock supplies. Firms must then engage in some mix of the following two options: Either cut prices or cut production to reduce inventories. Because they are unaware that consumers are still consuming at the same rate (but predominantly out of their stock, not from flow purchases), they may suspect that demand is now lower for their product. They could reduce production (perhaps through temporary layoffs) and work off excess inventories while they wait to see what happens to demand. In this way they will not lose money on goods already in inventories, they will not have to incur any expenses from lowering prices, and should demand pick up again, they will be prepared to increase production. Unfortunately, the layoffs (and reduced raw material orders) lead to the usual demand-diminishing feedbacks in the aggregate economy. Thus, stock-and-flow interactions importantly affect macroeconomic conditions, and the latter cannot be well understood without reference to the former.

As taught today, economics presents the perceptive student with a schizophrenic view of the economic system. In the microeconomic portions of principles, an intermediate microeconomics supply and demand analysis is presented as "the truth," with the usual treatment implicitly converting all demands to flows.

If supply and demand in fact "works," however, the bright student must surely wonder why half of principles books are devoted to a "nonproblem." The answer, of course, is that neither macroeconomics nor microeconomics, as usually taught, "work." The simple Keynesian macroeconomic model virtually ignores market-clearing entirely, while the standard microeconomic supply-and-demand model in Chapter 3 assumes perfect market-clearing. The approach to supply-and-demand analysis presented here provides a bridge between microeconomics and macroeconomics and should make both models seem more relevant.

SUMMARY

1. A flow variable has a time dimension (a day, a month, a year), while a stock variable refers to a quantity at a particular moment of time and, hence, has no time dimension.

2. Businesses and households both hold stocks of commodities called inventories. Households have purchases for use (flow) and purchases to hold (stock). Businesses have production for sale (flows) and production for stockpiling (stocks).

3. Individuals hold stocks of inventories for various reasons: to accumulate a reserve against future predicaments, to hedge against inflation, and to avoid frequent exchanges.

4. The stock demand for any commodity varies inversely with the market value of the commodity. That is, when you are holding high-priced commodities in inventory, the cost is higher than holding the same quantity of low-priced commodities.

5. Stock supply cannot change at any moment of time; it is a mere "snapshot" of what is on hand.

6. Stock excess demand and excess-stock supply are zero at only one price. At any other price, individuals will desire to alter their existing holdings.

7. Actual stocks may be different from desired stocks, and actual stocks can be altered by changing the flow.

8. Stocks always increase if inflows are greater than outflows, and stocks always decrease if inflows are less than outflows. But, for the market *as a whole*, stocks can only decrease if consumption exceeds production, and vice versa.

9. The market supply (demand) of any commodity is a function of its current market price and stocks currently held by prospective sellers (buyers).

10. In order for market equilibrium to occur at one particular moment, the following conditions must be met: Stock excess demand and stock excess supply must be zero flow excess demand and flow excess supply must be zero, and actual production must be equal to actual consumption. (The last condition is guaranteed if the first two hold.)

WORDS AND CONCEPTS FOR REVIEW

flow variable	stock variable
inventories	disequilibrium
stock excess supply	stock excess demand
stock demand	excess flow demand or supply
desired stock	actual stock
market demand	market supply
undesired inventories	

REVIEW QUESTIONS

1. Which of the following represents a stock? A flow?
   a. speed of a car
   b. distance traveled on a trip
   c. water draining from a sink
   d. water standing in a bathtub
   e. electricity consumption in June
   f. a skyscraper
   g. the mass of the moon
   h. temperature
   i. wind velocity

2. Is national income, measured as a flow, likely to be the same on June 1 of a given year as on July 1? Explain.

3. What is meant by the term *stock supply*? *stock demand*? What are the determinants of each?

4. What would be meant by the phrase "stock demand for money?" What could one infer about a person's excess-stock demand for money at the instant when the person chases a six-pack of soft drinks? Discuss.

5. Describe what is meant by the terms *flow supply* (market and production) and *flow demand* (market and consumption). What factors would be most important in determining the magnitude of each quantity?

6. If flow demand is equal to flow supply, what does this imply about the behavior of stock supply? What if flow supply exceeds flow demand? Explain carefully.

7. Can a market be in equilibrium when flow demand differs from flow supply? When stock demand differs from stock supply? Discuss.

8. Can a market be out of equilibrium when both flow excess demand and stock excess demand are zero? Explain carefully.

SUGGESTED READINGS

Ackley, G. "Commodities and Capital: Prices and Quantities," *American Economic Review*, 73 (March 1983), 1–16.

Clower, R. W. "An Investigation into the Dynamics of Investment," *American Economic Review*, 44 (March 1954), 64–81.

"Stock-Flow Analysis," *International Encyclopedia of the Social Sciences*, 1968, pp. 273–77.

Harrison, G. "The Stock-flow Distinction: A Suggested Interpretation," *Journal of Macroeconomics*, (Spring 1980), 111-28.

Sexton, R., R. Clower, P. Graves, and D. Lee, "Incorporating Inventories into Supply and Demand Analysis," *Atlantic Economic Journal* 20 (December 1992), 41–45.

Part 2

CONSUMERS, PRODUCERS AND COMPETITIVE OUTPUT DETERMINATION

CHAPTERS

Part 2, "Consumers, Producers and Competitive Output Determination," presents the core of microeconomics. This section contains Chapters 5 and 6, which will deal in depth with the optimizing behavior of individuals in their roles as consumers. Specifically, Chapters 5 and 6 include the standard consumer behavior model. Chapters 7 and 8 "The Theory of Production" and "The Costs of Production," cover the output and supply side of final product markets. In Chapter 9, "Competitive Price Determination," we merge consumer theory with the theory of production and costs, to describe price and output determination in competitive markets.

Chapter Five

THE THEORY OF CONSUMER BEHAVIOR

Questions to Think About

1. What is the difference between cardinal and ordinal utility?

2. What is the law of diminishing marginal utility?

3. How does a consumer allocate income among purchases of goods?

4. What is the marginal rate of substitution, and how does it relate to an indifference curve?

5. What do the following indifference curves look like: perfect substitutes, goods that are not substitutable, two unrelated goods, and a good and a bad?

6. What is a budget line?

7. What is a consumer's optimum consumption bundle?

8. How does an in-kind gift such as food stamps, a subsidy, or a cash grant affect a consumer's budget line, optimum consumption bundle, and utility?

5.1 INTRODUCTION

The representative household is a seller of factor services such as labor, a holder of money balances and other assets and a buyer of consumption goods. In principle, we should deal simultaneously with all these activities, for it should be intuitively clear that what a household spends on consumption must be limited in the long run by its income. For purposes of exposition, however, we shall treat the representative household as if it consisted of two virtually independent decision units: (1) a shopping specialist whose task is to decide how any given amount of currently available funds should be allocated among purchases of commodities for current consumption. (2) an asset manager whose task is to decide what factor services the household will offer for sale in each period and how its current receipts will be divided between consumption and saving. This chapter is concerned with the activity of the shopping specialist, a topic usually referred to as the theory of consumer demand. The asset management aspect of household behavior and its relation to consumption planning will be considered in Chapter 19, Asset Management and Intertemporal Income Allocation.

Keeping in mind the major concepts relating to demand-and-supply analysis, we now address the underlying determinants of demand and demand elasticity. Recall from Chapter 2 that the analysis of consumer behavior is based on the assumption that consumers act rationally, seeking to maximize satisfaction from given incomes. According to the law of demand, the quantity demanded increases as the price declines; thus, demand curves slope downward from left to right. This relationship is strongly supported by extensive empirical evidence. The analysis usually assumes that (1) consumers seek to maximize satisfaction; (2) incomes are limited; and (3) the marginal utility—the addition to satisfaction from acquiring an additional unit of a good—falls as additional units of a good are acquired. The law of demand can be explained in rather simple terms on the basis of diminishing marginal utility or, in slightly more general terms, by using indifference curves and the concept of diminishing marginal rate of substitution.

5.2 CARDINAL UTILITY ANALYSIS

One approach to the consumer choice problem is to suppose that the satisfaction of the household is directly measurable in units of "utility" in much the same way as temperature is measurable in terms of the height of a column of mercury in a thermometer. On intuitive grounds, we may suppose that the household derives some increment of potential pleasure from every increment in planned consumption; that is to say, total utility may be regarded as an increasing function of quantities demanded for purchase. Less plausibly, but without violating common sense, we might argue that the increase in potential pleasure that results from an increment in planned consumption declines steadily as the rate of planned consumption increases. This proposition is traditionally referred to as the law of **diminishing marginal utility**.

Diminishing marginal utility describes the behavior of marginal utility as the change in the quantity of a good possessed by an individual varies during a particular time period. According to this "law", as a person obtains additional units of any good, marginal utility declines; that is, each successive unit adds less to the person's satisfaction than did the previous unit. The first automobile that a consumer acquires may yield a great deal of satisfaction by providing a form of transportation more suitable for many purposes than alternative forms. If the person acquires a second car (in the same period of time), it will increase his or her satisfaction to a certain extent because, for example, two members of the family can now use cars at the same time. But the marginal utility—the increase in satisfaction resulting from the acquisition of the second car—is likely to be far less than that resulting from the purchase of the first car.

The law of diminishing marginal utility involves the mutual interaction of two ideas: Individual wants are satiable, and different goods are not perfect substitutes for one another in satisfying particular wants. As a person uses more and more units of a good to satisfy a given want, the intensity of the want diminishes. Units of the good cannot be transferred to other wants and produce as much satisfaction as they yielded initially in satisfying the first want. This is because the good is not a perfect substitute (and possibly not one at all) for goods best designed to satisfy the second want. For example, as a person consumes more and more water in various time periods, the desire for it to drink is eventually satisfied within any of those periods. Additional amounts can be used for other purposes, such as watering lawns or washing cars, but these units will yield less satisfaction than the initial units used to quench one's thirst. (See Problem 5–1.)

The preceding assumptions about the relation between planned quantities of consumption and household satisfaction are illustrated in Figure 5–1. While total utility steadily increases with every increase in quantity demanded, the marginal utility associated with each increment steadily diminishes.

FIGURE 5–1

Total utility rises with increasing consumption, but it does so at a decreasing rate. Hence, marginal utility, the additional utility from another unit, diminishes.

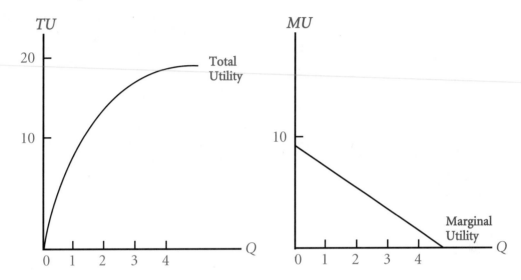

5–1 Why do most individuals take only one newspaper from covered coin-operated newspaper racks?

While ethical considerations keep some people from taking additional papers, the law of diminishing marginal utility is also at work. The second newspaper adds practically zero satisfaction or utility to most individuals on most days. The exception might be on Sundays when supermarket coupons are included. While the marginal utility is still lower for the second paper than the first, the marginal utility of the second paper may be large enough to tempt some individuals to take an additional copy.

THE ALLOCATION OF CONSUMER INCOME

Because marginal utility diminishes as additional units of a good are acquired, a person maximizing satisfaction from limited income must avoid making purchases of any one good beyond the point at which other goods will yield greater satisfaction for the amount spent. Hence, consumers must exercise care in allocating income among various goods. To **maximize satisfaction**, they must allocate income in such a way that the marginal utility of a dollar's worth of any good is the same for every good. When this goal is realized, one dollar's worth of gasoline will yield the same increment to satisfaction—the same marginal utility—as one dollar's worth of additional bread or apples or theater tickets or soap. If the marginal utilities of additional units are not the same, the person can increase total satisfaction by buying more of some goods and less of others. If, for example, the marginal utility of one dollar's worth of apples is 4 and that of a dollar's worth of bread is 8, total satisfaction can be increased by buying more bread and fewer apples. This equilibrium is shown by the equation:

$$\frac{MU_1}{P_1} = \frac{MU_2}{P_2} = \frac{MU_3}{P_2} \cdots = \frac{MU_n}{P_n}$$

This equation tells us that utility maximization requires that the ratios of marginal utility (MU) to price (P) are the same for all goods.

Alternatively, consumers achieve maximum satisfaction by allocating income in such a way that the ratios of marginal utilities of units of the various goods purchased are equal to the price ratios of the goods. That is, if oranges cost twice as much per pound as apples, consumers adjust their purchases of the two commodities until the marginal utility of a pound of oranges is twice as great as the marginal utility of a pound of apples. Viewed this way, the equilibrium can be shown by a modified version of the previous equation:

$$\frac{MU_i}{MU_j} = \frac{P_i}{P_j} \ (i,j, = 1 \cdots n)$$

(See Problems 5–2 and 5–3.)

5–2 True or False? Because many goods are not available in sufficiently small, inexpensive units, perfect adjustment of marginal utilities is impossible.

True. Large consumer goods and almost all durable goods (automobiles, refrigerators) are indivisible, and that complicates the process of equating marginal utilities. With durable goods, however, we are concerned with *flow* demands, which are much more divisible than stocks. That is, the flow of services from an automobile is what gives utility in a given period, and that *service* flow can be varied smoothly by getting a slightly better or worse automobile or varying the miles driven. Indeed, throughout this chapter think of all goods as being flows entirely consumed within the period, unless otherwise specified.

5–3 Suppose you currently buy one loaf of bread and one pound of cheese each week. Your marginal utility of bread is 10 and your marginal utility of cheese is 5. The price of bread is $1 and the price of cheese is $2. Can you benefit from any changes in your consumption patterns?

The marginal utility per dollar for bread is 10/1, and the marginal utility per dollar for cheese is 5/2, or 2.5. Because the marginal utility per dollar is greater for bread than for cheese, you would increase your total utility by buying more bread and less cheese. A consumer who spent one dollar more on bread and one dollar less on cheese would increase utility by approximately 7.5 utils (10 utils - 2.5 utils).

5.3 THE INDIFFERENCE CURVE TECHNIQUE

Once the concept of an indifference curve is introduced, we will learn that the notion of utility in a cardinally measurable sense is essentially irrelevant to the decision problem of the shopping specialist. All that will matter is that we are able to rank commodity bundles in order of increasing satisfaction, not that we should be able to say by how much satisfaction increases as we move from one market bundle to another. In other words, it is an **ordinal** rather than a **cardinal** measure. For example, a person can compare the satisfaction gained from a second car with that obtained from the first car, and with the satisfaction from a trip to Europe.

Let us begin by saying that the amount of money a representative household has available for expenditures on consumption goods during a given time period, say a week, has already been determined by some kind of budgeting arrangement. Then the decision problem of the shopping specialist is simply to decide how the total sum of money available for shopping should be allocated in the purchases of various consumption goods. This allocation decision depends on two sets of factors: (1) the consumption preferences of the household, as viewed by the shopping specialist; and (2) the money prices of the various commodities and the amount of money available for expenditure.

THE INDIFFERENCE SCHEDULE

An indifference schedule lists various combinations of two goods that yield a consumer the same total utility. For example, a household may obtain the same satisfaction from 8 loaves of bread and 4 pounds of steak a week as from 6 loaves of bread and 5 pounds of steak, or 15 loaves of bread and 2 pounds of steak, and so on. The consumer's indifference schedule, that accompanies Figure 5–2, contains various possible combinations of the two commodities that will yield the same total utility (or satisfaction).

The curve connecting the various equally satisfying bundles of X or Y is known as an **indifference curve**. *The indifference curve itself indicates nothing about the absolute amount of satisfaction obtained but merely identifies various combinations that will yield equal satisfaction.*

Our indifference-curve paradigm assumes that a consumer prefers more of a good to less of a good and that the consumer's tastes are never satiated. This implies that we are restricting the consumer's choice to goods, not bads. If the model incorporated bads such as garbage pollution, congestion, and crime, then less would be preferred to more. The model also assumes that the consumer has the ability to and does choose "consistently" among alternative bundles of goods. That is, for any two bundles of goods, say A and B, a consumer must either prefer A to B, prefer B to A, or be indifferent to both A and B. In addition, if the consumer is indifferent to both 1 apple and 2 oranges and between 2 oranges and 1 cantaloupe, the consumer must also be indifferent to both 1 apple and 1 cantaloupe. That is to say, the consumer's preference ordering must be *transitive*.

The Theory of Consumer Behavior   111

THE FAMILY OF INDIFFERENCE CURVES

We have just specified how to construct a single indifference curve representing a given level of satisfaction. For each consumer and for each pair of goods, however, there is actually a whole family of indifference curves, each indicating different levels of satisfaction. A family of three indifference curves representing part of an indifference map is presented graphically in Figure 5–3.

DISTINCT PROPERTIES OF INDIFFERENCE CURVES

Indifference curves such as those depicted in Figure 5–3 have several distinct *properties*.

1. *Indifference curves cannot intersect.*

Successive indifference curves on an indifference map never intersect, because each portrays various combinations that yield a particular degree of satisfaction. If they did intersect, then there would be points on either side of the intersection such that a point on the higher curve had more of *both* goods than a point on the lower curve. This point would thus be *preferred*. However, this would contradict the existence of the intersection point, which by definition expresses the fact that the same level of satisfaction must be achieved on both curves, because all points on the intersecting curves are indifferent to the intersection point. The principle that indifference curves cannot intersect is a property of a consistent preference ordering and is illustrated in Figure 5–4.

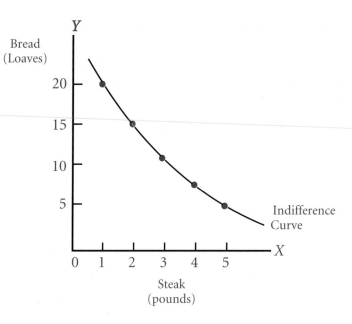

Various Combinations of Bread and Steak
Yielding a Given Level of Satisfaction to a Consumer

Bundle	Steak (pounds)	Bread (loaves)
A	1	20
B	2	15
C	3	11
D	4	8
E	5	6

FIGURE 5—3
A FAMILY OF INDIFFERENCE CURVES OF A CONSUMER FOR STEAK AND BREAD

This indifference map shows a series of indifference curves, each representing a different level of utility. The most northeasterly indifference curve, I_2 designates the highest level of utility, and indifference curve I_0 designates the lowest level, because some bundles on I_2 contain more bread and steak than some bundles on I_0. Note that the consumer need only be able to rank bundles ordinally: assigning a numerical (cardinal) value to the level of satisfaction associated with each indifference curve is *not* necessary.

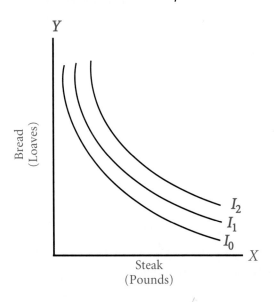

FIGURE 5—4
NONINTERSECTING INDIFFERENCE CURVES

Because points A and B are both I_0, the consumer must be indifferent to both bundles A and B. Similarly, A and C are on I_1 the consumer is indifferent to both A and C. Transitivity of preferences implies the consumer is indifferent to both B and C. Bundle B, however contains more of both goods, Y and X. Because more is preferred to less, B is preferred to C. Thus, an inconsistency occurs.

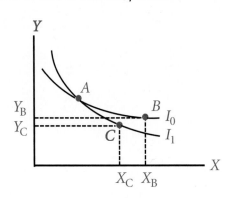

2. Indifference curves are negatively sloped.

Indifference curves slope downward from left to right under the assumption that, as more units of one good are added, fewer units of the other will be needed to maintain the same level of satisfaction. The slope of an indifference curve measures the *marginal rate of substitution* (MRS) between the two goods. The marginal rate of substitution of good X for good Y is the number of units of good Y that must be sacrificed to add a unit of good X and maintain the same level of satisfaction.[1] Thus, in Figure 5–5, in moving from bundle B to C implies the consumer is willing to give up 4 loaves of bread in exchange for an additional pound of steak. The marginal rate of substitution is -4/1 = -4. However, if we multiply by -1 we can treat MRS as a positive value as we have done in the table that accompanies Figure 5–5. Moving down the indifference curve, we see that the consumer is willing to give up less and less bread for an additional unit of steak. For example, in a move from bundle D to E, the consumer is now willing to give up only 2 units of bread for an additional unit of steak. Note that the marginal rate of substitution is declining as we move down along the indifference curve. (See Problems 5–4 and 5–5.)

---

[1]Let $U = U(X,Y)$ and totally differentiating

$$dU = \frac{\partial U}{\partial U} dX + \frac{\partial U}{\partial U} dY$$

we see how total utility changes and X and YY change. Holding utility constant at some level of indifference involves setting $dU = 0$:

$$0 = \frac{\partial U}{\partial U} dX + \frac{\partial U}{\partial U} dY$$

therefore,

$$\frac{dY}{dX} = \frac{\dfrac{\partial U}{\partial X}}{\dfrac{\partial U}{\partial Y}} dY$$

represents the marginal rate of substitution.

FIGURE 5–5
INDIFFERENCE CURVES ARE NEGATIVELY SLOPED

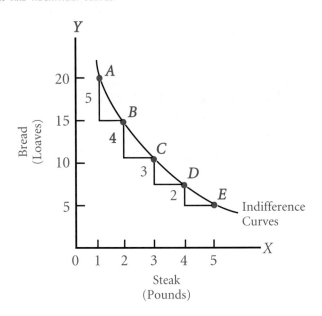

The Marginal Rate of Substitution between Bread and Steak for a
Particular Consumer

Bundle	Steak (pounds)	Bread (loaves)	Marginal rate of Substitution* of Steak for Bread
A	1	20	
B	2	15	5
C	3	11	4
D	4	8	3
E	5	6	2

*The number of units of bread necessary to replace a unit of steak and maintain
a given level of satisfaction.

5–4 Using indifference curves, demonstrate that the consumer's indifference curves between two goods (generally) have a negative slope.

We have just learned that all bundles on a particular indifference curve yield the same level of satisfaction. That is, individuals should be indifferent between bundles A and B on I_0, bundles A and C on I_1, and bundles A and D on I_2. But how can that be without violating the assumption that more of a good is better? If X and Y are goods, then bundles B, C, and D all must be preferred to bundle A because bundles B, C, and D have either more of X, more of Y, or more of both X and Y. Thus, we must conclude that indifference curves for two *goods* will generally be negatively sloped.

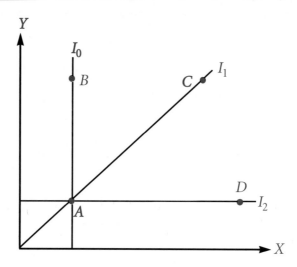

5–5 True or False? When only a small amount of bread is needed to replace a large reduction in steak, the indifference curve is nearly horizontal; if the number of units of bread required to replace a unit of steak is relatively large, the curve will be nearly vertical.

True. In Figure (a) it is easy to see that when the indifference curve is nearly horizontal, a move along the indifference curve from a to b requires only a small amount of additional bread to compensate this consumer for a large reduction in steak. This person is clearly not a steak lover. In Figure (b), when the indifference curve is nearly vertical, we see that with a move along the indifference curve from a to b, even a small reduction in steak would require a large amount of bread to make the individual equally well off. This is a steak lover.

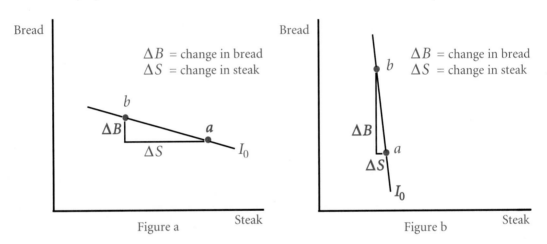

Figure a   Figure b

3. Indifference curves for goods are convex to the origin.

Aside from being downward sloping, indifference curves are convex to the point of origin; that is, the left-hand portion is relatively steep while the right-hand portion is relatively horizontal. In terms of the bread/steak trade-off, this means that the more units of bread a consumer has, the fewer the units of steak necessary to replace a unit of bread in while maintaining the same total satisfaction. Likewise, the more units of steak, the fewer units of bread necessary to replace a unit of steak. This relationship is known as the principle of **diminishing marginal rates of substitution**. Reiterating, as additional units of one good are added, the marginal rate of substitution of this good for the other falls; that is, as we move down along the indifference curve, the consumer needs progressively fewer loaves of bread to replace units of steak to maintain the same level of satisfaction.[2]

---

[2]Note that the principle of diminishing marginal rate of substitution, unlike the downward slope of an indifference curve, cannot be "proven." Rather, it is based on an empirical regularity that we shall assume; this assumption is however, quite plausible.

One way to analyze diminishing marginal rate of substitution is to think in terms of diminishing marginal utility. If you have relatively large amounts of bread (as on the upper left portion of the indifference curve in Figure 5–6), bread has a low marginal utility. To get an additional unit of steak (which has higher marginal utility at low quantities), you would be willing to give up a large amount of bread. However, at the lower right on the indifference curve in Figure 5–6, you would be very reluctant to give up much of the small amount of bread (which has high marginal utility) for even larger quantities of low-marginal-utility steak.[3]

Note, however, that while this discussion of diminishing marginal rate of substitution in terms of diminishing marginal utilities is appealing, it is not at all necessary. We need not assume diminishing marginal utility to arrive at the principle of diminishing marginal rate of substitution. Indeed, the marginal utility of goods could be increasing and one could still have a diminishing marginal rate of substitution. The key to the distinction between the two is that your willingness to substitute one good for another depends on relative quantities consumed. If you have lots of something, you will give up more (regardless of marginal utility) to get something else than you would if you only had a little. Because diminishing MRS is less restrictive than diminishing marginal utility, we shall adopt this assumption in the discussion that follows.

---

[3]Recall the derivative of footnote [1]:

$$0 = dX = \frac{\partial U}{\partial X} dX + \frac{\partial U}{\partial Y} dY$$

This can be rearranged, solving for the slope of the indifferent curve:

$$\frac{dY}{dX} = - \frac{\partial U/\partial X}{\partial U/\partial Y} = - \frac{MU_X}{MU_Y}$$

If one has large amounts of Y, the ration on the right is large since MU_Y is small—you would give up a great deal of Y to get additional X, holding satisfaction constant along an indifference curve. The opposite holds true, if one has relatively small amounts of Y.

On the upper portion of the indifference curve bread has a low marginal utility and steak has a high marginal utility. To get an additional unit of steak, the consumer would give up lots of bread. However, on the lower portion of the indifference curve, the consumer would be very reluctant to trade small amounts of bread (high marginal utility) for large quantities of steak (low marginal utility).

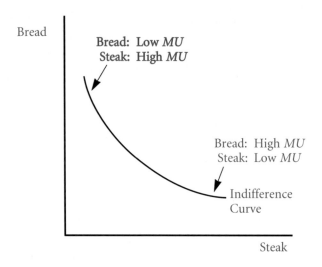

The diminishing MRS principle follows as a matter of logical necessity from the assumptions that particular wants are satiable, that various goods are not perfect substitutes for one another, and that increased quantities of one good do not increase the want-satisfying power of the other. As more units of one good are added, the ability of additional units of this good to satisfy wants falls because the want for which the good is best suited becomes more completely satisfied. Thus, a relatively small quantity of the other good (the desire for which is relatively intense, per unit, with a few units being acquired) is necessary to replace a unit of this good and maintain satisfaction. As indicated by the steak/bread example, when the consumer has relatively little of the first good and large quantities of the second, a large additional amount of the second is needed to replace a unit of the first in order to maintain the same level of satisfaction. (See Problem 5–6.)

5–6 If indifference curves are in fact convex to the origin, how can one tell whether either or both the goods are actually "bads"?

Consider the odd-looking circular indifference curves I_0, I_1, and I_2. These preferences look typical in Region I (the lower left) which depicts the usual downward-sloping, diminishing marginal rate of substitution behavior. The other regions have unusual directions of increasing utility, as indicated by the arrows pointing in the direction of increasingly preferred bundles. Point b is commonly referred to as the "bliss point or the satiation point"—the point of maximum satisfaction in terms of goods consumption. At point b we can see from the figure that we are at Y_{MAX} and X_{MAX}.

Given diminishing marginal rate of substitution, we can now see that Region II represents a case where Y is the bad (say, pollution), while Y is the good (say, coal production). When the curve bends the other way, as in Region IV, Y would be the bad and Y the good. The intuition in these cases, and in that of Region III, where both goods are bads (say, living without free disposal in a small condominium with $Y = 1,000$ watermelons and $Y = 500$ chairs), is not as immediately obvious as in the Region I case. Consider Region II at the left boundary. Y is just becoming a bad, and very little of the good would be needed to compensate for an additional unit of a bad. As we get more and more of the bad, however, it requires larger and larger quantities of the good to compensate for additional amounts of the bad.

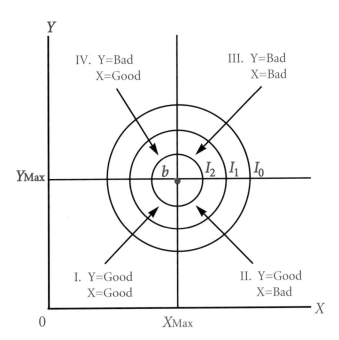

COMPLEMENTS AND SUBSTITUTES

The ability of one good to satisfy a want for a consumer will often depend on the quantities of other goods consumed. Many goods are **complements** to each other; that is, the use of more units of one encourages the acquisition of additional units of the other. Gasoline and automobiles, baseballs and baseball bats, snow skis and bindings, bread and butter, and coffee and cream are examples of complementary goods. When goods are complements, units of one good cannot be acquired without affecting the want-satisfying power of other goods. Some other goods are **substitutes** for one another; that is, the more you have of one, the less you desire the other. (The relationship between substitutes is thus the opposite of the relation between complements.) Examples of substitutes include coffee and tea, sweaters and jackets, and home-cooked and restaurant meals.

The degree of convexity of an indifference curve—that is, the extent to which the curve deviates from a straight line—depends on how easily the two goods can be substituted for each other. If two commodities are perfect substitutes (such as, for example, "left" and "right" socks of the same size, quality, and color), the indifference curve is a straight line (in this case, of slope -1). This is depicted in Figure 5–7, because the marginal rate of substitution is the same, regardless of the extent to which one good is replaced by the other.

At the other extreme are two commodities that are not substitutes, in other words, that are perfect complements, as are left- and right-hand gloves. For most people, these goods are never used separately but are consumed only together. Because it is impossible to replace units of one with units of the other and maintain satisfaction, the marginal rate of substitution is undefined; thus, the indifference curve is a right angle convex to the graph's origin, as shown in Figure 5–8 and in the boxed example. The left portion is vertical, in that an infinite amount of Y is necessary to replace one unit of X. The right portion is horizontal because an infinite amount of X is necessary to replace a unit of Y. In more typical cases, in which the two commodities can be substituted for one another but are not perfect substitutes, the indifference curve will be shaped as depicted at the outset. The more easily the two commodities can be substituted for one another, the nearer the curve will approach a straight line; in other words, it will maintain more closely the same slope along its length throughout. (See Problems 5–7 and 5–8.)

FIGURE 5—7
AN INDIFFERENCE CURVE OF PERFECT SUBSTITUTES

When two goods are perfect substitutes, the indifference curve is linear. In this example, the consumer is equally satisfied by 6 units of *X* and 1 unit of *Y*, and 6 units of *Y* and 1 unit of *X*. The consumer will always trade 1 unit of *X* for 1 unit of *Y*, so the marginal rate of substitution in this case is constant at -1. Although the MRS is always constant for perfect substitutes, it is not necessarily -1.

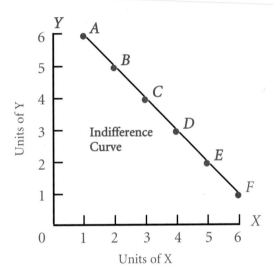

Indifference Schedule of Perfect Substitutes

Bundle	*X*	*Y*	MRS
A	1	6	
B	2	5	1
C	3	4	1
D	4	3	1
E	5	2	1
F	6	1	1

FIGURE 5–8
AN INDIFFERENCE CURVE OF GOODS THAT ARE NOT SUBSTITUTABLE

Two goods are perfect complements when they are always used together, such as right gloves and left gloves. A consumer is indifferent to both 1 right glove and 1 left glove, and 1 right glove and 5 left gloves, as nothing is gained from the addition of 4 left gloves. Similarly, the consumer is indifferent to both 1 right glove and 1 left glove, and 5 right gloves and 1 left glove. Hence, perfect complements are represented by L-shaped or right-angled indifference curves.

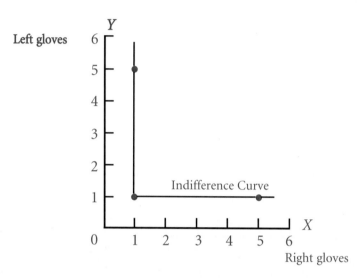

5–7 Draw a *set* of indifference curves for left and right shoes.

Left and right shoes are perfect complements. For perfect complements, indifference curves are L-shaped. For example, point *a* (2 left shoes and 2 right shoes) and point *b* (4 left shoes and 2 right shoes) would be equally satisfying. The reason is that the 2 left shoes without mates would be presumably worthless to most individuals. In contrast, point *c* (3 left and 3 right shoes) on a higher (or further northeast) indifference curve would be preferred to both points *a* and *b*.

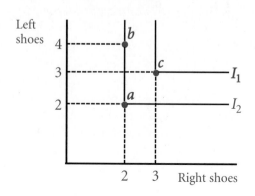

5–8 Draw an indifference curve for money and pizza when pizza has to be eaten on the spot.

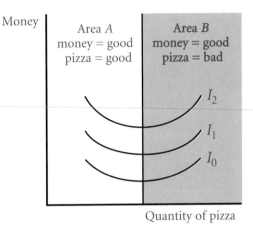

In Area *A* both money and pizza are goods. To have another piece of pizza, one would be willing to give up some money. In shaded Area *B*, this is not the case. The individual has "had his or her fill" of pizza, and now he or she would have to be paid to eat more. Hence, it is possible that some goods may become bads after a certain quantity has been consumed.

5.4 THE BUDGET LINE

A person's preference ordering as represented by a family of indifference curves for various goods, exists apart from the feasible opportunities he or she has to act on those preferences. Actual purchases, however, depend on the consumer's total quantity of money budgeted for expenditures and on relative commodity prices, with prices affecting the way the consumer allocates money for expenditures among different goods. Possible patterns of expenditures of a given sum of money on two commodities may be illustrated on the indifference graph by the use of a **budget line**. Such a line shows the various combinations of the two goods that can be purchased with a certain expenditure, given the prices of the two goods. For example, say that $20 is to be spent on bread and steak, and bread costs 80 cents a loaf and steak $4 a pound. The consumer can purchase 25 loaves of bread and no steak, 5 pounds of steak and no bread, or various combinations of the two, such as 3 pounds of steak and 10 loaves of bread or 1 pound of steak and 20 loaves of bread. The various combinations are shown in Figure 5–9.

The Y intercept and the X intercept can easily be found by dividing the money for expenditures by the price of good Y (bread) and the price of good X (steak), respectively. That is, the Y intercept is $20/$.80, or 25, and the X intercept is $20/$4 or 5.

The slope of the budget line is equal to $-P_X/P_Y$. The negative coefficient of the slope indicates that the budget line is negatively sloped. For example, the slope in Figure 5–9 would be -$4.00/$.80 = - 5. That is, for every additional pound of steak the consumer must give up 5 loaves of bread.

The budget line has several distinct *properties*:

1. The budget line is negatively sloped.

2. As long as the prices of the goods are fixed to a consumer independent of the quantities purchased, the budget-constraint line will necessarily be linear.

3. The budget line shifts outward if the amount of money available for expenditures increases and inward if the amount of money available for expenditures decreases, maintaining the same slope in each case.

4. The slope of the budget-constraint line will only change when different relative prices change.

FIGURE 5–9

The budget line shows all the possible combinations of bread and steak that can be purchased with $20.00 when the price of bread is $.80 per loaf and the price of steak is $4.00 per pound. If the consumer spends all $20.00 on bread, 25 loaves of bread may be purchased ($20.00/$.80) and if the consumer spends all $20.00 on steak, 5 pounds can be purchased. The slope of the budget line in *absolute value* is the price of steak, divided by the price of bread, or 5. That is, to obtain another pound of steak the consumer must forego 5 loaves of bread.

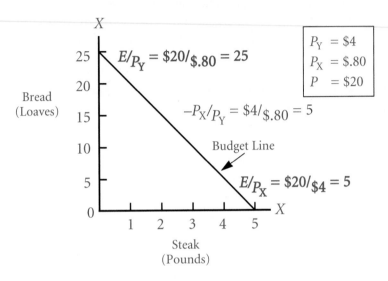

Expenditure Schedule on Bread and Steak,
Total Expenditure of $20.00

Bread (Price $.80) Loaves	Steak (Price $4) Pounds
25	0
22.5	0.5
20	1
17.5	1.5
15	2
12.5	2.5
10	3
7.5	3.5
5	4
2.5	4.5
0	5

Suppose a consumer can choose to spend a given budget on two goods, X and Y. We can specify an equation which states that the consumer's budget devoted to expenditures (E) is exhausted on X and Y. That is, expenditure on X equals its price, P_X, times the amount of X; expenditure on Y is its price, P_Y, times the amount of Y. If we equate the sum of these two expenditure components to E, we form the equation of the budget line. Thus, $E = (P_X \cdot X) + (P_Y \cdot Y)$, which can be rewritten in the form of the equation of the budget line is $Y = E/P_Y - P_X/P_Y \cdot X$. The Y intercept (setting $X = 0$ and solving for Y) is E/P_Y; the X intercept is E/P_X, and the slope is $- P_X/P_Y$.

Figure 5–10(a) shows how the budget line rotates inward from L_0 to L_1 when P_X rises. That is, if the consumer spent all of her income on X, she would not be able to buy as much X as she would have before the price increase. In addition, the feasible or possible set of goods the consumer can now buy has become smaller. Figure 5–10(b) shows how the budget line rotates outward from L_0 to L_1 when P_X falls. The consumer would be able to buy more X now that the price of X has fallen and the feasible consumption set would expand. Figure 5–10(c) depicts a parallel outward shift in the budget line when the total budget increases. Figure 5–10(d) depicts a parallel inward shift when the total budget falls. (See Problems 5–9, 5–10 and 5–11.)

FIGURE 5–10
BUDGET LINE CHANGE

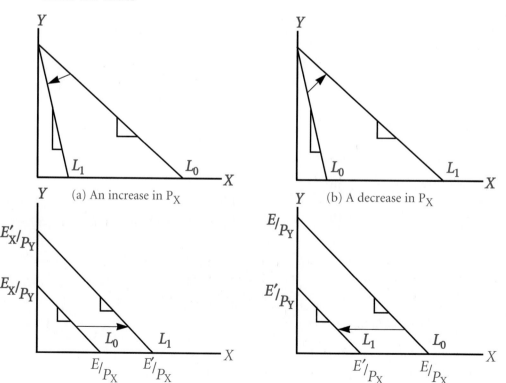

(a) An increase in P_X

(b) A decrease in P_X

(c) An increase in money available for expenditures

(d) A decrease in money available for expenditures

5–9   True of False? The slope of the budget line shows the size of the budget, while the position shows us the relative prices (or price ratios).

False. The position of the budget line indicates how much of both goods one can obtain. The farther the line is from the origin the better for the consumer because this implies the capacity to buy more of both goods. A changing slope refers to a change in the relative price between the two goods. If magazines and cheeseburgers are the two goods on the graph, which relative price has risen when the budget line shifts from L_0 to L_1?

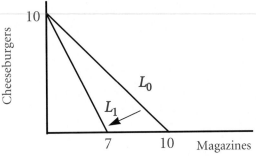

The relative price of magazines has risen. Put simply, with the same money you could have had either 10 magazines or 10 cheeseburgers before but now can have either 7 magazines or 10 cheeseburgers; therefore, the price of magazines must have increased relative to the price of cheeseburgers. Moreover, unless the consumer was consuming zero magazines before the price rise, the consumer is worse off (utility is lower) after the price rise because the new budget constraint represents a smaller feasible set of bundles from which to choose.

5–10   Draw the budget line for a situation in which a consumer's money available for expenditure rises between 1995 and 1996 while the relative price of videocassette recorders falls?

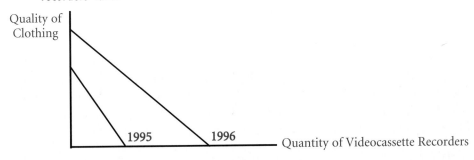

Remember: the slope of the budget line is determined by relative prices and reflects the opportunity cost of adjusting purchases, because a movement along the budget line measures the cost of one item in units of the other. On the other hand, the position of the budget line measures the money available for expenditures. The graph shows that the consumer can buy more of both goods in 1996 than in 1995. Simply put, the farther the line is from the origin, the better for the consumer, since this implies the capacity to buy more of both goods.

5–11   If you had a budget of $200, and the P_Y is $5 and the P_X is $10, draw the budget line. Draw the budget lines when the P_X falls to $8. Show the budget line when the money available for expenditures increases to $400. What is the slope of the budget line when P_Y is $5 and P_X is $10? How about when P_X falls to $8?

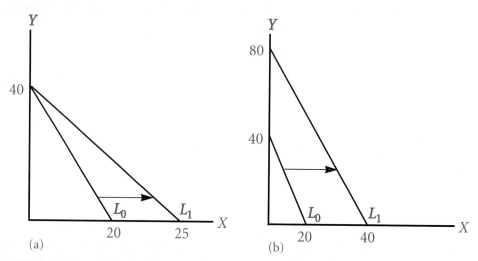

(a)   (b)

The Y intercepts in Figure (a) are E/P_Y, or $200/$5 = 40 and E/P_X or $200/$10 = 20. When P_X falls to $8, the budget line rotates outward from L_0 to L_1; and now E/P_X is $200/$8 or 25. In Figure (b), the intercepts are E/P_Y, or $400/$5 = 80, and E/P_X or $400/10 = 40. Figure (b) shows that budget line L_0 is parallel to L_1. The slope of this budget line is $-P_X/P_Y$ = -$10/$5 or -2. The slope of the budget line when P_X falls to $8 is -8/5 or -1.6.

QUANTITIES PURCHASED

Given the consumer's indifference curves for two goods, together with the budget line showing the various quantities of the two that can be purchased with the allocated expenditure, the optimal quantities of each good to be purchased can be determined. The point of tangency between the budget line and an indifference curve indicates the quantities of each good that will be purchased in order to maximize total satisfaction.

At that point of tangency, -MRS (the slope of the indifference curve) equals $-P_X/P_Y$ (the slope of the budget line).[4] In Figure 5–11 the budget line is tangent to indifference curve I_1 at point a: The consumer will acquire 2.5 pounds of steak and 12.5 loaves of bread. To maximize satisfaction, the consumer must acquire the most *preferred*, attainable bundle—that is, reach the highest indifference curve that can be reached with a given expenditure of money. The highest indifference curve that can be reached is the one to which the budget line is tangent at point a. Any other possible combination of the two goods either would be on a lower indifference curve and thus yield less satisfaction or would be unobtainable with the given expenditure. For example, point b is affordable but would place the consumer on a lower indifference curve. In other words, an individual at point b could be made better off moving to point a by consuming less Y and more X. (See Problems 5–12, 5–13 and 5–14.)

---

[4]The point of tangency can be derived mathematically:

$$\text{Maximize: }_{X,Y} \quad U = U(X,Y)$$
$$\text{s.t. } E = P_X X + P_Y Y$$

Lagrange provides a clever way to incorporate the income into what then becomes a free optimization problem. Rewrite the problem as:

$$\text{Maximize: }_{X,Y,\lambda} \quad \mathcal{L} = U(X,Y) + \lambda(E - P_X X - P_Y Y)$$

The first-order conditions for a maximum (or minimum for that matter, although we shall not be unduly concerned about such possibilities) are that the partial derivatives of $\mathcal{L}$ with respect to the choice variables be zero. That is, at the top of the constrained utility "hill," the slope is zero in every direction:

$$\frac{\partial \mathcal{L}}{\partial X} = \frac{\partial U}{\partial X} - \lambda P_X = 0$$

$$\frac{\partial \mathcal{L}}{\partial Y} = \frac{\partial U}{\partial Y} - \lambda P_Y = 0$$

$$\frac{\partial \mathcal{L}}{\partial \lambda} = E - P_X X - P_Y Y = 0$$

Forming the ratio of the first two equations gives the text result that $\text{MRS}_{XY} = -P_X/P_Y$

Note that the third equation, the "trick" of the Lagrangean method, guarantees that the income constraint is satisfied in the neighborhood of the optimum, and thus, that the consumer must be on their budget constraint.

In the text graphs, it will be apparent that the tangency of the indifference curve with the budget constraint determines the quantities of the goods purchased when utility is maximized. If a specific function is chosen to represent preferences, the optimal quantities can be derived formally from the simultaneous solution of the first-order conditions above.

FIGURE 5—11
THE OPTIMAL COMBINATION OF PURCHASES OF TWO COMMODITIES

The consumer's most satisfactory, affordable bundle *a*, occurs where the indifference curve is tangent to the budget line. Bundles on I_2 and I_3 are more appealing to the consumer but are not affordable. The consumer can purchase bundles on I_0, but these provide less satisfaction than at point *a*.

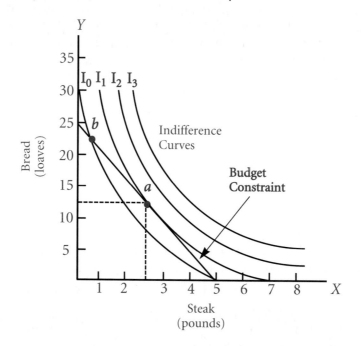

5-12 Joe buys more clothes than Jim.

    a) Using indifference curves, show how Jim's consumption of clothing and food may differ from Joe's because they have different tastes, *ceteris paribus*.

    b) Suppose that Jim and Joe have the same tastes and income. Joe's father manages a clothing store, and Joe is able to buy all his clothes at wholesale prices. Show why Jim's choices of food and clothing differ from Joe's in this situation.

    c) Now suppose that Jim and Joe have the same tastes and face the same prices, but that Joe has more money to spend than Jim. Demonstrate how this affects Joe's consumption pattern compared with Jim's.

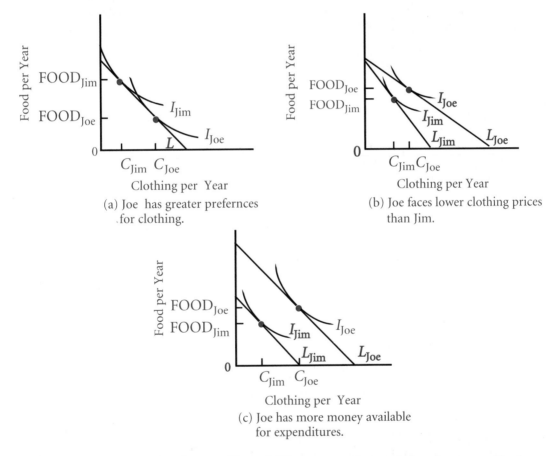

(a) Joe has greater prefernces
.for clothing.

(b) Joe faces lower clothing prices
than Jim.

(c) Joe has more money available
for expenditures.

Figure (a) shows that Joe and Jim have different indifference curves because Joe's preferences are biased toward clothing and thus Joe purchases more clothing than Jim. Note that because the indifference curves are from separate preference maps, they can intersect. In Figure (b), Joe can buy clothes at a reduced price, so his budget line rotates outward from Jim's and he buys more clothes. Joe has more income than Jim in Figure (c), so Joe's budget line is positioned to the right of Jim's.

5–13 Graph a family of indifference curves for someone who has no preferences for steak (derives no positive or negative utility from additional steak). In which direction will the consumer's more preferred combinations lie? Where will the point of consumer optimum occur? Would the optimal consumption point change if the price of steak decreased?

The consumer will be better off only by moving eastward, as designated by the arrows. Steaks are useless, providing the consumer neither utility or disutility. The consumer will not be willing to trade any amount of bread for any amount of steak—this is the case of infinite MRS_{XY}. In this situation, the consumer's optimum is always be a *corner solution* on the bread axis (point a in the graph, where no steaks are consumed). Notice that even when the relative price of steak falls (the budget line shifts up on the steak axis), the consumer's optimum remains unchanged.

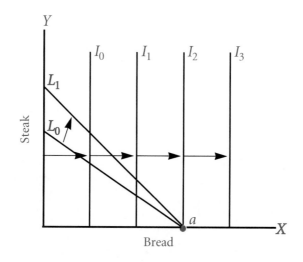

5–14 Stephanie cannot distinguish brand X peanut butter from brand Y. In other words, she gets the same amount of utility from one ounce of brand X as from one ounce of brand Y. Suppose brand X is more expensive than brand Y. Graph Stephanie's indifference curves, budget line, and optimal bundle of brand X and brand Y peanut butter.

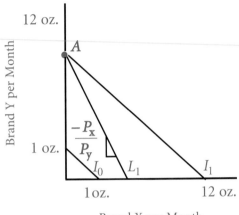

Brand X and brand Y are perfect substitutes for Stephanie. As the figure shows, Stephanie's indifference curves are straight lines. She is willing to trade 1 ounce of X for 1 ounce of Y, so her marginal rate of substitution, the slope of the indifference curve, is 1. Because the price of brand X is greater than that of brand Y, $P_X/P_Y > 1$, and the budget line is steeper than the indifference curve. The optimum is the corner solution, at point A, with Stephanie buying only brand Y. Because she cannot tell the difference between X and Y, Stephanie buys only the lower priced brand Y.

.

In cases where the principle of diminishing marginal returns is not valid, and thus indifference curves are not strictly convex to the point of origin, there may be no single optimal combination of goods corresponding to a particular set of prices and level of expenditures. For example, consider the unlikely possibility that an indifference curve such as I_0 in Figure 5–12(a) is convex in part and concave in part. With budget line L_0, there are three distinct points of tangency, a, b, and c, and thus three optimal points, all yielding the same level of satisfaction; the analysis, however, does not indicate which of these the consumer will select. Suppose, perhaps more realistically, that the indifference curve and budget line appear as in Figure 5–12(b). Here there is one optimal point, a, but this is not a point of tangency. Under such circumstances as these (so-called **corner solutions**), the earlier analysis does not describe the optimum of the consumer, and additional assumptions are required. Lastly, consider Figure 5–12(c) where the indifference curve is concave throughout. In this case the MRS_{XY} increases rather than decreases as we move down along the indifference curve. This specification implies that the more an individual has of any good, the more units of the other good he or she would be willing to sacrifice for an additional unit of that good. Figure 5–12(c) shows that moving from *a* to *b* requires giving up greater amounts of Y to obtain each additional unit of X; yet the consumer already possesses a large quantity of X. The result would also lead to a *corner solution,* where an individual would consume either only good X or only good Y.

FIGURE 5–12
ODDLY SHAPED INDIFFERENCE CURVES

Non-convex indifference curves yield unusually utility maximizing solutions for the consumer. Multiple optima points *a, b,* and *c,* in figure (a). Figure (b) shows a *corner solution,* an optimum bundle that contains only one commodity and none of the other commodity. Figure (c) shows a concave indifference curve. In this case, the more the consumer has of a particular good the more he or she *will* value an additional unit of that good. This violates the assumption of diminishing marginal rate of substitution, and will ensue a consumption optimum that is a corner solution because point *f* is preferred to point *e.*

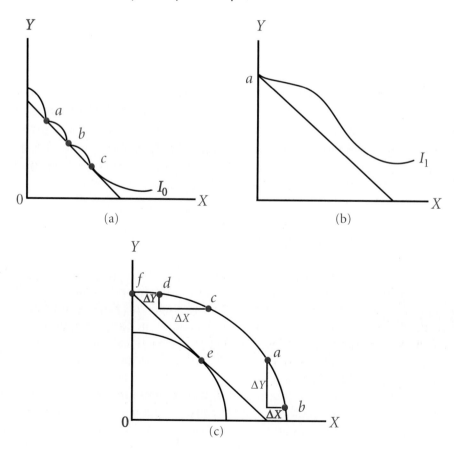

With "well-behaved" preferences, however, the optimal combination is an inferior solution defined by a point of tangency between the budget line and an indifference curve, where the marginal rate of substitution between the two commodities is equal to the ratios of their prices and where indifference curves are nonintersecting, convex to the origin, and negatively sloped. As shown in Figure 5–11, the marginal rate of substitution between bread and steak at point *a* is 5 to 1. That is, 5 loaves of bread must be added if 1 pound of steak is eliminated; this is equal to the price ratio 100/20, or 5/1. This relationship follows from the fact that because the curves are tangent at this point, they have the same slope. If this relationship did not hold, the consumer could gain satisfaction by purchasing more of one good and less of the other. Assume, for example, that the consumer were buying a combination of steak and bread for which the marginal rate of substitution was 12 to 1, while the price ratio was 5 to 1. The addition of 1 pound of steak, then, would require the loss of only 5 loaves of bread, whereas the person would be willing to sacrifice 12 loaves to gain the pound of steak. This substitution would obviously increase that satisfaction of the person and additional substitutions would continue to increase the individual's satisfaction until the two ratios became equal. The rule of maximizing satisfaction by equating marginal rates of substitution with price ratios applies to each pair of goods purchased, and thus must occur across all pairs of goods.

INDIFFERENCE CURVES WITH MORE THAN TWO COMMODITIES

The relationships portrayed in this analysis for two goods are similar to relationships between all of the various goods a person is interested in acquiring. This relationship can be illustrated by following the procedure of showing one commodity on the horizontal axis and all other goods (represented by dollars of expenditure on all other goods—AOGs) on the vertical axis. The **composite good** is the amount of money the consumer has left after buying good X. Prices of all other goods are assumed to be given and unchanged during the analysis. The indifference curve then shows various combinations of purchases of the good under consideration and total expenditures on all other goods (the "composite" good) that yields the same satisfaction. The curve's slope shows the person's marginal rate of substitution between this good and the expenditure on all other goods. As was the case in the two-good model, the consumer optimum occurs when the consumer reaches the highest indifference curve attainable with a given expenditure of money. (See Problems 5–15 and 5–16.)

5–15 Using indifference curves and a budget constraint show the impact of emission controls on the consumption of automobiles.

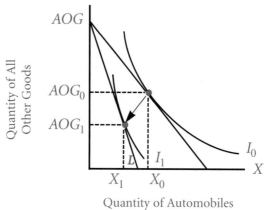

The imposition of emission controls on automobiles increases the relative price of automobiles. Hence, we would expect that fewer automobiles would be purchased.

5–16 Fertility rates in developing countries are higher in rural areas than in urban areas. Using indifference curves and budget lines, explain why you think this might be so, assuming that urban and rural families have the same preferences for children versus other goods.

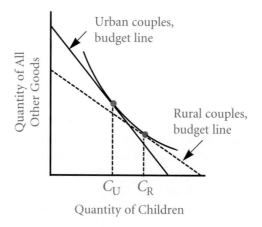

The relative price of children is higher in urban areas than it is in rural areas for at least two reasons. First, food and housing are generally more expensive in cities. Second, children have fewer opportunities to be productive in an urban setting. Rural children are quite productive at an early age, doing chores such as planting, weeding, gathering, and fence building. This is not the case in urban areas, where a child's contribution to the family's output is generally quite low.

The indifference curve is a convenient tool to aid in our understanding the effects of subsidies on individual consumption behavior. In this final section, we will consider two examples comparing the effects of an income subsidy to a price subsidy. The first question is whether the poor would be better off with a cash gift or food stamps. The second example examines the more general question of subsidizing the price of such goods as buses or trains.

Using the indifference curve approach, we can show that the poor would be at least equally as well off receiving cash rather than a subsidy such as food stamps.

Consider Figure 5–13. Point a represents a poor persons optimal position before a food-stamp subsidy program is introduced. Here the person consumes F_0 amount of food, an amount society deems insufficient. The introduction of a food-stamp program that allows the recipient to spend an additional $100 per month exclusively on food would make the consumer better off (bundles on indifference curve I_1 are preferred to those on I_0). For the same expense, however, this individual might be made even better off by receiving $100 in cash. The reason is that the shaded triangle is unobtainable to the recipient of food stamps but not to those receiving a cash payment. Unless the individual intended to spend *all* of the next $100 of additional income on food, he or she would be better off with a choice.

FIGURE 5–13
CASH GRANT VERSUS FOOD STAMP INCOME SUBSIDY

With no government assistance, the poor person chooses bundle a. The availability of food stamps increases the budget and allows the buyer to purchase bundle b, consuming more food and more other goods and attaining a higher level of utility. A cash grant, however, expands the budget set further. The recipient would purchase bundle c which contains more nonfood items and less food than bundle b, The person reaches a higher level of utiltiy with a cash grant than with food stamps.

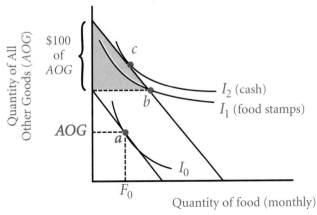

Similarly, subsidizing the price of a good (such as education, postal services, mass transportation, or medical services) is usually *not* the best method to assure that society's scarce resources will be efficiently allocated. Subsidizing the price of a good distorts market signals and results in output levels of the subsidized good that are inefficiently large. In other words, the opportunity cost of other goods that could have been produced with those resources is greater than the (marginal) value of the subsidized good. (Recall the ordinary supply-and-demand diagram for a subsidy from your introductory economics course.) Figure 5–14 shows that if the whole budget line is shifted parallel by an amount equivalent to the price subsidy, *ab* (*ab* = *cd*), then a higher indifference curve can be reached. Because reaching the highest indifference curve subject to the budget constraint maximizes consumer satisfaction, this simple diagram shows that it is better to subsidize income (parallel shift) than to subsidize price (altering the slope), if society is interested in making some group better off.[5] Of course, if society wants certain groups (say, the poor) to consume more of *particular* goods (housing or food), rather than just raising their utilities, the appropriate policy would not include unconstrained income subsidies. Recall that economists can never, in their role as economists, recommend one approach over the other, but they can point out the implications of alternative choices. (See Problems 5–17 and 5–18.)

---

[5] *Note also*: A prerequisite for even this analysis to be correct is that the group being subsidized must be small—if the graph referred to society as a whole (subsidizing everyone's food or transportation), the budget constraint (really, production possibilities curve in this case) will not shift at all. There are no free lunches.

FIGURE 5–14
CASH GRANTS VERSUS PRICE SUBSIDIES

A subsidy lowers the price paid for the goods, pivoting the budget line to the right, whereas a cash grant causes a parallel shift of the budget line to the right. The consumer chooses bundle A with the subsidy but attains a higher level of satisfaction under a cash grant program. More units of the subsidized good and fewer units of other goods are consumed with a subsidy than with a cash grant of equivalent value.

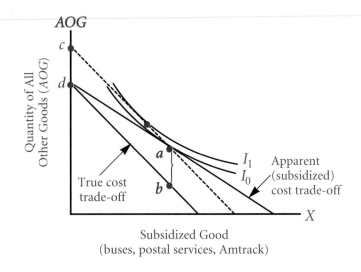

5–17 Evaluate the impact of subsidized food stamps on the recipient's budget line, level of utility, and choice of all other goods and food. Compare this to the outcome from an equivalent cash grant. Under what circumstances would a recipient be indifferent to equivalent values of food stamps and cash?

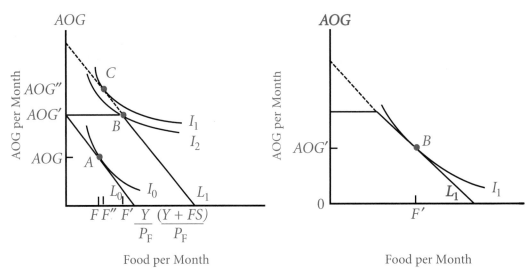

(b) Cash grants yield greater satisfaction than food stamps.

(b) Cash grants and food stamps yield the same level of satisfaction.

In Figure (a), L_0 is the consumer budget line, F is the optimal commodity bundle of food, and AOG is all other goods without any government assistance. Food stamps enable the consumer to increase consumption possibilities according to the kinked budget line, purchase more food (F') and more other goods (AOG'), and increase utility. An equivalent cash grant expands the consumer's opportunities further along the dotted line. This consumer purchases more of other goods (AOG'') and less food (F'') than with food stamps and achieves a higher level of utility.

Figure (b) shows the preference of a consumer who attains the same level of satisfaction and buys the same amount of food and other goods with food stamps as with an equivalent cash grant. This buyer's preferences are strongly biased toward food.

5–18 Government can support college education for veterans in two ways. One is to pay tuition for full-time enrollment directly to the university; the other is to give each veteran an equivalent amount in cash. Which method would encourage the most education? Which method would probably give the recipient the most utility?

The figure shows the student's budget line with no assistance, L_0. If tuition is paid, the budget line becomes L_1, and the student consumes E' education. With an equivalent cash grant the budget line becomes L_1 extended to the vertical axis. Here the student consumes less education but receives greater utility because the student is now on a higher indifference curve.

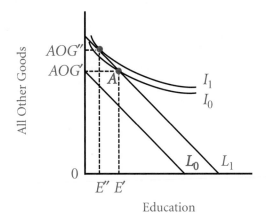

SUMMARY

1. When a specific number of utils can be attached to goods and services, utility is said to be measured cardinally. When goods and services can be ranked, we say that utility is measured ordinally.

2. The law of diminishing marginal utility states that marginal utility declines as successive units of a good are acquired.

3. The interaction of two factors are important in the explanation of diminishing marginal utility: Individual wants are satiable, and different goods are not perfect substitutes in satisfying particular wants.

4. Maximization of satisfaction requires that income must be allocated so that the marginal utility of a dollar's worth of any good is the same for every commodity. Alternatively, maximization requires that the ratios of marginal utilities of the various goods purchased equal the respective price ratios of the goods.

5. An indifference schedule (and curve) indicates the various combinations of two goods that yield a consumer the same total satisfaction. The indifference curve shows us nothing about the absolute amounts of satisfaction obtained. It merely indicates the various combinations that yield equal satisfaction.

6. More of a good is preferred to less of a good and transitivity of preferences is assumed with the indifference curve approach. Consistency of preferences requires that if bundle A is preferred to bundle B and bundle B is preferred to bundle C, then bundle A is preferred to bundle C.

7. Indifference curves cannot intersect. Intersecting curves would yield the inconsistent result of points on a higher indifference curve being equally satisfying to points on a lower indifference curve.

8. Indifference curves for two goods are negatively sloped. The slope of the indifference curve measures the marginal rate of substitution. The marginal rate of substitution is the number of units of one of the commodities necessary to replace one unit of the other good in order to maintain the same total satisfaction.

9. Indifference curves (for two goods, as opposed to a bad and a good, for example) are convex to the point of origin. The shape of indifference curves arises from the principle of diminishing marginal rate of substitution.

10. The budget line shows the various combinations of the two quantities of the two goods that can be purchased with a certain budget or given expenditure.

11. To attain the highest level of satisfaction one must reach the highest indifference curve obtainable with a given expenditure of money.

WORDS AND CONCEPTS FOR REVIEW

utility	diminishing marginal utility
ordinal measures/cardinal measures	indifference curve
transitivity	nonintersecting indifference curves
marginal rate of substitution/ diminishingmarginal rate of substitution	complements
substitutes	budget line
corner solution	composite good

REVIEW QUESTIONS

1. Explain the concept of marginal utility.

2. What is the law of diminishing marginal utility? Explain the underlying rationale.

3. Explain, in terms of the marginal utility approach, the pattern of allocation of consumer income that is necessary to allow maximization of satisfaction.

4. Why does optimal allocation require that the marginal utilities of the various goods purchased be proportional to their prices?

5. Explain the law of demand in terms of the marginal utility approach.

6. What is meant by an indifference schedule?

7. Why do indifference curves slope downward from left to right? Why do they not intersect?

8. What is meant by the term *marginal rate of substitution?* What is its relation to the slope of an indifference curve?

9. Why are indifference curves convex to the point of origin? What principle is involved in the explanation?

10. What determines the degree of convexity of an indifference curve?

11. Explain the budget line. What happens if the budget line rotates inward? Outward?

12. Explain why the point of tangency of the budget line and an indifference curve is the point of optimal satisfaction?

13. What is the relationship between the ratio of the prices of two goods and the marginal rate of substitution between them at the point of optimum satisfaction? Explain.

14. Which of the following statements is more accurate, and why?
    a.) "Bundle A is most preferred because it gives highest utility."
    b.) "Bundle A gives highest utility because it is most preferred."

SUGGESTED READINGS

Baumol, W. *Economic Theory and Operations Analysis*, 4th ed. Englewood Cliffs, N.J.: Prentice Hall, 1977, Chapter 9.

Cooter, R., and P. Rappoport. "Were the Ordinalists Wrong about Welfare Economics," *Journal of Economic Literature*. (June 1984), 507–30.

Henderson, J. M., and R. E. Quandt. *Microeconomic Theory*, 3rd ed. New York: McGraw-Hill, 1980, Chapter 2.

Hicks, J. R. *Value and Capital*, 2nd ed. Oxford: The Clarendon Press, 1946, Chapters 1 and 2.

Stigler, G. *The Theory of Price*, 4th ed. New York: Macmillan, 1987, Chapter 4.

Chapter Six

CONSUMER THEORY
AND DEMAND

Questions to Think About

1. What is a price-consumption curve?

2. What are the income and substitution effects of a price change?

3. What is the difference between normal, inferior, and Giffen goods?

4. What is the relationship of cross-elasticities to substitutes and complements?

5. What is the relationship between price elasticity of demand and the price-consumption curve?

6. What is an income-consumption curve?

7. What is an Engel curve?

6.1 INTRODUCTION

With an understanding of how individuals make decisions founded on their preferences (represented by indifference curves) and constrained by scarcity (reflected in the budget line), we can expand consumer theory to examine consumer behavior when prices and money available for expenditures are made variable. Indeed, this analysis lies at the heart of any effort to understand changes in consumer behavior.[1]

In this chapter for convenience we equate expenditures to income, bearing in mind that in this context income refers to budgeted expenditure available to the shopping specialist rather than the total income of the household.

6.2 THE PRICE-CONSUMPTION CURVE

The tangency relationship between a budget line and an indifference curve indicates the optimal amounts of each of the two goods the consumer will purchase, given the money prices of both goods and the consumer's available money income. At different possible prices for one of the goods, given the price of the other and given total income, a consumer would optimally purchase different quantities of the two. A change in the price of one of the goods alters the slope of the budget line because a different amount of the good can be purchased with a given level of income. If, for example, the price of X falls, the budget line becomes flatter because more of X can be purchased than previously with a given income. Likewise, at all points except that at which no units of X are purchased, the new budget line lies to the right of the old one: As Figure 6–1 shows, it rotates outward, from L_0 to L_1, as a result of the price reduction. Thus, the new point of tangency with an indifference curve will be on a higher indifference curve. The point of tangency moves from a to b as a result of the decline in price of X from \$20 to \$10; the equilibrium quantity of X purchased increases from 2 to 5 units.

Figure 6-2(a) shows a series of points of tangency of the budget line with indifference curves. The graph shows budget lines for various possible money prices for X (\$50.00, \$20.00, \$13.30, and \$10.00), the price of Y remaining unchanged at \$10.00. A relation known as the **price-consumption curve** (PCC) may be drawn through these points of tangency, indicating the optimum quantities of X (and Y) at various possible prices of X (given the price of Y). From this price-consumption curve, we can derive

---

[1]With stable preferences (an unchanging utility function), it is *only* changes in prices or income that can lead to changed behavior. This is the economist's somewhat restrictive approach; yet without good predictive theories of how tastes *change* (from perhaps sociology or psychology), the economist's approach is the only one available to those interested in prediction.

the usual demand curve for the good. Thus, Figure 6–2(a) shows that if the price of X is $10, 5 units will be purchased. These data may be plotted, as in Figure 6-2(b), to derive a demand curve for good X. Note that in Figure 6–2(b), the price of X is measured on the vertical axis and the quantity purchased on the horizontal axis, whereas the axes of Figure 6–2(a) refer to quantities of the two goods. Note also that the quantities demanded, as shown in Figure 6–2(b), are those with the consumer's expenditures in equilibrium (at his or her optimum) at the various prices. (See Problem 6–1.)

6–1 Derive an ordinary demand curve for compact discs (CDs) from the price-consumption curve given below. Assume a $20 budget line and a price of $1 for good Y.

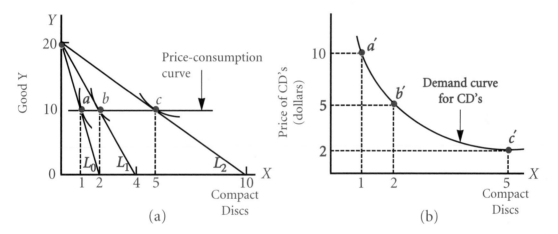

(a)   (b)

Starting with budget line L_0, if we spend the entire $20 on CDs and none of it on good Y, we can buy two CDs; this implies that the price of CDs is $10 each. When the price of CDs falls to $5 per unit, the budget line moves to L_1 (because $20 would, if spent entirely on CDs, buy 4). At L_2 CDs are $2 each. According to the indifference curves and budget lines in Figure (a), the consumer will buy one CD at $10 (*point a*), 2 when the price falls to $5 (*point b*), and 5 when the price is $2 (*point c*). In Figure (b) we convert the consumer's equilibrium points into a demand curve, with a′, b′, and c′ representing the price and quantity-demanded points for prices of $10, $5, and $2, respectively. In Figure (a), the price-consumption curve is perfectly horizontal, indicating that the demand curve is unitary elastic. Later in this chapter, we will discuss the implications of different slopes of the price-consumption curve for the elasticity of demand.

FIGURE 6–1
THE EFFECT OF A PRICE DECLINE

When the price of X falls from $20 to $10, the budget line rotates outward from L_0 to L_1. With $100 of income, the consumer can now afford to buy 10 units of X if all income is spent on X. The optimum bundle of X and Y changes from a to b and the consumer increases consumption of X from 2 to 5.

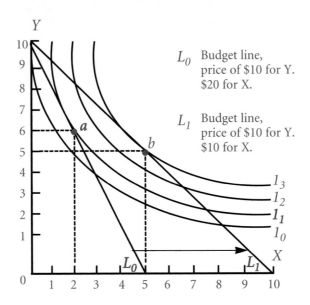

FIGURE 6–2

In part (a) the price-consumption curve, PCC, charts the equilibrium combinations of *X* and *Y* at different prices of X. In other words, the PCC connects the points of tangency between succeeding budget lines and indifference curves. The desired quantity of *X* for a given price can be read directly from the price-consumption curve diagram. For example, *point a* indicates that the consumer will buy 1/2 of a unit of *X* when the price of *X* is $50.00 (along budget line L_0). Because the demand curve shows the quantity demanded at various prices, *X* = 1/2 at price of *X* = $50.00 is one point on the demand curve in part (b). Similarly, the other points on the demand curve can be plotted.

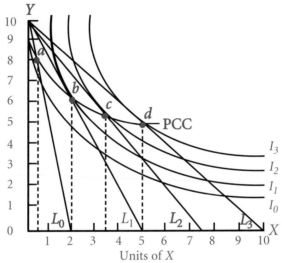

(a) The various combinations of goods *X* and *Y*
which will be purchased at various prices of *X*

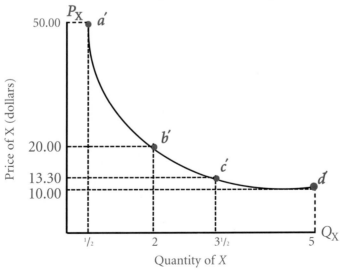

(b) The demand schedule for good *X* derived
from the price-consumption curve in graph (a)

Essentially, the demand curve is constructed from the optimal price and quantity points. That is, the demand curve indicates the quantities of a particular good the consumer will buy at various prices when he or she has attained optimal adjustment of expenditures among the various goods. However, one difficulty in constructing demand curves by observing actual consumer behavior is that observation alone does not indicate whether the consumer is at an optimum, and thus whether the observed price-quantity point lies on or off the demand curve. Rather, it is assumed that individuals attempt to maximize satisfaction or utility; hence, observed purchases are assumed to occur where (unobserved) indifference curves are tangent to the (observed) budget line.

6.3 THE INCOME EFFECT AND THE SUBSTITUTION EFFECT

With indifference curves, we can easily see the two ways through which a price reduction influences the quantity demanded. When the price of a good declines, the **income effect** enables the person to buy more of this good (or other goods) with a given income; the price reduction has the same effect as an increase in money income. That is, the consumer can now move onto a higher indifference curve. For example, in Figure 6–2, if price falls from $20 to $13.30, the consumer can move from indifference curve I_1 to curve I_2, and thus to a higher level of satisfaction. Of course, the entire amount of purchasing power freed might be used to purchase other goods. The typical effect, however, is to increase the consumption of good X as a result of the income effect, because income increases lead to an increase in demand for all normal goods.

The second influence of the price decline on the quantity demanded is the **substitution effect**. The lower price encourages the consumer to buy larger quantities of this commodity to replace units of other goods. The substitution effect is always negative. That is, price and quantity demanded are negatively correlated; lower prices mean higher purchased quantities and vice versa.

Figure 6–3 shows the income and substitution effects for an increase in the price of good X. Because the relative price of X increases, the budget line rotates inward from L_0 to L_1. (Note that the Y intercept has not changed, because neither income nor the price of good Y has changed. Hence, if all income is spent on Y before and after the price increase of X, the same amount of Y can be purchased). The total effect of the increase in the price of X is indicated by *point c*, that is, a reduction in the quantity of good X from X_0 to X_1.

Within the total effect, however, are both the substitution effect and the income effect. First, consider how much of the total effect is the result of substituting away from the now higher-priced good X, holding real income constant. This can easily be determined by taking the new budget line, L_1, and drawing a new hypothetical budget line, L^*, parallel to L_1 but tangent to the initial indifference curve I_0. Why? This shows the effect of the new relative price on the old indifference curve—in effect, the consumer is compensated for the loss of welfare associated with the price rise by enough income to return to the original indifference curve, I_0. Remember that as long as L_1 and L^* are parallel, the relative prices are the same; the only difference is the level of income. Thus, we are able to isolate the one effect—the amount of substitution that would prevail without the real income effect—which is the movement from a to b—the substitution effect.

The movement from b to c is a change in the real income when the relative prices are constant, because this move requires a parallel shift in the budget line. Thus, the movement from b to c results from the decrease in real income because of the higher price of good X while all other prices have remained constant—the income effect. Remember that the slope of the budget line indicates relative prices; thus, by shifting the new budget line tangent to the old indifference curve, we can see the change that took place holding real income (measured by utility) constant. Then when we make the parallel shift, we see the change in income, because the size of the parallel shift measures only the amount of real income change, with relative prices remaining constant.

Two cases that show the income and substitution effects of a reduction in the price of good X are considered in Figures 6–4(a) and (b). In Figure 6–4(a), the decrease in the price of X causes the budget line to rotate outward on the X axis from L_0 to L_1. As a result of the price decrease of X, the consumer would apparently wish to increase purchases of X by moving to bundle a^* from a. That is to say, if we somehow offset the real income effect of the reduction in price, the consumer would increase rather than decrease planned purchases of X, substituting the now cheaper good X for the relatively more expensive good Y, as required by common-sense accounts of the law of demand. In this case, however, we see that an increase in income (prices constant) would lead to a decrease in the equilibrium quantity of X demanded for purchase (going from a to b). In other words, the negative income effect has dominated the substitution effect. While this possibility of a so-called Giffen good is theoretically interesting, it has extremely limited empirical significance.[2]

Clearly, even if the income effect of a price reduction is negative, the total effect will still be to increase quantity demanded if the negative substitution effect is sufficiently large. Alternatively, if the quantity purchased is rather small, then the real income change associated with a price reduction will be small and the substitution effect of the price reduction will outweigh the income effect. We do not expect to turn

---

[2]The possibility that a price reduction could lead to a quantity reduction, and vice versa (upward-sloping demand curves), is however of only theoretical interest; there has never been a properly conducted empirical analysis in real market settings recording such a good referred to as a "Giffen good". However, it is possible that a Giffen good might be observable in experimental settings. The normal downward-sloping demand curve stems from the fact that a price change for most goods will generate a relatively small income effect because most goods must be both strongly inferior and important in the budget to offset the substitution effect, which always leads to downward-sloping demand.

up cases in practice in which the overall effect of a reduction in price is to decrease the quantity demanded of a good whose price has declined; that is, an upward-sloping demand curve.

The usual case for inferior goods is more like that represented in Figure 6–4(b). Here the lines and points are labeled precisely as in Figure 6–4(b), but the consumer's preferences are different. Again, good X is inferior with respect to changes in income but only to a limited degree. The substitution effect of the price change thus outweighs the income effect, and the overall result of a price reduction is to increase the quantity of X demanded for purchase. It is thus clear that the law of demand applies in all cases where (1) the good whose price declines is a normal good or (2) the total expenditure on the good whose price declines is small in relation to total expenditure on all goods— that is, the good is only weakly inferior with respect to changes in income. (See Problems 6–2 and 6–3.)

FIGURE 6–3
THE INCOME AND SUBSTITUTION EFFECTS

An increase in the price of good *X* causes an inward rotation of the budget line. The substitution effect, *a* to *b*, is measured along the original indifference curve. The income effect is measured by a parallel shift of the budget lines, *b* to *c*.

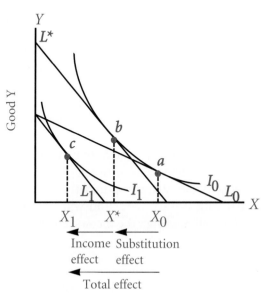

FIGURE 6–4
TOTAL EFFECT OF A PRICE REDUCTION FOR INFERIOR GOODS

As shown in part (a), a reduction in the price of *X* can decrease the quantity desired of *X* only if *X* is an inferior good and the negative income effect (*a** to *b*) dominates the substitution effect (*a* to *a**). In part (b), *X* is also an inferior good because the additional purchasing power resulting from the price decline (*L** to L_1) reduces the quantity of *X* desired (*a** to *b*). The net effect of the decreased price, however, is to increase purchases of *X* because the negative substitution effect exceeds the negative income effect, as will virtually always be the case even for inferior goods.

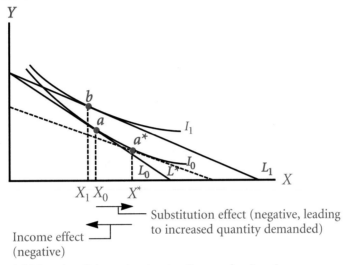

Substitution effect (negative, leading to increased quantity demanded)

Income effect (negative)

(a) Negative: Price reduction implies a reduction in quantity demanded

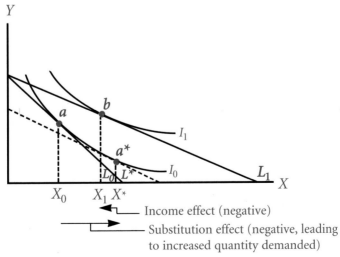

Income effect (negative)

Substitution effect (negative, leading to increased quantity demanded)

(b) Positive: Price reduction implies an increase in quantity demanded

6–2 Cigarette and alcohol taxes are imposed to discourage the consumption of "socially undesirable" goods. Using indifference curves, show the effect of a higher tax on alcoholic beverages. What is the total effect? How much of the change is the result of the income effect? The substitution effect?

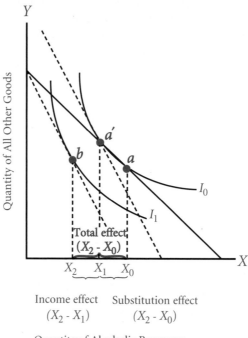

The effect is to reduce the consumption of alcoholic beverages by increasing their relative price. The total effect of the reduction in consumption is $X_0 - X_2$. The distance between X_0 and X_1 represents the reduction resulting from the substitution effect. That is, substitution occurs, which favors other goods relative to the now more-expensive alcoholic beverages. The other component of the total effect is the income effect. The income effect shows the loss in real income resulting from the price increase. When the price of all other goods and income remain fixed, the consumer *loses* real purchasing power.

6–3 Show graphically the income and substitution effects for an increase in the price of Y.

An increase in P_Y is reflected by the rotation of the budget line from L_0 to L_1. The total effect of the price change is from A to C. The substitution effect is determined by noting the change in the consumption of Y that would result from the change in the relative prices along the original indifference curve, or the change from A to B. The income effect is the lower amount of Y desired, resulting from the reduction in purchasing power corresponding to the movement from B to C.

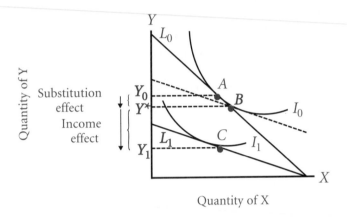

Quantity of X

DETERMINANTS OF PRICE ELASTICITY OF DEMAND: SUBSTITUTABILITY

The price elasticity of demand for a good depends primarily on the degree which it can be substituted for other goods in the satisfaction of wants. When consumers regard several goods as more or less equally desirable in satisfying particular wants, the demand curve for each tends to be relatively more elastic, because changes in their relative prices will cause substantial shifting of relative purchases. For example, an increase in the price of oranges would cause many consumers to purchase more apples, grapefruit, or bananas and fewer oranges. When less satisfactory substitutes are available, price changes have less effect on the quantity demanded.

The effects of **substitutability** on the elasticity of demand may be illustrated using an indifference curve. The greater the degree to which the good in question can be substituted for others (and other goods may be substituted for it), the less the curvature of the indifference curve; that is, the curve more closely approaches a straight line. The flatter the curvature, the greater the extent to which the point of tangency of the budget line with an indifference will shift to the right when the price of the good falls; thus, the more the purchases of the good increase in response to the price reduction.

The significance of the curvature is illustrated in Figure 6–5(a) and (b). To show exactly the significance of substitutability, we have to eliminate the income effect on utility. We do this by drawing a budget line (L^*) parallel to the new budget line (L_1) after the price change, at a location such that L^* is tangent to the old indifference curve (I_0).

In Figure 6-5(a), where the curvature of the indifference curve is slight, the tangency of L^* with I_0 (where X_1 is purchased) is much farther to the right of the original tangency of L_0 with I_0 (where X_2 is purchased) than it is in Figure 6-5(b), where the curvature is greater because the goods are poor substitutes. (See Problem 6–4.)

FIGURE 6–5
SUBSTITUTABILITY AND ELASTICITY

When X and Y are close substitutes, indifference curves are nearly linear. A decline in the price of X induces a large increase in the purchases of X as the consumer substitutes X for Y. Corresponding demand curves tend to be relatively more price elastic. When X and Y are not readily substitutable, indifference curves approach the L-shape, and a change in the price of X evokes a much smaller change in the quantity of X desired. In this case, demand curves are relatively price inelastic.

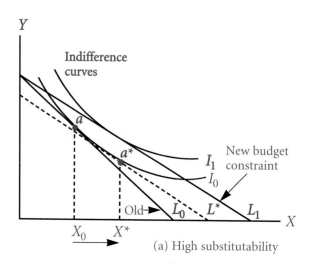

(a) High substitutability

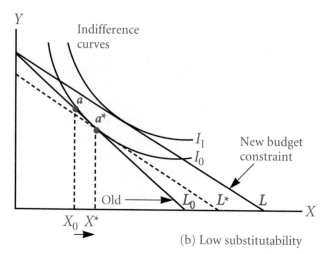

(b) Low substitutability

6–4 Elizabeth always consumes potato chips and dip in fixed proportions, never consuming one without the other. Using a diagram, show an optimum combination of chips and dip for Elizabeth. Suppose the price of chips rises. Show the new equilibrium. How does a change in the price of chips affect the demand for dip?

Chips and dip are perfect complements for Elizabeth. In the figure her original consumption of dip is X_D. When the price of potato chips rise she consumes fewer chips and less dip, X'_D. The combinations (P_D, X_D) and (P_D, X'_D), where P_D is the price of dip (which has not changed on this example), represent points on two different demand curves for dip (see Figure (b)). Hence, the price of the complementary good chips is a demand-curve shifter for dip.

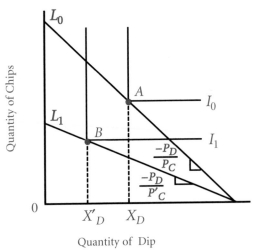

(a) An increase in the price of chips

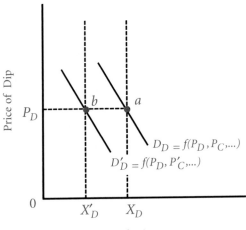

(b) The demand for dip

The same relationships may be expressed in terms of marginal rates of substitution. If the rate falls rapidly, as it will if the goods are poor substitutes, a decline in the price of one good results in only a relatively slight readjustment in quantities of the two goods purchased to restore equality of the price ratios and the marginal rate of substitution. If the marginal rate of substitution falls slowly, a much greater readjustment in relative purchases is optimal.

OTHER INFLUENCES ON PRICE ELASTICITY OF DEMAND

The price elasticity of demand is likewise affected by the nature of the want for which the good is being acquired or, in terms of utility, the rate of decline in marginal utility as additional units of the good are acquired. The more quickly the want is satiated, and thus the more rapidly the marginal utility (or the marginal rate of substitution) falls, the less elastic is the demand. The marginal utility of bread, for example, generally falls more quickly than the marginal utilities of various forms of recreation. When a good has alternate uses, however—that is, when a good can be used to satisfy other wants—marginal utility declines at a slower rate.

Price elasticity is affected by two closely related considerations: product durability and the time interval for which the demand schedule is relevant. When goods can be used for a number of years, individual consumers are not in the market for additional units for a considerable period of time after they have been purchased. If the goods are not durable, however, consumers can adjust their rates of purchase at any time and thus are more immediately sensitive to price changes. As a consequence, demand curves for durable goods are more elastic the longer the period of time over which demand is defined; that is, demand would be more elastic for a price change lasting for a year than for a month.

The demand for nondurable goods used in conjunction with durable equipment is affected in a similar manner. If someone has purchased a diesel-engine automobile, she cannot quickly shift from diesel to gasoline without substantial additional expense. Thus, changes in relative prices of diesel and gas do not cause an immediate switch from one fuel to the other. When the automobile is replaced, however, substitution of the cheaper fuel for the more expensive one may occur, *ceteris paribus*.

Apart from considerations of durability, the importance of habit in consumer purchasing causes the demands for many goods, durable or not, to be more elastic over a longer period of time than they are in a shorter period. People become accustomed to buying certain articles and do not frequently reconsider the desirability of adjusting their purchases. Thus, price changes may bring little immediate response. Over a longer period, however, there is greater likelihood (indeed *requirement*, if prices are higher or income is lower) of reconsidering the desirability of purchases and of seeking substitutes, and the effects of changes in relative prices is greater. Thus, if the price of beef falls greatly, most consumers at first may not consider replacing chicken or fish with beef. If the price remains at a low level over a period of time, more and more people may revise their purchase patterns to take advantage of the lower price of beef. Furthermore, over a longer period, consumers are more likely to become better informed about the existence of lower prices.

The elasticity of the market-demand curve for a good is determined by the elasticities of the individual-demand curves that underlie it. As the price of a good falls, much of the increase in quantity demanded may come from new purchasers—persons who would buy none of the good at higher prices. These may be people with relatively low incomes or those whose desires for the good are relatively weak. For some products, the demand curves of individual buyers are extremely inelastic, yet the market demand is elastic because many additional buyers will enter the market at lower prices. Thus, the demand for compact disc players may be relatively elastic, even though few individuals buy more than one regardless of the price.

6.4 THE LEVEL OF MARKET DEMAND

As noted in Chapter 3, a given *market*-demand curve relating price and quantity demanded is valid only when the prices of other goods are given and a host of other "shift" parameters (income, population, tastes, and so on) are held constant. It is useful to consider the relationships between changes in those "givens," which result in shifts in the position and form of the individual-demand curve. The problem may be approached by considering the relationship between these variables and the quantity demanded, price now being regarded as given instead of variable.

PRICES OF OTHER COMMODITIES

The first major determinant of the demand for a good is the prices of other related goods. The influence of the prices of other goods in part depends on the good whose price changes. Price changes of close substitutes are far more significant than are those of goods not closely related to the good in question. The demand for oranges is affected much more by the prevailing price of tangerines than by that of theater tickets.

The nature of the cross-elasticity of demand between two goods depends on the relative influences of the income and substitution effects. You may recall from Chapter 3 that the *cross-price elasticity* formula is as follows:[3]

$$E_{O,A} = \frac{\Delta Q_O / Q_O}{\Delta P_A / P_A} = \frac{\Delta Q_O}{\Delta P_A} \cdot \frac{P_A}{Q_O} \qquad \begin{array}{l} O = \text{Oranges} \\ A = \text{Apples} \end{array}$$

---

[3]In terms of derivatives,

$$E_{Y,PX} = \frac{dY}{dP_X} \cdot \frac{P_X}{Y}$$

As with ordinary price elasticities, we must be careful to consider whether real income is being held constant. When the price of one good falls, the income effect (the freeing of purchasing power due to the price reduction) encourages the consumer to purchase more units of both goods. However, the fact that the price of the first good has fallen relative to the price of the second encourages people to substitute the first for the second and, thus, to buy less of the second. If the substitution effect outweighs the income effect, the cross-elasticity is positive, and the two goods are regarded as **gross substitutes** for one another.[4] This situation is illustrated in Figure 6–6. If the price of good X fell, consumers would substitute away from good Y as they buy more X. The price of good X, fell, consumers would substitute away from good Y as they buy more X. The higher the cross-elasticity, the greater is the ease of substitution. If the articles are perfect substitutes (and thus essentially the same good, from the users' standpoint), the cross-elasticity is infinite.

In two types of situations cross-elasticity is negative; that is, a decline in the price of one good will lead to an increase in the quantity of the other good purchased. In the first case (shown in Figure 6–7), the income effect of the price change may outweigh the substitution effect. As the price of X falls, if little substitution occurs and the demand for X is inelastic, less of a given budget will be spent on X than before, and the amount of Y purchased may increase.

The other case of negative cross-elasticity is when the goods are *complementary*, such as tennis rackets and tennis balls, where the increased use of one induces the increase in the use of the other. A decline in the price of tennis rackets stimulates increased use of tennis balls. This raises the marginal utility of tennis balls and increases the quantity of tennis balls purchased. If total expenditure on the two items rises, of course, then purchases of other goods must decline to free the necessary purchasing power.

---

[4]The term *gross* includes the real income effects; that is, moving down the PCC as the price of *X* falls, holding money income and the price of *Y* constant, real income is rising. Therefore, when either the term *gross complement* or *gross substitute* is used it includes both the substitution and real income effect. If, on the other hand, we were to use the term *net substitutes* or *complements*, then we are exclusively referring to the substitution effect.

FIGURE 6–6
POSITIVE CROSS-ELASTICITY

A decrease in the price of X reduces the amount of Y desired from a to b. The cross-elasticity, the percentage change in purchases of Y divided by the percentage change in the price of X is positive and the two goods are *gross substitutes.*

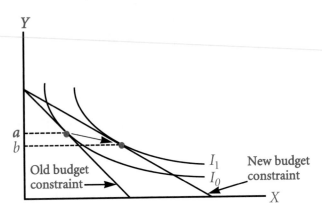

FIGURE 6–7
NEGATIVE CROSS-ELASTICITY

Purchase of Y increase in response to a decrease in the price of X when the two goods are *gross complements.*

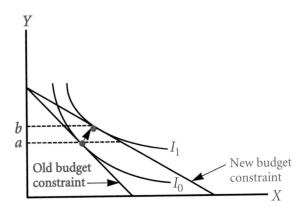

The slope of the *price-consumption curve* reveals the individual's price elasticity of demand. With fixed money income I, we vary the price of X in Figure 6–8.

In Figure 6–8(a) the PCC is horizontal. There is *no change* in expenditure on Y (the same amount is bought, and the price of Y is unchanged); hence, there is *no change* in expenditure on X. That is, when the PCC is flat, price changes lead to proportional changes in consumption of the good whose price changes; the price elasticity is 1, or unit elastic. But what about the cross-price elasticity when the PCC is flat? It must be zero! Because there is no change in Y consumed when the price of X changes and the PCC is flat, there is said to be an "independence of wants" between the goods. Good X and good Y are neither substitutes nor complements.

What about the upward- or downward-sloping portions of the price-consumption curve?

If the PCC is downward sloping, as in Figure 6–8(b), the lowering of the price of X results in less of Y being bought. Because the price of Y has not changed, less is spent on Y; hence, *more* must be spent on X. It must be the case, then, that at lower prices the proportional increase in X consumption more than offsets the price reduction. That is, the percentage increase in quantity is larger than the percentage price reduction, which means the demand for X is *price elastic* over this range. Hence, when the PCC curve is falling, the price elasticity must be greater than 1. What about the cross-price elasticity? Because lowering the price of X decreases the quantity of Y demanded, X and Y are gross substitutes.

If the PCC is upward sloping, as in Figure 6–8(c) the argument reverses: Because more Y is bought when the price of X falls, expenditures on good Y increase and expenditures on good X decrease. Hence, the proportional price reduction of good X is larger than the proportional increase in demand for X at lower prices. Thus, the demand for X is *price inelastic* if the PCC slopes upward. Hence, when the PCC is rising, the price elasticity must be less than 1. As for the cross-price effect, the price reduction of X causes more Y to be purchased; hence, X and Y are **gross complements.**

FIGURE 6–8
THE PRICE-CONSUMPTION CURVE AND ELASTICITY OF DEMAND

The price elasticity of demand will be equal to 1 if the PCC is horizontal (figure a.), greater than 1 if the PCC has a negative slope (figure b.) and less than 1 if the PCC has a positive slope (figure c.).

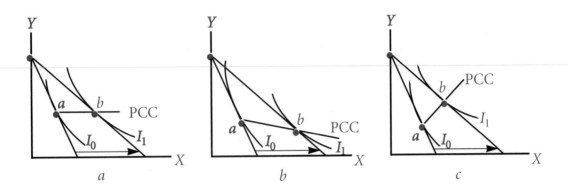

CHANGES IN INCOME

A second major determinant of the household's consumption demand is income. The functional relationship between quantity demanded and income (*ceteris paribus*), and thus the income elasticity of demand, varies greatly between different goods. These differences arise from the nature of consumer preferences and the behavior of marginal utility (or marginal rate of substitution) as additional units are acquired. The more rapid the rate of decline in marginal utility (or the marginal rate of substitution) as income rises, the lower the income elasticity. High positive income elasticity is characteristic of many so-called luxuries, items not imperative for a minimum living standard but highly desired once incomes reach a certain level. Low income elasticity is characteristic of goods the desire for which is quickly satisfied.

The response of demand to income changes can be illustrated with the use of indifference curves by showing progressively higher budget lines (drawn *parallel* to indicate unchanged relative prices). With a given pattern of indifference curves, larger amounts available for spending result in an **income-consumption curve** (ICC) connecting the optimal consumption points (tangencies) at each income level. Figure 6–9 shows goods of **high positive**, **low positive**, and **negative income elasticity**.

As Chapter 3 noted, income elasticity is negative for inferior goods; the quantities purchased fall as income rises. These are goods such as cheap cuts of meat or second-hand clothing, which consumers generally buy only because they cannot yet afford more expensive substitutes. As incomes rise, buyers shift to preferred substitutes and decrease their demand for the inferior goods. Such a case is shown in Figure 6–9(c), where good X is inferior. (See Problems 6–3 and 6–4.)

FIGURE 6–9
INCOME ELASTICITY

An increase in income, shifting the budget line to the right and parallel to the original budget line, increases the amount of X desired from a to b in part (a). The income-consumption curve, ICC, shows the optimum combinations of X and Y as income changes. The relatively flat slope of the ICC signifies a large response in the demand for X as income changes and a high income elasticity. In part (b), the rise in income induces a smaller increase in the demand for X (a to b). The ICC is steeper, and the income elasticity is lower. The downward-sloping ICC in part (c) indicates that an income boost reduces the demand for X from a to b. Thus, in part (c), X is an inferior good and the income elasticity is negative.

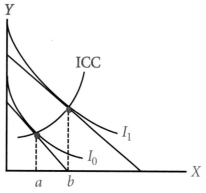

(a) High positive income elasticity

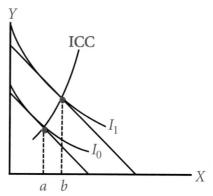

(b) Low positive income elastic-

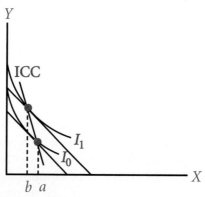

(c) Negative income elasticity

6–5 Can an income-consumption curve be constructed for a good that is initially normal at low income levels, but becomes inferior at higher levels?

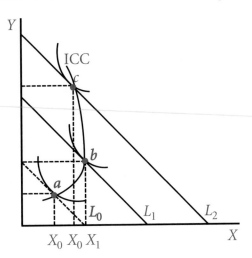

Yes. As the budget line moves out from L_0 to L_1, this consumer desires more of both goods and increases consumption of good X from X_0 to X_1 and increases consumption of good Y from Y_0 to Y_1. However, when income rises to the level reflected by budget line L_2, the consumer reduces consumption of good X from X_1 to X_2 and increases consumption of good Y from Y_1 to Y_2. Thus, as income increases, this consumer has reduced consumption of good X. For example, this might be the case with hamburgers; if income increases slightly, you might consume more hamburger at home. However, if income increases still more, you might switch to New York steaks.

6–6 Katherine, a five-year-old, doesn't care whether commodity X, (a super hero "action" toy) exists. She neither gains nor loses from this good; that is, the super hero "action" toy is a neutral commodity. Graph Katherine's indifference curves for X and good Y (dolls), and show her equilibrium bundle. Graph Katherine's income-consumption curve for X and Y.

In the figure Katherine's indifference curves for X and Y are horizontal; that is, she derives no additional utility from additional units of good X (super hero "action" toy). Her only preference direction is north, where she reaches a higher indifference curve and more dolls. When Katherine's budget line is L_1, her equilibrium bundle is A, consuming all of Y and none of X. As income increases (birthday money), she purchases more Y but never purchases any X. Hence, Katherine's ICC is the vertical axis.

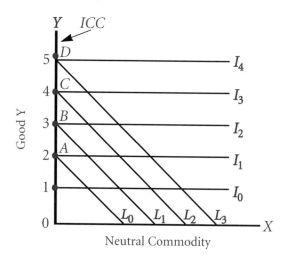

ENGEL CURVES

Studies of income elasticity of demand for various goods were among the first empirical studies in economics. The pioneer work was that of Engel, who discovered the relationships now known as Engel's laws (or, graphically, as Engel curves). In recent years, greater availability of data has allowed much more exhaustive research on the question. One of Engel's laws—that food consumption rises less rapidly than income—has been confirmed many times. Most studies have found elasticities approaching unity for clothing and education, and high elasticities for recreation, personal care, home operation, and other services. There are, of course, significant variations based on family characteristics and preferences.

The derivation of an **Engel curve** is straightforward, as shown in Figure 6–10(a) and (b). At the initial money income level $20, 6 units of X are consumed, as seen in Figure 6–10(a). This point is plotted as point a′ on the Engel curve for good X in Figure 6–10(b). Doubling income from $20 to $40 leads to a somewhat less than doubled demand for good X, and this combination of income and demand for good X is plotted as point b′ in Figure 6–10(b). An equivalent further increase in money income to $60 leads to a further increase in demand for X, as drawn in Figure 6–10(a); this increase is proportionately smaller than the increase in money income. This is plotted as point c′ in Figure 6–10(b); connecting all such points yields the Engel curve. (See Problems 6–7 and 6–8.)

FIGURE 6–10
THE ENGEL CURVE

The relationship between money income and demand for a commodity is depicted by the Engel curve. Each budget line in part (a) corresponds to a different income level, and each tangent point on the ICC shows the optimum amount of goods X and Y for a consumer. The combination of good X and income along the Engel curve in part (b) can be read directly from the ICC diagram.

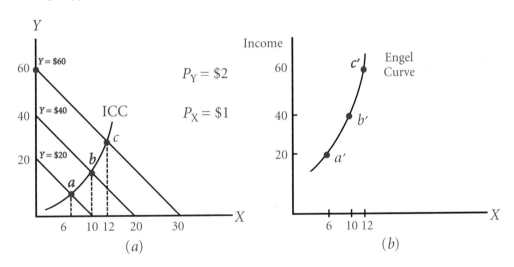

6–7 Diagram the ICC for a normal good on the Y axis and an inferior good on the X axis, and the corresponding Engel curve for an inferior good. Can both goods be inferior in a two-good world? What factors must be held constant when diagramming an Engel curve?

Figure (a) charts the ICC. Good Y is normal, because an increase in income, demonstrated by a shift in L_0 to L_1, increases purchases of it; conversely, X is inferior, since less is desired when income rises. If there are only two goods, assuming the consumer must spend all income, increases in income necessitates greater purchases of at least one of the goods. If this were not the case, it would violate one of the indifference curve assumptions: More of a good is preferred to less of a good. Thus, both goods cannot be inferior. The Engel curve showing the equilibrium quantity of X for each income level is drafted in Figure (b). The price of X, the prices of related goods, tastes, and price expectations must be held fixed to graph an Engel curve.

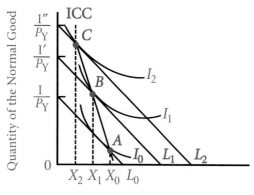

(a) The income-consumption curve: Inferior Good

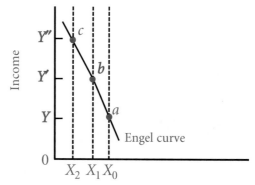

(b) The Engel curve: Inferior Good

6–8 Using indifference curves and budget lines, show how the prices of substitute and complementary goods, income (normal good), and tastes affects the demand for good X.

Figure (a) shows that an increase in the price of a substitute good Y raises the demand for X_0 to X_1. In Figure (b), the demand for X falls to X_1 when the price of a complementary good Y rises. If X is a normal (inferior) good as in Figure (c), an increase in income raises (lowers) demand. A change in tastes that favors X shifts the indifference curves as in Figure (d).

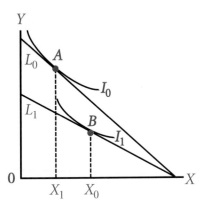

(a) Increase in the price of a
substitute group

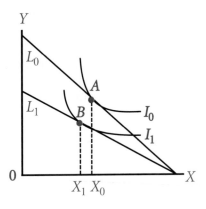

(b) Increase in the price of a
complementary group

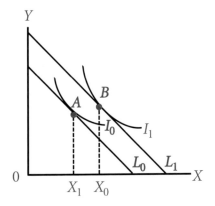

(c) Increase in income for
normal goods

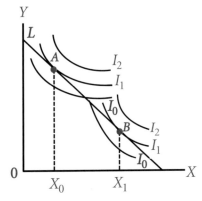

(d) Change in tastes

SUMMARY

1. The price-consumption curve is derived by connecting the tangency points of the indifference curves and budget lines as the price of X changes (holding money income, tastes, and other prices constant).

2. When the price of a good falls (rises) the consumer is able to buy more (less) of this good and other goods. Thus, the price reduction (increase) has the same effect as an increase (decrease) in money income. The income effect is usually positive.

3. The substitution effect results in a consumer substituting a less expensive good for a relatively more expensive good as the relative price changes.

4. Price elasticity of demand is influenced by the relative substitutability between goods, the satiability of wants (i.e., the more quickly the want is satiated, the less elastic the demand), the durability of the product, time intervals, and so on. The price elasticity of the market demand schedule is determined by the individual demand schedules that underlie it.

5. The level of the market demand schedule is determined by shift parameters such as the price of other goods (i.e., substitutes and complements), income, and taste.

6. The nature of cross-elasticity of demand between two goods depends on the relative influences of the income and substitution effects. The higher the cross-elasticity, the greater is the ease of substitution. A negative cross-elasticity means that either the goods are complements or the income effect of a price change outweighs the substitution effect.

7. The income-consumption curves connect the optimal consumption points (tangencies) as the income level is varied. Inferior goods have an income elasticity that is negative. Goods with low income elasticity are those for which the desire is quickly satisfied. High positive income elasticities usually denote so-called luxury goods.

WORDS AND CONCEPTS FOR REVIEW

price-consumption curve   income effect

substitution effect   high (low) substitutability

gross substitutes   gross complements

income-consumption curve   high and low positive income elasticity

negative income elasticity   engel curve

QUESTIONS

1. Distinguish between the price-consumption curve and the demand curve.

2. Explain how the demand schedule can be derived from an individual indifference curve map and budget lines.

3. Distinguish between the income and substitution effects of an increase in the price of good X when X is a normal good. Illustrate your answer graphically.

4. Distinguish between the income and substitution effects of a decrease in the price of good X when X is an inferior good. Illustrate your answer graphically.

5. What is a Giffen good? Illustrate your answer graphically.

6. It has been said the utility-maximizing approach to the theory of consumer demand merely tells us that the household acts as it wishes to act—which is not a theory at all. Do you agree or disagree? Explain.

7. List some of the determinants of the elasticity of demand.

8. Using indifference curves, show the difference between gross substitutes and gross complements.

9. Derive an income-consumption curve from an indifference-curve map.

10. Draw an income-consumption curve and an Engel curve for good Y, a normal good, and a luxury good such as gourmet restaurant meals.

SUGGESTED READINGS

Friedman, M. *Price Theory*. Chicago: Aldine Publishing, 1976, Chapter 2.

Henderson, J. M., R. E. Quandt. *Microeconomic Theory*. 3rd ed. New York: McGraw-Hill, 1980, Chapter 2.

Hicks, J.R. *Value and Capital*. 2nd ed. Oxford: The Clarendon Press, 1946, Chapters 1 and 2.

Stigler, G. *The Theory of Price*. 4th ed. New York: Macmillan, 1987, Chapter 4.

Chapter Seven

THE THEORY
OF PRODUCTION

_____ *Questions to Think About* _____

1. What is a production function?

2. What are total product, average product, and marginal product? How are they related?

3. What are the three stages of production?

4. What is an isoquant?

5. What is the marginal rate of technical substitution?

6. What are increasing, constant, and decreasing returns to scale?

7.1 INTRODUCTION

*H*aving completed our discussion of consumer demand, we turn now to the output and supply side of final product markets—the theory of production and cost. Our point of departure is the assumption that the object of the business firm is to maximize the profit stream over a number of periods, as discussed in Chapter 2; that is, we assume that firms attempt to maximize the difference between total revenue and total cost. Achieving this object requires, among other conditions, that the firm purchase and combine factor inputs in such a way that the total cost of producing a particular level of output is as low as possible, given existing technological and institutional conditions. This chapter examines the reactions of output to changes in inputs of various factors.[1]

The typical business firm manages a substantial portfolio of financial and physical goods, equipment, machinery, land, and buildings. The financial management side of a firm's activities is not rigidly linked with its production activities. A firm that requires additional space does not need to purchase a building outright, for it may buy a plant from another business firm or lease space from one of its divisions to provide space for another. Similarly, in deciding how to divide earnings between payments to owners and savings on its own account, a business firm's actions seldom impinge directly on current production decisions. An efficient management will attempt to conduct its production, marketing, and financial management activities so that joint returns are optimized. We first examine the theory of production as an essentially separate branch of the general theory of business behavior.

7.2 THE PRODUCTION FUNCTION

The maximum amount of a product that a firm can produce with any given collection of factor inputs is determined by its unique circumstances and by existing technology. The relationship between the inputs and the outputs is expressed symbolically by a **production function** of the general form

$$q = f(V_1, V_2 \cdots V_n)$$

Where the variables V_1, V_2, $\ldots$, V_n represent quantities of various factor inputs such as labor, capital, and natural resources. The variable q represents the firm's maximum output for a given technology. We may assume that an increase in any of the input

---

[1]The behavior of cost in response to changes in output will be discussed in Chapter 8. The determination of market prices through the interplay of demand and output-supply considerations will be examined in Chapters 9 – 12.

variables will, at least up to some limit, increase output. We may also assume that the proportions in which various factor inputs can be combined to produce a given quantity of output are normally variable. Of course, certain chemical processes require fixed proportions (at least among ingredients); but experience indicates that apart from this (and perhaps a few other minor exceptions), input proportions can be varied significantly while maintaining output at a constant level. Thus, one material can be substituted for another in the production of houses or automobiles; capital equipment may be substituted for labor in the production of long-distance phone calls, secretarial services, and so on.

7.3 TYPICAL OUTPUT BEHAVIOR:
ONE VARIABLE INPUT

Suppose that the input of just one factor is varied, while all other inputs are held constant. What will be the behavior of total output in these circumstances? Common sense suggests that output will start at a low (possibly zero) level and increase—perhaps rapidly at first and then more slowly—as the amount of the variable input increases. It will continue to increase until the quantity of the variable input becomes so large in relation to the quantity of other inputs that further increases in output become more and more difficult or even impossible. Beyond this point, additional units of the variable input may even result in a decline in total output. The implied pattern of output behavior is illustrated in Figure 7–1 by the total product curve (TP). The intuitive plausibility of this pattern may be strengthened by considering alternative interpretations of the variables V and q.

Suppose that q represents the output (in horsepower) of an electric motor and V represents the input of electric energy (in watts). At zero input, the motor does not turn; as energy input rises, the motor turns with increasing speed and delivers evergreater amounts of mechanical power until the capacity of the motor (a fixed factor) is reached. Beyond that, power output does not increase and may even decrease through overheating of bearings or actual breakdown.

Alternatively, suppose that q represents your cumulative grade-point average while V represents your average weekly input of study hours. Depending on your intelligence, the quality of your personal and college libraries, the competence of your teachers, the personality of your roommate, and other factors, the curve relating your input to your output may be relatively steep or relatively flat, but its general shape will surely be as illustrated in Figure 7–1.

FIGURE 7–I
TOTAL PRODUCT CURVE: ONE VARIABLE INPUT WITH FIXED INPUT(S)

The graphical representation of the production function when one input varies and all others are fixed is the total product curve. It shows the potential output produced by various quantities of the variable input V and the fixed inputs.

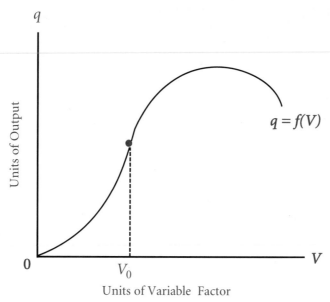

7.4 AVERAGE AND MARGINAL PRODUCTS

To facilitate later analysis, it is convenient to introduce two new concepts at this point: *average product* and *marginal product*. The **average product** (AP) of an input is defined as the ratio of total output to the quantity of the input used; in symbols:

$$AP = q/V$$

The magnitude of this ratio corresponding to any given value of V can be obtained graphically from the total product curve. The average product curve can be determined by finding the slope of a straight line (a ray) connecting the origin with any point on the total product curve. The slope of such a line obviously varies continuously with variations in V. Because the slope of the ray from the origin to any point on the total product curve is $0q/0V$, the slope represents the average product. For example, in Figure 7–2, we see as we move from ray 1 to ray 2 to ray 3 that the slope of the rays that connect to points A, B, and C on the total product curve first rises and then falls. That is, the AP curve must first rise and then fall with a normal-shaped TP curve.

The **marginal product** (MP) of any single input is defined as the change in total output resulting from a small change in the input.[2] In symbols:

$$MP = \Delta q / \Delta V$$

That is, the marginal product of an input can be described as the ratio of *small change* in output (denoted by Δq) to a *small change* in input (denoted by ΔV). The slope of the total product curve is the change in total product divided by the change in V. This is also the marginal product, the change in total product when V changes by one unit along the TP curve. The slope of the tangent to the total product curve obviously varies with variations in V, and this slope shows the rate at which output increases for small changes in V at various levels of V. This is illustrated by the marginal product curve, MP, as shown in Figure 7-2. You can see that the MP is at a maximum when the slope of the total product curve is greatest, at its inflection point, A, where the slope of the total product curve begins to increase at a decreasing rate. Thus, the MP curve must first rise and then fall.

The relation between the AP, MP, and TP curves in Figure 7–2 and Table 7–1 merits close examination. Where the MP curve lies *above* the AP curve, the AP curve rises with additional inputs. This reflects the familiar fact that adding a larger than average number to a sequence of numbers increases the average value of the sequence. For a similar reason, whenever the MP curve lies *below* the AP curve, the AP curve declines with added inputs. Hence, MP intersects the AP curve at the highest point of the latter; where the MP curve lies neither above nor below the AP curve, the AP curve can be neither rising nor falling. Note also that where the TP curve reaches its peak, the MP curve intersects the horizontal axis (the slope of TP is zero); that is, further increases in the input cause total product to decline.

Figure 7–2 shows the relationship between the TP, AP, and MP curves. The MP is at a maximum when the slope of the TP is greatest, at its inflection point A. The AP is at a maximum when a ray drawn from the origin is the steepest possible. This occurs at point B. It is also the point on the TP where the slope of the ray and the slope of the TP curve are identical. Thus, at point B, MP = AP. Where TP is flat, at point C, MP = 0.

The intersections of the MP curve, first with the peak of the AP curve and then with the horizontal axis, demarcate three stages that are typical of most production processes; (1) an initial stage of *increasing average returns* (where MP exceeds AP); (2) an intermediate stage of *diminishing average returns* (where MP is less than AP but MP is positive); (3) a terminal stage of *negative marginal returns* (where total product declines). The three stages are indicated in Figure 7–2 by the broken lines, one passing through the highest point of the AP curve and the other passing through the highest point of the TP curve. (See Problem 7–1.)

---

[2]The marginal product, then, is the partial derivative of the production function with respect to one input, the values of all other inputs being held constant. If $q = f(V)$, the marginal product is

$$\frac{\partial q}{\partial V} = f'(V)$$

TABLE 7–1

Typical Output Behavior with One Variable Factor

Units of Variable Factor V	Total Output q	Average Product q/V	Marginal Product $\Delta q / \Delta V$
1	12	12.00	12
2	28	14.00	16
3	52	17.33	24
4	74	18.50	22
5	91	18.20	17
6	104	17.33	13
7	114	16.29	10
8	120	15.00	6
9	121	13.44	1
10	115	11.50	-6

FIGURE 7–2
OUTPUT BEHAVIOR AS ONE VARIABLE FACTOR INPUT IS INCREASED WITH OTHER FACTORS FIXED

The MP, or slope of the TP curve, reaches a maximum when the TP curve is steepest at its inflection point (Point A on TP; Point a on MP). MP equals zero when the TP curve is flat at its maximum (Point C on TP; Point c on MP). The AP, or slope of a ray from the origin to the TP curve, is at a maximum at the steepest ray which is tangent to the TP curve (Point B on TP, Point b on AP). Thus, AP = MP when AP is at a maximum. A rising AP curve characterizes stage one, whereas positive but declining average productivity designates stage two. Stage three exhibits a negative MP.

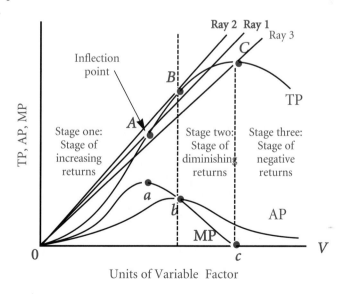

7–1 If output is 70 units a day with 9 workers, and rises to 73 units if a tenth
     worker is added, what is the marginal product of the tenth worker?

Three units. More precisely, the marginal product of 3 units is a result of the change in workers from
9 to 10. (It doesn't matter who was first or last if labor is "homogeneous," but customarily we speak
of it in relation to the additional factor unit added—the tenth worker in this example.)

7.5 THE BEHAVIOR OF OUTPUT WITH
VARYING PROPORTIONS:
THE LAW OF DIMINISHING MARGINAL RETURNS

It is customary to attribute the S-shape of the total product curve to two main causes:
(1) It is impossible to use certain factor units efficiently except in combination with a
minimum quantity of other factor inputs; for example, without any brains it would be
useless to study; (2) The operation of a famous principle called the law of diminishing
marginal returns.

The first explanation is merely an alternative way of saying that total product rises
at an increasing rate over a certain initial range of input values. It explains very little.
The second seems to say something more, for it involves a "law" which gives it a certain
status even before we say what it asserts. Set out in full, the law of diminishing marginal
returns runs as follows: As the amount of a variable input is increased—the amount of
other (fixed) inputs being held constant—a point ultimately will be reached beyond
which marginal product will decline. The empirical validity of this proposition can be
supported with endless maxims: "Too many cooks spoil the broth," or "You can't grow
the entire world's supply of wheat in a single flowerpot."

The **law of diminishing marginal returns** is based upon two premises. First, the
level of available technology is given: the law is relevant to the behavior of output when
factor inputs are varied within the framework of available methods and techniques.
Second, it is assumed that units of the various factors employed are homogeneous; that
is, any unit is of equal efficiency and thus interchangeable with any other unit.

The point of this discussion, however, is that most production functions conform
to the pattern illustrated in Figure 7–1. If an apparently contrary pattern ever were discovered, we should merely conclude that (1) some fixed factor originally thought to
limit a process was not, in fact, essential, (2) some fixed factor was not held constant,
or (3) the point of diminishing returns had not yet been reached.
(See Problems 7–2 and 7–3.)

With this preliminary survey of the law of diminishing returns completed, we can
now analyze the behavior of average and marginal product in the successive stages of
increasing average, diminishing average, and negative marginal returns.

7–2 What is responsible for the operation of the law of diminishing marginal returns?

Essentially, marginal physical product decreases beyond some point because each successive unit of the variable factor has a smaller quantity of fixed factor units with which to work. Once the point is reached at which the number of variable units is adequate to use the available fixed factor units efficiently, further increases in the variable factor will add progressively less to total product.

7–3 A technological advance allows a firm to produce the same level of output with fewer inputs. Illustrate how that would impact the total product curve.

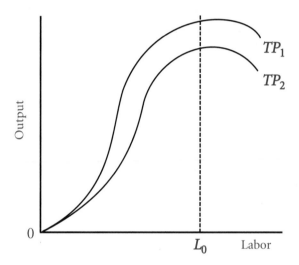

The total product curve would shift upward. That is, using the same amount of labor and capital, more output can be produced.

STAGE ONE: INCREASING AVERAGE RETURNS

The initial rise in marginal and average product is the result of more effective use of fixed factor units, and possibly of other variable factor units, as the number of units of the variable factor under consideration is increased. A conveyor belt is of little value with a single worker; as additional workers are added to the assembly line, marginal and average product initially rise.

When the number of variable factors is extremely small, the the quantity of the fixed factor can be so great that it interferes with efficiency of operation; production could be greater if some of the fixed factor units were eliminated. Put differently, there may be so many units of fixed factors that, in effect, they get in the way of other factors. For example, if one man tried to operate a large department store alone—doing work of all types necessary in the store—his energies would be spread so thinly in so many directions that total output (sales) might be less than if he were operating a smaller store (that is, working with less capital). As successive workers are added, up to a certain number, each worker can add more to total product than the previous one.

More significantly, the stage of increasing average returns comes about because certain fixed and variable factor units are used more efficiently as they are combined with large quantities of other factors. For example, certain types of capital equipment may require a minimum number of workers for efficient operation, or perhaps for operation at all. With a small number of workers (the variable factor), some machines cannot operate at all or can only operate at a very low level of efficiency. As additional workers are added, machines are brought into more efficient operation, and thus the marginal product of the workers rises sharply.

Similarly, additional units of the variable factors may permit more effective use of their services. Some tasks are inherently difficult for a single person to perform; adding a second person may more than double the output. This is true, for example, of bricklaying. Without a helper, a bricklayer will waste a great deal of time and energy climbing up and down a ladder with bricks. Similarly, with given equipment and techniques, two persons can get the hay crop into a barn in much less than half the time necessary for one person.

In sum, the firm will always want to hire more of the variable input in stage one, since AP is rising. That is, in stage one, the firm could hire ten workers instead of five and more than double their output. Therefore, it would be increasingly profitable to expand the use of variable inputs anywhere in stage one. Wouldn't you take an optional exam if you knew your average grade would rise as a result? (See Problem 7–4.)

7–4 True or False? In some lines of production, the stage of increasing average returns may never manifest itself at all.

True. If the variable factor units cannot be obtained in small units (for example, if workers cannot be hired for periods shorter than a day or a week), the first unit of the variable factor may carry production out of the increasing returns stage, and thus the firm is never aware that such a stage exists. Only if the variable factor could be added in much smaller units would the stage be noticeable. In a small store, therefore, adding one worker may carry operations into the decreasing returns stage, and the marginal product of a second worker will be less than that of the first. Likewise, if the fixed factor units are divisible into very small units, increasing returns may never be encountered because it may be possible to set aside a portion of them and concentrate the work of variable units on only a subset of the fixed factors.

Stage two is the only stage where the firm will knowingly operate. In stage two, the average product and marginal product are falling, but total product is still rising; that is, additional units of the variable input increase total product. In this region the firm will neither underutilize its fixed factors (stage one) or overutilize its fixed factors (stage three). The actual point in stage two where the firm will operate will depend on input prices and output prices discussed in chapters 9–12.

The third stage, one that a firm *never* knowingly allows itself to reach, is that in which the use of additional variable factor units actually reduces total output, and marginal product is therefore negative. In such a situation, there are so many units of the variable factor that efficient use of the fixed factor units is impaired. Too many workers in a store make it difficult for customers to shop; too many workers in a factory get in one another's way. In such a situation, reducing the number of variable units actually *increases* total output.

7.6 OPTIMAL FACTOR COMBINATIONS: TWO VARIABLE INPUTS

If the production manager had to deal with just one variable input, decision problems would be relatively easy. Given the output target, the production manager would purchase the minimum quantity of input needed to produce the assigned output and would inform the output manager of the costs incurred. However, the production manager's job becomes much more complicated when the output can be produced with several alternative combinations of inputs. For the sake of simplicity, we shall confine ourselves to two variable inputs, capital and labor.

The various combinations of two factors that allow the firm to produce a given quantity of output can be illustrated graphically. The curve showing the various factor combinations that can produce a given level of output is known as an **isoquant**. Figure 7–3 shows that units of capital are measured on the vertical axis, and units of labor on the horizontal axis; isoquant q shows the various combinations of capital and labor that allow the firm to produce a given level (20 units) of output.

The Theory of Production   183

Isoquants, like indifference curves, have several important properties. Isoquants are negatively sloped, nonintersecting, convex, and they increase in value as we move in a northeast direction from the origin. However, unlike indifference curves, isoquants are measured cardinally. That is, an output of 40 is twice as large as an output of 20.

THE MARGINAL RATE OF TECHNICAL SUBSTITUTION

Explanation of the optimal factor combination can be facilitated by discussing the concept of the **marginal rate of technical substitution of labor for capital**, MRTS (to distinguish it from the marginal rate of substitution along an indifference curve). The slope of the isoquant is the number of units of one factor necessary to replace a unit of another factor, in order to maintain the same level of output, $-\Delta K/\Delta L$. If we remove the negative sign on the slope we have the MRTS.

Suppose that various combinations of labor and capital (together with given quantities of other factors) are used to produce a given level of output, as illustrated in Figure 7–3. There are various combinations that will produce 20 units of output per day; for example if 2 units of labor are used, 6 units of capital will be needed (Combination B); and if 3 units of labor are used, then 3 units of capital will be required (Combination C). Note that the various combinations are alternative possibilities for the production of a given quantity of the product, 20 units of output per day in this example.

The MRTS measures the quantity of capital that can be given up by using one additional unit of labor, while still producing the same level of output. For example, if 2 units of labor (and 6 units of capital) are now being used, 3 units of capital can be given up by using 1 additional unit of labor. (See Problem 7–4.)

As the data in Figure 7–3 illustrates, the isoquants are convex. That is, the MRTS diminishes as we move down along the isoquant. We also see that labor becomes more abundant and capital more scarce. Hence, it becomes increasingly difficult to substitute even more labor for capital.

As the quantity of one factor, say labor, is increased relative to the quantity of the other, say capital, output being constant, the number of units of capital that can be replaced by one unit of labor falls. This is because the marginal product of labor falls as we use more of it, and the marginal product of capital rises as we use less of it.

Under ordinary circumstances, the isoquant will be convex to the point of origin because of the principle of diminishing marginal rate of technical substitution. The greater the quantity of labor used, the smaller is the quantity of the capital needed to replace a unit of labor and maintain output. Thus, the right-hand portion of the isoquant is almost parallel to the horizontal axis, while the left-hand portion is almost parallel to the vertical axis.

FIGURE 7–3
ISOQUANT SHOWING VARIOUS COMBINATIONS OF LABOR AND CAPITAL THAT CAN BE USED TO PRODUCE 20 UNITS
OF OUTPUT PER DAY

The isoquant q indicates that 20 units of output can be produced with 10 units of capital and 1 unit of labor
(combination A), or 3 units of capital and 3 units of labor (combination C). All other combinations of capital
and labor capable of producing 20 units of output are also charted along isoquant q.

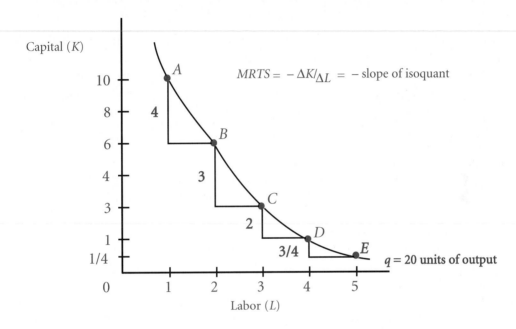

Combination	Labor (L)	Capital (K)	Marginal Rate of Technical Substitution
A	1	10	
B	2	6	4
C	3	3	3
D	4	1	2
E	5	1/4	3/4

The marginal rate of technical substitution is equal to -ΔK/ΔL, which is the slope of the isoquant. Recall that all combinations on a given isoquant yield the same level of output. Thus, if labor is substituted for capital, with output remaining constant we know that:

$$(\Delta K)\ (MP_K)\ +\ (\Delta L)\ (MP_L)\ =\ 0$$

Rearranging the terms in this equation we have:

$$MRTS\ =\ -(\Delta K)/(\Delta L)\ =\ MP_L/MP_K;$$

that is, the slope of the isoquant at any point is equal to the ratio of the marginal product of labor to the marginal product of capital.

The MRTS is a measure of the extent to which the two factors are substitutes for each other. If they are perfect substitutes—that is, if either factor can be used equally well to produce the product—the marginal rate of technical substitution will be a constant. If capital and labor can be used equally well, the MRTS will remain unchanged, regardless of the extent to which substitution is carried in either direction, as seen in Figure 7–4. For example, a woven rug or a sweater could either be done almost exclusively by machine or with a few tools and hand labor.

At the other extreme, two factors may not be substitutes for a particular purpose (such as carpenters and hammers or taxicab drivers and taxicabs). Here, the MRTS is undefinable, because output cannot be maintained if one factor is replaced by the other. If this relationship exists between all factors the firm uses, the factor combination the firm employs is dictated entirely by technological conditions, and no substitution is possible. The curve in Figure 7–5 is a right angle indicating that the same output would be forthcoming if more of either (but not more of both!) of the inputs were used. That is, you are equally well off producing q_1 output using factor combination A as you would be using factor combination B. However, you can clearly produce more output, q_2, if you increase both labor and capital, a move from A to C. This type of production relationship is called a **fixed-proportions production function**. (Problem 7–4)

7–4 True or False: A firm would never choose a factor combination on a positively sloped portion of an isoquant.

The figure below reveals two isoquants with positively sloped sections. If the amount of input V_2 is fixed at $\overline{V_2}$, 1 unit of output can be produced at with either V_1 or V_1'' amount of V_1. The input combination at point C would clearly be less efficient than point A because C uses more of input V_1 and would be more costly. Note that the positively sloped segment of an isoquant corresponds to stage three of production because an increase in V_1 from V_1' to V_1'' when V_2 is fixed at $\overline{V_2}$ results in a lower quantity of output (q falls from 2 to 1).

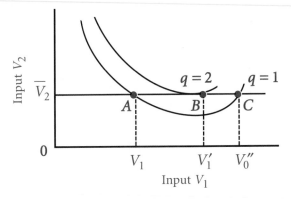

Isoquants with Positively Sloped Segments

7–5 True or False: If two factors are partial substitutes for one another, the marginal rate of substitution will vary as factor proportions are altered, ranging from infinity from values to, or equal to, zero.

True. Suppose for example, that in the production of VCRs, either metal or plastic can be used for most purposes, but metal is essential for some purposes because plastic lacks sufficient strength for performing the task. In this case, once the quantity of metal has been reduced to the minimum amount required, the *MRTS* will become infinite, because output cannot be maintained if substitution is carried further.

FIGURE 7–4
PRODUCTION FUNCTIONS WHEN INPUTS ARE PERFECT SUBSTITUTES

When the production isoquants are straight lines, the two inputs are perfectly substitutable. The *MRTS* is constant along a given isoquant; that is, either combination *A* or combination *B* could be used equally well to produce Q_3.

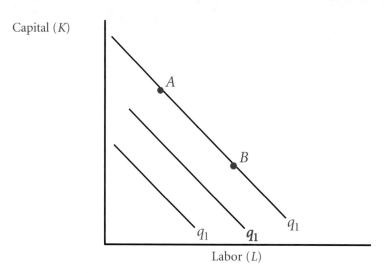

FIGURE 7–5
PRODUCTION FUNCTIONS WITH FIXED PROPORTIONS

If the production function is L-shaped, it is a fixed proportions production function. The addition of more labor (A to B) does not produce more output. You can, however, produce more output (q_2) if you increase both labor and capital (A to C).

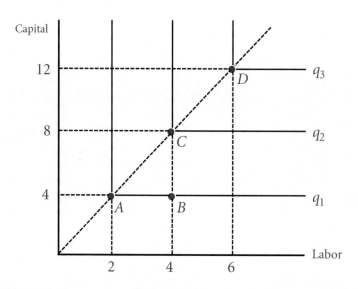

7.7 ADJUSTMENTS IN ALL FACTORS: RETURNS TO SCALE

Having considered various changes in factor proportions, we turn to the other major segment of the theory of production, which analyzes the behavior of output when all factors are varied. For example, if all factors are doubled, will output double, or will the new output be more or less than twice as great? Returns to scale covers the three possible relationships between an increase in inputs and a consequent increase in outputs when all factors are increased:

1. Constant returns to scale: A proportionate change in all inputs results in an equal proportionate change in output.

2. Increasing returns to scale: An equal increase in all inputs results in a more-than-proportionate increase in output.

3. Decreasing returns to scale: An equal increase in all inputs results in a less-than-proportionate increase in output.

It is widely believed that in a typical production activity, when the scale of operations is first increased, returns to scale are increasing; then, with the exhaustion of all economies, returns to scale are constant; if expansion is carried far enough, decreasing returns to scale set in.

AN ISOQUANT REPRESENTATION OF RETURNS TO SCALE

With **constant returns to scale**, the isoquants representing successive unit increases in output (with adjustments of all factors) are equidistant on any line extended from the point of origin. Figure 7–6 depicts segments *Or, rs, st,* and so on, as segments of equal length; doubling the inputs results in a doubling of output. As shown in the lower output ranges of Figure 7–7, with **increasing returns to scale**, the segments between isoquants (each successive isoquant representing the same increase in output) decrease in length. Finally, Figure 7–7 also shows that, with **decreasing returns to scale**, the segments increase in length for the larger output levels.

Representing *constant, increasing,* and *decreasing returns to scale* on a graph does not shed much light on when one would be expected to observe each case. What causes increasing returns to scale?

FIGURE 7–6
CONSTANT RETURNS TO SCALE

Equidistant isoquants indicate that proportionate increases in inputs—for example, from *r* to *s*—boost output by the same proportion.

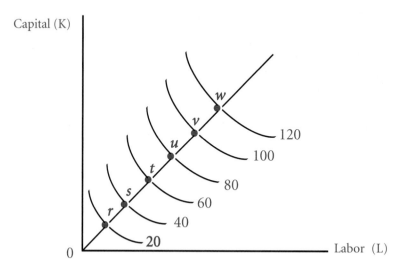

FIGURE 7–7
FIRST INCREASING RETURNS TO SCALE, THEN DECREASING RETURNS TO SCALE

Doubling the amount of the factors from *p* to *r* raises output from 20 to 60, implying increasing returns to scale. At point *s*, however, doubling inputs to point *u* increases output from 80 to 120, indicating decreasing returns to scale.

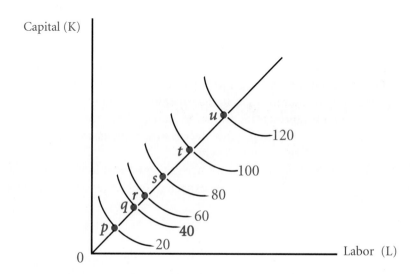

Increasing returns to scale are based, most importantly, on **indivisibilities** of some factors and on advantages of **specialization**.

1. Indivisibilities

Certain factor units cannot be divided into smaller units without either complete loss of usefulness in production or partial loss in efficiency. The result is a relatively low output per unit of input when operations are conducted on a very small scale. (In some instances, it is not possible to adjust all factors in the same proportion upward or downward.) Certain types of capital goods (for example, presses and road-construction equipment) do not perform their function if they are built on too small a scale, because weight is important in their operation.

    With other capital equipment, small units can be made, but the output per unit of factors used to make and operate them is low. A 5-horsepower engine cannot be built for 1 percent of the cost of a 500-horsepower engine. For physical reasons, larger machines require less material per unit of output for their construction than smaller machines; they likewise require less labor for their construction per unit of product, because it takes little or no more time to assemble a machine designed to produce 100 units a day than to assemble a similar machine designed to produce 50 units. If the machine is very small, more time may actually be required because of the difficulty of working with small parts and obtaining the necessary precision in measurements. In warehouse construction, doubling the building material will more than double the amount of usable space. With a rectangular building, costs of walls need increase only 50 percent for the capacity of the area to double. (See Problem 7–5.)

7–5 True or False? Indivisibilities are confined to capital goods?

No, labor units are not completely divisible either. One operator may be required for each machine, regardless of its size. A freight train requires one engineer, regardless of the tonnage of the train; there is no way to use a fraction of an engineer on a train of light tonnage. Within limits, employees in small enterprises may be used to perform several different tasks. But as a practical matter, there are severe limitations to such possibilities. A sales clerk in a store may be busy only one third of the time; yet the clerk must be paid for the entire day. In any type of business, it is difficult to use each worker to the maximum of his or her productivity at all times. As an establishment grows from a very small level, the percentage of labor time not used should fall if management policies are effective.

2. Specialization

The other, closely related cause of increasing returns to scale is the advantage offered by specialization. In a very small business, employees must perform a wide variety of tasks. As the size of the enterprise increases, employees can be used in more specialized jobs, with a consequent increase in output per worker. The advantages of labor specialization have been recognized at least since Adam Smith analyzed the manufacture of pins more than 200 years ago.[3] The primary advantages of specialization are that employees acquire greater skill, they avoid wasted time in shifting from one task to another, and they do the types of work for which they are best suited.

In managerial activity as well as in other phases of work, advantages of specialization are encountered. In larger firms, personnel relations are conducted by a specialist; traffic management is in the hands of a full-time traffic expert instead of someone with a half-dozen other tasks. The owner of a small retail store may select the location for the store primarily through guesswork, placing it where sales volume should be high or where an empty low-rent building is available. In contrast, larger chains have store sites selected by experts who have experience in analyzing the factors that make different locations relatively more desirable.

Specialization is also possible with capital equipment. As a firm increases its scale of operations, it can replace nonspecialized equipment capable of performing a number of tasks with specialized equipment designed for various specific operations. This results in a consequent increase in output per unit of input.

The importance of the phase of increasing returns depends in large measure on the type of production process involved. When almost any type of business expands from a very small initial size, returns are likely because of indivisibilities. If, however, a business uses relatively little capital equipment, and if labor specialization has few advantages, increasing returns may very quickly come to an end. On the other hand, if a firm uses large amounts of capital goods of types that cannot be used efficiently on a small scale, returns may increase substantially over a great range of output. Thus, increasing returns are very important in steel, cement, and automobile production but less important in agriculture and retailing.

Constant Returns to Scale – As a firm continues to expand its scale of operations, it gradually exhausts the economies responsible for increasing returns. The firm will eventually grow to the point at which it is using the best type of capital equipment available and is gaining full advantages of labor specialization. Beyond this point, further increases in the scale of operations are likely to produce approximately constant returns for a substantial range of output. In this range, if the entire scale of operations doubles, output will approximately double also.

Decreasing Returns to Scale – As a firm continues to expand its scale of operations beyond a certain point, returns to scale tend to decrease. A given percentage increase in the quantities of all factors, therefore, brings about a less-than-proportional increase in output. In some types of production, decreasing returns may follow directly after the increasing returns phase with no significant intervening period of constant returns. However, on the basis of limited evidence, it appears that a long phase of constant returns is common.

---

[3]See his *Wealth of Nations*, Modern Library ed. (New York: Random House, 1937), pp. 7–8

Decreasing returns to scale for a particular plant must be distinguished from such returns for an entire firm. Those for a particular plant are attributable almost entirely to physical relationships. As the area over which production operations must be coordinated and the territory from which labor supplies must be drawn are increased, this will ultimately result in lower product per unit of input in a given plant. A classic historical example of failure to consider decreasing returns to scale was provided by the Portuguese vessels in the East Indian trade in the sixteenth and seventeenth centuries. As trade flourished, the Portuguese continued to increase the size of their ships to provide greater cargo space. But they could not maintain strength and maneuverability as the vessels became larger, and the ships became increasingly vulnerable to storms and attractive to pirates. As a consequence, losses of vessels increased disastrously, and the Dutch, with smaller, faster ships, proceeded to capture the trade.[4]

Decreasing returns to scale for the firm itself are usually attributed to increased problems and complexities of large-scale management. Beyond a certain point, continued increases in entrepreneurial labor activity encounter more and more serious difficulties. An increasing percentage of the total labor force is required in administrative work to coordinate the firm's activities and control the large numbers of employees. As the firm reaches substantial size, final authority for basic policy remains in the hands of a group that controls the operation of the business, yet is far removed from actual operations. Managers are forced to make decisions on the basis of second-hand information, and on subjects with which they have no direct contact. Furthermore, substantial delay can occur in decision making because the request for decision, plus necessary information, must pass up through the chain of command to the managerial group, whose decision must then pass down to the operating unit.

To minimize the amount of red tape and delay in making decisions by those out of contact with the situation, responsibility for many decisions must be delegated to subordinate officials. Decisions are thus made by persons who lack knowledge of general business policy, experience, or the incentive of those at the top-level management positions. As a result, various parts of the enterprise may lack coordination and unity of policy. Modern business management attempts to delegate decisions while maintaining a reasonable unity of policy, but the problem can never be eliminated. Scientific management principles merely lessen its seriousness.

The growth of a business likewise increases the amount of division of responsibility and serves to lessen initiative, especially on the part of persons in lower-level jobs who are in a position to note desirable changes. With increased size can come a loss of personal contact between management and workers, with a consequent loss of morale and an increase in labor strife.

---

[4]See Ralph Davis, *The Rise of the Atlantic Economics,* (New York: Cornell University Press, 1973).

SUMMARY

1. The relationship between inputs and outputs is called the production function.

2. When the input of just one factor is varied (other inputs held constant), output starts at a low level and increases as the amount of the variable input increases. At some point, as more inputs are added, it becomes increasingly difficult to increase output, and a decline in output may ultimately result.

3. Average product is total product divided by the quantity of the input used. Marginal product is the change in total output that results from a small change in the amount of the input.

4. The behavior of output as a variable factor is increased relative to some fixed factors can be separated into three stages. In the first stage (increasing average returns), average product increases, with marginal product being greater than average product. In the second stage (diminishing average returns), marginal product declines and eventually reaches zero while average product declines throughout. In the third stage (negative marginal returns), total product diminishes; marginal product is, therefore, negative while average product continues to decline.

5. As the amount of a variable input is increased, the amount of other inputs being held constant, a point is reached beyond which marginal product declines. This is the law of diminishing returns. It is assumed that technology is given and that factors employed are homogeneous.

6. An isoquant shows the various factor combinations that produces a given output.

7. The marginal rate of technical substitution is the number of units of one factor necessary to replace a unit of another factor and maintain the same level of output. The slope of the isoquant at any one point indicates the marginal rate of technical substitution between the two factors.

8. The principle of diminishing marginal rate of technical substitution states that as the quantity of any one factor is increased relative to the quantity of another, output being constant, the number of the units of the second that can be replaced by one unit of the first falls.

9. There are three possible outcomes with regard to the relationship between an increase in inputs and the consequent increase in outputs when all factors are increased in proportion: *constant returns to scale*, where a doubling of all inputs results in a doubling of output; *increasing returns to scale*, where an increase in all inputs results in a more than proportionate increase in output; and *decreasing returns to scale*, where an increase in all inputs results in a less-than-proportionate increase in output.

WORDS AND CONCEPTS FOR REVIEW

production function

average product

marginal product

law of diminishing marginal returns

marginal rate of technical substitution

isoquant

fixed-proportions production function

constant returns to scale

increasing returns to scale

decreasing returns to scale

indivisibilities

specialization

REVIEW QUESTIONS

1. Why do firms engage in production?

2. What is a production function?

3. What is the difference between production functions with fixed coefficients of production and those with variable coefficients? Give an example of the former.

4. How do average physical product and marginal physical product differ?

5. How would you graph the typical behavior of total product as the input of one factor is increased (with given quantities of the other factors)?

6. Why is marginal product equal to average product at the highest level of average product?

7. Why does marginal product fall if the rate of increase in total product falls?

8. Can average product be rising while marginal product is falling? Explain.

9. Upon what premises is the law of diminishing returns based?

10. Explain the concepts of increasing returns and increasing returns to scale. Indicate the causes of each.

11. a. Contrast the causes of the stage of diminishing returns and those of decreasing returns to scale.
    b. Distinguish between decreasing returns to scale for the plant and for the firm. Why is the latter the more significant of the two?

12. What is meant by the stage of negative marginal returns? What can be responsible for negative returns if a firm expands far enough?

13. How does one explain the meaning of the term *marginal rate of technical substitution* with respect to factors?

14. Why may the marginal rate of substitution of *y* for *x* fall as the quantity of *y* is increased? Why may it rise initially?

15. What is the relationship between the marginal rate of technical substitution and the degree of substitutability of the two factors for each other?

SUGGESTED READINGS

Baumol, W. J. *Economic Theory and Operations Analysis*, 4th ed. Englewood Cliffs, N.J.: Prentice Hall, 1977, Chapter 11.

Ferguson, C. *The Neoclassical Theory of Production and Distribution*. London: Cambridge University Press, 1969.

Henderson, J. M., and R. F. Quandt. *Microeconomic Theory*, 3rd ed. New York: McGraw Hill, 1980, Chapter 3.

Chapter Eight

THE COSTS
OF PRODUCTION

——— *Questions to Think About* ———

1. What is the difference between implicit and explicit costs?

2. Why would a firm ever operate if economic profits were zero?

3. What are fixed costs? Variable costs?

4. What is average cost? Average fixed cost? Average variable cost? Marginal cost?

5. What are the reasons for the shapes of the average-variable-cost curve and the short-run average-cost curve?

6. What is the difference between the short run and the long run?

7. What is an isocost line?

8. What is the optimal input or factor combination?

9. What is the long-run average-cost curve? long-run marginal-cost curve?

8.1 INTRODUCTION

To obtain factor inputs for use in production, a firm must compensate factor owners. These payments are *income* to the factor owners and costs to the firm. The quantity of output that a firm decides to produce and offer for sale depends on the relationship between prices and costs. Costs, in turn, depend on the quantities of various factors the firm needs to produce a given output and on the prices it pays for factor units. The cost per unit as the firm varies output is determined by the extent of the required changes in inputs. The relationship between price and cost not only governs the firm's decisions about output, but also influences its decisions on undertaking new business enterprises and liquidating old ones. Thus, a discussion of what determines output and supply must begin by introducing the relevant concepts of cost and describing how different types of costs vary with changes in output.

8.2 THE NATURE OF COST

The term *cost* has a wide variety of meanings. In *business*, items that are costs for the purpose of some decisions might not be costs for other purposes. In determining accounting profit, for example, cost includes only the usual business expenses (including depreciation, interest, rent, and taxes). However, when a firm is calculating the potential profitability of undertaking an expansion or buying new equipment, cost also includes the return on the financial capital used for the investment, even though the money is supplied by the firm itself. The same procedure is often followed in pricing various products.[1] For yet other purposes, the firm might take a much narrower view of costs. If a firm with an idle plant considers whether to accept additional orders that can be sold only at a very low price, it considers only the direct out-of-pocket costs that result from the additional output. When an airline decides whether to continue operating a particular airplane, it considers only the cost resulting directly from operating that airplane and not the plane's share of administrative expenses, interest on investment, and so on.

For purposes of *economic* analysis, the most satisfactory definition of cost is broader than the concept used in *financial accounting*, but similar to the concept business firms use for general purposes. Specifically, the term **cost** refers to *the compensation that must be received by the owners of financial capital and the units of the factors of production used by a firm, if these owners are to continue to supply financial capital and factor units to the firm.*

---

[1]This is not meant to imply that firms can set their prices on a basis of cost considerations alone. But cost is an element considered, and for this purpose, cost usually includes a "profit" on the firm's own capital.

Two elements in this definition require explanation. The phrase "compensation that must be received by the owners" is used rather than "payments that must be made to the factor owners" because in some instances no formal payment occurs. Business owners do not usually "pay" themselves interest on funds that they invest in their own businesses. Yet, if they do not receive a return on such funds equivalent to the amount that they could get by lending the funds to others, they will probably end up liquidating the businesses.

Likewise, the definition says "continue to supply the factor units" rather than "supply the factor units," because factor owners may supply inputs for a period of time even though they are getting little or no compensation. The firm will not be able to obtain factor inputs indefinitely, however, if it cannot offer a return comparable to that available in other industries. The owners of a business that is not yielding a normal return often continue to operate it for some time because they cannot quickly exit the industry without incurring substantial financial losses. A slower exit, say, by allowing capital goods to wear out, may be less costly. (See Problem 8–1.)

8–1 True or False? From the standpoint of a particular business firm, the amount of compensation that owners of factor services must receive is determined by the other opportunities they have.

True. The opportunity is measured by the amounts which they could obtain by supplying factor inputs to other business firms. Thus, if the market price for copper is $1 a pound, a manufacturer who wishes to use copper must pay this price, because sellers of the input will not supply it to him for less, when they can get $1 from other buyers. If the current wage rate for laying brick is $80 a day, a contractor must pay $80 a day to obtain bricklayers. The same principle applies to factor inputs owned by the firm itself or supplied to it by the owners of the firm. A businessperson who invests $50,000 in his or her own business could have bought stock, perhaps in General Motors, and for this sum received $2,000 a year in dividends and a (risky) chance of additional capital gains. This sum constitutes a cost for which the business is responsible.

8.3 EXPLICIT AND IMPLICIT COSTS

Total cost consists of two elements: (1) **explicit costs**, such as wages or rents, which take the form of contractual payments by the business firm to factor owners; and (2) **implicit costs**, which, when covered, accrue directly to the firm itself or its owners with no contractual obligations for payment.

EXPLICIT COSTS

The first group of costs consists of the items usually treated as costs in financial accounting: wages and salaries; payments for raw materials, fuel, and goods purchased for resale; payments for transportation, utilities, advertising, and similar services; interest on borrowed capital; rent on land and leased capital equipment; and taxes. However, not all the payments that firms make are costs. Those made to purchase capital equipment involve merely a change in the form of the firm's assets. They are not, therefore, costs of producing the output charged to the period in which the assets are purchased. Rather they are charged to capital account, and a depreciation charge—an implicit cost—is set up to recover the amount paid over the period of years during which the equipment will be used. Similarly, payments of dividends to stockholders are not explicit costs, but merely withdrawals of profits from the firm by stockholder-owners. Taxes are not true social costs of production, since they do not represent compensation to an input with alternative uses (like labor, capital and other inputs). However, taxes are costs from the perspective of the firm.

IMPLICIT COSTS

Costs are implicit when factor units are owned by the firm or its owners. Although the firm is not obligated to make a contractual payment for these factor units, their use involves an opportunity cost, because they could be supplied to other producers if they were not used in the business.

In the typical large-scale corporate enterprise, the two major implicit costs are depreciation and an average return on money capital that stockholders have supplied. **Depreciation** charges are sums that must be recovered over the life of a capital good to maintain the capital sum invested in the item. The sums involved, if actually earned, may be used by the firm for any purpose. The charges, however, constitute costs and must be earned if the firm is to continue to operate indefinitely.

Similarly, the firm's owners must earn an adequate rate of return on their invested money capital, that is, a rate equal to the figure they could obtain from other investments of comparable risk. If the owners of a firm have invested $500,000 in the business, they are forgoing a return on this money that they could otherwise have made by lending the money (directly or through bond purchases), by purchasing stock in other corporations, by buying land or buildings, and so on. (See Problems 8–2 and 8–3.)

8–2 True or False? In smaller businesses, especially those organized as partnerships or individual proprietorships, implicit costs,—such as the wage that the owner of the firm could make by hiring himself out to another business—are not important.

False. A grocer must be able to earn as much from his own store as he could by working for, say, a supermarket chain, or, more exactly, the wage he could get at the chain less the value that he attaches to the privilege of working for himself. A person may be satisfied with a somewhat smaller return from his own business because he prefers to be his own boss, but this preference has a definite value: If the differential between the store's earnings and the available wage exceeds a certain figure, the alternative of taking a job will become preferable.

8–3 A firm has the following balance sheet for the previous year:
Revenue = $100,000
Labor Costs = $50,000
Capital Costs = $5,000 ($50,000 plant depreciated evenly over 10 years, the expected life of the plant)
Rental Value of Capital = $6,000
Entrepreneur's salary = $40,000.
Calculate economic and accounting profit for this firm.

Economic profit = $100,000 - $50,000 - $6,000 - $40,000 = $4,000
Accounting Profit = $100,000 - $50,000 - $5,000 = $45,000

When a firm earns an amount in excess of all opportunity costs, including implicit costs, the additional amount constitutes "excess profit" or "economic profit."

8.4 THE ADJUSTABILITY OF COSTS IN RESPONSE TO CHANGES IN OUTPUT

Of fundamental importance for cost behavior is the extent to which a firm is able to adjust the inputs of various factors and, therefore, the total amount of its costs as it varies output. This ability, in turn, is affected by the length of time involved. Over a period of time long enough for the firm to adjust all factors, called a **long-run period**, all costs are *variable*; that is, they are free to change as output changes. The time necessary for adjustments to be made in all factors varies according to the lifespan of the capital equipment, the firm's ability to obtain additional skilled workers and managers, and the extent to which capital goods are specialized (usable only for particular purposes). In general, it takes longest to adjust specialized and relatively indivisible capital equipment—nuclear plants, dies used to make automobile parts, railroad tracks, hydroelectric plants, steamships, grain elevators, and so on. Note that firms *never* actually operate *in* the long run, where everything is variable. At any point in time, source inputs are fixed—either at zero or at some positive amount. Thus, the long run is always a *planning horizon* that is long enough for the firm to vary all inputs.

In the **short-run period**, the amount of some factor units is not adjustable. New capital equipment cannot be obtained or built overnight. Additional skilled labor and management personnel often can be secured only by training new workers. Likewise, with a downward adjustment, specialized capital equipment rarely can be sold for the amount of money invested in it; the firm has the alternative of suffering a heavy loss of invested funds or using the equipment over a long period at a low return. The latter alternative is often preferable.

Fixed factors—those not readily adjustable—consist primarily of capital equipment and top management personnel, and are often designated by the term **plant.**

FIXED COSTS

The costs for which fixed factor units are responsible are known as **fixed costs**, while those arising from the use of variable factors are known as **variable costs**. More precisely, fixed costs may be defined as costs that are the same in total amount regardless of the volume of output, even if nothing is produced. The costs that are usually fixed in the short run may be classified into two major groups: **recurrent** costs and **allocable** costs.

RECURRENT COSTS

Recurrent fixed costs involve an actual outlay of money during the period. They include interest payments on money borrowed; taxes that are independent of output, such as capital stock taxes; the general property tax (to a large extent); the portions of heat, utility, and insurance costs that are independent of output; most rent; and the portions of labor cost (generally salaried managers, as opposed to production workers) not affected by output changes. Even if a plant produces nothing at all, some labor will be necessary: night patrol, maintenance employees, clerical and accounting personnel, portions of the administrative staff. These recurrent fixed costs require cash outlays; the firm must obtain the funds from some source—current revenue, accumulated cash surplus, disposition of noncash assets, or borrowing.

ALLOCABLE COSTS

Allocable fixed costs do not usually require cash outlays during the period, the total outlay having been incurred at one time for the benefit of production in several later time periods. The firm can continue to operate for a time even if these costs are not covered. Nevertheless, these items constitute costs in the sense that they must ultimately be covered if the firm is to continue operations. One major example of this type of fixed cost is the portion of depreciation that is a result of the *passage of time* rather than use. The economic life of capital equipment is in part independent of usage; for example, the development of new techniques can render old equipment obsolete. The portion of depreciation that depends on use is a variable cost, but many firms make no effort to separate the time and usage element in total depreciation. They assign the entire amount on the basis of time alone, thus in effect treating depreciation entirely as a fixed cost.

The other major allocable fixed cost is the necessary return on capital supplied by owners. This sum does not have to be earned or paid out in any particular period, but it must be earned over a period of time if the firm is to continue operation. Given the average rate of return and the quantity of financial capital invested by the owners, the necessary profit is the same for each year, regardless of the volume of output. The actual profit earned may fluctuate widely, but the necessary return is essentially a fixed cost.

VARIABLE COSTS

Variable costs depend on the volume of output. If nothing is produced, there are no variable costs. The major short-run variable costs are those for materials, fuel, electric power, and transportation; most wages, especially for work in direct physical production; and taxes that vary with output, such as those levied upon sales and gross receipts.

As indicated earlier, the distinction between fixed and variable costs is significant only in a short-run period, because over the longer period all factors—and all costs—are variable. In the long run, the firm can either get out of business or expand all inputs to produce more. Note that firms are always in some particular short-run stage (they have some existing fixed plant). The long run is a planning horizon that the firm is never "in."

8.5 COST SCHEDULES

A **cost schedule** indicates the total cost of producing various volumes of output. It shows the response of cost to changes in output. A long-run schedule shows the costs of producing various amounts of output during a time period long enough to allow the firm to adjust all factors to obtain the optimal factor combination for each output level.

The costs of producing various amounts of output depend primarily on three considerations: (1) *the technique of production,* (2) *the efficiency of the factor units employed,* and (3) *the prices paid for factor units* (including the necessary compensation for factor units owned by the firm).

1. Profit maximization requires the firm to use production techniques that allow the optimal combination of factors. In the short run, the optimal combination for any given level of output is the least-cost combination possible with the fixed factor units that the firm has on hand. Over a longer period, all factors can be varied, so the firm firm is free to select the short-run combination that is absolutely optimal.

2. Cost levels are affected not only by available methods of production, but also by the efficiency of factor units: the quality of natural resources employed, the types of capital goods available, and the skill of all types of labor, including managers. The better the resources, for example, the greater the output obtained from a given quantity of resources and the lower the cost of production. (This assumes that the efficiency of more inputs is not offset by their higher cost.)

3. Finally, factor unit prices influence cost in monetary terms. The cost of factor units to any one producer is the price that the owner of the unit could obtain from making it available in the next-best use—that is, the opportunity cost.

8.6 SHORT-RUN COST SCHEDULES

Table 8–1 is **a short-run cost schedule** for an individual firm. It shows the behavior of cost when output is varied with a given plant and fixed factor prices. For most purposes, unit (or average) cost data are more convenient to use than total cost data. **Average cost**[2] is equal to total cost divided by the number of units of output; it consists of two elements, **average fixed cost** (total fixed cost divided by the number of units of output) and **average variable cost** (total variable cost divided by the number of units of output).

---

[2]For simplicity, the term average cost is used rather than average total cost.

TABLE 8–1
DAILY SHORT-RUN COST SCHEDULE OF A PRODUCER

Units of Output	Total Fixed Cost	Total Variable Cost	Total Cost	Average Fixed Cost	Average Variable Cost	Average Cost	Marginal Cost
0*	$ 20	$ 0	$ 20	—	—	—	—
1	20	30	50	$ 20.00	$ 30	$ 50.00	$ 30
2	20	56	76	10.00	28	38.00	26
3	20	75	95	6.67	25	31.67	19
4	20	80	100	5.00	20	25.00	5
5	20	105	125	4.00	21	25.00	25
6	20	132	152	3.33	22	25.33	27
7	20	182	202	2.86	26	28.86	50
8	20	320	340	2.50	40	42.50	138
9	20	720	740	2.22	80	82.22	400
10	20	3,000	3,020	2.00	300	302.00	2,280

*If no units are produced, total fixed cost is the same as it would be if production were carried on. No variable costs are incurred. The unit cost columns are blank for zero units because the concept of cost per unit has no meaning if no units are produced.

The last column in Table 8–1 shows data on marginal cost—the increase in total cost that results from the production of an additional unit of output. For example, with 5 units of output, total cost is $125; with 6 units, it is $152. Thus, the marginal cost of the sixth unit—the amount that the production of the sixth unit adds to total cost—is $27 ($152 - $125). Marginal cost depends solely on changes in total variable cost, because total fixed cost is, by definition, the same for every level of output. Table 8-1 shows a typical pattern of cost curves for a firm.

The analysis of short-run cost behavior is based on the following assumptions:

1. The firm has only a fixed quantity of certain factors, and therefore certain cost items are fixed in total.

2. The fixed factor units require a certain minimum quantity of variable factor units for efficient operation but have at least some degree of adaptability for use with varying quantities of other factors.

3. Some types of variable factors cannot be acquired in infinitesimally small units. For example, workers often cannot be hired for periods of less than one day.

FIGURE 8–1
SHORT-RUN COST CURVES OF A FIRM

SRAC, composed of AVC and AFC, decreases initially because of specialization and indivisibilities of inputs at low levels of output, then rises because of diminishing returns at higher levels of output. AFC declines throughout, as fixed expenses are spread over more units of output. The SRMC curve eventually rises due to diminishing returns, and intersects the SRAC and AVC curves at their minimum points.

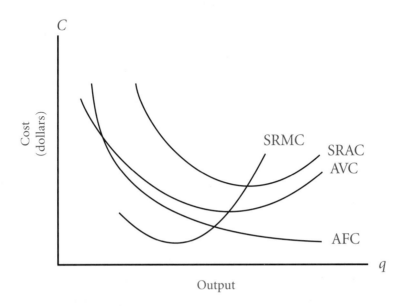

Under these assumptions, as output is increased, short-run average cost (SRAC) first declines and then increases, giving the curve an overall **U-shape**. The reasons for this behavior can best be explained in terms of the reactions to changes in output of the component parts of average cost—average fixed cost (AFC) and average variable cost (AVC).

AVERAGE FIXED COST

As output increases, AFC declines continuously, because a given sum of total fixed cost is being spread over successively larger volumes of output. As a result, the curve is a rectangular hyperbola.

AVERAGE VARIABLE COST

Under the assumptions made, AVC declines initially but ultimately increases. Its precise behavior depends on the behavior of the average product (AP) of the variable factors, under the assumption of given prices for the factor units. If AP increases as more units of the variable factors are added, then AVC falls: As each additional unit of output is produced, the quantity of variable factors required per unit of output falls. Conversely, if AP falls, AVC must rise. If AP is constant, AVC is unaffected by output changes. Table 8–2 illustrates these relationships.[3] Each unit of the variable factors (consisting, perhaps, of one worker plus a certain quantity of materials and electric power) is assumed to cost $20. Because the AP of the variable factor rises when the number of factor units is increased from one to three, total variable cost rises at a slower rate than output; therefore, AVC falls. In the range from 3 to 5 units of the variable factor, AP remains constant; total variable cost and total product rise at the same rate, and thus AVC remains constant. With 6 or more units of the variable factor, diminishing average returns are encountered, AP falls, and AVC rises. We now consider these phases in more detail:

---

[3]Because $AVC = \dfrac{TVC}{q}$, where q is the output of the firm, then letting (for simplicity) labor (L) be the only variable input (paid a wage, W) we have:

$$AVC = \frac{TVC}{q} = \frac{W \cdot L}{q} = \frac{W}{q/L} = \frac{W}{APP_L}$$

Hence, when the AP of the variable factor is rising, AVC must be falling, and vice versa. Costs are, then, inevitably intertwined with the production function relationships discussed in detail in Chapter 7.

TABLE 8–2

RELATIONSHIP OF AVERAGE PRODUCT OF THE VARIABLE FACTORS AND AVERAGE VARIABLE COST

	Productivity Schedule			Schedule of Variable Costs	
Units of Variable Factor	Output	Average Product per Unit of Variable Factor	Output	Total Variable Cost	Average Variable Cost
1	5	5.00	5	$ 20	$ 4.00
2	15	7.50	15	40	2.67
3	30	10.00	30	60	2.00
4	40	10.00	40	80	2.00
5	50	10.00	50	100	2.00
6	54	9.00	54	120	2.22
7	56	8.00	56	140	2.50
8	57	7.125	57	160	2.81

Under the assumptions made, AVC passes through three successive phases as output is increased:

1. The Phase of Declining Average Variable Cost

We assume that fixed factor units cannot be used effectively until a certain minimum quantity of variable factor units have been added. AP thus rises as additional variable units are added, because more effective use is made of fixed factor units. AVC falls because the rate of increase in output exceeds the rate of increase in variable factor units. A plant, for example, may have a certain set of machines that requires 5 workers for efficient operation. With only 2 or 3 workers, the machines are ineffective, and the output per worker is relatively small. As the fourth and fifth workers are hired, however, operation of the machinery reaches a high level of efficiency, so that output per worker is higher and variable cost per unit of product is lower.

The tendency for AVC to fall will be strengthened if the variable factors must be acquired in relatively large indivisible units. It is difficult, for example, to hire workers for only a few hours or to use particular workers on a large number of different tasks. Accordingly, when output is low, a portion of the work force is not being fully used. If the firm wants to increase output, it may not have to hire proportionately more additional workers. Thus, output per worker rises, and AVC falls. (See Problem 8–4.)

8–4 True or False? A bus driver or a cashier at a movie theatre might experience declining average variable costs when coupled with greater output per worker.

True. Extreme examples are found in certain service industries. One bus driver is required whether 1 passenger or 50 are carried in a bus; and as the load increases, the cost per passenger falls. A movie theater must have at least 1 cashier on duty while the theater is open, regardless of the number of customers.

2. The Phase of Constant Average Variable Cost

When the inputs of variable factors have reached such levels that the fixed factors can be employed effectively, and when each variable factor unit is likewise fully used, the AVC of further increases in output may be more-or-less constant over a considerable range. Through this range of output, doubling the variable factors approximately doubles output, and thus the AP and AVC are roughly constant. This stage may be encountered at relatively low levels of output, but only if fixed factor units are divided into small units, each requiring only a small number of variable units to operate it. If a plant consists of a large number of small identical machines (such as those used in some lines of textile production), efficient operation with a small volume of output can be obtained with only a small labor force. As output is increased, more workers are added and more machines brought into use, and variable cost will be more or less constant per unit of output. If the nature of a production process is such that operations can be carried on in three shifts of eight hours each, output can be tripled (more or less) from what it was when the plant was fully used on an eight-hour basis, without any significant change in AVC. The ability to vary the speed at which production is carried on likewise increases the range of constant AVC.

Empirical studies of cost functions have confirmed the importance of the phase of constant AVC. The phase is not always encountered, however. If the fixed capital requires a certain number of variable units for efficient operation, yet further increases in the number of variable factor units increases output very little, then the initial phase of decreasing AVC will be followed directly by the phase of increasing AVC.[4]

3. The Phase of Increasing Average Variable Cost

Eventually, in any type of business, as output is increased with a fixed plant, the AP of the variable factors will decline because of the law of diminishing returns. The plant is designed for a certain volume of production; when output is carried beyond this level, the increase in the variable factors necessary to produce the additional output is relatively greater than the output increase. As a result, AVC rises. In some production

---

[4]If we were to abandon the assumptions that fixed factors require a certain minimum quantity of variable factors for efficient operation and that variable factors cannot be obtained in very small units, then the phase of constant AVC could be encountered initially. It is widely believed, however, that these assumptions are realistic ones, though their significance varies widely in different lines of production.

processes the increase is gradual, as equipment is used longer hours than intended, machinery is operated at a faster rate, and obsolete equipment will be placed in use. These adjustments involve some increase in AVC, because maintenance costs rise more than proportionately when machinery is run at a higher rate and older equipment is used. Nevertheless, such adjustments make possible further increases in output without large changes in cost. In some lines of production, however, it may be almost impossible to produce more than the quantity for which the plant was designed; AVC rises rapidly because a substantial increase in the quantities of the variable factors is needed to produce a few more units of output. Once absolute capacity[5] is reached, there are no meaningful AVC figures for larger volumes of output, because such quantities of output cannot be produced. (In such cases, AVC is said to be infinite.)

THE BEHAVIOR OF AVERAGE COST

Because average cost (AC) is the sum of AVC and AFC, its behavior reflects the combined influence of changes in the two constituent elements. As a firm first increases output, AFC must necessarily fall; under the assumptions above, AVC also falls. As a consequence, AC must fall as well, as illustrated in Table 8–1 and Figure 8–1. The rate of decline depends on the relative importance of fixed and variable cost elements, the extent to which fixed factor units consist of large unadaptable units requiring several units of variable factor for efficient operation, and the extent to which the variable factors can be obtained in small units. The rate of decline in AC will be particularly great in large manufacturing establishments with heavy fixed costs and equipment that requires a relatively large labor force to operate effectively.

If AVC does not decline initially or becomes relatively constant once output has reached a certain level, AC still declines because of the fall in AFC, but the rate of decline is very low once output has expanded to the point at which fixed costs are a minor element in total cost.

If production is expanded far enough, AC must eventually rise. Once the minimum of the AVC curve is reached, AVC increases and eventually offsets the continuing decline in AFC. The speed at which AVC and AC rise depends primarily on the nature of the production process, and particularly on the flexibility of the fixed plant—the ability to expand production without a substantial increase in variable factors.

In summary, the **short-run average cost** (SRAC) curve is **U-shaped**. Figure 8–2 illustrates the case in which AC falls and rises sharply because the nature of the capital equipment requires a substantial number of workers for efficient operation. Once the equipment is brought into effective operation, additional output cannot be obtained

---

[5]The term *capacity* refers in some cases to the "optimum" or "low-cost" level of operation (the minimum of the AC curve); and in other cases to the absolute maximum output level possible with the plant. The appropriate meaning should be clear from the context.

except by using substantially greater quantities of the variable factor. The U becomes broad and flat when AVC is more-or less constant over a substantial range of output, as Figure 8–3 illustrates.

FIGURE 8–2
SHORT-RUN AVERAGE COST CURVE, WITH INFLEXIBLE PLANT

Inflexible fixed factors become much more efficient when variable factors are initially utilized, but once a sufficiently large level of output is reached, large numbers of the variable factors must be added to raise output. The SRAC curve declines sharply and then rises sharply as output increases.

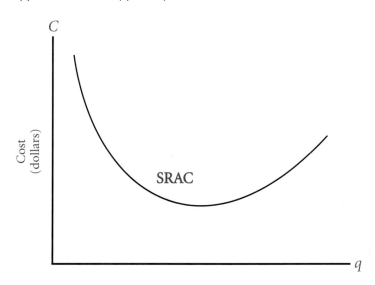

FIGURE 8—3
SHORT-RUN AVERAGE COST CURVE, WITH FLEXIBLE PLANT

When plant size is fixed but "flexible," the SRAC curve is relatively flat with a large horizontal segment.

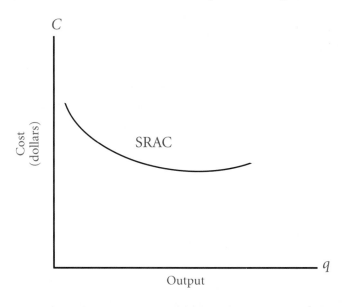

THE BEHAVIOR OF MARGINAL COST

Because the behavior of marginal cost (MC) depends on changes in total cost, its determinants are the same as those of AVC. Certain relationships between MC and AVC should be noted, however. When AVC is falling, MC must be less than AVC (but not necessarily falling); likewise, when AC is falling, MC must be less than AC. On the other hand, when AVC is rising, MC is greater than AVC, and when AC is rising, MC must of course exceed AC. Marginal cost is equal to AVC at the lowest point of AVC and is equal to AC at the lowest point of AC. Thus, the MC curve intersects both the AVC curve and the AC curve at their respective low points.

This relationship is simply a matter of arithmetic; when a number (the marginal cost) being added into a series is smaller than the previous average of the series, the new average will be lower than the previous one; when the number added is larger than the average, the average will rise. (See Problem 8–5.)

8–5 True or False? If the marginal amount rises, the average rises.

This is true only if the marginal amount is *greater* than the average. For example, if you have taken two intermediate microeconomic exams and received a 90 percent on your first exam and 80 percent on your second exam, you have an 85 percent average. After some serious "studying," you get a 100 percent on the third exam (the marginal exam). What happens to your average—it rises to 90 percent. It is possible, however, that the marginal amount could fall and the average would still rise. What if your fourth exam was a 94 percent? The marginal amount, then, has fallen (you had a 100 percent on your last test), but the average has risen from 90 percent to 91 percent.

If AVC is constant, MC and AVC have the same value, because the production of an additional unit adds to total cost the same amount as the previous average of the variable cost. Clearly, adding an amount equal to the previous average will not alter the average.

On the assumption of constant factor prices, the behavior of MC bears a definite relationship to the behavior of the marginal product (MP) of the variable factors. When MP is rising, MC is falling because each successive unit of the variable factors adds more to total product than did the previous unit. Thus, the increase in total cost resulting from the production of another unit of output is less than the increase resulting from the production of the previous unit. If the addition of a sixth worker raises output by 45 units a day and the addition of a seventh worker raises output by 65 units, the marginal cost of each of those 65 units is less than that of each of the previous 45. When MP is constant, MC is constant; when MP is declining, MC is rising, because successive factor units add progressively less to total output.[6] (See Problems 8–6 and 8–7.)

---

[6]Using differentials, and again simplifying as in footnote[3] to the case of labor as the only variable cost component:

$$MC = \frac{dTC}{dq} = \frac{dTVC}{dq} = \frac{W \cdot dL}{dq} = \frac{W}{dq/dL} = \frac{W}{MP_L}$$

This establishes the text result.

8–6 Derive the algebraic relationship between SRMC and MP. Explain why SRMC is U-shaped, given your equation.

Let V be the variable input, P_V the price of V, and assume all other inputs are fixed. Then,

$$SRMC = \Delta TVC / \Delta q$$
$$= \Delta (P_C \cdot V) \Delta q$$
$$= (P_V \cdot V) \Delta q \quad \text{(Since } P_V \text{ does not change with output in competitive markets.)}$$
$$SRMC = P_V / MP_V \quad \text{(as } MP_V = \Delta q / \Delta V)$$

The short-run marginal cost is equal to the price of the variable input divided by its marginal product. Specifically, SRMC varies directly with the price of the variable input and varies inversely with the marginal product of that input. Consequently, when MP rises, SRMC falls; when MP is minimum, SRMC is maximum; and when MP declines, SRMC rises. The hill-shaped MP curve gives rise to the U-shaped SRMC.

8–7 Consider a short-run production process with one variable input. In Figure (a), the marginal product (MP) and the average product (AP) curves are depicted. At what levels of output will AVC and SRMC be minimum?

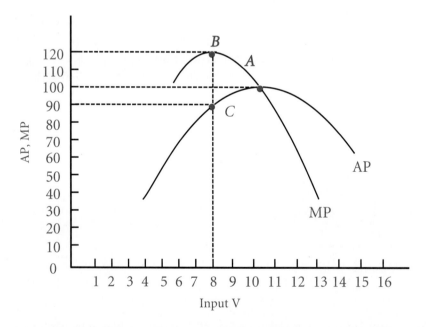

Input V

We know from Problem 8–6 that when SRMC is at a minimum, MP is at a maximum (Point B in Figure (a)). To find the level of output at B, note that AP = 90 and V = 8 when MP = 120. Recall that AP = q/V, so that AP $\cdot$ V = q. Thus, q = 90 $\cdot$ 8 = 720 when SRMC is at a minimum.

In addition, $AVC = (P_V \cdot V/q = P_V/AP$. When AP is a maximum, AV is a minimum. This occurs at point A, when $AP = 100$, $V = 10$ and $q = 1,000$. AVC and SRMC corresponding to the AP and MP curves of Figure (a) are sketched in Figure (b).

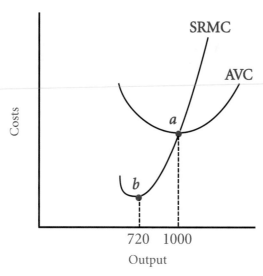

The SRMC and AVC Curves Corresponding to the MP and AP Curves in Figure (a).

THE APPLICABILITY OF THE ASSUMPTIONS

The usefulness of short-run cost analysis depends on how applicable the underlying assumptions made earlier are to actual situations. The first assumption—that certain factor units are fixed in quantity—follows from the definition of a short-run period and describes the situation that confronts a going concern in relatively short time intervals.

The second and third assumptions relate to the nature of fixed and variable factor units. We assume that a certain minimum quantity of variable units is required to use the fixed factor units effectively. This assumption is relevant to many types of capital equipment in manufacturing; an automobile assembly line, for example, cannot be used without a certain minimum numbers of workers. In other lines of production, however, this consideration is of less importance. In retailing, for example, there is typically no equipment that requires a substantial number of workers. In this type of industry, therefore, there is less likelihood of an increase in APP, and thus an initial decline in AVC from this cause. AFC will, of course, fall as output increases.

The third assumption that variable factor units (especially workers) cannot always be obtained in very small units is more likely to be realized in practice. It is usually difficult to hire a worker for less than a day, and it is of course impossible to hire "half a worker." Accordingly, the time of the first workers added will not be fully utilized initially; as output is increased, proportionate increases in inputs of variable factors will not be required, and AVC will fall.

It is necessary to treat technological conditions, factor unit efficiency, and factor prices as given. Otherwise, we are unable to distinguish the relationship between output and unit cost from cost changes resulting from variations in technology, factor prices, and efficiency. In some instances, however, the price paid for various factor units changes *as a result* of changes in output by the firm; hence, the changes are relevant for the nature of a particular cost schedule. When firms purchase materials in larger quantities, they often can get lower prices. Rate schedules for electric power often provide lower rates per unit for larger quantities than for smaller amounts; shipping in truckload quantities reduces freight costs per unit. When quantity discounts are available, the net cost per unit of the variable factors falls as more units are acquired, and the decline in AVC resulting from the initial rise in APP per unit of the variable factors is reinforced. In retailing and some other lines of business, the quantity discount feature is of particular importance; it is likely to be of greater significance in bringing about an initial decline in AVC than the behavior of APP because of the relative unimportance of capital equipment in these lines of business.

As a firm continues to expand, however, eventually all available quantity discounts will be obtained, and further increases in factor purchases may drive factor prices upward. For example, if a large firm is the principal employer of skilled labor in a certain area, it may eventually exhaust the local supply of this type of labor. Further increases in output will require the firm to pay higher wages to draw workers from other plants or from more distant areas. To the extent that factor prices are increased as output increases, AVC tends to shift upward. This effect reinforces the increase produced by the decline in APP. (See Problem 8–8.)

8–8 True or False? While factor prices may rise as a firm increases output, the additional factor units may be less efficient.

True. The assumption of homogeneous factor units is by no means necessarily realized in practice. Presumably a firm will hire the most efficient workers first. As additional workers are hired, successive workers are likely to be less skilled and less capable. Thus, the decline in APP and the rise in AVC will be greater than would result from the law of diminishing marginal returns alone, unless the prices paid for less-efficient factor units are proportionately lower than those paid for better units. But often they are not.

EMPIRICAL STUDIES OF VARIABLE COST BEHAVIOR

Determining the actual cost schedule data of a particular firm is a difficult task, far more so than might appear at first glance. A firm usually knows with reasonable accuracy the average variable cost at existing output levels, but has little more than a rough estimate of costs at other output levels. Serious attempts to ascertain these data are rare, and the difficulties involved in doing so prevent the results from being entirely accurate. The firm must, however, base its production decisions on *some* estimate of cost behavior. Various studies of business policy suggest that firms rarely attempt to ascertain marginal cost as such, seeking instead to determine equilibrium price and output levels with the use of total and average cost and revenue data. On the whole, however, firms probably know more about their cost schedules than their demand schedules, because the latter depend on often unpredictable reactions of customers and competitors.

A number of studies have been made of cost functions in particular industries, primarily to determine whether the pattern of cost behavior developed by economic analysis accords with actual behavior. Such studies have encountered serious problems. A major one arises because the underlying determinants of cost behavior—factor prices, techniques of production—never remain constant during the period under study. Statistical techniques to isolate cost changes due to output changes resulting from changes, due to shifts in other factors, are not entirely satisfactory. Also, in any particular period, costs may be affected by the *rate* at which output changes; a sudden increase may cause temporary additions to cost that can be avoided once production is adjusted to the higher volume. Another problem involves the time periods in which costs are recorded. Raw materials might be purchased in large quantities and charged as expenses in a period in which output is low (but is expected to increase) and then used in a later period when few materials are purchased. The measurement of units of output likewise is a source of difficulty. Most firms produce several types of products, the relative importance of which is likely to change. Finally, the range of output may be relatively narrow, such that only a small segment of the schedule can be computed; the data obtained cannot safely be projected into ranges of output for which no data are available. (See Problem 8-9.)

A most important discovery is the importance of the phase of constant AVC. Within the ranges of output for industries for which data were available, AVC and thus MC were frequently found to be relatively constant—as depicted in Figures 8–4 and 8–5. Therefore, the typical AVC curve would appear to contain an extensive horizontal section rather than being sharply *U*- or *V*-shaped. (See Problem 8–9.)

FIGURE 8-4
A TYPICAL SHORT-RUN AVERAGE COST CURVE

Empirical studies generally find that the SRAC curve is constant for some output levels.

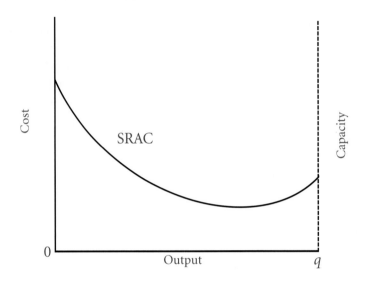

FIGURE 8-5
ANOTHER PATTERN OF SHORT-RUN AVERAGE COST

In this example, the SRAC curve is constant over an even greater range of output.

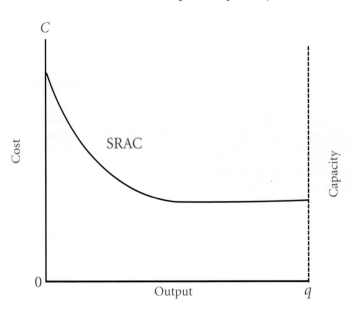

8–9 Illustrate how the SRMC curve is affected by the following:

    a. A tax on each unit of output.

    b. A license to operate fee.

    c. An increase in marginal product due to technological change.

    d. A decrease in wage rates.

    e. An increase in output.

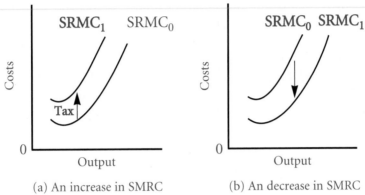

(a) An increase in SMRC   (b) An decrease in SMRC

Any particular cost schedule is based on the assumption that factor prices and production technology (represented in the production functions of Chapter 7) are given. When these underlying determinants change, the costs of the firm will be shifted.

a. Figure (a) shows how a per-unit tax increases the marginal cost of each unit of output, shifting the SRMC curve up by the amount of the tax.

b. A license-to-operate fee is a fixed cost and does not affect the marginal cost curve.

c. The marginal cost and marginal product are inversely related. An increase in marginal productivity lowers the marginal cost of each unit of output and shifts the SRMC curve downward as in Figure (b).

d. Lower wage rates reduce marginal costs, shifting SRMC downward as in Figure (b).

e. An increase in output is shown by a movement along the SRMC curve.

8.7 COST SCHEDULES WITH
LONG-RUN ADJUSTMENTS COMPLETED

The long-run period has been defined as a period sufficiently long for a firm to adjust all factors of production. The long run, as emphasized earlier, is always a *planning period*, because at any moment, firms are inevitably in some short-run situation. In the long run, however, a firm can choose any short-run plant configuration. The actual time interval depends on the nature of the production processes and particularly on the extent to which specialized capital equipment, requiring a substantial period to construct and having a certain lifespan, are used. The time a firm needs to adjust all factors is much greater for a steel mill or a railroad than for a service station or a grocery store. Over a long-run period, because all factors are adjustable, all costs are variable.

In the long run, the firm can alter all its inputs. Thus, the manager must choose among alternative inputs that minimize the cost of producing a given output. In addition we need to obtain information on long-run costs and output levels.

ISOCOST LINES AND THE OPTIMUM FACTOR COMBINATION

The optimal factor combination can be shown graphically by combining isoquants (Chapter 7) with **isocost (equal cost) lines** each of which shows the various possible quantities of the two factors that can be purchased with a given outlay of money. Figure 8–6 shows isoquants when isocost lines are added. Specifically, Figure 8–6 shows the various quantities of capital and labor that can be purchased with a given outlay of money, assuming that the prices of labor and capital are $6 and $3 per unit, respectively. If the given outlay is $210, for example, the isocost line is represented in Figure 8–6 by line A, which indicates that 70 units of capital can be purchased if only capital is purchased, 35 units of labor if only labor is purchased, and 20 units of labor if 30 units of capital are used. The isocost relation is a straight line as a matter of mathematical necessity as long as prices paid for factor units are the same regardless of the quantities purchased. The various possible isocost lines, one for each potential level of outlay on factors, are parallel to each other (see lines A, B, and C in Figure 8–6). The farther to the right an isocost line is located, the higher is the level of outlay that it represents.

FIGURE 8–6
THE OPTIMAL COMBINATION OF CAPITAL AND LABOR

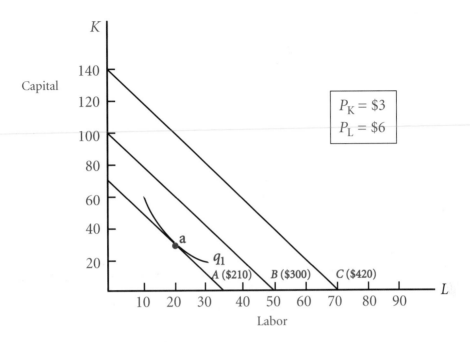

The isocost lines contain factor combinations that can be hired at the same expense. Minimizing the cost of producing q_1, output involves chooses a factor combination that coincides with q_1 output. The optimum input combination occurs at point a, where 20 units of labor and 30 units of capital are utilized to produce q_1 output.

Minimum cost is achieved when the firm chooses the least expensive combination of factor inputs for a given level of output. This combination is represented graphically by the lowest isocost line (the farthest one to the left) that touches the isoquant representing the quantity to be produced. Thus, the **optimum factor combination** is represented by a point of tangency between the given isoquant and the lowest possible isocost line, point a in Figure 8–6.

The isocost line that is just tangent to the isoquant allows a firm to acquire the necessary factor units with the lowest possible outlay.[7] Any lower line would not allow the firm to purchase enough factors to produce the desired output, while any higher isocost line would entail unnecessarily high factor costs. At any point on the isoquant other than the point of tangency, the outlay on the factors to produce the given output would be higher than that at the tangency point. At the tangency, the slope of the isoquant (which represents the marginal rate of technical substitution between the two factors)

---

[7]Remember that an isoquant shows the various quantities of the two factors necessary to produce a given output, while each isocost line shows the various quantities of two factors which can be acquired with the expenditure of a given sum of money.

is equal to the slope of the isocost line (which represents the ratio of the prices of the two factors), and thus the marginal rate of technical substitution is equal to the ratio of the factor prices.[8] (See Problem 8-10.)

Therefore at the tangency points, the isoquant and the isocost line will have identical slopes. Because the slope of the MRTS is equal to the ratio of the factor prices

$$MRTS_{LK} = w/r \quad \text{where } w = \text{wages (the price of labor)}$$
$$\text{and } r = \text{rental rate of capital}$$

---

[8]Formally, to minimize costs, subject to the constraint of producing a fixed quantity,

$$\text{minimize} \quad_{L,K} wL + rK \quad \text{where } L \text{ and } K \text{ are labor and capital and } w \text{ and } r \text{ are wages and rental cost}$$
$$\text{s.t. } f(L,K) = \bar{q} \text{ of capital for the same period.}$$

Forming the Lagrangean ($\mathcal{L}$):

$$\text{Minimize} \quad_{L,K,\lambda} = wL + rK + \lambda(q - f(L,K))$$

At the optimum least-cost point—the "bottom" of the "valley of costs", we know that small changes in L or K will have a negligible impact on costs or

$$\frac{\partial \mathcal{L}}{\partial L} = w - \lambda f_L(L,K) = 0$$

$$\frac{\partial \mathcal{L}}{\partial K} = r - \lambda f_K(L,K) = 0$$

$$\frac{\partial \mathcal{L}}{\partial \lambda} = \bar{q} - f(L,K) = 0$$

Forming the ratio of the first two equations gives the text result that MRTS = ratio of input prices at the cost minimizing solution. It should be noted that λ is equal to the marginal cost of an added unit of output.

8–10 **True or False?** **Minimizing the cost of producing a given level of output and maximizing output for a given level of cost are equivalent optimization solutions.**

True. Figure (a) shows that to minimize the cost of producing 100 units of output, the firm should produce at point A, where the isoquant is tangent to the isocost line. Point B is an input combination that can produce a 100 units of output. However, B costs more than A. Point C represents a cheaper factor combination, but it is impossible to produce 100 units of output with so few inputs. Figure (b) illustrates the alternative optimization process, maximizing output for a given level of costs. The producer attempts to reach the highest isoquant for a given isocost line. Again point a, the tangency point between the isoquant and the isocost line, gives the optimum factor combination. Point b is feasible, but produces a lower level of output. Greater output is attained at point c, but costs are too high. Hence, both strategies result in the same optimization conditions: the isoquant and the isocost line are tangent, and the MRTS equals the ratio of input prices.

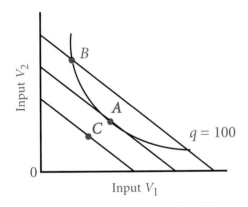

(a) Minimizing the cost of producing a given output level

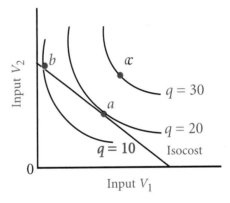

(b) Maximizing output for a given level of expenditure

Recall from Chapter 7 that MRTS is a measure of the extent to which the two factors are substitutes for each other. Also recall that the MRTS is equal to the ratio of the marginal product of labor to capital. So we can rewrite our previous equation as:

(slope of the isoquant) $- MP_L / MP_K = -w/r$ (slope of the isocost line).

or $MP_L / MP_K = w/r$

Rearranging our terms, we find that $MP_L / w = MP_K / r$

In other words, at the tangency solution, the ratio of the marginal product to input price must be the same for all inputs used in production. (See Problem 8–11.)

8–11 A firm is producing 50 units of output. The marginal rate of technical substitution at the current usage rates of V_1 and V_2 is 1. The price of $V_1 = \$8$ per unit, and the price of $V_2 = \$9$ per unit. Should the firm change its purchases of V_1 and V_2?

The firm can substitute one unit of V_1 for one unit of V_2 and still produce the same output level, but the price of V_1 is less than the price of V_2. Thus, the firm should decrease the amount of V_2 and increase the amount of V_1. The situation is depicted in the Figure. The input price ratio, 8/9, is less than the MRTS, 1, which is demonstrated by the flatter slope of the isocost than the isoquant at point A, the current factor combination. The firm can, however, lower its expenditure by moving to point B and hiring more V_1 and less V_2.

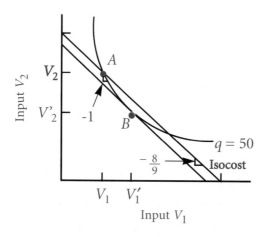

FACTOR PRICE CHANGES AND FACTOR SUBSTITUTION

The explanation of the optimal factor combination in the preceding section has, of necessity, been based on the assumption that factor prices are fixed. It is important, however, to extend the analysis to consider changes in the relative prices of the two factors and the consequent changes in quantities of the two factors acquired. As may be suspected, this discussion is very similar to that of the consumer decision to buy more or less at changed relative prices.

A change in the price of any factor, assuming that total output and the prices of the other factors remain unchanged, leads to readjustment in factor proportions, because the price change destroys the equality of the price ratio and the marginal rate of technical substitution.[9] The readjustment will continue until this equality is restored. The

---

[9]In general, desired total output will be affected by the factor price change. The parallel between the consumer and the firm break down a bit here in that the firm, unlike the consumer, does not maximize output (the analog of utility). Rather, it maximizes profit.

slower the rate of decline in the marginal rate of technical substitution between two factors, the relatively greater is the extent of substitution of one factor for another as their relative prices change.

In graphical terms, a change in the price of one factor changes the point of tangency between the isoquant and the isocost line and thus results in a new optimum combination. If the factors are good substitutes over a wide range of input combinations and, thus, the isoquant has little curvature, the shift of the point of tangency will be substantial (from 0a to 0b in Figure 8–7) and the increase in the usage of the factor that has become cheaper will be relatively great. If the two factors' ability to substitute deteriorates rapidly as input combinations are changed, as in Figure 8–8, the curvature will be sharp and the shift in the quantity of the factor acquired will be relatively slight (from 0a to 0b). (See Problems 8–12 and 8–13.)

8–12 Suppose a union raises earnings for workers, and management decides to continue to produce the same output level. How will the firm's optimum combination of labor and capital change, assuming only two inputs? Illustrate graphically. Under what conditions will the effect be large?

The original factor combination is L and K at point A in the figure. A pay raise increases the slope of the the isocost line, the price of labor divided by the price of capital. If the firm continues to produce along the same isoquant, the new quantities of labor and capital are L' and K'. If labor and capital are roughly equally good substitutes over a wide range of input combinations, the isoquant will have little curvature, and the substitution of capital for labor will be great.

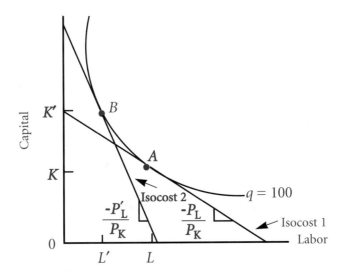

8–13 Use isoquants to demonstrate how technological advance allows a firm to produce the same level of output with fewer inputs.

In the figure, a technological advance is illustrated by the inward shift of the isoquant from $q' = 100$ to $q' = 100$. Both isoquants represent the same level of output, but q' demonstrates that the new technology requires fewer inputs to do so. Thus, the same level of output can be produced at lower costs.

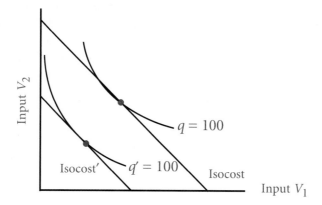

FIGURE 8–7
READJUSTMENT OF THE OPTIMUM FACTOR COMBINATION IN RESPONSE TO A CHANGE IN THE PRICE OF ONE FACTOR: HIGH SUBSTITUTABILITY

The isoquant for two readily substitutable inputs is nearly linear. An increase in the relative price of input V_2 decreases the slope of the isocost line. The firm will increase its usage of input V_1 substantially form a to b while continuing to produce the same level of output.

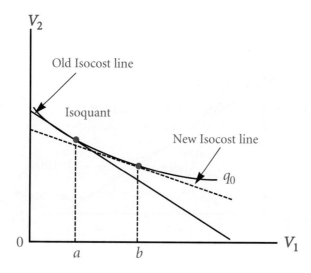

FIGURE 8–8

READJUSTMENT OF THE OPTIMUM FACTOR COMBINATION IN RESPONSE TO A CHANGE IN THE PRICE OF ONE FACTOR. POOR SUBSTITUTABILITY

The curvature of the isoquant is more pronounced when the two inputs are not easily substituted for one another over a wide range of input combinations in production. When the relative price of input V_2 rises, the firm's additional employment of V_1 from a to b is not as great as in Figure 8–7.

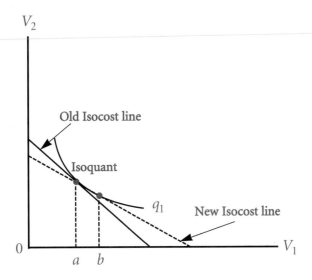

THE EXPANSION PATH

In Figure 8–9, the optimal factor bundles are presented for different levels of output. For example, the least-cost method for producing 100 units of output is using L_1 units of labor and K_1 units of capital, while the least-cost method of producing 120 units of output would be combining L_2 units of labor and K_2 units of capital. The expansion path is the line that connects these least cost input combinations, holding input prices constant.

The **expansion path** provides us information regarding the long-run total cost curve. Specifically, it shows the least-cost input solutions for providing a given output, or equivalently, the lowest long-run total cost for producing each level of output. The connection between long-run total cost and the expansion path is seen in Figure 8–10. Points A, B, and C are the cost minimizing input combinations along the expansion path in part (a). The corresponding points on the long-run total cost curve are a, b, and c in part (b). Long-run total cost is simply the optimum amount of labor times the wage plus the optimum amount of capital times the price of capital.

FIGURE 8–9
THE EXPANSION PATH

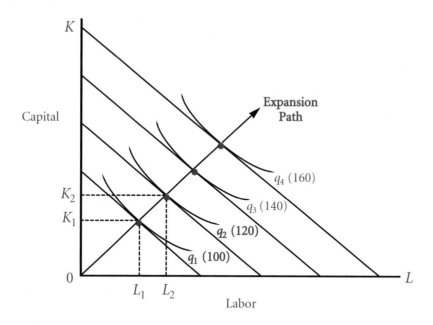

An expansion path connects the firm's least-cost input combinations of producing each level of output in the long run, when all inputs can be varied. The least-cost input combination for producing 120 units of output is K_2 units of capital and L_2 units of labor.

FIGURE 8–10
DERIVING LRTC FROM AN ISOQUANT-ISOCOST MAP

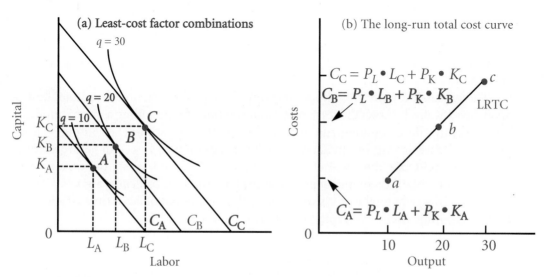

For each level of output, the long-run cost schedule shows the *lowest possible cost* of production, given a sufficient time interval for the firm to adjust all factors and attain the optimum factor combination. In Table 8–1, the total cost of producing 10 units is $3,020 with the particular plant. This plant, however, was designed for *4* units per day, a much smaller volume of output. With a considerably larger plant suited for 10 units, the total cost of producing 10 units per day might be $190. This figure, because it is the lowest possible cost of producing 10 units, is the appropriate cost figure for this level of output in the long-run cost schedule. Similarly, for other levels of output, there are certain figures of lowest possible total cost, each with the plant size—a combination of all factors—best suited to the particular output level.

A typical long-run cost schedule for a firm is presented in Table 8–3. The long-run cost data are obtained from a number of short-run cost schedules, one for each possible plant size. The data from each of the short-run schedules are the cost figures for the lowest-cost levels of output at the most satisfactory factor combination. From the short-run schedule shown in Table 8–1, the cost data for 4, 5, and 6 units of output might go into the long-run schedule, because the plant allows a lower cost for this output range than any other. For a daily output of 7 or 8 units, however, a somewhat larger plant would be needed. Moreover, the long-run cost figures taken from the short run cost data for the larger plant would be lower than the figures for producing the same output with the smaller plant. For an output of 3 units or fewer a day, a plant smaller than that for which data are given in Table 8–1 would allow still lower cost.

TABLE 8–3
TYPICAL LONG-RUN AVERAGE COST SCHEDULE OF A FIRM

Typical Long-Run Average Cost Schedule for a Firm

Units of Output	Total Cost	Average Cost	Marginal Cost
5	$ 125	$ 25.00	—
10	190	19.00	13.00*
15	263	17.35	14.60
20	340	17.00	15.40
25	418	16.72	15.60
30	498	16.60	16.00
35	579	16.54	16.20
40	664	16.60	17.00
45	751	16.69	17.40
50	845	16.90	18.80

*The increase in total cost of $65 resulting when 5 additional units are produced, divided by 5.

By employing isoquant analysis, we can easily see why short-run costs are generally higher than long-run costs. Consider Figure 8–11, which depicts at (K_0, L_0) the optimal long-run (and short-run) input bundle to employ if q_0 is the desired output. Any other way of producing q_0 will involve greater cost as long as relative input prices are constant. Suppose that the firm has been producing q_0 and now wishes to produce q_1, a larger output. This would happen, for example, if the price of the good being produced were to rise.

Clearly, the least-cost way to produce q_1, if all inputs were adjustable as they are in the long run, would be to employ (K_{LR}, L_{LR}), as shown by the tangency of the isocost line. By definition, however, the short-run period is too short to vary all inputs. Suppose that the stock of capital (plant and equipment) is fixed in the short run at K_0. In this case, the least-cost way to produce q_1 is by employing (K_0, L_{SR}). (See Problem 8–14.)

8–14 A firm hires only labor (L) and capital (K). The price of labor is $10 per hour and the price of capital is $5 per hour. Given the information in Figure (a), draw the corresponding portions of the LRTC and SRTC curves on one graph and the segments of the the LRAC and the SRAC curves on another graph. In the short-run, 10 units of capital are available.

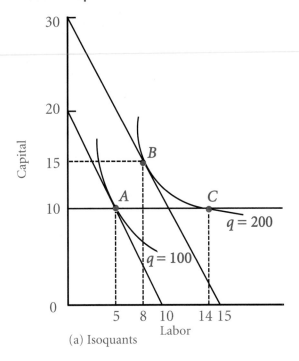

(a) Isoquants

Figure (b) charts the SRTC and LRTC for the data provided in Figure (a), and Figure (c) maps the average cost curves.

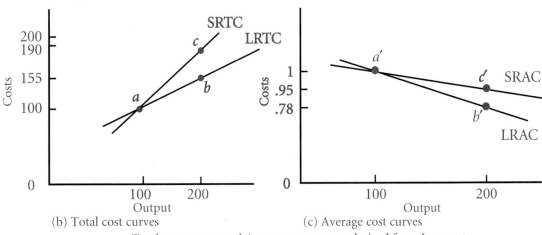

(b) Total cost curves   (c) Average cost curves

Total cost curves and Average cost curves derived from Isoquants

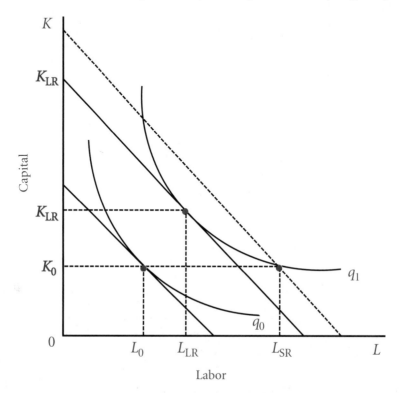

FIGURE 8–11

A GRAPHICAL ILLUSTRATION OF WHY SHORT-RUN COSTS ARE GENERALLY GREATER THAN LONG-RUN COSTS

In the short run, capital is fixed at K_0. To produce q_1, the firm will hire LSR labor. The short-run cost, represented by the dashed isocost line, exceeds the long-run cost, represented by the isocost line passing through K_{LR}, L_{LR}.

LONG-RUN AVERAGE COST

Long-run average cost (LRAC) is defined as the lowest possible average cost of producing a particular amount of output, with the optimal plant size (thus the optimal factor combination) for that particular amount of output. The long-run average cost for any output level is determined by dividing the long-run *total cost* for this output by the number of units of output.

Each firm has many alternative scales at which it could operate (plant sizes it can build). For each of these, there is an appropriate SRAC schedule and curve. These curves for various scales of operation may be drawn on a single graph, as illustrated in Figure 8–12. For simplification, cost curves of only three possible scales are shown, under the assumption (not unrealistic for many industries) that indivisibilities of some factor units prevent the use of intermediate scales of operation.

Certain relationships among the successive curves should be emphasized. For very small output levels, costs are lowest with plant size $SRAC_1$. Costs with plant size $SRAC_2$ or $SRAC_3$ are relatively high for these low levels of output, because those plant's fixed costs are far too high for low levels of output—machinery, buildings, and so on would be poorly utilized. Beyond this low level of output, however, costs with plant size $SRAC_2$ are lower that those with $SRAC_1$. If output levels in this range were produced with plant $SRAC_1$, the plant would be operated beyond designed capacity, and AVC would be high. In contrast, plant $SRAC_2$, designed for a larger volume of output, would be operating at close to optimal capacity. For still higher volumes of output, cost is lower with plant $SRAC_3$.

For each level of output, LRAC is represented by the lowest point on any SRAC curve for that particular output. If a perpendicular line were extended upward from the output axis on a graph containing the various SRAC curves for different size plants, the point at which it first struck an SRAC curve would indicate the relevant value of LRAC for that output level. Thus, in Figure 8–13, for low levels of output the lowest average cost point is on curve $SRAC_1$; at high levels, it is on $SRAC_3$, and so on. The LRAC curve is identical with $SRAC_1$ up to a certain level of output (the intersection of $SRAC_1$ and $SRAC_2$), and so on. The entire long-run average cost curve LRAC (for the output range covered) is indicated in Figure 8–12 by the heavily shaded, scallop-shaped line. If the LRAC curve is plotted directly from an LRAC schedule, such as that in Table 8–3, the only portions of the short-run curves that will appear are those which make up portions of the long-run curve itself. It is important to note that the long-run schedule contains no data that are not to be found in the firm's various short-run schedules.[10]

---

[10]In mathematical language, the long-run curve is the lower envelope of the short-run curves.

The LRAC curve shows the minimum cost per unit of each level of output. The firm chooses the plant scale coinciding with the lowest SRAC curve for each output level. The LRAC curve, therefore, is the *envelope,* or lower boundary, of the feasible SRAC curves.

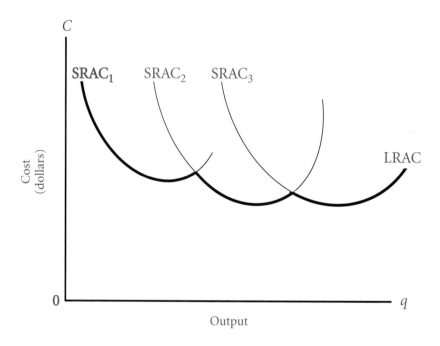

When all factors are divisible into small units, the successive scales of operation will be close to one another, as in Figure 8–13. The LRAC curve will therefore be smooth, as it is in Figure 8–14. When indivisibilities prevent small adjustments in plant scale, the short-run curves are farther apart and the long-run curves will be irregular, as in Figure 8–12.

To sum up, the LRAC curve is often called a *planning curve* because it represents the cost data relevant to the firm when it is planning policy relating to scale of operations, output, and price over a long period of time. At a particular time, a firm already in operation has a certain plant and must base its current price and output decisions on the cost schedule with the existing plant. When the firm considers the possibility of adjusting its scale of operations, however, long-run cost estimates are necessary.

FIGURE 8–13
PATTERN OF SHORT-RUN AVERAGE COST CURVES, WHEN ALL FACTORS ARE DIVISIBLE

When fixed factors are easily divisible, SRAC curves are close together. In the limit each SRAC curve contributes just one point to the LRAC curve. Divisibility implies an infinite number of plant scales and a smooth LRAC curve.

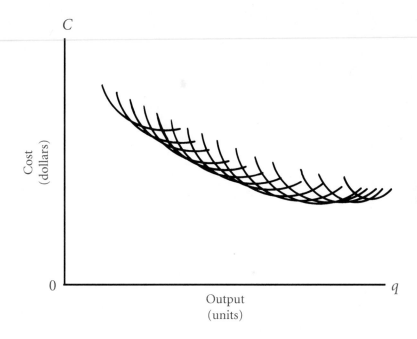

The LRAC, or envelope, curve is smooth when numerous feasible plant scales are available. Long-run marginal costs are derived from the short-run marginal cost associated with the least-cost way of producing each quantity. (See Figure 8–15.)

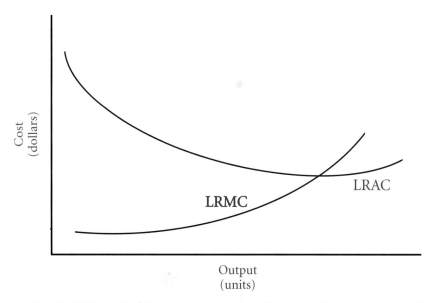

Note that the LRAC schedule does *not* consist of historical data showing what cost has been in the past with various size plants; it shows alternative possibilities at the *present* time—what cost would be for various levels of output if various sized plants were built.

THE BEHAVIOR OF LONG-RUN AVERAGE COST

The behavior of LRAC in response to changes in output is controlled by considerations substantially different from the considerations that affect cost behavior when a firm operates at a particular plant size. Short-run cost behavior is conditioned largely by the presence of constant quantities of some factors. These factors are responsible not only for certain costs being fixed, but also for the nature of the reactions of variable costs to output changes. In the long run, a period of time sufficiently long for the scale of operations to be adjusted, all factors are adjustable, and the consideration of fixed factors is no longer relevant for cost behavior.

The analysis of long-run cost behavior is therefore based on the following assumptions:

1. All factors are variable.

2. Certain factors may be indivisible; that is, they cannot be obtained in infinitesimally small units, or they are relatively inefficient if reduced in size below a certain figure.

3. An increase in the quantities of all factors allows greater specialization in the use of particular factor units.

4. The managerial factor cannot be multiplied in the same manner as other factors because of the need to maintain unified control over the entire enterprise.

The major "givens" are the same as those for the short-run schedules: factor prices, technological conditions, and equal efficiency of successive factor units (homogenous inputs).

With these assumptions, the behavior of LRAC is determined by the manner in which the principle of returns to scale operates in the particular production activity and, thus, by the behavior of changes in output as the inputs of all factor units are changed. As indicated in Chapter 7, a firm typically experiences increasing returns to scale as it expands its operations initially, in part because of indivisibilities of some factors, especially capital equipment, which make operation inefficient and costly on a small scale, and in part because of the advantages of specialization of labor. Because output with increasing returns to scale rises at a faster rate than the rate of increase in factor units, total cost rises at a slower rate than output, and average cost falls. Typically, as a firm expands, the low cost points for successively larger plants are progressively lower. This is illustrated in Figure 8–12; here the low segment of $SRAC_2$—the segment that constitutes a portion of the LRAC curve—is lower than the low segment of $SRAC_1$; that of $SRAC_3$ is lower than that of $SRAC_2$. The LRAC curve, therefore, slopes downward from left to right in the initial stage.

Eventually, however, the *economies of large-scale production* are exhausted; otherwise, there would just be *one* firm in every industry (whichever grew biggest first). The best available types of capital equipment are employed and used to capacity, and full advantage is gained from specialization. Once a point is reached at which all workers are performing tasks sufficiently limited in scope, further increases in output merely require additional workers doing the same tasks. When output reaches the level at which the stage of increasing returns to scale is succeeded by that of constant returns, total cost and output increase at the same rate, and average cost is constant. Especially in industries where little capital equipment is used and thus few economies of large-scale production are available, the stage of constant average cost may be encountered at relatively low levels of output and may extend over a very substantial range. By contrast, wherever there are important indivisibilities and gains from labor specialization, constant average cost will be encountered only after a long phase of decreasing cost.

If expansion is carried far enough, decreasing returns to scale (caused, as explained in Chapter 7, primarily by the complexities of large-scale management) eventually cause LRAC to become progressively greater for successively larger output levels. This rise is likely to be very gradual, however, and is not at all comparable with the rapid rise in average cost in the short run, when expansion of output beyond the designed capacity can cause a sharp increase in variable cost and therefore in average cost.

Under these assumptions, the LRAC curve will be shaped like the one in Figure 8–14, the rate of decrease on the left portion is much greater in some industries than in others, and the rate of increase in the right portion is very gradual. The exact shape of the curve in any particular case depends on the extent to which economies of scale are available, the level to which output must be expanded before economies are completely exhausted, and the extent to which complexities of large-scale management are encountered. Thus, industries in which the lowest possible cost can be obtained with a small volume of output, such as bakeries, are characterized by a large number of small firms. In other industries, such as automotives, where low cost is obtained only when output reaches a substantial figure, firms tend to grow large and small firms have difficulty competing. (See Problem 8–15.)

8–15 **True or False?** If forced to sell larger outputs in more distant markets, a firm's average cost may rise as output expands.

True. As a firm increases its output, it often must sell to buyers at greater distances from the plant. As a consequence, transportation costs increase and raise the average cost of production and (joint) distribution. The firm may seek to avoid this by building additional plants in other areas, but if the original location was the one most suited to the particular type of production, costs will be higher in the new plants. A good example of this geographical property is provided by electric-power-generating plants; despite substantial scale economies of production, costs rise with output that must be sold over larger market areas when distribution costs are, as they should be, considered.

LONG-RUN MARGINAL COST

The concept of **long-run marginal cost** (LRMC) refers to the increase in total cost that occurs when a shift is made to a one-unit-higher scale of production, with optimal factor combinations both before and after the change. (See the two representative tangencies in Figure 8–11.) Because changes in scale ordinarily cannot be made economically in small increments, LRMC may be regarded more realistically as the increase in total cost that occurs when a transition is made from one scale of output to the next highest scale, divided by the number of units of increased output that results. Assume, for example, that for a plant designed for 20 units per day, the total cost is $340. At the next largest feasible scale, one designed for 25 units, the total cost is $418. LRMC is, therefore, $15.60 a unit ($78 increase in total cost divided by 5 units increase in output).

Long-run marginal cost bears the same relation to LRAC as does short-run marginal cost (SRMC) to short-run average cost (SRAC). Generalization about the relationship of LRMC to SRMC schedules for the various possible plant sizes is more difficult. For any given plant size, SRMC will be lower than LRMC for ranges of output up to a certain level. This is because SRMC is affected only by cost elements that are variable in the short run, whereas all cost elements enter into LRMC. Beyond a certain point, however, SRMC will be greater than LRMC. This is because SRMC is affected by the effort to get more and more output from a given plant capacity and, therefore, is subject to the law of diminishing marginal returns.

The relationship between LRMC and SRMC is subtle and requires further explanation. First, to derive the LRMC curve, see Figure 8–15. The LRMC curve is derived, at each output level, from the short-run marginal cost of production at that output level, *if* the least average cost plant is being used to produce that output. At output level q_0, therefore, the short-run marginal cost of production provides one point on the long-run marginal cost curve. Similarly, other points on the SRMC curves corresponding to the least cost of producing q_1 and q_2 (and all other output levels) are used to flesh out the full LRMC curve. Remember that the LRMC shows the cost changes under optimum- or least-cost input combinations. (See the LRMC curve in Figure 8–15.)

A puzzle emerges from examining points like q_0, q_1, or q_2: Unlike the average cost curves, the LRMC is *not* an envelope of the corresponding SRMCs. Looking at output levels to the left of each of the output levels, q_0, q_1, and q_2, depicted in Figure 8–15, we see that the short-run marginal cost is *less* than the long-run marginal cost. How can this be?

The answer to the puzzle is most readily seen by returning to an isoquant diagram corresponding to, say, q_0 in Figure 8–15. This isoquant is shown in Figure 8–16. Isoquant q_1 shows the combination of labor and capital that can produce a smaller amount of output than q_0. The marginal expenditures that are saved from reducing output from q_0 to q_1 are seen in Figure 8–16 by the changing position of the isocost line. Because capital is fixed in the short-run at K_0, the reduction in costs are smaller as we move from the original isocost L_0 to isocost L_{SR} than if we moved to isocost L_{LR} when all inputs are variable. That is, in the *short run* the firm moves from A to B, while in the *long run* it moves from A to D, an added short-run cost saving denoted by the distance C to B. Alternatively, a move from q_1 to q_0, with a plant designed for q_0 (going from B to A—a short-run move) has lower marginal costs than moving from q_1 to q_0 with a plant designed for q_1 (moving from D to A—a long-run move). Hence, short-run marginal costs are less than long-run marginal costs at output levels that are themselves less than the designed capacity.

An alternative explanation is that for output levels smaller than designed plant capacity, labor (which is variable) has relatively large amounts of fixed capital with which to work. That is, at these lower levels of output, capital is fixed at a level higher than would be the case of the cost-minimizing level for that lower output in the long run. The marginal product of labor would, therefore, be higher with the larger amounts of capital, and the marginal cost of an output expansion would therefore be lower in the short run. The higher marginal product of labor means that fewer units of labor are needed to get any given output increase—say, from q_1 to q_0.[11]

FIGURE 8–15
DERIVING THE LRMC CURVE FROM THE SRMC CURVES

The SRMC corresponding to the optimum SRAC for each output level equals the LRMC. For example, $SRMC_0$ coincides with the minimum cost plant given by $SRAC_0$ of q_0. Thus, the short-run marginal cost along $SRMC_0$ at q_0 is the long-run marginal cost of producing q_0.

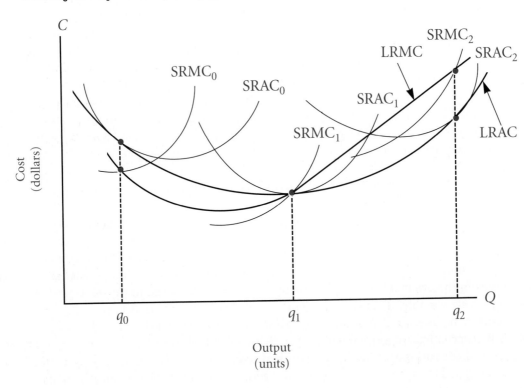

[11]We are assuming that capital (the fixed input in the short run) is a noninferior input, that labor and capital are complementary inputs, and that we are dealing with two inputs—one fixed and one variable.

FIGURE 8-16
SRMC CAN BE LESS THAN LRMC

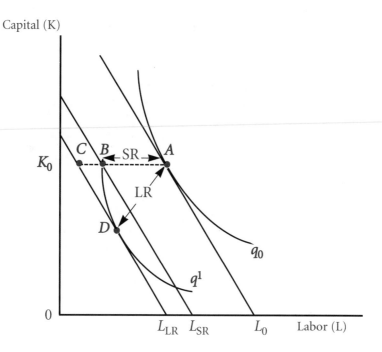

The additional cost of increasing output from q_1 to q_0 (with a plant designed for q_0) in the short run is illustrated by the increase in cost from the isocost L_{SR} to the isocost L_0 (*B* to *A*). In the long run, a greater increase in cost occurs from the isocost L_{LR} to L_0 (*D* to *A*). Thus, LRMC > SRMC for output levels below the designed plant capacity.

THE SIGNIFICANCE OF THE ASSUMPTIONS

The significance of the analysis of long-run cost depends on how applicable the assumptions on which it is based are in particular situations. Each of the assumptions will be examined briefly.

1. Variability of Factors
The assumption that all factors can be varied in the long run is valid except in rare cases of unique, specialized resources.

2. Factor Indivisibility
The assumption that small units of certain factors cannot be obtained or are relatively inefficient appears to be applicable in many lines of production. It is not possible, for example, to build all types of capital equipment on a small scale. Some types, while they

can be built this way, provide relatively low output per unit of input. Labor often cannot be obtained in very small units, such as by the minute. While these considerations are more important in some lines of production than in others, both casual observation and careful empirical studies suggest that some indivisibilities are encountered in virtually all lines of production.

3. Gains from Specialization of Factor Units
Economies typically appear to be obtainable by the more use of specialized labor and other factor units at larger output levels.

Despite the obviously extensive validity of assumptions 2 and 3, it must be recognized that if, in a particular instance, neither assumption is valid, LRAC cannot be expected to decline initially.

4. Adjustment of the Managerial Factor
The assumption that the managerial factor cannot be adjusted in the same manner as other factors, with consequent increasing complexities and cost of management as an enterprise grows, is subject to greater question. The problems of large-scale management are, of course, very real: As business firms grow in size, attention is given to the development and application of the principles of management in an effort to overcome these problems. By this means, firms may succeed in preventing an increase in average cost for a very substantial range of output. Whether this increase can be prevented indefinitely as output is extended farther and farther is doubtful. However, a rise in average costs is by no means inevitable over substantial output ranges.

EMPIRICAL STUDIES OF LONG-RUN COST SCHEDULES

Few producers have precise data about long-run cost behavior. But only a small segment of the cost schedule directly concerns a producer at any time. Producers know that costs with a very small plant would be prohibitively high, but they do not care exactly how high. A firm in imperfectly competitive markets knows that there is no need to consider the costs with a plant ten times the present size because that plant could not possibly sell the increased output at a profitable price. Attention centers on a much narrower range of plant sizes. If a firm suspects that a change might be desirable, it will attempt to figure the cost with various scales of operation, aided by engineering estimates and by data on costs of other firms with larger or smaller scales of operation than its own. Once a plant adjustment is made, the decision is irrevocable for a period of time, even if the cost estimate upon which it is based proves to be erroneous. This is because additional time is required for further changes.

Empirical studies have been made of long-run cost behavior, but the results have not been at all conclusive. The problems encountered are even more serious than those that arise with short-run cost studies. Any attempt to determine the actual long-run cost functions of a single firm from observations of cost with different scales of operation over a period of time is almost entirely futile. Because of the time needed to get any substantial number of observations, other determinants of cost—particularly methods of production—change so much that statistical adjustment for them is difficult. As a consequence, actual studies for the most part have taken cost data for several firms of different sizes at a particular time in an effort to build up a cost schedule typical of firms in the industry. This approach also encounters serious problems. Some firms may operate closer to capacity than others, and so the cost differences will reflect variations in the degree of plant usage as well as variations resulting from differences in plant size. Differences in age of equipment, quality of product, management efficiency, cost accounting methods, and prices paid for factors also skew the results, because the effects of these differences cannot be satisfactorily eliminated.

It is likely that LRAC declines as the scale of operations is increased from a very small size. There is little evidence, however, to prove (or disprove) the thesis that long-run average cost must eventually rise as the scale of operations is expanded, because of increased complexities of management and consequent decreasing returns to scale. Some evidence suggests that LRAC does *eventually* rise in some industries as operations are expanded, but they do so primarily as a result of the tendency of factor prices and distribution costs to rise.

8.8 FURTHER COMPLEXITIES OF COST

The cost analysis of this chapter has been based upon two simplifying assumptions; effects of changes in certain cost elements upon demand schedules for the product have been ignored, as well as the fact that firms frequently produce more than one product. The cost elements for activities that affect sales are known as **selling costs**, in contrast to *production* costs, those arising from the actual production of the goods. Selling costs are incurred for the purpose of influencing the choice of the buyer for the product he or she buys or the firm from which the buyer makes the purchase. Their existence creates an interrelationship between cost schedules and demand schedules, which will be considered in Chapter 12.

The production of more than one product by a firm—a practice which is almost universal—gives rise to **common costs**, those which are incurred for the production of two or more products, no one of which is responsible for any particular part of the cost. The cost of maintenance of a railroad line, therefore, is a common cost for freight and passenger traffic. The concept of average cost for each product is no longer precise when common costs are allocated among the various products produced.

8.9 THE PROBLEM OF DISEQUILIBRIUM

The last two chapters we have tacitly assumed that the cost and revenue estimates of business firms are unaffected by realized results. More specifically, we have ignored possible inconsistencies between the input and output plans of business firms and the factor-supply and consumption plans of households. In effect, therefore, we have developed the entire theory of business behavior on the supposition that no individual firm ever confronts market disequilibrium.

If, however, we assumed that the normal state of a market economy is one of disequilibrium, the first victim would have been our assumption that revenue and cost conditions as seen by business firms are stable functions of time. Without this assumption, we could not have derived even the simplest cost and revenue curves nor stated any simple rules for profit-maximizing behavior. This would have been merely the beginning of a long list of consequences, the total impact of which would have been analytically disastrous.

In defense of the procedure we have followed, we might say, first, that it is traditional; second, that the situation described is conceivable (if not likely); third, that a theory of virtual equilibrium is a necessary and natural point of departure in the development of theories of disequilibrium. The last of these arguments is the most compelling, but the first two are not without force. If further justification is required, we should add that some theory is better than none. As social sciences go, economics is quite old, but professional concern with short-run problems of economic adjustment is a relatively recent phenomenon, and the development of theoretical models to deal with such problems is still in its infancy. The theory we have is certainly not complete. Provided we recognize its limitations, however, it represents our best hope for something better.

SUMMARY

1. The broad definition economists use for *costs* is the compensation that must be received by the owners of money capital and the units of the factors of production used by a firm if these owners are to continue to supply money capital and factor units to the firm.

2. There are two types of total costs: explicit and implicit. Explicit costs are the direct costs of the firm, such as wages, fuel, and raw materials. Implicit cost refers to the opportunity costs of employing resources that could be employed elsewhere.

3. In the long run, all costs are variable. That is, all costs can vary with output. However, in the short run, some costs are fixed, such as capital equipment, taxes, and insurance. These fixed costs are independent of output.

4. The cost of producing various amounts of output depends primarily on three considerations: the technique of production, the efficiency of the factor units employed, and the prices paid for factor units.

5. Short-run cost schedules for a firm show the behavior of cost when output is varied with a given plant, when factor prices are fixed.

6. Average cost is equal to total costs divided by the number of units of output. Average fixed cost (total fixed costs divided by the number of units of output) *plus* average variable cost (total variable cost divided by the number of units of output) equals average total costs.

7. Average variable costs pass through three successive phases as output is increased: declining average variable costs, constant average variable costs, and increasing average variable costs.

8. The optimum factor combination occurs at the tangency of the isoquant with the isocost line. The isocost lines show the various possible quantities of the two factors that can be purchased with a given outlay of money.

9. A change in the price of any one factor, holding output and other factor prices constant, requires a readjustment in factor proportions until the equalities of factor price ratios and marginal rates of technical substitution are again met. A fall in the price of any factor will lead to its increased use, and vice versa.

10. The long run is a planning period, because at any point in actual time, firms are always in some short-run situation. The long-run average cost curve is a planning curve, because it represents the data that are relevant to the firm when it is planning policy. The long-run cost schedule shows, for each level of output, the lowest possible cost of producing the particular amount of output, given a sufficient time interval The long-run average cost curve shows alternative possibilities at the *present* time.

11. The primary determinant of the behavior of long-run average cost is the manner in which the principle of returns to scale (i.e., increasing constant or decreasing returns to scale) operates in the particular production activity, and thus the behavior of changes in output as all factor inputs are changed.

12. Long run-marginal cost is the increase in total costs that occurs when a transition is made from one scale of output to the next highest scale, divided by the number of units of increased output that results.

WORDS AND CONCEPTS FOR REVIEW

cost	explicit costs
implicit costs	long-run period
short-run period	plant
fixed costs	variable costs
cost schedule	short-run cost schedule
marginal cost	average (total) cost
average fixed cost	average variable cost
short-run average (total) cost	planning period
isocost	optimum factor combination
factor price changes and factor substitution	expansion path
long-run average cost	long-run marginal cost
selling costs	common costs

REVIEW QUESTIONS

1. Explain the meaning of the concept of cost as used in economic analysis.

2. Distinguish between explicit and implicit costs, and give examples of each.

3. What payments made by business firms are not regarded as costs, at least during the period in which they are made?

4. Which implicit cost is treated as a business expense under usual accounting principles?

5. Distinguish between the short run and the long run.

6. Distinguish between fixed costs and variable costs. The latter are variable with respect to what?

7. List the major fixed and variable cost items.

8. Why are all costs variable in the long run?

9. What are allocable costs.

10. Is depreciation a cost? Explain.

11. What is the opportunity cost to you of attending college? Of taking a vacation this summer, instead of working?

12. In typical short-run cases would you expect each of the following to be fixed or variable costs?
    a. sales taxes
    b. property taxes
    c. rent on a factory building
    d. interest on money borrowed to buy additional materials
    e. fire insurance
    f. cost of goods sold
    g. the salary of the company president

13. List the major assumptions in short-run cost analysis. Do assumptions make the analysis less realistic? Compare these with the assumptions used in the analysis of long-run cost behavior.

14. A firm with a particular plant has daily fixed costs of $400. Total variable costs for successive quantities of output, per day, are as follows:

Output	Total Variable Cost	Total Variable Output	Cost
1	$ 200	6	400
2	250	7	450
3	275	8	550
4	300	9	750
5	350	10	1,500

Determine average fixed cost, average variable cost, average cost, and marginal cost for the output levels given.

15. Why does marginal cost solely reflect variable cost?

16. Why does the MC curve intersect the AC curve at the lowest point of the latter?

17. If AVC is falling, must MC be falling? Must MC be less than AVC under these conditions? Explain.

18. Why does AFC decline continuously as a firm increases output?

19. Under what circumstances does AVC decline initially as a firm increases output?

20. Why does AVC eventually rise as a firm continues to increase output?

21. Why is the SRAC curve generally U-shaped?

22. What significance does the law of diminishing returns have for the behavior of SRAC?

23. Why does AVC fall if the APP of the variable factor is rising?

24. As a firm adds successive units of variable factors, costing $50 per unit, output increases as follows:

    Units of Factor   Total Output
        1 8
        2 20
        3 45
        4 54
        5 60
        6 63
        7 64
    Determine AVC for the range of output for which information is available.

25. Under what circumstances is a firm likely to experience a wide range of constant AVC?

26. Why may AVC fall even though the APP of the variable factors is constant?

27. In what respect does the ability to operate an enterprise in more than one shift affect the behavior of SRAC?

28. What difficulties are encountered in making empirical studies of short-run cost behavior?

29. What is meant by the term *optimum factor combination*?

30. Define carefully the term *long-run average cost*.

31. How is the long-run cost schedule built up from the short-run cost schedules?

32. Why may the LRAC curve be irregularly shaped?

33. Under what conditions will LRAC decline as a firm first expands its scale of operations? Compare the causes of this decline with the causes of decline in SRAC as a firm expands output with a given plant.

34. Under what circumstances would LRAC not fall as a firm first increases its scale of operations?

35. What may cause an eventual increase in LRAC if a firm continues to expand?

36. What are common costs?

SUGGESTED READINGS

Baumol, W. *Economic Theory and Operations Analysis.* Englewood Cliffs, N.J.: Prentice Hall, 1977, Chapter 11.

Clark, J.M. *Studies in the Economics of Overhead Costs.* Chicago: University of Chicago Press, 1923.

Ferguson, C.E. *The Neoclassical Theory of Production and Distribution.* Cambridge: Cambridge University Press, 1969, Chapter 6.

Sexton, R. L., P. Graves, and D. Lee, "The Short and Long Run Marginal Cost Curve: A Pedagogical Note," 24, no. 1, Winter 1993, *Journal of Economic Education.*

Viner, J. "Cost Curves and Supply Curves." *In Readings in Price Theory,* G.J. Stigler and K.E. Boulding, eds. Homewood, Ill.: Irwin, 1952.

Chapter Nine

COMPETITIVE
PRICE DETERMINATION

———————————— *Questions to Think About* ————————————

1. What conditions are necessary for perfect competition?

2. What are the three stages of competitive price determination?

3. Why is the demand curve for a perfectly competitive firm perfectly elastic? What does this imply about the firm's average revenue and marginal revenue curves?

4. Why will a perfectly competitive firm maximize profits by equating marginal costs and price?

5. Why will a firm shut down if the price falls short of average variable costs? Why does a firm continue to operate in the short run when average cost exceeds price?

6. What is the long-run profit-maximization condition for a perfectly competitive firm? Why are economic profits for such firms zero in the long run?

7. What is the long-run industry supply curve?

8. What is an increasing cost industry? Constant cost industry? Decreasing cost industry?

9.1 INTRODUCTION

H aving completed our analysis of demand and cost, we proceed to describe price and output determination in various market structures: perfect competition, monopoly, monopolistic competition, and oligopoly.

The determination of prices and outputs of various commodities is affected by the structure of the markets. The price and output will obviously be different if the entire supply is controlled by one firm than if it is provided by a large number of small sellers, all acting independently of one another. The number of buyers and the relationships prevailing among them will likewise affect price and output.

This chapter examines **perfect competition**—a market structure in which market prices are treated as known and given to all buyers and sellers, who are assumed to be perfectly informed about the tastes and technology that underlie all prices, and that the output of each seller is homogeneous. Moreover, in perfectly competitive markets, buyers and sellers are assumed to be perfectly mobile, assuring they can act on their information when it is in their interests to do so.

9.2 GENERAL CONSIDERATIONS

In practice, the perfectly competitive market is likely to be approximated most closely in highly organized markets for securities and agricultural commodities, for example, the New York Stock Exchange or the Chicago Board of Trade. Of the conditions for perfect competition mentioned in the introduction, the most crucial is the requirement that transactors (buyers and sellers) regard prices as something over which they have so little control that for all practical purposes they simply ignore the influence of their choices on the market price.

THE STAGES OF COMPETITIVE PRICE DETERMINATION

Competitive price determination falls into three stages: the market period, the short-run period, and the long-run period. The **market period** is so short that *total stock* of the good available for sale is *fixed*. The length of the market period depends on the kind of good traded and on conditions affecting its production and consumption. For goods such as Christmas trees on Christmas Eve, the market period may be less than 24 hours; for others the market period may be anything from a few days to a month or longer. In general, one may think of the market period as being so short that *no* inputs can be varied, with the result that the quantity available remains fixed.

In the next stage, the **short-run period**, the period is long enough to vary *some* inputs, but not all; output, therefore, can vary to some extent. This means that existing stocks can be altered by production and consumption flows; that is, existing inventories can be altered. Certain production and consumption features, however, are prohibitively expensive to vary quickly and are simply treated as fixed. The plant size of firms or the housing or net worth position of households are good examples.

In the final stage, the **long-run period**, buyers and sellers have had enough time to fully adjust their asset levels and composition as desired, taking into consideration items such as taste and technology. The long-run period might be a year or a decade. Technically speaking, it is a period in which all inputs are variable and adjustments are made to bring the economy toward stationary equilibrium.

Of course, any theory or procedure that separates economic decision processes into overlapping time periods and simultaneously treats decisions associated with longer periods as if they were independent of decisions associated with shorter periods must appear artificial. Indeed, it is artificial to an extent. However, this simplifying assumption helps our models to yield significant practical fruit. (See Problem 9–1.)

9–1 Why are stock and securities markets good examples of a perfectly competitive market structure?

In these markets, a large number of investors (buyers and sellers) trade with relatively low information costs, because information about stock prices and companies' profit-and-loss statements are readily available. New information is quickly understood by buyers and sellers and incorporated into the price of the stock, while old information (often only as old as a few minutes) is already reflected by current market prices. For example, if a news story breaks on an infestation of the cotton crop, the price of cotton futures will rise immediately, and only those who speculated before the news or had inside information will make profits. Thus, prices move rapidly in response to news, and it is difficult for any individual to make exorbitant profits when information about products and prices flows so freely. Even the best analysts on Wall Street have only a *slightly* better-than-average record over the long haul.

9.3 THE DEMAND CURVE OF AN INDIVIDUAL SELLER

In a perfectly competitive market, a change in the individual seller's output does not alter the expected market price. The seller believes he can sell as much as he wishes to place on the market at the prevailing price. In other words, the demand as seen by the seller is perfectly elastic. A wheat farmer assumes that he can dispose of his entire crop at the current market price, for he knows that any change he makes in the quantity offered for sale will have no appreciable effect on market price. Likewise, he knows that he cannot dispose of his wheat at any figure higher than the market price; if he attempted to charge a higher price, prospective buyers would simply purchase their supplies from other sources. Also, he would not knowingly charge a lower price, because he can sell all he wants at the higher current market price. Thus, if the prevailing market price of the product were $6, the farmer's demand curve would be represented graphically by a horizontal line at that market-determined price, as shown in Figure 9–1.

How is it possible that the demand curve of an individual seller is horizontal when the market-demand curve for the product is not? Why will a wheat farmer believe that he can sell as much wheat as he pleases without affecting the market price if the total quantity of wheat demanded at each price is a finite amount and larger quantities can be sold only at lower prices? This is possible because of the very large number of sellers, all selling identical (homogeneous) products. Each producer provides such a small fraction of the total supply that a change in the amount he or she offers does not have a noticeable effect on the market price, and the producer, therefore, anticipates that his or her sales have no effect on it. In other words, the effect is imperceptible. Thus, the farmer's demand curve appears to be horizontal over the entire range of output that he could possibly produce.

To say that producers under perfect competition regard price as a given is not to say that price is constant. The *position* of any individual firm's demand curve, as distinguished from its elasticity, varies with every change in the current market price. In effect, sellers are provided with current information about market demand-and-supply conditions through the medium of market prices. It is an essential aspect of the perfectly competitive model that sellers respond to the signals provided by such price movements. That is to say, sellers alter their behavior over time in the light of actual experience, revising their decisions in conformity with changes in market price. In this respect, the perfectly competitive model is quite realistic, for unlike other models of market-price determination, it does not assume any knowledge on the part of individual buyers and sellers about market demand or cost functions. The force of this characteristic will become clear in later chapters when we deal with price formation under conditions of monopoly, monopolistic competition, and oligopoly.

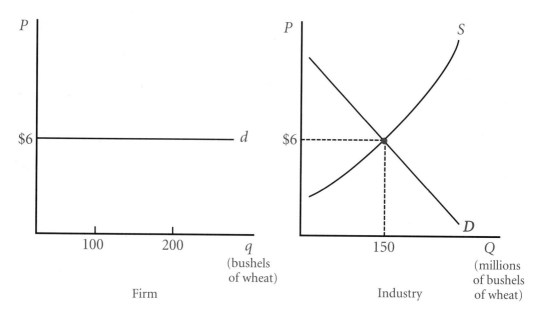

FIGURE 9–1
THE DEMAND CURVE OF A SELLER OF WHEAT

At the market price for wheat, $6, the individual farmer can sell all the wheat he wishes. Because each producer provides only a small fraction of industry output, any additional output will have an insignificant impact on market price. The firm's demand curve is, therefore, assumed to be perfectly elastic at the market price.

The concept of marginal revenue must now be introduced, because it is vital to our analysis of all firms' decision making. **Marginal revenue** is the addition to total revenue resulting from the sale of an additional unit of output.[1] In a perfectly competitive market, because additional units of output can be sold without reducing the price of the product, marginal revenue for each unit of output is identical to the price of the product. For example, in Figure 9–2 if the price of the product is $5, the marginal revenue is $5. Because total revenue is (P • q), as we add one additional unit of output, total revenue will always increase by the amount of the product's price, $5. As will be explained in later chapters, in *imperfectly competitive* markets (monopoly, monopolistic competition, and oligopoly), marginal revenue and demand are not identical.

---

[1]Formerly, marginal revenue is the derivative of the total revenue function. *Total revenue,* TR, is defined simply as the quantity sold times the price at which it is sold:

$$TR = P \cdot q$$

If price is given (constant with respect to output changes at the firm level) to the firm:

$$MR = \frac{dTR}{dq} = P$$

Figure 9-2
Marginal Revenue Equals Market Price in Perfect Competition

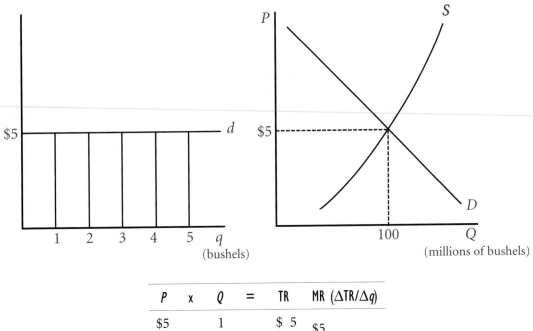

P	x	Q	=	TR	MR (ΔTR/Δq)
$5		1		$ 5	$5
$5		2		$10	$5
$5		3		$15	$5
$5		4		$20	$5
$5		5		$25	$5

Each additional unit sold by the producer will increase total revenue by the market price of $5. Because marginal revenue is defined as the addition to total revenue resulting from the sale of an additional unit of output, marginal revenue must equal the market price.

9.4 OUTPUT AND PRICE IN THE MARKET PERIOD

Because we have defined the market period as a time interval that is too short to alter existing stocks of a commodity through production or consumption, the forces that determine current price are primarily stock supply and stock demand, concepts discussed in Chapter 3. Thus, **market-period supply** consists of existing stocks of inventories of finished goods held by business firms and households.

The quantity of any good actually held by individuals at any given moment is a legacy from the past, as is the aggregate stock of the good available to the economy as a whole. At any moment of time, therefore, the aggregate stock is "frozen" and cannot be changed. Of course, an individual can increase stock of a good right now by acquiring it in exchange from somebody else, but the economywide (aggregate) stock of that good is not affected. Although the future magnitude of a stock supply of a commodity can be altered by human action, its current level is simply a fact. Figure 9–3 illustrates the stock-supply curve, S_0, as a vertical line, to indicate that the quantity of existing stocks does not respond to the current market price. Costs of production now sunk, are not relevant in price determination. Specifically, supply determines quantity and market demand determines the price at which that quantity can be sold.

For example, when a good such as fresh fish or fresh-cut flowers cannot be stored, the entire stock will continue to be offered for sale regardless of price, and higher prices will bring forth no larger quantities in the time period under consideration. Sellers will unload their stock of flowers for whatever they can get because the fresh flowers will be worthless tomorrow (it is unlikely that your price would fall to zero, however, as you would presumably take flowers home for your or your family's enjoyment before giving them away). This reasoning would generally apply to all perishable goods, not just flowers.

We can see that in the case of a perishable good such as flowers, price only acts to ration demand: if the market demand increases, the price will be higher; if the market demand falls, the price will be lower but the quantity is fixed in the market period.

FIGURE 9–3
OUTPUT AND PRICE DETERMINATION IN THE MARKET PERIOD

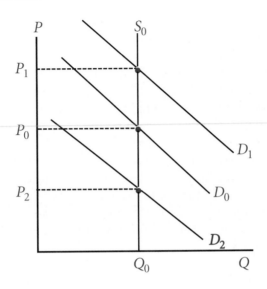

Price only acts to ration demand in the market period. Market supply is fixed whether market demand is high, D_1, or low, D_2.

9.5 OUTPUT AND PRICE IN A SHORT-RUN PERIOD

Over time, firms can adjust their output, so the supply function depends on the rate of output rather than merely on a firm's willingness to sell from a given stock of goods. In all situations in which output is adjustable—short run or long run—attaining maximum expected profit requires the firm to adjust output so that any additional increase in output, however small, increases total revenue more than it increases total cost, and any reduction in output reduces total revenue less than it reduces total cost. Thus, marginal profit—the additional profit resulting from the sales of an additional unit of output—is positive for units of output less than the profit-maximizing level, zero at the **profit-maximizing level of output,** and negative for increases in output beyond that point. Thus, supply depends on those items that influence marginal cost of production at various levels of output.

The short-run period is defined as an interval long enough to allow the firm to adjust some inputs (and therefore, to adjust output) but not all inputs (particularly plant size).

The **short-run-supply function** is the relationship between various prices and the quantities that will be offered for sale at those prices during an interval long enough to allow the existing firms to adjust output with given plant capacity. As noted previously, because firms can adjust output, a new determinant of supply becomes significant—namely, the cost of production.

The firm does not produce at all unless the price it can obtain at least covers *average variable cost* (AVC). Variable costs would cease if production were suspended; operation at a price that does not cover them therefore worsens the firm's financial position.[2] If a firm cannot obtain enough revenue from the sale of the product to cover the direct wage, raw material, and power costs necessary to produce it, then each additional unit produced reduces the firm's wealth. Even if the owners of a business desire to continue operation under such circumstances, they cannot do so for very long. Firms continue to operate when price is below AVC only if the owners believe that prices will rise in the near future and wish to avoid the costs associated with closing and reopening the plant and losing experienced personnel.

---

[2]Proof: when $\pi(0) > \pi(q^*)$, then firm will shut down. This equivalent to: $-\text{TFC} > Pq^* - \text{TC}(q^*)$ or $-\text{TFC} > Pq^* - \text{TFC} - \text{TVC}(q^*)$ or $0 > Pq^* - \text{TVC}(q^*)$ or dividing by q^* and rearranging: $\text{AVC} > P$. Therefore profit at zero output is greater than profit at the optimal positive quantity of output if price does not cover average variable cost.

FIGURE 9–4
EQUILIBRIUM OUTPUT OF THE FIRM IN THE SHORT RUN

When marginal cost equals marginal revenue, the corresponding output level maximizes firm profits (or minimizes losses) as long as price is at least as great as average variable cost. Because price exceeds average cost for the firm in this example, the firm reaps positive economic profits in the short run.

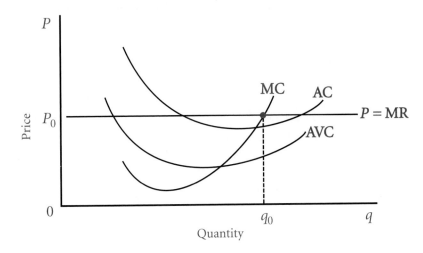

At price levels equal to or higher than AVC, a firm produces in the short run even if average total cost is not completely covered. Because fixed costs continue whether the firm produces or not, it is preferable to earn enough to cover a portion of these costs rather than earn nothing at all. In the short run, it is not economically feasible to liquidate the business, curtailing fixed costs. A major reason is that money capital invested in specialized equipment cannot be withdrawn quickly except at great loss, because used capital goods, as a rule, have little resale value.

In the range of prices at which production is carried on (those equal to or above AVC), the firm adjusts its output to a level at which *marginal cost* (MC) with the existing plant is equal to *marginal revenue* (MR). Recall that in perfect competition, marginal revenue is equal to market price. Until this volume of output is reached, each additional unit produced results in a greater *addition* to the total revenue of the firm (marginal revenue) than to its total cost (marginal cost) and hence is profitable to produce, provided that price covers AVC. If output is carried beyond the level at which MR = MC, additional units add more to total cost than to total revenue and thereby either reduce profits or increase losses.

Figure 9–4 illustrates the level of operation of a firm in perfect competition in the short run. The short-run cost schedule, comparable to those discussed in Chapter 8, is plotted on the same chart with the revenue schedule. The demand curve is a horizontal line at the level of the current market price, P_0. This line also indicates marginal revenue, which is identical to market price in perfect competition. Because, in this illustration, price is higher than AVC for the level of output under consideration, the firm operates;

it produces that number of units q_0, such that MR = MC = P_0, as indicated on the graph by the intersection of the MC and MR curves. Price in this instance also exceeds AC. In contrast, Figure 9–5 illustrates a case in which price is less than AVC at all ranges of output; therefore, the firm does not produce ($q_2 = 0$). Figure 9–6 shows price as less than AC but more than AVC ($q_1 > 0$). In this case, the firm produces in the short run, but at a loss. To shut down would make this firm worse off, because it can cover at least *some* of its fixed costs with the excess of revenue over variable cost. (See Problem 9–2.)

9–2 True or False? The owner of a summer camp may choose to shut down during the off-season because he cannot pay his fixed costs.

The issue is not whether you can pay your fixed costs. The decision to shut down or operate depends on variable costs. If the owner cannot pay his variable costs, he should shut down. Recall that the owner has to pay his fixed costs whether he operates or not. Because the demand for summer camps will be lower during the off-season, it is likely that the price may be too low for the camp to pay its variable costs, and the owner will choose to shut down. The owner will still have to pay his fixed costs: property tax, insurance, the implicit costs associated with the camp structures, and so on. However, if the camp is not in operation during the off season, the owner will not have to pay the variable costs, such as, salary and benefits for the seasonal camp staff, food, and electricity.

SHORT-RUN EQUILIBRIUM USING THE TOTAL APPROACH

The short-run profit-maximizing equilibrium output can also be shown using the total revenue and total cost curves in Figure 9–7. Because total profits equal total revenue minus total costs, the firm will attempt to produce that output level where the difference between total revenue and total cost is the greatest. In Figure 9–7, total profits are maximized at q^*, where the vertical distance between points A and B are the greatest. The total-revenue curve is a straight line (constant slope) because for the given market price, total revenue increases proportionally with output. The total-revenue curve begins at the origin because total revenue will be zero if desired sales (output) are zero. The slope of the total-revenue curve is the marginal-revenue curve. The slope of the total-cost curve is marginal cost. The total-cost curve, however, is not a straight line because total costs include both fixed and variable costs and are subject to the law of diminishing returns, as discussed in Chapter 7. At low levels of output we can see that profits are negative because total revenues are insufficient to cover total costs.

At the optimal (profit maximizing) level of output, q*, we have maximized the difference between total revenue and total cost, or in other words, we have equated marginal revenue and marginal cost. That is, at q*, the slope of the total-revenue curve (marginal revenue) at point a is equal to the slope of the total-cost curve (marginal cost) at point b.

At each possible price above the level of lowest AVC, the firm places on the market the number of units that equates MC to price. The firm's supply schedule can, therefore, be derived directly from its MC schedule, as Figure 9–8 illustrates. The right-hand portion of the table indicates the supply schedule of the firm on the basis of the cost data presented on the left-hand side. At any price below $20, nothing would be produced because AVC would not be covered. A price of $20 would just cover AVC, and the firm would therefore be indifferent between operating and shutting down in the short run; if it operated, 4 units would be produced, because with a price of $20, MC = MR at an output of 4 units. At $25, with an output of 5 units, the firm just covers average total costs, and would be willing to continue producing in the long run. If the price were $27, 6 units would be supplied; if it were $50, 7 units; and so on. For output levels 6 and 7, the firm is earning economic profits; this will, as we shall see, tempt others into this industry.

In graphical terms, the short-run supply curve of an individual competitive seller is identical with that portion of the MC curve that lies on or above and to the right of the point at which the MC curve intersects the AVC curve. As a cost relation, this curve shows the marginal cost of producing any *given output*; as a supply curve, it shows the *equilibrium output* that the firm will supply at various prices in the short run. Figure 9-8 shows that the portion of MC above its intersection with AVC is the supply curve. The declining portion of the MC curve has no significance for supply because greater profit can be made by extending production to the quantities at prices on the rising portion of the curve.[3] All units of output in the intervening range add more to total revenue than to total cost.

---

[3]Indeed, setting price equal to marginal cost when the latter is downward sloping corresponds to a profit minimum (given positive production) rather than the profit maximum. At a maximum, the rate of increase of marginal profit is negative (marginal profit is declining as one moves through the point at which P = MC). Therefore, the second derivative of the profit function must be negative:

$$\pi = TR(q) - TC(q)$$

Marginal profit $\dfrac{d\pi}{dq} = MR(q) - MC(q)$

$\qquad\qquad = P - MC(q)$ in competition

$\qquad\qquad = 0$ at the top, (or bottom) of the profit "hill." (that is, P = MC(q) at the optimum)

and $\quad \dfrac{d^2\pi}{dq^2} = \dfrac{-dMC(q)}{dq} < 0$ if at the top, rather than the bottom, of the profit hill.

If marginal costs are increased as output increases (dMC(q)/dq > 0), this condition is met, in light of the minus sign. Therefore, marginal cost must be increasing in the neighborhood of the optimum.

FIGURE 9–5
REVENUE AND COST CURVES OF A FIRM IN THE SHORT RUN, PRICE LESS THAN LOWEST AVC

The firm ceases to produce in the short run when average variable cost exceeds price. In the long run, this firm would also leave the industry. Not even variable inputs can be paid out of revenues, and the firm cuts losses by discounting production.

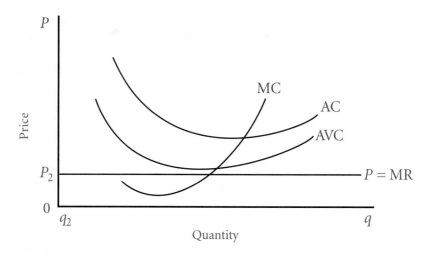

FIGURE 9–6
REVENUE AND COST CURVES OF A FIRM IN THE SHORT RUN, WITH PRICE ABOVE AVC BUT BELOW AC

In this case, the firm operates in the short run but incurs a loss because average cost exceeds price. Nevertheless, price is greater than average variable cost, and revenues cover variable costs and partially defray fixed costs. This firm would still leave the industry in the long run unless price rose through exit of other firms.

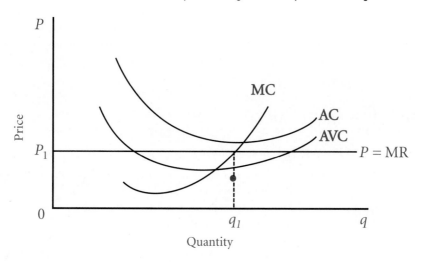

FIGURE 9–7
SHORT-RUN EQUILIBRIUM—THE TOTAL APPROACH

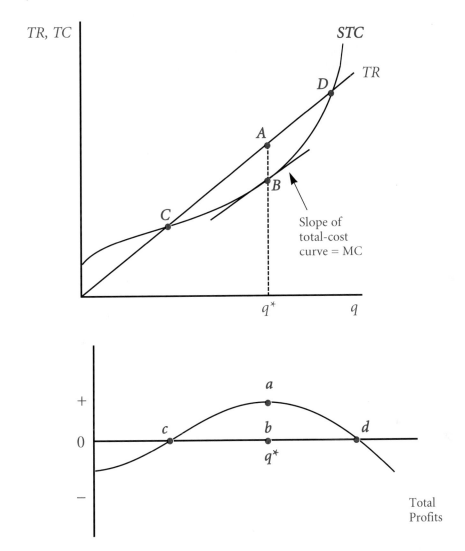

The firm chooses output, q^*, where the vertical distance between TR and STC is greatest (points *A* and *B* in top graph and points *a* and *b* in the lower graph). This is the output where total profit is maximized. At q^*, MR = MC, because the slope of the total-revenue curve (MR) is equal to the slope of the total-cost curve (MC).

FIGURE 9–8
SHORT-RUN COST CURVE AND SUPPLY CURVE OF A FIRM

	Daily Cost Schedule			Daily Supply Schedule	
Units of Output	Average Variable Cost (dollars)	Average Cost (dollars)	Marginal Cost (dollars)	Price (dollars)	Quantity Supplied
1	$30	$50.00	$30	$ 8	0
2	24	34.00	18	12	0
3	20	26.67	12	15	0
4	20	25.00	20	20	4
5	21	25.00	25	25	5
6	22	25.53	27	27	6
7	26	28.86	50	50	7
8	40	42.50	138	138	8

The quantity supplied by the firm for a given price is the quantity which maximizes profits. Profit maximization requires that MR = MC, and because P = MR in perfect competition, P will equal MC at the optimum quantity. The $P \geq$ AVC condition ensures that the firm will operate in the short run. Thus the MC curve on or above the AVC curve is the short-run supply curve for the firm.

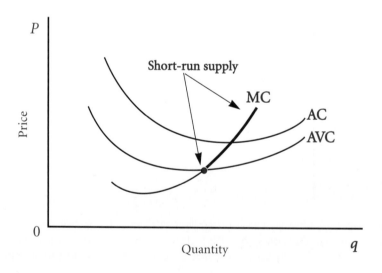

Because beyond the point of lowest AVC, the marginal costs of successively larger amounts of output are progressively greater, the firm will supply larger amounts only at higher prices. The absolute maximum that the firm can supply, regardless of price, is the maximum quantity that it can produce with the existing plant.

By definition, the short run is too brief for new firms to begin production; the total short-run supply schedule is, therefore, closely related to, and sometimes is, the sum of the individual schedules of existing firms. A potential difference arises from the possible effect that higher levels of output may have in raising prices that must be paid for factors of production used by existing firms. If factor prices rise, the quantities supplied at higher prices will be somewhat less than they would appear to be on the basis of a summation of existing individual schedules at current factor prices.

In summary, the **determinants of short-run market supply** include:

1. the number of firms

2. the short-run cost functions of firms (costs being viewed as a function of quantity produced only), and

3. factor prices

RELATIONSHIPS BETWEEN PRICE AND COST IN THE SHORT-RUN PERIOD

As a consequence of firms' ability to adjust output in the short run, certain relationships must exist between equilibrium price and costs, once all adjustments are complete. Specifically,

1. $P = MC$ for each firm, as required for short-run profit maximization;

2. $P > AVC$ for each firm, because firms will not operate unless AVC is covered at the short-run equilibrium output.

At the short-run equilibrium output, market price may be either above or below AC, for fixed costs do not have to be covered except in the long run. The actual relationship between short-run equilibrium price and AC in each particular case depends on the relationship between market demand and short-run supply. If demand is sufficiently great, price will be above AC; if demand is relatively low, price will be in the range between AC and AVC.

SHORT-RUN PROFITABILITY

Figure 9–9 presents three short-run equilibrium positions. Each of these alternatives represents the firm maximizing profits in the short run at different market prices. That does not necessarily mean that the firm is making an economic profit. However, it does mean that the firm is operating as profitably as it can, given its current circumstances.

Figure 9–9 also lists three alternative prices, $6, $5 and $4, for a firm with given costs. Figure 9–10(a) has the firm charging $6 per unit at an equilibrium level of output (MR = MC) of 120 units. Total revenue (price • output) is $6 • 120 or $720. The average total costs at 120 units of output is $5 and the total cost (ATC • output) is $600. This firm is earning short-run economic profits of $120.

The market price has fallen in Figure 9–10(b) to $4 per unit. At the new equilibrium level, the firm produces 80 units of output at an average total cost of $5 per unit. The total revenue is now $320 ($4 • 80), and the total cost is $400 ($5 • 80). The firm is now incurring economic losses of $80. However, the firm should continue to operate, because it is covering average variable costs.

Figure 9-10(c) shows the firm "breaking even." The market price is $4.90, and the average total cost is $4.90 per unit for 100 units of output. In this case, economic profits are zero because total revenue, $490, minus total cost, $490, equals zero. This firm is just covering all its costs, both implicit and explicit. (See Problems 9–3 and 9–4)

FIGURE 9–9
THREE ALTERNATIVE SHORT-RUN EQUILIBRIA

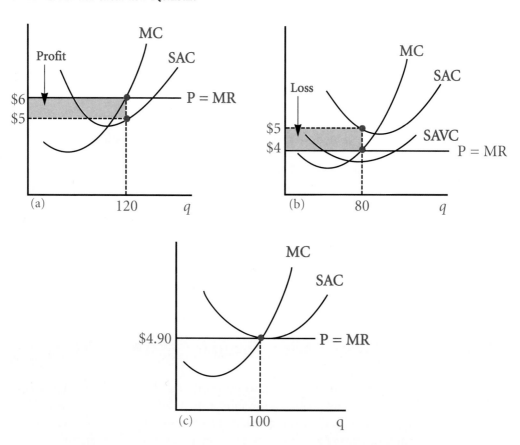

In Figure (a), the firm is earning short-run economic profits of $120. In Figure (b), the firm is suffering losses of $80, but would continue to operate, because the firm is covering AVC. In Figure (c), the firm is breaking even, with the price just equal to short-run average cost.

9–3 In Table (a), if the price of output is $50, what is the quantity supplied by the firm in the short run? How much profit is earned at that price? If the price is $150, what are the short-run quantity supplied and profits? What are the short-run quantity supplied and profits for the firm if the price is $200? What is the short-run supply schedule?

Table (a)

Output	Total Cost	Average Cost	Average Variable Cost	Average Fixed Cost	Marginal Cost
1	50	—	—	—	—
2	250	250	200	50	200
3	400	200	175	25	150
4	450	150	133.3	16.7	50
5	600	150	137.5	12.5	150
6	800	160	150	10	200

To maximize profits, P = SRMC and P > AVC. If P = $50, P = SRMC when q = 3. AVC, however, is 133.33 when q = 3 which exceeds P. Thus, when P = $50, then q = 0 and profits = $50. If the firm produced 3 units, the firm would lose $300 (at q = 3, TR = $150 and TC = $450). When P = $150, q = 4, and profits are $0, 4 units will be offered when P = $150. When P = $200, q = 5, and profit = $200. The short-run supply curve for the firm is SRMC on or above AVC. Table (b) displays the supply schedule.

Table (b)

Quantity Supplied	Price
0	<150
4	150
5	200

9–4 Graph the Short Run AC, AVC, MC, and MR curves and the equilibrium output levels for a perfectly competitive firm operating at a loss. What is the output level that minimizes losses?

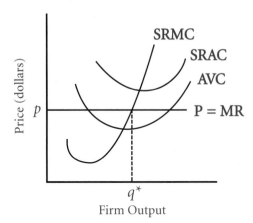

The Cost for a Firm Operating at a Loss

The figure shows the cost curves of the firm that is producing q^*, the loss-minimizing level of output. The firm stays in business because $P >$ AVC but incurs an economic loss because $P <$ SRAC (because by multiplying both sides of the inequality by q: TR $<$ SRTC).

9.6 OUTPUT AND PRICE IN THE LONG-RUN PERIOD

At any one time, adjustments in output with existing plant tend to bring the market price to the short-run equilibrium figure. But over a longer period—one that allows firms to adjust all factors of production, including plant size, and allows new firms to enter the market and unprofitable ones to leave—the various adjustments bring both the market period price and the short-run equilibrium price to the long-run equilibrium level. If all long-run adjustments are completed, the short-run and long-run equilibrium prices are the same, and the market price is equal to them.

   The long-run equilibrium price is determined by the relationship between demand and long-run supply. This relationship is the schedule of total amounts that would come onto the market at various prices in each time interval, given a period of time long enough to allow firms to adjust the quantities of all the factors they use. Demand requires little further consideration. As indicated previously, demand schedules are more elastic over a longer period than they are at a given time; this is because buyers make greater adjustments to price changes over a longer time interval than they do immediately after the change. Long-run supply, however, requires more detailed analysis, because its determinants are not identical with those of supply in the short period.

LONG-RUN SUPPLY SCHEDULES

In the long run, output adjustments of existing firms differ from those made in the short run for two reasons: first, because firms are able to adjust the quantities of all factors employed and they can thereby alter costs that affect short-run equilibrium levels of output; second, because the number of firms in the industry may change, which will alter total quantities supplied at various prices and which may also alter the cost curves of existing firms.

LONG-RUN ADJUSTMENTS BY EXISTING FIRMS

Price in the short run needs to cover only average variable cost to ensure that firms continue production. Over a long-run period, however, price must cover *all costs*—and thus be at least equal to average total cost—or the owners will liquidate the enterprise and reinvest in other fields. At price levels equal to or higher than the minimum average total cost (AC), a firm adjusts plant capacity until long-run marginal cost (LRMC) and short-run marginal cost (SRMC) both equal marginal revenue (MR) and, therefore, price. Plant size is adjusted to allow equality of LRMC and MR and so permits the lowest cost-factor combination for any given volume of equilibrium output. The firm produces at the point at which SRMC with this plant is equal to price. The **long-run output equilibrium** position of an existing firm is illustrated in Figure 9–9. At the price P_0, the firm has adjusted all factors until it attained the plant represented by curve SRAC, and it produces q_0 units of output. At this level of output, both SRMC and LRMC equal MR at the prevailing market price, P_0.[4]

---

[4]There is one sense which this reasoning is faulty: If firms really know everything required of them by assumption in perfect competition, they will know that the positive profits depicted in Figure 9–10 cannot last due to entry of new firms. They may instead build the long-run least-cost plant associated with long-run equilibrium *after* entry of new firms.

FIGURE 9–10
Long-Run Output Equilibrium of Individual Firm

In the long run, the firm chooses the plant scale and output level for which LRMC = MR. If price covers average cost, the firm will stay in business. P_0 is not the long-run equilibrium price because the firm is making
excess profit, which will attract entry.

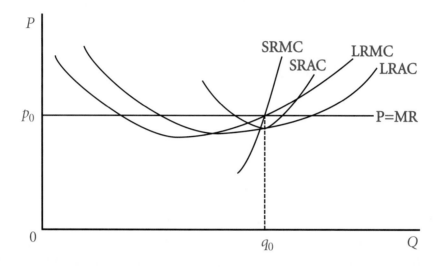

ADJUSTMENT IN THE NUMBER OF FIRMS

As illustrated in Figure 9–10, the prevailing price more than covers the firm's long-run
average costs. In these circumstances, the prevailing price cannot represent a long-run
equilibrium price because it permits the individual firm to earn economic profits. The
existence of economic profits (more precisely, the situation in which price is above the
minimum point on the LRAC curve of any potential producer) will attract new entrants
into the industry and possibly additional resources from existing firms. The additional
output therefore offered for sale depresses the price in the short-run period and so
forces existing firms to adjust long-run output. The number of firms in the industry
becomes stationary only when price attains a level at which no firm is able to earn economic profits. Figure 9–11 illustrates this equilibrium . When long-run adjustments in
the number of firms have been completed, price is at a level, P_1 where the firm's demand
curve (which is equal to MR in perfect competition) is tangent to the LRAC curve at its
lowest point. At this point, the equilibrium level of output, q_1, is such that price is equal
to LRAC, to SRAC with the optimum-size plant, and to both SRMC and LRMC.

Positive economic profits attract new firms into the industry. Short-run industry supply increases, and equilibrium price declines. Entry continues until economic profits are zero—that is, until price equals the minimum long-run average cost for each firm.

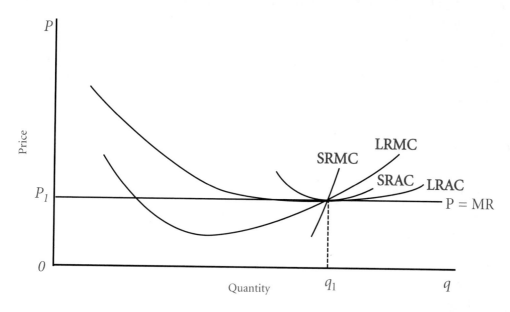

The principles discussed in the preceding paragraphs apply to all firms in the industry. The number of firms in the industry tends to change over time as long as price differs from the minimum level of LRAC for any firm. Because there is a single market price for the commodity, LRAC must be equal to this price for all firms. It follows that only those firms that are capable of producing at a LRAC that is no greater than that of any other firm can survive. The contradiction between this conclusion and common knowledge about differences in costs of various firms arises because the statement is not applicable in any given time period in which long-run adjustments have not been completed. Many apparent cost differences are short-run phenomena that disappear over a longer period. Firms that have high costs because of obsolete techniques or poor management must either lower their costs (by paying lower salaries to the poor managers, for example) or go out of business. Firms that appear to have lower costs because of particularly good resources or higher than average management ability do not actually have lower cost schedules, if all implicit cost elements are considered. The owners of superior factor units can command a higher price for them than for standard-quality units. The price differential will, in general, reflect the difference in productivity. (See Problems 9–5, 9–6, and 9–7.)

9–5 True or False? The costs to the firm (either implicit or explicit) of using superior factor units are higher than those of firms using standard units; and average cost, including both explicit and implicit elements, is not lower for firms using superior units.

True. For example, a farmer whose land is particularly fertile has lower labor and capital costs per unit of output than other farmers, but based on its yield, she could rent the land to others at a price considerably higher than the rent that the owners of poorer land could get. The rent element in total cost is greater by the amount of the reduction in her other costs resulting from the use of the good land, and her average cost will be the same as that of neighbors using poorer land once rents have been included.

9–6 Explain why the following conditions characterize long-run competitive equilibrium:
  a. LRMC = MR
  b. Minimum LRAC = P
  c. SRAC = LRAC and SRMC = LRMC

a. LRMC = MR ensures that the firm is maximizing profits. If LRMC > MR, the cost of the last unit exceeds the revenue from producing it, and the firm could increase profits by reducing output. If LRMC < MR, then the firm could raise profits by selling another unit of output because the additional revenue from doing so would be greater than the additional cost. If LRMC = MR, then the firm cannot increase profits by either increasing or decreasing output. This is called *allocative efficiency.*

b. *P* = Minimum LRAC in long-run equilibrium means that economic profits are zero and no firms have incentive to enter or exit the industry. If *P* > minimum LRAC, then TR > LRTC, and profits are positive, which would attract firms into the industry. If *P* < minimum LRAC, then firms are incurring losses, and some will leave the industry. Only if *P* = Minimum LRAC is there no tendency for change. This is called *productive efficiency.*

c. SRAC = LRAC and SRMC = LRMC indicate that the firm is in short-run as well as long-run equilibrium. If the firm has chosen the optimal combination of inputs in the long run when all inputs are variable, it must also have chosen the optimal combination of inputs in the short run, that is, given the fixed plant selected. The second equation means that the firm is maximizing profits in the short run as well as in the long run (assuming that MR = LRMC).

9–7 Evaluate the following statements. Determine whether each is true or false and explain your answer.

    a. If a firm uses only one variable input, given information on its marginal and average product schedules, the only additional information needed to determine the firm's short-run supply curve is the price of the variable input.

    b. If economic profits are zero, firms will exit the industry in the long run.

    c. A firm in a competitive industry earns profits 5 percent above the average profit rate in other industries. Each firm produces 200 units of output at a price of $1 per unit, and there are 5,000 firms in the industry. Therefore, the long-run equilibrium price equals $1.

    d. A firm cannot maximize profits without minimizing costs.

    e. If a firm is minimizing costs, it must be maximizing profits.

a. True. The firm's short-run supply curve is the SRMC on or above the AVC. The SRMC is the variable input price divided by the MP, and the AVC is the variable input price divided by the AP.

b. False. Zero economic profits indicates that the owners of the firm are earning as much as they could earn with their resources (financial or labor) in any other endeavor. There is no incentive to leave the industry, as they cannot earn more elsewhere.

c. False. Because firms are currently earning positive economic profits (more profits than could be earned in other industries), the current price is not the long-run equilibrium price. Firms will be attracted into the industry, increasing short-run supply and lowering price until economic profits are zero.

d. True. If a firm is spending more than is necessary to produce a given level of output, profits will be lower than they would have been if the cost-minimizing input combination had been employed.

e. False. The long-run average-cost curve charts the minimum per-unit cost of producing each level of output. In the long run, only one level of output, however, maximizes profit: that which corresponds to the equality of MR and LRMC.

9.7 LONG-RUN INDUSTRY SUPPLY FUNCTIONS

The preceding sections have considered the behavior of cost for the individual firm as it varies output on the assumptions that prices paid for factor units are given, except insofar as they may be influenced by changes in the output of the firm itself, and that the efficiency of factor units is given. There is much greater likelihood of changes occurring in factor prices and in factor efficiency when the output of an entire industry changes.

There are three possible industry cost conditions—constant, increasing, and decreasing.

CONSTANT COST INDUSTRIES

Constant cost conditions, in which the cost schedules of the firms are not affected by changes in the output of the entire industry, will occur when the industry does not use its factors in sufficient quantities for their prices or efficiency to be affected by changes in the output of the industry.

As explained earlier, once long-run adjustments are complete, each firm operates at the point of lowest LRAC. Each firm, therefore, supplies the market with the quantity of output that it can produce at the lowest possible LRAC.

Figure 9–12 shows the impact of an unexpected increase in market demand. When the price increases from P_0 to P_1 the firm increases output from q_0 to q_1 and industry output increases from Q_0 to Q_1. The increase in demand generates a higher price and positive profits for existing firms. The existence of economic profits will attract new firms into the industry and the short-run supply curve shifts from SRS_0 to SRS_1, lowering price until economic profits are zero. This shift results in a new equilibrium point C in Figure 9–12. Because the industry is one of constant costs, industry expansion does not alter firm's cost curves, and the industry long-run supply curve is horizontal. That is, the long-run equilibrium price is at the same level that prevailed before demand increased; the only long-run effect of the increase in demand is an increase in industry output, as Figure 9–12 indicates.

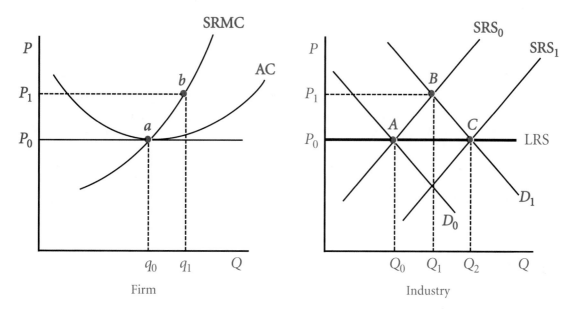

FIGURE 9–12
LONG-RUN SUPPLY—CONSTANT COST INDUSTRY

An unexpected increase in market demand leads to an increase in the market price. The new market price leads to positive profits for existing firms, which attracts new firms into the industry, shifting SRS_0 to SRS_1. This increased the short-run industry supply curve intersects D_1 at point C. Each firm is again producing at q_1 and earning zero economic profit.

INCREASING COST INDUSTRIES

In an increasing cost industry, the cost schedules of the individual firms rise as the total output of the industry increases.

Increasing cost conditions result from **external diseconomies** of large-scale production. Specifically, increases in factor prices (upward shifts in cost curves) occur as larger quantities of factors are employed in the industry. When an industry utilizes a large portion of a factor whose total supply is not perfectly elastic, factor prices will rise when the industry uses more of the factor. External diseconomies of scale should not be confused with diseconomies of scale. The former refers to upward shifts in the cost curves as the industry expands, and the latter refers to an upward movement (moving left to right) along a given LRAC curve caused by internal forces, such as bureaucratic problems associated with firm size.

Increasing cost conditions are typical of the "extractive" industries, such as agriculture, fishing, mining, and lumbering, which utilize large portions of the total supply of specialized natural resources, such as land or mineral deposits. As the output of such an industry expands, the increased demand for the resources raises the prices that must be paid for their use. Because additional resources of given quality cannot be produced, greater supplies can be obtained (if at all) only by taking them away from other industries or by using lower-quality (and thus higher-cost) resources. Wheat production is a typical example of an increasing cost industry. As the output of wheat increases, the demand for land suitable for the production of wheat rises, and so the price paid for the use of land and the sales value of the land increase. Farmers owning their own land prior to the output increase do not experience an increase in their expenditure costs, but their total costs increase just as do those of tenant farmers; the opportunity cost of using the land for their own production instead of renting it to others is now greater than before. (See Problem 9–8.)

If in Figure 9–13, there were an unexpected increase in the demand for wheat, then the market demand curve would shift from D_0 to D_1. Consequently, price would increase from P_0 to P_1 in the short run. The typical firm would have positive short-run profits and expand output from q_0 to q_1. With the presence of short-run economic profits new firms would enter the industry, shifting the market-supply curve to the right. The prices of inputs, such as, farmland, fertilizer, seed, farm machinery, and so on would be bid up by competing farmers, causing the marginal and average cost curves to rise. Consequently, the LRAC would shift up from LRAC_0 to LRAC_1, thus the term *increasing cost industry*. The new long-run equilibrium would be at a higher price P_2 and a greater industry output, Q_3. The long-run supply curve would have a positive slope; that is, the industry must receive a higher price to produce more output because of the higher input costs that would result. (See Problems 9–9 and 9–10.)

9–8 True or False? Increasing cost conditions may also arise from a reduction in efficiency of production as the total output of the industry increases.

True. For example, in an agricultural area irrigated from wells, increased production—and pumping of water—will lower the water table and increase pumping costs for all farmers in the area. Similar problems arise in oil production: an increase in the number of wells in a field will lessen the pressure and increase the difficulty and cost of getting the oil to the surface. As more and more planes use New York area airports, the greater is the delay in landing, with higher costs and accident hazards. These costs are "technological" rather than "pecuniary," as in the earlier discussion. More will be said about the former in later discussions of externalities.

9–9 Graph and explain the long-run equilibrium adjustments from a decrease in market demand for an increasing-cost industry.

The figure below illustrates the effects of a decrease in industry demand from D_0 to D_1 in figure (b). Industry price falls; firms earn negative profits. Some firms leave the industry, and others contract output. This has two effects: (1) the short-run industry supply curve shifts to the left (from SRS_0 to SRS_1), in figure (b) and (2) declining production lowers demand for inputs, and input prices fall, shifting firm cost curves down in figure (a). The new equilibrium price, P_{LR}, is established at the new firm minimum long-run average cost, point c, where profits are zero. The long-run effects of a demand decrease in an increasing-cost industry are price and output reduction in the industry.

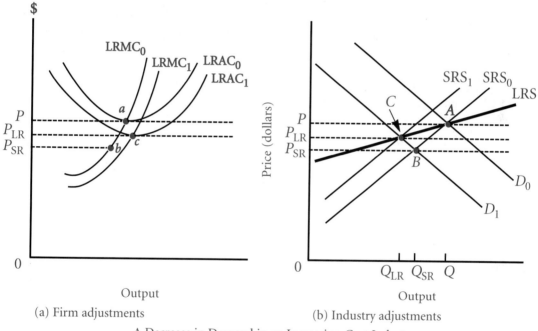

(a) Firm adjustments (b) Industry adjustments

A Decrease in Demand in an Increasing-Cost Industry

9–10 Suppose a tax per unit of output were levied on producers in an increasing-cost industry. How would this affect a firm and the industry in the long run?

In Figure (b) a per-unit output tax raises the firm's LRAC curve to $LRAC_1$ initially. Because $LRAC_1 > P_0$, firms incur losses and some exit the industry while others cut back on production. Short-run supply decreases as firms exit (from SRS_0 to SRS_1 in Figure (a)), and costs decline to $LRAC_2$ because of a decrease in input prices from the reduction in industry output. The new equilibrium price, P_1, equals the minimum of $LRAC_2$. Both short-run supply and long-run supply have decreased to SRS_1 to LRS_1. LRS permanently shifts because the minimum LRAC is now higher for every level of output. Price rises and output declines when an output tax is levied on producers in an increasing cost industry.

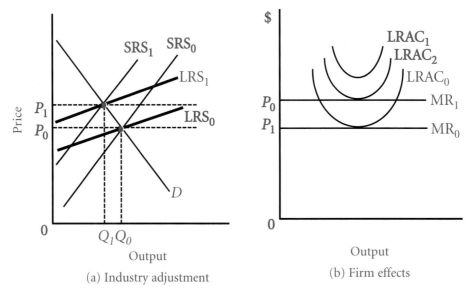

(a) Industry adjustment   (b) Firm effects

A Per-Unit Output Tax Levied on Producers in an Increasing-Cost Industry

DECREASING-COST INDUSTRIES

In a decreasing-cost industry, the cost schedules of the firms fall as total output of the industry increases because of external economies of large scale production, as illustrated in Figure 9–14. External economies should not be confused with economies of scale. Economies of scale occur as the firm moves down a given LRAC. **External economies** occur because the cost curves of the firm have shifted downward as industry output expands.

Consider a new mining region, developed in an area remote from railroad facilities in the days before the motor vehicle. So long as the total output of the mines was small, the ore was hauled by wagon, an extremely expensive form of transport. But when the number of mines increased, and the total output of the region rose substantially, it

became feasible to construct a railroad to serve the area. The railroad lowered transportation costs and reduced the cost schedules of all the firms. No one mine could possibly
have increased its output sufficiently to warrant the building of a railroad; but when the
total output of the industry increased sufficiently, construction of the road became
profitable.

As a practical matter, decreasing-cost industries are rarely encountered, at least
over a large range of output. However, some industries may operate under decreasing-
cost conditions in short intervals of output expansion when continued growth makes
possible the supplying of materials or services at reduced cost.

FIGURE 9–13
LONG-RUN SUPPLY—INCREASING-COST INDUSTRY

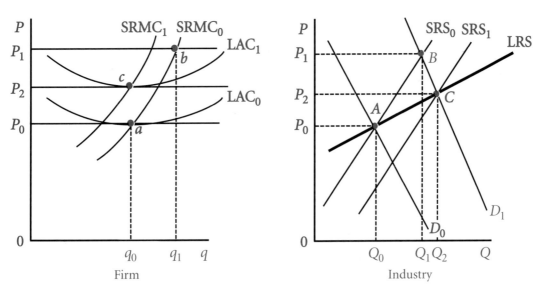

The unexpected increase in demand for wheat shifts D_0 to D_1 and P_0 to P_1. The typical firm will experience
short-run profits at $P_1 q_1$ with the existence of economic profits, firms enter the industry shifting SRS_0 to SRS_1.
However, as farmers compete, the price of inputs are bid up, sending $SRMC_0$ to $SRMC_1$ and $LRMC_0$ to $LRMC_1$.
The new long-run equilibrium output for the firm will be at $P_2 q_0$. The LRS is positively sloped; this means that
the industry must receive a higher price to produce more output, Q_2 because that increased output causes input
prices to rise.

FIGURE 9–14

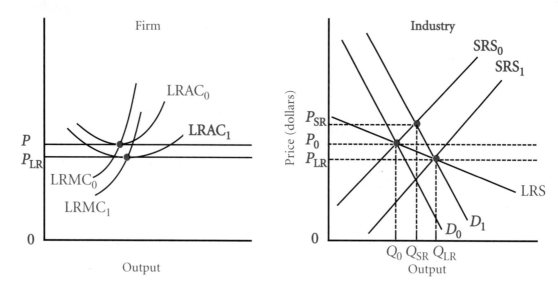

An increase in demand generates a higher price and positive profits for existing firms. New firms enter the industry and, as the industry expands, costs decline. Adjustments continue until profits are zero.

9.8 IMPERFECTIONS IN ADJUSTMENTS IN PERFECTLY COMPETITIVE INDUSTRIES

Our analysis of price and output determination in perfect competition has been based on the assumption that no **imperfections** interfere with adjustments. Because imperfections are likely to be of considerable significance in some instances, reference to some leading examples is in order.

KNOWLEDGE OF FUTURE PRICES AND TIME LAGS IN SUPPLY ADJUSTMENTS

In industries with large numbers of small producers, two imperfections may interfere seriously with market adjustments: lack of knowledge of market conditions, coupled with the substantial time lag that often occurs between change in inputs and actual change in output reaching the market. Farmers, for example, must base output plans on forecasts of future prices at the time crops are planted, and these may largely reflect the current price. They may be unaware, however, of the actions of other firms relative to output. Thus, when crops actually reach the market, the total increase or decrease in output made by producers may prove to be too large or too small to result in the price forecast when the crops were planted. (See Problem 9–11.)

9–11 An extreme example of time lapse in the production process is in the growing of certain types of fruit. Apple and walnut trees, for example, do not reach full bearing until 10 to 20 years after planting. In an industry of this type, when the market price exceeds the long-run equilibrium figure, is there a tendency for too many trees to be planted?

When the crops of all new producers reach the market, the supply may be so great that market price will fall below average cost. As a result, some of the firms will be forced to retire from business. A good example of this reaction is provided by the apple industry in the Pacific Northwest during the 1920s and 1930s. During the early 1920s, apple prices exceeded average cost and many new orchards were developed. By the end of the 1920s, the increased supply from the new orchards began to reach the market and prices fell below average cost. The problem was greatly aggravated by the general business depression, which reduced demand at the same time that the increased supply reached the market.

COBWEB MODELS

A similar reaction, but one of a recurrent nature, may occur with crops that require only one season to reach maturity. If price exceeds average cost at harvest time in any year, the next year's crop may be so large (based on *overoptimistic* price expectations) that when it comes to market the price falls below average cost. As a result, in the following year, production may be reduced so much (based on *overpessimistic* price expectations) that price will rise above average cost and so on. This type of behavior is described by a so-called **cobweb model**.

The name originates from the appearance of the graphical presentation of price quantity behavior in a situation of this sort. Figure 9–15(a) illustrates a case in which the amplitude of the excessive production adjustment in alternate years is declining. The D curve is the usual demand curve; it shows the quantities that will be produced at various prices in a particular year or, in other words, the prices at which various quantities placed on the market can be sold. Curve S shows the quantities that will be produced and placed on the market in the second year, on the basis of various prices prevailing during the first year; it is a "lagged" supply curve. If, in the first year, the actual market price (determined by that year's current supply-demand relationships) is P_0, the quantity that will be supplied the next year is Q_1, as indicated by the curve S. In that year, because of the increased supply, the price will fall to P_2. Supply the following year will then be Q_2, and price will rise to P_3, only to fall to P_4 the next year, and so on. Eventually, final equilibrium will tend to be reached at price P_0 and quantity Q_0 because each year the amplitude of the fluctuations is reduced. Figure 9–14(b) illustrates a case in which the demand and "lagged" supply curves have the same slopes (but of opposite sign). In this case, the fluctuations continue indefinitely at the same amplitude. Figure

9–15(c) shows a case in which the fluctuations grow in amplitude, because the slope of the demand curve is greater in absolute value than that of the lagged supply curve. There is no evidence that this case is found in practice.

For the purpose of illustrating the cobweb model, suppose that during the current year potato prices exceed average cost. As a result, next year many farmers will shift acreage from other crops to potatoes. When next year's crop is harvested, market supply will be considerably greater than it is this year. The increase may be so great that market price will fall below average cost. As a result, the following year potato acreage will be reduced substantially as farmers shift back to other crops. The reduction may be so great that prices will again rise above average cost and lead to another excessive increase in supply. (See Problems 9–12 and 9–13.)

FIGURE 9–15
COBWEB MODELS

Part (a) exhibits a lagged supply function S and a demand function D. At price P_1, quantity supplies in the next period expands to Q_1. Consumers, however, are only willing to pay P_2 for Q_1. Producers reduce quantity supplied in the next period, only to find that buyers will pay P_3 for Q_2. This process eventually equilibrates at P_0 and Q_0. In part (b), demand and supply have the same slope, and oscillations continue indefinitely. The amplitude of the fluctuations grows when demand is steeper than supply in part (c).

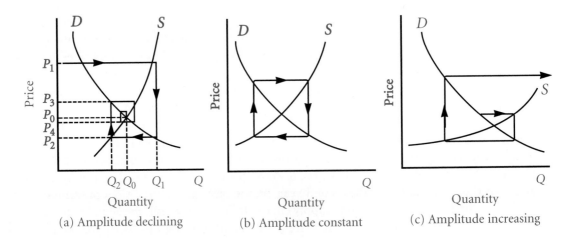

(a) Amplitude declining   (b) Amplitude constant   (c) Amplitude increasing

9–12 Why are there no good examples of cobwebs in which fluctuations grow in amplitude.

There are several reasons. First, farmers would be expected to learn from past experience—the basic assumption of a supply curve based strictly on last year's price is at odds with profit maximization in a world in which farmers possess "rational expectations." Some "crafty" farmers would perceive the price pattern and would plant more in years following low prices, in anticipation that most farmers would plant less. This behavior to be expected in the real world would greatly smooth price fluctuations.

Also, for many crops (such as apples and potatoes) there are multiple uses of varying "durability." Apples can be dried, canned, or frozen during low fresh-apple price periods and placed on the market when fresh-apple prices are high, effectively eliminating a large portion of the demand for fresh apples. Frozen french fries, powdered "mashed" potatoes, and the like perform a similar price-smoothing function in the fresh-potato market. Such effects, taken together, greatly reduce the price fluctuations one would otherwise expect to observe in the real world.

9–13 Assume that the annual industry supply curve for corn is given by $Q_s = .4P - 100$, and the annual demand curve for corn is $Q_d = 300 - .4P$. This year the price is $300. What will be the excess supply (demand) this year? What will happen to the demand price at the quantity supplied? How much will producers supply next year at this year's demand price? Trace the adjustment process using a cobweb model. What will happen if some farmers opportunistically behave counter to the other farmers (that is, produce more for next harvest when current demand price falls)?

When $P = \$300$, $Q_s = 20$ and $Q_0 = 180$, so excess demand $= 160$. This is represented in the Figure below by the segment *ad*. If Q is only 20, the demand price is 700 (point *b*). Producers, expecting the high price to continue, produce 180 in the next period [(.4 · 700) - 100] at point *c*. When $Q = 180$, however, buyers are only willing to pay 300 at point *d*. Disequilibrium, therefore, continues indefinitely when the slopes of the demand-and-supply curves are equal in absolute-value terms. Nevertheless, if some farmers come to understand how the market is behaving at point *d*, they will anticipate the price increases following low price and supply slightly more in the period following low prices. The market will adjust along to the dotted line *defghi* and eventually come to equilibrium at *i*.

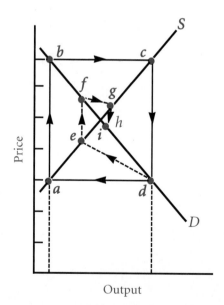

A Cobweb Model with Rational Expectations

Knowledge of Cost

Another source of imperfection is lack of knowledge by sellers of their costs. The typical production unit in perfect competition is small; the average farmer, for example, has very incomplete records and inadequate knowledge of his costs (for example, as caused by unpredictable weather patterns). As a result, output is frequently not completely adjusted to the level that will maximize profits, and short-run supply is different from what it would be if farmers knew their marginal cost more accurately.

Immobility of Producers

Another source of imperfection can be the unwillingness of small producers, particularly farmers, to abandon their jobs and turn to other types of activity when they are unable to cover costs. They frequently are not skilled in other lines of work and job opportunities elsewhere may not be plentiful; and their personal attachment to farming or optimistic expectations that future conditions will improve may prevent them from leaving even though prices have fallen dramatically. Farmers and other producers may typically shift quickly from one crop or product to another in response to relative price and profit situations, but they can be very slow to leave farming or other production entirely. As a consequence, when prices of large numbers of farm or other products fall below current average cost, readjustment to long-run equilibrium may be very slow.

Governmental Intervention

Federal agricultural-support programs have introduced another type of imperfection. The federal government has sought to prevent prices of various farm product from falling below certain levels by purchasing the commodities and by other programs designed to reduce supply.[5] Other examples of government intervention include guaranteed loans, and preferential treatment to small businesses and general regulatory activity. (See Problems 9–14, 9–15, and 9–16.)

---

[5]Recall that supply reductions will raise revenue in cases such as farming, where demand is inelastic. The combination of higher revenues and lower costs clearly makes farmers as a group better off if supply is restricted. Any individual farmer, however, will still wish to supply where marginal cost equals the (higher) price. Such programs obviously interfere with supply adjustments and serve to raise consumer food costs, while actually not greatly helping poor farmers who sell less of their output in the market. Such policies also perpetuate maladjustments in allocation of farmland to various crops. When production becomes excessive in certain lines, consequent price declines should bring about a reduction in production. But if the government artificially holds prices up, the supply adjustment fails to occur.

Competitive Price Determination   285

9–14 Since the Great Depression, there have been several agricultural programs devised to assist the farmers. How would you graph a price-support program using supply and demand? Who gains and who loses under price-support programs?

With the price-support system, the farmer is guaranteed a certain price for products, let's say $4 a bushel. The reasoning is that the equilibrium price of $3 is "too low" and would not provide enough revenue for the farmer to maintain a "decent" standard of living. This situation is depicted below.

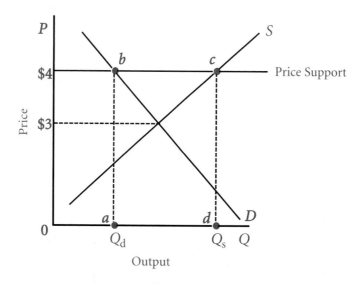

With the support price at $4, consumers would like to purchase $0Q_d$ and farmers would like to sell $0Q_s$. There is a surplus of *abcd* which the government must absorb. In sum, the consumer pays a higher price and higher taxes (that is, the government has to pay for the buying and storing of the extra wheat), and the wheat producer benefits by selling at a higher-than-equilibrium price. This is especially beneficial to farmers and owners of larger plots of agricultural land, because this translates into an even greater subsidy.

9–15 Technological change in agriculture has increased productivity (average product and marginal product). In the absence of government intervention, how would technological change affect the industry in the short run? In the presence of price supports, what would be the effect of productivity improvements?

Increases in MP and AP reduce SRMC and AVC. Firms' cost curves shift down, $P_0 >$ SRAC, and firms enter the industry. The short-run supply curve shifts to the right from SRS_0 to SRS_0 in the figure below. With no price supports, equilibrium moves from point A to point B, price falls from P_0 to P_1, and quantity rises from Q_0 to Q_1. If price supports are in effect and the farmer is guaranteed the price P_S, quantity demanded will be Q_d, quantity supplied will be Q_s, and the surplus will be CD, before the technological change. After the productivity improvements, quantity supplied rises to $Q's$ and the surplus expands to CE.

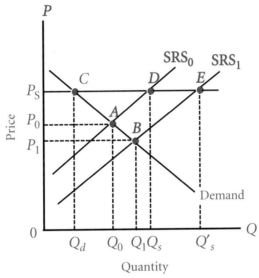

Technology Change and Price Supports

9–16 What are the implications for efficiency and equity of rent controls? *Hint*: Think about such controls both in the context of the market period when housing supply is fixed and the long run.

Rent controls have had a long history and are politically appealing. Their appeal stems from the pronounced difference between the short-run equity effects (which are viewed as positive by political entrepreneurs) and the long-run efficiency effects (which, while clearly undesirable, occur in a future period of little relevance to the next election). The lower, controlled rent price has only a modest impact on the market period supply; it therefore transfers wealth from owners (few in number) to renters (many in number). Because housing is viewed as an important good, and because it represents a major share of the budget, voting support for rent controls is often substantial. In the long run, of course, there will be less of this important good in existence and the quality of the housing stock at any point in time will deteriorate steadily, if slowly.

Figure (a) shows the impact of rent control in the long run, assuming that rental units are an increasing cost industry. If the price ceiling is set below the market price, the quantity demanded will increase to $0Q_2$ from $0Q^*$ and the quantity supplied will fall to $0Q_1$ from $0Q^*$. The rent-control policy will therefore create a shortage, the difference between Q_1 and Q_2.

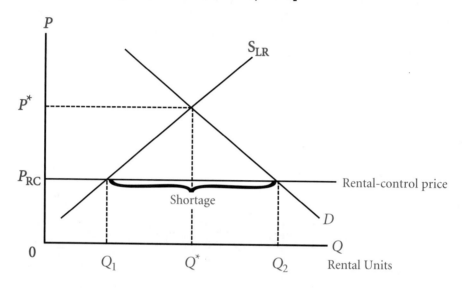

SUMMARY

1. Perfect competition is a market structure with the following conditions: there are numerous buyers and sellers of a homogenous products, buyers and sellers have perfect mobility and information, and individual buyers and sellers believe that they cannot influence price by varying their purchases or sales.

2. There are three stages in the competitive price-determination model: the market period, the short-run period, and the long-run period. The market period is so short that total stocks of the commodity available for sale are fixed. The short-run period is long enough for existing stocks to be altered, but short enough so that some production and consumption features are prohibitively expensive to vary and are thus treated as fixed.

3. The sum of individual-supply schedules is equal to the total or market-supply schedules (unless industry expansion changes the prices of some factors of production). At higher relative prices additional amounts will be placed on the market.

4. The firm will not produce at all in the short run unless the price obtainable at least covers average variable cost (AVC).

5. At price levels equal to or in excess of average variable costs, a firm will produce in the short-run period even if average total costs are not completely covered.

6. The perfectly competitive firm will adjust its output to a level where marginal cost with the existing plant is equal to marginal revenue.

7. Marginal revenue and the seller's demand curve are identical in perfect competition, and both are equal to price.

8. The competitive firm's short-run supply curve is the upward sloping portion of the marginal-cost curve on or above the intersection of the average-variable and marginal-cost curves.

9. The determinants of the market short-run supply schedule are the cost functions of existing firms, the number of firms presently in existence, and the size of the industry relative to the size of markets in which factor inputs are purchased.

10. Over the long-run period, price must cover all costs and therefore must be at least equal to average total costs. The plant will be adjusted to a size that allows equality of LRMC and MR, and the perfectly competitive firm will produce at the point at which SRMC with this plant is equal to price.

11. Because there is a single market price for the commodity, LRAC must be equal to this price for all perfectly competitive firms.

12. The nature of the long-run industry supply depends on the cost conditions in which the industry operates: constant cost, increasing cost, or decreasing cost.

13. Imperfections are likely to interfere with adjustments in many instances. Some examples are imperfect knowledge with regard to future prices, time lags in supply adjustments, lack of knowledge by sellers of their costs, factor immobility, the inability to predict future government regulation, varying climatic conditions, and so on.

WORDS AND CONCEPTS FOR REVIEW

perfect competition	market period
short-run period	long-run period
marginal revenue	market-period supply
profit-maximizing level of output	short-run supply function
determinants of short-run supply	long-run output equilibrium
external diseconomies	external economies
imperfections	cobweb models

REVIEW QUESTIONS

1. What is meant by the term *perfect competition*? Is it possible for a situation that does not conform to the assumptions of perfect competition to still be described by the perfectly competitive price theory? Discuss.

2. Does the analysis of pricing in perfectly competitive markets assume that sellers have perfect knowledge of total demand-and-supply conditions? Explain.

3. Explain the concept of a "market period." For what types of products is the concept of the market period, as distinguished from the short-run period, significant?

4. What is meant by short-run supply?

5. a) Why must price cover AVC if firms are to continue to operate?
    b) If firms are covering AVC but not all of their fixed costs, will they continue to operate in the short-run period? Why or why not?
    c) Why is it possible for price to remain above average cost in the short-run period?
    d) Why would one expect price to equal marginal cost in the short-run period?

6. Explain the relationship between marginal cost and the firm and industry short-period supply functions.

7. If market price is above the short-run equilibrium level, by what process will it be brought to the latter? What determines the length of time that this adjustment will take?

8. On the basis of the data given below, can you determine the supply schedule of the firm in the short-run period? If not, why not?

Output	Total Variable Cost	Output	Total Variable Cost
1	$ 22	6	85
2	32	7	115
3	40	8	155
4	50	9	205
5	65	10	310

9. Why does the short-run supply curve slope upward from left to right?

10. If long-run adjustments are complete, why will firms in perfectly competitive markets necessarily operate at the point of lowest average cost?

11. Why in an increasing-cost industry is the long-run industry supply curve identical to the long-run industry cost curve?

12. Draw the long-run supply curve for the industry on the basis of the cost data given below:

Total Output of Industry	Lowest Average Cost Figure for Each Firm
500,000	$ 47
1,000,000	52
1,500,000	55
2,000,000	58
2,500,000	63
3,000,000	66

13. What determines actual long-run output in a constant-cost industry, as distinguished from potential output?

14. Under what circumstances in perfect competition is long-run price dependent upon demand considerations alone? Upon cost considerations alone? Illustrate graphically. Which case is most generally relevant?

15. Explain the cobweb model. If you were a farmer producing a product whose price is subject to cobweb-model fluctuations, what could you do to increase your profits from a long-run standpoint, provided other farmers do not do the same thing?

16. Why do many farm product prices fluctuate greatly from year to year?

SUGGESTED READINGS

Adams, Walter. *The Structure of American Industry*, 7th ed. New York: Macmillan, 1986.

Friedman, Milton. *Price Theory*. Chicago: Aldine, 1976.

Marshall, Alfred. *Principles of Economics*, Book V, 8th ed. London: MacMillan, 1927.

Scherer, F.M., and David Ross. *Industrial Market Structure and Economic Performance*, 3rd ed. Boston: Houghton Mifflin, 1990

Stigler, George. "Perfect Competition, Historically Contemplated." In Edwin Mansfield (ed.), *Microeconomics: Selected Readings*, 3rd ed. New York: Norton, 1979.

Part 3

IMPERFECTLY COMPETITIVE MARKETS

CHAPTERS

10. MONOPOLY

11. MONOPOLISTIC COMPETITION

12. OLIGOPOLY

Part 3, Chapter 10, 11, and 12, present the theory of markets that are imperfectly competitive. As in competitive price determination, we merge the theory of consumer behavior with the theory of production and costs to determine price and output in imperfectly competitive markets. "Monopoly" is presented in Chapter 10, "Monopolistic Competition" in Chapter 11, and "Oligopoly" in Chapter 12.

Chapter Ten

MONOPOLY

_____ *Questions to Think About?* _____

1. What is a monopoly?

2. What is the position of the marginal-revenue curve relative to the demand curve for a monopolist?

3. How is the market-period price determined in monopoly?

4. What is a monopolist's profit-maximizing criterion?

5. How are short-run price and equilibrium determined in a monopoly?

6. What is the difference between monopoly and perfect competition with regard to long-run price and equilibrium conditions?

7. What are the different forms of price discrimination?

8. What is peak-load pricing?

9. What are the alternative pricing policies for regulated monopolists?

10. How will a per-unit tax, a lump-sum tax, and a profit tax affect a monopolist?

10.1 INTRODUCTION

As Chapter 9 noted, the essential condition for perfect competition is that sellers believe that prices are determined by forces outside their control. In contrast, the distinctive characteristic of imperfectly competitive markets is that individual sellers consider themselves able to exert a noticeable influence on market price by varying the quantity they offer for sale, by advertising or other sales promotion activities, by lobbying for favorable legislation, by buying out or otherwise eliminating competing sellers, and so on. A second distinction between perfect and imperfect competition is based on the demand curve. The demand curve of perfectly competitive firms consists of the market prices they face; their only decision is how much to produce. The demand curve of imperfectly competitive firms, however, involves both price and sales as variables, and is influenced by a number of considerations. Accordingly, a central problem in the general theory of imperfect competition is to explain the demand and marginal-revenue curves of individual firms—that is, the relationships, as seen by the sellers, between the amounts of goods that sellers place on the market, the prices at which they can sell these amounts, and the revenues that they would earn as a result.

Identifying empirically relevant and theoretically consistent demand and marginal-revenue curves is particularly difficult in oligopolistic markets. This is because sellers are so few that each seller's revenue prospects necessarily depend directly on the actions, whether anticipated or not, of all other sellers. Such mutual interdependence cannot be entirely ignored even in monopoly and monopolistic competition, but it is not important enough in those situations to require explicit theoretical attention. For this as well as other reasons, therefore, it is convenient to deal separately with different types of imperfectly competitive markets. This chapter analyzes monopoly—markets in which buyers are numerous but total output of the good offered for sale is controlled by a single firm. Monopolistic competition and oligopoly are discussed in later chapters.

DEMAND, MARGINAL REVENUE, AND TOTAL REVENUE

In monopoly, the market-demand curve may be regarded as the demand curve for the firm's product because the monopolist is the only seller of that particular product. The demand curve indicates the quantities the firm can sell at various possible prices. As Chapter 9 noted, marginal revenue is the addition to total revenue resulting from the sale of an additional unit of output. Figure 10–1 shows a hypothetical demand curve for a firm's product and the related marginal-revenue curve.

The demand curve for the firm's product declines as additional units are placed on the market.[1] As a result, marginal revenue is less than price for all units except the first. Therefore, Figure 10–1 shows the MR curve lying below the demand curve and declining at a more rapid rate. Each additional unit sold adds less to total revenue than the price received for it because the firm has to lower the price on all the units the firm would have been able to sell at a higher price, in order to sell additional units. In the example, to sell 8 units instead of 7, the firm must lower the price on those seven units from $10 to $9, while the eighth unit sells for $9; it therefore adds only $2 (the difference between $70 and $72) to the firm's total revenue, and so, marginal revenue ($2) is below price ($9). This is true for any negatively sloped demand curve. Marginal revenue must be below price.[2]

---

[1]For imperfectly competitive market structures, price depends on quantity sold (recall the downward-sloping demand curves of earlier chapters):

$$P = f(q) \quad \text{where} \quad \frac{df(q)}{dq} < 0$$

Hence $TR = P \cdot q = f(q) \cdot q$, and marginal revenue approaches (using the product rule for derivatives):

$$MR = \frac{dTR}{dq} = f(q) + f'(q)q$$

$$= P + \frac{dP}{dq}\, q$$

This can be rewritten as

$$MR = P\left(1 + \frac{dP}{dQ}\, \frac{q}{P}\right)$$

$$= P\left(1 + \frac{1}{\frac{dq}{dP}\, \frac{P}{q}}\right)$$

$$= P\left(1 + \frac{1}{n}\right) \quad \text{where } n \text{ is the price elasticity of demand (negative).}$$

Note that as the price elasticity approaches infinity, MR approaches P; otherwise it is less than P when demand is downward sloping.

[2] For linear-demand curves, it is easy to establish that marginal revenue falls at exactly *twice* the rate at which demand falls, both beginning at the same point. Let $P = a - bQ$ represent the demand relationship. Then $TR = P \cdot Q$ or $(a - bQ)Q = aQ - bQ^2$. But the marginal revenue, MR, is just the derivative of total revenue with respect to quantity:

$$MR = \frac{dTR}{dQ} = a - 2bQ$$

Therefore, both starting at a, the marginal-revenue curve has twice the slope of the D curve. This is, of course, consistent with other related characteristics of linear-demand functions. For example, the midpoint is the point of unitary price elasticity; that is, for small changes in price, $P \cdot Q$ (or TR) does not change. But that means that TR is either maximized or minimized at the point; and, indeed, MR > 0 for the quantities smaller than this and MR < 0 for larger quantities, so TR is *maximized* at the midpoint.

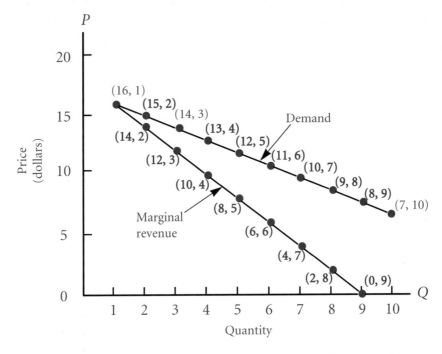

FIGURE 10–1
DEMAND AND MARGINAL REVENUE FOR A MONOPOLIST

The industry-demand curve shows the price at which each unit of output can be sold. Price exceeds marginal revenue because selling additional units of output requires lowering the price on preceding units.

The relationship between the elasticity of demand and marginal revenue are shown in Figure 10–2, in which elasticity varies along a linear-demand curve. Above the midpoint the curve is elastic (e > 1); below the midpoint it is inelastic (e < 1); and at the midpoint of the curve it is unit elastic (e = 1). How does elasticity relate to total revenue? In the elastic portion of the curve, when the price falls, total revenue rises (marginal revenue is greater than zero). In the inelastic region of the demand curve, when the price falls, total revenue falls (marginal revenue is less than zero). Thus, at the midpoint of the linear-demand curve, where MR = 0, the total revenue function reaches its highest point. (See Problem 10–1.)

Along a linear-demand curve, the elastic segment lies above the midpoint, the inelastic segment lies below the midpoint, and the point of unitary elasticity is the midpoint. A high price elasticity of demand indicates that small price reductions will increase quantity considerably. Total revenue rises as a result, and marginal revenue is positive. At unit elasticity, total revenue is at a maximum. Price and quantity change by the same percentages so that total revenue does not change with output and marginal revenue is constant. A modest output response to a price decrease occurs when demand is inelastic. Total revenue declines as a result, and marginal revenue is negative.

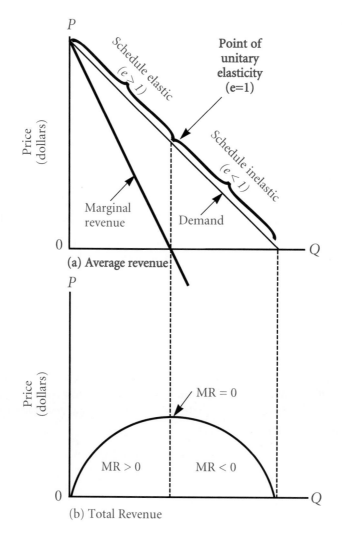

10–1   Would a monopolist ever operate on the inelastic portion of the demand curve?

No.   On an inelastic region of a demand curve, total revenue is declining as price is lowered to increase sales, so that marginal revenue is negative.   Profit maximization requires that LRMC = MR.   Because MR < 0 when demand is inelastic, a monopolist would produce in that region only if LRMC < 0.   Negative LRMC implies that factor owners pay the firm to use the factors!   Thus, the monopolist always operates on the elastic portion of the demand curve, barring free or negatively priced inputs.

10.2 PRICE AND OUTPUT DETERMINATION: UNREGULATED MONOPOLY

A *monopoly* is defined, for purposes of economic analysis, as a single firm that supplies the entire quantity of a good offered to buyers in a particular market. Monopolies are virtually nonexistent in basic manufacturing industries, although they did exist around the turn of the century in steel, tobacco, aluminum, and other industries. They occur most commonly now in regulated public utilities and in particular geographic areas where transportation costs or similar factors allow a local seller (for example, a lumber-supply firm, a lawyer, or a fabric store) to act as a monopolist within a certain range of prices. (See Problem 10–2)

10–2   True or False?   Because every commodity has a number of more or less close substitutes, monopoly implies complete absence of competition from other commodities.

False.   Monopoly does imply an absence of competing sellers in the particular market, and a relatively low cross-elasticity of demand between the product and other products.   The lack of seller competition leads us to emphasize aspects of market behavior different from those emphasized in our analysis of perfect competition (and monopolistic competition considered later) and also to extend the analysis to include certain kinds of activities (such as advertising and price discrimination) that are absent in perfectly competitive markets.   Our treatment of monopoly is nevertheless similar in broad outline to our treatment of perfect competition.   Major similarities and differences between the two kinds of markets will be emphasized.

MONOPOLY PRICE DETERMINATION IN THE MARKET PERIOD

The market period for monopoly, just as for perfect competition, is an interval of time so short that adjustments in output are impractical. Here, however, we assume a given output rate, not a given stock of goods on hand, as in the market period of the perfectly competitive model. If, as is usually assumed, the monopolist deals directly with its customers and so sets its own asking price, the price that it sets is the market price, and demand conditions are important only insofar as they affect the monopolist's view of revenue prospects.

If quantity demanded at the current price is greater than the firm's current output, the monopolist may either meet demand by selling from previously accumulated stock or choke off excess demand by increasing the asking (and the market) price. The alternative the monopolist adopts depends on its estimation of the relative advantages of each policy. If, for example, the monopolist believes that demand is currently running at an abnormally high level, it may maintain the prevailing price in order to retain customer goodwill and avoid possible expenses from revising price. If, however, the monopolist believes the current level of demand is permanent, it will probably raise the asking price. The exact amount would depend on its estimate of demand elasticity, the danger of attracting attention from antitrust authorities, the possibility that high prices may encourage buyers to gravitate toward substitute commodities offered for sale in other markets, and so on.

Similar considerations apply when quantity demanded at the prevailing price falls short of current output. The monopolist either may hold price at its current level and watch inventories mount or may cut price in an attempt to reduce storage and other current costs.

In a short-run period (a period sufficiently long to permit output to be adjusted with existing plant), the monopolist's problem is therefore to choose a profit-maximizing level of output such that MR = MC.[3] The monopolist's formal decision problem is the same as that of a competitive seller. There is a practical difference, however: Whereas for a competitive seller, knowing the current market price is equivalent to knowing marginal revenue (because MR = P) for each unit that could be sold, a monopoly seller may find it difficult to estimate marginal revenue accurately.

The only objective basis on which a monopolist can estimate its revenue prospects is by referring to past information about actual sales at various prices. If demand conditions are completely stable over time, a little experimentation with different asking prices would provide the firm with an accurate estimate of the position of the market-demand curve and its elasticity in the neighborhood of previously observed price/sales points. However, if demand conditions fluctuate constantly (for example, because of changes in other prices or consumer preferences), the monopolist can form only a rough statistical estimate of the probable position and form of short-run demand and marginal revenue functions.

How, then, does a monopolist determine the short-run equilibrium output and price? Assuming that the monopolist arrives at an estimate of the relevant short-run demand curve, it determines the equilibrium level of output and price using the relations shown diagrammatically in Figure 10–3. The monopolist's demand curve is represented by the line D; the marginal-revenue curve corresponding to the given demand

---

[3]The proof that setting marginal cost equal to marginal revenue maximizes profit is straight forward. By definition, profit equals total revenue minus total cost:

$$\pi(Q) = TR(Q) - TC(Q)$$

At maximum (or minimum) $d\pi(Q) = TR(Q) = 0$ or

$$0 = \frac{dTR(Q)}{dQ} - \frac{dTC(Q)}{dQ}$$

But this is exactly the assertion to be proved, that MR (Q*) equals MC (Q*) at a maximum (or minimum). To guarantee that a maximum, rather than a minimum, is found, the second derivative of (Q) must be negative at Q*, (that is, profits must be falling for output levels a bit above or below Q*). Imposing this condition yields

$$0 = \frac{d^2TR(Q)}{dQ^2} - \frac{d^2TC(Q)}{dQ^2} < 0$$

This, however, merely says that for a maximum, the slope of the marginal revenue function at Q* is less than the slope of marginal cost. Because the slope of marginal revenue is normally negative (or zero in perfect competition), being on the upward-sloping portion of the marginal-cost curve is sufficient to meet this condition.

curve is represented by the line MR. The factors governing short-run costs of production in monopoly are assumed to be similar to those of an individual seller operating under conditions of perfect competition; we may therefore regard the short-run variable-cost function a given, and from it derive the average variable-cost curve (AVC) and the corresponding short-run marginal-cost curve (SRMC). Finally, we obtain the short-run average-cost curve (SRAC) by adding average fixed cost to average variable cost at each possible level of output.

Given the relations shown in Figure 10–3, the firm's short-run equilibrium level of output, Q_0, is defined by the intersection of the MR curve and the MC curve—that is, by the requirement that output be such that MR equals MC, provided AVC is covered by the resulting price. The short-run equilibrium price is given by the D curve as that price P_0 at which buyers are willing to purchase that quantity of output Q_0—that is, the price at which short-run output is just equal to short-run quantity demanded.

Another approach to finding the equilibrium monopoly output uses the short-run total-cost and total-revenue curves, as depicted in Figure 10–4. The output level Q_0 is identical to the output level determined using the marginal approach in Figure 10–3. However, using the total cost and revenue approach, maximum profit is determined at the output level where the vertical distance between the SRTC and the TR curve is greatest, Q_0. At this level of output, the slope of the total-cost curve (marginal cost) is equal to the slope of the total-revenue curve (marginal revenue).

One similarity between monopoly and the perfectly competitive model should be noted. As in perfect competition, the equilibrium value of output in monopoly is defined by the requirement that MR equal MC. However, because the demand curve of the monopolist is downward sloping rather than horizontal, marginal revenue is less than price at the equilibrium level. In contrast, marginal revenue is equal to price in perfect competition.

One difference between perfect competition and monopoly is that the short-run equilibrium output of a monopolist, unlike that of a competitive seller, is a determinant rather than a function of market price. The theory of monopoly output determination does not, therefore, lead directly to a definition of the short-run supply function, as does the theory of competitive output determination.[4]

---

[4]On closer inspection, however, it is clear that this supposed difference between perfect competition and monopoly is more apparent than real. *Under perfect competition, there is just one equilibrium value of output corresponding to any given demand function; the same is true in the theory of monopoly.* The supply curve of a competitive seller is generated by varying the position of the demand function; it indicates, for each set of values of the parameters defining the demand function of an individual seller, the corresponding equilibrium level of output. A similar relation could be established between the equilibrium output of a monopolist and various levels of the parameters that define the monopolist's demand function. But such a function is not particularly useful for purposes of analysis (because supply will depend on both cost *and* demand parameters) and thus is not typically established.

FIGURE 10—3
SHORT-RUN ADJUSTMENT OF PRICE AND OUTPUT

Like the perfectly competitive firm, the monopolist's output level coincides with the equality of marginal revenue and marginal cost, providing that the price at which that quantity can be sold is at least as great as average variable cost. The equilibrium price charged the consumers is P_0. Because price is greater than average cost in this case, this monopolist receives positive profits.

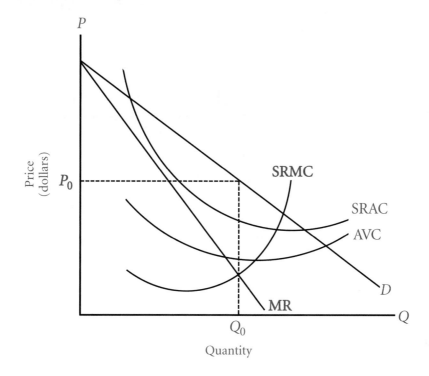

FIGURE 10–4
TOTAL REVENUE AND TOTAL COSTS: THE SHORT RUN

Total revenue less total costs (implicit and explicit) equals profit. Geometrically, the vertical distance between the total revenue and short-run total-cost curves designates profit. Profit is maximized when the slopes of the two curves—that is, marginal revenue and short-run marginal cost—are equal.

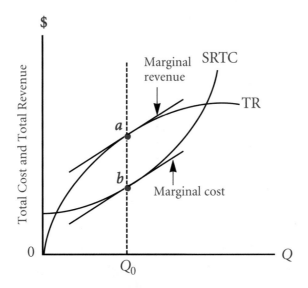

An important difference between monopoly and perfect competition concerns the welfare implications of the fact that under monopoly conditions, price exceeds marginal cost. Provided that the monopolist's demand curve accurately reflects actual market-demand conditions, a monopoly seller's failure to equate marginal cost with price implies that, compared with perfect competition, equilibrium output is restricted and price is higher. Figure 10–5 illustrates this difference.

FIGURE 10–5
PERFECT COMPETITION VERSUS MONOPOLY

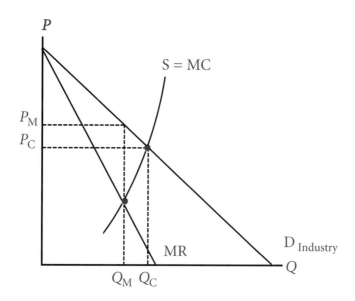

Compared with perfect competition, the monopolist's equilibrium price is higher, P_M, and its equilibrium output is lower, Q_M.

LONG-RUN ADJUSTMENTS

As long as a firm remains a complete monopoly, long-run price and output adjustments involve nothing more than adjustments to bring about equality of LRMC and MR; that is, the firm adjusts plant to a level such that MR = SRMC = LRMC at the long-run equilibrium level of output.

To earn maximum profits at a given time, the firm has to operate at the level at which MC with the existing plant equals MR. Over a longer period of time, however, the firm may be able to increase profits by adjusting plant size. When this adjustment is complete, MR will equal both SRMC and LRMC. If MR does not equal SRMC, the firm has failed to operate at the most profitable output level with existing plant. If MR does not equal LRMC, the firm has failed to complete all profitable plant adjustments.

Figure 10–6 indicates the long-run adjustment. Initially, with plant size $SRAC_0$, the firm produces Q_S units (for equality of MR and $SRMC_0$ with plant $SRAC_0$) and sets a price of P_S. But MR does not equal LRMC at the point of most profitable operation because the plant is too small relative to the demand for the product. Accordingly, the firm increases its plant size to that associated with $SRAC_1$. With this plant, MR = $SRMC_1$ = LRMC at the point of most profitable operation, Q_L, with corresponding price P_L.

Because the firm is a monopoly, no new firms can enter the industry, and, therefore, no other long-run adjustments can take place. Figure 10–6 shows the monopolist earning economic profits per unit of output equal to the difference between P_L and C_L. Economic profits are not inevitable, however, because a monopolist may or may not have sufficient sales potential to earn more than a normal return on invested capital. If a monopolist's potential sales volume is so limited that it does not earn even a normal return, then the owners will eventually liquidate the business. A monopoly position in itself is no guarantee of economic profits. If demand is inadequate, then a lack of competitors is of little benefit to a seller. (See Problems 10–3 and 10–4.)

FIGURE 10–6
LONG-RUN ADJUSTMENT OF A MONOPOLIST

The monopolist chooses the scale of plant for which MR = LRMC, the scale represented by SRAC$_1$ in this example. In the long run, the monopolist produces Q_L and sells this quantity at price P_L.

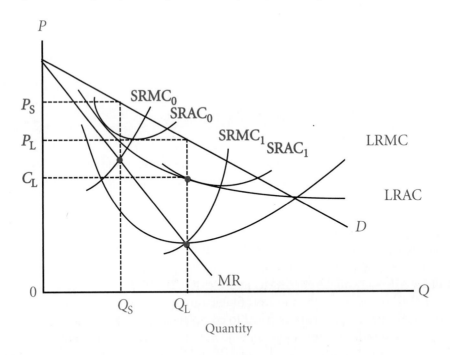

10–3   Would a monopolist stay in business if economic profits were zero? Draw the
        long-run cost curves for a monopolist operating with zero economic profits. Why
        is it possible for a monopolist to earn positive economic profits in the long run?

Yes. Zero economic profits implies that the monopolist is earning as high a return on its investment as
it could in alternative endeavors. The accompanying figure depicts the cost and revenue curves for a
monopolist earning zero economic profits. Positive economic profits may persist in the long run, unlike
in the perfectly competitive case, depending on demand and cost conditions, because new firms cannot
enter the industry.

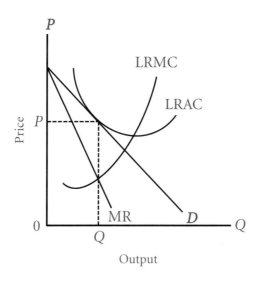

10–4 Given demand, marginal revenue, and marginal-cost curves D_0, MR_0, and LRMC in the accompanying figure, what is the profit-maximizing level of output and the equilibrium price for the monopolist? Determine quantity and price when consumer preferences are described by D_1 and MR_1. Can you derive a supply curve for the monopolist? Explain.

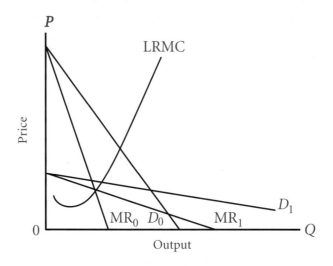

The figure below shows that P_0 and Q are the profit-maximizing output level corresponding to D_0 and MR_0. The equilibrium price for D_1 and MR_1, however, is P_1, although quantity remains at Q. A supply curve shows the relationship between price and quantity supplied. In this example, Q may be offered for sale at P_0 or P_1, depending on demand conditions. Thus, a given Q does not coincide with a unique price, and a supply curve cannot be drawn.

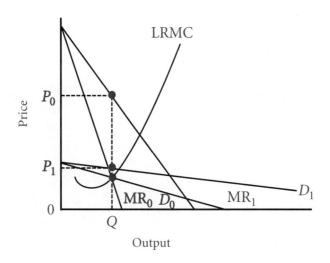

10.3 PRICE DISCRIMINATION

The discussion to this point has been based on the assumption that a firm sells a given product to all buyers at the same price. Under monopoly conditions, however, such a policy is not always necessary and is usually not profit maximizing for the monopolist. Monopolists often find it profitable to discriminate (where possible) among various buyers, charging higher prices to those willing to pay more and/or charging individual buyers on a sliding scale (lower average prices for larger purchases) for units purchased. Such policies are known as *price discrimination*, defined more precisely as the practice of charging various customers different prices that are not based on differences in the costs of producing and handling the goods. Discrimination also includes the practice of charging identical prices to various customers when costs differ.

THE CONDITIONS NECESSARY FOR DISCRIMINATION

Price discrimination occurs only under three conditions. First, discrimination is possible only with monopoly or where members of a group of firms (colluders or oligopolists, to be considered later) follow similar pricing policies. When a large number of competing firms follow independent pricing policies, discrimination is impossible because competitors will undercut prices charged by others in the high-price markets.

Second, discrimination is possible only if resale from one market to another is impractical; otherwise, goods would flow from the low-price market to the high-price market.

Finally, price discrimination can only occur if the demand curves for different markets, groups, or individuals are different. If they are not, then $MR_i = MR_j = MC$ at the same price, and a profit-maximizing monopolist would charge the same price in both markets. (See Problem 10–5.)

10–5 True or False? Price discrimination is advantageous for the firm because some buyers are willing to pay more for a commodity than others, and because some buyers are willing to pay more for initial units than for subsequent units.

True. One buyer may be willing to pay $12,000 for a copying machine, while another buyer will take the same machine only at $10,000; the first buyer may be induced to acquire a second copying machine, but only if it can be bought for $8,000. With a single, uniform price, some buyers are pushed out of the market completely, others buy fewer units than they would at a lower figure, and many of those buying the product at the prevailing price would be willing to pay more for some of the units they are currently buying. Discrimination is designed to gain additional revenue by varying the price according to the demand elasticities of customers.

PERFECT-PRICE DISCRIMINATION: AN EXTREME BUT INFORMATIVE CASE

Perfect-price discrimination (sometimes called first-degree price discrimination) requires that each buyer be induced to pay the maximum possible sum he or she is willing to pay for any given quantity, rather than forgo use of the good entirely; that is, the consumer will be stripped of all consumer surplus.

Suppose, for example, that each week a person buys 1 quart of orange juice if the price is $1.00 a quart, 5 quarts if the price drops to 50 cents, and 10 quarts if the price drops to 25 cents. The objective of perfect-price discrimination (assuming the marginal cost of a quart of orange juice is less than 25 cents) is to get the buyer to pay $1.00 for 1 quart, 50 cents each for the next 4 quarts, and 25 cents each for the last 5, and thus to pay $4.25 instead of $2.50, the price if the buyer could obtain all 10 quarts at 25 cents each. In this manner, the buyer's individual demand schedule effectively becomes the seller's schedule of marginal revenue from the particular buyer. This is because the seller does not have to lower prices on earlier units to sell more. The equilibrium amount to be sold to each buyer is still that at which marginal cost is equal to the sellers marginal revenue from the sale to the particular buyer, but as indicated above, in this case marginal revenue coincides with the buyer's demand curve.

The charge for the entire group of units sold to the customer is the sum of the buyer's demand prices for each successive unit ($4.25 in the example above); the buyer is required to pay this sum and take the entire amount under an all-or-nothing bargain. Because the seller will not sell the buyer a smaller number of units, the buyer has only two alternatives: paying $4.25 for the 10 units or not buying the good at all. Or, in terms of the usual marginal-revenue/marginal-cost diagram, the monopolist extends production and sales up to the point at which the MC curve intersects the demand curve, because the monopolist can sell additional units at successively lower prices without lowering the price on all units sold. The-all-or nothing price charged all but marginal buyers is therefore greater than that indicated by price at which MC equals D (equals MR, in the case of perfect-price discrimination).

Market conditions obviously do not permit perfect discrimination to be carried out to any significant extent. One example on a partial scale may be found in the practice of doctors who vary charges according to their customers' insurance coverage or income status. A breeder of fine horses, dealing individually with relatively uninformed buyers in different parts of the country, may be able to carry on perfect discrimination. Apart from such isolated cases, however, the analysis of perfect discrimination is useful primarily to illustrate a type of price-setting procedure that would be more profitable to the firm if it could be employed.

MULTIPART-PRICE DISCRIMINATION

Multipart-price discrimination (sometimes known as second-degree price discrimination) is much more common than perfect discrimination. This method of discrimination, where discounts are given to buyers who purchase larger quantities, is often used by public utilities and wholesale traders, and even by stores that sell six packs of soda for less than six single cans.

Specifically, this form of discrimination allows the monopolist to sell blocks of its output at different prices, charging the greatest amount for the first block and less for successive blocks. Figure 10–7 depicts how the monopolist might sell the first block of output from 0 to Q_1 at price P_1 and then sell the second block, Q_1 to Q_2, at the lower price of P_2. Ultimately, the monopolist would allow the customer to buy Q_3 at the lowest price it offered (P_3 in Figure 10–7).

The reasoning for multipart pricing is simple. Imagine that the monopolist's single-price maximization point (MR = MC) would result in price P_3. If the monopolist charged this price for all its output, total revenue would be the rectangle $0P_3aQ_3$. In contrast, the multipart-discriminating monopolist would be able to transfer the shaded areas of consumer surplus to total revenue raising its profits. The consumer's loss, in this way, is the monopolist's gain.

FIGURE 10–7
MULTIPART-PRICE DISCRIMINATION

The monopolist charges P_1 for units of output up to Q_1, P_2 for units from Q_1 to Q_2, and P_3 for any additional units. In the absence of multipart-price discrimination, P_3 would be charged for all Q_3 units of output. Thus, this type of discrimination transfers the portion of consumer surplus in the shaded area to the monopolist.

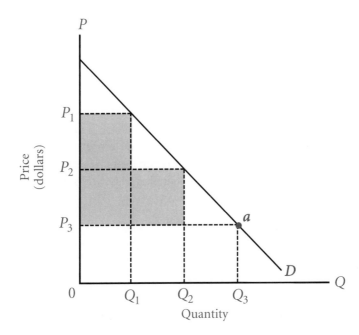

A firm can seldom exploit fully its profit possibilities in dealings with individual buyers. It may, however, be able to segment its total market into several parts on the basis of demand prices and elasticities. It can then charge different prices to different groups of buyers. As Figure 10–8 shows, relatively high prices will be charged in segments where demand is more inelastic (market A) and relatively low prices will be charged in segments where demand is more elastic (market B). Accordingly, the firm can advantageously sell a larger quantity than it can under a uniform-price policy (as fewer sales will be lost by a price increase to a more inelastic demand market segment than will be gained by an equivalent price reduction in a more elastic demand market segment). Such a policy is known as segmented-market price discrimination (sometimes called third-degree price discrimination); here the equilibrium price is obtained from groups of buyers rather than from each individual buyer.

When segmented-market price discrimination is possible, profits are maximized by adjusting total output to the level at which the marginal cost of the entire output equals the horizontal sum of the marginal revenues in the various markets. The marginal revenue in each market segment is then set equal to the marginal cost of the last unit produced. Figure 10–8 illustrates the case for two segmented markets. In market A, the D curve is D-A and the MR curve is MR-A; in market B the two curves are D-B and MR-B, respectively. Curves D-T and MR-T show the horizontal sums of the D and MR schedules in the two markets. If profits are to be maximized, total output is Q_T, as determined by the intersection of the MC curve and MR-T, the curve showing the sum of the marginal revenues in the two markets. The amount sold in each market (Q_A and Q_B, respectively) is the quantity at which marginal revenue in the market is equal to MC at the output level at which MC and the MR_T are equal. This figure is indicated by the point of intersection of the market's MR_T curve with a line drawn horizontally through the intersection of MC and MR-T.[5] The price charged in each market (P_A in A, P_B in B) is indicated by the point on that market segment's D curve directly above this intersection. It is, of course, the price at which the firm can sell the output that yields maximum profit in the market. The greater the difference in the elasticities of the demand curves in the various markets, the greater the optimal price differences and the larger the profit increase resulting from this form of price discrimination. If demand elasticities are the same in all market segments, there can be no gain from discrimination.

---

[5]The output sold in each market is not that at which marginal revenue in that market is equal to the marginal cost of producing the particular amount of output sold in that market; the significant marginal cost figure is that of the entire output sold in the two markets.

FIGURE 10—8
SEGMENTED-MARKET PRICE DISCRIMINATION

Total output for a segmented-market price-discriminating monopolist is that which corresponds to the equality of MC and the total MR curve, the horizontal sum of the MR curves for the two markets. The output is allocated between markets by setting MC on the last unit produced by the entire firm equal to MR in each market.

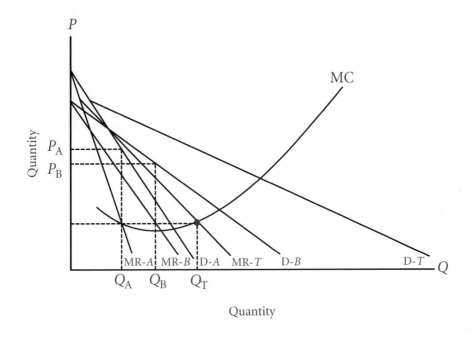

Quantity

The basis upon which markets are segregated depends primarily upon the nature of market conditions and the seller's ability to prevent resale between market segments. The seller seeks to segregate customers in a way that produces the maximum difference in elasticity between the various markets. Typically, customers are segregated in one of four ways.

1. In some instances the basis for segregation is use. Railroad freight rates, for example, vary among goods shipped, largely on the basis of demand conditions.

2. Markets are frequently segregated geographically. Products may be sold in a more distant area at a price lower (or higher) than that charged near the site of production because more (or fewer) substitutes are available in distant areas or demand is more (or less) elastic because of competition.

3. A third basis for segmentation is the direct attempt to group customers on the basis of buying preferences and incomes either by charging different prices to different groups directly or by providing several brands of a product (sometimes physically identical), each intended for a certain buying group, with prices adjusted to reflect anticipated differences in the elasticity of demand. Price differentials may bear little relationship to cost differences. For example, seats in various portions of a baseball stadium are priced in a manner designed to attract different income groups. With a uniform price, fewer from lower income groups would come, and those in higher income groups would pay considerably less than they were willing to pay. While it is true that the various seats are not the same "good," the differences in price are often larger than differences in seat "quality."

4. A fourth basis is the size of the order. Sellers often find it advantageous to make substantial price concessions to large buyers to obtain their business—concessions that are not necessary to sell to customers buying smaller amounts. While some of this behavior is cost based (for example, it may cost about as much for a bank to make a very large loan as to make a small loan), much of it is not. (See Problem 10–6.)

10–6 When airlines offer discounts on transcontinental flights, it is often mandatory to purchase tickets at least two weeks in advance. Why do you think this is an effective pricing strategy?

This strategy allows the airlines to charge more to business travelers, who often need a flight on the spur of the moment. Thus, the business traveler has a more inelastic demand curve (fewer substitutes). If the airlines cut prices for these clients, their revenues and profits would fall. However, the planned traveler (perhaps a vacationer) operates on a much more elastic demand curve. For these travelers there are many substitutes: other modes of transportation, different destinations, different times, and so on. The airlines, therefore, charge lower prices to this group of travelers contingent upon their making earlier reservations. In this way, the airlines can make more money by segmenting the market according to each group's elasticity of demand, rather than charging all users the same price.

PEAK-LOAD PRICING

Peak-load pricing is a variant of third-degree price discrimination. Different groups of buyers are still charged different prices for the same good or service, but with peak-load pricing, buyers are segmented into groups on the basis of when they consume the good or service. That is, buyers are charged a higher price for the good or service during peak periods and lower prices during nonpeak periods.

Examples of firms that use peak-load pricing include: restaurants, ski resorts, amusement parks, airlines, movie theaters, and telephone companies. In all of these cases, demand fluctuates considerably and predictably between the peak and nonpeak periods.

Consider an electric-utility company that plans to change its pricing strategy from constant pricing to peak-load pricing. Figure 10–9 presents the utility company as charging 5 cents per kilowatt hour, 24 hours a day. This constant price is based on the average cost to the electric company in the combined peak and nonpeak periods. Under a peak-load pricing scheme, the company will charge 6 cents per kilowatt hour for 600,000 kilowatts per hour during peak periods (afternoons) and 4 cents per kilowatt hour during nonpeak periods (early morning and evenings) for 200,000 kilowatts per hour. However, at the quantity that would be demanded at 5 cents per kilowatt hour in the off-peak period, we can see from our demand (marginal benefit) curve that during the nonpeak period the marginal benefits, 5 cents, exceed the marginal costs, 3 cents (A-B). This is clearly not an efficient solution; society would be better off if more electricity were supplied during the nonpeak period, because the marginal benefits outweigh the marginal costs at 200,000 kilowatts per hour, point C. The optimal solution in the nonpeak period would be to supply 300,000 kilowatts per hour at 4 cents per kilowatt hour, point C.

It is also economically inefficient to charge the same 5-cents-per-kilowatt-hour price during peak periods. In the peak period, the marginal benefit of an additional unit is 5 cents, but the marginal cost is 7 cents, (E-F). In this case, society would be better off if the electric company sold fewer units at 6 cents per kilowatt hour, point D.

In sum, the most economically efficient solution is to charge the lower price during nonpeak period and the higher price during the peak period. The gain from peak-load pricing compared with constant pricing can be seen graphically as the sum of the two shaded triangles in Figure 10–9.

FIGURE 10–9
PEAK-LOAD PRICING

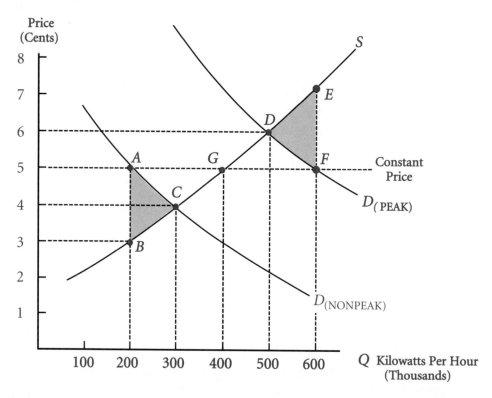

Demands for some goods and services fluctuates considerably and predictably between peak and nonpeak periods. It is more efficient to charge a higher price, 6 cents, during peak period (higher marginal costs) and a lower price, 4 cents, during nonpeak periods (lower marginal costs) than charging a single price, 5 cents, at all times.

10.4 ADJUSTMENT OF
PRODUCT AND SELLING ACTIVITIES

The discussion to this point has assumed that the product is a standard item, not subject to variation, and that the firm does not do anything to affect the demand for the product. Actually, however, the firm can adjust both the product and its selling activities in search of higher profits.

ADJUSTMENT OF THE PHYSICAL PRODUCT

Once the firm has selected the type of product or products it will produce, it must select the exact variety or quality of the product that allows maximum profit. For each potential form of the product, there is a certain cost schedule and a certain demand schedule and, therefore, a certain possible profit at the level of output for the product where marginal revenue equals marginal cost. In general, the higher the quality of the product, the greater the potential sales at various prices, but the cost per unit for producing various quantities is also higher. The firm often earns greater profits if it offers several forms of the product, each with different equilibrium price and output levels.

Unfortunately, it is very difficult for the firm to estimate sales corresponding to each of various forms of the product because of the difficulty of predicting consumer reaction. Experimentation is sometimes possible (test marketing in target populations), but usually the firm is forced to select the forms that, on the basis of rough estimates, appear to yield the greatest net return.

A firm seldom limits itself to one quality, finding it advantageous to carry several different varieties of the same product with differences in quality and price. With several different qualities, the firm may be able to use its plant more effectively and gain greater advantages of large-scale production. The importance of having a "full line," so that shoppers can satisfy their wishes for various types of items (colors and varieties of paints, for example) may also encourage the firm to carry a wider variety of qualities.

SELLING ACTIVITIES

Profit maximization also requires the firm to optimally adjust its selling activities designed to influence its demand. The costs of these activities are known as selling costs, as distinguished from production costs. In practice, a precise line cannot be drawn between the two classes of cost; expenses of packaging, for example, and the salaries of sales personnel fall partly into each category. But the distinction is useful for purposes of analysis.

Selling activities, in turn, may be grouped into two major classes: quality-service competition and direct sales promotion. The former involves either improving the quality of the product (or giving the impression of improving it) without altering its basic nature, or adding to the service rendered in conjunction with the sale of the product. A major aspect of quality-service competition is the emphasis on style and deliberate changes in styles which make existing models obsolete. Whenever style changes can be profitably emphasized, as with clothes and automobiles, firms will employ them.

No sharp line can be drawn between the process of selecting the optimum physical product and that of adjusting quality and service as methods of increasing sales. Both actions affect sales and cost schedules and, if successful, increase the demand for the product. The distinction is essentially one of degree.

Almost universally in monopoly (as in all imperfectly competitive markets, even those with relatively standardized products), firms find it advantageous to increase their sales by using sales representatives, advertising, and other selling activities. Sales promotion, if successful, can increase demand for the firm's product. Consequently, the firm can sell a greater volume at the existing price (perhaps with lower production costs per unit because of economies of scale), or it can raise prices and thus increase profit per unit. If the addition to total cost resulting from selling activities is less than the increase in receipts (net of any change in production cost), the firm's profits will increase. (See Problem 10–7.)

10–7 Why do you think sales promotion is effective?

Sales promotion is effective primarily because consumers have limited knowledge of the quality of the goods they are contemplating buying and their desires are subject to influence. They are not aware of many commodities and frequently have no satisfactory way of even judging the relative desirability of products with which they are familiar. Furthermore, consumer wants are themselves subject to modification. Persons have certain basic desires for food, clothing, shelter, and so on. But the exact nature of the wants—whether they wish to eat meat or fruit, for example—is subject to change. Finally, many persons have incomes well in excess of the amounts necessary to satisfy the basic needs of life. Great opportunity exists for producers to influence these persons to use a portion of their income to make luxury purchases.

The Level of Selling Activities

Selling activities are influenced by how much sales respond as expenditures on selling activities are increased—the "promotional elasticity" of advertising. Apparently, as a firm first increases sales effort, returns typically increase because additional dollars spent on advertising produce successively greater increases in sales. There are two reasons for this. First, successful advertising requires repetition; that is, repeated suggestions are frequently necessary to influence the actions of buyers. If total expenditures on advertising are small, they may therefore have hardly any effect on sales; thereafter, a relatively limited increase may produce a sharp increase in sales because of the repetition effect. Second, as selling expenditures are increased, more effective means can sometimes be used. Division of labor produces advantages in selling as well as in other forms of business activity. Firms, for example, can hire advertising experts and employ nationwide media coverage.

Eventually, however, additional dollars spent on sales promotion produce progressively smaller increases in sales. Economies of scale are eventually exhausted, along with the exploitation of the best portions of the potential market. Additional sales can be made only to persons who are less interested in the product than those who bought it initially, and so greater effort is required to induce them to buy. Frequently, additional customers are more expensive to contact. Old customers can buy additional units only by sacrificing other purchases that offer greater utility than those forgone in order to buy initial units of the good. To buy one automobile, for example, a person may need to sacrifice only a portion of the year's savings and a trip to Hawaii. To buy a second car, however, the buyer may have to forgo some of the food and clothing to which he or she has become accustomed. Thus, maximizing profits requires the firm to select the optimum profit level of selling activities, as well as the most advantageous types of selling activities. This level, however, cannot be determined independently of decisions on product, output, and price, because the level of selling activities that maximize profit is not the same at alternative quality, quantity, or price levels. Likewise, product, output, and price cannot be determined independently of the volume of selling activities, because the latter affects both cost and revenue schedules.

Imperfections in the Determination of Selling Activities

Any firm is likely to have extreme difficulty in jointly adjusting price, selling activities, and product to levels that allow maximum profits. It is especially hard for firms to determine optimum selling expenditures. The results of sales efforts cannot be predicted in advance; even after sales expenditures have been made, the firm cannot be sure of their exact effect upon its demand schedule. Thus, as a practical matter, the firm's estimate of the optimum sales effort is largely guesswork, more so than decisions in virtually any other phase of business policy. Many firms spend more or less constant amounts annually for sales promotion; others adjust sales expenditures to a certain percentage of expected gross sales; and still others are influenced by current net-profit figures. In recent years the so-called objective-and-task method has become widely used. With this method the firm selects certain sales objectives and attempts to estimate the amount of advertising expenditure necessary to obtain them. None of these methods is likely to yield the exact optimum amount, but they are employed because of the lack of more precise techniques.

10.5 OBJECTIONS TO MONOPOLY
AND WELFARE COST OF MONOPOLY

Monopoly is often considered "bad." What is the basis in economic theory for concerns about monopoly power? To begin with, observe that Figure 10–10 show that the equilibrium output need not be achieved where the average total cost of producing the good is minimized. Per-unit costs of production are at their lowest point where the MC curve crosses the ATC curve, at output 0G. This profit-maximizing monopolist, however, produces a smaller output, 0A, an output that requires more resources per unit of output than is possible at higher outputs. Under perfect competition, firms in the long run produce at the minimum point on their average total-cost curves. Monopoly, then, can sometimes promote inefficiency by using more resources per unit of output than are used in perfect competition and by failing to produce units of output having marginal benefits greater than marginal costs. The major objection to monopoly, therefore, is that, under certain assumptions that are very often realistic, monopoly leads to a lower output and to higher prices than would exist under perfect competition.

Figure 10–10 shows why this is so. In monopoly, the firm produces output 0A and charges a price of 0D. Suppose, however, that the market was perfectly competitive and that the industry was characterized by constant returns to scale, meaning many small firms could produce output with the same efficiency (at the same cost) as one large firm. The marginal-cost curve, then, is the sum of the firms' individual marginal-cost curves, and the upper portion of that curve can be considered the industry-supply curve. Equilibrium price and quantity would be determined where the MC, or supply, curve intersects the demand curve, at output 0F and price 0J. Thus, equilibrium in perfect competition provides for more output (AF more) and lower prices (DJ lower) than the equilibrium in monopoly.

FIGURE 10–10
PROFITS DERIVED BY A MONOPOLIST

In a perfectly competitive constant-cost industry, price and output would be 0J and 0F. The monopolist, however, sets a higher price, 0D, and restricts output of 0A. Per-unit profits equal D minus ATC (C-B) and total profits equal the area BCDE. Because firms are not free to enter, these profits will not be eliminated in the long run.

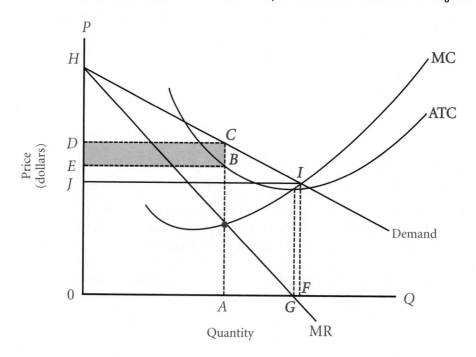

Opponents of monopoly regard these differences as unfair and inefficient. Consumers bear the burden of higher prices, and goods producible at costs lower than consumer benefits are not produced. In monopoly, the consumer's surplus (the value to consumers from getting the good for less than they would be willing to pay for all units except the last) is area DCH, while in perfect competition it is the much larger are JIH.

Secondary objections to monopoly are sometimes also raised. One is that monopoly involves a concentration of economic power. The monopolist controls significant quantities of inputs and output. Some think that in a democratic society, bigness itself is bad for reasons related to justice and equality.

In addition, it is argued that a lack of competition tends to retard technological advance. According to this view, the monopolist becomes comfortable, reaping monopolistic profits, and so it does not work hard at product improvement, technical advances designed to promote efficiency, and so forth. Sometimes, American railroads are cited as an example. Early in this century, railroads had a considerable amount of monopoly power; yet they did not spend much on research or development or aggressively try to improve rail transport. As a consequence, technical advances in other transport modes (such as trucks and airplanes) led to a loss of monopoly power. A more contemporary example sometimes cited is the United States Postal Service, a government monopoly. Mail is delivered in much the same way today as it was 75 years ago. Only very recently have efforts been made to use electronic and computer advances to speed transmission of written messages, but these efforts have been stimulated largely by competing private firms. (It is debatable, in this case, whether the lack of research and development reflects complacency or instead the absence of the profit motive because of government ownership.)

The belief that monopoly retards innovation can be disputed, however. Many near-monopolists are in fact important innovators. Companies such as Polaroid and Xerox—with very strong market positions that in some instances approach monopoly secured by patent protection—are important innovators. Indeed, innovation can actually help firms obtain a degree of monopoly status because patents give them a monopoly on cost-saving technology. Even monopolists wants more profits, and any innovation that lowers costs or expands revenues creates profits. The incentive to innovate exists, therefore, in monopolist as well as competitive market structures. (See Problems 10–8 and 10–9.)

10–8 The output level set by the monopolist is inefficient from society's standpoint, but the profits are not. Why?

The net loss resulting from lower output is what economists call the welfare cost of monopoly. However, society as a whole does not lose from monopoly profits. Why? Because the income is not lost, but is transferred from consumers to producers, with monopolists (stockholders and workers) gaining at the expense of consumers that pay a higher price for a monopolist's product than they would if the product were produced by a perfectly competitive firm. This is depicted in the accompanying figure.

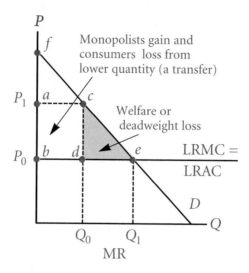

The welfare loss is graphically represented by the area *cde*. It is the difference between how much consumers value quantity Q_1 minus Q_0, which is $Q_0 ceQ_1$, and how much they would have to give up for it, $Q_0 deQ_1$. You may recall from Chapter 2 that this is called *consumer surplus*. Under perfectly competitive conditions, however, the area abcd would also be part of the consumer's surplus. In sum, the loss to society from monopoly is the area *cde*, and the area *abcd* is merely a transfer of consumer surplus to monopoly profits. The actual amount of the welfare loss caused by monopolists is a subject of considerable debate among economists. Estimates vary from between 1/10 of 1 percent to 6 percent of national income. The variation depends on the researchers' estimates of elasticities of demand, whether the researcher used firm or industry data, whether adjustments to profits were made (by including royalties and intangibles for example), and whether the researcher included some proxy for scarce resources used in attempting to create a monopoly.

10–9 Why is there no social-welfare loss when a monopolist practices perfect-price discrimination?

A perfect-price-discriminating monopolist obtains the maximum price along the demand curve for each unit of output. For example, in the figure below, the monopolist charges $10 for the first unit of output, $9 for the second, $8 for the third, and so on. The demand curve represents the firm's marginal-revenue curve, and profits are maximized at the output level at which the LRMC equals MR, or in this case, LRMC equals *P*. (Constant costs are assumed for simplicity.) The marginal social benefits, represented by the demand price of the last unit sold ($5), equal marginal social costs, LRMC, and social welfare cannot be improved by increasing or decreasing output. Thus, the perfect-price-discriminating monopolist charges the competitive price on only the last unit sold and produces the competitive output level, 6 units. The consumer surplus that would have arisen in perfect competition, the area *ABC* (the difference between what consumers are willing to pay and what they actually pay), is transferred to the monopolist as profits.

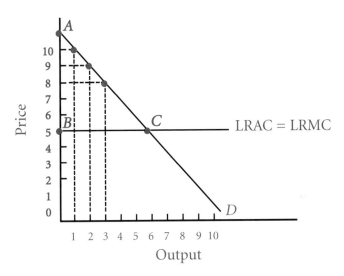

10.6 RESTRAINTS ON MONOPOLY PRICE

Even in industries where the monopolist is not subject to regulation, various considerations may deter it from seeking maximum profits and induce it to set a price lower than the one allowing absolute maximum gains.

First, barriers against entry are never absolute. If a monopolist sees a chance of new firms developing, it may deliberately hold price below the profit-maximization figure to make entry by new firms less attractive and more difficult. Thus, the monopolist sacrifices temporary gains in hopes of greater long-term gains.

Second, the firm may be deterred by fear of government regulation. Especially in the United States and Canada, where there are long-standing policies maintaining competition and public attitudes to monopoly are basically hostile, a firm may be extremely careful to avoid exploiting its monopoly position, thereby warding off antitrust prosecution.

Third, pressures toward the goal of profit maximization are less severe on a monopolist. Competitive firms are compelled to undertake measures to maximize profit because failure to do so will likely lead to losses and possible bankruptcy. In contrast, a monopolist earning a good rate of profit has much less need to exploit every opportunity to increase profit, especially if the enterprise is a large, widely held corporation. Quite apart from fear of regulation, the monopolist may wish to appear "respectable"—to avoid behavior that seems to customers like ruthless monopolistic exploitation.

Today the desire to be regarded as fair about not exploiting monopoly or semi monopoly positions, like the desire to avoid being regarded as a price chiseler, seems to play some part in molding business behavior and in modifying the profit-maximization goal.

10.7 REGULATED MONOPOLIES

In a public utility industry, a single firm is ordinarily allowed a monopoly in its market area because operation of more than one firm would prevent the attainment of full economies of large-scale production and interfere with complete use of capacity (which often must be extended in advance of needs). However, these monopolies are subject to regulation by governmental agencies, which seek to set general rate levels such that the rate (the price) is equal to average cost—which includes a "fair," or average, rate of return on investment—and to guarantee that all customers can buy all they wish at this price. Thus, Figure 10–12 sets the rate (assuming no discrimination) at P_1, as indicated by the intersection of the D curve with the AC curve. Because of the difficulty of estimating the elasticity of demand and of defining a "fair" return, the actual rate level would only approximate this figure.

Some critics feel that setting the rate at the level of average cost is contrary to the principles of economic welfare (as outlined in Chapter 18) unless the utility were operating at the point of lowest average cost and unless the marginal cost happened to equal average cost. These critics argue that optimum use of resources requires extension of the output of each good to the point at which MC equals P (Q_2 in Figure 10–11). If, at the point at which AC equals P, marginal cost is below price, as it would be if the utility were operating on the downward portion of its AC curve, then additional units of output would add less in cost to the economy (in the sense of resource use) than the price charged for them. Thus, optimum use of resources requires production of these additional units, moving from Q_1 to Q_2.

FIGURE 10–11
RATE ADJUSTMENTS OF A REGULATED MONOPOLY

Pricing difficulties arise in regulated monopolies because of declining average costs. If regulators choose P_1, economic profits are zero, but social welfare is not maximized because the marginal benefits exceed the marginal costs of producing additional units of output. Although optimum social welfare is achieved at P_2, the firm incurs losses and must be subsidized by taxpayers. Two-tiered pricing can recover the losses by charging a fixed fee to users.

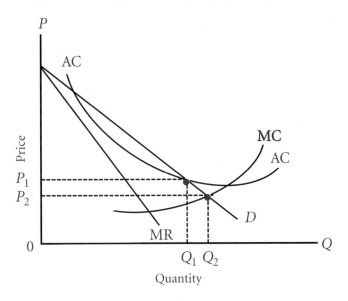

In practice, however, output is more likely to be set at the point Q_1 where AC equals P rather than at Q_2 where MC equals P. If price is set at the level of marginal cost, the utility will not be able to earn a normal return on its investments, nor perhaps even cover all of its explicit costs. A subsidy, therefore, would be required to keep the enterprise in operation. Government subsidies to private enterprise give rise to a host of difficulties, and the taxes needed to pay the subsidies themselves interfere with resource allocation. As long as the production of utility service remains in private hands, the use of an average cost basis for regulation of price and output is likely to continue. An alternative approach in such cases is to levy a fixed charge for use of the good (say, any use of electricity or any trips on a bus), but then only charge marginal cost prices for any particular use. The charge could be, for example, an annual charge to electricity users or an annual fee for a photo-ID for bus users. With this type of "two-tiered pricing," the fixed fee can cover the losses associated with marginal-cost pricing. (See Problems 10–10 and 10–11.)

10–10 The actual implementation of a rate (price) that permits a "fair and reasonable" return is more difficult than the analysis suggests. Why do you think this is so?

Calculating capital costs and values is difficult, particularly in periods of inflation. In permitting a normal rate of return to the utility's capital, do the regulators value it at its original cost minus depreciation, or do they value it at replacement cost, specifically the cost of replacing the capital today? In other words, do the rate setters account for the impact of inflation and changing real relative scarcity? This is but one problem that regulators face.

Also, in the real world, consumer groups are constantly battling for lower rates while the utilities themselves lobby for higher rates to obtain monopoly profits. Decisions are not always made in a calm, objective, dispassionate atmosphere free of outside involvement. It is precisely the political economy of rate setting that disturbs some critics of this approach to dealing with the monopoly problem. Some critics argue that in the long run, the utility companies end up controlling the regulators (The companies have much at stake). Rate-making commissioners become friendly to the companies, perhaps believing that they can obtain a nice utility job after their tenure as a regulator is over. The temptation is therefore great for the commissioners to be generous to the utilities. On the other hand, other observers usually express concern over the recent tendency of regulators to bow to pressure from consumer groups. A politician who wants to win votes might succeed by attacking utility companies and promising lower rates. If zealous rate regulators listen too closely to the consumer groups and push rates down to levels below average costs, the industry may be unable to attract capital for expansion.

While the public regulation of private monopolies has its difficulties, the relevant question is whether any other option is better. Breaking up utility monopolies and permitting multiple firms to operate seems undesirable, given the declining-cost nature of many such industries. It makes little sense to have five companies running electric transmission lines from power plants to every area of a city. Nationalization often leads to politicization of business enterprises and inefficiency of its own. For that reason, most Americans accept public regulation of private utilities as being the best, or perhaps the "least bad," of the various alternatives.

10–11 True or False? There are cases in which price is equal to marginal cost but average cost is not covered; all costs of production, therefore, cannot be recovered.

True. An obvious example is a public utility that has a monopoly in a particular geographical area but does not have a market large enough to allow it to reach the point of lowest cost. As explained in earlier chapters, in ranges of output less than that of lowest average cost, marginal cost is less than average cost. An extreme example is provided by a toll bridge that is not used to capacity. The marginal cost of another car using the bridge may be almost zero; yet the average cost may be substantial. If prices are set at a level equal to marginal cost, the deficit must be made up by a subsidy financed by taxation. Because virtually all taxes have some adverse effects upon the economy, the decision about pricing must be made on the basis of a weighing of the relative disadvantages of taxes versus those of departure from marginal-cost pricing.

DISCRIMINATION

The possibility of rate discrimination greatly complicates the task of controlling utility rates. From the standpoint of the average cost of providing utility services and the optimum use of resources, discrimination may have merit because it allows the utility to gain business that it would not otherwise get, lowers the cost per unit for all output (assuming operation under decreasing-cost conditions), and encourages operation nearer the point at which marginal cost equals price. In some instances, especially railroads, firms would probably be unable to cover costs if discrimination were not practiced. If a single uniform rate were charged on all freight, shipments able to bear only a low rate could not move, and shipments able to bear high rate would be subject to a lower rate than the shippers would be willing to pay. The consequence would be overall reduction of volume and railway revenue. But rate discrimination raises significant questions of equity and economic effects upon customers, questions to which answers are not easily supplied by the theory of economic welfare. Especially in the transportation industry, some of the most difficult problems of rate regulation center around questions of discrimination among shippers of different goods, shipments between different points, and shipments of different individuals.

10.8 MONOPOLY CONTROL: TAXATION

One way to regulate any inequities associated with the profits of monopoly is through taxation. The three methods of taxation used most often are a per-unit tax, lump-sum tax, and profit tax.

PER-UNIT TAX

A per-unit tax is a tax on each unit sold. Figure 10–12 shows the before-and-after effects on price and output of a per-unit tax. The before-tax profit-maximizing position of the monopoly firm is denoted by quantity Q_B and price P_B. The key to understanding this tax is that it appears to the firm as a variable cost increase because it is attached to each additional unit of output. As you recall from Chapter 8, an increase in variable cost affects both the long-run average cost and the marginal cost of the firm, vertically shifting both curves upward to $LRAC_A$ and MC_A. The new price and output are P_A and Q_A, respectively. A glance at Figure 10–12 shows the profit before tax (the difference between P_B and C_B times Q_B) to be higher than the profits after tax (difference between P_A and C_A times Q_A).

Who pays this tax? The producer pays part in the form of reduced profits, and the consumer pays part in the form of higher prices for lower output. The proportion that each pays depends on the elasticity of the demand and marginal cost curves. The tax has one important drawback, however, for it causes the monopolist to further reduce output (compared to the competitive case), leading to worsening resource allocation. This approach to controlling monopoly is inefficient (for still more goods having benefits greater than cost go unproduced), though administratively it is straightforward. (See Problem 10–12.)

10–12 Suppose a monopolist faces constant costs. If a per-unit tax is levied on the monopolist, who bears the burden of he tax? Who bears the tax burden in perfect competition?

In Figure (a), the equilibrium price and quantity before the tax levy are P_0 and Q_0 for the monopolist. Because the tax varies with output, it raises LRAC and LRMC by the amount of the tax. The post-tax price and quantity are P_1 and Q_1. As the price increases—but by less than the tax—consumers and the monopolist share the burden of the tax. In perfect competition, the industry price and output are P_0 and Q_0 in Figure (b) before the tax. The cost increase is depicted by the upward shift in LRAC, and post-tax equilibrium occurs at P_1 and Q_1. In perfect competition with constant costs, consumers pay the entire tax, for the price increase equals the tax.

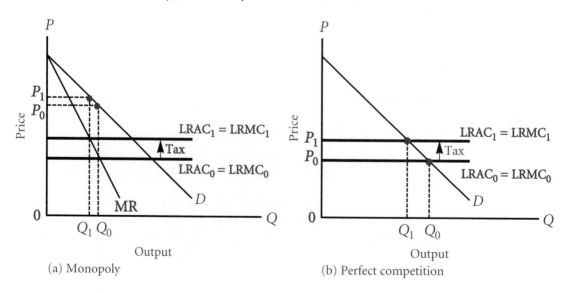

(a) Monopoly (b) Perfect competition

From the firm's perspective, a lump-sum tax resembles a fixed cost, in that it is levied on the firm's total output whether that output large or small. The firm must pay this lump-sum tax if it wishes to stay in business. Figure 10–13 shows the tax shifting the LRAC$_{Before}$ up to LRAC$_{After}$. However, the marginal cost curve is unaffected, because the tax is the same whether the firm produces 1 unit a year or 10,000 units a day; that is, marginal costs do not rise with this type of tax. Because the demand and marginal-revenue curves are also unaltered, profit-maximizing price and output do not change, as Figure 10–13 shows. Therefore, a lump-sum tax does not reduce allocative efficiency, though it does reduce the monopolist's profits.

FIGURE 10–12
PER-UNIT TAX

A per-unit tax raises the average and marginal cost of producing each unit of output. LARC and MC curves shift up, output declines to Q_A, and price rises to P_A. The monopolist and the consumers share the burden of the tax.

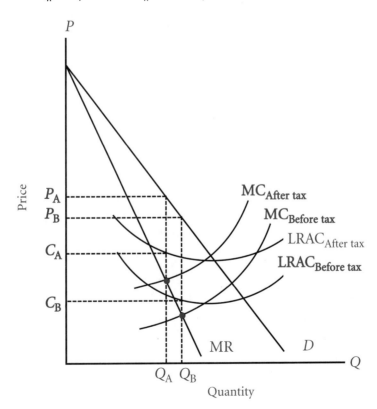

FIGURE 10–13
LUMP-SUM TAX

Since the lump-sum tax is fixed regardless of the level of output, it increases average costs but not marginal costs. Equilibrium price and quantity are unaffected, but profits are reduced.

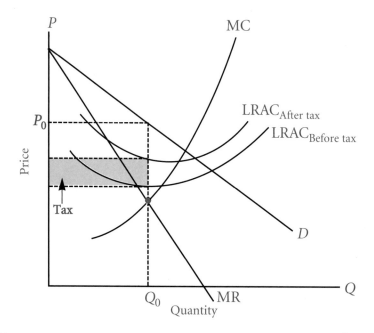

FIGURE 10–14
PROFITS TAX

A percentage tax on profits does not affect price or quantity but simply transfers part of the profit to the government.

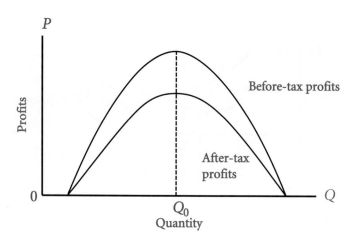

A profits tax does not affect either marginal cost or marginal revenue curves if the profit base is properly calculated (that is, on economic profits, not accounting profits). Although it does not affect the equilibrium price and quantity (Q_0 is the profit-maximizing output before and after the tax), it does affect profits, lowering them in proportion to the size of the tax at each output level. (See Figure 10–14, where a tax of about 50 percent is depicted.)

10.9 THE CASE FOR MONOPOLY

The analysis presented above clearly suggests that monopolies are economically inefficient. Noneconomic considerations such as the concentration of power also contribute to opposition to the existence of monopoly. Remember, however, that the notion that monopoly leads to higher prices and reduced output hinges on the assumption that the monopolist has no inherent efficiencies related to size. To the contrary, as Figure 10–15 shows, there may be economies of scale, so that very large firms are more efficient than smaller ones. It is likely that, given demand conditions, the market will accommodate only one such large, low-cost firm. In this case, prohibiting monopoly would not lead to higher output and lower prices. The marginal costs of many small producers at any given output would be higher than the marginal cost of the monopolist, so that the supply (MC) and demand curves could intersect at higher prices and lower output in competition than in monopoly.

The decreasing-cost industry case depicted in Figure 10–15 is conducive to the formation of a natural monopoly such as an electric-power company. In some cases, the average total-cost curve may decline over a wide range but then begin to increase again at an output level that would permit two or three firms to operate efficiently, suggesting a "natural oligopoly;" this may be the situation that existed, for example, for many years in the American automobile industry. The growth of world demand and international trade has resulted more recently in a more competitive structure for this industry. (The lesson, of course, is that free international trade, in addition to comparative advantage arguments favoring it, also reduces monopoly inefficiency worldwide.)

FIGURE 10-15
APPROPRIATENESS OF MONOPOLY

In Figure 10–15, economies of scale exist relative to market demand and small firms are inherently inefficient. A good case for monopoly exists, although society may be still better served by effective regulation in such cases.

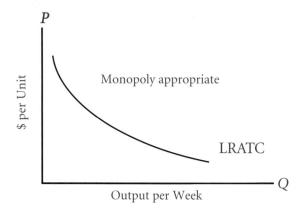

SUMMARY

1. Imperfectly competitive firms can influence the market price by such actions as advertising, lobbying for legislation, and varying quantities available for sale.

2. A monopoly is a market in which buyers are numerous but the total output of the commodity, which has no close substitute, is controlled by a single firm.

3. The demand curve for a nonprice discriminating monopolist is downward sloping, meaning that the monopolist must lower its price to sell more output.

4. Marginal revenue for a nonprice discriminating monopolist is less than price for all units except the first.

5. In the market period, if quantity demanded at the current price is greater than the firm's current output, the monopolist may either sell from accumulated stocks or increase the asking price. If quantity demanded falls short of current output at the prevailing price, the monopolist may either cut prices or increase inventories.

6. The monopolist attempts to equate MR and MC in the short run. However, the monopolist may find it more difficult to estimate marginal revenue than does the perfectly competitive firm.

7. A monopolist's price is higher and its output is lower than those of a perfectly competitive firm.

8. The long-run equilibrium level of output for the monopolist is where MR = LRMC = SRMC.

9. Having a monopoly is no guarantee of excess profits. If demand is inadequate, lack of competitors is of little benefit to a seller.

10. Price discrimination occurs when a monopolist charges various customers different prices that are not related to differences in costs.

11. Perfect-price discrimination requires that each buyer pay the maximum sum he or she is willing to pay—that is, the reservation price—for each quantity unit.

12. Multipart discrimination allows the monopolist to sell different parts of its output at different prices, charging more for the first block than for successive blocks.

13. Segmented-market price discrimination allows the firm to separate its total market into several parts on the basis of demand prices and elasticities. The firm then charges different prices to different groups of buyers.

14. Firms must select the exact variety or quality of the product that allows maximum profit. Demand schedules and cost schedules differ for each different form of the product.

15. The firm must optimally adjust selling activities to maximize profits.

16. Common methods of regulating monopolies include taxation (per-unit tax, lump-sum tax, and profit tax) and price controls. The profits tax and the lump-sum tax are preferred to the per-unit tax because they do not reduce output and raise the price paid by consumers, *ceteris paribus*.

17. The smaller output produced in monopoly markets represents a misallocation of resources and, therefore, causes a welfare cost to society. Goods having benefits greater than (opportunity) cost of production are not exchanged.

WORDS AND CONCEPTS FOR REVIEW

imperfectly competitive markets

price discrimination

multipart-price discrimination

selling costs

per-unit tax

profits tax

monopoly

perfect-price discrimination

segmented-market-price discrimination

welfare costs of monopoly

lump-sum tax

REVIEW QUESTIONS

1. Suppose that a firm is the sole supplier of a particular product, but the cross-elasticity of demand between this product and other products is very high. Is the monopoly analysis useful in explaining behavior in this industry? Explain.

2. Suppose that in a market period, a monopolist finds that the demand for its products at the price set exceeds the market-period current output rate. What will it do? Explain.

3. How does a monopolist estimate the demand curve?

4. Why is the equilibrium output level where marginal cost equals marginal revenue?

5. In both monopoly and perfect competition, the equilibrium output is at the level at which MR = MC, but only in the latter is P = MC. Why?

6. What is the difference between the short-run and long-run adjustments of a monopolist?

7. Can a monopolist always set a price that covers average cost? Explain.

8. What is meant by price discrimination? What conditions are necessary for price discrimination?

9. Why can price discrimination not occur in perfectly competitive markets?

10. Suppose that all buyers have precisely the same demand schedules for a commodity. Is price discrimination profitable? Explain.

11. What is the difference between perfect-price discrimination and other forms of price discrimination?

12. In segmented-market price discrimination, why are the equilibrium output levels in each market not the levels at which marginal revenue in that market equals marginal cost of the product sold in that market?

13. Determine whether or not price discrimination occurs in each of the following situations. If it does, indicate why discrimination is advantageous and how customers are segregated.
    a) family fares on airlines and railroads
    b) lower admissions charges for children or senior citizens than adults at the movies
    c) lower fares for commuters on railroads and bus lines
    d) higher prices for foreign periodicals to American subscribers than to residents of the source countries (the differences exceeding differences in postal charges)

SUGGESTED READINGS

Harberger, Arnold. "Monopoly and Resource Allocation," *American Economic Review* 44, (May 1954), 77–87.

Posner, Richard A. "The Social Cost of Monopoly and Regulation," *Journal of Political Economy* 83, (August 1975), 137–169.

Scherer, F. M., and David Ross. *Industrial Market Structure and Economic Performance,* 3rd ed. Boston: Houghton-Mifflin, 1990.

Chapter Eleven

MONOPOLISTIC
COMPETITION

_____ *Questions to Think About* _____

1. What are the characteristics of monopolistic competition and how is it different from perfect competition? How is it similar?

2. What is product differentiation?

3. Why is the demand curve for a monopolistically competitive firm more elastic than for a monopolist, but less elastic than for a perfectly competitive firm?

4. What is a proportional-demand curve?

5. How are price and output determined for a monopolistically competitive firm in the short run?

6. How does the monopolistically competitive firm adjust to long-run equilibrium when economic profits are earned in the short run?

7. Why does excess capacity arise in monopolistic competition?

8. How do such selling activities as advertising affect product differentiation and the price elasticity of demand?

11.1 INTRODUCTION

*T*he models of monopoly and perfect competition outlined in the two preceding chapters directly apply only to the analysis of limited sectors of the contemporary economy—the former to regulated industries and a few isolated markets, the latter to markets for basic agricultural products and securities. With some modifications the models are applicable to a much wider range of markets in which conditions approach, but do not agree entirely with, the assumptions on which the models are built. Two major types of these models involve elements of both monopoly and perfect competition in varying proportions. This chapter discusses the first of these models, monopolistic competition; Chapter 12 discusses the second, oligopoly.

11.2 GENERAL CHARACTERISTICS OF MONOPOLISTIC COMPETITION

The theory of monopolistic competition is based on three primary assumptions: (1) products of various sellers are differentiated; (2) the number of sellers is sufficiently large for each to act independently of the others; and (3) entry of new firms is relatively easy. Thus, unlike perfect competition, individual sellers can influence their price. They can increase their sales by lowering prices in part by taking sales from their competitors; yet they do not consider any individual competitors as rivals whose policies will be influenced by their own action. Because of the relatively free entry of new firms, long-run price-and-output behavior is similar to that of perfect competition; because the firm produces a product that is different from others, there is also some degree of monopoly power. In a sense, each seller in monopolistic competition may be regarded as a "monopolist" of its own particular brand of a good—but unlike the firm of the monopoly model, there is competition by firms producing similar brands.

PRODUCT DIFFERENTIATION

One required characteristic of monopolistic competition is product differentiation—when a group of similar products are close but imperfect substitutes. The significant feature of product differentiation is the buyers' belief that the products of the various sellers are not the same, whether the products are actually different physically or not. There are various sources of differentiation, depending on the product. (1) Actual physical differences constitute one source. Brands of apparently similar ice cream, beer, or wine differ significantly in taste to many buyers. The physical differences among various makes of cars lead some buyers to prefer one make, some another.

(2) Prestige considerations can be significant. Many persons prefer to be seen using the currently popular make, while others prefer the "off brand." Prestige considerations are particularly important with gifts. (3) In retailing, location is a major factor. People are not willing to travel long distances to shop for items that are minor in their overall expenditure pattern, thus the growth in convenient stores such as 7-Eleven and gas station/minimarts. (4) Service considerations are likewise significant. Speedy service is very important to some people, less so to others or at other times. Reliability or "no-hassle" return policies lead many people to buy at department stores instead of at discount houses, even though the latter may have lower prices. The personal attitudes of storekeepers and clerks is also an important influence. The attitude of waiters, for example, may significantly affect choice of restaurants. Even though many buyers believe that there is no significant difference between brands of gasoline, their choice of gasoline might be influenced by credit terms or the location of the service station.

PRICE

Despite differentiation, many buyers simply select sellers who offer the lowest prices, and all prefer lower prices to higher prices. Accordingly, sellers in a monopolistically competitive market discover from experience (if not common sense) that relatively small changes in price can produce relatively large changes in sales. Each seller therefore regards the demand for its product as relatively elastic. By the same token, an individual seller who fails to follow price trends initiated by competitors or fails to respond to the entry or exit of other sellers in his industry experiences substantial variations in quantity sold at any given price. The effect is to encourage individual sellers to revise their estimates of their demand curves in the light of actual sales experience. Thus, a seller will act on the assumption that the maximum price that can be charged for any given level of output is restricted to a range of values in the neighborhood of the prevailing "product group" price level. The seller revises the estimate of the position of the demand curve with significant changes in sales or in the typical price level. Thus, sellers behave as "competing monopolies." Each firm has a less than perfectly elastic demand in its own "market," but the demand curve is very elastic, and its position shifts significantly as conditions change in other "markets"—that is, as competing firms change prices or other policies.

FREE ENTRY

By the nature of monopolistic competition, entry into a given industry is unrestricted. New firms may easily start up production of close substitutes for existing products, although they cannot produce products that appear identical to existing ones in the eyes of prospective purchasers. Because of this relatively free entry, economic profits tend to be eliminated in the long run. As we shall see later, however, this tendency is moderated in a variety of ways. Some firms can earn economic profits even in the long run, and other firms that have earned economic profits often lose them not because prices are forced down, but because costs are forced up. (See Problem 11–1.)

11–1 If you were opening up a new restaurant and wanted to make your restaurant different from others, how would you differentiate your product? Can you think of any additional costs associated with differentiated products?

You could use any of a number of methods to make your restaurant different: location, service, type of menu, quality of food, ambiance, and so on. It should be noted, however, that there are some costs to differentiated products. First, the more differentiated the product, the greater the potential monopoly power. As we learned in the last chapter, monopolies generally produce a lower output at a higher price than competitive firms. Second, the abundance of variety can conflict with economies of scale. For example, average costs would be lower for one restaurant with a limited menu rather than four restaurants each with a large and varied menu..

11.3 MARKET-PERIOD PRICE DETERMINATION

The market period in monopolistic competition is an interval of time so short that orders to suppliers or other determinants of output cannot be altered. A seller in this period has a strong incentive to adjust price to ensure that sales coincide with the current rate of output or purchases, particularly to avoid accumulation or depletion of inventory. Because the seller is (by hypothesis) merely one among many, it does not have to be concerned about possible direct reactions by competitors to a temporary change in its asking price.

If a change in demand causes sales to lag significantly behind current output, the seller may reduce price sharply to bring about a quick adjustment of sales to output. Although demand may be very elastic in the short run, additional customers can be found immediately only if the seller makes important price concessions. Accordingly, special sales of goods at attractive discounts, combined with advertising that is designed to attract temporary rather than regular customers, is a characteristic feature of monopolistic competition.

If, in contrast, a change in demand causes current sales to exceed current output, different considerations apply. The seller normally distinguishes between regular and casual customers, and is reluctant to run the risk of losing a regular customer for the sake of a temporary and probably minor increase in revenue. Thus, sellers are hesitant to increase prices in the market period. Instead, the seller often adjusts sales to output by simply failing to meet demands by casual customers, rationing available output to regular customers at the prevailing price. For example, several years ago, Cabbage Patch dolls were very hard to come by. Consequently, many toy store owners had an incentive to lay away new shipments for their most valued customers rather than "jacking the price up" to clear the market. This asymmetry in price behavior (that is, lowering the price when output exceeds sales but holding the price when sales exceed output) in the market period could not occur in perfectly competitive markets. Moreover, frequent temporary price reductions are unlikely to be found in monopoly or oligopoly. Yet this kind of behavior is so familiar in actual retail markets that it demonstrates the usefulness of the monopolistic-competition model for market-period price determination in such markets. (See Problem 11–2.)

11–2 Imagine that you own a clothing shop. Lately, demand for your clothing has been tremendous. In the market period, will you increase your price to ration off the available supply of clothing?

Probably not. It is much more likely that if sales exceed output you would give preferential treatment to your steady customers instead of raising price.

11.4 OUTPUT AND PRICE DETERMINATION IN THE SHORT RUN

Because sellers in conditions of monopolistic competition have some ability to set prices, they must make decisions about short-run levels of output. These decisions are based on estimates of the probable prices at which various levels of sales can be made and on estimates of cost. Output and price determination is complicated by the fact that the position of the seller's demand curve depends on the average level of prices in the industry.

INDUSTRY PRICE AND COSTS

On what basis do the firms estimate what the "industry" price level will be? There are various approaches. One is recent price experience: If other fast food chains are charging $1.50 for hamburgers and $1 for milkshakes and have been doing so in recent months, each fast food establishment will assume that other firms will typically continue to charge these figures, and it will estimate its own potential sales at various price levels on this assumption. Alternatively, a firm may reasonably assume that the industry price level will be somewhat above average variable cost (AVC), using a markup that has become more or less traditional. It may be assumed that because entry of new firms is relatively easy, variable costs (such as, cost of goods sold) constitute the major element of total costs. Each seller knows that these costs must be covered if firms are to stay in business. Each seller also knows that certain markups above variable cost are regarded as traditional and are needed to cover fixed costs. Given its estimates of variable costs, the firm can therefore estimate the typical price level that it expects to prevail, and thus the position of its own demand curve.

Given the position of an individual's demand curve, we can describe the determination of short-run equilibrium output and price in terms similar to those used in the analysis of monopoly output and price determination. The relevant cost and revenue curves of a typical seller are represented in Figure 11–1. The intersection of MR and SRMC indicates that the short-run equilibrium output is q_{SR} and the short-run equilibrium price is P_{SR}. Because the demand curve is relatively flat, the excess of equilibrium price over marginal cost may be relatively small as compared with the monopoly model. Because different sellers will form different estimates of the level and position of the demand curve, equilibrium prices can differ among firms. The differences are unlikely to be extreme, however, because all firms are likely to have rather similar MC curves under the assumed conditions. As in perfect competition, this conclusion is subject to the requirement that price must cover AVC. If, however, the firm regards its failure to cover AVC as temporary, it may continue to operate for a time in order to avoid losing customers, a consideration not relevant in perfect competition.

FIGURE 11–1
INITIAL SHORT-RUN ADJUSTMENT OF PRICE AND OUTPUT

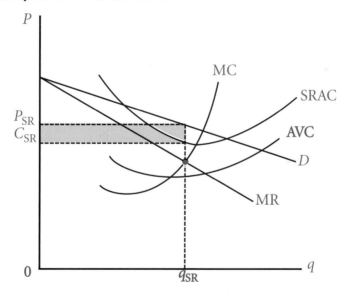

In monopolistic competition, the short-run optimum is similar to monopoly except that the D curve is relatively more elastic. The profit-maximizing output level, q_{SR} is determined where MR = SRMC, and the corresponding price on the demand curve. P_{SR} is the profit maximizing price. The firm continues to produce as long as AVC is less than or equal to price. This firm earns positive profits, as price exceeds SRAC at the current output level.

An individual seller determines output on the basis of its current estimate of demand prospects. The equilibrium value of this output varies over time in response to changes in the general level of prices in the industry. The mechanism by which such adjustments occur can be illustrated most conveniently by supposing that the actual sales of a typical individual seller at any given price are indicated not by the individual seller's demand curve, d, that the firm anticipates, but rather by an objective sales curve, represented in Figure 11–2 by the relation D. The definition of the curve D poses some logical problems because the curve cannot be obtained except by making specific assumptions about the prices charged by all other sellers. For the sake of simplicity—and not too unrealistically—we may suppose that the D curve shown in Figure 11–2 describes for each level of price what the sales of a typical seller would be if all other firms were charging exactly the same price. That is, the demand curve facing a typical firm—which may be thought of as a "proportional" demand curve—is $1/n$ of the product group's overall demand curve if there are n firms. Our analysis of the probable sequence of adjustments in short-run equilibrium output and price by a typical seller (supposing that other sellers always match the given seller's current price) can then proceed as follows:

Starting with an individual sellers' initially expected demand curve d_0, the seller chooses a value of output $\bar{q}_0$, as indicated by the intersection of the marginal revenue curve MR_0 and the marginal cost curve MC. But if price is thus set at P_0, actual sales are only q_0, or less than $\bar{q}_0$. The seller therefore revises its estimate of demand. Let us assume that the firm now regards d_1 rather than d_0 as the relevant demand curve. Curve d_1 reflects the requirement that the curve that is currently relevant must contain the currently "observed" sales-price point (q_0, P_0). Equilibrium output is then changed from $\bar{q}_0$ to q_1, and the price is revised downward from P_0 to P_1. Again, however, sales are less than output $(q_1 < \bar{q}_1)$, so there is still another expected firm d curve. This process continues until the seller arrives at an estimate of demand represented by the curve d_2 in Figure 11–2. This curve represents an equilibrium value of output; price is P_2, and output q_2 is consistent with actual sales.

FIGURE 11–2
FINAL SHORT-RUN ADJUSTMENT OF PRICE AND OUTPUT

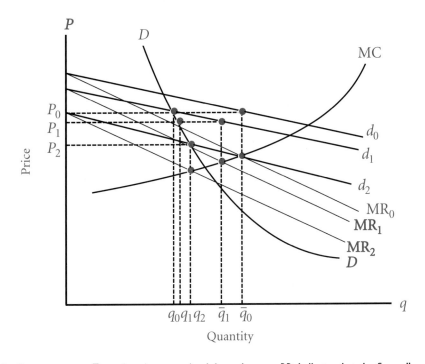

At P_0, the firm expects to sell q_0, but the proportional-demand curve, *DD*, indicates that the firm sells only $\bar{q}_0$. Industry demand is less than expected by the firm. The monopolistic competitor adjusts expectations until equilibrium is established at P_2 and q_2, and the anticipated demand is equal to actual demand on *DD* when the firm sets MR_2 equal to MC.

Although this adjustment process is based on very special assumptions, the general character of the process can be shown to be much the same under less restrictive conditions. Of course, the precise nature of the process depends on the factors assumed to govern each seller's output and price behavior. The simplified analysis presented here contains, however, an important element of truth about the way competing sellers adapt to sales experience in almost any imperfectly competitive market. Of particular interest is the conclusion that the seller's expected-demand curve shifts over time as long as the perceived optimal output at the current price differs from actual sales at the same price. *This elementary consistency condition is an essential requirement for any empirically meaningful model of output and price determination.* The same condition is implicit in the theory of perfect competition, for in perfect competition, market equilibrium occurs if—and only if—price is such as to equate quantity demanded with quantity supplied. (See Problem 11–3.)

11–3 Suppose that the demand for restaurant services increases. The monopolistic competitor sells more than expected at the the current price. Using the proportional demand curve, trace the adjustment process to short-run equilibrium.

The figure below illustrates that the firm incorrectly anticipates its demand curve to be d_0. At the current price P_0, the firm is able to sell more than anticipated, q_1 instead of q_0. The firm adjusts its anticipated d curve until equilibrium quantity and price are q_2 and P_2, and expected sales revenue equals actual sales revenue (that is, d_2 and DD intersect at the equilibrium price).

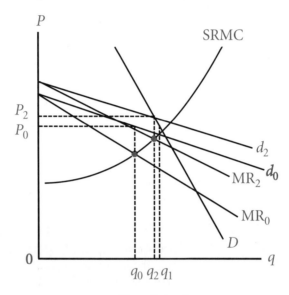

Firm Output
Adjustment to an Increase in Industry Demand

11.5 LONG-RUN PRICE AND OUTPUT ADJUSTMENTS

In monopolistic competition, as in monopoly and perfect competition, adjustment of plant size will be made by existing firms over a long-run period in an attempt to minimize long-run costs for any given level of output. At a given time, maximum profits are sought by establishing output at a level such that MR equals SRMC with the existing plant. This level of output, however, maximizes long-run profit only if the existing plant permits the short run equilibrium output to be produced at minimum cost. Plant size is adjusted over time, therefore, as long as SRMC differs from LRMC. Exactly as with monopoly, attainment of long-run equilibrium requires that MR, SRMC, and LRMC are equal.

While these conditions for long-run equilibrium are necessary, they are not the only conditions that must be met. While individual firms are adapting their plant sizes to reduce long-run costs, other firms may be considering entry into the industry. Because, as noted earlier, capital requirements are likely to be low and economies of scale rather insignificant in such industries, entry is fairly free. The main barrier to newcomers is the established reputation of existing firms. The rapid flow of firms into and out of the restaurant field provides a good illustration of this characteristic of monopolistic competition.

When new firms enter the industry, any prevailing gap between price and average cost tends to close. To build up sales volume, newcomers may find it advantageous to set prices lower than those charged by older firms. Older firms may then find it necessary to reduce prices to maintain their sales at a satisfactory level. However, price reductions brought about in this fashion will not have a significant effect on total market sales unless total demand for the product is sufficiently elastic. This is because the existing sales volume may merely be divided among more firms. Whether or not prices fall, each firm's decline in sales is likely to force operation to a point farther away from the point of lowest cost, and excess profits will therefore be eliminated in part because of the rise in average cost.

THE TANGENCY CASE IN THE LONG RUN

If entry is free enough to lead to complete elimination of economic profits, long-run equilibrium occurs when D is equal to AC for each firm at a level of output at which each firm's D curve is just tangent to its AC curve. For if the demand curve cuts the average-cost curve at any point, profits will continue to be earned. The adjustment is illustrated in Figures 11–3 and 11–4. Figure 11–3 shows the short-run equilibrium output at q and economic profits being earned. As a consequence, new firms enter, and the demand curve of each firm moves to the left until it is tangent to LRAC, as indicated in Figure 11–4. The point of tangency is, of necessity, at the same level of output as that at which MC—both short and long run—is equal to MR. The tangency point thus coincides with the point of maximum profit, with "competitive" entry or exit ensuring that the maximum equals zero. (See Problem 11–4.)

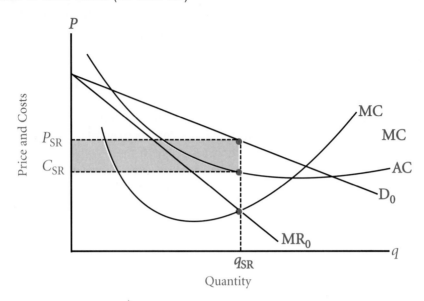

FIGURE 11–3
A SITUATION OF EXCESS PROFITS (THE SHORT RUN)

In the short run, the monopolistic competitor operates the plant that produces the level of output for which MR = MC. This firm earns positive economic profits because $P >$ AC.

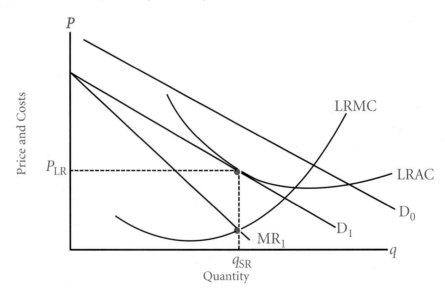

FIGURE 11–4
THE TANGENCY CASE—THE LONG RUN (ZERO PROFIT)

Excess profits attract new firms into the industry. The firm's share of the market declines, and D shifts left from D_0 to D_1. Profits are eliminated when $P =$ LRAC, that is, when LRAC is tangent to D_1.

11–4 Describe the adjustment to long-run equilibrium in monopolistic competition when firms are incurring losses.

The firm in Figure (a) incurs losses because price is less than LRAC at q_0, so some of the firms in the industry will exit. The remaining firms will experience an increase in their share of the market, and their d curves will shift right and become less elastic. The exodus will continue until price rises enough to cover average costs. Equilibrium is established at P_1 and q_1.

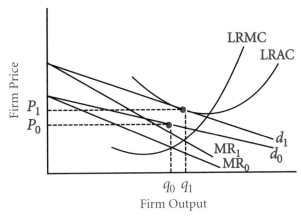

Long-Run Adjustment to Economic Losses

Because the demand curve slopes downward, its point of tangency with LRAC is not at the lowest level of average cost. When long-run adjustments are complete, firms operate at levels that do not permit them to fully realize economies of scale. The existing plant, even though optimal for the equilibrium volume of output, is not used to capacity—that is excess capacity (downward sloping SRAC curve) exists at that level of output. Any attempt to increase output to attain lowest average cost would be unprofitable because the price reduction necessary to sell the greater output would exceed the cost reduction that it makes possible. In industries of this type, there is a chronic tendency toward "too many" firms, each producing a volume of output less than that which would allow lowest cost. Note that the optimal-size plant, while underutilized, is itself smaller (with higher minimum-average cost) than would be the case in perfect competition. Thus, there may be too many grocery stores and too many service stations in the sense that if the total volume of business were concentrated in a smaller number of sellers, average cost and price would be less. (See Problem 11–5.)

11–5 A T-shirt store owner hires primarily teenagers as salespersons. Minimum average cost for the store is \$5 per T-shirt and price = \$5.50. Suppose the minimum wage of teenagers declines, and minimum average cost falls to \$3 per unit. What will be the new price?

The cost decline has two effects: It shifts cost curves down and it raises profits, which attract new firms. Demand for existing firms declines and becomes more elastic, and the new price coincides with the tangency of the new demand curve and the new LRAC curve. Price falls to a level between \$5.50 and \$3, P_1 in Figure 11–5. The exact price depends on the shapes of the new demand and cost curves.

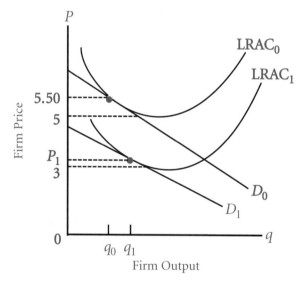

The Impact of a Decline in Average Cost

The significance of the difference between the relationship of LRMC to price in monopolistic competition and in perfect competition can easily be exaggerated. As long as preferences for various brands are not extremely strong, the demand schedules for the products of firms will be highly elastic. Accordingly, the points of tangency with the AC curves are not likely to be far above the point of lowest cost and there is only a small amount of excess capacity, as Figure 11–4 illustrates. Only if product differentiation is very strong will the difference between the long-run price level and that which would prevail under perfectly competitive conditions be significant. (See Problem 11–6 and 11–7.)

11–6 True or False? The greater the product differentiation, the less elastic the perceived demand curve.

True. Recall the discussion of elastic demand curves in Chapter 2, where it was claimed that an elastic demand curve implied may close substitutes. Greater differentiation means more monopoly power, which in turn means fewer substitutes, hence a less-elastic demand curve with more-strongly differentiated products. This also implies that the point of tangency of our demand curve and average-cost curve will be further to the left than otherwise at a lower level of output, as seen in the figure below. This difference between the minimum point of the average cost curve and the tangency point is called excess capacity. Excess capacity is the price we pay for product differentiation. Have you ever thought about the many restaurants, movie theaters, and gasoline stations that have "excess capacity?" Can you imagine a world where all firms were working at full capacity? After all, choice is a good, and most of us value some choices dearly. Excess capacity, therefore, is the price we pay for differentiated goods, and many of us are willing to pay this price. How do you feel about the choice between low-priced homogenous (similar) goods versus higher-priced but differentiated goods? That is what would you think about everyone wearing the same drab shirts or driving the same car?

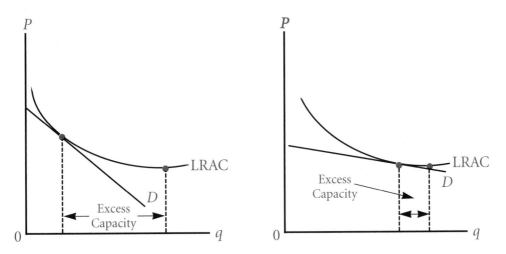

11–7 Compare the market characteristics and long-run equilibrium conditions of monopolistic competition with perfect competition and monopoly.

Both perfect and monopolistic competition have many independent sellers and free entry. Product differentiation, however, allows the monopolistic competitor some discretion over price. Thus, the monopolistic competitor, like the monopolist, faces a downward-sloping demand curve, although the demand curve is much more elastic in monopolistic competition.

In long-run equilibrium, zero profits are earned in perfect and in monopolistic competition. In all three market structures, LRAC = SRMC = MR. In perfect competition, P = LRMC = minimum LRAC. In contrast, P > minimum LRAC in monopoly and monopolistic competition, and there is a social-welfare loss because P exceeds LRMC, although inefficiency is potentially more severe in monopoly.

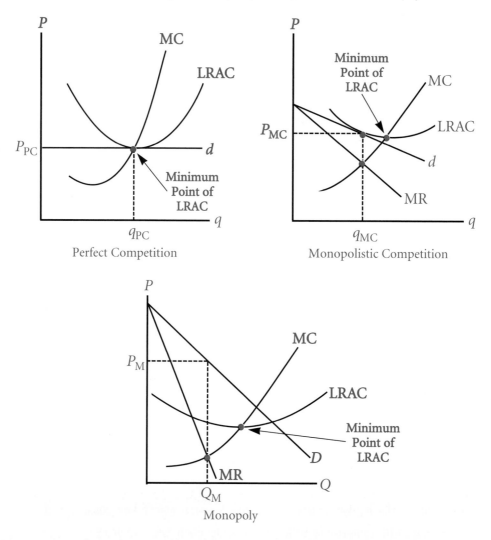

Perfect Competition

Monopolistic Competition

Monopoly

EXCESSIVE ENTRY OF NEW FIRMS

In industries in which relatively low capital requirements make entry of new firms comparatively easy, it is possible that so many firms may enter the industry that few sellers, if any, can earn even normal profits. The extremely high rate of mortality among firms in some lines of retailing, especially in the first two years of operation, suggests a chronic tendency toward excessive entry of newcomers. In part, excessive entry may result when economic profits have been earned temporarily. Because of the time required for operation to get under way, too many firms may start operations, just as farmers may plant too many apple trees when apple prices are high relative to costs. Even when only normal profits are being earned, there may be a tendency for new firms to start, either because newcomers optimistically believe they can operate more profitably than existing firms or because they lack adequate knowledge of profit possibilities but are anxious to develop their own businesses. (See Problem 11–8.)

11–8 True or False? Many restaurants fail every year despite their attempts to equate marginal revenue and marginal costs.

True. Remember that marginal revenue and marginal costs are based on expectations of the future. Because information is imperfect and costly to obtain, people can and do make mistakes. Nobody opens up a new restaurant expecting to go out of business. The owner attempts to equate expected marginal revenue and expected marginal costs, but those expectations might not be realized.

RESTRICTIONS ON COMPLETELY FREE ENTRY

Complete adjustment toward equality of price and average cost may be checked by the strong reputations of some established firms. Firms that are particularly successful in their selling efforts may create such strong consumer preferences that newcomers— even though they are able to enter the industry freely and cover their own costs—cannot take enough business away from them to eliminate their economic profits. Thus, a restaurant that has been particularly successful in promoting customer goodwill may continue to earn economic profits long after the entry of new restaurants has brought about equality of price and average cost for others, or even losses. Adjustments toward a final equilibrium involving equality of price and average cost thus do not proceed with the certainty characterizing perfect competition.

INDUSTRY (OR PRODUCT-GROUP) COST CONDITIONS

An industry's cost conditions have the same general significance for monopolistic competition product groups as they do in perfect competition. A product group is a collection of producers of similar (but differentiated) goods (for example, retail apparel or gasoline). If these producers were homogeneous, they would be considered an industry in perfect competition. In an increasing- or decreasing-cost industry, the height of the cost schedule of each firm is affected by changes in the total output of the entire industry. The actual average cost to which price is equal when long-run adjustments have been completed in a situation of free entry will depend on the volume of output for the industry or product group. Thus, in part, it depends on the total demand for the product. A single precise set of product-group-cost curves that would have empirical significance cannot be drawn, however, because firms do not operate at levels of lowest average cost, and because costs at actual points of operation are not uniform among firms. Likewise, products of different firms are not homogeneous.

11.6 *ADVERTISING AND MONOPOLISTIC COMPETITION*

Differentiation is a key characteristic of monopolistic competition. Thus, advertising plays a major role, because consumers must be aware of differentiation for it to matter. Differentiation is created by adjusting the product, including branding and packaging, and reputation is largely created by advertising. Increased advertising not only increases demand for the firm's product, it also makes demand less elastic by attaching customers more closely to particular brands. Also, advertising is likely to be much more significant than it is for a monopolist, because of the possibility of taking business away from competing firms.

The effect of advertising on prices in monopolistic competition is complex, and generalizations are not as obvious as they might appear to be. Expenditures on advertising are costs, which must be covered by revenues if a normal rate of profit is to be earned. To business firms, advertising costs are not significantly different from production costs. Successful advertising campaigns, however, also alter demand schedules. The combined effect of higher cost and higher demand is almost certainly higher prices. There are possible exceptions, however, such as in the toy and eyeglass industries and the legal profession, where advertising has led to reduced prices. This can happen because advertising may allow monopolistically competitive firms to increase sales so that sellers can operate closer to the point of minimum cost. Therefore, it is possible that the decline in production cost (through economies of scale) exceeds the advertising cost per unit of output, allowing the firm to sell its product at a lower price (see Figure 11–5). Unless total demand for the product is significantly affected by advertising, other firms may be forced out of business, and sales may be concentrated in the hands of a smaller number of firms. It should be noted, however, that the new price is lower only compared with the price under monopolistic competition without advertising. The price cannot be lower than would prevail with perfect competition, for in a competitive market there is no advertising, because products are assumed to be homogeneous.

Firms in monopolistic competition are not likely to experience substantial cost reductions as output increases. They cannot, therefore, generally offset advertising costs with lower production costs, particularly if advertising costs are high. The chances of significant reduction in per-unit cost are much greater in oligopoly, as discussed in Chapter 12. (See Problem 11–9.)

FIGURE 11–5
THE EFFECTS OF ADVERTISING

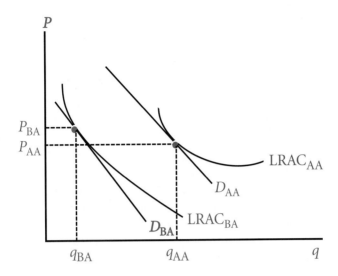

The LRAC before advertising is $LRAC_{BA}$. After Advertising, the curve shifts to $LRAC_{AA}$. If the demand increase from advertising is significant, economies of scale from higher output levels may offset the advertising costs, allowing the firm to sell its product at a lower price.

11–9 A monopolistic competitor believes advertising is very important. Why is it particularly important to advertise in this type of market structure?

For a clothing shop to compete with many other clothing shops, it must advertise to demonstrate that its clothing or store is somehow different. Remember: monopolistically competitive firms differ from competitive firms because of their ability, to some extent, to set prices and to alter other traits of the product (color; design; packaging; service before, during, or after the sale; and so on). Advertising is therefore important, because it informs consumers of the differences (real or artificial) between one firm's product and those of its rivals.

11.7 THE SIGNIFICANCE OF MONOPOLISTIC COMPETITION

The three primary assumptions on which the analysis of monopolistic competition is based—(1) large numbers of sellers and absence of recognized mutual interdependence, (2) differentiated products, and (3) relatively free entry of firms—are most likely to be approximated in industries in which specialized capital equipment is of relatively minor importance in production. In these fields, comparatively little money capital is required to commence production, and economies of scale in production are of limited importance, because they are largely attained at relatively low levels of output. Various lines of retailing and small handicraft production and repair are therefore the types of activity most likely to operate under conditions of monopolistic competition.

However, the study of these fields raises some doubt about the applicability of the assumptions. Despite the large numbers of retailers, each particular market area rarely has a substantial number, and feelings of mutual interdependence do not appear to be entirely absent, for firms recognize that their policies have some effect upon the policies of competing retailers.

Some economists regard the assumption of free entry as incompatible with the assumption of product differentiation. They argue that when consumers have preferences for the products of particular firms, the flow of new firms into a field is inevitably restricted. Thus, the principle that price tends to equal average cost, with the demand curve tangent to the AC curve at a point to the left of lowest average cost, is not valid. They also argue that the concept of an industry is ambiguous when products are differentiated and that the empirical implications of an equilibrium analysis of such an "industry" are correspondingly vague.

Finally, it can be argued that monopolistic competition can exist only when the initial decline in average cost is of limited magnitude. Thus, the principle that firms do not operate at the point of lowest average cost, once long-run adjustments have been completed, is of little significance, because the difference between price and lowest average cost is slight.

Accordingly, even though the demand curves of these firms are not perfectly elastic, the model of perfect competition describes these firms adequately for many purposes, and we do not need a separate model.

It must be admitted that these criticisms have some merit. Few markets are completely free of oligopolistic influence, and established reputations undoubtedly are a frequent obstacle to complete elimination of economic profits. However, monopolistic competition is valuable as a limiting case in which interdependence is relatively weak and entry of new firms is relatively easy. Moreover, the fact that some criticisms of existing monopolistic competition analysis are valid does not mean that we should condemn all conceivable models of this type. Here, as in most other areas of economic analysis, further research is in order.

SUMMARY

1. A monopolistically competitive market is characterized by a large number of independent sellers, relatively low barriers to entry, and differentiated products (perceived or actual).

2. Product differentiation stems from many different sources: location, physical differences, perceived differences through heavy advertising and service, and so forth.

3. Individual sellers in a monopolistically competitive industry view demand for their product as relatively elastic. That is, small price changes are expected to have more than proportional effects on quantity sold.

4. Relatively free entry into monopolistically competitive markets has a tendency to eliminate excess profits in the long run.

5. In the market period, a decrease in demand causes sales to lag behind output and prices to fall. If an increase in demand causes sales to exceed output, the seller will most likely ration output to regular customers at the prevailing price.

6. In the short run, the seller's demand curve depends on the average level of prices in the industry. Estimates of industry price can be derived from either recent price experiences or some traditional method of markup above average variable costs.

7. In the long run, maximum profits are reached when the level of output is such that MR = SRMC = LRMC. But this is not the only condition that must be met. With the threat of new entrants, older firms may find it necessary to reduce prices to maintain a certain level of sales, and economic profits may be maximized at zero.

8. Because of the downward slope of the demand curve in the monopolistic competitive model, its point of tangency with LRAC is not at the lowest level of average costs.

9. Low barriers to entry make it possible many firms to enter the industry, making it difficult for many firms to earn abnormal profits.

10. Firms with strong reputations and customer loyalty may earn economic profits despite new entrants.

11. Advertising may increase demand and also make demand more inelastic by creating strong preferences.

WORDS AND CONCEPTS FOR REVIEW

monopolistic competition

tangency case

excessive entry of newcomers

product differentiation

excess capacity

restrictions to free entry

QUESTIONS

1. What are the assumptions on which the model of monopolistic competition is based?

2. In what sense is monopolistic competition a hybrid of monopoly and perfect competition?

3. Suppose that you are considering the purchase of each of the following items. The prices charged by various sellers are the same. What considerations would influence your choice of the particular seller or brand?
   a. a new car—make of car
   b. shoes—make of shoe
   c. gasoline in your home area—dealer and brand
   d. gasoline while on a trip—dealer and brand
   e. a motel while on a trip
   f. a restaurant in your home area
   g. an airline for a trip to Europe
   h. a classical record

4. Contrast the characteristics of a firm's demand curve in monopolistic competition with those in (a) monopoly and (b) perfect competition.

5. In a market period in which the seller in monopolistic competition cannot adjust rate of purchases or output, will the seller be more willing to reduce prices if sales lag behind current output or to raise prices if sales outrun current output? Explain.

6. In setting price in a short-run period, how would a firm estimate the "industry" price?

7. Why are fixed costs not likely to be a significant portion of total cost in monopolistic competition?

8. Explain the tangency of D and AC in monopolistic competition.

9. Why can firms in monopolistic competition be operating at the point of lowest long-run average cost, if all excess profits have been eliminated? Illustrate with a graph.

10. What leads to excessive entry of new firms in some monopolistically competitive markets?

11. Why do some firms in monopolistic competition continue to earn economic profits for long periods, even though new firms may easily start up?

12. Explain the effect of advertising on prices in monopolistic competition.

SUGGESTED READING

Chamberlin, Edward H. *The Theory of Monopolistic Competition*, 8th ed. Cambridge, Mass.: Harvard University Press, 1962.

Robinson, Joan. T*he Economics of Imperfect Competition*, London: Macmillan, 1933.

Scherer, Frederick, and David Ross. I*ndustrial Market Structure and Economic Performance*, 3rd ed., Boston: Houghton Mifflin Company, 1990.

Stigler, George. "Monopolistic Competition in Retrospect." *Five Lectures on Economic Problems*. New York: Macmillan, 1950.

Chapter Twelve

OLIGOPOLY

Questions to Think About
---

1. What is mutual interdependence? How does it generate uncertainty in oligopoly?

2. What is differentiated oligopoly?

3. What is collusion? What is spontaneous coordination and how does it occur?

4. What is the difference between complete and partial oligopoly?

5. Why does a complete oligopoly achieve the same equilibrium position as a monopolist?

6. Why is the kinked demand curve kinked?

7. Why are cartels unstable?

8. How do you find equilibrium price and output in price leadership models?

9. What is average cost pricing?

10. What is game theory? Noncooperative games? Dominant strategy? Nash equilibrium?

11. How do firms deter entry?

12.1 INTRODUCTION

*L*ike monopolistic competition, oligopoly is a market structure that lies somewhere between perfect competition and monopoly. Yet oligopoly differs from monopolistic competition in several important ways. Oligopoly involves only a few firms, while monopolistic competition involves many. Whereas product differentiation is critical to monopolistic competition, it may or may not be important to oligopolists, some of whom sell standardized products such as steel. Whereas in monopolistic competition, the behavior of one firm usually has little impact on the behavior of other firms in the industry, in oligopoly, each firm's behavior can affect the behavior of other firms. Only in one vital respect are oligopoly and monopolistic competition similar: Firms in both market structures are price searchers who have some control over product prices.

Another feature of oligopoly is mutual interdependence among firms. Each seller shapes its policies with an eye to the policies of other firms. Oligopoly is likely to occur whenever the number of firms in an industry is so small that any change in output or price by one firm materially affects the sales of competing firms. Almost inevitably, a firm with rivals that react directly takes these reactions into consideration when determining policy.

What is responsible for the prevalence of oligopoly? Primarily it results from the relationship between technological conditions of production and potential sales volumes. For many products, such as automobiles and steel, a firm cannot attain a reasonably low cost of production of many products unless it produces a large volume of output. The result of such economies of scale may be that only a few efficient scale companies can supply the entire market demand.

12.2 CLASSIFICATION OF OLIGOPOLY: PURE VERSUS DIFFERENTIATED OLIGOPOLY

An oligopoly can be classed into one of two groups, depending on whether the product is differentiated. In pure oligopoly, the products of various firms are identical. This model is approximated in some capital goods industries, such as cement production. Mutual interdependence is greater when products are identical than when they are differentiated, because any price change by one firm produces substantial changes in its competitors' sales, causing them to alter their policies.

In contrast, in differentiated oligopoly, products are not identical, so price changes may have less direct effect on competitors. Each firm can, in effect, isolate its market. The stronger the differentiation, the weaker the mutual interdependence. Differentiated oligopoly makes up a very large portion of the total economy, including most manufactured consumer goods and retailing in most areas. The degree of differentiation and the strength of mutual interdependence, therefore, vary widely among industries. This makes it difficult to develop general models for price and output analysis in oligopoly. (See Problem 12–1.)

12–1 Imagine you have a friend who is a cosmetic surgeon; one of many in the country. She specializes in face-lifts. Recently, she developed a procedure for her patients that is less painful, results in less scarring, and has a faster recovery time. Price changes by other cosmetic surgeons will have a major impact on the price your friend charges for facial surgery.

False. Because the products are not identical, there is less likelihood that other cosmetic surgeons will have a major impact on your friend's prices. If all surgeons were producing identical face-lift operations, then perhaps the rivals' actions would have to be more closely watched.

COLLUSION VERSUS SPONTANEOUS COORDINATION

Oligopolies can also be classified on the basis of whether mutual interdependence results in outright collusion or merely in spontaneous coordination of the firms' policies through each firm's recognition of the effects of its actions on its competitors.

Collusion involves direct negotiation and agreement among competitors, and increases the stability of oligopoly. It decreases the direct rivalry in the market; without it, firms might base their actions on mistaken estimates of their competitors' behavior.

Collusive agreements may cover various matters. Some may extend to price only, others to both price and output. Sometimes, oligopolists merely agree on the method of price determination, such as the rule of following prices set by one firm, which economists call price leadership.

Frequently, however, oligopoly involves spontaneous coordination rather than outright agreement, particularly because the latter is illegal in the United States and many other countries. Each firm simply takes into consideration its competitors' expected responses to its own actions, and determines its policies accordingly. With each firm following similar practices, price and output figures may eventually adjust to figures that are acceptable to all firms. With spontaneous coordination, various firms may independently adopt pricing practices comparable to those agreed on in collusion, they may accept one firm as a price leader, or they may adopt methods of price setting, such as the markup system common in retailing. These pricing practices are discussed later in the chapter.

Oligopoly is complete oligopoly if interdependence among firms is so strong that the profits of the firms as a group are maximized. Otherwise, it is called partial oligopoly. As explained later, complete oligopoly is in all likelihood rare, and varying degrees of partial oligopoly are more typical. Analysis of complete oligopoly is important, however, because it represents the firms' ultimate ideal—maximum profits.

The wide variety of possible situations in oligopoly makes analysis of price and output determination difficult. A broad theory, with assumptions so general that they cover all possible oligopoly situations, offers little specific guidance in analyzing particular situations, while developing separate theories based on all possible assumptions is an impossible task. At present, it is possible to consider only those cases that appear to be of primary importance.

Because of the complexities and diversity of oligopoly, it is necessary to divide the analysis of price and output determination in such markets into several sections. As a convenient starting point, we shall deal first with complete oligopoly; then we shall examine partial oligopoly.

12.3 COMPLETE OLIGOPOLY

Complete oligopoly exists when relationships among the firms are close enough to permit them to maximize their joint profits. This condition may result from spontaneous coordination of the firm's policies or, more likely, from outright cooperation among their officials. This model does not differ fundamentally from that of monopoly, except that there is more than one firm and their costs are likely to be different.

Maximizing joint profit requires firms to determine price much as would a single monopolist, based on the total (or market) demand schedule for the product and the horizontal sum of the marginal cost schedules of the various firms, as shown in Figure 12–1. With outright agreements—necessarily secret because of antitrust laws—firms that make up the market will attempt to estimate demand-and-cost schedules and set optimal price and output levels accordingly. If one firm sets prices and all others follow, the price setter acts on the basis of total schedules rather than its own, and other firms abide by the decision. Without collusion, oligopolists can obtain maximum joint profits only if each firm, acting independently, correctly estimates and sets the price that is optimal from the standpoint of the group.

FIGURE 12–1
SHORT-RUN ADJUSTMENT AND OUTPUT FOR COMPLETE OLIGOPOLY

A complete oligopoly maximizes joint profits by equating marginal revenue for the market and the sum of the marginal cost schedules for all firms. The optimum price, P_0, is determined at the profit-maximizing output level Q_0, along the market-demand curve. A complete oligopoly achieves the monopoly price, quantity, and profits.

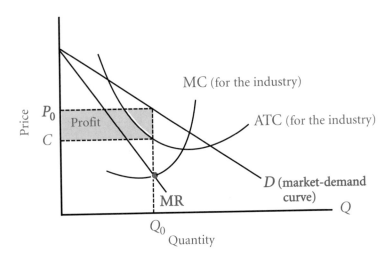

The way firms in the industry share total profits depends in part on relative costs and sales of the various firms. Firms with low costs and large sales obtain the largest profits. Sales, in turn, depends in large measure on consumer preferences for various brands if the oligopoly is differentiated. With collusion, firms may agree on market shares and the division of profits. The division of total profits will depend on each firm's relative bargaining strength, which is influenced by its relative financial strength, its ability to inflict damage (through price wars) on other firms if an agreement is not reached, its ability to withstand similar actions from other firms, relative costs, consumer preferences, and bargaining skills.

OBSTACLES TO JOINT-PROFIT MAXIMIZATION

Many obstacles prevent firms from maximizing joint profit through complete oligopoly. The major one is the unwillingness of firms to surrender all freedom of action, combined with the desire of each to increase its own share of total sales and profits. This unwillingness shows up in a variety of ways.

First, the maximum joint-profit price is optimal (that is, at the best position) for each firm as well as for the firms as a group only if marginal cost-and-demand schedules; and therefore, marginal revenue, are the same for all the firms. If this is not the case (and it is unlikely), firms that would be worse off at the joint-profit maximum must be compensated by other firms or frightened into compliance by threats of punitive action, or they will not accept the optimal price and output levels P_0 and Q_0 in Figure 12–1. In some instances it would be necessary to close down high-cost firms to attain the highest joint profit, but these firms may resist such a policy. In the absence of adequate compensation, the best that can be obtained is a compromise: a level of profits tolerable to all the firms, but not the joint-profit maximum.

Second, not only is it difficult to determine the exact form of the demand curve, different firms will also have different opinions about it, making compromises inevitable.

Third, profit maximization may be checked by one firm's strategic moves designed to force other firms to take certain actions or to discourage them from carrying out policies detrimental to the interests of the given firm. Thus, a firm may take action to drive rivals out of business completely or to test their strength and bargaining power.

Fourth, attaining maximum group profits may be hampered when firms are unable to agree on product changes, advertising policies, and new techniques. Typically, it appears that agreements relate only to price. Firms are highly conscious that price changes lead to changes by competitors, so agreements on prices appear highly desirable. Agreement on nonprice elements, however, is particularly difficult. Each firm may be confident that it will be able to outdo other firms in selling activities and therefore will be unwilling to reach an agreement about them. Firms often believe, too, that they will be able to do better than competitors with new methods, products, and advertising. With spontaneous coordination (basing decisions on expected responses of rival firms), firms are likely to be much more conscious of competitors' reactions to price changes than to changes in other variables that affect profits.

A fifth deterrent to the setting of maximum-profit prices is the fear that such prices will stimulate the growth of new firms. Although most oligopolistic industries (such as steel, automobiles, and airlines) have significant barriers to entry by new firms, newcomers may nevertheless seek to enter. High prices and economic profits not only provide great incentive, they make such entry easier. High prices ease the problem of covering heavy initial costs of operations, and good profit prospects make it easier to raise necessary funds from investors. As a consequence, existing firms may deliberately hold prices below the short-run maximum-profit level, preferring instead a "reasonable" profit that will continue longer because it does not encourage prospective entrants.

Finally, difficulties in coordinating actions discourage firms from changing prices frequently in response to changing conditions. Continuous maximization of joint profits is clearly out of the question, however, if firms do not alter prices from time to time. (See Problems 12–2 and 12–3.)

12–2 True or False? Joint-profit maximization is more likely in a growing industry than in a declining industry.

True. If firms are close to full capacity (which is more likely in a growing industry than a declining industry), that is, using their employees and plants intensively enough so that average costs are as low as possible, they are less tempted to lower prices secretly or offer special discounts to certain customers. In contrast, when there is much excess capacity, as is usual in a declining industry, average costs can be lowered by increasing production. Firms are therefore more strongly tempted to cheat on the agreement.

12–3 What are the equilibrium price and quantity of a complete oligopoly? Why do you think collusion is illegal in the United States?

Equilibrium price and quantity for a complete oligopoly, like that of a monopoly, are determined according to the intersection of the MR curve for the market and the horizontal sum of the SRMC curves for the oligopolists. The figure below shows the equilibrium price, P, and quantity Q.

Collusion facilitates joint-profit maximization for the oligopoly. Like monopoly, if the complete oligopoly is maintained in the long run, it charges a higher price, produces less output at a higher per unit cost, and fails to maximize social welfare, relative to perfect competition.

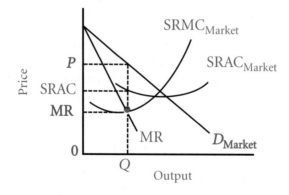

A Complete Oligopoly

12.4 PARTIAL OLIGOPOLY

While complete oligopoly may be the ultimate goal of a group of firms, it is not typically achieved. Partial oligopoly, in which joint profits are not maximized, is far more common. Spontaneous coordination is probably more common than collusion in partial oligopoly. Firms set their own prices on the basis of estimates of demand schedules while taking into consideration possible reactions on the part of their competitors and their own cost schedules. The critical difference between the price setting of oligopolists and that of other firms is the attention oligopolists give to possible reactions by competitors. If competitors tend to follow price changes, fewer customers will shift among firms, and each oligopolist's demand elasticity will be controlled primarily by the elasticity of total demand for the product. As oligopoly develops in an industry, prices may be expected to rise as the demand schedules of firms become less elastic. As in other competitive situations, a firm's maximum profit is determined by the level of operation at which marginal cost equals marginal revenue. The problem for oligopolists is that marginal revenue depends on the price reaction of others when any one firm changes price.

The mutual interdependence that characterizes oligopoly creates great uncertainty. Even if a firm suspects that competitors will react to changes in its price, it cannot know the extent of these reactions. A small price reduction may cause a large increase in sales if competitors do not reduce their prices, but only a slight increase if competitors meet the cut, or even a reduction in sales if competitors exceed the cut. Under such circumstances, the firm is in a sense confronted not by one demand curve, but by an infinity of potential curves, and the appropriate one in a particular instance depends on the exact (but unknown) reactions of competitors. However, the firm must act; it must set some price and accept one of the potential demand curves. However, the uncertainty is itself a major influence on the firm's policy, encouraging it to develop pricing and marketing techniques that minimize the danger of following policies based upon mistaken estimates of competitors' reactions. Uncertainty also encourages firms to minimize the frequency of price changes because of possible dangers (such as price wars) arising from changes in the status quo.

What means does a firm have to find out what its relevant demand schedule is? One possibility is to study actual sales data over a period during which different prices have been charged. Such a study must be made with great care, because other determinants of sales—consumer incomes and preferences, price of substitutes, weather conditions, and so forth—are constantly changing. Isolation of the effects of price changes from the effects of other changes is difficult, but careful analysis may yield useful information. Study of sales volumes of competitors charging different prices (when information is obtainable) and analysis of the nature of the market in order to estimate elasticity of total demand may also help. Many large firms devote considerable effort to market research, either by their own personnel or by independent firms specializing in this work. Market research today, however, is devoted primarily to such problems as estimating sales potential in geographical areas, determining new uses and outlets for a product, discovering consumer reaction to quality changes, checking on the effectiveness of advertising and other selling campaigns, and estimating the probable response of a firm's sales to changes in national income. Little attention has been given specifically to price/sales relationships primarily because of the great difficulties involved. The information obtained and techniques employed in present market research are, however, valuable in providing further information about price/sales relationships.

Another approach to determining the demand schedule is experimentation with price changes. Firms must use this procedure with great care, however. Other determinants of sales may change during the period. Far more serious is the danger that if the change proves unprofitable, the firm may be unable to recover its original sales volume if it returns to the old prices. Competitors may meet or even exceed reductions and may not follow the change back to the earlier level. Consumers might resist returning to the old figure; they may consider the low price appropriate and may shift to other brands or products should the firm attempt to raise it again. Experimental price increases are less dangerous than decreases, because they are less likely to produce defensive reactions on the part of competitors; they may, however, drive customers permanently into the arms of competing firms. A final difficulty with price experimentation is that the entire effect of the change does not occur instantaneously. When prices are raised, buyers may not shift away immediately, but many may do so over a longer period. Alternatively, reductions may cause only temporary sales increases from buyers stocking up in anticipation of the return of prices to the original level. Because of these problems, most firms consider experimentation with price changes hazardous. Seldom do they deliberately experiment; rather, they will make changes only when they are reasonably certain that the new prices will be more profitable than the old. (See Problem 12–4.)

12–4   Imagine you are an executive working for Ford Motor Company. You think it might be appropriate to cut prices on your autos across the board. How do you know whether you should or not?

You don't! If you cut 5 percent and General Motors reacts by cutting 10 percent, then you might actually sell fewer cars at lower prices. Thus, with so much uncertainty about rival behavior, there is a strong incentive to collude.

12.5 THE CASE OF THE KINKED DEMAND CURVE

It has been suggested—more on the basis of common-sense observations than on careful empirical study—that oligopoly demand curves frequently exhibit a sharp bend, or kink, at the level of the existing price. This kinked demand curve, illustrated in Figure 12–2, is produced by the greater tendency of competitors to follow price reductions than price increases. A price reduction takes business away from other firms and forces them to cut prices to protect their sales; an increase does not, however, necessitate them to react because they gain customers if rivals increase their price. At the point of the kink, the MR curve is discontinuous; thus, in a sense, marginal revenue is not defined. At higher and lower levels of output, however, the figure is defined, being equal to or greater than r'' for lower output levels and equal to or less than r' at higher levels of output. (See Figure 12–2.)

FIGURE 12–2
PRICE AND OUTPUT ADJUSTMENT: KINKED DEMAND CURVE

Assuming rivals do not follow price increases, a firm will lose customers by raising price and the demand curve will be relatively elastic above the prevailing price. If rivals follow price cuts, a firm cannot capture many of its rivals' clients by lowering price, so the demand curve tends to be relatively inelastic below the current price. The resulting kink at the prevailing price yields a gap in the marginal-revenue curve. Equilibrium price and quantity, P_0 and q_0, correspond to the equality of short-run marginal cost and marginal revenue within the discontinuity of the marginal-revenue curve, r'' to r'

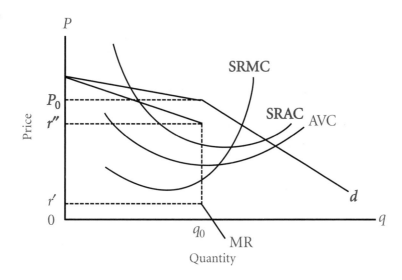

The point of maximum profit for the firm is almost of necessity at the output level at which the sharp change in elasticity occurs (q_0 in Figure 12–2). It is likely that marginal cost will not equal marginal revenue at a lower volume of output because the MR curve is so high (and nearly horizontal) in this output range. At output levels to the right of the kink, the MR curve drops—perhaps to a negative figure—and almost certainly lies below the MC curve. The optimal price (P_0 in Figure 12-2) is indicated by the point at which the firm's demand curve changes slope. It is obvious to the firm that any other price would be unprofitable, given the assumptions about rival behavior, because increases would cause great losses in revenues (as many other firms fail to follow the price increase), while reductions would yield little additional business (because most of the other firms are presumed to follow price cuts). The more standardized the product, the sharper the kink, because customers shift more readily and competitors, therefore, react more quickly and precisely.

One important consequence of the kink in the demand curve is that the firm may be slow to adjust price in response to cost changes. Because of the discontinuity in the MR curve, the MC curve can move up or down over a substantial range without affecting the optimum level of output or price.

While the kinked demand curve may be useful for explaining sellers' reactions to various changes, the analysis of the case in itself contributes little to the explanation of existing price and output levels, because it does not explain why the kink came to be where it is. Without any general principle to explain this level, appeal must be made to historical price trends and to particular techniques used by the firms in setting prices, as noted in later sections. (See Problems 12–5 and 12–6.)

12–5 Why does the kinked demand curve have a kink? Illustrate graphically the equilibrium price and output level for an oligopolist according to the kinked demand curve.

The kinked demand model assumes that rivals follow a firm's price cuts but do not follow price increases. If a firm raises price above the current level, it loses customers to lower price competing firms, and demand is relatively elastic. Below the prevailing price, demand is fairly inelastic because any price reduction will be matched by rivals, Therefore, a kink exists at the current price. The figure below depicts equilibrium according to the kinked-demand-curve model at P and q.

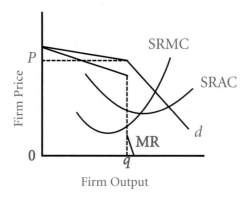

12–6 How does a cost decrease affect price and quantity, according to the kinked-demand-curve model?

When costs fall, $SRMC_0$ shifts to $SRMC_1$ and $SRAC_0$ to $SRAC_1$. Price and quantity do not change in this example, because SRMC did not fall below the discontinuity in MR.

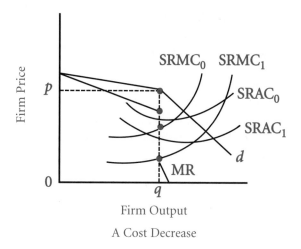

A Cost Decrease

12.6 COMPLETE OLIGOPOLY REVISITED: COLLUSION

The potential for disastrous pricing decisions is substantial in partial oligopoly, because a firm may misjudge the behavior of rivals. This uncertainty has led some economists to suspect that oligopolists change their prices less frequently than perfect competitors, as implied in the kinked-demand-curve analysis. It is unclear from examination of the data, however, whether prices are in fact significantly less variable in oligopoly.

The temptation is, however, great for firms to reduce price uncertainty through collusion. Their goal would be to behave as a complete oligopoly, because collusion reduces uncertainty and increases the potential for monopoly profits. However, collusive oligopoly, like monopoly, leads to an inefficient allocation of resources (goods having benefits greater than costs are not produced) and to inequitable wealth transfers from consumers of the good in question to the owners of oligopoly firms.

A complete oligopoly acts as the equivalent of one firm from the standpoint of pricing and output decisions. The economic effect is therefore exactly the same as a multiplant monopolist's: a single demand curve for the group of firms jointly determines the profit-maximizing price and output (the latter allocated in principle according to marginal costs). Disagreements about allocating the output, however, are at the heart of the instability of complete oligopolies.

Complete oligopoly agreements on sale, pricing, and other decisions are usually called cartels. We can illustrate the instability of cartel arrangements with the Organization of Petroleum Exporting Countries (OPEC).

For collusion to work, each firm must agree to some share of the restriction in overall output to maintain the profit-maximizing price. However, at the profit-maximizing price, the temptation for each of the firms to cheat on the agreement of the complete oligopoly is great. Because collusive agreements are illegal in the United States and in some other countries, the other parties are extremely limited in their ability to punish the offender, although legal considerations do not apply to OPEC.

Organized more than a decade earlier, OPEC began acting as a collusive oligopoly in 1973, in part because of political concern over American support for Israel. For two decades prior to 1973, the price of crude oil had hovered around $2 a barrel in nominal terms, falling substantially in real terms during that period. In 1973, OPEC members agreed to quadruple of oil prices in nine months; later price increases pushed the cost of a barrel of oil to more than $20. Prices then stabilized, actually falling in real terms between 1973 and 1978, as the profit-maximizing price was sought and politics remained relatively calm. By the early 1980s, however, prices were approaching $40 per barrel—success from OPEC's perspective, but quite difficult for consuming nations, although the wealth of Western oil companies actually rose because their oil inventories soared in value.

The OPEC nations were successful with their pricing policies between 1973 and the early 1980s for several reasons. First, the worldwide demand for petroleum was highly inelastic with respect to price in the short run, for reasons which should be fairly obvious. Second, OPEC's share of total world oil output had steadily increased from around 20 percent of total world output in the early 1940s to about 70 percent by 1973, when OPEC became an effective cartel. Third, the price elasticity of supply of petroleum from OPEC's competitors was low in the short run: Ability to increase production from existing wells is limited, and it takes time to drill new ones.

More recently, OPEC oil prices have again fluctuated in real terms because of increases in non-OPEC production and the uncertain willingness of key suppliers (such as Saudi Arabia) to restrict supply. Moreover, at the higher prices of the 1970s, long-run substitution possibilities caused oil consumption to fall almost 5 percent per year, with conservation and alternative energy easing the demand for OPEC oil. (See Problem 12–7.)

12–7 How does each firm's share of output in a cartel compare to the desired output level for the firm? Under what circumstances would a firm be more likely to cheat?

Figure (b) shows the equilibrium price and output level for the cartel, where MR = the horizontal sum of the SRMC curves for the firms. A firm's allocation is q_0 in Figure (a) and occurs where the cartel's MR = the firm's SRMC. In the firm's view, however, MR = P because each unit of output sold yields

$P to the firm. The firm's profit-maximizing level of output equals q_1, where the firm's MR = the firm's SRMC. At the cartel allocation, q_0, the firm's MR > SRMC, and the firm can raise its profits by producing more output. Thus, each firm has an incentive to cheat. It is easy to cheat: the smaller the firm is relative to the industry, the greater the number of firms in the cartel, and the higher the monitoring costs. Of course, if all firms cheat, industry output increases, price falls, and profits fall.

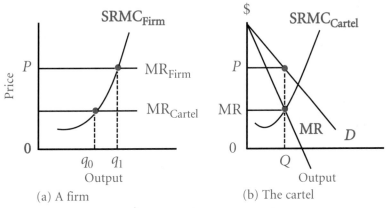

(a) A firm   (b) The cartel

A Firm's Incentive to Cheat on a Cartel Arrangement

12.7 OTHER APPROACHES TO PRICING: PRICE LEADERSHIP

Firms may lessen the significance of oligopolistic uncertainty by avoiding independent price changes, instead adopting prices or policies set by other firms. If this is so widespread in an industry that all firms follow the prices set by one firm, price leadership is said to occur.

Price leadership is most likely to develop when one firm produces a large portion of total output, the remainder being distributed over several relatively small firms. Almost inevitably, the large firm is the one to dominate pricing, leaving the small firms in a position to sell what they can at the price set by the "dominant" firm. For maximum profits, the large firm sets its price on the basis of its own cost schedule and the total demand schedule for the product, less the expected amounts to be sold by other firms. Price may approach the maximum profit figure, where MR derived from the total market demand equals MC, unless deliberately kept lower to discourage growth of smaller firms.

The easiest way to view this model is shown by the two graphs in Figure 12–3, one for the price leader and the other for the smaller firms. Here we assume that there is only one large firm (the dominant firm) and many smaller firms, all selling a homogeneous product. The dominant firm is the price leader; it sets the price at P_{DF} and, then allows the smaller firms to sell all they want at that price. The dominant firm then sells the residual demand—that is, the excess demand in Figure 12–3(a). It is therefore, the excess demand in Figure 12–3(a) that determines the position of the dominant firm's demand curve. (The distance between 1 and 2 in both graphs is equal.)

FIGURE 12–3
PRICE LEADERSHIP: DOMINANT FIRM
1. MARKET-DEMAND CURVE AND   2. DOMINANT FIRM'S
    SMALL FIRM'S SUPPLY CURVE   DEMAND AND COST CURVES

The dominant firm's demand curve in Figure (b) is market demand less the expected sales of all other firms in the industry. The corresponding marginal-revenue curve intersects the dominant firm's marginal-cost curve at the equilibrium level of output for the dominant firm, q_0. The industry price, P_{Df}, is the dominant firm's price at Q_0 on d_{Df}. The followers sell the quantity supplied on S in Figure (a) at P_{Df}, and the excess demand is supplied by the dominant firm. Note that because the followers are price takers, their supply curve is the horizontal summation of their marginal cost curves.

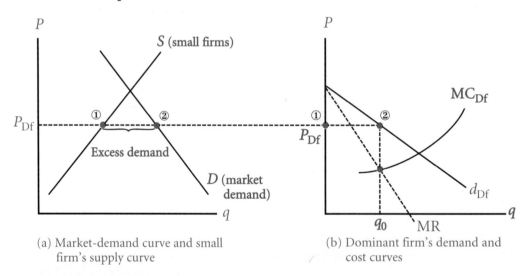

(a) Market-demand curve and small firm's supply curve

(b) Dominant firm's demand and cost curves

In other cases, price leadership might fall to the lowest-cost firm. One firm in a group of firms of more or less comparable size may play the role of price leader, not because of its dominant position in the market, but because other firms regard its actions as a suitable barometer of changing market conditions. They are thus willing to follow its policies to minimize competitive disturbances.

To visualize price leadership by the low cost firm, most simply assume that just two firms produce a homogeneous product and agree to split the market equally (see Figure 12–4). The market demand curve is D and the relevant demand curve for each firm once the market is split is d. Firm 1's cost curves are AC_1 and MC_1; Firm 2's cost curves are AC_2 and MC_2.

Figure 12–4 shows that the profit maximizing price and output for each firm considered separately would be P_1, q_1 for Firm 1 and P_2, q_2 for Firm 2. If both are selling a homogeneous product, then the higher-priced seller, Firm 2, would clearly lose customers to Firm 1. According to this model, therefore, Firm 2 will lower its price, accepting the P_1 price set by the low-cost firm. The amount sold by Firm 2 (and whether the overall market will have shortages or surpluses at P_1) depends on where MC_2 intersects P_1.

FIGURE 12–4
PRICE LEADERSHIP: LOWEST-COST FIRM

Assuming a homogeneous product, two firms in the industry, and an agreement to share the market equally between the two firms, the market demand curve, D, is twice as great as the demand curve for either firm, d. The price leader, Firm I, equates its own marginal cost and marginal revenue and sets the price along d accordingly at P_1. To maximize profits independently, Firm 2 would have changed P_2. Given that Firm I sells the same product at a lower price, however, Firm 2 would have lost all sales at that price. Firm 2 follows its lower cost rival by charging P_1, and sells the level of output for which P_1 and MC_2 are equal, because P_1 is its marginal revenue under these circumstances. Because overall market demand and supply may not be equal at P_1, there may be some "fine tuning" of this price (raising it if $D > q_1 + q_2$, lowering it if $q_D < q_1 + q_2$).

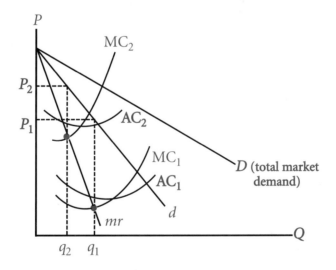

Of course, Firm 1 could lower its price enough to drive its competitor out of business (any price below AC_2 would cause Firm 2 to shut down in the long run), but it does not. Why the benevolence? One answer might be the fear of being the sole seller in the market, because a monopoly is more at risk of being prosecuted under antitrust laws and perhaps even being nationalized in some countries. (See Problems 12–8 and 12–9.)

12–8   True or false?   In an industry like the steel industry where there are dominant firms, it is likely that the firms will settle on maximizing joint profits.

False.   Joint-profit maximization is not as likely when a dominant firm is present.   The reason is that higher profits can be made by the dominant firm if it sets its output at the profit-maximizing level, while others with less-desirable cost conditions follow the lead of the price setter.   Of course, in the presence of substantial international competition, one could question whether a dominant firm exists in any one home country without international tariff or quota barriers.

12–9   How do equilibrium price and output respond to a demand increase when there is a dominant-firm price leader?   A low-cost price leader?

The figure below illustrates the initial price and quantity sold by the dominant firm, Figure (b), and by the remaining small firms, Figure (a).   An increase in the market demand to D_1 also raises the demand curve of the dominant firm to D'_{DF} and price to P_1.   Quantity sold increases from q_0 to q_1 for the small firms and from Q_0 to Q_1 for the dominant firm.

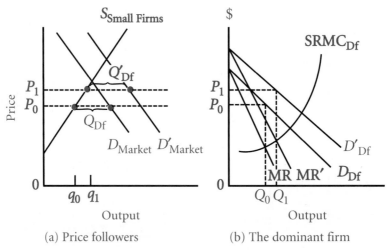

Dominant-Firm Price Leadership and a Demand Increase

The situation of low-cost price leadership is drawn in the figure below. Market demand rises and the leader's share of demand increases from d to d_1 (assuming two firms producing a homogeneous product). Price rises from P to P', quantity supplied by the leader rises from q_1 to q'_1, and the quantity supplied by the follower increases from q_2 to q'_2.

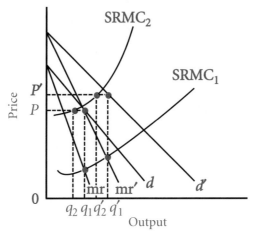

The Impact of a Demand Increase when
Prices are Led by the Low-Cost Firm

12.8 PRICE FOLLOWING OR IMITATIVE PRICING

In an industry with price leaders, the other firms inevitably are followers. Even in industries without price leaders, however, firms frequently deliberately adopt no independent pricing policy of their own, merely adapting to the prices of others. Such an imitative pricing policy avoids the necessity and cost of calculating prices, avoids any danger of upsetting competitive conditions, and allows the firm to concentrate on nonprice competition.

Price following in some instances involves the selection of a price higher or lower than the typical figure in the industry. A firm stressing high quality and prestige may, therefore, price at a percentage higher than the typical industry figure, while cut-rate firms may deliberately set prices below the competitors.

12.9 THE COST-PLUS, AVERAGE-COST, OR MARKUP APPROACH

Empirical studies suggest that the most common approach to pricing is the use of an estimate based on average cost. Average cost, in turn, is computed by adding to direct cost a markup that includes the rate of profit regarded as normal or attainable by the firm. This approach is often called the cost-plus or target-return method.

CALCULATION OF PRICE

The markup approach to pricing involves several basic steps. First, the firm estimates the direct separable cost per unit of output for which the product is responsible, primarily labor and material costs. These are usually assumed to vary proportionately with output, so that the amount per unit is the same regardless of the volume of output (that is, variable cost curves are flat). Second, when (as is typical) the firm produces more than one product, it must allocate among the various products the common costs, that is, costs incurred for the production of more than one product. Indirect labor costs—costs of labor not directly engaged in physical production—are often allocated on the basis of hours of direct labor cost per unit of various products. Finally, there is added a markup, usually expressed as a percentage, to cover a return on investment.

The rate of profit included in cost calculations depends on the attitude of firm officials about the rate the firm can attain and that appears to them to offer the best long-range profit possibilities. On the basis of experience over the years, a number of firms have set up target return figures that, on the average, they believe they can earn.

MARKUPS IN RETAIL PRICING

Some firms, particularly retailers, use customary markup figures, which they rarely recalculate. Under usual retail pricing techniques, the markup percentage, applied to the purchase of goods sold, is set high enough to cover all overhead costs in retailing—heat, lighting, rent, the wages of clerks, and the like—plus expected profit. In some fields of retailing, a uniform markup percentage is used on all items, but more typically there are variations. Items requiring refrigeration may be subject to a higher markup to cover additional separable costs for which they are responsible. Prices on other goods are adjusted to bring them to certain price lines at which the goods are traditionally sold; for example, neckties might be carried only at $15, $20, and $25. Other articles, such as electrical appliances and some lines of clothing, are typically priced at figures ending in 95 or 99 cents, in the belief that these prices have significant psychological advantages. The retailer has no control over the prices of some goods, because the manufacturer establishes the resale price. In recent years, however, as a result of the rise of discount houses and the lessened role of state legislation sanctioning minimum prices, substantial shading of manufacturers' suggested prices has become common. Finally, demand considerations may force a retailer to vary a standard markup; some staple goods, for example, have come to bear markups typically smaller than the average.

RIGID VERSUS FLEXIBLE MARKUPS

In a few industries, firms typically set prices by adding a fixed markup to average cost. More commonly, though, markups are flexible; that is, average costs serve as a point of departure in price setting, but do not finally determine the actual price. In this way, the firm considers demand as well as cost. If the calculated price is higher than prices charged by other firms, the seller must consider whether it can charge more than competitors; if not, the seller must adjust the price downward. If, on the other hand, average cost plus customary markup is less than prices other firms are charging, the firm may find it advisable to increase its price above that level because rivals may otherwise reduce their prices and all firms in the industry may be worse off. If demand appears to be inelastic, price increases may be in order. For example, retailers often apply higher-than-average markups to luxury food items, and automobile manufacturers apparently load expensive cars with a greater share of overhead than cheaper cars, whose buyers are more price conscious.

THE ADVANTAGES OF THE AVERAGE-COST APPROACH

The widespread use of the average-cost (versus marginal-cost) approach to pricing indicates that it must offer significant advantages. An obvious one is simplicity: When firms have thousands of products, some workable rule-of-thumb pricing technique is imperative. Second, as long as the method is widely employed, it leads to greater uniformity of pricing, and thus lessens the danger of price wars and breakdown of oligopolistic stability. Especially when markups are customary and uniform among firms— and materials, labor, and other direct costs are comparable—firms set similar figures.

    The average-cost approach to price setting is also furthered by a belief on the part of businesses that it is reasonable and fair. Although there are many exceptions, the notion that all goods should bear their "share" of overhead and that prices should be set at a figure that includes a fair profit is widely accepted in the business community.

AVERAGE COST PRICING AND PROFIT MAXIMIZATION

Economists disagree about the extent to which average cost pricing departs from the assumption of profit maximization. Obviously, any method of pricing involving the addition of a fixed percentage to variable costs can maximize short-run profits only by sheer accident. Nevertheless, the average-cost method, properly employed, may allow firms to come closer to maximum profit under certain circumstances than other pricing systems for several reasons.

First, as noted earlier, the average cost technique is an effective way to stabilize rivalry and lessen the price uncertainty of oligopolistic markets. Second, as long as demand elements are taken into consideration, price may not differ too greatly from the figure that it would select on the basis of marginal revenue and marginal cost. Adjustments made in average-cost estimates in setting actual prices bring demand aspects into the picture, and thus lead to a price that more closely approximates the maximum-profit level.

Third, once firms in an industry have set price on an average-cost basis, the price may actually seem to yield maximum profits, where marginal revenue equals marginal cost for any given firm, because the kink in each firm's subjective demand curve is at this level. The price at this level may not yield maximum profit for the firms as a group, and it may be substantially different from the price firms would set by estimating marginal revenue and marginal cost. Given prevailing rivalries and the inability to maximize true joint profits, however, the price arrived at by average-cost methods may represent a relative if not absolute optimum.

While the use of average-cost pricing may be broadly consistent with profit maximization in oligopolistic industries, firms that rely totally on average cost figures may sacrifice profits, particularly if relatively small price reductions would lead to large increases in sales. As indicated above, although most business firms consider these factors in setting prices rather than using average-cost techniques alone, some continue to overemphasize the significance of average cost.

THE SIGNIFICANCE OF AVERAGE-COST PRICING

From the standpoint of resource allocation and reactions to demand and cost changes, the use of the average-cost pricing techniques has considerable significance:

Effect on Prices
In the first place, the use of this technique results in a different allocation of common cost (or overhead costs, as in the retail example) among various products than would occur with direct use of marginal techniques, and thus in different prices and outputs of particular goods.

Effect on Price of an Increase in Demand
With the establishment of prices based on estimates of marginal cost and revenue schedules, an increase in demand will usually lead to price increases, as illustrated in Figure 10–5, when the revenue curve shifts from P_0 to P_1. But when the average-cost approach is used, the decline or constancy of average cost consequent on increased sales

will lessen the likelihood of price increases and in some cases actually leads to price reductions. Reductions would be more common if average cost were calculated on the basis of estimated sales instead of normal sales. Likewise, when demand falls, strict adherence to average-cost price, with actual sales used as a basis for calculating average cost, will tend to bring about price increases.

Reaction of Price to an Increase in Cost

With marginal-cost pricing, price will not (except under unlikely assumptions) be raised immediately by the full amount of a cost increase. A firm readjusts output until marginal cost and marginal revenue are again equal, thus increasing marginal revenue by the amount of the increase in marginal cost. Price is raised by a smaller amount, as shown in Figure 12–6. Price rises from P_0 to P_1, while the amount of the cost increase is the vertical distance between AC_0 and AC_1. When price is set on the basis of average cost, however, firms are likely to raise price immediately by the full amount of the cost increase.

FIGURE 12–5
SHORT-RUN ADJUSTMENT TO AN INCREASE IN DEMAND

The strategy of pricing according to marginal cost and marginal revenue results in price and quantity increases when demand rises. Average-cost pricing, however, may lead to price decreases when demand rises, because of economies of scale.

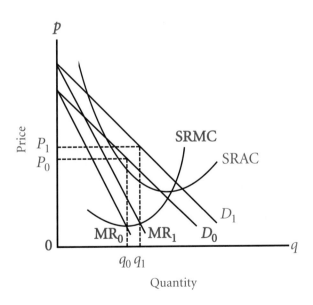

Price rises by the amount of the average-cost increase when markup pricing is employed. Under a marginal cost-marginal revenue pricing policy, however, price will rise (P_0 to P_1), but by less than the full amount of the cost increase (AC_0 to AC_1).

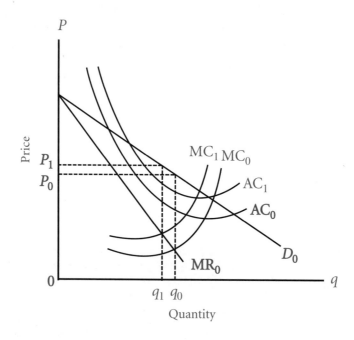

Suppose, for example, that wages paid by all firms in an industry increase. Average cost for all of them goes up by the amount of the wage increase per unit of output; accordingly, price is likely to be raised by the same amount. If all firms follow the same policy, all will be better off (unless they have already attained maximum joint profits) than they would have been had they raised price by a smaller amount. If the total demand for the product is at all elastic, firms will not cover average cost despite the increase (assuming average profit before the wage rise), but they will approach doing so more closely than if they raise price by a smaller amount. Some departure of firms from the industry is still necessary to restore average profits. It should be noted that such a price increase would have been profitable even without the wage increase. Given the competitive situation, however, no one firm could raise price because there was no assurance that others would follow. When costs increase for all firms, however, each may feel that others will raise prices if it does, and the increase will take place accordingly. (See Problem 12–10.)

12–10 The owners of a regional cement company might merely mark up their prices on cement. How is the firm's behavior in the face of a cost increase likely to differ from that of a firm employing marginal-cost pricing?

If the owners are concerned both about rivals and about new entrants in the cement industry, they might be reluctant to pass on additional costs, especially if the firm is the only one to incur these higher costs (perhaps they suffered higher costs because of an equipment breakdown). If they raised their price, competitors or new entrants might take away some of their business. However, if there are high barriers to entry, the firm would be tempted to pass on the cost in the form of higher prices. Remember: the company cannot charge as much as it would like, because customers can always find substitutes for cement. (Substitutes for cement might include asphalt, steel, wood, and so on.) Thus, instead of equating expected marginal revenue and expected marginal cost in the short run, the owners may increase price or not change their price, depending on the extent of their perceived competition (from existing competitors as well as potential entrants).

12.10 INTRODUCTORY PRICING

For established products, the task of determining prices involves merely asking how much to change them from existing levels. With introductory pricing of entirely new products, the problem is more complicated, however, and the firms' policies may vary widely. Some firms simply apply their standard pricing techniques. Others set relatively high prices in an effort either to recover very quickly the costs of developing the new product or to take advantage of the temporary lack of competition. Drug manufacturers have tended to price new products relatively high in order to recover heavy research costs in a short period of time, and in so doing they have incurred substantial public criticism. Other firms have followed the opposite policy, pricing below average cost (which is typically high until volume becomes substantial) in an effort to stimulate widespread use of new products. The policy a firm chooses no doubt reflects differences in how well the firm is protected from potential rivals by patent laws, goodwill, and so forth.

12.11 ADJUSTMENT OF PRODUCT TO PRICE

In some product lines, firms may follow a policy of selecting a price and then adjusting quality and thus cost to allow profitable production at the price selected (provided volume is adequate). The classic example was the 10-cent candy bar, which many firms retained for long periods, despite rising costs, by reducing size. Some firms varied quality from year to year in conformity with fluctuating prices of cocoa, sugar, and other ingredients. This phenomenon is encountered in other industries as well. Producers of household electrical appliances and farm implements frequently select a price at which they believe a product will sell in profitable amounts and then adjust the quality of the product to obtain a cost that allows an adequate profit.

12.12 STRATEGIC MOVES IN OLIGOPOLY

In some respects, partial oligopoly resembles a military campaign or a poker game. Firms take certain actions, not because they are advantageous in themselves, but because they improve the position of the oligopolist relative to its competitors and may ultimately improve its financial position. A firm may deliberately cut prices, sacrificing current profits either to drive competitors out or to scare them enough to discourage them from undertaking actions contrary to its interests. On the other hand, the desire for security and the ability to hold out against aggressive action on the part of competitors may lead a firm to take action that is itself contrary to profit maximization. Thus, a firm may expand to increase the absolute size of its financial resources or to ensure supplies of materials or market outlets during periods of competitive struggle, even though these actions are not in themselves profitable.

Some economists have suggested that the entire approach to oligopoly price and output should be recast. They replace the analysis that assumes firms' attempts to maximize profits with one that examines firm behavior in terms of a strategic game. This point of view, called game theory, stresses the tendency of various parties in such circumstances to minimize damage from opponents. With this approach, there is a set of alternative solutions (with respect to price and output levels, for example); the actual one chosen in a particular case depends on the specific policies each firm follows. The firm may also seek to ascertain competitors' most likely countermoves to its own policies and formulate alternative defense measures.

Games can either be cooperative or noncooperative. An example of a cooperative game would be two firms that decided to collude in order to improve their position through joint profit maximization. However, as we discussed earlier, often there are too many firms and enforcement costs are too high to keep all firms from cheating on collusive agreements. Consequently, most games are noncooperative games where each firm is independent to set its own price. The primary difference between cooperative and noncooperative games is the ability to contract. For example, players in a cooperative game can talk and set binding contracts, while those in noncooperative games are assumed to act independently, with no communications and no binding contracts. Because antitrust laws forbid firms to collude, we will assume that most strategic behavior in the marketplace is noncooperative.

The firm's decision makers must map out a strategy based on a plethora of information. They also must decide whether their strategy will be effective only under certain conditions regarding the actions of competitors, or whether the strategy will work regardless of the competitor's actions. When a strategy has been devised that will be optimal regardless of the opponents' actions, it is called a dominant strategy. An example of a famous game that has a dominant strategy and demonstrates the basic problem confronting colluding oligopolists is known as the prisoners' dilemma.

Imagine that there is a bank robbery and two suspects are caught. The robbers are placed in separate cells in the county jail and are not allowed to talk with each other. Table 12–1 presents the payoff matrix, which summarizes the possible outcomes from the various strategies. There are four possible alternative: both confess, neither confess, Prisoner A confesses but Prisoner B doesn't, and Prisoner B confesses but Prisoner A doesn't. Looking at the payoff matrix, we can see that if both prisoners confess to the crime, they will each serve three years. However, if neither confesses, each prisoner may only get a year on a different charge because of insufficient evidence. If Prisoner A confesses and Prisoner B does not, Prisoner A gets six months and Prisoner B gets six years. Alternatively, if Prisoner B confesses and Prisoner A does not, Prisoner B gets six months and Prisoner A gets six years. So you can see that the prisoners have a dilemma. What should they do?

Looking at the payoff matrix, we can see that if Prisoner A confesses it is in the best interest of Prisoner B to confess, because this means that Prisoner A would get three years rather than six years. To confess is also the best strategy for Prisoner B, if he knows that Prisoner A is going to confess. This would mean a lighter sentence for Prisoner B; three years rather than six years. It is also clear that both would be better off confessing if they knew for sure that the other was going to remain silent, since that would lead to a six month rather than a one-year sentence. But can they take the chance that their conspirator will not talk? The dominant strategy, while it may not lead to the best joint outcome, is to confess; that is, the prisoner's know that to confess is the best of a bad situation. No matter what their counterpart does, the maximum sentence will be three years.

TABLE 12–1
THE PRISONERS' DILEMMA PAYOFF MATRIX

		Prisoner B	
		Confesses	Doesn't Confess
Prisoner A	Confesses	3 Years (A) 3 Years (B)	6 Months (A) 6 Months (B)
	Doesn't Confess	6 Years (A) 6 Months (B)	1 Year (A) 1 Year (B)

To demonstrate how the prisoners' dilemma can shed light on oligopoly theory, let us consider the pricing strategy of two firms. Table 12–2 presents the payoff matrix—the possible profits that each firm would earn under different pricing strategies. Assume that each firm has total production costs of $1 per unit. When both firms set their price at $10 and each sells 1,000 units per week, then each earn a profit of $9,000 a week. If both firms set their price at $9, each sells 1,100 units per week, for a profit of $8,800. However, suppose one firm charges $10 and the other firm charges $9. The low price firm increases its profit through additional sales. It now sells, say, 1,500 units, for a profit of $12,000, while the high-price firm sells only 600 units per week, for a profit of $5,400.

When the two firms each charge $9 per unit, they are said to have reached a Nash equilibrium. At a Nash equilibrium, each player is said to be doing as well as it can given the actions of its competitor. For example, if each firm believes the other is going to charge $9, then the best strategy for both firms is to charge $9. For example, if Firm A charges $9, the worst possible outcome is a profit of $8,800. However, if Firm A prices at $10 and Firm B prices at $9, Firm A will have a profit of only $5,400. The choice that minimizes the risk of the worst scenario, therefore, is $9. The same is true for Firm B; it, too, minimizes the risk of the worst scenario by choosing to price at the Nash equilibrium, $9. In this case, the Nash equilibrium is also the dominant strategy. The Nash equilibrium takes on particular importance because it is a self-enforcing equilibrium; that is, once this equilibrium is established, there is no incentive for either firm to move away from it.

In sum, we see that it will be in their best interest for the two firms to collude and set their price at $10. Each firm, however, has a strong incentive to lower its price to $9 if this pricing strategy goes undetected. However, if both firms defect from the joint-profit maximization decision, both will be worse off than if they had colluded, but at least each will have minimized its potential loss if it cannot trust its competitor. This is the oligopolist's dilemma.

TABLE 12—2
THE PROFIT PAYOFF MATRIX

Firm B
Pricing Strategy

		$10	$9
Firm A Pricing Strategy	$10	$9,000 Firm (A) $9,000 Firm (B)	$5,400 Firm (A) $12,200 Firm (B)
	$9	$12,200 Firm (A) $5,400 Firm (B)	$8,800 Firm (A) $8,800 Firm (B)

A NONDOMINANT STRATEGY GAME

There are also situations where a firm might find itself in a position where there is no dominant strategy. Perhaps the decision makers of a large firm are deciding whether or not to wage an advertising campaign against its rival. According to the payoff matrix in Table 12–3, Firm B has no dominant strategy—that is, an optimal strategy regardless of the rival's actions. In this case, Firm B is better off advertising only if Firm A advertises. Specifically, profits for Firm B will rise from $12,000 to $16,000 if Firm A and Firm B advertise. If Firm A advertises and Firm B does not advertise, profits for Firm B will be $12,000. If Firm A does not advertise, and Firm B does advertise, Firm B will earn profits of $10,000. Therefore, the optimal strategy for Firm B depends on what Firm A does.

Can we predict a likely outcome if Firm B does not have a dominant strategy? We can if we can predict what Firm A will do. The dominant strategy for Firm A is to advertise (using the same reasoning we used in the prisoners' dilemma model), and if Firm B knows that Firm A will advertise, it will advertise too.

TABLE 12—3
A NONDOMINANT STRATEGY GAME

Firm B

		Advertises	Doesn't Advertise
Firm A	Advertise	$14,000 (A) $16,000 (B)	$18,000 (A) $12,000 (B)
	Doesn't Advertise	$ 8,000 (A) $10,000 (B)	$12,000 (A) $12,000 (B)

12.13 OTHER OBJECTIVES OF OLIGOPOLISTS

Some students of oligopoly pricing have argued that profit maximization is not in accord with the objectives of managing large-scale, widely owned businesses. William Baumol, for example, has stressed the importance of maximizing sales, provided that profits are adequate at the maximum sales figure. Thus, output is extended until MR is zero instead of equal to MC, and selling activities are extended to the point at which they bring no further increase in gross revenue. The point of operation, therefore, in Figure 12–7 is q_1. Baumol defends this thesis on two grounds: Management regards total sales, and therefore its share of the market, as the prime measure of success; and salaries of management are more closely related to gross sales than to profits. Adherence to this goal is strengthened by emphasis on "satisfactory," or "fair," profit, instead of maximum profit.

Other writers, such as Oliver Williamson, have stressed the personal goals of corporation management. In widely held corporations, management has certain "expense preferences"—types of expenditures that yield benefits to management over and above those yielded to the firms. Thus, they carry these expenses beyond the profit-maximizing level. Additional expenditures for staff constitute a major example: Each subordinate executive seeks to increase the staff working under him, because doing so increases his own salary, prestige, and security. This is a phenomenon frequently attributed to government agencies. It is also argued that management at all levels seeks to increase perquisites—supplements to their salaries that yield direct benefits to the recipients. Management likewise regards the amount of funds available for investment use at their discretion as important. These considerations may lead to price and output policies different from those based on profit maximization.

The significance of nonprofit-maximizing goals is an empirical question. Further studies of decision making and development of more elaborate models of behavior under diverse and multiple goals are clearly required. (See Problem 12–11.)

FIGURE 12–7
EQUILIBRIUM OUTPUT: GOAL OF MAXIMUM SALES REVENUE

Providing that profits are satisfactory, management may choose to maximize sales revenue. As discussed in prior chapters, total revenue peaks when marginal revenue is zero at q_1. Equilibrium quantity is higher and price is lower when management's goal is sales revenue maximization than when it is profit maximization, because MC is never zero.

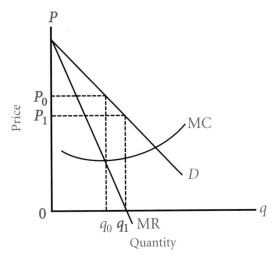

12–11   If an oligopolist maximizes sales revenues rather than profits, how are equilibrium price and output affected? Which strategy is less detrimental to the consumer?

As long as additional output raises revenue and profits are satisfactory, a revenue-maximizing firm produces the output level for which MR equals 0, q_0 in the figure below. The profit-maximizing solution produces a lower output level, q_1, at a higher price, P_1, compared to P_0. The consumer is better off maximizing sales revenue, because consumer surplus expands from ABP_1 to ACP_0.

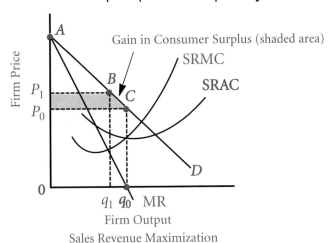

Sales Revenue Maximization

12.14 PRODUCT VARIATION AND SELLING ACTIVITIES

Oligopoly provides a particularly fertile ground for product variation, advertising, and other selling activities. Price tends to stabilize at a certain figure; and although firms are eager to increase sales to lower average cost, price reductions may not be profitable because of the danger that other firms will also reduce prices. Firms therefore turn to various selling activities, primarily because competitors' reactions are likely to be less disastrous to the firm than reactions to price reductions. A price cut is a definite conspicuous act that competitors can match or exceed if they wish. Sales activities are less obvious in their effects on competitors. Competitors can meet price cuts almost instantly, but they need time to follow selling activities. By the time competitors discover the success of nonprice policies and attempt to duplicate them, customers may be so well attached that they do not return to the competing firms. Moreover, there is always a chance that competitors are unable to devise equally satisfactory selling methods. Furthermore, the widespread attitude that price cutting is unethical encourages the firms to use selling activities instead of price adjustments. Legislative action, such as sanctioning resale price maintenance or placing restrictions on selling below "cost," may also direct competition into nonprice activities.

MUTUAL INTERDEPENDENCE IN SELLING ACTIVITIES

Firms are less interdependent with selling activities than with price changes, but they are not entirely independent. Oligopolists have a wide range of possible relationships in product policy and selling activities. At one extreme there may be perfect collusion: The firms agree implicitly or explicitly to select product and selling policies that maximize profits for the group. Substantial evidence suggests, however, that complete collusion on product and sales activities is rare. From all indications, firms are much less willing to agree on these matters than on price, partly because each believes it can carry on these activities more effectively than competitors, partly because the results of failure to agree appear to be less disastrous.

Without complete collusion on product and selling activities, firms almost certainly conduct more selling activities than they would with collusion. Each firm attempts to increase its share of the market at the expense of other firms. Because competitors follow the same policy, much of the activity cancels out, with none of the firms gaining anticipated sales volumes. All firms might be better off if all would cut the volume of advertising, yet no one firm can do so independently.

On the other hand, if firms consider the effects of changes in their own selling activities on the policies of competitors, their level of selling activities will be lower than they would be if firms ignored those effects. If, for example, a firm believes that initiating an extensive sales campaign will induce its competitors to follow suit; that belief might inhibit it from taking any action at all. If competitors follow increases in selling activities but not decreases, a firm will find it difficult to retreat from a high level of selling activities.

The success of an oligopoly's selling activities has a major influence on how competing firms share the total market. The largest shares may go to firms that do the best selling job rather than to those that attain the lowest manufacturing costs. The firms that fail may be those that make mistakes in the adjustment of product (such as introducing changes in style that are too revolutionary) or fall behind in selling activities. Furthermore, the tendency of firms in oligopoly to stress selling activities as a means of increasing sales may lead to a higher level of selling activities than would be carried on in other market structures, making average cost (including selling cost) higher. On the other hand, to the extent that firms consider the effects of their selling activities on the sales policies of competitors, the overall level of selling activities may be less than if the market were one of monopolistic competition. Moreover, successful selling activity may concentrate the total business in the hands of a smaller number of firms and allow operation nearer the point of lowest average cost. Thus, the price of the product could be lower than it would be if no selling activities were carried on.

12.15 PRICE DISCRIMINATION

Price discrimination is, in all likelihood, necessary for maximum joint profits. It is not possible, however, unless the various firms follow uniform pricing policies, because prices in the higher-price markets would tend to be pulled down to those in the lower-price markets. Firms must either agree on the prices to be charged in the various markets or spontaneously follow uniform practices. Because complete cooperation is difficult to obtain, effective discrimination is less likely to occur in oligopoly than monopoly.

Some of the most significant instances of price discrimination in the United States have arisen from devices designed to lessen price competition, rather than from a pricing policy introduced to adjust prices in terms of demand elasticities in various markets. One of the most important of these devices has been the basing point system, under which the price of the product in each locality was calculated by adding the freight from the basing point to the locality to the price at the basing point, regardless of the actual origin of the goods. For many years, steel prices in all parts of the country were determined by adding to the Pittsburgh price the freight from Pittsburgh, regardless of the actual origin of the steel. A Chicago buyer obtaining steel from a Gary mill would be quoted the Pittsburgh base price plus freight from Pittsburgh, even though steel was shipped only a few miles from Gary. In later years, several basing points were used instead of one. The single-point system provided a uniform quoted price in each area for all firms, regardless of the location of the plant and served as a device to lessen price competition. Ultimately, Supreme Court decisions interpreting antitrust laws brought an end to most basing-point techniques. The use of a uniform price for the entire country, followed frequently in industries in which freight is a relatively unimportant expense, also facilitates the avoidance of price differences and price cutting, yet is seldom interfered with under the antitrust laws.

12.16 LONG-RUN ADJUSTMENTS

In oligopoly, just as in other types of markets, equilibrium price and output are different in the long run than at any particular time. The difference arises partly from internal adjustments designed to attain the optimum sized plant, and partly from changes in the number of firms in the industry.

LONG-RUN COST ADJUSTMENTS

Over the long run, firms adjust their plant size to expected demand. Thus, LRMC, including plant and current operating costs, becomes a primary determinant of output and price policies. Just as with monopoly, long-run adjustment requires MR to equal both LRMC and SRMC with the plant that is optimal under the circumstances.

TENDENCIES TOWARD THE ELIMINATION OF EXCESS PROFITS

Mutual interdependence is, in itself, no guarantee of excess profits, even if the firms in the industry succeed in maximizing joint profits. The extent to which excess profits disappear depends on the ease with which new firms can enter the industry. When entry is easy, newcomers are attracted by excess profits. They may break down existing price institutions and agreements as they cut prices to establish themselves in the industry. Older firms may reduce prices to avoid excessive sales losses, and the general level of prices will approach average cost more closely. If the firms' perceived demand curves are kinked, the action of newcomers in setting lower prices lowers the level of the kink for all firms.

FIGURE 12–8
ADJUSTMENT OF PRICE TOWARD AVERAGE COST, FREE ENTRY

In the left panel of Figure (a), an oligolopist earns economic profits because price P_1 exceeds long-run average cost at the equilibrium quantity, q_1. If entry is free, firms will be attracted into the industry and the firm's demand curve will shift to the left. Entry continues until profits are zero and the D and LRAC curves are tangent. In the kinked-demand-curve framework shown in Figure (b), as long as the entrants stand by the pricing policies of established firms, the price will remain the same. The kink will shift to the left, however, as firms lose some of their customers to newcomers. Equilibrium is established when excess profits are eliminated and the LRAC curve is tangent to the D curve.

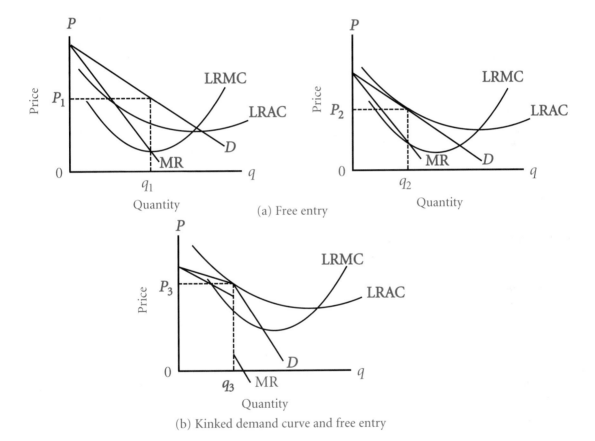

(a) Free entry

(b) Kinked demand curve and free entry

On the other hand, new firms may follow the same pricing policies as existing firms, either initially or after a period of price cutting. As a consequence, at least some firms will attain equality of price and average cost through an increase in average cost rather than a decline in price. The result of an increase number of firms is that total business is divided among a larger number of firms, and so each has a smaller sales volume. If loss of sales forces a firm to operate at a higher point on its AC curve, it may lose excess profits without reducing price.

Figure 12–8(a) illustrates how the entry of new firms eliminates excess profits: As new firms enter, the D curve moves to the left until excess profits are eliminated and D is tangent to LRAC at a price of P_2. Figure 12–8(b) illustrates a completed adjustment with a kinked demand curve. If the curve is kinked, the chances of a price reduction as new firms enter is particularly slight. As long as new firms follow the prices of the old, none finds a price reduction (or increase) desirable; the point of the kink, therefore, gradually moves to the left but stays at the same horizontal level until it is just tangent to LRAC. The use of average-cost pricing techniques also increases the likelihood that excess profits will be eliminated without a price cut. The loss in sales to new firms raises average cost (if it is calculated on the basis of actual sales) and discourages price reductions.

Existing firms may sometimes deliberately constrain their profits, sacrificing them for greater long-run security. If they earn excess profits and new firms enter, there is always a danger that too many new firms will commence operations, with consequent losses (for a period) for many of the firms. To avoid this danger, existing firms may deliberately set prices to yield only a more-or-less average rate of return, and price may be only slightly above or equal to lowest average cost.

ENTRY RESTRICTION

To the extent that entry is relatively free, empirical studies of firms' actual levels of operation should indicate that they typically operate on the downward-sloping portions of their LRAC curves, as explained in the previous section. However, Joe Bain's study of 20 major, long-established manufacturing industries reveals that most firms had reached a scale of plant and firm size great enough to allow lowest cost of operation, and many were well beyond the minimum necessary for low cost. Their positions are shown graphically in Figure 12–9. The maximum-profit price is represented by P_0. Typically, the rate of profit in these industries at actual price was higher than the figure regarded as average for the economy as a whole.

This phenomenon can be explained in two ways. First, the firms may deliberately hold prices below the maximum-profit point (p', which is less than p in Figure 12–9) as a means of discouraging newcomers from entering, or because of general acceptance of the idea of a "fair" profit rather than the maximum one. This attitude undoubtedly plays some role. Second, restriction of entry may prevent an increase in the number of firms. The profit rate in these industries suggests that this explanation is the primary one.

FIGURE 12–9
LONG-RUN EQUILIBRIUM, ENTRY RESTRICTION

With barriers to entry, oligopolists may earn excess profits in the long run. Theoretically, profit maximization occurs at P_0 and q_0. Empirical work, however, suggests that oligopolists actually charge a lower price than the profit-maximizing price (such as P_1). This strategy discourages entry and appears more equitable to consumers.

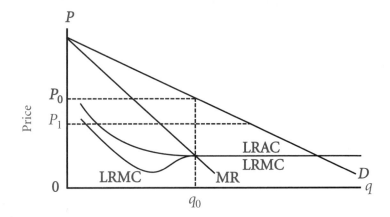

The Bain study examined entry barriers and found three to be of primary importance:

1. Economies of Large-scale Production

These economies make operation on a small scale during the early years of a new firm extremely unprofitable. A firm cannot build up a large market overnight; in the interim, cost per unit is so high that losses are heavy. Recognition of this feature discourages new firms from entering.

2. Product Differentiation and Established Reputations

These make the development of an adequate market by new firms very slow and, particularly when coupled with economies of scale, may make entry almost impossible. Bain concludes that, on the whole, differentiation is more significant as a barrier than economies of large-scale production. Among the major features of differentiation are the durability and complexity of product, which makes consumer appraisal of new brands difficult and leads to reliance on established reputation. A second is dealer relationships; exclusive dealerships and the reluctance of retailers to carry a large number of lines can seriously impede the development of a new product. Finally, conspicuous consumption, the desire to be seen using the popular make or brand may play some role.

3. The Absolute Magnitude of the Investment Required

A firm's ability to obtain financing depends primarily on its credit standing. New firms without established credit often have difficulty obtaining necessary capital, even when loan funds are generally plentiful. New businesses may have to be developed primarily with the capital of the owners plus reinvested earnings; persons lacking adequate resources of their own, therefore, find it extremely difficult to establish a business, even with good profit prospects. This type of restriction is particularly serious for lines of production that require heavy initial capital investment, such as steel.

Additionally, there are certain absolute restrictions to entry found by Bain to be of little significance in the industries which he studied, but undoubtedly of greater importance in other sectors of the economy:

1. Limited Raw-material Supplies

When necessary specialized resources, such as ores of a certain type, are found only in limited areas and existing firms control the entire supply, it is impossible for new firms to commence operation. Entry into nickel production and diamond mining, for example, is severely restricted by this consideration.

2. Legal Restrictions

Government activity may restrict entry of new firms. Patent rights may interfere with the ability of new firms to develop competing products. Trademarks protect various differentiation devices. Tariffs and quotas interfere with foreign competition in domestic markets. Cities may limit the numbers of certain types of enterprises (taverns, for example) or prevent peddlers from operating. Licensing requirements for various trades are often used to restrict numbers. The most severe legal restrictions are applied to public utilities; new firms are not permitted to enter without approval of regulatory agencies. In general, sanction is not given without substantial proof that the service of existing firms is inadequate.

Some of these legal restrictions are established in the interests of general welfare. For example, control of entry into public utility industries might be necessary to prevent excess plant capacity and higher rates. Many of the restrictions, however, such as most tariffs and many licensing requirements, result from the political activity of interested groups.

COMMON COSTS AND THE LEVEL OF AVERAGE COST

When a firm is producing several products and some of the costs are common, there is no determinate average cost for each product, that is, no average cost figure which price must cover in the long run and which price will equal if there is completely free entry. The enterprise as a whole must cover common as well as separable costs, and with free entry, total receipts will equal costs for all products together, including common costs and a necessary profit. Further, each particular product must sell for a price which covers its average separable costs, or the firm will cease producing it. But there is no necessary way in which common costs must be shared among the various products. In practice, some articles may carry more than a proportionate share of overhead and others less; but it is advantageous for the firm to continue to produce even items contributing relatively little to common cost, provided they make some contribution. The actual distribution of common costs among the various articles will depend primarily upon the techniques employed by firms in allocating common costs, the nature of consumer demands for the various products, and the extent of competition in various markets.

ELIMINATION OF LOSSES

Mutual interdependence among the firms in an industry does not ensure that all of them can earn even an average rate of profit. This is because the number of firms may be so great relative to demand that at each possible output level, average cost exceeds the price. Firms can make two possible adjustments when they incur losses. First, if price and output are not at the level at which joint profits are maximized, increased cooperation on the part of firms may produce enough of an increase in price to cover average cost. The NRA (National Recovery Administration) period of the 1930s was characterized by extensive activity of this sort, when for a short period such cooperation was not illegal. Without greater cooperation, firms can make another adjustment: They can restore price to the average-cost level, forcing some firms to leave the industry. These are most likely to be the ones that fall behind in the race for customers because of poor selling success. They may, however, be firms whose equipment wears out first or whose owners are most pessimistic about the future. As some firms leave, the increased sales volumes of remaining firms allows them to cover cost (assuming that their average cost declines as they increase sales). Prices may not rise at all, as they would under similar circumstances in pure competition; the losses of survivors may be eliminated entirely by the decline in the average cost.

NONUNIFORMITY OF PRICE

With differentiation, the prices of the various sellers are not likely to be uniform, even after long-run adjustments. Differentiation often involves deliberate quality differences, designed to appeal to different income levels. As a consequence, both cost schedules and the height of demand schedules differ. Even with outright price agreements, price differentials are essential if low-quality product firms are to remain in business. In other situations, firms without established reputations must maintain lower prices if they are to continue to sell. Most of these sources of differences are not eliminated by the passage of time. Even if all firms in an industry are making a normal rate of profit, prices may vary substantially from one firm to another.

12.17 PURE OLIGOPOLY

The analysis in preceding sections rests on the assumption that products are differentiated. In pure oligopoly, however, the product standardized. Pure oligopoly is most closely approximated in markets for capital equipment, building materials, and so forth, which are purchased by expert buyers to meet specific uses in production. Markets for lumber, cement, brick, railroad equipment, industrial machinery, steel, copper, and aluminum provide examples. Rarely, however, is differentiation completely absent, primarily because of differences in service rendered in conjunction with sales, the personal relation between officials of various companies, and the efforts of sales staffers.

With a standardized product, mutual interdependence and the tendency toward outright cooperation are greatly strengthened. With no differentiated products, prices must be uniform, or the high-price firms sell nothing. Accordingly, independent price determination on the part of each firm, with no attention paid to competitors' actions, would be suicidal, with price fluctuations and frequent periods of losses as firms sought to increase sales by price reductions. Some type of coordinated action is, therefore, imperative—much more so than with differentiated products, in which each firm has an established clientele and quality differences lessen the severity of price competition. The forms which coordinated action may take are, in general, the same with standardized products as with differentiation. Price leadership or outright agreements are more likely, because the use of standard pricing techniques may not give the necessary degree of uniformity. Price agreements are, of course, illegal, but they nevertheless exist; their secret nature preventing effective enforcement of the antitrust laws. Occasionally, with the advent of a newcomer into an industry or in a period of severe depression, when firms are anxious to increase sales, established pricing institutions break down and a period of price competition ensues. Such action is not frequent, however.

The same considerations of price and output determination apply to pure oligopoly as to differentiated oligopoly, although the greater degree of cooperation may ensure joint profits that are closer to the maximum. Lack of differentiation makes the entry of new firms easier, but in many capital equipment industries, the heavy capital investment and large volume of output necessary for low-cost operation impose formidable obstacles to the free flow of firms into the field. (See Problems 12–12 and 12–13.)

12–12 Suppose there is a pure oligopoly and each firm does not realize that rivals will react to a price change. What do you think would be the long-run equilibrium when some firms exit? What response to losses is possible in an oligopoly that is impossible in other market structures?

If an oligopolist believes that rivals will not respond to pricing policies, each producer expects to capture rivals' customers by reducing price. Rivals will cut prices as well, and if they do not understand the mutual interdependence among firms, they will attempt to undercut prices. A price war, therefore, ensues until economic profits are zero and price equals average cost. Under the conditions of constant returns to scale, equilibrium price and quantity (P, q) are depicted in the figure below. The outcome is equivalent to equilibrium in perfect competition in this case.

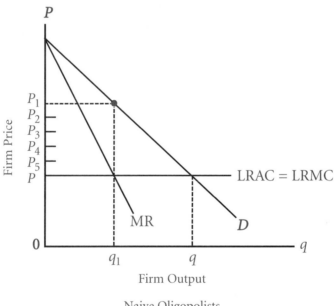

Naive Oligopolists

12–13 With all the different models of oligopoly—the joint-profit-maximization model, the kinked demand curve, the entry-limit model, game theory, and so on—it appears that the theory of oligopoly is groping for firmer ground. Why is the theory of oligopoly so vague?

It is very difficult to predict how firms will react when there is mutual interdependence. No firm knows what its demand curve looks like with any degree of certainty and therefore has a very limited knowledge of its marginal-revenue curve. In order to know anything about its demand curve, the firm must know how other firms will react to its prices and other policies. Thus, in the absence of additional assumptions, equating marginal revenue and expected marginal cost is regulated to guesswork.

SUMMARY

1. Oligopoly involves a few firms, each controlling a large segment of the market. Product differentiation may or may not be important, but the actions of rival firms is very important.

2. Products are identical in a pure oligopoly. Price changes are extremely important to rivals in this type of market.

3. Products are not identical in a differentiated oligopoly. In this type of market, price changes have a smaller impact on rival firms.

4. Spontaneous coordination may occur when a firm bases its decisions on the expected actions of its competitors.

5. Firms face many obstacles in maximizing joint profit and attaining complete oligopoly.

6. Partial oligopoly, where joint profits are not maximized, is the general rule.

7. Most oligopolistic firms consider experimentation with price changes dangerous.

8. Oligopoly equilibrium resembles that of monopolistic competition, except that the firm is uncertain about the location of its demand- and marginal-revenue curves, whose positions depend on pricing and other decisions of competitors.

9. Collusive oligopolies or cartels can act much like monopolists, although such oligopolies often break down, because one of the price-fixing members cheats on the agreement in an attempt to enhance its profits.

10. One of the most successful collusive oligopoly, the OPEC cartel, benefited from a price-inelastic demand for oil, an inelastic short-run supply of oil on the part of non-OPEC members, and a large share of the international petroleum market.

11. Price leadership may lessen uncertainty in oligopolistic industries.

12. The cost-plus, average-cost, or markup approach is computed by adding a markup that includes profits to the direct costs of the firm.

13. Important barriers to entry may ensure long-run profits including: economies of large-scale production, product differentiation, established reputations, the absolute magnitude of investment required, limited raw-material supplies, and legal restrictions.

WORDS AND CONCEPTS FOR REVIEW

pure oligopoly	differentiated oligopoly
collusion	spontaneous coordination
complete oligopoly	partial oligopoly
mutual interdependence	kinked demand curve
collusive oligopoly	cartels
price leadership	imitative pricing
cost-plus, average-cost, or markup approach	introductory pricing
game theory	noncooperative games
dominant strategy	payoff matrix
Nash equilibrium	

REVIEW QUESTIONS

1. What is the difference between pure and differentiated oligopoly? Between collusion and spontaneous coordination? Between complete and partial oligopoly?

2. Explain the requirements for establishing price and output at the maximum joint-profit level.

3. What are the major obstacles to the attainment of maximum joint profit?

4. Explain the kinked-demand-curve model and indicate why the optimum (best) price point is at the level of the kink.

5. Explain the average-cost approach to pricing.

6. Considerable empirical evidence as well as casual observation suggests that firms typically increase prices by the amount of an increase in excise or sales tax. Does this reaction suggest the use of an average cost or an MC-MR approach to pricing? Explain.

7. Explain the goal of maximizing sales revenue and its significance for price-output policy.

8. What is the Williamson "managerial discretion" hypothesis?

9. Suppose that entry into an oligopoly field is relatively easy. By what process do excess profits tend to be eliminated?

10. Some writers maintain that free entry and oligopoly are inconsistent; if entry is free, oligopoly will break down. Discuss.

11. Explain briefly the major barriers to free entry.

12. What are the primary barriers to entry into the following industries in the United States?
    a. farm-machinery production
    b. cement production
    c. bus operation
    d. soft drink production
    e. quicksilver mining
    f. beer manufacture
    g. computer manufacture

13. What is the significance of the absence of differentiation for oligopoly policy?

14. What factors have permitted the OPEC cartel to have been so successful in the past? What would this chapter suggest about the future of this cartel?

SUGGESTED READINGS

Adams, Walter. *The Structure of American Industry*, 7th ed.New York: Macmillan, 1986.

Bain, J.S. *Barriers to New Competition*. Cambridge, Mass.: Harvard University Press, 1956.

Okun, A.M. "Inflation: Its Mechanics and Welfare Costs," *Brookings Papers on Economic Activity 2*, (1975), 351–401.

Plott, C.R. "Industrial Organization Theory and Experimental Economics," *Journal of Economic Literature*, December 1982, 1485–1527.

Scherer, F.M., and D. Ross. *Industrial Market Structure and Economic Performance*, 3rd ed. Boston: Houghton Mifflin, 1990.

Stigler, G.J. "The Literature of Economics: The Case of the Kinked Demand Curve," *Economic Inquiry*, April 1978, 185–204.

Part 4

FACTOR MARKETS

In Part 4, we explain how factor inputs are allocated across production activities in a market economy. This section offers thorough coverage of factor markets: "Factor Pricing and Labor Markets" in Chapter 13, "The Theory of Interest and Capital Markets" in Chapter 14, "Rents and Quasi-Rents" in Chapter 15 and the "Theory of Profits" in Chapter 16.

Chapter Thirteen

FACTOR PRICING
AND LABOR MARKETS

Questions to Think About

1. What is the basic rule of optimum factor use?

2. What is total factor cost? Average factor cost? Marginal factor cost?

3. How does monopsony, perfect competition, and quantity discounts affect the average- and marginal-factor-cost curves?

4. What is marginal revenue product?

5. What is the firm's factor-demand curve and how can we find the firm's optimizing condition for hiring an input?

6. What are the principal determinants of the elasticity of factor demand?

7. What causes the factor-demand curve to shift?

8. Why is an industry's demand curve for labor less elastic than a firm's demand curve?

9. Why might a factor-supply curve bend backward?

10. What is the individual's labor-supply curve? How is the the indifference-curve, budget-line framework used to derive an individual's labor-supply curve?

11. How do you determine the labor market equilibrium when there is a monopsony?

12. What is bilateral monopoly?

13.1 INTRODUCTION

Much of the analysis of the pricing of consumption goods is also applicable to the pricing of factor inputs used in production. In contrast to consumption goods, however, factor units are acquired by business firms for use in production rather than by individuals to satisfy personal wants. As a result, the determinants of factor demand are different from those of demand for consumption goods. To be sure, the demand for factor inputs is derived indirectly from households' demand for goods. However, the interrelationship of product demand to factor demands are complex, for a wide variety of factor-input combinations and production technologies may be used. Moreover, the determinants of factor supply are significantly different from those of consumption goods because many factors (other than capital goods) are supplied by individuals rather than business firms.

    This chapter analyzes the demand for and supply of factor inputs and develops some general principles of price determination that are broadly relevant for all kinds of factors. In subsequent chapters, these principles are applied to particular types of factors: labor, land, capital goods, entrepreneurship, and money capital.

13.2 FACTOR PRICES AND INCOME DISTRIBUTION

In a market economy, the prices paid by producers for factor units are the primary sources of income available to consumers for purchasing consumer goods. Wages, for example, are costs from the standpoint of producers, but represent income for workers and provide them the means to buy consumption goods. Wage levels, therefore, not only affect costs, prices, and relative outputs of various goods but also determine the share of national income received by workers, thereby affecting the demand for consumer goods. (See Problem 13–1)

13–1 Does the explanation of factor pricing completely describe the manner in which individuals share in the national income?

Factor pricing tells us nothing about how property rights to resources are distributed among individuals and, therefore, how property incomes are distributed among individuals. Likewise, factor pricing reveals nothing about nonmarket income transfers. Even though many people may supply no factor units for use in production, they may share in the national income by receiving old-age pensions, aid to families with dependent children, federal scholarships, and other transfer payments. Others lose portions of their incomes through tax payments, or they voluntarily relinquish funds by making gifts to charitable organizations.

A description of the forces governing such transfers lies beyond the scope of this chapter. Our purpose is to analyze factor pricing in order to provide a basic framework for explaining those aspects of income distribution that are market determined.

13.3 FACTOR DEMAND

The theory of **factor demand** is predicated on the assumption that the goal of a business firm is to maximize profit. To maximize profit, a firm must produce a given quantity of output at minimum total cost. To do that, the firm has to choose the level of output at which total revenue exceeds total cost by the greatest amount. Thus, there is a close relationship between the theory of demand for individual factor inputs and the theory of production and cost developed in Chapters 7 and 8. A similar relationship exists between the demand for factors as a whole and the theory of output and price determination developed in Chapters 9 through 12.

THE BASIC RULE OF OPTIMAL FACTOR USE

The kernel of the theory of factor demand is contained in the general principle that *a firm finds it profitable to hire any factor unit that "pays for itself."* More precisely, it is profitable for a firm to hire a factor unit if the addition to total cost resulting from its acquisition is equaled *either* by an equivalent increase in total revenue or by an equivalent decrease in total outlay on other factor inputs. In this context the precise meaning of the terms *addition to total cost—marginal cost* and *increase in total revenue—marginal revenue* depends on the structure of the markets in which factor inputs and commodity outputs are traded, and on the nature of the firm's production function. To develop the implications of the principle stated above, we must first examine the nature and significance of these background conditions.

AVERAGE AND MARGINAL FACTOR COSTS

The costs that a firm seeks to minimize in producing a given level of output depend partly on the quantity purchased of each variable factor input, and partly on the unit price, or *average factor cost* (AFC), that the firm expects to pay for various kinds of factors. If the letters $V_1, \ldots V_i, \ldots V_n$ represent quantities of relevant inputs, and $W_1, \ldots W_i, \ldots W_n$ represent expected prices of these same inputs, then the total (variable) factor cost (TFC) of any given set of price and input variables is

$$TFC = W_1 V_1 + W_2 V_2 + \cdots + W_i V_i + \cdots + W_n V_n.$$

The input quantities in this equation are, of course, decision variables for the firm—variables over which the firm has control. In contrast, the values of the average factor cost (price) variables depend on numerous influences over which the firm has little or no control. In particular, if the firm purchases factor i in a perfectly competitive market, then it would regard W_i as fixed—equal to the prevailing market price of the factor. If, however, it purchases the factor in an imperfectly competitive market, the value of W_i may depend partly on the quantity of the factor input that the firm purchases as well as on the factor's current selling price.

When factor *i* is purchased in a perfectly competitive market, the addition to total cost, or the *marginal factor cost* (MFC_i) of a unit increase in purchases of a variable input *i*, is equal to the market price of factor *i*. Thus, marginal factor cost is equal to average factor cost: $MFC_i = AFC_i$. The "supply curve of the factor as seen by the firm"—the firm's *average-factor-cost curve*—is therefore represented by a horizontal line such as AFC (= MFC = W) in Figure 13-1; the same line will also represent the firm's *marginal-factor-cost curve*.

When a factor is purchased in an imperfectly competitive market, MFC differs from AFC in one of two ways. If the firm is a *monopsonistic*—that is, an exclusive buyer of the factor (see Chapter 14)—AFC is an increasing function of quantity purchased, as illustrated by the curve AFC_1 in Figure 13-1. The corresponding MFC curve (MFC_1 in the figure) lies above AFC_1 at every level of factor purchases. Alternatively, if the firm receives quantity discounts, AFC is a decreasing function of quantity purchased (AFC_2 in Figure 13–1), and the corresponding MFC curve (MFC_2) lies below the AFC curve.

As will become clear later, imperfectly competitive conditions in factor markets create serious problems for the definition of factor demand functions. For the sake of simplicity and convenience in the argument that follows, therefore, we shall temporarily assume that AFC curves are represented by horizontal lines, with AFC equal to MFC.

In competitive input markets, the firm views the input as given. Average factor cost, marginal factor cost, and factor price are equal, constant, and represented graphically by a horizontal line. In the case of monopsony, the factor price increases as the firm hires more of the factor. Marginal factor cost rises, average factor cost rises, and marginal factor cost exceeds average factor cost at all input levels, on the other hand, input declines as factor employment rises when the firm has access to quantity discounts. The marginal-factor-cost curve lies below the average-factor-cost curve, and both curves decline throughout.

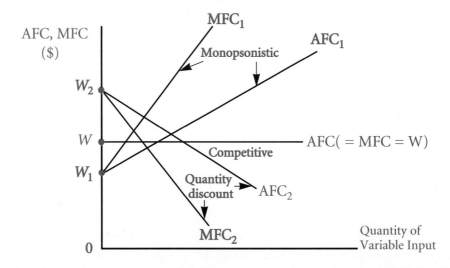

MARGINAL REVENUE PRODUCT

The addition to total revenue that the firm expects to realize by purchasing and using an additional unit of any factor input is simply the marginal product (MP) of the input multiplied by the additional revenue generated from an extra unit of output; that is, marginal revenue. In general, of course, price varies with the amount of product offered for sale, so MR differs from the firm's demand curve, except in the case of perfect competition where MR = P. In every instance, whether the output market is competitive or not, the addition to total revenue that is of concern to the firm when it is considering buying an *additional* unit of any factor input is the **marginal revenue product** (MRP) of the factor input. The marginal revenue product is described by the formula:

$$MRP \ = \ MP \cdot MR$$

THE BEHAVIOR OF MARGINAL REVENUE PRODUCT IN THE SHORT RUN

Because a firm's plant capacity is assumed to be fixed in the short run, the MRP of a factor may be expected (based on the theory of production outlined in Chapter 7) to rise initially and then fall. That theory assumes that, as units of a factor are first added, the firm makes more efficient use of both fixed and variable factor units, and MRP rises.

Beyond a certain point, however—and perhaps at a fairly early stage of the addition of units of the factor—MRP diminishes. That is, when additional factor units are used to increase output, MP eventually diminishes. Because some factors, such as capital, are fixed in the short run as the firm adds further units of other factors, it eventually encounters diminishing returns.

The MRP curve takes on different characteristics depending on whether the output market is competitive or imperfectly competitive. First, assume that the product market is perfectly competitive. Recall from Chapter 9 that in competitive output markets, the firm will sell all its output at the market price. Consequently, the marginal revenue from the sale of an additional unit is also equal to the market price. When output markets are perfectly competitive, therefore, the marginal revenue product of a factor is equal to the marginal product times the price of the product the firm is selling:

$$MRP = MP \cdot P$$

The MRP will take on a slightly different characteristic when the firm is selling its product in an imperfectly competitive market. Under imperfectly competitive output market conditions, the price of the product must be reduced as greater quantities of output are placed on the market. Thus, as additional factor units are added, MRP (MP · MR) declines, even if MP remains constant, because the marginal revenue associated with the larger output is declining. Given MP, if MR < P, then MP · MR is less than MP · P. That is, the imperfectly competitive firm's MRP curve (MP · MR) not only declines but it will be lower than the perfectly competitive firm's MRP (MP · P), as seen in Figure 13–2.

THE BEHAVIOR OF MARGINAL REVENUE PRODUCT IN THE LONG RUN

Over a period of time long enough for the firm to adjust the quantities of all factors, the MRP of each factor is substantially different than it is in the short run, primarily because MP behaves in a different manner. In general, however, both in the long run and in a period in which plant capacity is fixed, MRP initially increases and then diminishes. The increase results from economies of large-scale production; the use of more-efficient types of capital equipment, learning by doing, and increased specialization all lead to an increase in the factor's MP. Eventually, however, just as in the short run, MRP is likely to start to fall, but at a different level of output. In part, the decline is the result of the fall in MP, which occurs once the firm encounters decreasing returns to scale (resulting from problems of large-scale management). In addition, just as in the short-run period, MRP falls because of the diminishing marginal rate of substitution between this factor and others, the tendency of costs of other factors to rise as more units are acquired, and the need to reduce the price of the product to sell more units (except in perfectly competitive conditions). (See Problem 13–2.)

13-2 True or False? Over time, income and population have grown in the United States and in many other developed nations, raising the demand for products and increasing MRP.

True. Rising product demand increases product price and the firm's marginal revenue, *ceteris paribus*. This in turn raises MRP and therefore increases the demand for inputs.

AN INDIVIDUAL FIRM'S DEMAND SCHEDULE FOR A FACTOR

The marginal product of a factor input tells us how much a firm will be willing to pay for an additional unit of input. The general rule is that it will pay a firm to continue hiring any (or all) inputs up to the point where cost on the factor is equal to its marginal product multiplied by marginal revenue.

$$MFC_i = MP_i \cdot MR \text{ where } MC = MR$$

Given the equilibrium condition MFC = MP · MR, it is a short step to the definition of factor demand functions. The right-hand term of this condition is the marginal revenue product of a factor (MRP); the value of the left-hand term corresponding to any particular quantity of an input is given by the MFC curve for the input.[1] Thus, we have only to describe the relation between the quantity of an input purchased and its MRP to determine the equilibrium input of the factor corresponding to any given MFC curve.

---

[1]The text discussion to this point is simple to characterize formally. Considering that the revenue and cost function can be written in terms of two inputs, labor (L) and capital (K), where the amount of K is fixed, rather than output, we have that profits (π) can be maximized as:

$$Max_{L,K} \pi = P\left[Q(L,K)\right] \cdot Q(L,K) - W(L) \cdot L - R(K) \cdot K$$

At a profit maximum, the slope of the "profit hill" with respect to both labor and capital will be zero. Looking only at labor (the condition for capital is exactly analogous) and employing the chain rule (Composite function theorem) and the product rule, we have:

$$\left[\frac{dP(Q)}{dQ} \cdot \frac{\partial Q}{\partial L}\right] \cdot Q(L,K) + P\left[Q(L,K)\right] \cdot \frac{\partial Q}{\partial L} - \left[\frac{dW(L)}{dL} \cdot L + W(L)\right] = 0$$

Taking the negative term to the other side and rearranging

$$P \cdot \left[\frac{dP(Q)}{dQ} \cdot \frac{Q}{P} + 1\right] \cdot \frac{\partial Q}{\partial L} = \frac{dW(L)}{dL} \cdot L + W(L)$$

The left side is marginal revenue times marginal product, while the right side is marginal factor cost. Note that with competitive input and output markets this expression simplifies to:

$$P \cdot \frac{\partial Q}{\partial L} = W$$

FIGURE 13–2
MARGINAL REVENUE

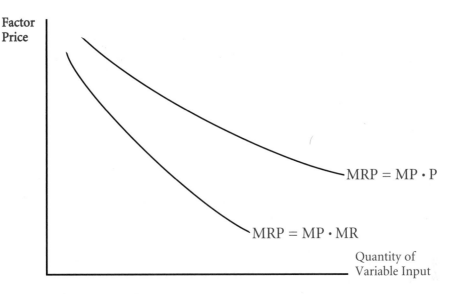

When output markets are perfectly competitive, the MRP = MPP • P. When output markets are imperfectly competitive, however, the MRP = MPP • P. Because MR < P in imperfectly competitive output markets, the graph of the MRP for the imperfectly competitive firm lies below the graph of the MRP for perfectly competitive firm.

It is now possible to complete the explanation of what determines an individual firm's equilibrium purchases of a factor. Our goal is to determine what quantity of an input a profit-maximizing business firm, corresponding to a short-run or long-run MFC curve, will purchase.

Three alternative MFC curves are shown in Figure 13-3. Applying the rule that units of a factor are hired up to the point where MFC equals MRP, V units are hired (in equilibrium) if MFC equals W; V_1 units will be hired at MFC_1, and V_2 units will be hired at MFC_2.

The effect of large firm size relative to input supply in driving up input prices in the factor markets (reflected by the marginal-factor-cost curve, MFC) is typically to reduce equilibrium purchases below the levels that would be purchased under conditions of perfect competition. Similarly, the effect of quantity discounts (MFC_2) is to increase equilibrium purchases compared with the level in perfect competition. (See Problems 13–3 and 13–4.)

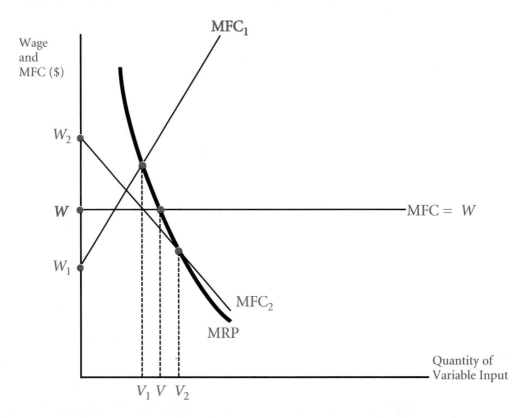

A profit-maximizing firm hires units of an input until the marginal factor cost equals the marginal revenue product. The monpsonist employs V_1 units of the factor, less than the amount hired under perfect competition, V,
whereas quantity discounts induce greater employment of the input at V_2.

13–3 A florist hires more workers during the week before Mother's Day. How does this affect the labor demand of the florist?

The quantity hired by the florist is determined by equating MFC to MRP. Mother's Day temporarily increases the demand for flowers. When demand increases, the marginal revenue product of labor also increases. Because MRP = MP • MR, the increase in MR also increases MRP, and the florist is willing to employ more workers. If the florist operates in a perfectly competitive market, the holiday boosts output price and therefore MRP. The florist's demand curve for labor shifts to the right.

13–4 During income-tax season, an accounting firm finds that by keeping one employee for an additional hour each day, $25 of additional revenue can be earned. After April 15, however, the additional work hour brings in only $15. If the employee's wage is $20 per hour, what is the optimal policy for the firm (assuming overtime payments are not necessary)?

During tax season the MRP ($25) of employing an additional worker hour is greater than the MFC ($20), so it is profitable to hire the worker. After tax season, however, MRP is less than MFC ($15 < $20), so it is not profitable to hire the extra hour of labor.

A firm's demand for labor or any other factor input therefore depends partly on the kind of market in which the input is purchased (the MFC curve), partly on production possibilities (the production function), and partly on the structure of the market in which the firm's product is sold (the MR curve). These various influences make it difficult to state any precise conclusions about the nature of "typical" factor demand curves except that they invariably slope downward from left to right. On the basis of the analysis so far, however, some general comments can be made about the factors that determine a firm's **elasticity of factor demand**.

1. The Substitutability of the Factors

The easier it is to substitute one factor for another in the production activity, the greater is the elasticity of the demand for the factor (that is, the smaller the degree of curvature of production isoquants). For example, if steel and aluminum are good substitutes for each other in the production of a certain product, the demand by the producer for either metal is likely to be fairly elastic; that is, any change in relative factor prices causes the firm to substitute one metal for the other with a substantial increase in purchases of the metal whose price has fallen (a significant shift in the point of tangency between the iso-cost curve and the equilibrium-isoquant curve).

2. The Rate of Decline of MP

The faster the rate of decline in MP when additional units of a factor are added to increase output, the lower the elasticity of each firm's demand curve for the factor. For example, suppose a farmer has a small plot of land under cultivation. If workers are added, it is possible that the MP of labor may fall so rapidly that hiring additional workers would be justified only if the factor price fell significantly. Alternatively, if the rate of decline is small and additional factor units add almost as much as do previous units to total output, small factor-price declines will generate substantial increases in the quantity of the factor used. The rate of decline in MP is less over a longer period, when all factors can be adjusted, than in a shorter period when some of the factors are fixed.

3. The Elasticity of the Demand for the Product of the Firm

The greater the price elasticity of the product, the greater the elasticity of demand for the factor that produces that product, *ceteris paribus*. For example, if demand for the firm's product is very elastic, a small price change would lead to a proportionately large change in quantity demanded. This would correspondingly lead to a large change in the quantity of the input needed to produce this commodity. If, however, the demand curve for the firm's product has a low price elasticity (that is, demand is relatively inelastic), a price change would have little impact on the quantity demanded of the product. There would therefore only be a very small change in the amount of input demanded for changes in the input price.

4. The Ratio of Variable Costs to Total Production Costs

The larger the proportion of total production costs accounted for by a particular variable input, the greater the elasticity of factor demand, *ceteris paribus*. For example, if the variable input, say labor, accounted for 100 percent of production costs, then an increase in wages of 20 percent would increase production costs by 20 percent. That is, if the variable input accounts for only a small part of the total cost of the product, a change in the input price will have only a small impact on total production costs.

CHANGES IN FACTOR DEMAND

Shifts in the demand schedules of business firms for a factor arise from changes in the parameters of the schedules, as demonstrated in Figure 13–4. Major causes of parameter changes include:

1. Technological Change that Influences the Marginal Product of a Factor

Computers, for example, increase output per worker and raise the marginal product of labor, shifting the factor-demand curve (in this case, shifting the labor-demand curve to the right). This of course assumes that labor and capital (computers) are complementary.

2. Changes in the Prices of Other Factors

An increase in the price of one factor increases the demand for substitute factors. For example, suppose the wages of low-skilled workers increase. The local pizza parlor might choose to sell soft drinks as all-you-can-drink rather than by the cup. It therefore substitutes beverage dispensers (capital) for additional low-skilled workers. When factors are complementary, a rise in the price of one reduces the demand for the other. For example, a rise in ditchdiggers' wages might lead to reduction in the demand for shovels, *ceteris paribus*.

3. The Demand for the Firm's Product

The greater the demand for the firm's product, the greater the firm's demand for factors. A higher demand for the firm's product affects the firm's marginal revenue, which increases the factor's marginal-revenue product. (Recall the factor-demand curve is MRP = MP · MR). Of course, if demand for the firm's product falls, the factor-demand curve (MRP) shifts to the left. (See Problems 13–5 and 13–6.)

FACTOR DEMAND WHEN INPUTS ARE VARIABLE

When the firm is hiring more than one input, it is a more more difficult problem because a change in the price of one factor input may change the demand for other factor inputs. For example, the marginal product of labor may depend on the amount of capital in the production process. Also, the amount of capital employed may depend on the price of capital relative to the price of labor. We learned in Chapter 8 that a change in the input price will change the focus of cost-minimizing input combinations. Specifically, the firm will minimize the cost of production of a given level of output by having an input combination that equates the ratios of of marginal physical product to input prices for all inputs. (See Problem 13–5.)

$$MP_1/MFC_1 = MP_2/MFC_2 = MP_3/MFC_3$$

Suppose a firm uses labor or capital in the production process. As wages fall from W_0 to W_1, more laborers will be hired even if capital remains fixed, at say 5 units. Figure 13–5 shows this as a movement along MRP_L from A to B. However, as labor cost falls, so does the marginal cost of production. Consequently, the firm can afford to expand output and purchase additional units of capital, say, 8 units. The additional units of capital to work with will lead to an increase in the marginal product of labor, causing a rightward shift in the MRP_L curve, a move from points B to C in Figure 13–5. The firm's demand curve for labor when capital is variable is therefore the demand curve for labor that connects points A and C. Because the demand curve for labor when capital is variable (the long run) is more elastic than the MRP_L curve when capital is fixed (the short run), we can conclude that the demand for labor is more elastic in the long run than in the short run.

FIGURE 13–4
SHIFTS IN THE FACTOR-DEMAND CURVE

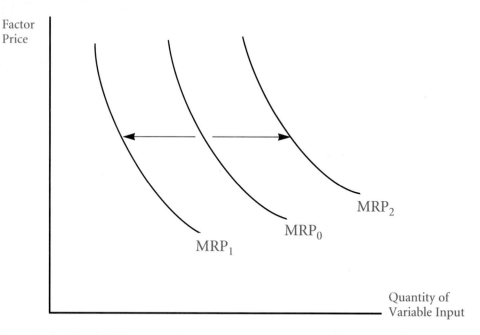

An increase in the product price (or marginal revenue) or and increase in the marginal product of the input will shift the MRP curve to the right. Alternatively, a decrease in the product price (or marginal revenue) or a decrease in the marginal product of the input will shift the MRP curve to the left.

13–5 A firm hires 30 units of factor 1 and 20 units of factor 2. The marginal products are 5 and 6, and the marginal factor costs are $2 and $3, respectively. Is the firm minimizing costs? If not, how should it adjust its expenditures?

Cost minimization requires that the MPP/MFC ratios of both factors be equal. For factor 1 MPP/MFC = 5/2 = 2.5. MPP/MFC = 6/3 = 2 for factor 2. Productivity per dollar is greater for factor 1, so the firm should hire more units of factor 1 and fewer units of factor 2.

FIGURE 13–5
DEMAND CURVE FOR LABOR WHEN INPUTS ARE VARIABLE

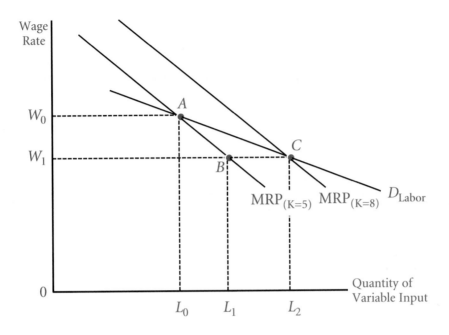

When wages fall from W_0 to W_1 (a movement from A to B), more laborers will be hired (L_0 to L_1) even if capital is fixed at 5 units. When labor costs fall, however, marginal costs of production fall and the firm can increase output and add units of capital, say 8 units. The additional units of capital cause an increase in MP causing MRP to shift to the right (a movement from B to C).

INDUSTRY DEMAND FOR LABOR[2]

The **industry demand for labor** can be precisely defined only if labor, or any other factor, is purchased in a perfectly competitive market. We should also note the important distinction between the firm's demand curve for labor and the industry demand curve for labor. Specifically, we assume that the product price is given when we derive the firm's demand curve for labor. Because the one curve allows the product price to vary and the other does not, we cannot merely take the horizontal sum of the individual firm demand curves to construct the industry demand curve for labor.

On the whole, the industry demand for labor or any other factor is likely to be much less elastic than demand for the typical individual firm (as shown in Figure 13–6). The primary reason for the different elasticities is that when all firms adjust output in response to a factor price change, the product prices of the firms are affected. For example, if the wage falls, the rational response of each firm is to hire more workers and increase

[2]The term *labor* refers to a particular type of homogeneous labor unit, not to labor of all types.

output, moving from point A to point B in Figure 13–6. Consequently, the market supply for output curve shifts to the right, implying a lower market price for the product, say $5 instead of $6. Because the output price is lower, MRP (MP • P) is also lower, resulting in fewer workers being hired. The change in MRP causes the sum of the firm labor-demand curves to shift left reducing their employment from L_1 to L_2 and moving from point B to point C in Figure 13–6. Therefore, the industry-demand curve for labor is constructed by connecting points A and C from the two summation curves in Figure 13–6.

FIGURE 13–6
THE INDUSTRY-DEMAND CURVE FOR LABOR

The industry-demand curve for labor, D, is less elastic than the sum of the firm's labor-demand curves, Σd_1. If the wage falls from W_0 to W_1, each firm anticipates hiring more labor as a result of product price reductions. Total employment along Σd_1 curve would rise to L_1. However, all firms (in attempting to hire and produce more) would collectively cause product price to fall and thus marginal revenue product to decline. The sum of firm labor-demand curves shifts to the left to Σd_2 as wage falls, leading to a smaller industry demand for labor increase, L_2.

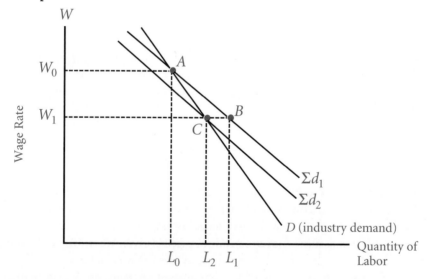

THE MARGINAL REVENUE PRODUCT PRINCIPLE AND BUSINESS POLICY

The principle that firms adjust the quantity of each factor purchased to the level at which MFC equals MRP follows logically from the assumption that firms seek to maximize profit. Actually, as previously indicated, this principle is merely a more precise way of expressing the rule that "workers will be hired only if they will pay for themselves." Obviously, however, firms do not always implement this principle.

One reason for this , as noted in earlier chapters, is that other motives besides profit maximization influence business decisions, and these motives may lead firms to depart from the MFC = MRP rule. If firms temporarily determine output and price on the basis of "satisfactory" rather than maximum profits, for example, output may be greater than the level at which MC equals MR, and the number of factor units acquired will be greater. A second reason is that in the desire to avoid taking action that will appear to aggravate an economic contraction, a firm may continue to employ more workers than the optimum number, if its finances permit. Third, in an effort to build a greater business empire, a firm may undertake unprofitable expansions involving the addition of factor units beyond the condition that MFC = MRP.

An analysis of factor demand built on the assumption of profit maximization, although not entirely adequate because of these exceptions, is nevertheless more satisfactory given the present state of knowledge than one built on any other assumption. (See Problem 13–6.)

13–6   Actual attainment of the goal of profit maximization in the hiring of inputs is obviously difficult. Why?

Determining MRP with any degree of accuracy is an extremely difficult task. Often, it is not even easy to determine the MPP of an additional factor unit (such as workers not directly involved in physical production). The firm's revenue schedule, knowledge of which is essential for determination of MRP, can at best only be estimated. The various determinants of marginal factor costs and marginal revenue product, such as the prices of other factors, techniques of production, and demand schedules, are constantly changing. As a consequence of these difficulties, all a producer can hope to do is to approximate the MFC = MRP rule. That is, if a firm expects that the hiring of an additional unit of a factor will bring forth marginal benefits that are greater than marginal costs, it will hire the unit. This is analogous to the difficulty firms have in precisely equating MR and MC. These models, however, while imprecise, can still be used to tell plausible and convincing stories.

13.4 FACTOR SUPPLY

For a theory of factor pricing, generalizations about factor supply must be very broad because the influences that affect supplies of particular factors are different.

The supply schedules of the various types of factors are considered in the next several chapters. At this point, though, one general statement may be useful. Decisions about the supply of factor units are made by the owners of these units, and the owners may have the option of using advantageously the units to satisfy their own wants. For example, a worker has the option of reserving his time for leisure instead of making it available for use in production, and a holder of money capital may gain the advantage of liquidity by holding the money. Thus, there is the possibility of a **"backward-bending" factor-supply curve**; that is, above a certain price level, owners may prefer to hold additional factor units to meet their own personal preferences for them because those units the owner does make available provide income that is regarded as adequate. At lower prices for the factor units, owners would supply larger quantities in order to obtain as much money income from the factor units as possible. Thus, the supply curve may appear as shown in Figure 13–7.

FIGURE 13–7
BACKWARD-BENDING FACTOR-SUPPLY CURVE

As the price of a factor rises initially, more may be offered for sale. Once the factor price reaches a certain point and factor owners obtain a particular income level, as factor price rises they may begin to offer fewer units for hire. Thus, the factor-supply curve may be positively sloped for lower prices, becoming negatively sloped at higher prices.

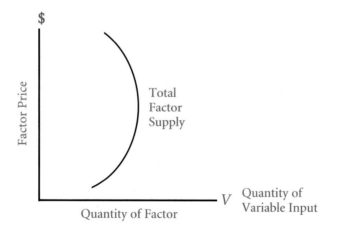

THE DETERMINANTS OF AGGREGATE LABOR SUPPLY

Labor services differ from other factor services in two primary respects: Workers are not produced on a profit-making basis, and the provision of labor services requires the direct participation of human beings. Thus, personal preferences between working and leisure as well as personal attitudes towards working conditions significantly influence supply. Accordingly, the determinants of the overall supply of labor available to the economy at any particular time include:

1. the total population capable of working.

2. institutional factors, such as educational requirements, minimum-age and wage legislation, compulsory retirement, and attitudes toward female workers. Compare, for example, two countries of equal population and similar age distribution. In one, women work, but in the other—say, a Moslem country—wives do not engage in labor outside the home. The market supply of labor will be much greater in the former than in the latter.

3. preferences for work as compared with leisure. There are only so many hours in a lifetime, and some of these are devoted to sleep and leisure rather than to work. Social customs and physiological requirements limit an individual's freedom of choice among the three alternatives, but much scope remains for individuals to decide for themselves what proportion of the total time to devote to each activity.

Given these considerations, what effect do wage changes have on the supply of labor? A higher wage may lure additional supplies into the labor market in one of two ways: (1) by causing those who are already working to work more hours per week—by working longer workdays, working on weekends, forgoing vacations, and so on; or (2) by luring into the labor market persons who would otherwise not work. These include persons who are able to subsist on nonlabor income or by depending on others, such as children or retired persons.

If wage changes have some effect on the labor supply, what is the nature of the relationship? Will the labor supply be greater at high wages than at low wages (as is true of the supply schedules of commodities)? The answer is by no means obvious, for rules that apply to commodities are not necessarily applicable to labor because workers have another use for their time—namely, leisure, an alternative not usually available to suppliers of commodities. Furthermore, wage increases have two conflicting effects on labor supply:

1. The Substitution Effect
When higher wages are offered, the cost of forgoing labor time to gain greater leisure time becomes greater; there is a tendency, therefore, to substitute labor for leisure. In other words, higher wages make leisure more costly—the opportunity cost of leisure rises.

2. The Income Effect
At higher wage levels, the income from a given quantity of labor is greater; the worker may therefore feel that he or she can afford more leisure. This assumes that leisure is a normal good because more is demanded at a higher income.

Because these forces operate in opposite directions, it is not possible to say what their net effect is and to define therefore the nature of the aggregate supply schedule of labor. The supply of labor is an empirical question that cannot be answered by deductive analysis. On the basis of available evidence, however, several observations can be made:

1. Most households must obtain wage income in order to maintain desired living standards; therefore, at least one family member ordinarily enters the labor market regardless of the wage rate. This consideration tends to make the supply schedule relatively inelastic.

2. Because of the requirements of modern production, most individuals have little control over hours worked. This is particularly true in manufacturing, where efficient production does not permit individual variance. This "all or nothing" consideration also tends to produce a more inelastic schedule.

3. Some variation in hours is possible through working overtime, moonlighting, and deferring retirement. Moreover, other members of the household may enter or leave the labor market at various times.

4. The portion of the schedule at relatively low wage rates is likely to be positively sloped, for higher wages bring forth additional labor hours. With wage rates very low, however, workers may not find it worthwhile to work additional hours; other members of the family may not find it worthwhile to enter the labor market at all, especially because doing so often results in additional costs for clothing, transportation, child care, and other expenses.

5. The upper portion of the schedule is more likely to show a negative relationship between wages and supply. As wages reach relatively high levels, people feel they can afford additional leisure because they can enjoy that leisure and yet maintain a relatively high standard of consumption. They refuse therefore overtime and will take more time off, and other family members may quit work.

6. The schedule is obviously affected by cultural patterns and goals. If maximization of income is paramount, higher wages bring forth additional labor hours. If, however, the primary goal is maintenance of a given standard of living, the reverse is true; as wages rise, persons work fewer hours to maintain the same living standard.

As a consequence of these considerations, it is possible that the supply curve of labor as a whole is backward sloping (or at least, very inelastic), as illustrated by the labor-supply curve in Figure 13–8. Labor-supply elasticity also varies according to the group being considered. For example, empirical studies have shown that the labor-supply curve for females slopes upward. This means that the substitution effect dominates the income effect. For older men, on the other hand, it is backward bending, meaning that the income effect eventually dominates the substitution effect.

How can we specify how much an *individual* is willing to work at different real wages? We can establish an individual's supply curve for labor by using indifference curves that place daily income on the vertical axis and hours of leisure per day on the horizontal axis. Recalling consumer theory (Chapter 4) we know that the shape of an indifference curve represents the individual's willingness to trade-off between income and leisure. Figure 13–9 depicts an individual's preferences between income (assuming for simplicity all income comes from wages) and leisure. Higher wages can entice someone to give up some leisure for more work, as shown in the movement from l_1 to l_2. This movement comprises an income effect and a substitution effect.

Figure 13–10 shows what happens when real wages rise, causing potential income (if zero leisure were bought) to rise from y' to y'', and then to y'''. As real wages (the slope of the budget constraint in Figure 13–10) rise from y' to y'', the individual again trades some leisure (l_1 - l_2) for additional income (y_2 - y_1); in this case, the substitution effect dominates the income effect. However, if real wages continue to climb (reflected by ever steeper budget constraints), this individual might cut back on the amount of work per day, presumably because he or she now feels wealthier and is in a position to demand more leisure. In this range the income effect dominates the substitution effect, as shown in Figure 13–11. (See Problem 13–7.)

FIGURE 13–8
AGGREGATE LABOR-SUPPLY CURVE

The aggregate labor-supply curve—the schedule of labor hours supplied from the total populous at different wage rates—bends back if all individual labor-supply curves (including those of the nonworking population) turn back at similar wage levels. Generally, the aggregate labor-supply curve slopes upward throughout.

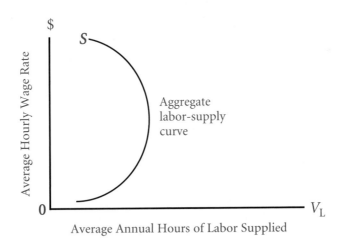

FIGURE 13–9
PREFERENCES BETWEEN INCOME AND LEISURE

The indifference curves chart the combinations of income and leisure that give the individual the same degree of satisfaction. The budget line shows the amounts of leisure and income the consumer can afford, given his or her daily income. The horizontal intercept (the hours of leisure if income is zero) is 24 hours per day; the vertical intercept (income earned with no leisure) is 24 times the hourly wage. The absolute value of the slope of the budget line is the hourly wage. The tangency of the indifference curve and budget line identifies the optimum amount of income Y_1, leisure l_1, and work hours $(24 - l_1)$. When the wage rises, the budget line becomes steeper and the individual consumes less leisure at l_2 and works more hours.

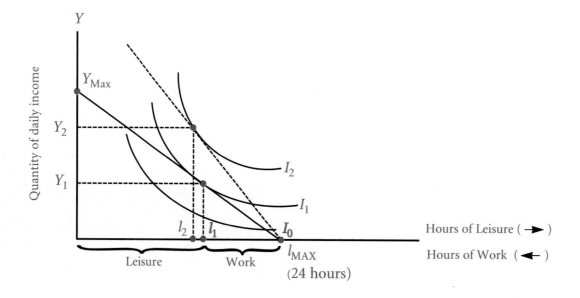

FIGURE 13–10
PREFERENCES BETWEEN INCOME AND LEISURE AS REAL WAGES RISE

The first wage increase rotates the budget line from Y' to Y''. The worker chooses to reduce leisure hours and increase work effort. Thus, the substitution effect dominates the income effect (the movement from *a* to *b*). A second pay raise pivots the budget line to Y''', raising leisure hours to l_3, and reducing optimum work hours (the movement from *b* to *c*). In this case, the income effect overwhelms the substitution effect.

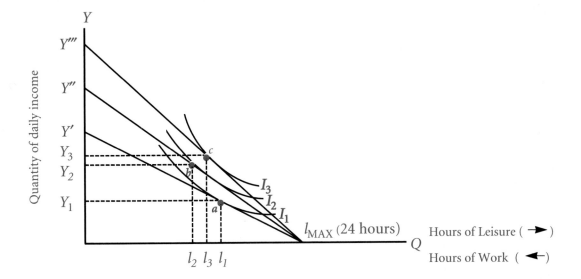

FIGURE 13–11
CONVENTIONAL LABOR-SUPPLY CURVE

This individual's labor-supply curve is derived from the preference mapping in Figure 13–10. The original wage rate, W_1, is the slope of budget line y'. The person is willing to work 24 - l_1 hours at that wage rate. When the wage rate rises to W_2, more work hours $(24 - l_2)$ are offered, but an additional pay increase reduces optimal labor hours to 24 - l_3. A backward-bending supply curve arises, therefore, from the dominance of the substitution effect at low wage levels and the dominance of the income effect at higher wage levels.

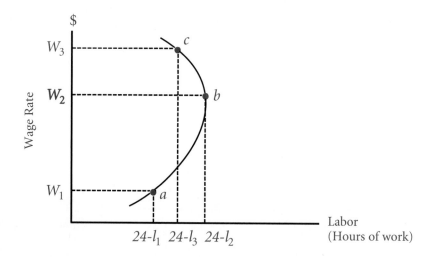

13–7 Mariah recently received a trust fund that pays her a daily allowance of $50. Using the work-leisure model, show how Mariah's hours of leisure and work are affected.

In the accompanying figure, Mariah's budget constraint shifts up by the daily amount of the trust fund, $50. The slope of the budget line, $-W$, is unaffected because her salary did not change, but the Y intercept shifts up to $24W + \$50$, the total income earned if Mariah worked 24 hours per day (where W is Mariah's hourly wage). If Mariah worked zero hours consuming 24 hours of leisure, she would still receive $50 (point C). Mariah's optimum combination of leisure and income before receiving the trust fund is A, but after she receives the trust fund it moves to B. Because Mariah increases her hours of leisure from l_0 to l_1, the trust fund reduces her labor hours supplied. Mariah's income increases from Y_0 to Y_1, and her utility also increases because she is now on a higher indifference curve.

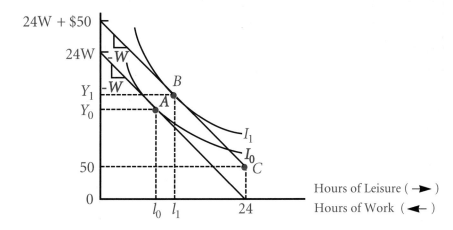

Figure 13–11 summarizes these changes in a conventional labor-supply-curve diagram. This one happens to be backward bending, as is the aggregate labor-supply curve depicted in Figure 13–8. (See Problems 13–8, 13–9, and 13–10.)

13–8 True or False? If all individuals have backward-bending labor-supply curves, this implies that the labor-supply curve to a particular industry or occupation is also backward bending.

False. Each individual may, above a certain wage (which depends on the individual), supply less labor of a given skill at progressively higher wages. However, this is extremely unlikely for any particular industry or occupation as a whole. As the wage rises within that industry or occupation, labor is attracted to it from other industries and from similar occupations. We may not wish to work more at higher wages, but we all want higher wages for the same work! This results in labor-supply curves of the usual, upward-sloping type.

13—9 Derive the labor-supply curve for an individual for whom the substitution effect dominates the income effect at all wage levels.

When the substitution effect always overwhelms the income effect, the individual always reduces the consumption of leisure and supplies more labor when wages rise. The accompanying figure depicts budget line and indifference curves for a person with such tastes. The corresponding labor-supply curve always slopes upward when the substitution effect outweighs the income effect.

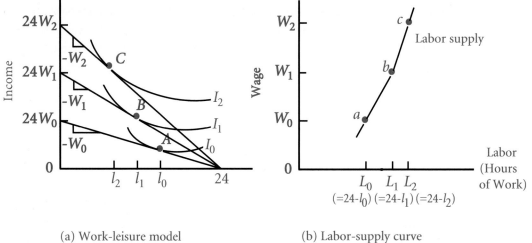

(a) Work-leisure model   (b) Labor-supply curve

Labor Supply when the Substitution Effect Exceeds the Income Effect

13–10 Lucy earns $\$W$ per hour and works 8 hours per day. Using the work-leisure model, show Lucy's current equilibrium. Now Lucy and Ricky get married, and Lucy figures her share of Ricky's income is one-half of his earnings, or Y^* per day. Show how Lucy's equilibrium hours of work are affected. How does this differ from her choice of hours worked if her wage had increased?

Lucy's original equilibrium (point A) is compared to her equilibrium after marriage (point B) in the accompanying figure. The extra income from Ricky reduces her labor hours supplied to 4 hours per day. The effect of a wage increase yielding the same income level for Lucy is shown as the movement from A to C. In this case, Lucy increases work hours to 10 hours per day because the substitution effect outweighs the income effect.

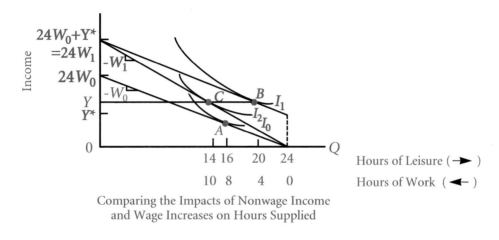

Comparing the Impacts of Nonwage Income
and Wage Increases on Hours Supplied

SUPPLY OF LABOR OF PARTICULAR TYPES

Labor is not homogeneous. The aggregate supply of labor consists of a set of supplies of workers with various skills and training. The schedule for any particular type of labor—clerical workers, mechanics, carpenters, and so on—is typically more elastic than the overall supply because workers can shift from one occupation to another. Whether they do depends on the degree of skill required, the number of persons in other occupations with relevant skills, the extent to which seniority and pension rights restrict mobility, and the importance of prestige and other nonmonetary considerations in various types of employment.

The supply of any particular type of labor is more elastic over the long run than in the short run because, given time, additional persons can gain the necessary training and skills. New workers more readily enter fields in which labor is relatively scarce and wage rates are correspondingly attractive. On the whole, however, regardless of the time period, the possibility that people can shift occupations creates a positive relationship between the wage rate and the quantity of labor supplied. Thus, if work/leisure considerations for a particular type of labor also produce a positive relationship, the combined effect of the two influences is sure to be positive. Higher wage rates not only lure workers from other occupations but will also induce additional persons to work or existing workers to work more hours. If the work/leisure relationship produces a negative effect, however, the net influence depends on the relative strength of the two conflicting forces. (See Problem 13–11.)

13–11   How might the supply curve for labor facing an individual firm differ from the supply curve for the total labor force?

While the labor-supply curve faced by an individual firm is quite elastic, the entire labor force supplies labor inelastically, as already indicated. For example, publishing firms might be able to attract additional employees from other industries by offering a slightly higher wage. Other things equal, people always wish to leave lower paying jobs for higher paying jobs, even if skill levels are somewhat different. However, the publishing firm's decision to pay higher wages does not affect the labor-supply curve for the whole economy. The decision to work or not and how many hours to work is not as much affected by wages as the decision of which industry to work in, which in some cases would involve new skills or training.

13.5 PERFECTLY COMPETITIVE WAGE LEVELS

If labor markets were perfectly competitive, the wages of each type of labor would tend to come to a level at which the demand for and supply of the particular type of labor were equal. If the wage level were temporarily higher, the number of workers available would exceed the number that employers wished to hire at that wage rate; wages would decline as workers sought the higher-wage jobs and offered to work for somewhat lower wages. If wages were temporarily below the equilibrium figure, employers would seek to hire more workers than were available; they would compete against each other for additional workers and therefore bid the wage up toward the equilibrium level. (See Problems 13–12, 13–13, and 13–14.)

In perfect competition, the intersection of the aggregate labor demand-and-supply curves identifies the equilibrium wage rate for a particular type of labor. Wage rates higher than W_0 create unemployment and downward pressure on the wage. If the wage falls short of W_0, there will be a shortage and wages will be bid up by firms. The labor market for each occupation is at full employment in a competitive equilibrium.

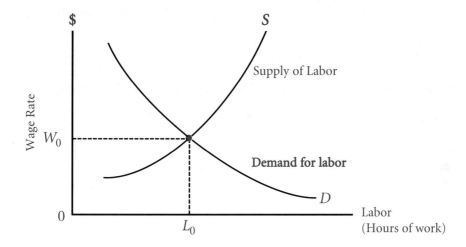

13–12 Professional athletes typically receive higher salaries than school teachers. Yet teachers, not athletes, are considered essential to economic growth and development. If this is the case, why do athletes receive higher salaries than teachers?

Individuals earn different wages for various reasons; they have different skill levels and educational backgrounds, some engage in life-threatening occupations (lumberjacks, firefighters, high-rise construction workers, and so on), and some have strong locational preferences (for example, they take a lower nominal wage to stay in a geographical area they love). Teachers and talented athletes are primarily in skills levels and are subject to supply and demand for those skills. For instance, extremely talented basketball players are in short supply relative to the demand for their services. On the other hand, while the demand for teachers is large, the supply of people who are willing to supply teaching services is also relatively abundant. These two labor markets are depicted in the accompanying graphs.

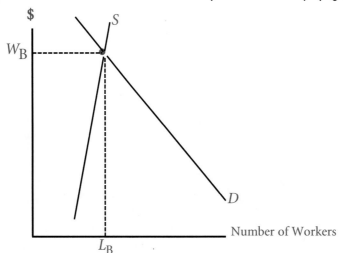

(a) Professional Basketball Players

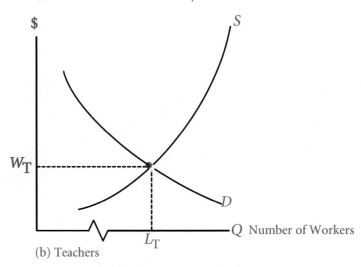

(b) Teachers

13–13 Many foreigners are motivated to migrate to the United States because of the higher real wages. Other things equal, what impact would a large influx of legal (or illegal) immigrants have on real wages?

Immigrants entering the United States would depress wages, as seen in the accompanying below. On the other side of the coin, however, consumers might benefit from lower prices as a result of falling factor (labor) prices. If consumers gain more than producers lose, the net economic effect may be positive.

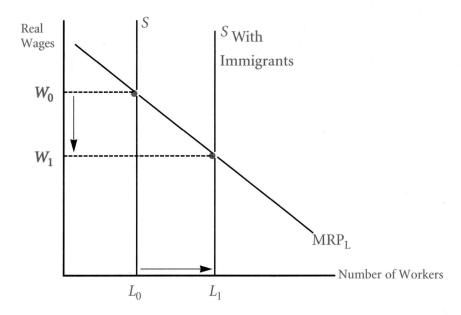

13–14 The formation of unions may increase wages in union jobs but lower wages in nonunion jobs. Discuss why this is or is not possible.

Suppose you have two labor sectors: the union sector and the nonunion sector. If unions are successful in obtaining higher wages either through collective bargaining or by limiting the number of workers admitted into the union sector (and thus bidding up wages), employment will lower in that sector. With a downward-sloping demand curve for labor, higher wages mean less labor is demanded in the union sector. Those unable to find union work will seek nonunion work, thus increasing the supply in that sector and in turn lowering wages for nonunion workers.

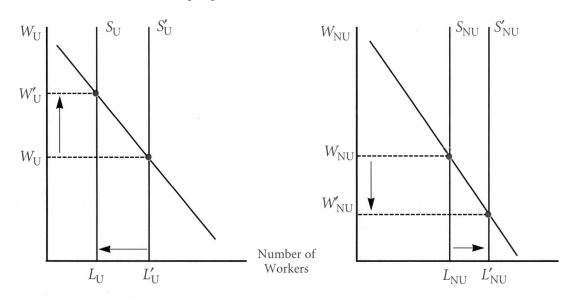

13.6 MONOPOLISTIC INFLUENCES IN LABOR MARKETS

The influence which an employer can exert on wages depends in part on the mobility of workers and in part on the extent of competition for workers by employers. If workers move freely from one firm to another, and if firms act independently in determining wage and employment policy, any one employer's control over wages would be small. In practice, however, the mobility of workers may be more limited. For example, many workers can not costlessly move in response to wage differentials because they are tied rather closely to a particular firm by various bonds. These bonds include privileges based on seniority in the present job, such as pension and continued employment rights; reluctance of workers to leave one job until they find another; preference for living in a particular locality and working with friends; and personnel and hiring policies that prevent effective competition between those seeking employment in the firm and those already employed.

LABOR IMMOBILITY AND MONOPSONY

Monopsony occurs when there is a single buyer of an input or resource. The basic feature of monopsony is the employer's recognition that the wage it must pay depends on the number of workers hired; that is, the supply schedule of labor is not perfectly elastic. The greater the immobility of workers, the less elastic the schedule will be.

Because additional workers (at least beyond a certain point) can only be obtained by offering a higher wage, the monopsonist's marginal factor cost exceeds the wage paid. Figure 13–13 illustrates the marginal-factor cost curve (MFC) as above the supply curve of labor (S). In hiring workers up to the point at which MFC equals MRP, the employer will not reach the point at which the wage is equal to MRP. The firm will thus hire only L_M workers in equilibrium at a wage rate W_1, whereas it would hire L_{PC} workers in equilibrium at the wage rate W_0, the rate which would prevail if the market were competitive.

FIGURE 13–13
DETERMINATION OF THE OPTIMAL NUMBER OF WORKERS WITH MONOPSONY

The monopsonist maximizes profits by employing workers until marginal factor cost equals the marginal revenue product at L_M. The labor-supply curve shows that these L_M workers are willing to work for only W_1, the wage rate paid by the firm. If the labor market had been perfectly competitive, the wage and employment levels would be W_0 and L_{PC}, respectively.

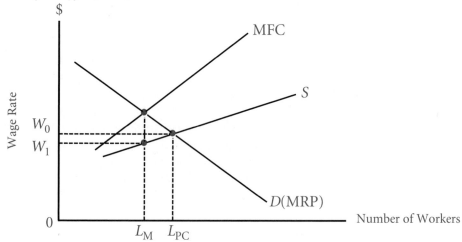

It must be emphasized that the supply price—the wage the employer must pay to get a given number of workers—depends primarily upon the exact degree of immobility of labor or, in other words, on the alternative opportunities of workers. Two extreme cases illustrate the concept. If there is only one employer in a certain market (perhaps in an isolated mining town) and workers cannot move, the necessary wage would be extremely low—one just high enough to induce the workers to seek employment instead of starving to death. At the other extreme, workers are highly (but not perfectly) mobile among employers; the supply schedule would be highly elastic, and competition among employers would bring the wage level close to the perfectly competitive figure, even though the initiative in the setting of wage rates rests with employers. Between these extremes, there is a wide variety of possible cases, differing on the basis of the elasticity of labor supply among firms. (See Problem 13–15.)

13–15   Why does the monopsonist face an upward-sloping supply curve for labor? Is the marginal amount it has to pay for an additional worker greater than the amount it has to pay all its workers?

Simple mathematics provides the answer to this one. Let's say our firm employs 5 workers at $50 each. However, the sixth worker will not take the job for less than $51; to hire the sixth worker the firm must pay all 6 workers $51. Thus, the marginal cost of the sixth worker is $56 [$51 to new worker + ($1 x 5 current workers)], while the average cost is $51 per worker. (Marginal cost of labor is greater than the average cost.) The supply curve is upward sloping because in order to attract new employees, employers must offer a higher wage.

BILATERAL MONOPOLY AND BILATERAL OLIGOPOLY

In the preceding section, it was assumed that the number of sellers was large. But monopsony or oligopsony on the buyers' side may be accompanied by monopoly or oligopoly on the sellers' side. Such cases are referred to as **bilateral monopoly** and **bilateral oligopoly**. If both oligopsony and oligopoly are complete, firms may succeed in setting a price that will maximize the gains of both buyers and sellers and split the gains on the basis of bargaining. But it is perhaps more likely that differences in bargaining strength will result in a figure relatively more advantageous to the stronger party than the amount of the maximum-joint-gain. No matter how strong buyers are, they cannot keep price below the average cost of the sellers or their supply will disappear. With prices above the maximum, sales of the product produced by buyers will drop sufficiently to cut profits all along the line. Subject to these limits, which may be far apart, the actual price may depend on bargaining, and no further generalization is possible. The theory of games, discussed in Chapter 12, has been of some use in analyzing the strategies that oligopolists and oligopsonists might follow in dealing with each other, but there are few settled questions in this area of economic theory. (See Problem 13–16.)

13–16 What would be the equilibrium wage and employment level for an oligopsony hiring from a large pool of labor?

For an oligopsony, the equilibrium wage and employment rate are indeterminate. We can, however, delineate the boundaries of the wage and employment rates. In the accompanying figure, W_0 and L_0 are the wage and employment rates for a collusive oligopoly acting as a monopsonist, and they represent the lower boundaries. If the oligopsony's power totally breaks down and firms compete for labor, the competitive wage and employment levels, W_1 and L_1, will result. Generally, the wage and employment levels will lie somewhere between these two extremes.

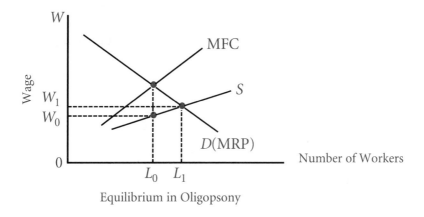

Equilibrium in Oligopsony

SUMMARY

1. In a market economy, prices paid by producers for factors are the primary source of income to households.

2. Factor price levels affect the costs and relative outputs of various goods; they also determine the share of national income persons receive.

3. Factor pricing does not tell us much about how any particular individual shares in the national income.

4. A firm finds it profitable to hire any factor unit that "pays for itself."

5. Marginal factor cost equals average factor cost only when there is perfect competition. If the firm is a monopsonistic buyer of the factor, average factor costs are an increasing function of quantity purchased. If a firm receives quantity discounts, average factor costs are a decreasing function of quantity purchased.

6. Except for the case of perfect competition, we must distinguish between the price at which a firm expects to sell an additional unit of product and the prevailing price.

7. At any least-cost combination of inputs, the firm's marginal cost of hiring an additional unit of any factor must be equal to the marginal product of the factor multiplied by the marginal revenue.

8. To maximize profit, the firm must (1) combine factor inputs to produce each given level of output at minimum total cost and (2) choose the level of output at which MR equals MC. In this way, we arrive at our general rule: it is rational for a firm to continue hiring any (or all) inputs up to the amount where MFC = MP • MR.

9. In general, MP rises initially and then declines, both in the short run, when plant capacity is fixed and in the long run.

10. A firm's demand for any factor input depends on the structure of market where the input is purchased, the firm's production function, and the structure of the market in which the firm's product is sold.

11. The elasticity of the factor-demand curve depends on the marginal rate of substitution between a given factor and all others, the rate of decline in the MP when additional units of a factor are added to increase output, the price elasticity of demand for the firm's product, and the ratio of variable costs to total production costs.

12. Major causes of changes in the factor-demand schedule include technological change, changes in the price of other factors, and changes in the demand for the firm's products.

13. The market demand for labor, or any other factor, is usually much less elastic than is the output demand facing a typical firm.

14. Factor supply (except in capital markets where the cost of production is relevant to supply) depends on the number of units of the particular type of factor in existence and on the willingness of factor owners to allow their factor units to be used in production.

15. It is possible to have a backward-bending supply curve in factor markets; that is, above a certain price (wage) level, factor owners may prefer to withhold additional factor units to meet their own personal preferences, especially for labor. At lower factor prices, larger quantities would be supplied in order to obtain sufficient factor income.

16. There are two opposing effects that determine the relationship of wages to an indi vidual's willingness to supply labor. At higher wages the substitution effect results in more work, while the income effects lead to less work. The shape of an individual's labor-supply curve depends on the relative strengths of these two effects.

17. If labor markets were perfectly competitive, the prevailing wage rate for each type of labor would occur at the level where the demand for and supply of the particular type of labor were equal.

18. The influence that an employer can exert on wages depends in part upon the mobility of workers and in part upon the extent of competition for workers by employers.

WORDS AND CONCEPTS TO KNOW

factor prices and the distribution of income	factor demand
rule of optimal factor use	average factor cost
marginal factor cost	marginal revenue product
elasticity of factor demand	industry demand for labor
factor supply	backward-bending factor-supply curve
the substitution effect	the income effect
perfectly competitive wage levels	monopsony
bilateral monopoly	bilateral oligopoly

REVIEW QUESTIONS

1. Why is it necessary to analyze factor pricing separate from the pricing of products?

2. Why is the theory of factor pricing often called the theory of income distribution?

3. Under what circumstances does the marginal outlay on a factor exceed the price paid for the factor? Under what circumstances is the marginal outlay less than the price paid for the factor?

4. What is marginal product? Average revenue product? Marginal revenue product?

5. Under what circumstances is each of the following true?
   (a) Marginal revenue product is less than average revenue product.
   (b) Marginal revenue product is zero; yet average revenue product is positive.

6. Complete the table below.

Units of Factor	Total Output	Marginal Product	Price of Product	Total Revenue	Marginal Revenue Product	Average Revenue Product
1	40	· · · · · · ·	$1.40	· · · · · · ·	· · · · · · ·	· · · · · · ·
2	90	· · · · · · ·	1.35	· · · · · · ·	· · · · · · ·	· · · · · · ·
3	130	· · · · · · ·	1.30	· · · · · · ·	· · · · · · ·	· · · · · · ·
4	150	· · · · · · ·	1.25	· · · · · · ·	· · · · · · ·	· · · · · · ·
5	165	· · · · · · ·	1.20	· · · · · · ·	· · · · · · ·	· · · · · · ·
6	172	· · · · · · ·	1.15	· · · · · · ·	· · · · · · ·	· · · · · · ·
7	175	· · · · · · ·	1.10	· · · · · · ·	· · · · · · ·	· · · · · · ·

7. For a given plant, why does MRP decline as units of the factor are added beyond a certain point? Why is the rate of decline faster where there is imperfect competition in the output market than it is with perfect competition (other conditions being the same)?

8. Construct a demand schedule for the factor for which the product data are given in Question 6 above.

9. Plot MRP and ARP data from Question 6, and connect the appropriate points to represent the firm's demand curve for the factor.

10. Why, if the firm's objective is to maximize profits, does a competitive firm expand the number of units of a factor used up to the point at which the MFC of the factor is equal to the MRP?

11. If MFC exceeds the factor price, will the firm hire more or fewer units with a given schedule of productivity relative to the case in which the MFC is flat? Why?

12. What will be the effect on the demand for a factor of each of the following?
    (a) increased substitutability of this factor for other factors
    (b) a decline in demand for the product of the industry
    (c) increased prices of other factors

13. Why is the market-demand curve for a factor likely to have a steeper slope than any one firm's demand curve for the factor?

14. Why, in practice, might firms not always expand the use of factor units up to the point at which the factor's marginal-revenue product is equal to its marginal cost?

15. What is the difference between the determinants of the supply of capital and other types of factors?

16. How do you determine the market price of a certain type of factor, assuming a perfectly competitive market for the factor?

17. Why, under competitive assumptions, must the equilibrium factor price equal the marginal revenue product of the factor?

18. How can the statement that the equilibrium factor price is equal to the marginal revenue product have precise meaning when the marginal revenue product varies with the number of factor units employed?

19. Explain the two conflicting considerations which influence the nature of the supply function of labor.

20. What is meant by a backward-bending supply curve? Under what circumstances will the supply curve of labor have this shape?

21. Why is the supply of labor believed to be relatively inelastic?

22. Empirical evidence shows that as real incomes have increased over the years, average number of hours in the work week have declined. What significance does this evidence have for the labor-supply curve?

23. What additional considerations influence the supply of any particular type of labor?

24. What are the major factors that influence the elasticity of demand for labor?

25. Explain the level to which wages would come in a perfectly competitive labor market.

26. What effect does the presence of monopsony in the labor markets have upon the determination of wage levels? Explain.

27. Why might employers deliberately pay higher wages than the minimum figures necessary to obtain the optimum number of workers?

SUGGESTED READINGS

Alchian, Armen, and William Allen. *Exchange and Production: Competition, Coordination and Control.* 3rd ed. Belmont, Calif.: Wadsworth, 1983, Chapters 14 and 15.

Baumol, W. J. *Economic Theory and Operations Analysis.* 4th ed. Englewood Cliffs, N.J.: Prentice Hall, 1977, Chapter 24.

Ehrenberg, Ronald G., and Robert S. Smith. *Modern Labor Economics: Theory and Public Policy.* 5th ed. New York: Harper Collins, 1994.

Sowell, Thomas. *Markets and Minorities.* New York: Basic Books, 1981.

Stigler, George. *The Theory of Price.* 4th ed. New York: Macmillan, 1987.

Chapter Fourteen

THE THEORY OF INTEREST AND CAPITAL MARKETS

Questions to Think About

1. What is the real interest rate? The nominal interest rate?

2. How is the equilibrium rate of interest determined?

3. What purpose does the interest rate serve?

4. How does the market for capital goods differ from other input markets?

5. What is the difference between capital widening and capital deepening?

6. What factors shift the demand for capital curve?

7. What is discounted present value? Internal rate of return? Payback period?

8. How do firms make investment decisions in light of risk?

9. How is equilibrium price and quantity determined in the capital-goods market?

14.1 INTRODUCTION

In this chapter we begin with a discussion of what interest rates are and how they are determined. Specifically, we will find that the supply and demand for money capital will determine market interest rates. Then we will examine how these market interest rates influence capital-investment decisions.

Most people think of interest as money that banks pay on savings deposits or that finance companies charge on installment purchases of products such as household appliances and automobiles. That understanding of interest is correct, but it is more accurate to think of interest generally as a rate of return implied by a loan contract or IOU. For example, when individuals loan money to banks in the form of savings deposits, the contract obligates the issuer of the deposit (a bank) to pay the buyer (the depositor) a stated percentage of the amount borrowed at regular time intervals. In this chapter, we shall speak (as is customary) as if just one rate of interest existed—the "market" interest rate, rather than many rates that prevail in the real world. This practice makes no substantive difference in the discussion because the interest rates tend to move together.

14.2 THE NATURE OF INTEREST

In a monetary economy where each individual held and used only assets that were saved and accumulated, interest payments would be nonexistent, for no person would ever be a borrower or a lender. However, interest payments would likely arise in a world without money. In biblical times, for instance, it was common for one person to lend another a stock of seed in return for the borrower's promise to return the wheat, with interest in the form of an additional quantity of wheat, at the end of harvest season. Accordingly, we may view **interest**, quite generally, *as any payment that is made by a borrower to induce a lender willingly to part with the use of an asset for a specified period of time.*

In modern times, interest seldom takes any form but money because it is normally more convenient to borrow money from one person and buy a physical asset from another than to borrow a physical asset directly from a potential lender. But the ultimate effect is much the same as if the lender of money purchased a physical asset and loaned it, rather than money, to a borrower. In many instances, indeed, the lender of money becomes the legal owner of a physical asset by requiring that it serve as collateral for the loan (a standard procedure in the case of automobile loans).

A person who currently has wealth in the form of money—currency (dollars and cents) or demand deposits (checking account)—is assumed to have three basic alternatives: (1) they can spend it on consumption, (2) they can continue to hold it in the form of money balances, or (3) they can lend it to another transactor such as a household, business firm, bank, or the government. In classical economic doctrine, interest was traditionally regarded as a payment to induce a person to save rather than to consume. It is more common today to regard interest as a compensation paid to holders of liquid wealth to induce them to make it available to others rather than to hold it idle or to use it to purchase resources for their own use. (See Problems 14–1 and 14–2.)

14–1 True or False? $1000 today is as good as $1000 a year from now.

False. Most people will prefer $1000 today to $1000 a year from now, even if they cannot earn interest. At worst, they can hold the $1000 until they have a use for it, whereas if they had to wait, they might be deprived of something they would like to buy in the interim. But few people have an insatiable lust for current consumption; when income rises above a certain level, therefore, almost every individual will put aside part of their current income for future use: to build a reserve for emergency purposes, to accumulate for old age, or for some particular use in the future, such as educating children, purchasing a home, or establishing a business.

14–2 What do pawnshops sell?

The typical response is that they sell used goods. In fact, they sell very few used goods. However, they do sell something that is even more important to their clientele. They sell liquidity—cash. When individuals hock their wares at pawnshops, they are usually desperate and are willing to pledge their watches, rings, or whatever as collateral. The pawnshop will allow you to buy your pawned item back in some specified time period for a higher price (that is, an interest charge). In this sense, pawnshops are like banks and will lend you money for a specified period of time if you are willing to pay the interest. But even if individuals don't buy their pawned item back, this behavior of selling and taking a lower price than could be obtained through the classifieds in order to get the money now demonstrates that buyers are willing to pay for liquidity.

INFLATION AND INTEREST RATES

Unanticipated inflation affects the nominal, or money, interest rate. The money or **nominal interest rate** is the one that is, implied on a IOU that promises to pay money, and is the rate quoted in the newspaper or on television. However, another, more important interest rate is the **real interest rate**, which is the nominal interest rate minus the rate of change in the price level.

The distinction between nominal and real interest rates is particularly critical during periods of unanticipated inflation. For example, in the late 1970s consumers were complaining about the "excessively high" interest rates of 15 percent. But the change in the price level was also close to 15 percent; the real interest rate, therefore, was only slightly positive. Remember: decisions about borrowing and investing are made on the basis of the expected real interest rate not the nominal interest rate. This chapter deals primarily with real interest rates.

14.3 THE EQUILIBRIUM INTEREST RATE

However, the important task is not to explain what interest really is but to describe how interest rates are determined. We must consider the supply and demand for loanable funds.

The *supply of loanable funds* may be defined as the amounts of funds available to borrowers (businesses and government) at various interest rate levels in a given period of time. There will be a positive relationship between the interest rate and the supply of loanable funds as illustrated in Figure 14–1. At higher interest rates, holding on to non-interest-bearing money becomes more costly and the propensity to save increases. The demand for loanable funds consists of the total amount of loanable funds that will be invested during the period by business firms (and governmental units) at various interest rate levels. At higher interest rates less will be borrowed simply because it is relatively more expensive to consume from borrowing funds.

The most important function that the interest rate performs in the operation of the economy may be summarized briefly. The interest rate acts to equilibrate the supply of loanable funds with the demand for it by inducing persons to make available their liquid wealth to finance business expansion.

Under the assumption of perfect competition in the market for loanable funds, the interest rate must come to a level at which the total demand for loanable funds is equal to the total supply available. Figure 14–1 indicates the determination of the basic equilibrium interest rate, r (5 percent in Figure 14–1). This equilibrium rate of interest will be maintained so long as there are no shifts in the demand-and-supply curves. If the interest rate is higher than r, the total supply of loanable funds will exceed the demand, and suppliers will lower the rate; if the actual interest rate is lower than r, demand will exceed supply, and the rate will be bid up by borrowers. (See Problem 14–3.)

FIGURE 14–1
THE EQUILIBRIUM RATE OF INTEREST

Under perfect competition, the equality of loanable funds supplied and demanded determines the equilibrium rate of interest, 5 percent in this example.

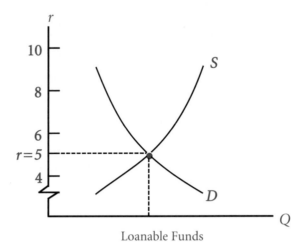

Loanable Funds

14–3 Suppose that the supply and demand for loanable funds are given by $S_{LF} = 2r$ and $D_{LF} = 15 - r$, where r is the percentage rate of interest and the prevailing interest rate is 7.5%. What would you expect to happen to the interest rate?

If $r = 7.5\%$, $S_{LF} = 15$, $D_{LF} = 7.5$ and there is excess supply of loanable funds, lenders will have to lower their interest-rate requirements in order to loan out their available funds. The interest rate will decline until it reaches 5%, the equilibrium rate which equates S_{LF} and D_{LF}. This is illustrated below.

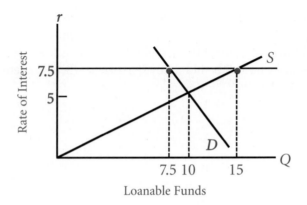

Loanable Funds

14–4 Explain how each of the following would influence the equilibrium rate of interest:
(a) a tax exemption on individual retirement accounts (IRAs)
(b) a rising federal budget deficit
(c) corporate income taxes
(d) a change of social attitudes favoring materialism

(a) Saving is less expensive when IRAs are exempt from taxation. Some people will save more, increasing the supply of available loanable funds and reducing the interest rate as in Figure (a).

(b) To finance a larger budget deficit, the federal government requires greater funding, increasing the demand for loanable funds and raising the interest rate—see Figure (b).

(c) Corporate income taxes lower the net returns from capital goods investment to the firm, decreasing the demand for loanable funds and reducing the interest rate—see Figure (c).

(d) When materialism becomes more fashionable, individuals may consume more today and save less, the supply of loanable funds declines, and the interest rate rises. Figure (d) below shows that rising product demand may also increase the marginal revenue product of capital through higher product prices, raising the demand for loanable funds and further boosting the interest rate.

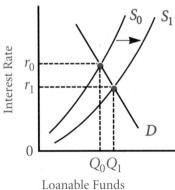

(a) An increase in supply

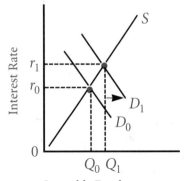

(b) An increase in demand

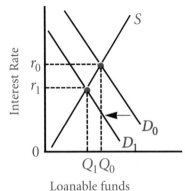

(c) A decrease in the demand

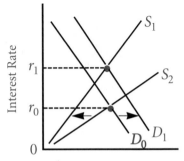

(d) A decrease in supply accompanied by an increase in demand

14.4 CAPITAL GOODS

Durable capital goods are distinguished from the so-called basic production factors—labor and land—in the sense that they are produced by people rather than supplied by nature. The use of such goods by firms introduces an important time element into the production process. This is because the services embodied in a capital good cannot be used at the moment the good is produced or purchased but must be drawn upon over an (often extended) interval of time. The discussion in this chapter focuses only on **fixed capital assets**—relatively long-lived capital goods such as plant, machinery, and buildings. Many other kinds of durable capital goods—previously processed materials, refined fuel, goods in process, stocks of finished goods—are produced and used up in the course of production processes and thus represent a kind of "circulating capital." Such goods are not necessarily short-lived, but in practice they seldom survive in that form for more than a few days or weeks. They are excluded from the analysis in this chapter not because they are unimportant (for they are important), but rather because to examine them effectively would require an explicit account of the dynamics of production processing and inventory adjustment—an area of analysis outside the scope of this book.

The theoretical analysis of the pricing of fixed capital assets involves some complications that do not arise—or that arise only to a minor degree—in connection with other kinds of factor inputs.

One of these complications is that fixed capital goods have to be financed before the final outputs produced with their services are sold. With labor, the opposite is usually the case. Payment for labor services is made only after those services have been used in production. Of course, a certain amount of loanable funds is needed to finance purchases of any kind of factor service, because in any production process some time typically elapses between the purchase of factor units and the sale of outputs produced with such units. However, financing requirements figure much more prominently in decisions about fixed capital goods than in decisions involving other kinds of factors.

A second complication is that fixed capital goods are commonly used over a period of several years. As a result, the risk that the firm will not achieve expected returns on the factor is much higher than it is on factors that are purchased and used on a more current basis. All production requires prediction, but predictions about sales and prices a week or month in the future obviously are much more likely to be accurate than predictions about more distant periods.

14.5 SOURCES OF PRODUCTIVITY OF CAPITAL GOODS

A firm may desire additional capital goods for several reasons:

1. To Replace Existing Capital Goods
A large portion of gross investment each year is designed to replace existing capital goods that have either worn out physically or become economically obsolete. A firm calculates the profitability of replacement investment in essentially the same way as it calculates that of new investment, except that it needs to consider the gain from continued use of old equipment relative to the gain from purchasing new equipment. For example, relative maintenance expenses of new and old equipment must be included in the calculation. (See Problem 14–6.)

2. To Permit Capital Widening
Capital widening refers to increasing the total stock of capital goods without changing capital intensity. An example would be a trucking firm with ten trucks adding another five trucks of the same capacity. Purchases of additional capital goods for widening— that is, to allow the firm to handle additional output—depend primarily on the *rate of change* of sales. If the capacity of existing equipment has been reached and sales continue to increase, it may be advantageous to purchase the additional equipment to handle the greater volume.

3. To Permit Capital Deepening
Capital deepening is the introduction of additional capital goods to allow more intensive use of capital relative to labor for a given volume of output. A firm may find such a change advantageous when wage costs increase while costs of new capital equipment remain unchanged.

14–5   True or False?   The original cost of existing equipment is a relevant factor in decisions to retain or replace it.

False. Once funds have has been "sunk" into a particular piece of capital equipment, it can be recovered (over and above its usually nominal salvage value) only by using up the equipment in which it is embodied. As with all wise decisions, the decision to retain or replace existing equipment is based on the comparison of expected marginal benefits and costs.

4. As a Vehicle of Technological Change

Each type of capital purchase noted thus far may be advantageous even when the state of technology remains unchanged. A large part of investment in new capital goods, however, is a product of technological change; in modern terminology, new capital goods embody the technological changes. Some embodying investments are made for replacement purposes; that is, new techniques may be introduced at the time old equipment is being replaced. So embodying investments may result in replacement well ahead of the original schedule. Many embodying investments are made, however, to produce new products, to achieve greater sales through improved quality or lower cost, or because of other dynamic forces. (See Problems 14–7 and 14–8.)

14–6 True or False? Early replacement of older capital with new capital embodying a technological advance occurs when the revenue added by the new machine exceeds both the cost of the new machine and the revenue that continues to be added by the old machine.

True. As always, the replacement decision depends on expected marginal benefits and costs. Note that the salvage value of the old machine, which the firm receives in either case does not figure into this decision (apart from the minor issue of when it is received).

14–7 Using isoquant and isocost curves, compare capital widening because of increased output with capital deepening because of high wage rates.

Figure (a) shows that capital widening involves purchasing more capital to produce more output. That is, the firm reaches a higher isoquant by using more capital and more labor without changing the capital-labor ratio.

   Capital deepening in response to an increase in wage rates is illustrated in Figure (b). The absolute value of the slope of the isocost line is the ratio of the input prices. A wage increase steepens the isocost line, and capital is substituted for labor at the same level of output.

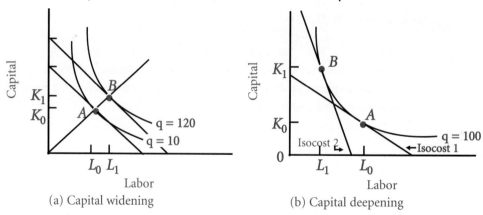

(a) Capital widening   (b) Capital deepening

14.6 DETERMINANTS OF INVESTMENT

The flow demand for capital goods is directly determined by the investment decisions of business firms. The same basic rule applies to capital goods as to other factor units: The purchase of units of capital will be extended to the point at which the marginal gain (marginal revenue product) is just equal to the marginal factor cost. The time and risk considerations, however, create additional complications that require the firm to choose from among a variety of decision-making techniques. Three distinct approaches to capital investment decisions warrant consideration: direct calculation of marginal efficiency, discounted present value, and the payback period rule.

DIRECT CALCULATION OF MARGINAL EFFICIENCY

One technique for deciding whether to invest in a capital good involves an assessment of the relative return on that capital good. The result of that assessment is often called the **internal rate of return**: the rate of return at which the discounted present value of the capital's good expected net future earnings are exactly equal to its initial cost. This rate is defined implicitly by the variable r in the equation:

$$\frac{y_1}{1+r} + \frac{y_2}{(1+r)^2} + \cdots + \frac{y_T}{(1+r)^T} - C = 0$$

where T is the life (in years) of the capital good, y_i represents the expected net return during the ith year (including salvage value in year T), and C represents the initial cost of the capital good. Given the net return figures $y_1, y_2, \ldots, y_T$, and given the cost of the capital good C, there is normally just one positive (real) value of r that satisfies the equation.[1]

For a simple example, suppose you were thinking about buying a machine that cost $50,000 and is expected to last five years. If in each of the years the MRP is $15,000 (a total undiscounted return of $75,000), then the internal rate of return is slightly more than 15 percent, the figure that, when applied to the various MRPs, yields a value of $50,000 when discounted. This figure in effect shows the net gain from the investment, discounting the MRP figure for each year the machine is used back to the present. Obviously, the projects that promise the highest rates of return are the most advantageous. However, the actual calculation of r can be a very complicated business, particularly if expected earnings figures fluctuate in value from one year to the next or if some values are negative. The calculation of r is a minor problem, however, in comparison with the task of estimating appropriate values for the y's, for these depend not only on

---

[1]There will be one value for the internal rate of return if costs are paid for the capital good prior to the receipt of returns

future prices and sales but also on expected future operating costs (which must be subtracted from gross revenues in estimating net returns) and on the expected salvage value of the equipment at the end of its life. Assuming that a firm somehow arrives at an estimate for the internal rate of return on a capital good, it will be potentially profitable, if the firm has funds available, to undertake all investments that yield an internal rate of return higher than the rate of interest that must be paid (or forgone) on loanable funds. Why? Because any investment that promises to yield a net return greater than this rate will add more to a firm's revenue than to its cost.

DISCOUNTED PRESENT VALUE

The principle alternative to the direct-calculation approach involves calculating the **discounted present value** of the future returns on the use of capital equipment (using a given interest rate equal to the current rate at which funds can be obtained). Any investment that will yield a discounted present value higher than the cost of the investment is advantageous. Under usual circumstances, this approach gives the same answer as the internal rate of return method. Any investment that shows an internal rate of return higher than the interest rate will also have present value higher than the original cost

In at least two situations, however, the two methods do not give the same answer. First, projects with highly irregular expected returns may, at certain interest rates, appear profitable with one method and not the other. Second, sometimes the firm cannot obtain all of the funds it needs to extend investment to the level at which the internal rate of return is equal to the interest rate; investment must be therefore rationed to a certain dollar amount. In this situation, the methods may give different answers about which projects are best. If the rationing is needed for some reason other than the shortage of financial capital, clearly the present value method is preferable because it indicates the largest potential gain. This is not necessarily true, however, if capital shortage is the cause, because the interest rate used in discounting future returns is not the true measure of opportunity cost of financial capital to the firm, and some version of the internal rate of return method must be used. (See Problem 14–9.)

14—8   Based on 1968 data and assuming an interest rate of 3 percent, the present value of estimated lifetime earnings from a bachelor's degree in various fields as estimated by Razin and Campbell are presented in the table below. Why do the present values of degrees in alternate fields differ?

First, the costs of investing to obtain degrees in various fields are not taken into account. It is possible that some fields require more expensive instruments, laboratory fees, computer equipment, tuition, and so on so that the net present value (present value of benefits minus costs) may be equal across fields. Second, tastes and aptitudes vary so that the nonmonetary benefits and costs of studying different fields are also different for different people. For those people who do not enjoy and lack the ability to understand advanced mathematics, for example, it would be costly (in terms of psychological stress and study time) for them to pursue a field that is mathematically intensive even if earnings are higher. If we could quantify the nonmonetary aspects of college, we would expect the net present value of the monetary and nonmonetary returns (over costs) to various fields would be equal.

Fields of Study	Lifetime Earnings x 1,000)
Mathematics	342
Economics	339
Computer Science	307
Political Science	300
Physics	283
Psychology	262
Biology	216
Sociology	214

Razin, Asaaf, and James D. Campbell, "Internal Allocation of University Resources," *Western Economic Journal*, September 1972, pp. 313-317.

RULE OF THUMB—THE PAYBACK PERIOD

Uncertainty about expected future yields leads many firms to use a third decision-making technique—the **payback-period rule**. With this rule, the firm calculates the number of years it will need to pay for a capital good from its earnings (before subtraction of depreciation). The firm gives priority to those goods having the shortest payback periods and does not undertake projects whose payback period exceeds a specified number of years—five or ten, for example. This method is obviously very crude for it completely ignores both yields from the investment in years beyond the payback period and the time distribution of earnings within the payback period. An investment that yields most of its net return in early years is normally preferable (having a higher present value) to one that yields an equivalent return only in later years However, this rule may be appropriate when a firm is operating in a politically unstable environment for which a short-term horizon is realistic..

Other firms may make capital-investment decisions primarily based on urgency of "needs," on the "need" for continued operation of the firm, or for an attainment of some other specific goal such as the integration of sources of raw-material supplies. Such criteria are clearly suitable in some instances; if a mile of railroad track is washed out, for example, it must be replaced if the line is to continue in operation. Excessive reliance on such methods, however, can result in piecemeal replacement of capital equipment that is not warranted by profit considerations. In the long run, this becomes self-destructive under reasonably competitive conditions and is at best undesirable under other market structures. Careless capital decisions are not only bad for profit-seeking firms but are also bad from the perspective of optimal social use of scarce resources. (See Problems 14–10, 14–11, and 14–12.)

14–9 A firm is considering three capital investments, Projects A, B, and C. Investment information for these projects is given in the table below. Each investment is expected to last one year with zero salvage value at the end of the year.

	Project A	Project B	Project C
Earnings	$10,000	$20,000	$35,000
Cost	$ 9,000	$19,500	$30,000

(a) Calculate the internal rate of return for the three projects. If the cost of financing is 5 percent, which investments will it be profitable for the firm to undertake?

(b) Calculate the present value of earnings for each project when the interest rate is 5 percent. Which projects will be undertaken according to the present value criterion?

(a) The firm will undertake Projects A and C. The rates of return are 11.1 percent for Project A, 2.6 percent for Project B, and 16.7 percent for Project C. Because the rate of return for Project B is less than the cost of its financing, it will not be funded.

(b) Again, the firm will invest in Projects A and C because the present value of the returns are $9,524 for A, $19,048 for B, and $33,333 for C.

14–10 Capital is sometimes interpreted more broadly to include human capital, the stock of skills and experience embodied in labor. How can we use the preceding analysis in deciding whether or not to pursue a college education?

As in all decisions, we must weigh the expected marginal benefits against the expected marginal costs. On the benefit side is a potentially higher lifetime income. Another benefit is the nonpecuniary aspect of a college education—the social life and the consumption value of education (benefiting from exposure to the classics of literature, art history, and so on). On the cost side are the direct costs of education (tuition, books, and room and board) and, especially, forgone employment opportunities. For example, let's say that instead of going to college you could have driven a truck for $30,000 a year. Over four years that translates into a $120,000 loss while you pursue a college education. College students, therefore, give up some income now for higher expected income later. But how do we find the value today of an investment that yields returns in the future? To look at the benefits over time, we can use the rate of return approach. The average rate of return for a college education has been estimated to be in the neighborhood of 7.5 to 10 percent a year. Although the rate of return has fallen in recent years, this is still a good investment considering that the average rate of return on stocks is between 5 and 7 percent and that education presumably offers greater nonmonetary returns than does stock ownership.

14–11 Given the data in the table below, if the firm uses the payback-period rule, how will the projects be ranked? Which investments will the firm undertake if it refuses to invest in projects with payback periods exceeding one year? If the rate of return were 5 percent, what would be the present value minus the cost of each project?

	Project A	Project B	Project C
Earnings Year 1	$10,000	$20,000	$35,000
Earnings Year 2	$ 5,000	$15,000	$30,000
Cost	$ 9,000	$25,000	$50,000

According to the payback-period rule, the priority ranking of the projects is A, B, and then C. If one year is the maximum payback period, the firm will invest only in Project A. The net present value of each project, however, is $5,059 for A, $7,653 for B, and $10,544 for C. By ignoring later periods, the firm may invest in the least lucrative endeavor.

14.7 RISK CONSIDERATIONS

In addition to the time dimension, another important and related consideration in investment decisions is the risk dimension. Investments in capital goods involve various types of risk. Market conditions may turn out to be substantially less favorable than anticipated: the expected return might not materialize, and the capital sum invested in the equipment might be lost. A new business may find that sales are much lower than anticipated, and an existing business may miscalculate the expected gain from a particular investment. Further, dynamic forces in the economy are difficult to predict; for example, technological change may render equipment obsolete far ahead of the expected time, or shifts in consumer preferences or the emergence of additional competitors may result in lower returns. History provides many examples; a classic case is the nation's investment of more than $1 billion in electric interurban railways, which were rendered obsolete by automobiles and buses long before the investment was recovered.

On the other hand, an investment may turn out to be much more profitable than anticipated. Sales may be greater, or the actual economic life of the capital good may prove to be longer than expected. It must be recognized, however, that forces of competition tend to set a limit on returns higher than expected, because such returns encourage new firms to enter the market.

Although it is obvious that capital investment involves risk, adjusting for risk in calculations of the profitability of the investment is quite another matter. The simplest method of adjusting for risk is to apply a **risk discount factor** to expected returns, reducing the returns accordingly. The obviously greater risk of later years is taken into consideration by the greater impact of the risk discount for these years. Although this approach does adjust for risk considerations, it suffers from a major limitation: There is usually no objective basis upon which to select a discount percentage, only sheer intuition. There are several reasons for this. Obviously, risk considerations differ with various types of industries. Electric-power generation on the one hand, and silver mining and restaurant operation on the other, are good examples of the extremes of risk. Furthermore, investors' attitudes toward risk differ significantly. Sources of funds affect a firm's risk; risks are greater if the funds are borrowed than if earnings are reinvested. A firm's financial situation also has an effect; for investments of a given magnitude, risks are greater for a small company with little reserve capital than for a large enterprise with substantial capital reserves.

Various attempts have been made to simplify or improve risk-discounting adjustments. Here are two that are widely used.

1. Use of a Cutoff Date or Finite Horizon

With this approach, the firm ignores potential returns beyond a certain date on the grounds that the degree of risk is so high that any attempt at prediction would be fruitless. This technique is arbitrary, of course, and could produce very poor results when it is reasonable to assume that there will be some benefit from predictions made about periods beyond the cutoff date, even if the attempt to predict identifies a set of possible future scenarios.

2. Probability Adjustments

A firm faces alternative investment possibilities with the expected return of each having a different probability, which is either projected from previous experience or estimated directly. For various alternatives, the most-certain-return projects are usually those offering the lowest potential yields; the least certain are typically those offering the potential of very high returns (as is also true, for example, of certain types of gambling). The difference may be illustrated by the indifference curves depicted in Figure 14–2. These indifference curves (iso-return curves) are between a good and a bad, where variance in the expected rate of return is the bad. Each curve indicates various combinations of risk (variance of returns) and earnings (rate of return) between which the firm is indifferent. The firm is assumed to prefer higher returns for any given level of risk (variance), or a lower risk for any given level of returns. Thus, all risk-return combinations that lie on a given iso-return curve are preferred to any combination that lies on a curve to the left of the given curve. The particular investment the firm chooses then depends on the alternative investments available to it. If, for example, the alternatives are represented by the set of risk-earning points included in the "choice set" shown in Figure 14–2, the investment alternative chosen will be that which is expected to yield a return of $\bar{r}$ at a level of risk $\bar{o}$.

In many instances, of course, risks cannot be projected from past experience with any degree of certainty; intuition and sheer guesswork are used to determine the relative probability of various returns. In estimating the risks of alternative investments, firms select those criteria that appear to be particularly critical and estimate the returns with various figures for these criteria. If the critical factor is the future price of raw materials, for example, at some price level the investment would be clearly unprofitable and can be eliminated from the choice set. Some estimate of the likelihood that raw materials prices will rise to that level therefore increases the quality of the predictions. (See Problem 14–13.)

14–12 The figure shows the probability distributions of the returns to two different investments for a firm, Project A in Figure (a) and Project B in Figure (b). Each distribution maps the relationship between the various possible earnings and the probability of achieving those earnings. The expected earnings (the probability—weighted average earnings) is *E*. Which investment would the firm prefer? Using an iso-return graph, plot a point representing Project A and one representing Project B.

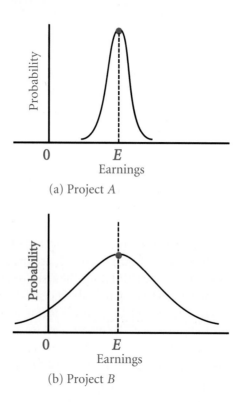

(a) Project *A*

(b) Project *B*

The Probability Distribution of Returns

The firm prefers investment A because it entails the same expected return E but it is associated with less risk. The range of possible returns is much less for Project A, and the chance of earning low or negative returns is much higher for Project B. The figure below shows that Project A is on an iso-return curve that is to the right of Project B, with a lower risk for the same expected return.

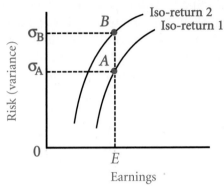

An Iso-Return Map for Projects A and B

FIGURE 14–2
RISK-RETURN ALTERNATIVES AND PREFERENCES

Indifference curves (iso-return curves) chart the combinations of expected earnings and risks of alternative investments which yield the same level of utility to the owners of the firm. The preferred investment plans are located in the southeasterly direction of the graph—that is, those with the greatest returns at the lowest risk. The firm will undertake the project associated with the tangency of the choice set (the set of projects available to the firm) and I_3.

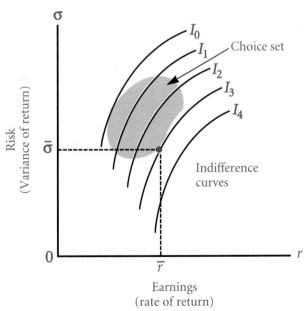

14.8 THE COST AND AVAILABILITY OF FINANCIAL CAPITAL

As just noted, if a firm is going to maximize profits, the crucial comparison it has to make in **capital budgeting** is between the internal rate of return and the cost of financial capital. The cost of financial capital—and thus the optimum level of investment for the firm—is influenced somewhat by the source of the funds. There are three possible sources of financial capital: borrowing money, selling stock, and retaining earnings.

1. Borrowing Money

The direct cost of borrowed money is the interest that must be paid for the loanable funds. Borrowing gives rise to an additional risk not incurred with other methods of financing, that of bankruptcy and loss of control of the company should the investment prove so unsuccessful that the firm cannot meet interest and repayment obligations. What is worse, the owners run the risk of losing their entire investment, not merely the additional investment made with the borrowed funds.

2. Sale of Stock

By selling stock, the firm incurs no contractual obligations to pay interest or repay principal, but the firm's earnings (on prior investments as well as on the new investment) are shared with the owners of the new stock. The cost, therefore, may be considered to be the current-yield figure on the additional stock issue. If new issues of stock that pay a $5 annual dividend can be sold at $100, the yield is 5 percent. Although the firm incurs no risk of bankruptcy, there is increased danger that it can lose control of the enterprise if it issues too much additional stock.

3. Reinvestment of Earnings or Plowback

The most important source of investment funds is often money accumulated internally from earnings, together with accumulated earned depreciation charges. The cost of such funds is the income forgone by not using them for other investments—to buy stocks of other corporations, for example. Because the cost of borrowing is higher than the cost of lending (due to transactions costs), this "opportunity cost" is lower than the cost to the firm of acquiring funds from outside sources. In addition, reinvestment of earnings creates no secondary costs such as greater danger of bankruptcy or loss of control. The only secondary cost is loss of liquidity, which could endanger the company's financial stability in the event of losses and which precludes the investment of the funds in more lucrative pursuits that might arise in the future. (See Problem 14–14.)

14–13 True or False? The cost of unds for additional investment differs with the source of the funds and the firm's general credit standing, which affects the cost of funds obtained from outside sources.

True. The actual choice of financing methods depends on the relative cost and availability of funds from various sources together with the firm's attitudes toward risk and dilution of control. Many firms as a matter of policy expand only when internal funds are available for the purpose. Others—particularly small enterprises—cannot raise funds by any but internal means, at least beyond a certain point. Thus, the availability of various sources of funds affects the total amount of investment.

A final but important point relates to the many cases in which firms engage in more than one or all of the preceding financing possibilities. In this case, for *marginal financing*, the firm must be indifferent between these financing options. Otherwise, the firm would not be observed choosing more than one financing option.

14.9 THE RELATIONSHIP BETWEEN THE AMOUNT AND COST OF FINANCIAL CAPITAL

In a perfect capital market, with no uncertainty, a firm could presumably borrow all it wanted at a given percentage rate. In practice, however, market imperfections and uncertainty create a positive functional relationship between the amount and cost of financial capital. As a firm obtains additional funds, beyond a certain point, it must pay a higher interest rate on borrowed capital or give a higher return to new stockholders. This is because the risks created by additional borrowing or stock financing as well as by reduced liquidity from the use of internal capital are increased. Thus, the marginal cost of additional investment rises.

One of the more significant peculiarities of the acquisition of financial capital is the prevalence of **capital rationing**. A firm may be required to ration capital because it is unable to raise funds at all beyond a certain point. Every firm has a limited amount of internal funds; lenders, leery of putting too many eggs in one basket, are frequently unwilling to lend more than a certain amount to a particular firm. Similarly, it may be difficult or impossible to sell stock beyond a certain sum. Many firms stop short of raising funds beyond the absolute maximum they can obtain from the outside.

The quantity of available funds thus limits some firms to an amount of investment that is less than optimal when the rate of return is higher than the cost of loanable funds. The investment decision under these conditions becomes one of selecting projects that offer the greatest potential return. More specifically, the amount of capital available is one of the constraints of the problem, and the firm's goal becomes that of maximizing the return from this amount of capital, taking risk into consideration. This problem can be solved rather simply by linear programming, a technique of managerial decision making that has been much in vogue within the business and economics community for a number of decades. Whether the decision proves to be the correct one or not depends on how accurately the firm predicts returns and on the appropriateness of the programming model that is used. (See the Appendix on "Linear Programming" at the end of the text.)

14.10 THE PRICE OF CAPITAL GOODS

There is an inverse relationship between the price of a unit of a capital good and the quantity demanded, as there is for any type of factor unit. Subject to special qualifications involved in calculations of MRP (noted earlier in this chapter) and the possible influence of capital rationing, the same considerations apply to the demand for capital goods as to the demand for other factor units. Higher prices of certain types of capital goods, *ceteris paribus*, causes firms to substitute alternative forms of capital equipment and to use more labor-intensive methods; total investment is therefore lower. For the economy as a whole, it is difficult for capital goods prices permanently to rise relative to wage rates because wage rates are primary cost elements in the production of capital goods. In the short run, however, capital goods prices (like stock-market values) may fluctuate wildly in relation to other prices because of changing views about the future profitability of such assets.

Because capital goods are produced by business firms on a profit-making basis, the same considerations are relevant to output, supply, and pricing policies as are relevant to consumption goods. For instance, many capital-equipment industries are oligopolies, with close implicit or explicit cooperation because of limited product differentiation. There are, however, no basic differences in pricing policies between these capital-equipment manufacturers and other kinds of firms.

CHANGES IN THE DEMAND FOR CAPITAL GOODS

Several dynamic forces affect the demand for capital goods and therefore the volume of investment. These forces include the supplies of other factors the supply of loanable funds, national income, technology, and expectations about the future.

Changes in Other Factor Supplies
An increase in quantities of other factors available tends to increase the demand for capital goods. Discovery of new natural resources, for example, leads to purchase of capital goods by firms that want to exploit the new resources or use products made from them.

Similarly, population growth makes available an increased supply of labor and requires the use of more capital equipment if least-cost combinations of factors are to be maintained, provided the increase in population does not lower the supply of the loanable funds that is available for investment. This qualification is particularly significant in underdeveloped countries in which families use so much of their income for consumption that little loanable funds is available for investment. In highly developed countries, in periods when people save more than the current rate of investment, the effect of population growth in increasing the percentage of income consumed stimulates investment by increasing sales of consumption goods. It also gives encouragement to investment by increasing the labor supply.

Changes in the Supply of Loanable Funds

The demand for capital goods and the demand for loanable funds are complementary because increased use of capital goods requires additional use of loanable funds. Accordingly, an increase in the supply of loanable funds, which tends (temporarily) to lower the interest rate, increases the demand for capital goods.

Increases in National Income Because of Greater Employment of Resources

As national income rises from recession levels through reemployment of idle factor units, additional investment is profitable because an increase in sales increases the expected MRP of capital equipment. When the recovery first begins, the effect on investment may be slight, because firms have substantial idle capacity. Once the capacity of existing equipment is approached, however, sharp increases in investment are to be expected.[2]

However, net investment because of a rise in national income continues only as long as the increase in output (or expectations of such increase) continues. As full employment is approached, the rate of increase in national income slackens; once full employment is attained, the rate of increase is limited to the rate permitted by increases in factor supplies and technological change. As a consequence, the volume of net investment must fall below the high levels possible during the period in which idle resources were being reemployed. Reinvestment will, of course, remain at higher levels because the total stock of capital goods is greater.

Technological Change

From a long-range point of view, the most important dynamic force influencing the volume of investment is technological change—the development of *new products* and *new methods of production*. The development of new products almost always temporarily produces new investment, although over a period of time investment to produce goods for which the new products are substituted is likely to fall. If the new articles

---

[2]If the various phases of cycles are fully anticipated, these effects will not be observed. Thus, so-called rational expectations will lead to investment based on "typical" growth over time.

require relatively large amounts of capital goods in their production—as, for example, automobiles—substantial net investment occurs during the period of their development and annual reinvestment will remain at a permanently higher level. During the past century, the significance for capital investment of a few major new products has been tremendous. The automobile, for example, has led to great investment in factories producing automobiles and their parts and accessories (such as tires), in the oil-refining industry, in service stations, and in highways.

In addition to new products, technical innovation leads to new methods of production. Over the last several centuries, most inventions have involved the use of more capital equipment relative to labor and natural resources. In general, inventions have provided means of accomplishing with capital-goods tasks formerly performed directly by labor. There have been exceptions, however; some technological developments have been capital-saving in the sense that they allow certain tasks to be performed economically with less capital investment per unit of output. The replacement of streetcars by buses in local transit service provides an example. Still, the general pattern of technological change has been accompanied by the use of progressively more capital goods and thus has made possible a continuous increase in net investment, except in years of sharp decline in national product.

New techniques have not only increased investment in industries directly affected, but by freeing labor and natural resources; they have often made possible increases in output and investment in other industries. Some developments have lessened the cost of producing capital goods and have increased the relative advantages of capital compared to other factors. While the introduction of a series of new techniques will permanently increase the volume of capital goods in use and the annual volume of reinvestment, net investment resulting from technological change will continue only as long as the development of new products and methods continues.

Changes in Expectations

Because capital equipment acquired in one period is used over succeeding periods of time, changes in expectations about the future affect both estimated MRP and the demand for capital goods. During a depressed period, increased optimism about the future, even if it is based upon no tangible changes in the current profit situation, can in itself stimulate recovery. Regardless of the initial cause of a recovery, once it gets under way, the tendency is for expectations to improve and for a general feeling of optimism to develop. This is likely to increase the volume of investment to a much higher level than would be justified on the basis of current sales. That such levels are not sustainable provides a significant cause for the next downturn. Capital theory in microeconomics, if properly understood, has much to say about the business cycle, a major concern in macroeconomics. Changes in expectations about future technological change can also alter present estimates of the MRP of additional capital goods. (See Problem 14–15.)

14–14 Using a graph, show how each of the following affects the MRP of a durable capital good and, therefore, the demand for the durable capital:

a. a decrease in the supply of a complementary input
b. a decrease in the supply of loanable funds
c. a recession in the national economy
d. the development of a capital-intensive technology
e. pessimistic expectations about the future
f. a decrease in the price of durable capital

An increase in the MRP of durable capital (and, thus, in the demand for capital) is illustrated in the figure below by a rightward shift from D_K to D'_K. Demand increases in case (d). The events in (a), (b), (c), and (e) reduce the demand for capital, shifting it leftward from D'_K to D_K. A decrease in the price of capital increases the quantity demanded of capital, case (f), illustrated by a movement along D_K from A to B.

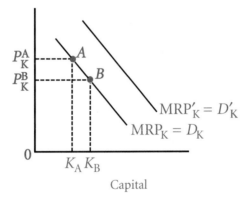

Factors Affecting the Demand for Capital

14.11 PAYMENTS FOR CAPITAL GOODS AND FACTOR INCOMES

The sums paid by business firms for new capital equipment do not in themselves constitute factor-income payments; they serve merely to cover the costs, explicit and implicit, of equipment-producing firms. These sums become factor-income payments when they are paid out by equipment producers in the form of wages, rent, interest, and profit to the persons supplying factor units to them, in the same manner as amounts paid to purchase consumption goods.

Capital-goods purchases by firms constitute production costs from a long-range point of view because the sums paid out must be covered if operation is to be carried on indefinitely. However, the cost of capital equipment acquired in any one year cannot be regarded appropriately as a cost for which the output of that year is wholly responsible because the equipment will be used to produce output over a period of years. Accordingly, the usual practice is to depreciate the purchase price of equipment over the years of its expected life. To do this, a formula is used to allocate a share of the total cost to each year. The allocation is inevitably somewhat arbitrary (especially in light of tax treatments that bear little relation to true depreciation) because there is no way of ascertaining exactly how much the value of the equipment declines in any given year or how long the equipment can actually remain in use. Moreover, these annual depreciation charges are not income; they merely reflect a decline in the value of a firm's capital equipment and therefore represent the recovery, in the form of financial capital, of earlier investment in equipment. The sums involved are available to repay loans to replace old equipment, to expand, or to increase liquid balances or securities holdings. Therefore, the amounts paid for capital equipment do not, in themselves, give rise to a form of income distinct from that which would arise if capital equipment were not used. The distinctive return that arises from the use of capital equipment can be discovered only by considering the financial capital that is required to obtain the equipment. For in the final analysis, it is the ultimate owner of the capital good (who may be a bondholder or a bank rather than the firm that uses the capital good) to whom the net income yield of the capital good accrues.

SUMMARY

1. The interest rate is the rate of return or yield implied by a loan contract and its sale price. Payment of interest is necessary to induce those persons who have loanable funds to temporarily relinquish their funds to those who wish to use it; therefore, interest is treated as a factor payment, as are wages.

2. The real interest rate is the nominal or money interest minus the expected rate of change in the price level.

3. There is a positive relationship between the interest rate and the supply of loanable funds and an inverse relationship between the interest rate and the demand for loanable funds. The equilibrium interest rate equates supply and demand.

4. The interest rate ensures that the flow of current saving is made available for investment in capital goods, instead of seeking to go into liquid balances, rations the total available amount of loanable funds among various possible uses, and establishes equilibrium between the amount of money already in existence and the amounts individuals wish to hold. As income to the recipient, interest rates also affect the demand for goods and services.

5. Fixed capital assets introduce some unique complications relative to other inputs: They must be financed before the outputs produced with their services are sold, and they involve a greater risk in the rate of return relative to the other factors.

6. Firms desire more capital goods for various reasons: to replace existing capital goods, to permit capital widening or deepening, and to facilitate technological change.

7. Investment decision making under the constraints of uncertainty can be made more precise by either the internal rate of return equation, the present value, or the payback-period rule.

8. To adjust for risk in calculating the profitability of a capital-goods investment, one can use a risk-discounting adjustment, such as a cutoff date or finite horizon, or probability adjustments.

9. The sources of financial capital are borrowing, selling stock, and reinvesting earnings.

10. The marginal cost of additional investments always rise; firms may not be able to raise funds at all beyond a certain point.

11. There is an inverse relationship between the prices of capital goods and the demand for them.

12. The demand for capital goods (and thus the volume of investment) is affected by changes in factor supplies, changes in the supply of loanable funds, an increase in national income because of fewer resources unemployed, technological change, and changes in expectations about economic conditions.

WORDS AND CONCEPTS FOR REVIEW

interest	nominal interest rates
real interest rates	fixed capital assets
capital widening	capital deepening
internal rate of return	present value or discounting
payback-period rule	risk-discount factor
capital budgeting	capital rationing

REVIEW QUESTIONS

1. Why is the payment of interest necessary?

2. What distinguishes capital goods from other factors?

3. What complications are created for the theory of factor pricing by the fact that durable capital goods are used over a period of years?

4. What is the difference between capital widening and capital deepening?

5. What is meant by embodiment of technological change? What role does technological change play in investment decisions?

6. What is the internal rate of return?

7. Why do many firms turn to "rule-of-thumb" methods for investment decision making?

8. What is the payback-period rule? What are its limitations?

9. Under what circumstances is use of the "urgency-of-investment rule" warranted? What danger is involved in its use?

10. Indicate the various approaches to managing risk in investment decision making, along with the limitations of these approaches.

11. Indicate the nature of the cost of financial capital under the borrowing, sale of stock, and plowback methods of financing investment.

12. Why are firms more likely to undertake marginal-investment projects if they have their own funds for the purpose than if they must borrow the money or sell additional stock?

13. What is capital rationing? Why does it arise? What significance does it have for investment decision making?

14. Indicate the major determinants of the total demand for capital goods.

15. What is the nature of the relationship between the price of capital goods and the quantity demanded? Why?

16. What are the major causes of changes in the demand for capital goods?

17. Why are payments for capital goods not in themselves factor payments? Do earned depreciation charges constitute factor incomes? Explain.

SUGGESTED READINGS

Alchian, Armen, and William Allen. *Exchange and Production: Competition, Coordination and Controls*, 3rd ed. Belmont, Calif: Wadsworth, 1983, Chapter 6.

Baumol, W.J. *Economic Theory and Operations Analysis*, 4th ed. Englewood Cliffs, N.J.: Prentice Hall, 1977, Chapters 25 and 26.

Fisher, Irving. *The Theory of Interest.* New York: Macmillan, 1930.

Friedman, Milton, *Price Theory.* Chicago: Aldine, 1976.283–322.

Harcourt, G. C. "Some Cambridge Controversies in the Theory of Capital," *Journal of Economic Literature*, June 1969, 369–405.

Hirshleifer, Jack. *Investment, Interest and Capital.* Englewood Cliffs, N.J.: Prentice Hall, 1970.

Jorgenson, D.W. "Econometric Studies of Investment Behavior: A Survey," *Journal of Economic Literature*, December 1971, 1111–1147.

Solow, R. M. *Capital Theory and the Rate of Return.* Amsterdam: North Holland, 1964.

Chapter Fifteen

RENTS AND QUASI-RENTS

————————— *Questions to Think About* —————————

1. What is the general meaning of the term *land*?

2. What is economic rent?

3. What is the marginal-productivity theory of land rent?

4. Why is there a fixed supply of land under perfect competition?

5. Why is the rental price of land solely demand determined?

6. How is the selling price of land determined?

7. How does land rent rise according to the differential-returns theory of land rent?

8. What is a quasi-rent?

15.1 INTRODUCTION

To attain optimal factor combinations, a firm in most instances has to use not only labor and capital inputs but also natural resources—inputs provided directly by nature. Natural resources, or **land**, to use the more common although less descriptive term, differ from capital in that their existence does not typically depend on human effort. Accordingly, the supply cannot be increased by deliberate action, although the usefulness of land for production purposes can be increased by various improvements—clearing, draining, introducing irrigation facilities, and so on—that require labor and that constitute capital goods. Because, however, land available for use is limited relative to demand, a price must be paid for its use, a price that constitutes an income to the owners in a society in which natural resources are privately owned. This return, which is a payment that is greater than its opportunity cost, is known as **rent**.

15.2 MARGINAL-PRODUCTIVITY ANALYSIS APPLIED TO LAND

The basic marginal-productivity analysis presented in Chapter 13 can be applied to land as well as to other factors. The demand for land of a particular type depends on the marginal-revenue-product (MRP) schedule of this type of land to various users of it. As is typical for all factors, land's MRP declines after a certain point as additional units are added.

The nature of the supply schedule of land is conditioned by the basic characteristics of this factor. For most business firms, this means that the quantity of land in use is not easily adjustable in the short run. Because land is fixed in quantity and cannot be increased by human activity, the potential supply to the economy is perfectly inelastic even over the long run. Relatively high prices paid for the use of the land of course stimulate owners to make improvements for irrigation, drainage, and so on, which will increase the output on given land. These improvements, however, are capital goods, and the higher output is attributable to them. Of course, these improvements raise the MRP of land because the land has more of other inputs with which to "work."

Not only is the potential supply of land perfectly inelastic, but so is the actual supply offered to users at positive prices, as long as the market is perfectly competitive. Because the owner of land gains virtually nothing by holding it idle, it is better for the owner to get the going market return for it, regardless of how low this figure is, than to get nothing at all. In contrast, the holders of financial capital gain the advantages of liquidity by holding their capital idle, and workers avoid the disutility of labor by not working. There is essentially no gain, however, from holding land idle.[1]

Under the assumption of perfectly competition, the rental payment for a particular type of land would adjust to the level at which the demand for and the supply of this type of land were equal. At this level, rent would equal the MRP of the land. Because supply is perfectly inelastic, changes in demand produce sharp changes in rent. For example, a substantial population increase (not offset by technological improvements in agricultural production) would result in a sharp increase in land rent, and thus in the share of national income going to the landowners. This tendency in the late eighteenth and nineteenth-century England led to great interest in the theory of rent, as reflected in the writings of Adam Smith, David Ricardo, and Thomas Malthus. (See Problems 15–1 and 15–2.)

15–1 Diagram economic rents captured from land in a supply-and-demand diagram. Would the same quantity of land be available at a low price (rent) as at a high price? Also if the supply of land is fixed, what must determine the amount of economic rent?

Because the supply for land is assumed to be fixed, the supply curve is perfectly inelastic as seen in the accompanying diagram. Even at some minimum positive price or at any other higher price, Q_0 of land will be available. The intersection of the vertical supply curve and the demand curve determines both the price and the amount of economic rent. If demand for land is strong (weak), economic rents will be large (small).

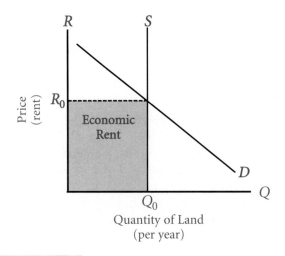

<hr />

[1]There are rare exceptions, for short periods. Some types of land become more productive if kept out of use for a few years. Alternatively, if land depreciates with use, at a sufficiently low rent it may be optimal to hold land idle.

15–2 David Ricardo states: "I think rent, and the increase of rent, is the necessary and unavoidable condition of an increased supply of corn for an increasing population." Using supply-and-demand analysis, illustrate Ricardo's statement.

In the market for corn, a population increase raises corn demand. Price rises, temporary profits are earned, new firms enter, and supply increases. A greater output is produced at a higher price, the latter due to increasing-cost conditions in the corn industry.

In the land market, the higher product price raises the MRP of land, thus increasing the demand for land. As shown in the accompanying figure, the original price and quantity of land are P_0 and Q, and rent equals the area $P_0 a 0$. When demand for land shifts from D_0 to D_1, land price increases from P_0 to P_1, and rent increases by the area $P_1 b a P_0$.

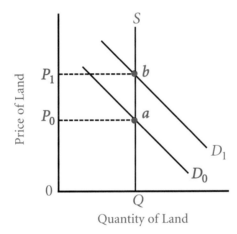

The Impact of an Increase in the Demand for Land or Rent

In the absence of imperfections in the land market, one would expect the price adjustment on a supply-demand basis to be rapid. Actually, the land market is somewhat imperfect. A particular market is limited in area, with a relatively small number of tenants and landlords. Knowledge of market conditions may be very limited, and the bargaining position of the various parties may be unequal. The small number of buyers and sellers may well prevent the markets from being perfectly competitive in many cases. The rent may be set by direct two-party bargaining, with results difficult to predict by general analysis. If monopoly elements develop, not all the available land may come into use; it may be advantageous for landowners to withhold a portion of their land in order to maximize revenue received. (See Problem 15–3)

15–3 Suppose there is a monopoly landowner in a particular town. Discuss the relationship between the price elasticity of demand for land and the landowner's incentive to restrict the amount of land in order to maximize rental income.

The figure below shows the demand and the marginal-revenue curve for the landlord. If Q_0 is supplied, price will be P_0 and rent will be $P_0 a Q_0 0$. It will be more profitable, however, for the monopolist to supply only Q_1, and earn $P_1 b Q_1 0$. The opportunity cost of the land is zero, so the owner maximizes rent or total revenue where marginal revenue is zero.

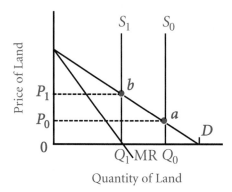

Monopolistic Restriction of Land Supply

15.3 THE SELLING PRICE OF LAND

A parcel of land may be purchased outright by the business enterprises using it. The selling price depends on the supply of and demand for the land at a particular time (assuming perfectly competitive conditions in this market). The price the buyer is willing to pay for a parcel and the price at which the present owner is willing to sell it are determined by the current and prospective rent that may be obtained from the land.

Suppose, for example, that the current market interest rate on loans is 5 percent. A parcel of land yielding, and expected to yield indefinitely, $600 a year in rent will sell for $12,000 if the market is perfect ($12,000 x .05 = $600). Any buyer who paid more for the land would be getting a return on wealth that was less than he or she could get elsewhere. If, for example an individual paid $20,000, this would amount to an annual return on the investment of only 3 percent ($600 / $20,000); whereas if the person had purchased bonds, then interest of 5 percent would have been earned. On the other hand, present owners would not sell for less than $12,000, or they would be getting a lower return after making the sale than they earn at present. (See Problem 15–4.)

15–4 True or False? The owner of a parcel of land has listed it for sale for $25,000. Its rental income is $1,000 per year and the interest rate on loans of comparable risk is 5 percent. A rational buyer would purchase the parcel.

False. The buyer could invest the $25,000 and earn $1,250 (5 percent) per year, which is more than could be earned on the land. The seller would have to lower the price to $20,000 to find a buyer because the return on $20,000 in comparable investments would be $1,000.

15.4 THE DIFFERENTIAL THEORY OF LAND

The supply-demand analysis of land-rent determination, as with the explanation of other factor prices, is not open to question on a logical basis. But for a long time an alternative approach, under which rent was explained in terms of **differential returns** on various grades of land, was regarded as a more satisfactory explanation of rent. This approach arose in part because of the wide variation in quality (and thus productivity) of different types of land, and in part from the fixed nature of the supply and the tendency, in many instances, for producers—particularly farmers—to regard acreage as a permanent fixed factor, to which quantities of other factors employed must be adjusted. This is not an unrealistic assumption from the standpoint of the firm in many countries in which, for reasons of law or custom, additional land cannot be purchased. Moreover, from the standpoint of an entire economy, the total supply of land is fixed in any country. This **differential-returns theory of land rent** is often called the Ricardian rent theory after David Ricardo, the early nineteenth-century economist who popularized it.[2]

DIFFERENCE IN FERTILITY AND LOCATION

The productivity differences of farmland are due largely to variations in the nature of the soil. With a given application of labor and capital, some types of soil will yield more output than others because of physical differences in content. Productivity is influenced also by temperature, rainfall, and other climatic factors, as well as by drainage and ease of cultivation. Productivity differences manifest themselves in differences in average cost figures (exclusive of rent) for the firms on various grades of land. On very fertile soil, well drained, with good rainfall and warm climate, the average cost of capital and labor per unit of output will be low because the farmer does not have to spend as much money on inputs such as fertilizers, seed, farm machinery, workers, and so on. The opposite will be true on poor land.

---

[2]See David Ricardo, *Principles of Political Economy* (1817).

Assume that land falls into certain definite grades, with successively higher cost schedules. In practice, the variation in the quality of land shades off gradually from the best to the poorest; but classification into grades, with the assumption being made that producers on all parcels of land in particular grades have identical cost schedules, will simplify the explanation without lessening its significance.

As long as the demand for the product is small, only the very best land—Grade A land—will be used. Once the demand is great enough to bring all Grade A land into use and the demand still cannot be satisfied at the price equal to lowest average cost on Grade A land, price will remain above the Grade A lowest-cost figure. As demand increases, market prices will eventually rise above lowest average cost on Grade B land, and units of this land will come into use. The increased market supply of the product will bring market price to the level of the lowest average cost on Grade B land. Price cannot fall below this figure with the demand at assumed levels, or all Grade B land will go out of use and the total supply of the good will be lower than the quantity demanded at the lower price level.

On Grade A land, production will be carried to the point at which price is equal to marginal cost. The differential between price (which equals average cost on Grade B land—the marginal land) and average cost (exclusive of rent) on the Grade A land is the land rent. The firms on Grade A land will be operating at a level of output at which marginal cost is equal to price. Note that the rent differential going to owners of Grade A land as demand increases makes these owners wealthier. But the owner-farmers do *not* have a cost advantage over those farmers who rent land from absentee owners! Recall that costs are opportunity costs regardless of whether explicit payments are made or not.

If the demand for the product continues to increase, eventually all Grade B land will come into use; further demand increases will raise the market price until it covers lowest average cost on Grade C land and the latter is brought into use. The price, which must now remain high enough to cover average cost on Grade C land if supply of and demand for the product are to be maintained at equality, will now exceed average cost on Grade B land, and rent will arise on the latter. Grade B land has ceased to be marginal land; Grade C, formerly submarginal, is now the marginal land. The rent on Grade A will be still greater.

Typical cost curves for the firms on each of the three grades of land are illustrated in Figure 15–1. So long as only Grade A land must be used, price will remain at $50.00. When demand has increased sufficiently to require the use of Grade B land to make supply and demand equal, the price must be $75.00, or all Grade B land will drop out of use and market demand will exceed market supply. Accordingly, a differential, a rent of approximately $24.00 per unit of output (*nr* in Figure 15–1) arises on Grade A land.[3] When demand increases still more, so that all B land is used and C land comes into cultivation, the price of the product must be $100.00. There now exists a rent of $24.00 per

---

[3]The figure is less than $25,00 because average cost rises slightly as output is pushed beyond the point of lowest cost.

unit of output (*ms*) on Grade B land and of $48.00 per unit (*n′r′*) on the Grade A land. The rent per acre would be the rent per unit of output multiplied by the average yield per acre on the particular grade.

In summary, price must equal long-run average cost on the marginal land, the poorest (in the sense of highest cost) land which will be used in production. On better grades of land the average cost (exclusive of rent) is lower. The difference between this lower-average-cost figure and the marginal-land average-cost figure is the amount of land rent on the better land. If land rent were less than this, farmers on poorer land would bid for the better land.

Once land rent has arisen, it constitutes a cost from the standpoint of the individual producer, regardless, as already emphasized, of whether the producer owns or rents the land. If the producer leases the land, rent will have to be paid to the landlord; if the producer owns the land, the cost includes the amount that could be made by leasing the land to someone else and must be covered (along with other costs) if the producer is to remain in business. Land rent may be regarded as a differential return from the standpoint of the economy but is a cost from the standpoint of the individual producer. (See Problems 15–5 and 15–6.)

FIGURE 15–1
LAND RENT FOR PARCELS OF LAND OF VARYING QUALITY

Long-run average costs are lowest for Grade A land, are higher for Grade B land, and even higher for Grade C land. If Grade A land is utilized, product price will be $50 in the long run. If product demand is sufficiently high to allow the use of Grade B land, price will stabilize at $75, and a rent of $24 per unit of output accrues for Grade A land. If price is $100, Grade C land will be cultivated, per-unit rent on Grade B land will be *ms* in Figure (b), and per-unit rent in Grade A land will be *n'r'* in Figure (a).

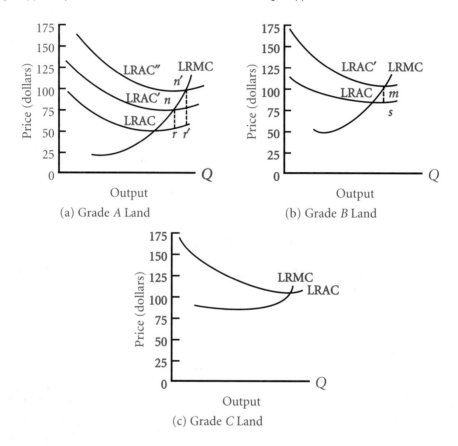

(a) Grade *A* Land

(b) Grade *B* Land

(c) Grade *C* Land

15–5   True or False? If farmers sell their product in the same central market, the location of their farm affects cost.

True. Because the products are sold in the same market areas, farmers using the more-remote land, or that land served by poor and costly transportation facilities have higher transportation costs of marketing their products than those producing on better-located land. Farmers in poorer locations, however, cannot sell at prices higher than those obtained by farmers located closer to the central market. Location advantages will therefore be incorporated into rents (and therefore, costs) in competitive markets; this differential pricing of land by location provides the theoretical foundation for urban economics.

15–6 Would land rent arise if the Law of Diminishing Returns did not operate?

No, if one could add additional units of capital and labor to a fixed quantity of land and obtain constant (not diminishing) increases in output, only the best parcel of land would be used. That this is implausible—say, the one most-fertile acre feeding the world's population—is testimony to the significance of diminishing returns.

NONAGRICULTURAL PRODUCTION

The differential approach to land rent has been explained in terms of agricultural production. A similar analysis can be applied to other types of industries. For manufacturing, rent is typically a minor element in cost while in retailing it is important. The cost differential in such uses arises solely out of considerations of location. Good locations in any city implies a lower cost of operation primarily because the rate of stock turnover is greater than for stores at less-desirable sites. Such locations are limited relative to the demand for them. The more rapid turnover lowers capital cost because a given amount of financial capital can be invested in a greater total volume of goods during a certain period of time. Faster turnover lessens loss from spoilage and obsolescence. Good locations usually allow better utilization of personnel and greater effectiveness of advertising. Other considerations are transportation and travel costs savings. (See Problem 15–7.)

15–7 True or False? In locations that are marginal for retailing activities, no rent will be earned over and above that which the land would yield from nonretailing use.

True. In better locations the average cost of operations (exclusive of rent) will be less. This differential is the additional rent arising out of the use of the land in retailing. Landowners will be able to extract this amount (plus, of course, the amount of rent that the land would yield in the next-best use) from retailers because the latter can pay this amount and still earn a normal return on their investment.

15.5 A MORE-INCLUSIVE CONCEPT OF RENT

Many economists expand the concept of rent to include all payments for factor units that are not cost elements from the standpoint of the industry or the entire economy. They are not cost elements because the payments to or earning of these factor units are not necessary to make the factor units available to the industry or the economy. For example, famous athletes and musicians would usually continue in their current occupations, even if demand for their sport or type of music declined, greatly lowering their earnings. Any return above opportunity cost would keep them in their current jobs. (See Problem 15–8.)

15–8 Some economics professors collect economic rents; that is, they enjoy their work so much that they would work for less than their current salary. Will the supply curve for economists be perfectly inelastic as it was for land? Draw the hypothetical supply-and-demand curves for economics professors and indicate which area is economic rent.

The difference between what the economics professor would be willing to work for and what he or she receives is the economic rent. However, with an upward-sloping supply curve for economics professors (that is, more will pursue professing economics at higher wages), part of the payment to the factor is required to keep the professor from pursuing another occupation and part is economic rent as indicated in the graph below.

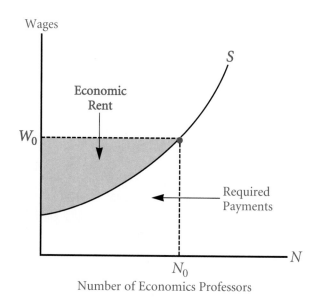

Number of Economics Professors

15.6 A FINAL NOTE ON RENT

The price paid for the use of land, in the sense of factor units provided directly by nature and therefore nonreproducible, may be regarded as a separate type of return designated as land rent, or it may be regarded simply as an interest return on the financial capital equivalent of the current sale value of the land. Regardless of the designation, the determination of the sum involved may be explained in terms of the marginal-productivity approach applied to each type of land or in traditional terms, as a differential between the average cost on the particular type of land as compared to average cost on marginal land.

These approaches are alternative methods of explanation, but there is no particular advantage of applying a method of analysis to land different from that applied to other factors.

The distinguishing feature of land is the fact that because it is provided by nature and is not producible, the supply is perfectly inelastic. The return, therefore, depends solely on demand for the land which in turn depends on the land's productivity or yield. In the short run, however, the supply of specialized capital equipment is likewise perfectly inelastic, and cost of production is not relevant once the equipment has been produced. In the short run, therefore, the return on capital goods depends solely on the yield of the equipment in production and is similar to land rent; it may be designated as a **quasi-rent**. But this is a short-run phenomenon only. Because capital goods are produced and wear out over a long period, the return depends on the cost of production of the equipment and must cover this cost plus an interest return on the money capital. If capital goods can be produced at constant cost, the long run is very different, indeed, from the short run; rather than price depending solely on demand, in the long run it depends solely on supply, with demand determining only how much is produced. (See Problem 15–9.)

15–9   True or False?   If professors' salaries rose as a result of a temporary increase in college attendance, the salary increases are called *quasi-rents.*

True. This occurred in the late 1960s as baby boomers and those attempting to avoid military service contributed to increased college enrollments. As a result of this temporary phenomenon, professors' salaries rose uncharacteristically. Until a larger supply of college professors (new Ph.Ds) hit the market, professors enjoyed higher-than-usual salaries because of these short-run rents called quasi-rents!

In recent years, then, the term *rent* has been extended to cover all returns attributable to specific factors that are surpluses, in the sense that payment for the use of a specific factor is not necessary to ensure that units of the factor will be available either to an industry or to the economy as a whole. (See Problem 15–10.)

15–10   On which types of land has land rent been increased by the development of the automobile? On which types has it been decreased?

The automobile has raised the demand for land more distant from urban centers. The lower full costs (i.e., money and time) of travel, such as commuting to central work, shopping, and entertainment areas lowers the cost of access to the center. Rents, therefore, have become relatively lower in central urban areas and higher in the suburbs and urban fringe.

SUMMARY

1. Rent is a consistent return to a factor of production that is greater than its opportunity costs. That is, rent is the excess of what the factor could earn in its next best alternative use.

2. In a perfectly competitive model, the supply curve for land is perfect inelastic.

3. An owner of land gains virtually nothing by holding it idle. Thus, it is best to get the market return on land even if that return is very low. This is not true for capital and labor.

4. The position of the demand curve determines the amount of economic rent when the supply curve is inelastic.

5. The land market is highly imperfect. Imperfect information, unequal bargaining powers of buyers and sellers, and the small numbers of buyers and sellers may reduce the competitiveness in the land market.

WORDS AND CONCEPTS FOR REVIEW

rent

differential returns

cost of land use

land-market imperfections

quasi-rent

marginal-productivity theory of land rent

differential-returns theory of land rent

cost of capital use

location and land costs

REVIEW QUESTIONS

1. How does land differ from other types of factors?

2. What is the nature of the supply schedule of land from the standpoint of the economy? From the standpoint of a particular industry?

3. Why is the market for the renting of land imperfect?

4. A piece of land is yielding $650-a-year rent and is expected to continue to do so in the future. What will be the approximate selling price of the land, assuming an interest rate of 4 percent on investments of comparable risk?

5. Why would the land in question 4 not sell for more than the figure given in the answer to that question? Why would it not sell for less?

6. Why will the sale price of a house not equal the capitalized sum of the figure for which it rents?

7. Would rent rise if all land were equally fertile and well located but limited in amount relative to demand?

8. Explain the term quasi-rent.

SUGGESTED READINGS

Stigler, George. *The Theory of Price*, 4th ed. New York: Macmillan, 1987, Chapter 16.
Worcester, Dean A. "A Reconsideration of the Theory of Rent," *American Economic Review* 36 (June 1946), 258–277.

Chapter Sixteen
THEORY OF PROFITS

_____ *Questions to Think About* _____

1. What are economic profits? How do economic profits differ from accounting profits?

2. What are the different types of implicit costs?

3. What are pure profits?

4. Are monopoly and monopsony profits pure profits?

5. Why are innovations and uncertainty considered a source of pure profits?

6. What are expected returns? How do they affect profits?

7. What important role do pure profits play in the economy?

8. What are the different types of losses that firms experience in the short run? What are the causes of these losses?

16.1 INTRODUCTION

The preceding chapters have analyzed how the prices that business firms pay for the services of factor units are determined. Demand schedules for factor units depend on marginal revenue products; supply schedules depend on particular circumstances affecting the availability of factor units and differ widely among various factors. If markets are perfectly competitive, factor prices depend directly on demand-and-supply relationships; if they are not, prices are affected by the exact nature of competition, the strength of monopoly and monopsony elements, and, in some instances, bargaining policies. Our final step in analyzing factor pricing and distribution is to explain the determination of residual income received by owners of businesses, known as profit.

16.2 ECONOMIC PROFITS VERSUS ACCOUNTING PROFITS

The term *profit* is used in two distinct senses: (1) in the business, or *accounting* sense, as the excess of revenues over all contractual costs and depreciation; (2) in the *economic* sense as the excess of revenues over all opportunity costs.

As used by accountants and the business community generally, *profit* refers to the sum available to a firm after it makes all payments for factor services it acquires on a contractual basis and after all other current obligations such as taxes and depreciation charges have been covered. During a given interval of time, a firm obtains a certain sum from the sale of its products. During this period, it also makes various contractual payments for labor services, materials, power, and so forth. It must also meet rent and interest obligations. Because capital declines in value during the period, the firm must regard a portion of its revenues, known as depreciation charges, as merely a return of capital and must charge them against revenues as a cost. Taxes must be paid. The excess of the total revenues over these various payments and charges is regarded as the profit of the business firm. In a proprietorship, this sum is directly available for the personal use of the owners; in a corporation, it may be paid out to the stockholders in the form of dividends or may be retained in the business. Essentially, **accounting profits** comprise the total income that accrues to the business firm as such and therefore to its owners (although in a corporation the owners may not have access to it).

One major problem in using accounting profits to measure a firm's success is that they fail to include implicit (that is, noncontractual) costs. These represent the opportunity costs of factor units and financial capital provided by owners of the enterprise. These are true cost elements, as explained in earlier chapters, in the sense that they must be covered over the long run if the firm is to continue to operate. They differ from contractual costs only in that the firm has no formal, legal obligation to pay the return. The implicit costs take the form of forgone earnings from other possible uses of factor units. Each of the major types of implicit costs will be reviewed briefly.

TYPES OF IMPLICIT COSTS

Interest Return on Financial Capital

In virtually all businesses, a portion of the financial capital is supplied by the owners, directly in partnerships and proprietorships, and indirectly through the purchase of stock or through retention of earnings in corporations. Because the owners forgo the advantages of liquidity or of a monetary return from placing funds in other investments, a return on the money is an essential cost from the standpoint of the business. Owners of financial capital would not invest in the business initially if they did not expect a return, and they will not retain their money in the business indefinitely if a return is not earned.

Implicit Wages

Especially in smaller firms, a portion of business profits may consist of noncontractual wages for work the owners perform in the enterprise. The typical farmer or small shopkeeper performs substantial amounts of ordinary labor for which he or she rarely receives a formal wage. A large portion of the sum that is regarded as business profit is an **implicit wage**, equal to the amount which he or she could obtain from selling labor services to other firms.

Implicit Rents

If rent is regarded as a distinct form of factor return arising out of the scarcity of non-reproducible assets, a portion of business profits may fall within the category of **implicit rent**. If a firm owns land, for example, a portion of its profits consists of the sum that this land would earn if rented out instead of being used in the business. Alternatively, an implicit-interest return on the current monetary value of the property may be regarded as an implicit cost. The sums involved are the same regardless of which approach is used. (See Problems 16–1 and 16–2.)

16–1 True or False? A firm located in a growing urban area can protect itself from rising rents by owning its own building.

False. The building the firm owns has an opportunity cost. That is, rising rents mean higher opportunity costs whether the firm owns or rents the building.

16–2 Which of the following are opportunity costs? Which are explicit costs? Which are implicit costs?
   a)   the depreciation charges on physical capital
   b)   the time the owner spends working for the firm
   c)   the rental value of the land the owner provides the firm
   d)   the wages of the workers
   e)   the interest forgone on monetary investments by the owner
   f)   the payment for physical capital

All of the costs are opportunity costs, but only (a), (d), and (f) are explicit costs. Explicit costs are contractual opportunity costs such as monetary payments to suppliers and workers. Implicit costs are the costs associated with the firm for which no actual monetary payment is made; they are the opportunity costs of the factor units and the financial capital that the owners of the firm have sacrificed.

16.3 ECONOMIC PROFITS

Any excess of revenues over and above implicit and explicit costs is regarded as excess or **economic profit**. **Pure profits** are present when economic profits are not capitalized into the firm's value. Only one segment of economic profit may be regarded as a truly pure profit; other segments, particularly those arising from monopoly or monopsony influences, constitute special forms and are therefore, in a sense, implicit costs. These segments of profit will be considered first, with subsequent attention to pure profit.

MONOPOLY PROFITS

When a firm is protected from entry of new firms, it will be able to earn profits over and above implicit costs, provided the price for the product is, in any range of output, above average cost, although the market structure may be one of oligopoly, monopolistic competition, or complete monopoly. This higher return protected by entry restriction is known as **monopoly profit**.

   Popular thinking attributes a large portion of excess profit to monopoly positions, and some economists have regarded monopoly as the primary source of pure profit. However, close examination of monopoly profits suggests that they differ in several respects from pure profits and should be distinguished from the latter on several grounds.

1. Imputation of Monopoly Profits

In the first place, unlike pure profits, monopoly profits can frequently be attributed to economies of large scale production or patents and licenses. Suppose, for example, that entry into a field is restricted because the firm possesses patent rights or established trademarks. Excess profits earned because of the inability of new firms to enter the industry are clearly attributable to the patent right or trademark. The firm could lease these rights to other firms for an equivalent return; the foregone return would therefore be in a sense an opportunity cost to the firm as the owner and user of the patent, instead of being a true or pure profit.

2. Capitalization of Monopoly Profits

When restriction of entry is the result of the large volume of business necessary to produce efficiently, monopoly profits are less clearly attributable to particular factors. However, the higher rate of profits tends to be capitalized if it is expected to continue, the sale value of the enterprise increasing by the capitalized sum of the monopoly return. Not only do new purchasers of the firm, or of stock in it, receive only an average rate of earnings on their investment, but the existing owners, who could dispose of the firm or their interest in it at the higher price, are also in a sense only earning a normal return on their investment represented by the potential sale price. The monopoly profit is therefore very similar to rent in the broad sense of that term and, from the standpoint of the firm itself, has some characteristics of a true imputed cost.

An example will illustrate the capitalization of monopoly profits. Suppose that a firm established with an investment of $500,000 succeeds in building up a strong reputation that competitors cannot duplicate and earns annual business profits of $200,000, year after year. If the firm is offered for sale, it may bring as much as $4,000,000 ($200,000 / .05) if investors regard 5 percent as an appropriate return on investment with the same degree of risk and if they expect the profits to continue indefinitely. The new purchasers would therefore earn only 5 percent on their investment, and the monopoly returns would appear to have vanished, having become an implicit cost. Actually, however, the return is much higher than is necessary to ensure continued operation of the firm. If entry barriers were broken and profits fell, the enterprise would continue to operate on a permanent basis as long as the business profits were as much as $25,000—representing a 5 percent return on replacement cost.

3. Monopoly Profits Distinguished from Other Returns

Monopoly profits have certain characteristics of rent because in large measure they tend to be capitalized. Thus, they resemble implicit costs from the standpoint of an individual firm. However, they may be distinguished from true implicit costs in at least three ways.

One, they are not necessary to ration economically scarce resources among competing units; most entry restrictions are artificial barriers to the establishment of new firms rather than true scarcity factors, that is, it is not a social cost because nothing is given up, but it is a private cost for the firm. For example, patent rights could be used by all firms in an industry if the law permitted, and brand names could be shared. Even when limited raw-material resources restrict entry of new firms, the restriction is a product of ownership of the available resources by existing firms.

Two, the monopoly revenues are not necessary to maintain output of the industry. If the earnings of firms drop to an average-return level through the breaking of barriers to entry, no firm will leave the industry.

Three, the existence of monopoly profits gives rise to constant striving on the part of the other firms to break entry-restricting barriers and enter production in the field. While monopoly profits must therefore be distinguished from pure profits, they must also be distinguished from true implicit costs even though they resemble the latter. (See Problem 16–3.)

16–3 True or False? Suppose that you buy the entire stock of a corporation that is earning and expected to earn monopoly profits. You will make a higher-than-average rate of return on the money you place in the enterprise.

False. Presumably the sellers of the stock that you purchased were aware of the extra-normal profits, and they would be foolish if they sold the stock for a price that did not include the capitalized flow of monopoly profit. The former owners may have earned rents from their stocks, but you will be earning the going rate of return (assuming the stock is sold under reasonably competitive conditions).

MONOPSONY PROFITS

When a firm is able to pay factor owners less than their competitive factor incomes, the owners of the firm effectively receive a portion of the factor income attributable to these factor units and thereby, in a sense, "exploit" other factor owners. For example, if one coal mine is able to hire workers more cheaply than other mines, the firm can earn a higher average rate of profit; the excess consists simply of the wage differential that the owners of the mine have been able to appropriate for their own use because of market imperfections. Only when markets are imperfect—when factor owners lack adequate knowledge of other possibilities or factor units are immobile—or when competition among various firms for factor units is not complete can monopsonistic profits be earned. It should be noted that if all firms in an industry gain similar advantage, profits tend to disappear. Only a differential advantage on the part of particular firms enables them to earn profit from this source.

Monopsony profits, though constituting an excess over implicit cost, tend to be capitalized in the same manner as monopoly profits and are therefore distinguishable from pure profit.

A third source of excess profit over and above usual implicit costs is the undertaking of **innovations**—deliberate changes in production and demand functions—by business firms. Some economists have regarded pure profits as solely the result of innovations; Joseph Schumpeter was the most famous advocate of this position.[1] Innovations may be classed into two groups: those affecting production and those affecting marketing. The first group includes all changes which alter techniques of physical production and distribution, and methods of organization and operation. If a firm is successful in introducing cost-reducing techniques, it will earn, at least temporarily, a higher rate of profit. The second type of innovation includes all changes that affect consumer demand for the product, such as the introduction of new products, new styles, advertising techniques, and so on. (See Problems 16–4 and 16–5.)

16–4 True or False? Profits resulting from any one innovation can be expected to continue indefinitely.

False. They will continue only until other firms succeed in duplicating the innovations successfully. If an innovation proves difficult to duplicate and other firms are restricted from entering the field, the continuing profits must be regarded as monopoly profits and will be capitalized. Any one firm can continue to make innovational profits, as such, only by continuing to introduce successful innovations.

---

[1] See J. Schumpeter, *Theory of Economic Development*, Cambridge: Harvard University Press,. 1934.

16–5 In the early 1970s, Schlitz Brewery introduced a cost-saving strategy, an accelerated batch-fermentation process that lowered fermentation from 12 days to less than 4 days. In 1976, expecting the Food and Drug Administration to require ingredient labeling, Schlitz changed to a new beer stabilizer that would filter the beer but not appear on the label. Then in 1977, Schlitz replaced the "gusto" advertising campaign with the "Drink Schlitz or else" slogan.[2] How do you think these innovations affected the profits of Schlitz?

Although these innovations may have seemed profitable beforehand, they proved to be detrimental to Schlitz. Consumers claimed that the quality of the beer had been altered by the new batch-fermentation process, and the beer stabilizer introduced in 1976 actually produced tiny flakes and a haze in the beer. Finally, the 1977 advertising campaign flopped. Schlitz was purchased by Stroh in 1981, unable to recover from its unsuccessful attempts to innovate. Accounting profits fell from $2.11 per barrel to -$1.44 per barrel between 1971 and 1981.

UNCERTAINTY AS A SOURCE OF PURE PROFITS

Pure profits may arise not only from deliberate innovations but also from windfalls, that is, from unexpected changes in revenues or costs. Examples include unanticipated shifts in consumer preferences or changes in raw material prices. If such changes are favorable, they give rise to profits; if they are unfavorable, they give rise to negative profits, that is, losses. If the concept of **uncertainty** is defined broadly, the outcome of innovations may be regarded as one case of uncertainty; uncertainty may therefore be regarded as the major source of pure profits. The tendency in recent years has been to explain profits in this way, following a classic work by Frank Knight.[3] In terms of the uncertainty thesis, *pure profits* may be defined as the difference between expected net revenues and actual net revenues during a given period—although, as noted later, the term *expected* is subject to more than one interpretation.

Uncertainty has two major sources: the circumstances directly affecting the costs and revenues of the firm, and changes in the general environment, such as national income, government policies, and so on, which indirectly affect cost-and-revenue schedules. A firm can never be certain about the behavior of sales, prices, and various cost items in the coming period; and pure profits are frequently earned because sales or prices rise or costs fall, without offsetting unfavorable changes. Even if a firm undertakes a deliberate change—for example, by introducing a new technique or product—it cannot be certain of the results. If expectations are exceeded, the firm earns pure

---

[2]For details see Tremblay, Victor J., and Carol Horton Tremblay, "The Determinants of Horizontal Acquisitions: Evidence from the U.S. Brewing Industry," *Journal of Industrial Economics*, 1988.
[3]See F. H. Knight, *Risk, Uncertainty and Profit.* Boston: Houghton Mifflin, 1921.

profits. On the other hand, pure profits may arise as a result of changes extraneous to the immediate circumstances such as, for example, changes in weather, government expenditures, taxes, government regulatory policies, tariffs, and so on. When the changes are adverse, of course, the firm suffers losses.

THE CONCEPT OF EXPECTED RETURNS

Clarification of the concept of pure profit requires interpretation of the term **expected returns**. If by this term is meant the prediction of the firm itself, any foreseen pure profits would not be pure profits at all—because the latter are defined as the difference between expected and realized revenues. If a firm undertakes an innovation in anticipation of a certain profit and actually attains this profit, the sum would not be pure profit, in terms of this interpretation of the term *expected*, but would be an implicit cost. The concept of profits is more useful, however, if the term *expected returns* is interpreted to mean a forecast accepted with certainty, not only by the firm but by general opinion in the market. Returns expected in this sense are reflected in factor prices and the selling or rental price of the firm as a whole, and, they are capitalized in the same manner as monopoly profit. They should not therefore be regarded as pure profit. Profits that the firm hopes to gain, however, but are not accepted by the market as certain, are not fully capitalized, and, if realized, constitute pure profits, even though the firm may have anticipated them. Gains from both innovations and windfalls, therefore, that are not market anticipated constitute pure profits. (See Problem 16–6.)

16–6 True or False? If profits arising out of uncertainty are foreseen by the market as a whole, they are pure profits if and when they are earned. They are also pure profits if they are anticipated by a particular firm.

It depends. If the profits are widely foreseen, this expectation causes the value of the firm to be bid up (perhaps resulting in rents being earned on capital in the short run). The profits must in fact occur, or, the owners of the firm will incur losses. Thus, profits will not be pure if the profits are widely foreseen. However, they are pure profits if anticipated only within the firm because they will not be capitalized on the market into a higher firm value.

16.4 THE ROLE OF PROFITS IN THE ECONOMY

Pure profits play an important role in the functioning of the economy. In the first place, pure profits are an important lure that lead firms to undertake innovations of all types and thus to sustain economic progress. Second, pure profits are a signal that the firm has to revise its behavior. Failure of expected and realized profits to coincide suggests that the firm needs to revise its estimates and policies. Third, pure profits and monopoly profits constitute a stimulus to other firms to attempt to duplicate the policies of successful firms or to develop other policies that will accomplish the same result. In a highly competitive field, firms dare not lag behind more successful firms or they will soon suffer losses; the pure profits earned by some firms constitute a warning to other firms to adjust policies if they are to avoid future trouble. Likewise, high profits in a certain field lead new firms to enter the industry and bring about a reallocation of resources in conformity with changes in consumer demand and other forces. (See Problem 16–7.)

16–7 Evaluate the following statements:
   (a) A profit is made, not because the industry produces more than it costs, but because it fails to give workers sufficient compensation for their toil. Such an industry is a social evil. (Simonde de Sismondi, 1819)
   (b) Men must have profits proportionable to their expense and hazard. (David Hume, 1754)
   (c) Profit, in some cases, may be more properly said to be acquired than produced. (James Maitland, 1804)
   (d) When wages are low, profits must be high. (David Ricardo, 1817)

a) De Sismondi has isolated only one type of profit, monopsonistic profit. This may be viewed as a "social evil" in the sense that labor is not paid its opportunity cost. Nevertheless, pure profit plays a positive role in the economy by promoting innovation, encouraging adaptability to changing economic conditions, and allocating resources according to consumer preferences.
b) Profits proportionate to expense represent pure interest, and profits proportionate to hazard represent the risk premium, the two components of the interest return on money capital. Revenues must cover these implicit cost (among other costs) for the firm to remain in business, as Hume states.
c) Monopoly and monopsony profits are acquired whereas innovative profits result from a productive contribution.
d) This is true for monopsonistic profits. Generally profits and wages are positively tied. For example, a marketing innovation that raises product demand (and profits) increases the marginal revenue product of labor and, therefore, the wage rate.

16.5 NEGATIVE PROFITS OR LOSSES

The preceding sections have been concerned with positive profits arising when actual results are better than expected. Actual revenues, however, may be less than anticipated, in which case pure profits will be **negative profits**. Economic profits are negative *whenever revenues are less than the sum of contractual obligations, depreciation charges, and implicit interest, wage, and rent costs.* If revenues are so low that they do not cover contractual obligations plus depreciation, the firm is experiencing business losses, or losses in the accounting sense. If the explicit costs are covered but all implicit costs are not covered, the firm is earning a business profit but is suffering negative economic profits or an *economic loss.*

TYPES OF ECONOMIC LOSSES

It is important to distinguish between losses that cause firms to cease operations immediately and those despite losses that continue to operate in the short run.

1. Failure to Cover Explicit (and Implicit) Variable Costs
If an enterprise is not taking in enough in current revenues to meet variable costs, continued operation is obviously undesirable unless an immediate improvement is expected. It is impossible unless the firm (or its owners) has adequate reserve funds to meet the deficit.

2. Coverage of Variable but not Contractual Fixed Costs
If revenues cover explicit variable costs but not explicit fixed costs, of which interest is likely to be the most significant, an enterprise will go into bankruptcy unless the reserves of the firm are adequate to meet the necessary payments or the owners of the firm are able and willing to supply necessary funds. Through reorganization in bankruptcy, creditors become the new owners of the enterprise and explicit interest costs can be reduced or eliminated; the situation thus becomes one of (3) or (4), below.

3. Coverage of Variable and Contractual Fixed Costs but not Depreciation Charges
 A firm may, before or after reorganization, be able to meet all contractual obligations involving both fixed and variable costs but not depreciation. The firm can obviously continue operations as long as existing equipment can be used; once its equipment wears out, it will lack funds for replacement and be unable to obtain them unless owners are willing to supply additional financial capital. They obviously will not do this unless an improvement in conditions is expected.

4. *Coverage of Contractual Costs and Depreciation but Failure to Earn all Implicit Costs*

A firm may have adequate revenues to meet all contractual factor payments and depreciation but not enough to cover all implicit costs, the most important of which is likely to be a return on the investment of the owners. Such a firm can continue operations indefinitely if the owners wish. However, it will not be advantageous for owners to permit continued operations once the point is reached at which cash earnings (revenues in excess of direct operating expenses, taxes, and the decline in salvage value during the period) fall below expected earnings that can be made on the salvage value if the enterprise is liquidated.

In practice, many firms operate far too long from the standpoint of the interests of owners. This is a product of continuing overoptimism about the future and of a reluctance by managers to discontinue an enterprise with which they have long been identified. As a consequence, depreciation funds and such business profits as are made are used to maintain or repair equipment, and eventually the equity of stockholders is destroyed.

CAUSES OF LOSSES

In general, losses may be attributed to uncertainty—to unanticipated events that adversely affect cost or revenue schedules. These events may include general changes in the economy, such as a fall in national income or altered government policy; or they may be changes in circumstances directly affecting particular firms, such as an adverse shift in consumer preferences, rises in materials costs, and so on. They may result from successful introduction of innovations by competitors, or failure of innovations attempted by the firm itself to produce desired results. Or they may result from plain bad management. Where losses are the result of obvious managerial errors, it may be argued that the source of the loss from the standpoint of the firm is overcompensation of management personnel (the opposite of monopsonistic exploitation). A frequent type of mistake is the establishment of new enterprises under circumstances in which profitable operation is impossible, promoters lack adequate knowledge of revenue and cost schedules, or managers are overoptimistic.

Losses lead to readjustments that may serve to eliminate them; losses constitute a warning to a firm to alter its policies to become more efficient, to develop innovations, and so on. Changes made may prove to be successful, and profitable operation may be restored; in other cases, a firm may be unable to escape the losses and thus must eventually liquidate. In large measure, continuing losses may be regarded as a penalty for failure to adapt to changing conditions.

SUMMARY

1. Business or accounting profits are defined as the excess of revenues over all contractual costs and depreciation. Economic profits are the excess of revenues over all opportunity costs.

2. Implicit wages and rents are measures of foregone income from labor and land respectively.

3. Barriers to entry can lead to monopoly profits provided that price is greater than average cost in the relevant output range. Often, monopoly profits exist because of property rights (patents, trademarks, and so on) established by the firm.

4. Monopsony profits arise when a firm is able to pay factor owners less than their competitive factor incomes. These profits exist as a result of market imperfections.

5. Pure profits may arise from innovations and uncertainty.

6. Pure profits are an important incentive to firms, a signal for firm behavior, and an important gauge to potential entrants.

7. Negative profits or losses exist when revenues are less than the sum of contractual obligation, depreciation charges, implicit interest, and wage and rent costs.

8. Losses for a firm may arise because of a firms failure to cover any of the following: explicit variable costs, contractual fixed costs, depreciation charges and/or implicit costs.

WORDS AND CONCEPTS FOR REVIEW

accounting profits

implicit wages and rents

economic profits

pure profits

monopoly profits

monopsony profits

innovations and profits

uncertainty and profits

expected returns

negative profits

types of economic losses

REVIEW QUESTIONS

1. Why does a large portion of business profits consist of elements that are costs from an economic standpoint?

2. Upon what base should the necessary return on the owners' investment be figured?

3. A farmer obtains $17,000 from the sale of his crop; his expenses, including taxes, are $4,000. His farm would sell for $50,000. He could obtain a job in a local feed mill at $10,000 a year, if he wished. Determine his business profits, the implicit cost elements in his business profits, and his pure profit, if any. Use a figure of 4 percent as a real rate of return.

4. Define *monopoly profit*. Why are monopoly profits, in a sense, implicit costs? Why are they not true costs from the standpoint of the economy?

5. What is the source of monopsony profits? Why are they not attained if monopsony powers extend to all firms in the industry?

6. Explain the meaning of the term *innovations*, and give examples. How do innovational profits differ from monopoly profits? From windfall profits?

7. What condition is necessary for monopoly profits to continue?

8. Indicate the major roles that profits play in the economy.

9. Suppose that a particular firm is covering all variable costs and depreciation but not an average return on investment. If the owners are seeking to maximize their gain, at what time will they discontinue operations? Explain.

10. Why do companies sometimes operate far beyond the optimum (from a profit standpoint) time of liquidation?

11. Indicate the major causes of losses.

12. How would you explain the following:
    a) frequent failure of small restaurants
    b) the losses of the New York subway system

SUGGESTED READINGS

Friedman, Milton. *Price Theory.* Chicago: Aldine, 1976.

Knight, F. H. *Risk, Uncertainty and Profit.* Boston: Houghton Mifflin, 1921.

Scherer, Frederic M., and David Ross. *Industrial Market Structure and Economic Performance*, 3rd ed. Boston: Houghton Mifflin, 1990.

Part 5

EFFICIENCY, EXCHANGE AND INTERTEMPORAL ISSUES

CHAPTERS

Part 5, Efficiency, Exchange and Intertemporal Issues, contains four chapters that present a diverse range of topics. Chapter 17, "General Equilibrium" and Chapter 18 "Welfare Economics" cover the interaction of related markets. In Chapter 19, "Asset Management and Intertemporal Income Allocation" choices that involve time are discussed. In Chapter 20 "Market Failures: Public Goods and Externalities" we find that market inefficiencies can be corrected through private bargaining and/or government intervention.

Chapter Seventeen

GENERAL EQUILIBRIUM

Questions to think About

1. What is the difference between partial-equilibrium and general-equilibrium theory?

2. How can general equilibrium be determined geometrically?

3. What is an exchange equilibrium? A production equilibrium?

4. What is a production-contract curve?

5. What are the limitations of the general-equilibrium model?

6. Under what circumstances is general-equilibrium theory particularly useful?

7. How do changes in consumer preferences, production techniques, factor supplies, and competitive relationships affect the economy?

17.1 INTRODUCTION

The preceding chapters analyze how the prices and outputs of *particular* commodities and the income and employment of *particular* productive factors are determined. We have been, in short, looking at the "trees" but ignoring how they go together to make up the "economic forest." This portion of economic analysis is known as **partial-equilibrium theory**—partial because it deals with adjustments in isolated sectors of the economy and makes only incidental reference to interrelations among different sectors.

Despite its somewhat restrictive assumptions, partial-equilibrium analysis is adequate for the study of a surprisingly wide range of practical problems. In analyzing the effects of a new excise tax on tobacco, for example, the assumption that prices are given in all markets other than the market for tobacco is not too unrealistic. Similarly, the effects of lower steel prices on the automobile and construction industries can be studied fairly effectively using partial-equilibrium methods, even though the total effect of these lower prices on the economy as a whole cannot be regarded simply as the sum of the separate effects on individual industries.

To obtain an adequate picture of the functioning of the economic system as a whole, however, and to develop analytical tools suitable for studying problems with ramifications through several sectors of the economy, economists need to know more about the interrelationships among the outputs and prices of various commodities and the prices and inputs of various factors. The portion of economic theory that deals with these interrelations is known as **general-equilibrium theory**. Before we examine the framework of general-equilibrium analysis, certain major interrelationships in the economy will be briefly presented.

17.2 CONSUMER-PRICE INTERDEPENDENCIES

The analysis of price and output determination in earlier chapters was based on the assumption that the prices of other goods were given; only occasionally did we refer to the direct effects that a change in the price of a particular good might have on the prices or demands of other goods. This type of modification, however, reflects only a small example of the **consumer-price interdependencies** that are possible. A change in the price of any one good inevitably alters the demand for and possibly the supply of many other goods. A rise in the price of butter, for example, increases the demand for substitutes such as margarine and leads to increases in the price and output of these goods if markets are perfectly competitive. If they are not, the price rise may affect only output, although the price of substitutes could also fall. Additionally, the prices of goods complementary to butter, such as bread, may fall because the demand for them will fall if butter becomes more expensive. The effects of a rise in the price of butter do not stop there. Changes in the outputs of these other goods affect factor supplies available for the production of bread and therefore its cost of production and supply, while shifts in the prices of other goods in turn affect the demand for bread. The changes in prices and outputs of substitute and complementary goods in turn affect the prices and outputs of other goods.

The prices of all goods can therefore adjust completely only when the various prices and outputs attain levels that are mutually consistent. Given the basic determinants of consumption-goods prices—namely, consumer incomes, consumer preferences, factor price schedules, production functions, and the nature of competition in various markets—such an equilibrium can be defined. A shift in some variable affecting any one good, however, may have widespread repercussions on the equilibrium prices and outputs of many other goods, reactions that are largely ignored in partial-equilibrium analysis.

Consumer prices are interrelated not only with one another but with factor prices. When we analyzed the pricing of consumption goods, we generally assumed that factor price schedules were given; similarly, in the discussion of how equilibrium-factor prices are determined, for the most part, we assumed consumption-goods prices were given. Actually, of course, the two sets of equilibrium prices are mutually dependent. For example, a major element in the cost of consumption goods is labor, making the wage level a significant influence on the prices of products. The demand for labor, however, and therefore wage rates depend on the marginal revenue product of various types of labor, which in turn depends on consumer-goods prices. No circular reasoning is involved in the analysis, as is sometimes claimed. Both wage (and other factor price) levels and commodity price levels must adjust to figures that are mutually consistent; until they do, one set of prices or the other will tend to shift.

17.3 A GRAPHICAL REPRESENTATION OF GENERAL EQUILIBRIUM WITH PRODUCTION AND EXCHANGE

Envision a family of "collective indifference curves" between goods X and Y for a society comprising two individuals, A and B, as represented in Figure 17-1.[1] There will also be a feasible production set showing combinations of goods X and Y that can be produced by our two individuals with their resources (labor, capital, and land).

At point (X*, Y*) in Figure 17-1 our society is producing the optimal relative quantities of goods X and Y. We know this because the marginal rate of substitution in consumption, MRS, is exactly equal to the marginal rate of technical substitution in

---

[1]There are severe problems with the idea of a "social-welfare function," but don't be unduly concerned at present. The discussion will be seen to have intuitive merit and will clarify what the "invisible hand" is really up to.

production, MRTS, at this point. Moreover, because we are on the production-possibilities curve rather than inside it must be the case that A and B are fully employed and all inputs are optimally allocated between the production of X and that of Y: that is, supply equals demand for each input, and marginal product per dollar spent on each input must be the same separately considering each good.[2]

FIGURE 17–1
A DEPICTION OF GENERAL EQUILIBRIUM WITH PRODUCTION AND EXCHANGE
(DASHED LINES DEPICT EXCHANGE DISEQUILIBRIUM)

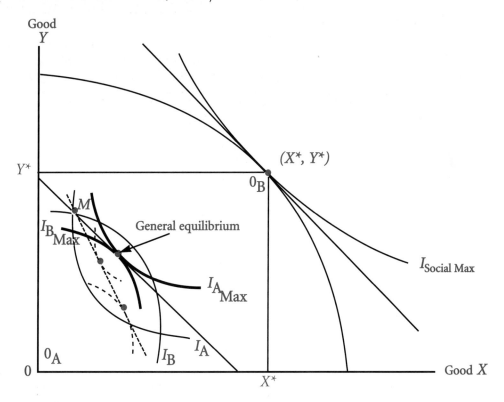

The point "General Equilibrium" represents exchange equilibrium (supplies equal demands and $MRS_A = MRS_B =$ price ratios) and production equilibrium (the MRS of each and all individuals in consumption equals MRTS in production). The socially optimal allocation (X^*, Y^*) occurs where the social indifference curve and production-possibilities frontier are tangent and $MRS = MRTS$. The distribution of output between individuals A and B falls within the box $O_A Y^* O_B X^*$. Being *on* the production possibilities frontier means marginal products per dollar factor cost are equated and supplies = demands in input markets. At point M, both individuals can reach a higher level of utility through a redistribution of X and Y.

_____

[2]An analogous graph with isoquants rather than indifference curves inside the box OAY* OBX* could be used to establish these points. The text discussion that follows will clarify how.

How about *distribution* of the output of our small economy? The bundle (X^*, Y^*) is produced, and any point inside the box $O_AY^* O_BX^*$ represents a possible allocation.[3] Suppose the marginal products of the resources owned by A and B are such that their earnings (they are paid in output, although money could be introduced and the analysis would still hold) are represented by point I in Figure 17–1. Individual B has a relatively large amount of good X and only a little Y (apparently B's resources were better suited, when optimally employed, to the production of X). Similarly, Individual A has relatively more Y and less X at M. Clearly, *any* point *within* the lens-shaped area contained by the indifference curves passing through M will be preferred to M; that is, for any interior point, both A and B can have greater satisfaction. Merely by *reallocating* existing supplies, both A and B are made better off; in other words wealth is created. Where will society end up? If relative prices were as indicated by the dashed line (X relatively expensive, because much Y must be given up to get more X), then individual A would wish to buy only a small amount of X relative to the amount individual B would wish to sell. The tangencies of the (utility-maximizing) indifference curves of A and B do not occur at the same point. The inconsistency would cause the price of X to fall, for there is excess supply at the price indicated by the dashed line. The price will continue to change until the utility-maximizing behavior is consistent, at "general equilibrium." At the General Equilibrium relative price of X, the amount individual B wishes to sell of X is exactly equal to the amount A wishes to buy and, indeed, A can pay for the X to be purchased with the proceeds from the Y that will be sold.

Notice that in some respects this case is *more* complicated than the real world. Here, prices adjust as if the economy were competitive; our example, however, had only two economic transactors, A and B. If there were, in fact, only two individuals, the final equilibrium position would be much harder to determine. Assuming voluntary exchanges (the stronger, meaner of A or B could just *take* the other's goods—the reason, at heart, for institutions such as courts and the police), we know only that the final outcome would be in the lens-shaped area. If A were a better bargainer, the final position would be further to the northeast; if B were more persuasive, the final position would be further to the southwest.

In the final equilibrium position—with price-taking, competitive behavior—the prices at which individuals exchange will be equal to the marginal rate of technical substitution in production. The price line passing through general equilibrium therefore must be parallel to that passing through (X^*, Y^*). This is because if exchange were occurring at other relative prices, it would be profitable to alter the relative amounts of what is being produced (ending up in a box with a different "shape" from that of Figure 17–1). (See Problems 17–1 and 17–2.)

---

[3]Note that one of the difficulties of talking of a "social-welfare function" yielding collective-indifference curves emerges here—each point of possible allocation represents a particular income distribution. Generally, we will have a different family bundle would be optimal. To get around this problem, assume identical preferences.

17–1 Adam and Eve go to Pizza Palace and order two minipizzas. Adam orders a taco pizza, and Eve orders a Hawaiian pizza. Using an Edgeworth box, show how Adam and Eve may allocate the pizza slices. Suppose Adam prefers taco pizza and Eve prefers Hawaiian pizza. How does your diagram and the optimal allocation change?

In the accompanying figure, 0_{ADAM} is the origin of Adam's indifference map and 0_{EVE} is the origin of Eve's indifference map. Eve's consumption of taco pizza increases from right to left from her origin, and her consumption of Hawaiian pizza increases from top to bottom from her origin. If Adam and Eve do not have strong preferences for one type of pizza, indifference curves will be similar to I_A and I_E in Figure (a). One potential allocation is at point A, although any point of tangency between Adam's and Eve's indifference curves may be optimal.

If, however, Adam prefers taco pizza, his indifference curves are fairly steep, similar to I_A in Figure (b). In other words, Adam would give up a lot of his Hawaiian pizza for one slice of taco pizza. Eve's strong preference for Hawaiian pizza results in relatively flat indifference curves. She will give up just a little Hawaiian pizza for one slice of taco pizza. In deciding how to allocate the two pizzas, one possible solution is point A in Figure (b). In this case, Adam's preference for taco pizza and Eve's preference for Hawaiian pizza are so strong that no trade takes place.

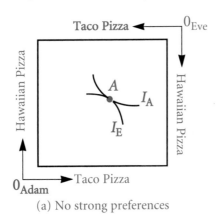

(a) No strong preferences

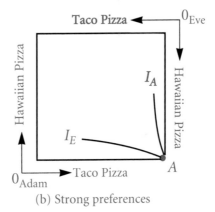

(b) Strong preferences

17–2 Elizabeth and Tom go to a Chinese restaurant for dinner one night. Elizabeth orders almond chicken and Tom orders moo goo gai pan. Using an Edgeworth box, show how Elizabeth and Tom might allocate servings of the two dishes assuming that Elizabeth and Tom like both dishes and have similar appetites.

The figure below shows the initial endowments of almond chicken and moo goo gai pan for Elizabeth and Tom at point *A*. The equilibrium allocation will be at a tangent point between indifference curves for Elizabeth and Tom, for example, point *B*.

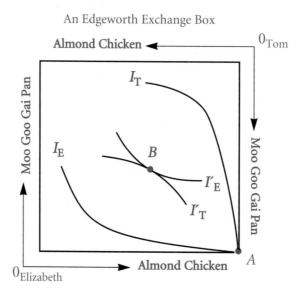

An Edgeworth Exchange Box

GENERAL EQUILIBRIUM IN PRODUCTION

Just as we have drawn an "exchange box" (called an Edgeworth box, in spite of having been invented by Pareto), we can also construct a "production box," as discussed at the outset. In the Edgeworth production box in Figure 17–2, the economy's labor is on one axis and capital on the other. The southwest corner represents zero output of good X with all the economy's resources devoted to Y, while the northeast corner represents zero output of good Y, with all resources devoted to X. We reach general equilibrium in production whenever the marginal rate of technical substitution between labor and capital is the same for the production of both X and Y. The isoquants must be tangent to each other for efficient production to occur. The curve joining the tangency points is called the **production-contract curve**. If the isoquants are not tangent, a higher production of X or Y or both can be obtained by reallocating of the inputs. However, once we are on the production-contract curve, we can achieve no further net gains in output.

It is easy to derive the **production-possibility curve** from the points we obtained on the production-contract curve; that is, the points on the production-contract curve are the boundaries on the production-possibilities curve as seen in Figure 17–3.

The final equilibrium (which would occur as we arrive at the General Equilibrium of Figures 17–1 and 17–2) would involve the value of marginal product of each input being the same in the production of either good.

Thus, general equilibrium ultimately stems from tastes, technology, and resource endowment. An economy with a great deal of accumulated capital, for example, would (abstracting from international trade and even grander notions of general equilibrium) tend to produce in relatively capital-intensive ways, and the lower relative price of capital-intensive goods would favor greater consumption of such goods. If preferences strongly favored good Y, the box in Figure 17–1 or Figure 17–3 would have a very different shape (tall and thin). Even with preferences unchanged, however, if technology (or resource endowment) were such that the production possibilities curve were flatter and lower, then relatively more X would be produced and consumed.

These concepts should already be familiar to you. Recall that even the most elementary discussions of supply and demand indicate that price and quantity are not determined by supply alone (technology, resource endowment) or by demand alone (preferences) but by their interaction, like scissors. (See Problems 17–3, 17–4, and 17–5.)

FIGURE 17–2
GENERAL EQUILIBRIUM IN PRODUCTION

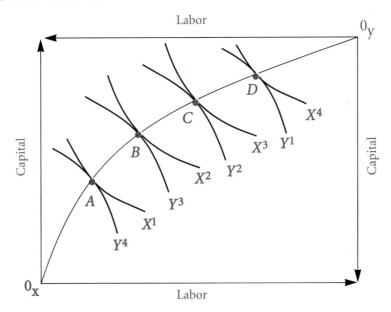

General equilibrium in production requires the equality of the MRTS for X and the MRTS for Y, that is the tangency of an X isoquant and a Y isoquant. The production contract curve maps all of the general-equilibrium combinations of labor and capital (A, B, C, and D).

FIGURE 17–3
PRODUCTION-POSSIBILITIES FRONTIER

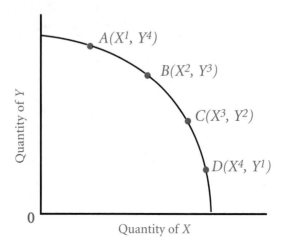

The maximum producible quantities of X and Y, depicted along the production-possibilities frontier, can be determined from the isoquants along the production-contract curve.

17-3 Given the production-contract curve in Figure (a), graph points on the corresponding production-possibility frontier.

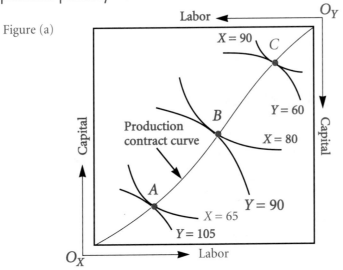

Figure (a)

In Figure (a), O_X is the origin for good X, and O_Y is the origin for good Y. The amount of labor used to produce good Y increases from right to left along the the top horizontal line, and the amount of capital used to produce Y increases moving down the vertical line. The total amount of capital available in the economy equals the distance along the vertical segment, while the total labor available equals the distance along the horizontal segment. Along the production-contract curve, the maximum output levels of X and Y are produced. At point A, 105 units of Y and 65 units of X are produced, which is plotted at point a in Figure (b). Similarly, the quantities of X and Y associated with point B in Figure (a) are charted at point b in Figure (b). Point C corresponds to point c. Points a, b, and c are on the production-possibility frontier. The dotted line sketches a possible production-possibility frontier.

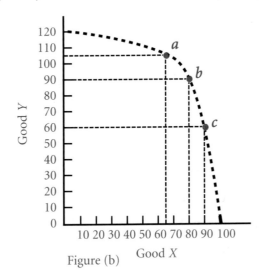

Figure (b)

17–4   Graph a general equilibrium for two individuals, Anne (A) and Bob (B), and two goods, milk (M) and wheat (W). Explain why general equilibrium is not possible when any of the following conditions are violated:

a. $MRS_A = MRS_B$

b. $MRTS_M = MRTS_W$ [This economy has two inputs, natural resources (R) and labor (L)].

c.   The slope of the social-indifference curve = the slope of the production-possibility curve.

One possible general-equilibrium allocation of goods and services is given by point E and A in Figure (a). O_A is Anne's origin and O_B is Bob's origin.

a.   At point B, where MRS_A does not equal MRS_B, the slope of Bob's indifference curves I_B exceeds the slope of Anne's indifference curve I_A, and Bob's utility is lower on I'_B than on I_B. Thus, they both can be made better off by moving to point E. At point B, Ann will trade milk for wheat and Bob will trade wheat for milk to move to E.

b.   Figure (b) shows production equilibrium at point E with 60 units of milk and 30 units of wheat. At point B, the slope of the milk isoquant is greater than the slope of the wheat isoquant, that is $MRTS_M > MRTS_W$, and only 20 units of wheat and 50 units of milk are being produced. By using more labor and fewer resources to produce milk, and using more resources and less labor to produce wheat (moving to point E), more units of milk and wheat can be produced. Point e in Figure (a) corresponds to point E in Figure (b) and lies on the production-possibility frontier because it is efficient; in contrast, point b, which corresponds to point B in Figure (b) lies inside the production frontier, because it is inefficient.

c.   In Figure (c), point A designates the optimal combination of milk and wheat. At point B, society's MRS is greater than the slope of the production-possibility frontier. Collective or social utility is lower at B than A, because B is on a lower collective-indifference curve. Social utility could therefore be increased by producing more milk and less wheat.

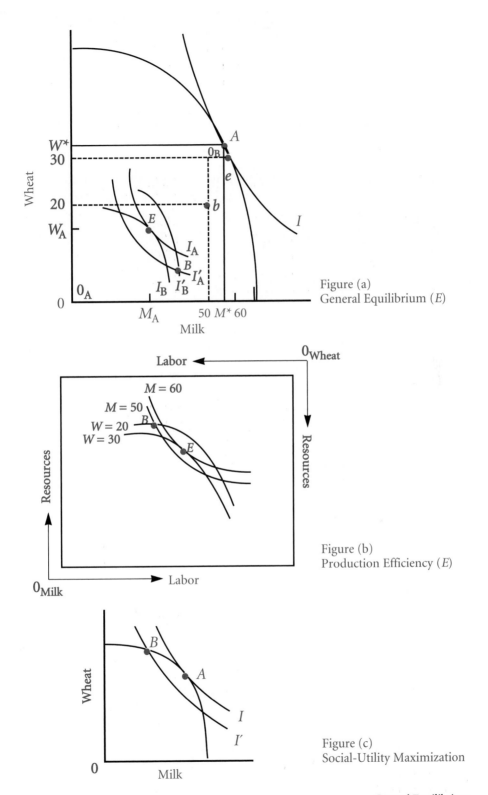

Figure (a)
General Equilibrium (E)

Figure (b)
Production Efficiency (E)

Figure (c)
Social-Utility Maximization

17–5 Explain how each of the following changes in economic conditions affects the general-equilibrium solution for Anne (*A*) and Bob (*B*), who produce wheat (*W*) and milk (*M*) with resources and labor:

a. an increase in preferences for milk relative to wheat

b. the development of a new technology that increases the efficiency of wheat production.

a. An increase in tastes favoring milk over wheat steepens the collective-indifference curve (and each individual's indifference curves) because society is willing to give up more wheat to obtain one more unit of milk. The increase in demand for milk raises the price of milk relative to the price of wheat. This is illustrated in the figure by the price line through the new equilibrium, *E′*, which is steeper than the price line through the old equilibrium, *E*.

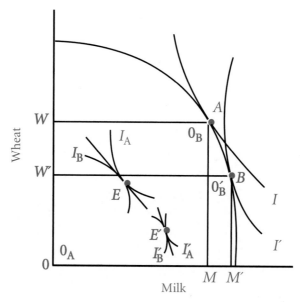

An Increase in Relative Preferences for Milk

b. Figure (a) shows the impact of a technological advance in wheat production using the production box. With the old technology, production efficiency occurs at point A, 60 units of milk and 30 units of wheat. With the new technology, the same amount of wheat can be produced with fewer inputs at point B, and more milk can be produced. Figure (b) illustrates how the technological change rotates the production possibility curve to the right. Points a and b correspond to points A and B, respectively, in Figure (a).

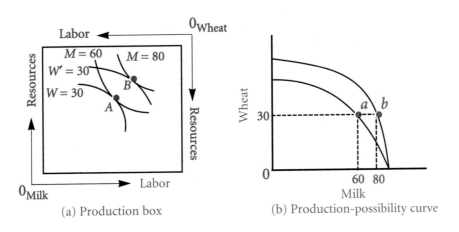

(a) Production box   (b) Production-possibility curve

17.4 FURTHER EXTENSIONS

In the preceding analysis, money was ignored as a medium of exchange. The price of X was "denominated" in Y production, and vice versa. It is a relatively simple matter, however, to extend the analysis so that it applies both to an economic system in which money serves as a medium of exchange and also to one in which individuals hold other kinds of assets (bonds, stocks, capital goods, and so on). Moreover, the assumption of perfect competition, which underlies the whole of the preceding analysis, can be replaced by the assumption of various forms of competition in all markets, and the analysis can thus be extended to monopolistic and oligopolistic markets. The analysis can also be generalized to consider geographically separated markets in which transportation and location variables are included among the unknowns of the general equilibrium system. Whatever the direction in which the analysis is extended, however, the basic conclusions would not change. The importance of these extensions—apart from their intrinsic theoretical interest—is that they may indicate the existence of often unrecognized interrelationships among economic quantities and so facilitate empirical research by providing a theoretical check on the consistency of observational data.

17.5 THE USEFULNESS OF
GENERAL-EQUILIBRIUM THEORY

General-equilibrium theory is of greatest value in stressing the interdependence of various portions of the economic system, which is easily lost from sight in partial-equilibrium analysis. Failure to recognize this interdependence is responsible for many errors in popular reasoning on economic questions.

General-equilibrium theory also provides a useful framework for the organization of empirical research. For effective study of concrete situations, it essential to approach data with a coherent sense of perspective. Preliminary examination of the data may indicate that only a small portion of one's total stock of theoretical knowledge is relevant for further analysis; but much foolishness and many serious mistakes can be avoided if provisionally relevant theoretical knowledge is retained for use until an explicit reason, based on factual knowledge, can be given for disregarding it. Even though general-equilibrium analysis does not itself lead to any directly useful conclusions, it is an extremely powerful instrument for the orderly arrangement of ideas about the real economic world. (See Problem 17–6.)

17–6 Tariff policy is often considered only in terms of its effect on output and employment in the particular industry protected (for example, employment in automobile production in Michigan). What else should be taken into consideration in deciding whether to enact a tariff?

The effects of the tariff in reducing exports and thus the demand for output and reduced employment in exporting industries should be considered. The analysis calls attention to the fact that changes in one portion of the economy will often have widespread repercussions in other segments, and that commodity and factor prices are mutually interrelated; wage changes, for example, almost inevitably affect output and prices.

17.6 LIMITATIONS OF GENERAL-EQUILIBRIUM THEORY

General-equilibrium theory is subject to two major limitations. First, it is essentially static in nature for it defines the overall equilibrium in terms of given determinants. While it offers a tool for studying the effect of changes in specific determinants (as illustrated in the following sections), it is of limited value for studying general economic trends. In recent years, increased effort has been given to the attempt to remedy this inadequacy by further analysis of the role of money and other assets and by work on the dynamics of general equilibrium. Much more work is required along these lines, however, before the analysis can become a truly useful tool for the study of dynamic situations.

The second limitation is a more practical one relating to the actual body of the theory as it now stands, namely, the difficulty of estimating various magnitudes in a general-equilibrium system so that the equations may be solved in quantitative terms and so that the theory may be used to predict precise quantitative results of various changes and policies. The tremendous complexity of the actual economic system and the inadequacy of data make this very difficult, although in the last decade various attempts have been made to do so with a simplified model.

17.7 CHANGES IN THE DETERMINANTS

Changes in any of the basic determinants of the system may have widespread repercussions in the system, as suggested in previous paragraphs, and will lead to the establishment of a new equilibrium pattern. The effects of several major sources of change will be considered briefly.

CONSUMER PREFERENCES

Consumer preferences constantly change as styles, tastes, and wants vary, partly as a result of deliberate efforts on the part of business firms, partly from endogenous (e.g., consumer income) and exogenous (e.g., government, technology) causes. Increased preference for one good (X) relative to another good (Y) increases the demand for X and reduces the demand for Y. Accordingly, firms find it advantageous to increase the output of X, while the output of Y falls. Thus, some resources are shifted from the production of Y to the production of X. If all factors involved are equally productive in the production of either good, factor prices may not change. However, this is unlikely; some factors are more efficient in the production of X, others in the production of Y. The prices of factors best suited for the production of X, therefore, tend to rise, and those best suited for Y fall. As a further consequence, the incomes of the owners of the former set of factors rise, and those of the owners of the latter group fall. These income changes, in turn, affect demands for goods and services at this second stage. Over a longer period, factors will shift from one use to another more easily than in a shorter period. Ultimately, the effects will dampen, resulting in new equilibrium—a new pattern of goods production, consumption, and distribution.

New inventions produce continuous changes in available techniques of production. These changes alter production functions, the quantities of various factors required to produce a unit of output of particular commodities in the optimal fashion, and the prices of finished products. Consequently, new production techniques affect how factors are allocated to the production of various commodities. They can also affect the prices of commodities and factors, in turn affecting the distribution of income. For example, suppose that a new, lower-cost technique is developed for the production of glass tableware. The technique lessens the amount of labor necessary per unit of output but also increases the amounts of certain chemicals required. The reduction in the cost and price of the glassware stimulates increased consumer use and greater use by the producers of the various ingredients. The quantities of those chemicals and other factors not affected by the technological change will increase; the quantity of labor used will decrease unless increased sales more than offset the substitution of chemicals for labor. Suppliers of chemicals and other materials will receive increased incomes, at least temporarily, and owners of nonproducible specialized resources used in their production will gain permanently higher incomes. Workers replaced by the new processes will experience declines in wages, unless their skills can be transferred to other industries. The net effects on factor prices and income distribution will be greatly affected by the ease of transfer of factor units from one line of production to another. (See Problem 17–7.)

17–7 How will the increased use of glassware affect the sales of other products?

Sales of direct substitutes, such as plastic dinnerware, will tend to fall, with consequent repercussions on output and factor prices. If the demand for the glassware is relatively inelastic, less money will be spent on the product, and purchases of other unrelated products will rise, with further repercussions on prices, outputs, and factor prices.

Technological changes that make new products available likewise produce modifications in the general equilibrium system. Such products alter consumer preference patterns, the output of substitute and complementary goods, and relative factor prices. The development of the automobile, for example, has had tremendous effects on the economy. The demand for and output of complementary goods (such as highways, gasoline, and tires), have increased greatly, together with facilities to produce them. The demand for and output of substitutes (such as horses and buggies, streetcars, and railway service) have declined. The location patterns of retail stores and of dwellings have been greatly altered, as have the nature and location of places of amusement and recreation. Incomes of owners of factors of particular importance in the production of automobiles and the other complementary goods have risen, while those of factor units used primarily to produce the substitutes (and not adaptable to other uses) have fallen. The owners of land containing oil have experienced great increases in their incomes, while owners of land primarily suited to growing hay for horses have experienced declines in income. The relative incomes only of the owners of completely adaptable factors have not been affected by the change.

FACTOR SUPPLIES

Changes in factor supplies, either in quantity or in quality, have much the same effects as technological developments. An increase in the available quantities of one factor compared with those of others alters relative factor prices, optimal factor combinations, and prices and outputs of consumption goods. The prices of goods using relatively large amounts of the factor that has increased in supply will fall relative to those of other commodities, and consumption and output will increase. The price of the factor that has increased in supply will tend to fall, but the total share of income going to the owners of this factor may rise, depending on demand elasticities. For example, a growth in the supply of capital goods relative to the quantities of other factors will increase the prices paid for labor and the incomes of the workers and increase the relative outputs of goods requiring relatively large amounts of capital goods for efficient production.

COMPETITIVE RELATIONSHIPS

Changes in competitive relationships also produce modifications in the equilibrium system. For example, if strong oligopoly replaces perfect competition in a particular commodity market, the relative price of the article will rise, and consumption and output will fall. The demand for other commodities will rise if the demand for this commodity is elastic and will fall if it is inelastic. The owners of firms producing this commodity will obtain greater incomes, as long as they are protected from the entry of new firms into the industry. The reduced employment of other factors in the industry will lead to readjustments in factor prices, in costs, and therefore in the outputs of other industries. Changes in competitive relations in factor markets alter relative factor and commodity prices and the relative outputs of various goods.

17.8 THE THEORIES OF CHANGE IN THE DETERMINANTS OF GENERAL EQUILIBRIUM

The preceding paragraphs indicate in a general way the types of readjustments that occur when the basic determinants of equilibrium change as a result of forces autonomous to the economic system. Relatively little attention has been given to the question of whether or not a theory of change in the determinants, one that relates this change to certain forces within or outside the economy, can be developed. A few such attempts have been made. Thomas R. Malthus, for example, developed a long-term relationship between wage levels and population growth, concluding that growth in population and thus labor supply were limited to the rate of increase in goods providing a subsistence level of income to workers.[4] This theory was accepted and developed by various English classical writers after David Ricardo. Joseph Schumpeter viewed the rate of change in the introduction of innovations as the primary factor determining the rate of economic development and thereby the rate and pattern of change in the determinants of the equilibrium system.[5] One of the most complete theories of economic development was that of Karl Marx. His basic principle of economic change was that each form of economic system develops within itself internal inconsistencies, which manifest themselves primarily in struggles between various groups in the economy. These ultimately destroy the particular form of economic system, which gives way to a new form, which in turn develops its own internal inconsistencies.

In recent years, renewed attention has been given to the establishment of theories of economic change and development, particularly the causes and processes of change in the level of employment and the determinants of the rate of long-term economic growth in both underdeveloped and more developed countries. For some time to come, however, this subject will probably continue to be one of the more underdeveloped areas of economic analysis. The problems are so complicated and the stock of established factual knowledge so slight that almost any theory has some degree of plausibility—or implausibility. As long as this is true, substantial progress in understanding concrete problems of economic growth is unlikely.

---

[4]Thomas R. Malthus, *Essays on Population.* London, 1798.
[5]Joseph Schumpeter, *Theory of Economic Development.* Cambridge: Harvard University Press, 1934.

SUMMARY

1. General-equilibrium analysis is the study of the interrelationships among the immense number of outputs and prices of various commodities and the prices and inputs of various factors.

2. A shift in some variable affecting any one good may have widespread repercussions on the equilibrium prices and outputs of many other goods.

3. General-equilibrium theory (like ordinary supply-and-demand theory) suggests that a market economy exhibits a consistent pattern of equilibrium prices, factor inputs, commodity outputs, and consumer purchases. However, the theory does not deal directly with the process of attaining an equilibrium position.

4. Graphically, we can depict general equilibrium. Exchange equilibrium exists on the consumption-contract curve (that is, the curve formed by points where indifference curves are tangent) where MRS_A equals MRS_B equals price ratios. Production equilibrium occurs when the isoquants are tangent along the production-contract curve. At this point $(MRTS_{LK})_X$ equals $(MRTS_{LK})_Y$.

5. General-equilibrium in production and exchange in the competitive model requires that the prices at which individuals exchange (that is, the slope of the line passing through the point where the indifference curves are tangent) be equal to the slope of the production-possibility frontier.

6. General-equilibrium analysis can easily be extended to an economic system in which money serves as a medium of exchange.

7. General-equilibrium theory is subject to two major limitations. One, it is static in nature. Two, it is difficult to estimate various magnitudes in a general-equilibrium system so the equations may be solved.

8. Several major sources of change may have widespread repercussions in the system: Consumer preferences, the techniques of production, factor supplies, and competitive relationships.

WORDS AND CONCEPTS FOR REVIEW

partial-equilibrium theory

general-equilibrium theory

consumer-price interdependencies

consumption-contract curve

production-contract curve

production-possibility curve

REVIEW QUESTIONS

1. Distinguish between partial- and general-equilibrium theory.

2. Trace the probable effects of an improved variety of orange, which allows a great increase in yield per acre, on:
   (a) the price of apples (immediate and long run)
   (b) the production of apples (immediate and short run)
   (c) the income of the owners of land best suited for production oranges
   (d) the income of the owners of land best suited for the production of apples

3. What are some of the probable effects of the development of nylon, Dacron, and Orlon shirts upon the prices and outputs of other commodities and on factor prices?

4. When will a change in consumer preferences permanently alter factor prices?

5. Specify the various assumptions on which the simplified general-equilibrium system is based, and indicate the extent to which these may be modified.

6. What are the advantages and limitations of general-equilibrium theory?

7. Trace the effects on the economy of an improved method of producing helicopters, which would allow them to be sold for $12,000 and would make them as safe as automobiles.

8. Trace through the effect of a shift in demand from oranges to apples.

SUGGESTED READING

Baumol, W. *Economic Theory and Operations Analysis*, 4th ed. Englewood Cliffs,N.J.: Prentice Hall, 1977, Chapter 21.

Kraus, M., and H. Johnson. *General Equilibrium Analysis*. Chicago: Aldine, 1975.

Quirk, J., and R. Saposnik. *Introduction to General Equilibrium Theory and Welfare Economics*. New York: McGraw-Hill, 1968.

Chapter Eighteen

WELFARE ECONOMICS

_____ *Questions to Think About* _____

1. What is the purpose of welfare economics?

2. What are alternative social goals?

3. What are the conditions that are required to maximize the satisfaction of wants in a society?

4. What is Pareto optimum?

5. What is the compensation principle?

6. What is a social-welfare function?

7. What is Arrow's impossibility theorem?

8. What difficulty arises with an equal distribution of income?

18.1 INTRODUCTION

The preceding chapters have directed attention to the operation of the economic system, without attempting to evaluate its performance by reference to standards of efficiency, justice, or morality. Put differently, we have considered how the economy works and why it works as it does, but we have not tried to judge whether particular features of the system are "good" or "bad." We have described, for example, how the price system determines output—and thus the composition of national product—without inquiring whether the results contribute to any worthwhile goal. We have considered the forces that determine the distribution of income without asking whether the resulting distribution is fair. Now, however, it is appropriate to raise some of these questions by surveying briefly the portion of economic analysis concerned with evaluation called **welfare economics**, this type of analysis seeks to judge whether the economic system leads to results that are "desirable" according to accepted social goals.

18.2 SOCIAL GOALS AND THE ECONOMIC SYSTEM

All applications of scientific knowledge give rise to ethical questions. The moral issues raised by the development of nuclear weapons or genetic engineering afford striking examples, but similar examples might be drawn from almost every field of human knowledge. Regardless of the field of study, evaluating an existing state of affairs or the consequences of a proposed action involves two distinct tasks. First, it is necessary to acquire a comprehensive understanding of the situation that is to be evaluated. Second, it is necessary to *select* and *apply* standards of evaluation. The first of these tasks, which is concerned with *what is* rather than *what ought to be*, is the main business of science as science. The first step in the second task, the **selection of standards**, is a part of the general field of ethics, because it involves value judgments about the personal and social desirability of alternative actions. The second step, the application of **ethical criteria** to evaluate particular situations, involves a mixture of science and ethics. It is this mixture that welfare economics explores.

For our purposes, we shall merely assume certain ethical goals that appear to reflect widely accepted attitudes in contemporary society. It must be stressed that these goals are assumed, not determined by economic analysis, and that the evaluations that follow are valid only in terms of these goals. If we were to assume other goals, the evaluations might produce different results. It is also worth emphasizing that what is being evaluated are situations described by economic models. The evaluations are relevant to the extent that these theoretical models provide an adequate description of the real world.

We assume that three primary social goals are desirable:

1. Maximum freedom of choice for individuals, consistent with rights for other individuals.

2. Maximum satisfaction of wants, which requires allocation and use of resources in a way that leads to maximum per capita real utility (often represented by income, for reasons that will become clear).

3. A pattern of income distribution regarded as most equitable according to standards of contemporary society.

The remainder of the chapter will more fully explain these possibly inconsistent goals, indicate the conditions necessary to attain them, and briefly evaluate the extent to which the conditions, and therefore the goals, appear to be satisfied in the present-day economic system.

18.3 FREEDOM OF CHOICE

Freedom of choice in the sphere of economic activity is the right of individuals to act as they wish in choosing employment and in purchasing and selling goods and services. This goal requires that individuals be free to select the commodities they prefer to satisfy their wants. They must also be free to make decisions about how to use the factor units they own: to make them available to business firms or not, to select the type and the place of work they prefer among available opportunities, to divide their time between work and leisure as they please, to establish a business if they wish to do so, and to make their own decisions in the operation of the business. Contemporary Western society regards freedom of action to be desirable in itself, apart from the role it may play in helping economies attain an optimal standard of living.

However, freedom of choice is relative. Absolute freedom would result in serious injury to others, so freedom of choice must be exercised within the framework established to protect the interests of society as a group and sometimes of individuals themselves. If all people were free to hunt deer without restriction, for example, there would soon be no deer to hunt, and the right to hunt would become worthless. The greatest overall freedom is obtained by establishing of certain restrictions in the interests of the group. Over the years, the number of restrictions of this type have tended to increase. Yet, in market economies such as in the United States, Canada, and much of the Western Europe, as well as in other areas, a substantial degree of personal freedom of choice remains. In general, persons are free to buy anything they please (with the exception of a few goods, such as certain drugs that could injure the consumer and/or others). Legally, they may work or not as they wish, obtain a job anywhere they can find one, and move from one area to another. People are free to start a business (with a few exceptions) and to select products, prices, methods of production as they desire.

18.4 MAXIMUM SATISFACTION OF WANTS

The second social goal is to maximize the **satisfaction of wants**, or in other words, to attain the highest possible level of economic well-being for society as a whole by using and allocating resources in a way that allows the highest per-capita real income, given the resources, technology, and the preferences of factor owners with regard to the use of their factor units. We assume that maximizing economic well-being requires maximum per capita real utility although it must be recognized that this in itself is a value judgment—one that would be rejected by some groups such as the Amish communities. If income increases (in a noncoercive society that does not make factor suppliers supply more than they wish), then utility will increase because more goods and services are consumed at higher incomes. Analytical problems arise relating to measurement of increases in per capita real income, particularly as the relative output of various goods changes. Also, significant questions arise about how the increase is distributed among the various individuals. For the moment, however, we disregard the question of the distribution of real income, discussing resource use and allocation with the prevailing pattern of distribution. The question of the optimum pattern of income distribution will be raised later in the chapter.

Given the existing pattern of income distribution, the requirements for optimum use and allocation of resources are often called the "marginal conditions". These conditions are discussed in the following paragraphs.

OPTIMUM EFFICIENCY IN THE USE OF RESOURCES

The optimum satisfaction of wants first requires that resources be efficiently used in production. This, in turn, requires firms:

1. to use the most efficient production techniques and methods of administrative organization and physical distribution systems available.

2. to attain least-cost factor combinations in short-run production, and in that way to adjust factor combinations until the marginal rate of substitution between any two factors is equal to the ratio of their prices.

3. to operate at the point of lowest long-run average cost; firms must not only expand plant to the size that allows lowest cost, but must also operate at the optimum capacity lowest cost point) of this plant.

Only if firms meet these requirements can they obtain maximum output from given resources. If firms use obsolete methods, fail to attain least-cost combinations, use plants that are too small, or do not operate at lowest average cost, total output obtained from given resources is less than the potential. (See Problem 18–1.)

18–1 To what extent do firms in a market economy attain the optimum organization of production?

This is not an easy question to answer. The profit motive provides a continuous incentive to reduce costs—one that is, of course, strongest when competition is effective, but that is present even with complete monopoly. The exact least-cost combination of factors, however, is rarely attained. It is an extremely difficult task for a firm to accomplish, especially with complex industrial processes.

When markets are perfectly competitive, firms theoretically operate at the point of lowest LRAC. However, imperfections—especially lack of knowledge—undoubtedly interfere with their ability to attain lowest average cost. In imperfectly competitive markets with free entry of new firms, operating at the lowest LRAC is impossible because the downward-sloping demand curves for the products of the firms cannot be tangent to the U-shaped average-cost curves at their lowest points. There are therefore too many firms for the market (but too few to permit the markets to be perfectly competitive), resources are poorly used, and costs could be lower if the market were divided among a smaller number of firms. The waste, however, may be less than is sometimes argued. This is because the demand curves of the firms in these industries are likely to be highly elastic, and the departure from perfectly competitive conditions may therefore not be very substantial. Furthermore, the product diversity of monopolistic competition may itself be valuable, and thereby worth some departure from least-cost production of a homogeneous good.

In imperfectly competitive markets in which entry is not entirely free, firms may, of course, be operating at the point of lowest cost (although price does not equal average cost); but there is no necessity for this to be so (indeed, it would be a fluke if MR equaled MC at this point). If an industry is dominated by a few large firms, they may easily expand to the point of lowest LRAC or even beyond. If the typical LRAC curve contains an extensive horizontal segment, as is now believed to be common, the likelihood that many firms may be operating at or near the lowest average cost figure in imperfectly competitive conditions is increased.

Whenever products are differentiated, a new cost element is introduced, namely, that of advertising and other selling activities. Though these activities inevitably raise costs above perfectly competitive levels, they do convey certain benefits to consumers. Evaluating the relative advantages of the higher costs and benefits is very difficult. In some instances, markets that would not be perfectly competitive even without selling activities, developing these activities may allow the firms to operate nearer the point of lowest average cost by increasing their sales volumes.

The second requirement for satisfying wants is to attain a pattern of outputs of various commodities that conforms to consumer preferences; that is, the composition of total output—and therefore the allocation of resources—must be one that best satisfies consumer preferences. If, for example, consumers desire some shoes and some luggage, all of the available leather should not be used for luggage production while people go barefoot or wear wooden shoes. The leather supply must be allocated so that consumer preferences for the two products are satisfied as completely as possible, given constraints. Similarly, if consumers desire both cake and bread, all flour should not be used to produce bread; but some should be used in cake production as well.

Optimum adjustment of production can be achieved only if, for each consumer, the *marginal rate of substitution* between the two commodities purchased is equal to the **marginal rate of transformation** between the two commodities in production, that is, to the number of units of one commodity that must be sacrificed if an additional unit of the other commodity is to be produced. If the two are not equal, consumer preferences will be more fully realized if some resources are shifted from the production of goods with excessive output to the production of goods with inadequate output. For example, the relative output of bread and cake must be such that consumers are indifferent between bread made with the marginal units of wheat going into bread production and cake made with the marginal units of wheat going into cake production. If the preference for bread is greater at the margin, more wheat must be used for bread production and less for cake production.

This relationship at the margin between rates of substitution and rates of transformation will be attained only if several requirements are met:

1. Consumers must allocate their incomes so that marginal rates of substitution between all commodities they buy are equal to the ratios of the prices of the commodities; in other words, the marginal utilities of all goods purchased must be proportional to their prices. The consumer who has failed to accomplish this adjustment has not reached the highest indifference-curve possible subject to his or her income, or, in other words, the consumer is not maximizing satisfaction.

2. Relative prices of various goods must reflect marginal rates of transformation between them; thus if consumers allocate incomes so that marginal rates of substitution are equal to price ratios, marginal rates of substitution also equal marginal rates of transformation.

Relative prices reflect marginal rates of transformation only if:

a) Factor prices equate the supply of and demand for the factors and are uniform to all producers. If factor prices exceed the levels at which supply and demand are equal, for example, they do not reflect the real costs of producing an additional unit of a commodity; in other words, they do not reflect the sacrifice of other goods necessary to obtain another factor unit for the production of the particular good. The same is true if factor prices are not uniform to all users.

b) A firm's marginal cost of producing a given product must reflect all costs to the economy arising out of its production; in other words, there must be no external diseconomies. If certain costs to society do not enter into the marginal production costs of the firms, the price of the commodity is too low and the firm produces too much of the good. The traditional example is the damage from factory smoke, which is not a cost to the firm operating the factory but which is a cost to society. As patrons pour out of a football-stadium parking lot at the end of the game, they congest traffic on the highway, cause accidents, and delay motorists and truckers. These are real costs for which the football game is responsible, but they are not borne by the firm operating the stadium and are not reflected in the prices charged the patrons. The air pollution caused by motor vehicles is yet another example.

3. All benefits from the use of commodities accrue to the person acquiring them; that is, there are no external economies of consumption. If others gain indirect benefits, too little of the commodity will be purchased and produced because the indirect benefits do not influence the purchasing decisions. If, for example, a person paints his house, his neighbors benefit as well, but homeowners are not likely to consider that (unless in the interests of neighborhood goodwill) when they decide whether to buy the paint supplies. The more significant examples of indirect benefits, however, are social or community goods such as national defense, which convey their benefits to the community as a whole rather than to individuals separately. (See Problems 18–2 and 18–3.)

18–2 Prove algebraically that in perfect competition:
  a. $MRS_A = MRS_B$ $A =$ Ann $M =$ Milk $R =$ Other Resources
  b. $MRTS_M = MRTS_W$ $B =$ Bob $W =$ Wheat $L =$ Labor
  c. $MRS = MRT$ (Hint: $MRT = MC_M/MC_W$ where $MC =$ marginal cost).[1]

  a. First, we know from demand theory that consumer equilibrium, maximizing utility within one's budget, occurs when $MRS = P_1/P_2$ for any two goods 1 and 2. This implies that for Ann, $MRS_A = P_M/P_W$, and for Bob, $MRS_B = P_M/P_W$. Because Ann and Bob face the same prices, $MRS_A = MRS_B$.
  b. The least-cost factor combination for every producer occurs at the tangency of the isoquant and isocost, that is, when $MRTS = P_{V_1}/P_{V_2}$ where P_{V_1} and P_{V_2} are the prices of inputs V_1 and V_2. In our two-good economy, $MRTS_M = P_L/P_R$ and $MRTS_W = P_L/P_R$. Therefore, as milk and wheat producers face the same labor and resource prices, $MRTS_M = MRTS_W$.
  c. In perfect competition, producers maximize profits when $P = MC$. For milk and wheat, $P_M = MC_M$ and $P_M = MC_W$. Dividing the first equation by the second yields: $P_M/P_W = MC_M/MC_W$. According to the hint, $MRT = MC_M/MC_W$. Thus $P_M/P_W = MRT$. For consumer equilibrium, $P_M/P_W = MRS$. Therefore, $MRT = MRS$.

---

[1]The MRT is the decrease in the output of wheat needed to produce one more unit of milk. For example, suppose the $MC_M = \$4$ and $MC_W = \$2$ at the current output levels. Producing one more unit of milk costs $4, and releasing $4 from wheat production decreases wheat output by 2. The MRT = 2 and $MC_M/MC_W = 4/2 = 2$.

18–3 Demonstrate graphically how at a point of general equilibrium, the marginal conditions for maximum well-being are attained. Use the following information:

a. $MRS_A = MRS_B$ A = Ann M = Milk R = Other Resources
b. $MRTS_R = MRTS_L$ B = Bob W = Wheat L = Labor
c. $MRS = MRT$

In figure (a), point B is a point of general equilibrium. $MRS_A = MRS_A$ because MRS is the slope of an indifference curve and Ann and Bob's indifference curves are tangent at point B. Second, $MRTS_R = MRTS_L$ because the allocation W^*, M^* is on the production-possibility frontier. $MRTS_R = MRTS_L$ guarantees efficient production of both goods and the production-possibility frontier shows only the maximum possible outputs. Finally, $MRS = MRT$ for society as a whole because I is tangent to the production-possibility frontier.

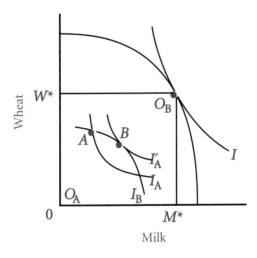

REALIZATION OF THESE REQUIREMENTS

Completely attaining these requirements would ensure an optimum allocation of resources—that is, an optimum "product mix," given the pattern of income distribution. In a perfectly competitive economy, with perfect knowledge on the part of consumers and business firms, with no external economies or diseconomies, these conditions would be attained. All consumers would allocate their incomes according to the MRS price-ratio rule; factor prices would equate factor supply and demand; prices of all commodities would be equal to their marginal-factor costs (which, in the absence of external diseconomies, would include all real costs); marginal rates of substitution would therefore equal marginal rates of transformation. This conditions essentially state the "invisible hand" doctrine first enunciated by Adam Smith in the eighteenth century: left to its own devices the economy will, under the assumed conditions, best serve the interests of society as a whole. It must be stressed, however that *the conclusions are valid only in a static context and assuming a given pattern of income distribution.*

The actual economy, however, is far removed from one of universal perfect competition and absence of external economies and diseconomies. Some of the major deviations and their significance for economic welfare are noted below:

1. *Consumers lack complete information in deciding how to allocate incomes.* Even though consumers may seek to maximize satisfaction from their incomes, they face many obstacles in achieving this goal. A major one is inadequate information about the ability of particular goods to meet various desires. In part this lack of information is inevitable because of the very nature of consumer wants: A person cannot tell if she likes guava pie until she tastes it; and if she does not taste it, she has not maximized satisfaction. The economic system, however, does not do as effective a job of informing consumers as it might. Advertising provides some information, but it is by no means complete and may be misleading. Some rules for labeling and describing contents have been imposed by governments, although the merits of such rules are debated.[2]

2. **a.** *Factor prices do not always equate supply and demand.* The most extreme deviation from perfect competition is mass unemployment: The real cost of additional units of output may be almost nil when unemployed workers and resources can be used to produce them. However, the marginal costs, reflecting existing factor prices, are much higher. These higher costs may be explained in part by imperfectly competitive elements in factor markets, but primarily by the inability of factor owners to adjust their real factor prices. If workers agree to work for lower wages, competitive forces may cause prices of products to fall; thus, real wages may change slowly, if at all.

   Similarly, factor prices are not always uniform to all users. Wages for a given type of labor may be higher in one area than in another, perhaps because of the varying strength of unions; the result is that the industries do not locate in the most economically beneficial locations. Price discrimination by monopolist or oligopolist producers of materials and monopsony influences exercised by buyers over price are also examples of deviations from perfectly competitive conditions.

   b. *Marginal costs do not always reflect all costs for which production of additional units is responsible.* Examples were given previously above in the discussion of this requirement; many others could be supplied. The social costs of alcoholism, for example, are not factor costs to liquor producers. If a factory is built in a residential area, the business firm does not have to pay for the decline in the value of surrounding property.

---

[2]For example, if labeling requirements have benefits to the consumer greater than costs, why would firms be required to label? It would be in their own interests to do so.

Governments have sought to meet this problem in several ways with varying degrees of success. They have prohibited the production of certain goods, such as narcotics, that have heavy social costs not borne by the producers. They have placed taxes on the sale of other products, such as liquor, to shift some of the additional social costs to the users and thereby reduce consumption. City zoning ordinances are primarily designed to prevent reductions in property values that result from the indiscriminate location of particular types of activities without reference to other property uses. The danger, of course, is "overcorrection," or correcting in inappropriate ways (ways having costs greater than benefits).

c) *Marginal cost equals price only if firms are selling in perfectly competitive markets.* From the standpoint of economic welfare the greatest advantage of perfectly competitive market conditions is equality of price and marginal cost. In imperfectly competitive conditions characterized by downward-sloping demand curves for the products of the individual firms, at the output level at which MR equals MC, price exceeds marginal cost, as illustrated in Figure 22–1. Therefore, the prices of commodities exceed the figures that reflect the real factor costs—that is, the sacrifice of output of other goods—and outputs of commodities are held to uneconomically low levels. These results are encountered whether excess profits are earned or not; the source of the difficulty is that the demand curve is downward sloping, which causes marginal revenue to be less than price at the point of most profitable operation.

In other cases, artificial deviations between marginal factor cost and price are caused by excise taxes on particular commodities. These taxes result in prices for the commodities that exceed their factor costs—and therefore in uneconomic reductions in output (if the other requirements for optimum economic welfare are attained). The exception, of course, is excise taxes that reflect costs to society that are not borne by the producers. Liquor taxes may perhaps be justified on this basis.

In imperfect competition, firms face downward-sloping demand curves. Consequently, price exceeds marginal cost and too little output is produced.

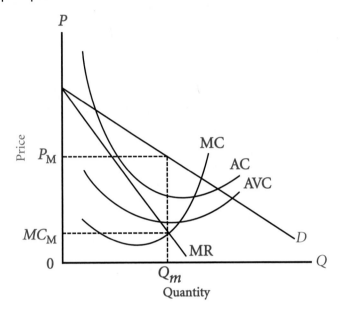

3. *The good yields important benefits to persons other than those who acquire them, or yields all or most of its benefits to the community as a whole, rather than separately to individuals.* National defense is the traditional example. By its nature, it cannot be broken up into small pieces and sold to individuals. Education directly benefits the recipients but also yields important community benefits in the form of greater social and political stability, more-rapid economic development, and cures for disease and other inventions that have benefits not captured fully by those responsible.

    Because of the importance of indirect benefits from many types of activities, governments (representing the community as a whole) provide such services to the community and cover the costs of producing them from compulsory taxes. Private enterprise cannot produce many of these services at all because they cannot be sold to individuals. Others, such as education, are both publicly and privately produced, but the total output would be uneconomically small if production were left entirely in private hands if there were no subsidies because the indirect benefits would not influence purchases. However, subsidies such as education vouchers could make the output optimal and open up the education industry to greater private competition.[3]

---

[3]This is not necessarily "good," although it might be a great improvement on our present educational system.

OPTIMUM DEGREE OF FACTOR UTILIZATION

A third general condition is necessary for attaining optimum satisfaction of wants, given the pattern of income distribution, is an optimum degree of utilization of factors. There are several aspects of this condition:

1. Avoidance of Cyclical Unemployment

Optimum use of factor units requires that all factor units whose owners wish to have them employed at the equilibrium-factor prices should find employment (perhaps after some optimal search process, in the case of frictional unemployment). Unemployment of factors obviously reduces the output of the economy and real income per capita below the optimum level. This affects savings levels and therefore growth. Furthermore, unemployment causes severe distress for the individuals concerned because their source of income vanishes.

2. Optimum Division of Time between Work and Leisure

Optimum economic welfare does not require the absolute-maximum-possible output but rather a level of output consistent with the allocation of time between work and leisure which persons prefer to make. Thus as real income rises as a result of increased productivity, optimum economic welfare does not require that the entire gain be taken in the form of greater output. Individuals may prefer to take a part or all of it in the form of increased leisure. The argument against shorter hours—that they reduce output—is not a convincing one. If society prefers more leisure and less output, it cannot be argued that it is inconsistent with the goals we have assumed.

In practice, the requirements of efficient production make it impossible for individuals to decide the number of hours they will work. In general, individuals must either accept the working period that is standard in their particular line of employment or work elsewhere. In recent years, however, as the economy has become increasingly less reliant on large-scale, mass-production industrial processes, the trend has been toward greater flexibility. In the 1990s, it is not unusual for individuals in many occupations to work some days at home, perhaps communicating via computer modem or fax machines to other centralized resources.

On the other hand, some economists argue that the growth in the importance of certain taxes has interfered with workers' ability to divide their time optimally between work and leisure. Income taxes apply to gains from work but not to those from leisure, and sales and excise taxes apply to gains from work to the extent that income is spent on taxable goods. Thus, these taxes alter the relative gains from work and leisure; some persons may seek to work more because of taxes (to maintain a standard of living), while others will seek to work less (substituting leisure for work). The consequent distortion interferes with the attainment of optimum economic welfare.

3. Optimum Rate of Capital Formation

The optimum rate of capital formation is particularly difficult to define. Economists maintain that economic welfare requires the division of total income between consumption and savings in a manner that conforms to the individuals' relative preferences for present and future consumption. However, this requirement is subject to certain modifications:

a) An increased rate of capital formation now leads to a more rapid increase in output of consumption goods in the future. Particularly in countries with very low per-capita incomes, relatively small increases in savings now may lead to very sharp increases in consumption in the future—increases not foreseen by the people of those societies. In such economies, a higher rate of capital formation than would occur on the basis of the preferred division of income between consumption and savings would greatly increase economic welfare, at least for future generations.[4]

b) The preferred allocation of income between consumption and savings may impede full employment and stable economic growth. If people save greater sums at high income levels than can be rapidly absorbed in investment, unemployment will develop, and optimum economic welfare will not be attained. Under such circumstances, a compromise is necessary between the requirement of allocation of income on the basis of individual choice and the desire for full employment.

4. Optimum Rate of Utilization of Scarce Natural Resources

Economic welfare requires an optimum rate of utilization of such scarce natural resources as oil and timber. This optimum rate, however, is difficult to define because of the conflicting interests of present and future generations. An extremely rapid rate of exploitation would exhaust supplies otherwise available for the future; an excessively slow rate involves heavy sacrifice of present welfare for future welfare, one that may prove unnecessary as new resources or alternative methods of production are developed in the future.

Some argue that the perfectly competitive outcome of the free market is short-sighted regarding the utilization of scarce natural resources. Greedy profit maximizers purportedly do not care about future generations in their single-minded pursuit of short-run profits. Is this view correct? It is not; indeed, the market efficiently allocates resources intertemporally in much the same way that it allocates resources efficiently at a point in time. Indeed, it is "greed" (attempts to maximize profit) that generates this desirable result. Let's see how.

---

[4]Issues of intergenerational equity are very complex and, of course, normative. Are large gains in consumption to future people sufficient justification for even small reductions in consumptions on the part of those living now? What is those in the future will be richer anyway, while present populations are desperately poor?

Suppose you own an oil well. If you believed that we were using scarce resources too fast, you would clearly expect the future price of oil to be very high as the larger future demand (from greater numbers of higher income households) confronts the smaller supply. Similarly, if we are using scarce resources too fast, won't present prices be relatively low? It would then be stupid for you to sell your oil *now* when by merely holding it in the ground, you can be much better off in the future. Presumably, you could borrow to finance "high living" today on the collateral of your oil wealth.

Of course, every other oil-well owner is just like you. They (and you) will, in fact, end up keeping just enough oil off the market (holding this asset) to guarantee that the oil "asset" earns the going risk-adjusted rate of return. How can oil earn *any* return when, in contrast to bonds, it has no coupon yield? The answer is that the price of oil (and other scarce natural resources) must rise at the rate of interest.[5] If some resource owners *were* to use them up too fast, prices would be depressed today and would be expected to be higher in the future; the "greed" of other resource owners would cause them, then, to hold their resources off the market to gain the extranormal rate of return. In sum, profit maximizing guarantees that resources *are* used efficiently over time. The value of scarce natural resources to future generations is indeed considered by present owners *as long as* they care about maximizing the present value of their wealth (which they do if they make the most discounted profits from future periods).

The preceding example should cause worry to those who believe that government intervention can improve the temporal pattern of resource usage. They would have to worry even if government were not shortsighted. Yet evidence suggests that our elected representatives have very short-time horizons (even a senator must face reelection every six years; all others more frequently). Political pressures to keep prices low *now* are more likely to cause intertemporal resource misallocation, harming future generations than are market forces.

ATTAINMENT OF AN OPTIMUM RATE OF ECONOMIC GROWTH

Traditional economic welfare theory has been based on static conditions; it has sought to define the requirements for optimum welfare in terms of given determinants of equilibrium positions. In recent years, however, economists have given increased attention to the significance of dynamic considerations for economic welfare. This attention has focused primarily on two elements: stable growth and increasing real national income.

1. The Maintenance of an Equilibrium, Full-Employment Rate of Growth
Generally speaking, an economy can continue to expand at a stable rate without continuing or frequently recurring unemployment only if balance is maintained among various determinants of the rate of development. In particular, aggregate demand for

---

[5]This is a bit of a simplification for it ignores marginal storage costs and so on. But the basic point is unaffected by various sophisticated "add-on" notions.

output must keep pace with growth in aggregate capacity to produce. The theory of economic development has not advanced to prescribe more fully the specific requirements for stability in growth.

2. The Attainment of an Optimum Rate of Increase in the Real Level of National Income

The economic system must provide maximum incentive for the discovery and introduction of new techniques, new methods of organization and operation, and new products. All of these increase the real level of national income and aid in maintaining the volume of investment at levels high enough to permit full employment.

One of the greatest advantages of the private enterprise market economy is that it encourages innovation. A major means by which firms can gain higher than average profits is to introduce innovations that yield excess profits until competitors are able to duplicate the change. If competitors are unable to duplicate the change, this may give rise to continuing monopoly profit. The pressures of competition likewise force other firms to meet innovations in order to escape losses.

Imperfectly competitive conditions may be somewhat more advantageous for economic growth than perfectly competitive ones, as long as some elements of competition remain. The typical firm selling in perfectly competitive markets may be too small to undertake the research and experimentation necessary for innovations. Largely for this reason, most agricultural research in the United States has been undertaken by the federal government. It is the larger firm, in situations of oligopoly and related cases, that may best be able to develop and introduce improvements that allow real increases in national income.

However, pressures toward improvement and efficiency slacken if the entry of new firms into various industries is limited and if existing firms gain monopoly or semimonopoly positions. Many innovations are made by newcomers. If new firms cannot enter the market and if existing firms are already making a high rate of profit, development may be checked. From the standpoint of overall economic welfare, restrictions on entry of new firms may be more detrimental than mere differentiation of product and the presence of relatively few firms in an industry. Similarly detrimental to economic progress are outright agreements among firms on methods of production, shares of output, and so on, as permitted in the cartel systems of some countries. (See Problem 18–4.)

18–4 How does each of the following affect the marginal conditions for maximization of social well-being?

a. Monopoly in the milk industry   b. Unionized labor in the milk industry
c. A per-unit-tax on milk production d. A lump-sum tax on milk production

a. Recall from Chapter 10 that a monopoly charges a price in excess of marginal cost. Suppose that in our two-good economy, milk is produced by a monopolist while wheat is produced competitively.

In that case, $P_M > MC_M$, but $P_W = MC_W$. Thus, $P_M/P_W > MC_M/MC_W$. Assuming consumer equilibrium, MRS $= P_M/P_W$. Recall from above, MRT $= MC_M/MC_W$. Combining equations yields MRS $>$ MRT. Therefore, the product mix is *not* in line with consumer preferences. The marginal utility of milk relative to the marginal utility of wheat exceeds the marginal cost of milk relative to the marginal cost of wheat. The economy should produce more milk and less wheat. Note that this result confirms the result in Chapter 10, that monopolies produce too little output.

b. Suppose that the milk industry (assumed to be perfectly competitive) is unionized but the wheat industry is not. $MRTS_M = P_L'/P_R$ and $MRTS_M = P_L/P_R$ for production efficiency, where P_L' is the union wage and P_L is the nonunion wage. Since $P_L'/P_R > P_L/P_R$, $MRTS_M > MRTS_W$. The economy is producing off the production contract curve as at point B in Figure (b), and inside the production possibility curve as at point b in Figure (a).

c. If a per-unit tax is imposed on the milk industry but not on the wheat industry, the price of milk increases, P_M/P_W increases, MRS increases, and thus, MRS $>$ MRT. The relative price of milk rises as a result of the tax, and consumers will decrease milk consumption and increase wheat consumption. Note that this (and the next) answer ignores the impact that government spending of tax revenues may have on the milk and wheat markets.

d. A lump-sum tax does not affect marginal costs (only fixed costs) and therefore does not affect the optimal allocation of milk and wheat.

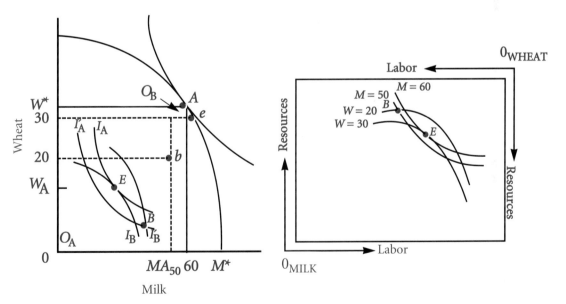

Figure (a) General Equilibrium (*E*)   Figure (b) Production Efficiency (*E*)

18.5 INTERPERSONAL COMPARISONS
AND WELFARE CRITERIA

The analysis thus far has abstracted from the problem of the relative economic positions of various individuals; we have, in effect, assumed that all individuals have the same capacity for satisfaction or, in other words, the same utility functions relating to money income. We have also assumed a given income distribution, an assumption that will be examined later in this chapter. The first assumption, if considered carefully, is seen to be essentially meaningless. Economists now universally recognize that with the present state of knowledge, it is not possible to make **interpersonal utility comparisons**—that is, to compare the relative satisfactions of different persons. The relative satisfactions gained by two persons drinking cups of coffee, for example, simply cannot be compared.

Once we recognize that interpersonal utility comparisons are impossible, it becomes evident that the principles advanced thus far in the chapter are not adequate to allow us to state with certainty that various changes in the economy will increase economic welfare, even many that are universally thought to do so. Almost any type of change benefits some persons and injures others—even, for example, readjusting factor combinations to bring them to the optimum or eliminating monopoly. Because the relative gains and losses of satisfaction by various individuals cannot be compared, we cannot say that the changes *necessarily* increase economic welfare, even though they bring the economy more closely in conformity with the rules of optimum efficiency and resource allocation. (See Problem 18–5.)

18–5 Suppose that building a new highway will bring benefits to thousands of motorists in the form of saved time, fewer accidents, and more-pleasant driving. The building of this highway, however, will necessitate moving the home of one family from a site for which it has strong preference and that it does not wish to leave, regardless of the compensation offered. Is there a way to compare the satisfaction received by the family and the motorists?

There is no scientific basis for stating that the total satisfaction gained by the thousands of motorists exceeds the dissatisfaction suffered by the one family, since interpersonal comparisons of satisfactions are not possible. An additional criterion is needed to determine appropriate policy on welfare grounds for building the highway. A common approach, benefit-cost analysis, compares the dollar willingness-to-pay of those affected. If, in the example, the aggregate willingness-to-pay of the motorists is $30 million and the cost of the road is $20 million, most people would suspect that the net benefit of $10 million is greater than the family's loss in satisfaction from having to move. There is no way to prove this, however, apart from bribery (and this would presume that the family would not lie!).

Thus, if welfare economics is to be at all meaningful as a basis for evaluating the economy and determination of economic policy, it is necessary to establish a suitable welfare criterion that overcomes this interpersonal comparison problem. Several approaches have been taken, including the Pareto optimum, the compensation principle, and the social-welfare function.

THE PARETO OPTIMUM

The **Pareto optimum**, as discussed in Chapter 17 on exchange, has played a major role in the development of general-equilibrium theory and welfare economics. According to Pareto optimality, a change may be regarded as desirable in terms of economic welfare only it benefits someone without injuring anyone else. This is, of course, a highly restrictive assumption; even elimination of monopoly, for example, while benefiting many persons, will injure the owners of the monopoly enterprise. Changes covered by the criterion might be restricted to such instances as the reduction of unemployment (if this could be done without costs to others), or alteration of factor inputs in a way that increases output with a given quantity of factor inputs, assuming no change in factor prices (and incomes) as a consequence. Thus, as a basis for judging efficiency or for policy recommendations, welfare economics is of little assistance if we hold rigidly to the definition of Pareto optimum.

THE COMPENSATION PRINCIPLE

In the years immediately after World War II, British economists Kaldor and Hicks and others developed a second approach for overcoming the interpersonal comparison problem, the so-called **compensation principle**, in an effort to broaden the applicability of welfare economics. This principle involved adding to the Pareto-optimum situations in which the persons benefiting from the change would be willing to compensate those losing enough that the latter would no longer oppose the change. Thus, for example, owners of business firms and consumers benefiting from improved technology might be willing to pay enough to induce the workers displaced by the technological change and having to take jobs at lower pay to end their resistance to the change. It is *willingness* to pay that is significant, not actual payment. If the latter occurs, the Pareto rule applies.

Economists have leveled various criticisms against this principle. One is a technical question, as noted by Scitovsky: In some instances once the change had been made, it would be advantageous for those who had allowed the change to compensate the other group to return to the original situation. Scitovsky argued that the rule was valid only if, after the first change, it would not be advantageous to change the situation back to the original. Other critics note that the compensation rule implicitly assumes that a given number of dollars represents equal utility to all persons; otherwise, the fact that those benefiting are willing to pay an amount more than the figure the injured would regard as adequate compensation for their injury does not demonstrate that there is a net gain in economic welfare. In effect, critics say, interpersonal utility comparisons have entered in. Finally, the principle cannot be implemented: The compensation that persons would be willing to offer and to accept could be easily ascertained, though much recent work has made progress in revealing demands in such situations.

SOCIAL-WELFARE FUNCTIONS

Today, the most widely accepted criterion for determining economic welfare is the **social-welfare function**, as developed by Bergson, Samuelson, Arrow, and others. The social-welfare function expresses the optimum pattern of distribution of benefits among individuals as viewed by the consensus in contemporary society.[6] The welfare function thus establishes a basis for weighing the benefits and injuries of various people—perhaps, for example, the relative numbers of people benefiting or losing or the nature of their gain or loss (such as cheaper products in preference to monopoly income). Ascertaining an overall social-welfare function that embraces all aspects of the economy is obviously impossible, given the present (or likely future) state of knowledge. It is not impossible, however, to develop major segments of such a function; this is constantly being done as people make judgments about the desirability or undesirability of certain economic and social policies.

Thus, to cite one application, we typically conclude that the benefits from the elimination of monopoly power, with consequent improvement of resource allocation, exceed the injury to those who lose their monopoly profits. Similarly, restricting of the right of smelters, refineries, or chemical manufacturers to pour out noxious fumes is accepted on the basis that the social-welfare function dictates that benefits to those living in the surrounding area are greater than the injury to the owners of the smelter and the consumers of the products made by the smelter, who must pay higher prices as a result of the costs of waste-control devices.

One merit of the social-welfare-function criterion is that it makes explicit the fact that virtually any change benefits some people at the expense of others and that society must weigh the benefits and injuries, not in terms of any scientific principle, but on a social-welfare function resting on value judgments. Unfortunately, ascertaining consensus is difficult, and the principle could lead to flagrant violations of the rights of a minority segment of the population. Given the present state of knowledge, however, there is no suitable alternative, and it is preferable to recognize that there is no scientific basis for the judgments than to make implicit assumptions that result in attaching scientific support to purely value judgments.

---

[6]The function could, of course, be based upon the opinion or a dictator or some other source.

According to Arrow, social-welfare functions are based on certain reasonable properties such as transitivity. You may recall from our discussion of indifference curves that transitivity holds that if, for example, policy A is preferred to policy B and policy B is preferred to policy C, then policy A must be preferred to policy C. Arrow, however, concluded that it is impossible to evaluate social welfare by democratic voting because it is possible that this transitivity assumption could be violated.

For example, assume that three individuals, Katherine, Elizabeth, and Tom, must make decisions regarding policies A, B, and C. The rankings of the three individuals are seen in Table 18–1. In this table, we see that both Elizabeth and Katherine (a two-thirds majority) prefer policy A to policy B, and that both Elizabeth and Tom prefer policy B to policy C. It is also true that a majority prefers policy C to A because Katherine and Tom prefer policy C to policy A. In this example, democratic voting therefore results in the majority preferring policy A to B, policy B to C, and policy C to A; that is, preferences are not transitive.

TABLE 18-1

Individual	Policy		
	A	B	C
Elizabeth	1	2	3
Katherine	1	2	3
Tom	1	2	3

18.6 THE OPTIMUM PATTERN OF INCOME DISTRIBUTION

The definition of optimum efficiency in the use and allocation of resources given in the preceding sections is based on the assumption of a given distribution of income; the assumption applies even to Pareto optimality and the compensation-welfare criteria. If conformity with the efficiency and allocation rules has been attained, the economy has attained optimum economic welfare in terms of the pattern of income distribution that prevails after all adjustments have been made—but only in terms of this pattern. Moving beyond this given, what can be said about the **optimum pattern of income distribution**?

AGGREGATE TOTAL SATISFACTION IS NOT MEASURABLE

Were utility measurable, and if interpersonal utility comparisons were possible, it would be meaningful to say, in conformity with the accepted goals, that the optimum pattern of income distribution would be one that would maximize aggregate satisfaction. However, satisfaction is not measurable and is not comparable among individuals, and such a statement is therefore meaningless. As a matter of practice, rough comparisons are frequently made. Most persons would accept the argument, for example, that the transfer of one dollar from a millionaire to a starving family would increase the satisfaction of the family more than it would decrease the satisfaction of the millionaire. However, this is strictly a value judgment; perhaps the millionaire became one because of his intense love for dollars or the things they can buy! Similarly, at least some of the poor could make themselves better off if they valued goods more intensely. In other words, we cannot maximize aggregate satisfaction, if for no other reason than we can not accurately define it.

THE LERNER ARGUMENT

Abba Lerner has argued that, in the absence of knowledge of the actual pattern of distribution that will maximize satisfaction, the most satisfactory assumption which can be made is that an equal distribution would be most likely to maximize satisfaction from a given level of national income. Lerner's argument is based on the assumption that capacities for satisfaction are distributed normally around the mode of a frequency distribution and that an equal distribution would involve only random error, whereas any other would involve a definite bias. However, this assumption likewise has no scientific foundation. Satisfaction may depend to a large extent on being able to outdo other people in consumption, or at least to keep up with them. Furthermore, an equal distribution is obviously not consistent with the maintenance of a high level of national income, neither because of effects on incentives,[7] nor with prevailing attitudes in contemporary Western societies.

THE ATTITUDES OF SOCIETY—THE SOCIAL-WELFARE FUNCTION

The only feasible approach to the problem is the principle that the optimum pattern is the one that is regarded as the most equitable by the consensus of opinion in the particular society—in other words, the one that is embraced in the social-welfare function.

---

[7]Indeed, if guaranteed $1/n$ of GNP (where n is the number of people) regardless of work effort, the realization that GNP will not be significantly affected by individual work/leisure decisions implies that GNP—therefore income—would go to zero!

This is a value judgment that cannot be derived from economic analysis, but it appears to reflect contemporary thinking on the question most satisfactorily. This criterion cannot be defined; it is simply one which accords with the concept of equity accepted in the particular society.

No precise method is possible for determining the consensus on the question of equal income distribution; evaluation of legislation, as reflecting (perhaps rather imperfectly) the will of society, represents the only tangible approach. On this basis, certain general statements about the current consensus of opinion are possible:

1. Excessive inequality of income is regarded as undesirable.

This point of view is reflected in the use of progressive taxation; in the provision of old-age pensions, relief, aid to housing; in antipoverty programs; and in the sentiment behind (if not the actual outcome of) minimum-wage legislation. Opinions differ on the question of what constitutes excessive inequality, but the general principle is widely accepted that the extent of inequality that develops in the absence of governmental interference is excessive.

2. Large incomes from monopolistic "exploitation" of the public are regarded as particularly objectionable.

An attempt is made to check this by antitrust legislation, public-utility regulation, and other legislation. From the standpoint of resource use, the basic objection to monopoly is that it restricts output below the level at which price is equal to marginal cost. Legislation, however, has been greatly influenced by the desire to eliminate monopoly profits.

3. Complete equality of income is regarded as undesirable because of its effects on production, and inequitable because it denies the more efficient, hardworking persons a higher reward for their skill and effort.

The lack of a more precise definition of the optimum pattern of income distribution reduces the significance of contemporary-welfare theory, the precision and strength of its conclusions, and the force of policy recommendations based on them. For example, on the basis of welfare principles relating to optimum use of resources, it can be argued that subway fares should be higher in rush hours than in nonrush hours because marginal cost is higher in the former (when extra cars and trains must be added to carry more passengers) than it is in the latter (when trains are half empty). However, the distribution of passengers by income group is not the same in the two periods, for there is a heavy concentration of workers in the rush hours. Thus, opponents of such a fare system condemn it on the grounds of its effects on distribution of the costs of providing subway service by income group. Welfare theory can offer no conclusive answer to this argument.

18.7 CONCLUDING OBSERVATIONS

Welfare economics is admittedly one of the least satisfactory portions of the overall subject of economics. The rules for attaining optimum efficiency in the use and allocation of resources—given the pattern of income distribution—are clearly definable and generally acceptable. Their significance though depends on the nature of the social-welfare function relating to gains and losses of particular individuals and groups and the optimum distribution of real income. The concept of a social-welfare function is clear enough; the determination of its empirical content—which must rest on consensus in the particular society—encounters serious theoretical and practical difficulties. Decision about the desirability or undesirability of certain features of the economy or policies therefore rests in part on the interpretations of particular persons about the nature of the social-welfare function. Here, differences of opinion are inevitable. Judgments are made and policies adopted, and welfare economics can make significant contributions to these actions, even if it cannot provide answers based entirely on scientific analysis. It is of utmost importance that the value judgments underlying these evaluations and recommendations be made explicit and that these not be given a scientific validity they do not possess.

SUMMARY

1. Welfare economics is the portion of economic analysis that evaluates the economic system by reference to generally accepted social goals.

2. Evaluation and consequences of an action can be separated into two distinct tasks: first, to acquire a comprehensive understanding of the situation; second to select and apply standards of evaluation.

3. Three social goals are assumed to be desirable: freedom of choice, maximum satisfaction of wants, and an optimum pattern of income distribution.

4. Freedom of choice is the right of individuals to act as they wish in choosing employment and purchasing and selling goods and services.

5. Another social goal is to attain the highest possible level of economic well-being for society as a whole, through the use and allocation of resources in such a fashion as to allow the highest per-capita real income given the resources, technology, and the preference schedules of factor owners with regard to the use of their factor units.

6. Optimum want satisfaction requires that resources be efficiently used in production.

7. Composition of total output must be such as to best satisfy consumer preferences.

8. Optimum adjustment of production can be obtained only if, for each consumer, the MRS between two commodities purchased is equal to the MRT between the two commodities in production.

9. It may be difficult to attain optimum product mix because of imperfect information in consumer and factor markets and external economies or diseconomies.

10. An optimum degree of factor use would include avoidance of cyclical unemployment, an optimum division of time between work and leisure, an optimum rate of capital formation, and an optimum rate of use of scarce natural resources.

11. Making interpersonal utility comparisons (comparing relative satisfactions received by different individuals) is not possible.

12. The Pareto optimum is desirable in terms of economic welfare only if the change benefits someone without injuring anyone else.

13. The social-welfare function expresses the optimum pattern of distribution of benefits among individuals as viewed by the consensus in contemporary society.

WORDS AND CONCEPTS FOR REVIEW

welfare economics

ethical criteria

satisfaction of wants

optimum adjustment of production

consumer allocation of incomes

optimum rate of economic growth

Pareto optimum

social-welfare function

optimum pattern of income distribution

selection of standards

freedom of choice

optimum efficiency in the use of resources

marginal rate of transformation

optimum degree of factor utilization

interpersonal utility comparisons

compensation principle

Arrow's impossibility theorem

REVIEW QUESTIONS

1. What is welfare economics?

2. How are the goals for evaluating welfare economics selected?

3. What major goals are generally employed as a basis for welfare economics?

4. Why can freedom of choice never be absolute?

5. What does the term *maximum satisfaction of wants* mean?

6. What are the requirements for optimum efficiency in the use of resources?

7. Why is the operation of firms at the point of lowest LRAC essential for optimum efficiency in the use of resources?

8. Why in perfectly competitive markets do firms operate at the point of lowest LRAC? Will they necessarily do so in imperfectly competitive markets? Explain.

9. Why does optimum adjustment of production require equality of the marginal rate of substitution and the marginal rate of transformation? What requirements must be fulfilled for this equality to be attained?

10. Indicate some examples, other than those given in the chapter, of divergence between costs to the economy and costs to the individual producer.

11. Give examples of external economies of consumption.

12. What is the significance for economic welfare of the failure of price to equal marginal cost in imperfectly competitive conditions?

13. How would you justify, in terms of welfare economics, the following government policies:
    a) high excise taxes on liquor
    b) municipal zoning ordinances
    c) financing subway construction by taxes on motor-vehicle use
    d) prevention of price discrimination
    e) restriction of entry of competing firms into the public-utilities field
    f) provision of funds for agricultural research

14. In what respects is perfect competition superior to imperfect competition from the standpoint of welfare economics? In what respects is it inferior?

15. Why is it difficult to state categorically that any particular change increases the economic welfare of society? What type of change is regarded as desirable in terms of Pareto optimum? Why is this a very restrictive rule?

16. What is the compensation principle? What are the limitations of this principle?

17. What is meant by a social-welfare function?

18. Explain the various approaches to defining the optimum pattern of income distribution.

SUGGESTED READINGS

Bator, Francis. "The Simple Analytics of Welfare Maximization," *American Economic Review* (March 1957), 22–59.

Baumol, W.J. *Economic Theory and Operations Analysis*, 4th ed. Englewood Cliffs, N.J.: Prentice Hall 1977, Chapter 21.

Bergson, A. *Essays in Normative Economics*. Cambridge: Harvard University Press, 1965.

Graff, J. de V. *Theoretical Welfare Economics*. Cambridge: Cambridge University Press, 1957.

Little, I.M.D. *A Critique of Welfare Economics*, 2nd ed. Oxford: Oxford University Press, 1957.

Scitovsky, T. *Welfare and Competition*. Homewood, Ill.: Irwin, 1957.

Chapter Nineteen

ASSET MANAGEMENT AND INTERTEMPORAL INCOME ALLOCATION

Questions to Think About
---

1. What is meant by intertemporal choice?

2. Why do households hold assets?

3. How does a rational household choose between the level of consumption in the present time period versus the future time period?

4. What is human capital?

5. What is the Coase Conjecture?

6. How can the monopolist cope with the problems associated with durability and the consumer's rational expectation?

7. What is the role of the speculator?

19.1 INTRODUCTION

U ntil recently, the theory of consumer demand constituted not just one branch but virtually the entire substance of the theory of household behavior. In recent decades, however, economists have increasingly recognized that the allocation of current expenditures among alternative purchases—the main concern of demand analysis—is only one part of the household story. By almost any practical reckoning, household problems of asset management and **intertemporal choice** (borrowing or saving to change consumption patterns) appear to be at least as important. Unfortunately, these problems do not lend themselves to precise analysis except at a high level of abstraction. In the discussion that follows, therefore, we shall be concerned more with clarifying particular kinds of asset- and income-management decisions than with elaborating a unified theory of household behavior.

19.2 INTERTEMPORAL CHOICE: BASIC IDEAS

The theory of intertemporal choice begins by recognizing that households are endowed with a few broad types of assets. The first includes consumer durables and financial assets. At any given time, a typical household possesses a certain amount (possibly zero) of previously accumulated wealth in the form of money balances and other financial assets. The household holds some part of this wealth (for example, stocks and bonds) mainly as a source of expected future income, which may consist partly of dividend and interest payments and partly of gains in capital value. It holds another part (including houses, cars, furniture, appliances) for the sake of current and prospective yields of consumption services. It holds a third portion (specifically, money and inventories of consumer goods) not for the sake of direct income or service yields but to avoid costs that would otherwise be incurred in synchronizing receipts and expenditures.

In addition to marketable physical and financial assets, the typical household also has a certain amount of human wealth (or capital)—personal services that members of the household can dispose of in exchange for payments of money income. Considered in the abstract, **human capital** is analogous to a parcel of land that cannot be sold outright (for legal or other reasons) but can be used to produce food for a household or rented out to others. Like such a plot of land, human capital can be improved in various ways (through vocational training or education, for example) to increase the market value of its services, but it can also be allowed to deteriorate (through laziness or lack of care). It differs from most forms of nonhuman capital in that its "capital value" can be realized only over an extended period of time and its "quantity" cannot quickly be altered.

Every asset (human or nonhuman) a household owns is a potential source of immediate purchasing power. In effect, therefore, a household that holds wealth of any kind incurs a certain cost in the form of forgone consumption. This is obvious in the case of currency, which yields no explicit income stream but which might be used to purchase interest-bearing bonds, the income from which could be used to finance a permanent flow of consumption expenditure. The proposition is no less true of interest-bearing bonds, however: These could be sold for money that could, in turn, be used to finance an immediate increase in consumption. One can even raise a certain amount of cash from human capital by borrowing against expected future earnings (as with student loans).

19.3 INTERTEMPORAL CONSUMPTION

To understand how a rational household chooses between the level of consumption in the present time period versus the future time period, it is convenient to begin by considering a simple model of intertemporal choice that is an extension of the indifference-curve approach presented in Chapter 5. The difference is that we are extending the model to show consumption decisions over two time periods. In the two-period model, households can either consume less in the current period (save more) and consume more in the future period or consume more in the current period (save less) and consume less in the future.

The **intertemporal budget line** L_0 in Figure 19–1 shows the maximum affordable allocation of current consumption and future consumption. The slope of the intertemporal budget line is $-(1 + r)$, the negative sign indicating that the budget line is negatively sloped. We can rearrange this to state that the absolute value of the slope is equal to $1 + r$ (where r is the interest rate). The slope means that every dollar the household borrows from future consumption, period 2, must be paid back with interest. That is, moving down the budget line the household is borrowing from future consumption and must pay interest. However, if the household were to save for future consumption, not consume as much in the present period, they could loan the money out—that is, one dollar saved in the first period would be equal to one dollar plus the interest rate in the second period. Therefore, moving up the intertemporal budget line the household is consuming less (saving more) in period 1 and earning interest on their savings. If capital markets are perfect and interest rates are the same for borrowers and savers, then the intertemporal budget constraint is a straight line.

FIGURE 19–1
POSSIBLE COMBINATION OF PRESENT AND FUTURE CONSUMPTION

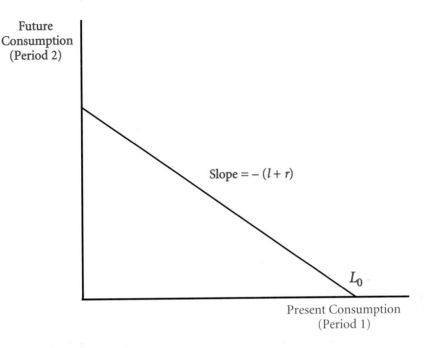

The intertemporal budget line L_0 shows the maximum affordable allocations of present consumption and future consumption. Present consumptions that are not spent in period I are available in period 2 with interest. Future consumption can be increased by decreasing present consumption and earning interest on the savings.

Figure 19–2 depicts an intertemporal preference ordering between current consumption on the horizontal axis and future consumption on the vertical axis. Which alternative the household selects depends (we assume) on its **time preference** between present and future consumption. The indifference curve shows all the combinations of present and future consumption that will yield the same utility for this individual household. Because the indifference curve is convex, we know that there is a diminishing marginal rate of substitution between **present and future consumption**. On the steep slope of the indifference curve, the household is willing to sacrifice a lot of future consumption for an additional unit of present consumption. While on the flat portion of the indifference curve, the household is willing to sacrifice very little future consumption to obtain an additional unit of present consumption. Recalling from Chapter 5, we know that the slope at any point along the indifference curve is the marginal rate of substitution. Because the slope of the intertemporal budget line is 1 + r, then the indifference curve must also be equal to 1 + r at the tangency or at the optimum. At the optimum, point A in Figure 19–2, the household will receive 1 + r units of future consumption for giving up a unit of present consumption. To the right of the optimum, point B in Figure 19-2, the household could increase their utility by saving more (currently consume less) because the marginal rate of substitution is less than the slope of the intertemporal budget line. (See Problem 19–1.)

Figure 19–2
Utility Maximization Between Current and Future Consumption

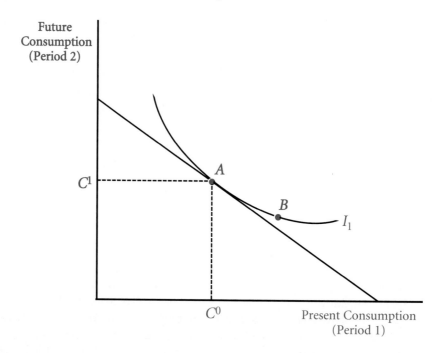

The indifference curves characterize a household's preferences between current and future consumption. The household maximizes utility at point A, consuming C^0 in the present period and C^1 in future consumption. The indifference curve and budget line are tangent, and the marginal rate of substitution is equal to $1 + r$, where r is the rate of interest.

19–1 Contrast the rate of time preference for Julie and Bob. Julie inherited a fortune but spent it all in the first few years. Bob inherited nothing but had a fortune when he retired.

Julie has a very high positive rate of time preference for current consumption over future consumption. On the other hand, Bob has a lower positive (or possibly negative) rate of time preference, preferring to save for the future rather than consuming in the present.

19.4 HUMAN CAPITAL

In principle, a household can achieve a positive consumption flow without earning any income from personal services, provided that it can somehow manage to acquire an initial endowment of income-earning nonhuman wealth. In practice, however, most households derive the bulk of their current income from personal services, for these result from the one kind of wealth with which every household is endowed from its inception, human capital.

If human capital were simply a matter of accident—that is to say, if the quality and quantity of services from human capital could not be altered by individual action—then describing the factors that govern a household's management of this portion of its asset portfolio would be a simple matter. The only choice confronting the household would be to decide what quantity of services to offer in exchange for money income in each period.

Unfortunately, we have little definite knowledge about matters of this kind or about related issues such as the effect of income taxes on work incentives. Generally speaking, people seem to be relatively insensitive in the short run to changes in wealth or real wage rates; habit and social circumstances tend to dominate work-leisure decisions over relatively short time periods (say, less than five years). The crucial question is whether economic factors significantly affect work-leisure decisions in the long run. If real wage rates are high and rising, decade after decade, for example, will this encourage people to work more to consume more, or will it encourage people to work less to enjoy more fully the pleasures of high-level consumption? If tax rates on incomes above a certain magnitude are maintained for a generation at very high levels, will this tend ultimately to discourage highly skilled people from working long hours, or will it encourage them to work even harder? Theory provides no clear answers to questions of this kind because theory allows for both income and substitution effects, which work in opposite directions in this case. Current empirical research is almost equally uninformative.

As a rule, human capital is not a fixed quantity; each individual, particularly early in life, can to some extent alter the future sale value of his or her services by investing resources in education and training. The factors governing choices at this level are extremely complex, and much work remains to be done before we understand even partially the technology and economics of such decisions. At a descriptive level, however, the problem is relatively easy to characterize.

At any given time, an individual has a choice between current work and investment activities that increase future earning power. The more currently available time that is devoted to work, the higher will be the current real income, but the smaller will be the difference between expected earnings in future years and the income currently received. If a person accepts a reduction in current income to devote some portion of current effort to education and training, that person can expect to realize a certain return on the investment, for in later years he or she will earn a higher wage rate (the amount of the increase depending on the nature of the education and training as well as the individual's natural ability).

If one could forecast exactly the consequences of alternative programs of investment in human capital, it would be relatively simple to compare expected returns with expected costs and decide whether the investment promised to be economically worthwhile. If the annual yield of an investment of $60,000 in a college education were equivalent to, say, $12,000 (20 percent) for 45 working years, a person obviously would be foolish to forgo the investment if one could obtain the necessary funds at something less than 20 percent, say, 15 percent per year. Similarly, a person would be unwise a pure financial sense to invest in a college education if the expected yield from it were less than the prevailing rate of interest on secure loans. (See Problem 19–2.)

19–2 Education and training are always undertaken purely with a view to financial considerations. True or False?

False. A person might well invest in a college education even if it yielded a negative return in money income, provided that is gave him or her personal satisfaction (an implicit income that might offset a very substantial loss of money income). Even if the individual does not benefit financially from increased education, society may benefit in cultural and other respects (for example, lower crime rates or more-informed voters) from having its members highly educated. Even if investment in human capital could be shown to be privately unprofitable, therefore, such investment might still be considered profitable from a social point of view. This may explain the prevalence of subsidized education in the United States and elsewhere.

The main difficulty in all discussions of investment in human capital is that both the costs and the returns are highly unpredictable. The problem is not simply that explicit costs and returns cannot be estimated; even without this complication, the far more serious problem of evaluating implicit (subjective and social) costs and benefits would remain. As matters stand, empirical studies stimulated by economic theory have contributed few answers to the many questions that might be posed. Proper strategy requires that research be directed first toward ascertaining explicit costs and returns, which involves (among other things) research into the technology of education and training. Work that has already been done in this direction has yielded much useful information about present patterns of private behavior in relation to investment in human capital and could also provide worthwhile guidance to social planners. It is of some value, after all, to be able to say more-or-less definitely whether a particular kind of educational program (such as free high-school education for all children) seems worthwhile from strictly an economic point of view. If it is, that should settle the issue (unless it is thought that educated people are undesirable, per se!). In the contrary case, policy decisions would have to be based on noneconomic considerations.

Based on data for 1990, the United States Census Bureau estimated that a male with a college education can expect to earn on average 1.75 times as much as a male with a high-school diploma. For women the difference is even more pronounced. A woman with a college degree is expected to earn 2.1 times as much as a woman with a high-school diploma. Given these figures, why don't all individuals attend college?

Before determining whether an investment is lucrative, one must consider the costs as well as the benefits and compare the net rate of return with alternative investments. Estimated rates of return on a college education vary from 5 to 15 percent. The rates of return are comparable to other investments in stocks, bonds, and so on. Those who obtain a college education of given quality at low cost (more gifted students) and who receive greater nonpecuniary gains from a college education (greater enjoyment from education or the jobs a college education brings) are most likely to go to college.

19.5 MONEY AND CONSUMER GOOD INVENTORIES

A typical household in the real world maintains sizable average inventories of canned foods, milk, soap, bread, coffee, gasoline, shirts, dresses, typing paper, toilet paper, paper towels, and other nondurable consumer goods. Indeed, the aggregate money value of such inventories may be anything from 2 to 20 times the amount of the household's average holdings of money balances. Such inventories are costly to hold, partly because of explicit expenses of storage and deterioration, partly because of implicit costs in terms of forgone interest income. To justify what might be regarded as uneconomic behavior, we have only to observe that if a household did not hold inventories of most of the goods that it regularly consumes, a household member would otherwise spend a great deal of time and effort making frequent trips to the market. Rational behavior on the part of the household implies that it maintain average inventories of nondurable consumption goods at a level such that the value to the household of marginal units of released energy and other resources that would otherwise be devoted to trading activity is just equal to the marginal storage and interest costs of such holdings.

In a money economy, it is possible to trade commodities in organized markets only by paying or receiving money in every exchange. The recurrent shopping activities of a household in a money economy thus involve certain indirect and direct inventory costs; in addition to holding inventories of physical goods, the household must maintain an inventory of cash to enter organized markets. In general, a household avoids holding large cash balances for much the same reasons as it avoids holding excessive inventories of goods. Very rarely, however, does a household attempt to do without cash by shopping and paying bills only on days when it receives cash income, for such a procedure would force the household to carry huge inventories of consumer goods, and the costs of such holdings would outweigh any real or monetary savings from lower cash balances and fewer trips to market. What the typical household does (and it is most likely a subconscious calculation) is to choose the frequency and timing of its shopping trips in the light of both the direct costs of holding inventories of goods and the related indirect costs of holding money balances.

19.6 THE COASE CONJECTURE

According to Professor Ronald Coase, in a two-period model, a durable-good monopolist will have very little market power if consumers form rational expectations about the monopolist's future behavior. For example, assume that the durable-good monopolist sells output at the traditional monopoly price, P_M, and output, Q_M in Figure 19–3. Once the monopolist has sold Q_M units, the monopolist could add to its total profit by lowering its price and selling additional units of output. In fact, in the extreme case it would sell its last unit at the competitive level, which is all the output above marginal costs, or Q_C in Figure 19–3. However, what if the prospective buyers know that the monopolist will rationally lower its price and sell additional units of the durable good in period 2? Consumers will balk at paying P_M in period 1. In other words, unless the seller commits not to reduce its future price, the monopolists initial-period sales at the monopoly price (or in the extreme, any price above marginal costs) will be significantly reduced, possibly to zero units. However, the "soon-to-be-lower-price" expectation problem can be eliminated. Suppose the monopolist is an artist who owns a master print of a popular lithograph that is being shown at an art show. She can promise not to produce more than M units, say by publicly destroying the master print so that additional lithograph prints would be impossible. Alternatively, she could rent the prints, that is, if the seller produced more output in future periods, the rental rate in the initial period would be unaffected. Lastly, she could sell each print with a repurchase agreement promising to purchase the print in the future at a fixed price which can be exercised at the option of the buyer.[1] All three of these options would allow the monopolist to cope with the problems associated with durability and the consumer's rational expectation that the seller will behave opportunistically by engaging in intertemporal price discrimination. (See Problem 19–3.)

---

[1] For an alternative to the repurchase agreement, see David Butz, "Durable-Good Monopoly and Best-Price Provisions," *American Economic Review*, 80, December 1990, 1062–1076.

FIGURE 19-3
THE DURABLE-GOOD MONOPOLIST

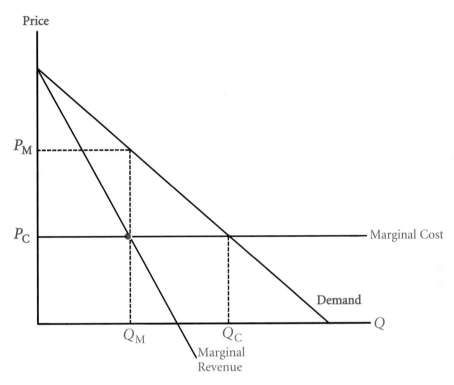

The durable-good monopolist initially sells output at the traditional monopoly price, P_M, and output, Q_M. Once the monopolist has sold Q_M units, the monopolist could add to its total profit by lowering its price and selling additional units of output. However, if prospective buyers know this, they will be reluctant to buy at P_M. In fact, in the extreme case no output would be sold at any price above marginal costs, or Q_C.

19-3   True or False?   If customers anticipated that airlines were going to reduce their ticket prices in a few weeks, many would not pay today's higher prices and defer their purchases.

True.   Only those that had urgent travel plans would buy now; others would wait to purchase a ticket in anticipation of a lower price.   That is, if consumers expect the airlines to lower their price in the future, these expectations affect their current demand for tickets.   Similarly, consumers might put off buying a new car for a couple of months if they expect the price of automobiles to fall at the end of the model year.   Both examples highlight the importance of expectations about future-period prices on the current-period demand, demonstrating the ability of consumers to shift their demands for goods intertemporaly.

19.7 SPECULATION AND TRADING COMMODITIES ACROSS TIME

It is often believed that speculators that carry goods from one period to supply in another provide little or no social function. After all, they are not buying these commodities to fulfill their own consumption; rather they have bought these products to hold off the market, anticipating (speculating) that prices will be higher in the future. If they are right, these gamblers, called **speculators**, can profit from selling their inventories of commodities at the higher price. In fact, on any weekday the trading of commodities, such as wheat, lumber, soybeans, copper, and so on, are traded across time as speculators buy and sell in the hopes of profiting by buying low and selling high. Speculators enter into what is called a futures contract when they agree to deliver or accept delivery of a certain amount of a commodity at today's futures price, at some specified date in the future. In some sense, most of us are speculators. If we expect the price of some nonperishable commodity to rise in the futures we may well stock up on that good now.

How can the often-maligned speculator possibly contribute beneficially to society? If speculators' transactions are on average profitable, then their activities will tend to smooth out the distribution of a commodity over time, and prices will in turn be stabilized over time as well. Society would therefore experience a net benefit from successful speculation because speculators are moving commodities across time from periods where the commodity is relatively less valuable to periods where the commodity is more valuable.

For example in Figure 19–4(a), assume that the supply of wheat harvested in the good year, period 1, is 8 million bushels and the supply of wheat harvested in the bad year, period 2, is 4 million bushels. Without speculation, we see that the price of wheat in the good year (period 1) is $6 a bushel and the price of wheat in the bad year (period 2) is $8 a bushel. Now if speculators buy the wheat for $6 in period 1 and then store it to sell in period 2 for $8, they are initially making profits of $2 a bushel (minus storage costs and interest and assuming that demand is the same in both periods). As speculators continue to buy in period 1 to sell in period 2, the period 1 price is driven up and the period 2 price is driven down. The process continues until the prices and output converge and speculative profits from additional transactions vanish. The price Figure 19–4(b) converges at $7 and the supplies converges to 6 million bushels per period. The final outcome of successful speculation is a stable price and output over the two periods and a shift of commodities from lower value to higher value.

FIGURE 19-4
TRADING COMMODITIES ACROSS TIME

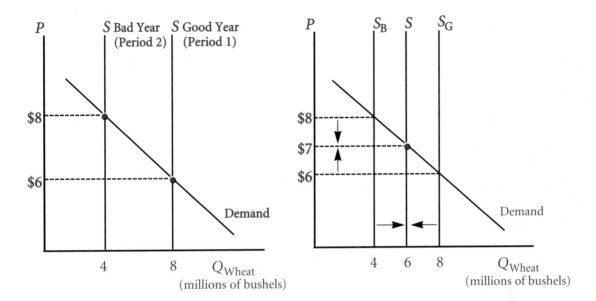

The supply of wheat harvested in the good year, period 1, is 8 million bushels, and the supply of wheat harvested in the bad year, period 2, is 4 million bushels. Without speculation, the price of wheat in the good year (period 1) is $6 a bushel and the price of wheat in the bad year (period 2) is $8 a bushel. If speculators buy the wheat for $6 in period 1 and then store it to sell in period 2 for $8, they are making profits of $2 a bushel (minus storage costs and interest). As speculators continue to buy in period 1 to sell in period 2, the period 1 price is driven up and the period 2 price is driven down. The price converges at $7 and the supplies converges to 6 million bushels per period.

19.8 PLANS AND REALIZATIONS

So far, our discussion of household problems of intertemporal choice has been concerned with states of equilibrium or, in the few instances where we have dealt with adjustment processes, with situations in which we assume that the household can execute its plans as scheduled. In a sense, therefore, we have been concerned with "virtual" rather than with "real" decisions; obviously a more realistic account of household behavior should provide for the possibility that plans cannot be realized—that quantities of consumption goods or assets demanded for purchase might exceed or fall short of quantities offered for sale at prevailing prices. To be sure, if the economic system always adjusted smoothly and quickly to remove prevailing inconsistencies in trading plans, it would hardly be worthwhile to analyze transition states of disequilibrium, for such states would be too short-lived to merit serious consideration. One does not have to be a professional economist, however, to have serious doubts about the validity of this view of economic adjustment. If the economic system worked as well in fact as it is customarily conceived to work in theory, the daily newspaper would not be full of worried editorials about unemployment and inflation.

19.9 UNSETTLED ISSUES

The deeper one goes into the details of household behavior, the more complicated the entire subject becomes. Economists often find themselves in the same position as physicists who have tried to explain the nature of the atom. Around the turn of the century, it seemed that the atom was like a miniature solar system, consisting of a hard central nucleus around which various electrons circled in regular orbits. Thirty years later, the nucleus no longer seemed hard; it appeared rather to consist of a large number of more basic particles—neutrons, protons, mesons, and other theoretically predicted objects. The electron no longer seemed to have any particular orbit, and it was associated with numerous other particles whose behavior could be characterized but not really explained. Physicists have not given up the search for order in the chaos that now seems to confront them, but most have given up the idea that the search will yield practical fruit and have turned their thoughts in the meantime to alternative ways of describing microphysical phenomena. Broadly speaking, they seek regularities in the average or statistical behavior of atomic processes and no longer attempt to describe the behavior of individual atomic particles in a literal fashion. Many economists have not yet reached the stage at which they are willing to confess their inability to characterize accurately the details of human-decision processes, but present conditions indicate that such a stage will be reached in the not-too-distant future. Modern work in this area tends to focus more and more on mathematically complicated descriptions of empirically trivial problems, such as the consumption and saving behavior of an individual with given and unchanging taste who has certain knowledge of all future income and prices. Such problems pose countless logical puzzles, but they do little to advance economics as an empirical science, except to the extent that they help to convince economists generally of the practical futility of such exercises.

These observations should not be interpreted as an attack on rigorous analysis of precisely defined models of human behavior. Even when such analysis has no direct payoff, it can produce useful negative results—as the physics example illustrates. It is not that economics can do without rigorous analysis but rather that economics cannot do without models that are designed to describe ongoing economic processes and are correspondingly endowed with empirical content. The existing body of theory dealing with household behavior may describe an imaginary situation and has much value in indicating where we are likely to run into problems in attempts to describe less-fanciful cases. It does not carry us very far, however, toward an understanding of actual household behavior, and it becomes seriously impaired when it is elaborated in finer and finer detail without reference to any kind of empirical data.

SUMMARY

1. Accumulated wealth is held in the form of money and other assets. These assets may be held for the sake of expected future income to provide a stream of consumption services (like cars), or to provide inventories of goods or money to ward off problems of uncertainty.

2. In addition to marketable physical and financial assets, households also possess a certain amount of nonsellable (but rentable) human wealth, called human capital.

3. Human capital differs from nonhuman capital because its "capital value" can be realized only over an extended period of time and because its "quantity" cannot quickly be altered.

4. The intertemporal budget line shows the maximum affordable allocation of current consumption and future consumption.

5. Intertemporal-indifference curves show the combinations of present and future consumption that will yield the same utility for individual households. Which alternative the household selects depends on its time preference between present and future consumption.

6. The household maximizes utility at the point where the indifference curve and intertemporal budget line are tangent, and the marginal rate of substitution is equal to $1 + r$, where r is the rate of interest.

7. At any given time, individuals have a choice between current work and investment in human capital. Because of future uncertainties, however, it is difficult to ascertain expected returns from expected costs of a particular investment in human capital.

8. Rational behavior on the part of the household requires that it maintain average inventories of nondurable consumption goods at a level such that the value to the household of marginal units of released energy and other resources that would otherwise be devoted to trading activity is just equal to the marginal storage and interest costs of such holdings.

9. In a two-period model, a durable-good monopolist will have very little market power if consumer's form expectations about future behavior. However, the monopolist can avoid the expectation problem by renting rather than selling, promising not to sell more than the original output, or agreeing to repurchase the good if the price drops.

10. Successful speculation leads to a stable price and output over the two periods and a shift of commodities from lower value use to higher value use.

WORDS AND CONCEPTS FOR REVIEW

intertemporal choice	intertemporal budget line
human capital	time preference
present and future consumption	Coase conjecture
speculators	

REVIEW QUESTIONS

1. How much do you think you could borrow from a bank on your present stock of human capital? From your parents? From a finance company?

2. Suppose that a person owns outright a house whose current market value is $100,000. If such a person told you that he lived "rent free," what might you say to him to correct his delusion?

3. What is meant by the term *time preference*?

4. Would the rate of interest on saving deposits be an appropriate measure of the rate of time preference to person who is currently paying an annual interest rate of 12 percent on an automobile loan? Explain your answer.

5. Each of us knows people who spend everything they earn as fast as they get it and also borrow as much as their friends will lend out. Does their behavior tell you anything about the probable magnitude of these individuals' rate of time preference?

6. Some people save a positive percentage of their income throughout most of their lives. Draw a diagram to illustrate the preferences of such people between present and future consumption.

7. What do you think would happen to the intertemporal budget line if the interest rate increased? Decreased?

8. During much of human history, some people have been "human capital" in a literal sense, that is, marketable as slaves. What factors would enter into calculations of the market value of such capital goods? Discuss.

9. Why are you going to college? Is it costing you anything but time (and forgone income)? What does it cost your parents? What does it cost your school? Will the value of your services be increased sufficiently as a result of your education to offset its cost to you and others?

SUGGESTED READINGS

Becker, G. *Human Capital.* New York: Columbia University Press, 1975.

Carlton, D., and J. Perloff. *Modern Industrial Organization,* 2nd ed., New York: Harper-Collins, 1994.

Coase, R. "Durability and Monopoly" *The Journal of Law and Economics,* 15, April 1972, 143–49.

Johnson, M. *Household Behavior: Income, Wealth, and Consumption.* London: Penguin, 1971.

Schultz, T. "Investments in Human Capital," *American Economic Review,* March 1961, 1–17.

Chapter Twenty

MARKET FAILURES: PUBLIC GOODS AND EXTERNALITIES

_____ *Questions to Think About* _____

1. What determines the socially optimal level of output?

2. When do private markets produce the socially optimal level of output?

3. Why does monopoly prevent the attainment of the social optimum?

4. What are positive externalities?   Negative externalities?

5. What are the characteristics of a public good?

6. What is a free rider?

7. Why is it difficult to ascertain the optimal amount of a public good?

8. How can government correct market failures?

9. What is the Coase Theorem?   What are its limitations?

10. How much information is optimal?

11. What is asymmetric information?   Adverse selection?

12. What is moral hazard?

13. What is signaling?   Screening?

14. What is public choice?   What are the similarities and difference between private and public choice?

20.1 INTRODUCTION

The forces of supply and demand perform an extremely complicated and valuable function. In concert, they coordinate the optimizing activities of a large, diverse set of economic agents and answers to the basic economic questions of WHAT? HOW? and FOR WHOM? Given an appropriate income distribution as discussed in Chapter 18, the answers to these questions are, moreover, often socially optimal in the sense that a larger output level has marginal costs greater than marginal benefits, whereas a smaller output level would leave unproduced goods having benefits greater than costs.

20.2 SUPPLY AND DEMAND REVISITED

Let us now examine more carefully the efficiency aspects of the supply-and-demand outcome under idealized conditions. Suppose that demand, or willingness to pay, accurately represents the marginal social values of additional output. Similarly, suppose that supply, or the marginal willingness to produce, represents the marginal social cost of output. Figure 20–1 shows the intersection of these two curves that indicates the quantity (Q^*) at which the marginal social value of the last unit produced is equal to the marginal social cost of the last unit produced. Figure 20–1 also shows that output levels higher than Q^*, say Q_{High}, have costs greater than benefits. On the other hand, at output levels below Q^*, say Q_{Low}, output having benefits greater than cost goes unproduced. In both instances, output levels are inefficient.

The demand curve purportedly depicts the **social marginal value** of various quantities of the good in question, while the supply curve is intended to reflect the **social marginal cost** (forgone opportunities) of alternative quantities of the good. Unfortunately, these curves do not always measure what they presume to measure in the usual supply—demand analysis. When they do not, the desirability of the Q^* outcome in Figure 20–1 is called into question. There are three important reasons why the invisible hand might leave a mess behind. This chapter considers one of these reasons in detail. First, however, let's briefly review two other major sources of resource misallocation.

FIGURE 20–1

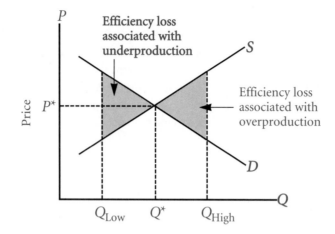

Equilibrium price and quantity (P^*, Q^*) are socially efficient when demand reflects marginal social benefits and supply reflects true marginal social costs. If output exceeds Q^*, marginal social costs exceed marginal social benefits, and efficiency requires a reduction in quantity. Conversely, at output rates less than Q^*, marginal social benefits exceed costs, and society would gain from additional output.

INCOME DISTRIBUTION

Suppose you believe that the current income distribution is "wrong". You might believe that income is distributed too equally, or merely that the wrong individuals have particular incomes (say, your own is too low). Specifically, you believe that income is distributed too unequally. Suppose, too, that you are able to redistribute income as you deem more fair. What difficulties would this income redistribution cause to the optimal provision of goods through market forces? To clarify how this question matters, further suppose that the good under consideration is yachts. Because this is a superior good over the relevant (high) income range, redistributing income would result in a leftward shift in the demand curve: With fewer millionaires, the number of yachts demanded would also be smaller. After your desired income redistribution, therefore, the optimal quantity of yachts would fall. You infer as a result that the predistribution quantity of yachts was not optimal.

Economists, in their role as economists, find little wrong with the preceding argument; in a sense, efficiency becomes a meaningless concept. But more can be said. First, under a representative form of government, the existing income distribution may fairly closely parallel what most people think appropriate. If income were unfairly distributed, either too equally or too unequally, politicians advocating various tax and other reforms would be elected. Such an evolutionary, or even revolutionary, outcome would push the system closer to the collective ideal.

Second, the income elasticity of demand for many goods is unity or close to unity. For such goods, redistributing income among people with similar preferences leads to reductions in the demand of those losing income that are completely offset by increases in demand from those gaining income, in other words, the market outcome for such goods is optimal, regardless of the income distribution. Note that because all income is spent (counting savings as a good), the collective income elasticity is 1, a figure that would represent your best guess of the income elasticity of any single good (lacking other information, such as, for example, the intuitive knowledge we have about yacht buyers). Not knowing whose ethical judgment about the appropriate income distribution is correct, economists therefore tend to treat the existing distribution as satisfactory, particularly because optimal overall quantities are often unaffected by any redistribution.

LACK OF COMPETITION

Another source of misallocation stems from noncompetitiveness on either the supply or the demand side of the market. With competition, demand (the marginal value of additional output to society) gets set equal to marginal cost, because demand equals marginal revenue to each firm. Monopolists, however, must lower their prices to sell additional output so that its marginal revenue is below its demand curve. Setting marginal revenue equal to marginal cost fails to produce output having value (the demand curve) greater than the marginal cost of production. Too little of those goods are therefore produced under monopolistic or oligopolistic conditions.

Our focus in this chapter, however, is on a third circumstance in which the unconstrained workings of the market lead to inappropriate quantities of goods produced. Even if the economy is competitive and the income distribution is correct, it is still possible for the market supply-and-demand curves to wrongly characterize the marginal social benefits and costs of production. How might this happen?

20.3 EXTERNALITIES

Consider first the false signals given by the market-supply curve. You recall that this curve is the (horizontal) sum of the marginal-cost curves (above the minimum of the average variable-cost curve in the short run) of each firm in the industry.[1] The marginal costs being summed are marginal *private* costs—firms' payments (explicit or implicit) to acquire the factors needed to produce various quantities of the good. These

---

[1]This ignores the possibility that industry expansion will drive up certain input prices that would be unaffected by an individual firm's expansion. This refinement does not materially affect the text discussion.

payments represent the opportunity costs of other goods that are forgone—as they are supposed to *if* the firm must pay for all of its inputs. Sometimes, however, unlike with labor and other inputs, the firm uses an input that is socially valuable (and thus, has an opportunity cost) yet costs the firm nothing. The classic example is the air used by an air-polluting factory. The firm uses clean air in production and returns dirty air to the atmosphere. The loss of air quality is felt by society as worsened health, material damage, and aesthetically unappealing views. Such damages are real costs of the firm's use of the air; yet because nobody owns the air (unlike other inputs), no charge is placed on its use. As a consequence, too much of it is used in producing too much of the polluting good.

Economists use the term **externality** to refer to these kinds of side effects. An externality is said to occur whenever a physical impact on third parties to a transaction takes place without compensation. This definition may be abbreviated to "uncompensated spillovers."

Figure 20–2 illustrates the presence of externalities and their implications for actual versus optimal resource use. $S_{PRIVATE}$ represents the private costs of the polluting good, say steel.[2] S_{SOCIAL} adds the cost of externalities to the private cost; this supply curve therefore reflects the true marginal social cost of steel. The actual competitive outcome, Q_A, occurs with steel selling for P_A. Notice, however, that the last unit of steel produced had a true social cost of P_S, greatly in excess of its price. The full efficiency loss is seen as the shaded region in Figure 20–2. This area shows the sum of the amounts by which full social costs exceed private benefits for the (excess) output from Q^* to Q_A. If the firm were to produce Q^*, marginal social cost would equal marginal social benefit; this ton of steel (and all inframarginal tons) would have social value equal to (or greater than) social cost.

The output level Q_0 represents the output level at which smokestack emissions first result in nonnegligible damages to people and things downwind. It is socially desirable to produce the steel between Q_0 and Q^* even though that production results in environmental damages. This results in the paradoxical assertion that there is an "optimal level of pollution" that is not generally zero! Some environmentalists find this assertion hard to swallow (though they themselves may use a product that directly or indirectly pollutes).[3] It is easy to see the efficiency loss to society of requiring steel producers to produce at Q_0; indeed, if we compare the appropriate efficiency loss triangles, it is clear that a zero pollution outcome would generally be much *less* desirable than would be the uncontrolled outcome.

While there are many similar examples of **negative externalities** in production, there can also be **positive externalities** on the supply side and especially on the demand

---

[2]While we suspect that the steel industry is competitive because of foreign competition, the skeptic may think of, for example, dry cleaners which emit carcinogenic benzene compounds, or even "mile of travel" with private automobiles (it is not just firms which pollute).

[3]Note that we are assuming that the social cost of production in Figure 20–2 includes all damages that are not compensated under the private-supply curve.

side. For many goods, the individual consumer does not receive *all* of the benefits of the purchased good. This is not the case for, say, a hamburger; if you buy it, you get all of its benefits. However, consider education, well-kept home exteriors, beautiful art, or even of praying mantises and ladybugs as an alternative to pesticides. Certainly, when you "buy" an education you receive many of its benefits: greater future income, more choice of future occupations, and the consumption value of knowing more about life as a result of classroom (and extracurricular) learning. These benefits, however, great as they may be, are not all of the benefits associated with your education. You may end up curing cancer or solving some other social problem of importance, or you may just be more interesting to everyone who talks to you for the rest of your life. These nontrivial benefits are the *positive* external-consumption benefits of education (see Figure 20–3).

FIGURE 20–2
NEGATIVE EXTERNALITIES AND RESOURCE MISALLOCATION

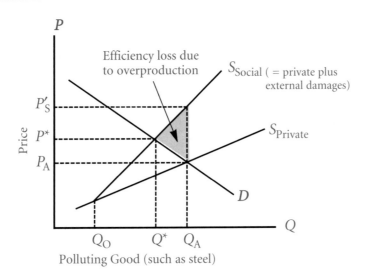

Polluting Good (such as steel)

The social-supply curve includes the marginal costs of production, reflected by the private-supply curve, plus the external costs (such as pollution). Market production is greater and market price is lower than is socially desirable. The shaded area designates the efficiency from overproduction.

When there are positive externalities, the private market supplies *too little* of the good in question (such as education). When there are negative externalities, the market supplies *too much*. In either case, the cause is that economic agents are receiving the wrong signals: The apparent benefits or costs of some action differ from the true social benefits or costs. The economic agents—producers and consumers—are *not* doing what they do because they are evil; rather, both well-intentioned and ill-intentioned people behave according to the incentives they face.

The free market, then, works fine in providing most goods but does badly without regulations, taxes, and subsidies) in providing others. The problem, at heart, lies with a concept closely related to the concept of externalities, that of public goods. (See Problem 20–1.)

20–1 How might a negative externality be internalized? A positive externality?

The private-supply curve lies below the social-supply curve for a polluting good such as steel. If a tax is imposed on the firm equal to the marginal social cost of the pollution, the firm's supply curve will shift up by the amount of the tax. The firm's supply curve becomes the social-supply curve, the socially optimal level of output equals the profit-maximizing output with the tax, and the firm has internalized the externality.

A positive externality can be internalized by subsidizing buyers of the good such as education. If students are subsidized, their demand curve shifts up by the amount of the subsidy, If the subsidy is sufficient to raise the marginal private value up to the marginal social value, the private-demand curve becomes the social-demand curve, and the socially optimal level of education will occur at Q_1.

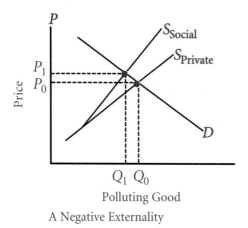

FIGURE 20–3
POSITIVE EXTERNALITIES AND RESOURCE MISALLOCATION

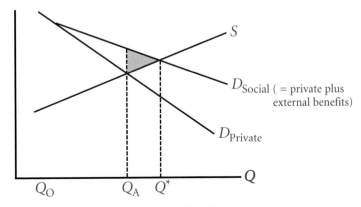

Positive Consumption Externality Good
(e.g. education)

The private-demand curve plus external benefits constitute the social-demand curve. The market price falls short of the socially optimal price, and the market underproduces the commodity. The shaded area indicates the associated efficiency loss.

20.4 PUBLIC GOODS, THE FREE RIDER, AND PROPERTY RIGHTS

Externalities are not the only culprit behind resource misallocations. Another source of market failure is what economists call *public goods*. As used by economists, the term refers not to how particular goods are purchased—by a government agency rather than some private economic agent—but to the properties that characterize them. A *private good* such as a hamburger has two critical properties in the present context. First, if you buy it, it is yours—nobody else can have it (unless you let them, in which case you no longer have it). This property is referred to as *excludability*, meaning that your use of the good excludes others from using the same good. Second, and closely related, is that the user of a private good receives all the benefits of its consumption. Consumption of a private good is therefore *rivalrous*.

PUBLIC GOODS

Many goods, however, have quite different properties. Such goods are said to be **public goods** whenever their consumption is (1) **nonexcludable** and (2) **nonrivalrous.**

Two classic examples of public goods are *national defense* and *lighthouses.* Whatever the level of national defense, we all get it (consumption is nonrivalrous) and we cannot be prevented from receiving it (consumption is nonexcludable).[4] The light emanating from a lighthouse exists for all boat owners; it is technologically impossible to keep certain boat owners from looking at it while letting others see it (nonexcludable). Similarly, one boat owner's decision to use the light as a guide does not diminish the ability of the light to guide other boat owners (nonrivalrous).

FREE RIDERS

Public goods are closely related to externalities and to something called the **free-rider** problem. Suppose the quality of the air where you live is undesirable, so you clean it up (say, by reducing your own pollution by substituting a cleaner wood-burning stove for a highly polluting one, or even by placing a huge filter upwind of your home). Because air quality (unlike land quality) is largely a public good, you know that others will benefit. It might well be advantageous from society's perspective for the air to be cleaned up in this way, but what incentive do your neighbors have to pay for the benefits they will receive?

The answer, of course, is very little. They know that if you choose to clean up the air, they cannot be prevented from receiving the benefits. They also know, individually, that no one of them would honestly be willing to pay enough to affect your decision. In other words, they may attempt to become what are known as free riders. Because you do not receive compensation for the benefits accruing to them, you will pollute more than otherwise, giving rise to externalities.

Now suppose a "Save the Whales" group came to your neighborhood to collect funds with which to lobby for protection of the blue whales (whose existence is a public good according to the definition). You may have a genuine interest in the whales' continued existence, but what incentives to contribute do you face? Suppose the whales' survival is actually worth $100 to you. If the 100 million households in the United States each made a similar contribution, this would add up to about $10 billion. You

---

[4]Actually, there are few "pure" public goods. National defense really is not identical everywhere, and at some very high cost it may be possible to exclude individual households from consuming defense. Indeed, many goods are mixed public/private goods—congestion at a national park or on the Santa Monica Freeway, for example, means that your consumption is rivalrous with others. Similarly, an endangered species may have a value both as a private good (for furs) and as a public good (for ecological stability or scientific research)

might write a check for $100, or you might reason as follows: "If I give $100, there is no guarantee that the whale will be saved because my contribution is negligible relative to the amount required to convene conferences, pass legislation, buy up existing boats, and so on. Furthermore, if I *don't* give $100, the whale may be saved anyhow, and I'll continue to receive the benefits of its existence plus the benefits of the $100." Taking the latter course represents a rational attempt to become a free rider. The rub is that if everyone attempts to take a free ride, the ride will not exist.

PROPERTY RIGHTS

It is easy to see by pursuing the previous examples how property rights figure into this discussion. If air quality were like land quality, where rights of ownership and use were easy to prescribe and enforce, each "owner" of air would have an incentive to protect the value of his or her asset just as people paint their homes, rotate their crops, and take similar actions to maintain the value of other assets. The nature of air, however, precludes this. (See Problem 20–2.)

20–2 Why are blue whales, condors, and bighorn sheep endangered when cows, chickens, and ordinary sheep are not?

The property rights associated with cows and similar animals give their owners the incentive to care for them. Nobody owns whales (or acts as if they did); whale users are therefore not charged a price to reflect the scarcity of whales, as they would be if cows were scarce. An ironic conclusion emerges: It is often believed that the price system of capitalist economies is responsible for our environmental woes, when in fact the opposite is true. The problem is a *lack* of prices (charging a zero price for the use of socially scarce air or wildlife); where prices work properly, we do not have environmental problems.

There is, however, a caveat to this assertion that there would be no environmental problems if the price system worked properly. The assertion takes, as seems appropriate to us, negative externalities to be synonymous with environmental problems. This means that it is human values that matter and that some environmental degradation may be optimal: When the benefits of producing a polluting good are greater than the full social costs, there are no "environmental problems" in the sense that efforts to improve the environment further make us worse off.

On both the supply and the demand side, it is clear that we will get too little of the public good without some intervention. On the supply side, nonexcludability precludes charging consumers for benefits received; producers are therefore not able to cover their costs of producing public goods from revenues. On the demand side, individual consumers have an incentive to be free riders, further reducing the likelihood that goods having benefits greater than costs will be produced. How, then, do we arrive at proper levels of public goods?

20.5 EFFICIENT PROVISION OF PUBLIC GOODS

The marginal social value of a pure public good is the vertical summation of individual-demand curves. Thus, it differs from that of a private good. For a private good the appropriate question is: "How much will be demanded at various prices in the market (**horizontal summation**)?" The corresponding question for the public good, because of its nonrivalrous nature, is: "How much will be offered in aggregate for various quantities (**vertical summation**)?"

We can show this graphically. Imagine a small coastal community of 10,000 people that considers investing in the services of a lighthouse. For simplicity, let us assume the three income groups in the community (the poor, the middle class, and the rich) have demand curves for the lighthouse represented by d_H (high income), d_M (middle income), and d_L (low income) in Figure 20–4. The low-income group, containing 1,000 individuals, are infrequent seafarers, but they would enjoy the aesthetics of a lighthouse on the point and are willing to pay 50 cents per person, or a total of $500, for the first lighthouse. The second group, which is the largest, is the middle-income class. Some members of the middle class fish; others enjoy boating. They are willing to pay $3 each; with 8,000 members, the middle class as a whole is willing to pay $24,000 for the first lighthouse. (This is why d_M is the d curve farthest to the right.) The last group includes the rich, who primarily use the services of a lighthouse while yachting. The group members, 1,000 individuals, are willing to pay $20,000, or $20 per person. In sum, the three groups are willing to pay $44,500 for a lighthouse. The social value (D_{SOCIAL}) is derived by summing vertically (at one lighthouse) each group's marginal benefit or demand curve.

With the construction of the social demand curve D_{SOCIAL}, we can determine the efficient output of lighthouses. To the left of the intersection of the MC curve (drawn horizontally for convenience) and the D_{SOCIAL} curve, the community is willing to pay more for a lighthouse than the marginal costs required to produce it; the lighthouse therefore should be built. This will continue to be the case until marginal social benefits fall to marginal social costs, at two lighthouses in Figure 20–4.

Note that two practical policy difficulties emerge from cases similar to this. First, it is difficult to get people to honestly reveal their preferences for the public good: They attempt to be free riders, trying to get the good for nothing (believing their individual valuations will have a negligible impact on the overall decision on the number of lighthouses). As a result, the right number of lighthouses will not be built. Second, the average cost per resident of the lighthouse is $3. Because the poor value the first lighthouse at 50 cents, they will be harmed by the decision to build one, unless equity is considered in choosing the financing mechanism (say, fees based on the assessed value of boats, rather than with general tax revenues). (See Problems 20–3, 20–4, and 20–5.)

FIGURE 20—4
THE EFFICIENT OUTPUT OF A PUBLIC GOOD

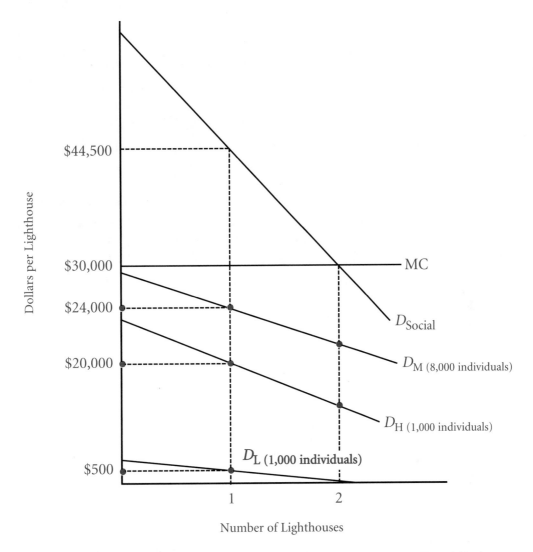

The social-demand curve for a public good is the vertical sum of individual-demand curves. The social optimum occurs when marginal social costs equal marginal social benefits, that is, two lighthouses at $30,000 each. In practice, consumers understate their willingness to pay, and public goods are often underproduced.

20–3 Suppose 10 residents of a condominium decide to hire a gardener. They have to decide how many days per month they want a gardener to work for them. Each resident values one gardener day per month at $10, the second day per month at $8, the third day at $6, and the fourth day at $3. Nevertheless, each reveals that he or she is only willing to pay $5 for the first day, $4 for the second, $2 for the third, and $1 for the fourth in hopes that the neighbors will make up the difference. If the cost of hiring a gardener for one day is $30, for how many days per month will the gardener be hired? What is the optimal number of days? What kind of good are gardeners, and what problem does this example illustrate?

The true marginal social value of each gardener day (P_s) and the revealed marginal private value of each gardener day (P_p) are listed in the table. Columns (1) and (2) show the social-demand curve, while columns (1) and (3) show the private-demand curve. At a price of $30 per day, the residents will hire a gardener for only 2 days per month, the number of days for which the private value exceeds the price. The optimal number of days, however, is 4 per month. In this example, gardener services are a public good and the residents are free riders.

Table 20-1

(1) Quantity of days	(2) P_S	(3) P_P
1	100	50
2	80	40
3	60	20
4	30	10

20–4 The accompanying figure shows demand curves for two people in an economy and a total-supply curve. What is the aggregate-demand curve and equilibrium price and quantity if the good is private? Suppose the good is a public good. What is the aggregate-demand curve and equilibrium price and quantity?

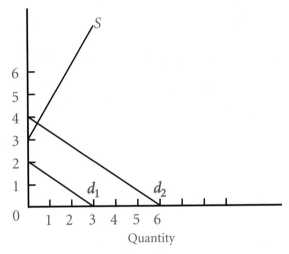

Individual-Demand Curves

The demand curve for a *private* good is the *horizontal* sum of the individual-demand curves. In other words, for private goods the demand curve maps the total quantity demanded at each price. Figure (a) shows the demand curve, equilibrium price, and equilibrium quantity for the private good shown in the figure above. If the good is *public* good, however, the *vertical* sum of the individual-demand curves constitutes the demand curve. For each quantity, the demand curve maps the total willingness to pay for a public good. Figure (b) illustrates equilibrium if the good were a public good.

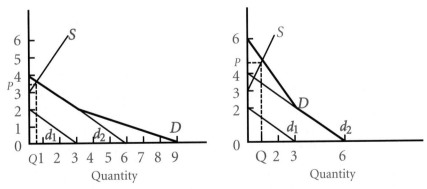

(a) Demand for a private good   (b) Demand for a public good

Horizontal and Vertical Summations of Individual-Demand Curves

20–5 Suppose an economist is attempting to determine the value of a public good, for example, a park. One approach is to ask people how much they are willing to pay for access to the park. Another is to ask them how much money it would take for them to give up access to the park. Do you think the two approaches would result in the same information? If not, which do you think would be more accurate?

Because of the free-rider problem, people tend to understate how much they are willing to pay for a public good if they think they will have to pay for it. If they will be compensated for giving up access to the park, they tend to overstate how much the park means to them. Thus, if people believe compensation will take place, willingness to pay represents a lower bound on the true value of the park while willingness to sell is an upper bound, the true value lying somewhere in between. Neither approach is accurate. It is best to use both estimates together.

FINANCING PUBLIC GOODS

Many public goods, such as national defense, are provided directly by governments. In other cases, combinations of taxes, subsidies, and direct regulations have been employed to move toward the socially optimal quantity of various goods. Consider, by way of another illustration, the case of air-pollution control. Airborne emissions come from many sources, including transportation, industrial stationary-source emitters, and power plants. Because uncontrolled emissions tend to lead to externalities,[5] the output of the polluting sources is too large and the public good "air quality" is underproduced. One might increase the level of air quality in ways that would be socially desirable, but some methods may have costs greater than benefits. The classic solution of Pigou, dating back to the early 1900s, is to tax the polluter per ton of emissions an amount equaling the external damages from a marginal ton of emissions. This would effectively internalize the externality, sending the appropriate signal to the producer that using air in a way that dirties it has an opportunity cost. The social-supply curve (S_{Social} in Figure 20–2) would then become the private-supply curve, and the market failure would be corrected in a way that largely maintains the desirable features of market exchange.

For other public goods, such as education, subsidies might be a desirable approach. Return to Figure 20–3 and note that by subsidizing the cost of education to certain individuals, the supply curve that represents the private marginal cost *to the education buyer* could be shifted down enough to encourage the purchase of the socially

---

[5]They will not always lead to externalities. The emissions may be so small relative to the large absorptive capacity of the environment (for example, squirrel droppings) that there is a negligible impact on environmental quality and, therefore on people. Also, as discussed in the text, the emissions that remain after optimal control policies are in effect will not represent externalities if the controls involve full compensation for those affected by the emissions. Recall that externalities are "uncompensated spillovers."

576   CHAPTER 20

desirable quantity of education, Q^*. Alternatively, private demand could be subsidized (through education coupons called vouchers). Such an approach would effectively lower the price to the education buyer enough so that he or she would desire the socially optimal quantity of education, Q^*.

In some cases, technological difficulties or cost considerations suggest the need for other approaches. It has historically been difficult or very costly to monitor actual emissions into the atmosphere or water bodies. As a result, environmental legislation introduced in the 1960s required that certain pollution-control devices be in place. Automobiles are therefore required to have exhaust gas-recirculation systems, catalytic converters, and so on, while certain industries must install wet limestone scrubbers, electrostatic precipitators, or baghouses on their smokestacks. Such approaches suffer from drawbacks that economic-incentives approaches such as taxing or subsidizing do not. First, the user has no incentive to be sure, even if it could be done at low cost, that the device is working properly.[6] The law requires only that it be present. This means that whatever environmental gains occur are more expensive than they should be. Second, polluters have no incentive to do *more* than required, even if some could do so at very low cost. There are many other problems with the direct-control-device approach that are more administrative in nature.

One approach sometimes advocated is of almost no help. "**Moral suasion**" (for example, in the form of television or newspaper ads exhorting people not to drive, to recycle, or to use less water) is hardly ever effective. This approach is useful in only two situations: in short-run emergencies, and when no other policy has benefits greater than costs. An example of the first type would be during unusual air-pollution-inversion conditions, when people would be asked not to drive and firms asked not to operate for a brief time. An example of the second would be policies dealing with litter in wilderness areas; not only would they not be "wilderness areas" if antilitter signs and police officers were present, but the cost would be prohibitive over the vast areas involved.

It is no doubt apparent by now that correcting market failures to provide public goods is a complex issue. The free-rider problem makes it difficult to determine values for public good. Lack of ownership and therefore lack of prices on scarce goods means that people do not face the proper incentive to economize on them. Policies commonly used to improve the situation sometimes make it worse! Are there any circumstances in which one can be more optimistic about market performance?

---

[6]Indeed, there is sometimes an incentive to ensure that control devices do *not* work. For example, unleaded gasoline is more expensive than leaded; a significant fraction (perhaps 10 percent) of drivers therefore put leaded gas in "unleaded only" cars. Two tankfuls ruin the catalytic converter, rendering the car about 100 times dirtier than if unleaded were used.

20.6 THE COASE THEOREM AND
THE IMPORTANCE OF TRANSACTION COSTS

Fortunately, environmental problems (and other public-good problems) are less numerous than one would initially suspect from the preceding discussion. In a classic paper, Ronald Coase observed that if benefits are greater than costs for some course of action (say, environmental cleanup), there must be potential transactions than can make some people better off without making anyone worse off.[7] To appreciate this important insight, consider the following problem:

A cattle rancher lives downstream from a paper mill. The paper mill dumps sulfurous compounds into the stream, which injures the rancher's cattle. If the rancher is not compensated, an externality exists. The question is: Why does the externality persist? Suppose the courts have established (perhaps because the paper mill was there first) that the property rights to the use (abuse) of the stream reside with the mill. If benefits are greater than costs of cleanup, the rancher should be willing to pay the mill owner to stop polluting. Let's assume the rancher's benefits from the cleanup (say $10,000) undertaken by the mill are greater than the cost (say $5,000). If the rancher were to offer $7,500 to the mill owner to undertake the cleanup activity, *both* the rancher and the mill owner would be better off than with continued pollution.[8] If, on the other hand, the property rights to the use of the stream resided with the rancher, and there was a sufficiently high benefit to the mill owner from polluting the river, then it would be rational for the mill owner to pay the rancher to adjust his cattle-raising activity up to the point where the marginal benefits to the mill owner of polluting equaled the marginal damages to the rancher from pollution. Apart from the wealth effect associated with the ownership right to use the stream (which would usually be fairly small), the outcome would be the same either way! Apart from property rights issues (about which there is much legal controversy), the socially desirable stream quality should therefore be attained.

The example hinges critically on low transaction costs between mill owner and rancher. **Transaction costs** are the costs of negotiating and executing an exchange, excluding the cost of the good or service bought. For example, when buying a car, it is usually rational for the buyer to spend some time searching for the "right" car and negotiating a mutually agreeable price.

Suppose that instead of one rancher there were a thousand, and that instead of one mill owner, there were ten—but, with the *same* total benefits and costs of cleanup. The

---

[7]This is the Pareto efficiency criterion. Note also that if an action exists that con make some people better off without making anyone worse off, it must also be possible to make *all* people better off by redistributing the benefits.

[8]In the terminology of the Edgeworth-exchange diagram, which is used to demonstrate the benefits of voluntary exchange diagram, which is used to demonstrate the benefits of voluntary exchange, the initial position is off the contract curve.

desirable outcome—that the workings of voluntary exchange will eliminate the externality—or, to say the same thing, that the optimal level of emissions will be present—would disappear. Not only would there be complicated issues of how to assign observed damages to specific mill owners, but each individual rancher might try to become a free rider. The $10,000 of benefits would now be only $10 per rancher, but the transactions costs of successfully dealing with the several polluters (either to bribe them or bring suit, depending on property rights assignment) would be far higher than that. Now imagine the complexities of more realistic cases: There are, for example, 12 million people within 60 miles of downtown Los Angeles. Each of them is damaged a little by each of a very large number of firms and other consumers (for example, automobile drivers).

It becomes apparent, therefore, why the inefficiencies resulting from pollution control are not eliminated by private negotiations. First, there is ambiguity regarding property rights in air, water, and other environmental media. Firms with historical ability to pollute resent controls, giving up their rights to pollute only if bribed; yet consumers feel they have the right to breathe clean air and use pristine water bodies. These conflicting positions must be resolved in court, with the winner being, of course, made wealthier. Second, transaction costs increase greatly with the number of transactors, making it next to impossible for individual firms and citizens to negotiate private agreements. Finally, the properties of air or water quality (and similar public goods) are such that additional people can enjoy the benefits at no additional cost and cannot be excluded from doing so. In practice, therefore, private agreements are unlikely to solve many problems of market failure.

It is, however, an easy jump to the conclusion that governments should solve any problems that cannot be solved by private actions. No solution may be possible, or that all solutions may involve costs that exceed benefits. In any event, the concepts developed in this chapter should enable those who wish to think carefully about such problems to formulate better policies than would otherwise be the case. (See Problems 20–6 and 20–7.)

20–6 A successful businessman has an aversion, arising from the death of several family members from lung cancer, to cigarette smoke. The costs of smoke in his mind are so great that if someone is smoking at a nearby table in a restaurant, he offers to pay the tab for their entire party if they will refrain from smoking. What levels of smoke pollution and food service would occur without his "bribe," and what levels occur with his "bribe?" Suppose the law changes and restaurants are required to have nonsmoking sections. What levels of smoke pollution from nearby tables and food service will result? How does the assignment of property rights to clean air affect the distribution of income?

In classroom experiments, nonsmokers have been willing to pay 10 to 100 times as much as smokers for their air rights.[9] It is therefore likely that the smokers in the restaurant would accept the bribe from the businessman. The level of pollution would be zero, and the level of food service may be greater than if the bribe had not been accepted because the businessman may otherwise leave the restaurant. This is an example of Coase's Theorem.

A nonsmoking-section requirement essentially shifts the property rights to air from smokers to nonsmokers. The businessman can eat in a smoke-free environment without having to make the bribe. The level of pollution and restaurant services is the same as with the bribe, but the income distribution has shifted in favor of nonsmokers.

---

[9]Lee Benham, "Comments of Lewit, Coate, and Grossman," *Journal of Law and Economics* 25 (December 1981), 571–573.

20–7 An economist claims that there is an "optimal" level of pollution, much to the chagrin of his wife, a nurse, who argues that pollution causes health hazards and should be greatly reduced if not eliminated. What is meant by the optimal level of pollution in the economist's view? Under what condition would zero pollution be optimal?

Pollution has costs and benefits. The benefits of pollution are lower production costs. The economist claims that the optimal level of pollution occurs where the marginal social cost and marginal social value of the polluting good are equal, as at Q_0 in Figure (a). For some pollutants such as plutonium, however, the potential health hazards are so great that the social costs may exceed the social value at all levels of output. In this instance, zero pollution is optimal as shown in Figure (b).

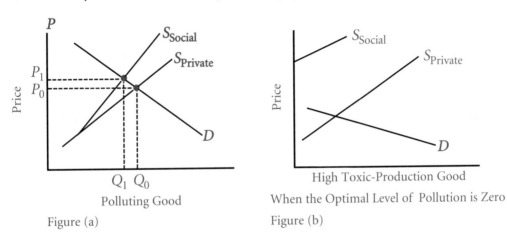

Figure (a)

Figure (b)

High Toxic-Production Good
When the Optimal Level of Pollution is Zero

THE ECONOMICS OF INFORMATION

As we discussed in Chapter 3, information is imperfect. Workers, for example, may be unaware of employment alternatives or a person planning to open a new restaurant does not have perfect information about the profit possibilities of different locations. Consumers cannot costlessly detect the precise quality of the product they are about to purchase. Nor do consumers know their exact preferences for goods for which they have no previous consumption experience. For example, how would consumers know in advance whether they liked mango pie if they had never tasted it before? Various imperfections in information is pervasive in the real world.

Information can be treated like most other scarce goods—it is desirable and limited, and people are willing to pay a positive price to obtain better information. Sometimes it is difficult to determine ex-ante whether the information you have received is worthwhile. You can protect yourself when you buy a new or used car with a warranty, but it is much more difficult to protect yourself when a stockbroker is offering to sell you a "hot tip."

Because information is usually costly to obtain, individuals will search for more information about a product or a job only if the expected marginal benefits of acquiring more information is greater than the expected marginal costs as seen in Figure 20–5. The costs of obtaining information about a product or job opportunities may be quite high. For example, let us say an individual is currently searching for a new employment opportunity. The associated search costs might include travel expenses, phone calls, placing "for hire" notices in newspapers, employment-agency fees, and, most important, the cost of the best alternative job offer that was rejected. It is rational to continue the search if the expected marginal benefits from continuing the search is greater than the cost of continuing the search. The **optimum level of search** occurs at Q* in Figure 20–5.

The marginal benefits of search decline as more time is devoted to search because after a certain period of time better jobs may become more difficult to find. As the search continues the marginal search costs rise as the individual finds higher paying (and higher amenity) jobs. How much information should an individual obtain before making a decision to accept a position? Enough information to establish that the expected marginal benefits of additional search are not greater than the expected marginal costs.

If information was perfect (costlessly available) searching for information would not be rational. However, in the real world, searching for "best" jobs or lowest product prices or services typically requires one to devote costly time and effort.

FIGURE 20–5
MARGINAL BENEFITS AND COSTS OF SEARCH

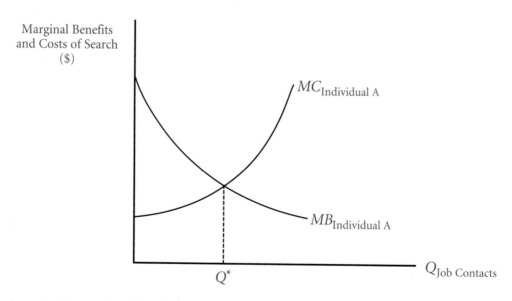

Consumers will search for additional information as long as the expected marginal benefits of further search are greater than the expected marginal cost—that is, until the consumer reaches Q*.

When the available information is initially distributed in favor of one party relative to another, there is said to exist an asymmetric distribution of information. One classic example of **asymmetric information** occurs in the used-car market where the seller of a used car has superior information about the car's condition than a potential buyer.[10] Suppose the seller of a defective used car (a "lemon") knows the car's defects and wants to sell the car. The problem is that the seller knows that the car has a specific defect in the transmission and that this defect is not costlessly detectable by a potential buyer. Without incurring significant quality-detection costs, like having it inspected by a mechanic, the buyer has an informational disadvantage relative to the seller. On the other hand, it is rational for the seller to claim that his car is in good shape and has no defects known to the seller—but the potential buyer cannot costlessly detect whether the car is a lemon or not. If the quality-detection costs are sufficiently high, a solution might be that used cars will be priced as if they were average quality. This means that the sellers of cars that are lemons will receive a payment that is more than the car is worth and the sellers of relatively high-quality cars will receive less than they are worth. However, if sellers of high-quality cars do not receive what the cars would sell for if the quality was known to the buyer, they would rationally withdraw their offers to sell their cars. Given the logical response of sellers of higher-than-average-quality cars, the average quality of used cars on the market will fall along with the price the potential buyers are willing to pay. In other words, the "bad cars have driven the good cars out of the market." This phenomenon is called **adverse selection**.

This distortion in the used-car market resulting from adverse selection can be eliminated by the buyer acquiring more information so that the two parties have equal information. In the used-car example, this might mean that an individual buyer would demand that an independent mechanic do a detailed inspection of the used car or that the dealership provide an extended warranty. This would help in eliminating the adverse-selection problem because buyers would have more information about the products they are buying.

The least-cost solution would have the seller reveal superior information to a potential buyer. The problem is that it is not individually rational for the seller to provide a truthful and complete disclosure, and this is known by a potential buyer. Only if the seller is punished for not truthfully revealing exchange-relevant information will a potential buyer perceive the seller's disclosure as truthful. (See Problem 20–8.)

---

[10]For more detail on asymmetric information, see George Akerlof, "The Market for 'Lemons': Qualitative Uncertainty and the Market Mechanism," *Quarterly Journal of Economics*, August 1970, 488–500.

20–8 True or False? Because individuals know a lot more about their health condition than an insurance company, we have another case of adverse selection.

True. Even after a medical examination, individuals know more about their health than the insurance company. After all, individuals have a better idea about their overall body condition and nutritional habits than an insurance company. However, the insurance company will set the premium for the average person, more-or-less meaning that the very healthy person will overpay and the unhealthy person will underpay. Insurance companies do, however, try to remedy the adverse-selection problem by requiring regular checkups, discounts for nonsmokers, charging different deductibles, different rates for different age and occupational groups, and so on.

MORAL HAZARD

Another information problem associated with the insurance market is **moral hazard**. If an individual is fully insured with fire, theft, auto, life, and so on, what incentives will this individual have to take additional precautions from risk? For example, a person with auto insurance will drive less cautiously than a person who does not have insurance. Those with health insurance will devote less effort and resources on preventive health maintenance than those who are not covered. The problem, of course, is that this could lead to much higher insurance rates if the insured are behaving more recklessly than they would if they were not insured. The moral hazard arises from the fact that it is costly for the insurer to monitor the behaviors of the insured party. For example, if individuals knew that their car was protected with a "bumper to bumper" warranty, they might have less incentive to take care of the car, despite the manufacturer's contract specifying that the warranty was only valid under "normal wear and tear". It would be too costly for the manufacturer to detect whether a product failure was the consequence of a manufacturing defect or the abuse of the owner-user. One method of controlling the user's potential abuse is to introduce a warranty agreement.

SIGNALING AND SCREENING

The existence of adverse selection may give rise to signaling behavior. For example, if a person is in the job market, the potential employer has little knowledge of the candidate's abilities. It would be in the best interest of the job candidate to supply as much valuable information as possible about her personal characteristics that are not on the resume. That is, it will be rational for the prospective job candidates to send a **signal** identifying their unique characteristics. The problem is that some of the candidates will possess superior characteristics, but which candidates? If knowledge and intelligence are important for the job, then years of education is one method of sorting out the candidates. Those that have performed well in school and have taken rigorous courses may be the company's best bet. While a college education may have increased the individual's productivity, the degree may send a more important signal about the person's intelligence and perseverance. In sum, education may be an important **screening** device that helps businesses make better choices about prospective employees.

Signals are important to employers because it cuts hiring costs. It would be very expensive to allow each candidate a "tryout". Hiring is a costly procedure, and to search, interview, and train each candidate to find out who is the best would be prohibitively costly.

PUBLIC CHOICE[11]

As we have discussed in this chapter, when the market fails as in the externality or the public-good case, it may be desirable for government to intervene and make public choices. However, according to Buchanan and Tullock, government actions in response to externalities may make matters worse.[12] Just because markets have failed doesn't necessarily mean that government can do any better.

Public-choice theory is the application of economic principles to politics. Public-choice economists believe that government is an outgrowth of individual behavior. Specifically, they assume that the behavior of individuals in politics, like that in the marketplace, will be influenced by self-interest. Bureaucrats, politicians, and voters make choices that they believe will yield expected marginal benefits that are greater than the expected marginal costs. There are, of course, differences between the private sector and the public sector in the "rules of the game." But the self-interest assumption is central to the analysis of behavior in both arenas.

Note that the self-interest assumption is not the only similarity between the market and public sectors. For example, scarcity is present in the public sector as well as the private sector. Public schools and public libraries come at the expense of something else. Competition is also present in the public sector as different government agencies compete for government funds and lobbyists compete with each other to get through favored legislation.

While there are similarities between market choice and political choice, there are also differences. For instance, the amount of information that is necessary to make an efficient decision is much greater in political markets than private markets. In a private market the only information that a potential buyer needs to know is how much he or she is willing to pay for the good and how much the seller is willing to accept for the good. The market price informs the buyer how much is necessary to entice the seller to supply the good. Only one question remains: Is the good worth more to the consumer

---

[11]My special thanks to Dwight Lee for his thoughts and suggestions in this section.
[12]See James M. Buchanan and Gordon Tullock, *The Calculus of Consent*, Chicago: The University of Chicago Press, 1962.

then he or she is willing to pay? If so, the consumer will purchase the good; if not, the consumer will not purchase the good. In either case, the consumer has enough information to make an efficient decision.

Information is much more difficult to obtain when a political good is being considered. The problem is that political decisions usually affect a lot of people. For example, if voters decide to increase national defense, everyone will receive more and pay higher taxes for the additional national defense. However, if this is an efficient political choice, it will require that we have information on everyone's preferences, not just the individual buyer and seller.

A similar problem occurs when the individual-consumption–payment link is broken. In private markets, when a shopper goes to the supermarket to purchase groceries, the shopping cart is filled with many different goods that the consumer presumably wants and is willing to pay for—this is the individual-consumption–payment link. The link breaks down when there is an assortment of political goods that have been decided on by majority rule. This might include such item as additional national defense, additional money for the space program, new museums, new public schools, and increased foreign aid. While an individual might be willing to pay for some of those goods, it is unlikely that he or she will want to consume or pay for all of them that have been presented in the *political shopping cart*. However, if the majority has decided that these political goods will be provided—whether the individual agrees or not—he or she will have to purchase the goods through higher taxes.

MAJORITY RULE AND THE MEDIAN VOTER

In a two-party system, the candidate with the most votes wins the election. Because voters are likely to vote for the candidate that who similar views, the candidates must pay close attention to the preference of the majority voters.

For example, in Figure 20–6, we assume a normal distribution, with a continuum of voter preferences from the liberal left tail to the conservative right tail. We can see from the figure that only a few are extremely liberal or extremely conservative. A successful campaign would have to address the concerns of the median voters if, as in this figure, most of the voters are in the moderate range then that would result in moderate policies. For example, if one candidate ran a fairly conservative campaign, attracting voters at and to the right of V_1, an opponent could win a landslide by taking a fairly conservative campaign just to the left of this candidate. Alternatively, if the candidate takes a liberal position, say V_2 then the opponent can win by taking a position just to the right of that position. In this case, it is easy to see that the candidate that takes the median position, V_M is less likely to be defeated. Of course, the distribution does not have to be normal or symmetrical; it could be skewed to the right or left. Regardless of the distribution, the successful candidate will still seek out the median voters. In fact, the model predicts there will be a strong tendency for both candidates to pick a position in the middle of the distribution, and therefore the election will be very close.

This, of course, does not mean that all politicians will find or even attempt to find the median. Politicians, for example, may take different positions because they have arrived at different predictions of voter preferences or merely misread the public sentiment, or they may think that they have the charisma to change voter preferences.

FIGURE 20–6
THE MEDIAN VOTER

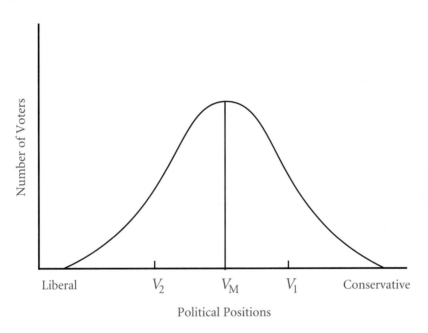

The median voter model predicts that there will be a strong tendency for both candidates to pick a position in the middle of the distribution, such as V_M, and that the election will be very close.

RATIONAL IGNORANCE

Representative democracy, has been a successful mechanism for making social choices in many countries. But there are some important differences in the way it is ideally supposed to work and how it actually does work.

One of the keys to an efficiently working democracy is a concerned and informed electorate. Everyone is supposed to take time to study the issues and candidates and then carefully weigh the relevant information before deciding how to vote. Although an informed citizenry is desirable from a social point of view, it's not clear that individuals will find it personally desirable to become politically informed.

Obtaining detailed information about issues and candidates is costly. Many issues are very complicated, and a great deal of technical knowledge and information is necessary to make an informed judgment on them. To find out how candidates really feel requires a lot more than listening to their campaign slogans. It requires studying their past voting records, reading a great deal that has been written either by or about them, and asking them questions at public meetings. Taking the time and trouble to do these things—and more—is the cost that each eligible voter has to pay personally for the benefits of being politically informed.

What are the benefits of being politically informed? Basically, there are two. Some people simply enjoy being informed. These people will be willing to make an effort to acquire some information on public issues just for the sake of knowledge. The other benefit from being informed has nothing to do with satisfying intellectual curiosity. By being politically informed, individuals have the knowledge to influence social decisions in directions that will yield them the greatest benefit. Unfortunately, this does little to motivate most people to become informed, because it isn't much of a benefit. The probability of one person's vote having any effect on an election is practically zero. With thousands voting in local elections and millions voting in state and national elections, each citizen is safe in assuming that his or her vote really doesn't count.

So, for most people, the costs of becoming politically informed are noticeable, while the benefits are negligible. As a result, most people limit their quest for political information to listening to the radio on the way to work, to conversations with friends, to casual reading, and to other things they normally do anyway. Even though most people in society would be better off if everyone became more informed, it isn't worth the cost for most individuals to make an effort to become informed themselves. There are obvious advantages to be realized if the public became more politically aware. Unfortunately, there doesn't seem to be any easy or desirable way of overcoming the problem of rational ignorance. Perhaps the government could require everyone to become politically well informed. If the government did that, however, how would they determine when an individual is adequately informed? Unfortunately, most of us find a close correlation between how much others agrees with us and how well informed they are. Pushing very far in the direction of having the government require and test political awareness might, therefore, lead to abuses that could offset the benefits of having a more-informed society. According to public-choice economists, political apathy is not the result of moral decay or lack of patriotism in our society. It's simply the result of individuals acting rationally. (See Problem 20–9.)

20–9 With only two out of three eligible voters registered, the "motor voter" bill has recently been passed which will use the Department of Motor Vehicles to increase voter registration. If voter registration is done in conjunction with drivers licenses it is estimated that 91 percent of the eligible voters will then be registered to vote. True or False? This will resolve the problem of rational ignorance.

False. According to public choice economists, the reasons for voter apathy have little to do with the number of voters registered and everything to do with individual incentives; that is, no matter how many voters are registered, individuals will still weigh their benefits and costs before voting.

SPECIAL INTEREST

This does not mean that public-choice economists think that everyone is politically apathetic or rationally ignorant. This obviously is not the case. Many have a large stake in being politically informed on particular issues. For example, individuals may have a strong motivation to organize a political pressure group. As a group they are more likely to influence decision makers and have a far greater impact on the outcome of a social decision than they would with just their one vote. Also, member of these special-interest groups will find it easier to organize because of the commonality of their goals and purpose. Finally, the smaller the group and the more specific their interest, the less costly it will become to organize and get everyone to contribute their share. It is not surprising, therefore, that special-interest groups are often able to bring a great deal of political pressure to bear on certain public decisions.

But what about those not in the special-interest group? They will pay the bill if the special-interest group is successful. Why can't the majority of citizens effectively counter the political power of a minority group? The answer to this question lies in the fact that the majority makes up such a large group. If the special-interest group is successful in getting everyone else to pay for a project that benefits them, the cost will be spread over such a large number of taxpayers that the amount any one person will have to pay is negligible. There isn't much motivation for an individual citizen to spend time and effort to resist an interest group, even if it were guaranteed that this resistance would be effective.

When a special-interest issue comes up that benefits the few at the expense of the many, it is likely that elected representatives will be solicited by special-interest groups. Because the special-interest activity will likely impose only small individual costs, those paying the bill may hear little or nothing. That is, if each representative believes that a favorable vote will be recognized and appreciated by those in favor of it and will go unnoticed by those paying the bill, then he or she might be willing to support the special-interest group. Because being reelected and receiving financial support is obviously important to elected representatives, special-interest groups will be very effective at influencing their voting behavior. The other side of the coin is that it is difficult to reduce government programs once they are in place. Government programs that arise because of the influence of special interests will generally be perpetuated by the influence of special interests. The elimination of such a program will deny a few significant benefits, while saving each general taxpayer but a few dollars in taxes. This might explain why it is so difficult politically to reduce government spending, even if the majority of the voters favored such a reduction in general. When people argue for cutting government spending, they invariably have in mind government programs other than the ones that benefit them. So any attempt to reduce government spending by isolating one program at a time generally meets strong resistance from those benefiting from the program under review and receives little support from the millions of taxpayers who will save but a few dollars each if the program were eliminated.

According to public-choice economists, the best hope for controlling government is by presenting a political package that calls for a simultaneous reduction in many programs. No special interest will be willing to sacrifice its program if it expects to be required to continue paying for the program of others. But if government has grown to the point where people feel that they are not getting their money's worth for the taxes they pay, then many groups will be willing to see their program reduced—if it means some savings on the taxes paid to support everyone else's programs. (See Problem 20–10.)

20–10   True or False? Many big cities have either built or are planning on building large sports arenas, largely at the taxpayers' expense. Sports arenas will bring recognition and fame to the city, and this will benefit everyone who lives in the city because they will be living in a more prestigious community. Everyone in the city should therefore contribute to the sports arena, whether they go to the games or not.

The people who receive the primary benefit from a sports arena are those who frequent them to watch ball games. It's easy to prevent a person from receiving this benefit if he or she doesn't pay at the gate. The assertion that everyone would benefit from the arena whether they go to the games or not has to be questioned. A sports arena will generate growth and congestion that many will find undesirable. To these people, paying for a big sports center makes no sense.

Perhaps some people who never go to a sporting event may feel a little bit better just knowing they can. This is what economists call option demand. But does this justify commandeering funds from everyone in the city to build a sports arena? What about fine restaurants? Certainly fine restaurants enhance the reputation of the city. Many people are happy to know that one is nearby, waiting to serve them, whether they visit it or not. But most people would find a proposal to publicly finance restaurants a little farfetched. If desirable side effects justified government subsidies, well-kept yards, car washes, toothpaste, deodorants, and smiles would all qualify for a handout.

Regardless of the desirability of requiring the public to pay for certain things, it should be noted that special-interest groups expend a lot of effort to obtain subsidies for those things from which they receive enjoyment and profit. Many of these efforts have been successful; the sports arena example is only one of many. The more "cultured," and usually wealthier, members of some cities have managed to obtain government support for symphonies, operas, ballet, and the performing arts in general. The stated justification for requiring everyone to pay for entertainment that caters primarily to the tastes of the cultured is similar to that given for subsidizing sports arenas. Supposedly, everyone in a community will benefit, even those who prefer to sit home with a can of beer and watch all-star wrestling on television. (See Problem 20–11.)

20–11   Many cities have decided that it is important to provide municipal golf courses yet many complain that there are still too few municipal courses. True or False? This may be a case where nongolfers are subsidizing golfers?

True. Many cities have decided that everyone benefits from golf courses, whether he or she plays golf or not. Consequently, people in many communities find themselves contributing to public golf courses and subsidizing golfers. Still, many golfers complain there are still too few municipal courses. One wonders how many golfers would complain of the insufficient number of golf courses if their green fees were raised to cover the full cost of providing these courses.

CLOSING THOUGHTS ON PUBLIC CHOICE

Public-choice economists are convinced that we can get more from government only by having less government. They recognize that the advantages of government are found in its ability to establish a legal and economic environment that provides general opportunity for people to benefit from their own efforts through productive cooperation with others. But they also see the threat of government if its power is captured by organized special interests and used to advance narrow objectives by imposing costs on the general public. Also if the government becomes a vehicle for promoting special interests, it fails in its primary responsibility of expanding opportunities for all; that is, instead of creating opportunities for people to benefit through productive cooperation with each other, government will have created the illusion that people can benefit at the expense of each other. Public-choice economists are not callously indifferent to the social benefits that government can provide. In fact, the difference between public-choice economists and those who see every social ill as justification for expanding government is not a difference in moral vision. Instead, it is a difference in interpretation or understanding of how government actually works. Public-choice economists lean towards less government, not because they want less from government but because they believe that it is important to get more from it.

SUMMARY

1. Sometimes the unconstrained workings of the market result in the "wrong" levels of output for particular goods. While monopoly, monopsony, income-distributional problems, and tax distortions may also be of importance, this chapter focuses on public goods and externalities as causes of resource misallocation.

2. Externalities are "uncompensated spillovers" that cause the private benefits or costs of an action to differ from the social benefits or costs. As a consequence, too little or too much is produced from society's perspective.

3. Because the use of a public good is nonexcludable, no private supplier receives sufficient incentive to produce it; producers would be unable to cover costs with revenues because of the free-rider problem.

4. Externalities and public goods are closely related: A firm that produces a good involving negative externalities (such as pollution emissions) tends to cause the level of some public good (air or water quality) to be low nonoptimally.

5. The efficient provision of a public good may be accomplished either by direct government production or by some method of making the private benefits and costs correspond to the true social benefits and costs (with subsidies or taxes, for example).

6. *If* property rights are well defined and transaction costs are small, externalities will tend to become internalized by either legal action (if rights to use the air or water reside with households) or "bribes" (if rights to use the environmental media reside with owners of firms). However, the large number of those emitting pollutants and, especially, of those being damaged greatly reduces the practical significance of this observation.

7. Information is scarce. Individuals will search for additional information if the expected marginal benefits of acquiring additional information are greater than the expected marginal costs.

8. When the available information is initially distributed in favor of one party relative to another, there is a asymmetric distribution of information problem.

9. The distortions caused by asymmetric information problems can be eliminated by the buyer acquiring more information so that the buyer and seller have equal information.

10. The moral hazard arises from the fact that it is too costly for the insurer to monitor the behavior of the insured party.

11. Public-choice theory is the application of economic principles to politics. Public-choice economists assume that the behavior of individuals in politics, like that in the marketplace, will be influenced by self-interest. Bureaucrats, politicians, and voters make choices that they believe will yield expected marginal benefits that are greater than the expected marginal costs.

12. The median-voter model predicts that there will be a strong tendency for both candidates to pick a position in the middle of the voting distribution and that elections will be very close.

13. Rational ignorance is the condition where voters tend to be uninformed because of high information costs and the low benefits of being politically informed. One benefit from being informed is satisfying intellectual curiosity. The other is to have the knowledge to influence social decisions in directions that will yield them the greatest benefit. Unfortunately, this does little to motivate most people to become informed because the probability of one person's vote having any effect on an election is practically zero.

14. Individuals may have a strong motivation to organize a political pressure group. As a group they are more likely to influence decision makers and have a far greater impact on the outcome of a social decision than they would with just their one vote. Also, member of these special-interest groups will find it easier to organize because of the commonality of their goals and purpose. Finally, the smaller the group and the more specific their interest, the easier it will become to organize and get everyone to contribute their share.

WORDS AND CONCEPTS FOR REVIEW

social marginal value	social marginal cost
externalities	negative externalities
positive externalities	public goods
nonexcludability	nonrivalrous
free rider	horizontal summation
vertical summation	transaction costs
moral suasion	optimal level of search
asymmetric information	adverse selection

moral hazard

signaling

screening

public-choice theory

rational ignorance

special-interest groups

REVIEW QUESTIONS

1. Why is the outcome of voluntary exchange in the market usually considered to be socially optimal? When would this outcome not be appropriate?

2. What properties characterize a public good? If such properties hold for a good, what is the socially optimal price to charge for this good? What problem results from actually charging the socially optimal price?

3. Why does recognition of the free-rider problem in providing public goods not cause people to contribute on the grounds that they know they will not get the good at all without doing so? Because they all know this, they might contribute enough to get the good. Would the likelihood of this happening be greater or less if a small number of people were affected?

4. How might one design a social policy relating to loud fraternity parties? Suppose the fraternity were taxed an amount per party that would just compensate those damaged (leaving them on the same indifference curve with the party and compensation, or without the party and compensation). Suppose further that the fraternities traditionally had two types of parties—either loud-rock-music/beer-bash dancing parties (now subject to tax), or quiet classical background-music/wine-and-cheese conversational parties (not subject to tax). What impact would you expect the tax to have on (a) the overall number of parties and (b) the ratio of beer bashes to wine-and-cheese parties? (Hint: Employ indifference-curve analysis.)

5. Would the results in Question 4 depend on whether the revenues from the loud-party tax were actually distributed to the neighbors? Or is that a value judgment about which people could have different opinions? (Hint: This is a complicated question. For simplicity, assume the tax revenue collected would be too small per neighbor to affect any neighbor's income negligibly, therefore, the demands for quiet.)

6. Can you think of any positive externalities from a firm's production?

7. Suppose there is substantial variation in air quality within an urban area. If people are aware of both the nature of pollution damages and the air quality at each location, will the resource misallocation be less severe or more severe than if the same average air quality were distributed uniformly everywhere? (Hint: If people are affected differently, with some greatly damaged and some harmed very little, will the bidding in land markets reduce external damages by, in effect, partly converting a public good to a private good?)

8. If you were in the market for a new car, how much information would you have to obtain before you made your decision to purchase?

9. How do you correct for the problems of adverse selection? What impact would better signaling, such as brand names and warranties, have on this problem?

10. How do insurance companies try to overcome the problem of moral hazard?

11. According to public-choice economists, it is possible that government policies designed to correct externalities could make matters worse. Why?

12. Using the idea of rational ignorance, make an analogy between rooting for your favorite politician and rooting for your favorite team. If voting is a consumption decision rather than an investment decision, how might this affect your decision to vote?

SUGGESTED READINGS

Coase, Ronald. "The Problem of Social Cost," *Journal of Law and Economics,* October 1960, 1–45.

Coase, Ronald. "The Lighthouse in Economics," *Journal of Law and Economics,* October 1974, 357–376.

Tietenberg, Tom. *Environmental and Natural Resource Economics,* 3rd ed. New York: HarperCollins, 1992.

Ruff, Larry E. "The Economic Common Sense of Pollution," *The Public Interest,* Spring 1970, 69–85.

Scherer, F. M., and David Ross, *Industrial Market Structure and Economic Performance,* 3rd ed. Boston: Houghton Mifflin, 1990.

APPENDIX A

ECONOMETRICS
AND SUPPLY AND DEMAND

INTRODUCTION

Econometrics is the branch of economics that employs economic theory and statistical methods "as analytical foundation stones and economic data as the information base."[1] The literal meaning of the word *econometrics* is "economic measurement," and this is the main task of all empirical research in economics. As a matter of practice, however, the word is ordinarily used to refer only to empirical research that is concerned with the measurement of economic relationships formulated in explicitly mathematical terms. From this point of view, econometrics is best regarded as an applied branch of mathematical economics. Any economic relationship that can be expressed as a mathematical equation may therefore be considered a potential object of econometric study. Such relations include supply-and-demand functions, production functions, cost functions, equations and inequalities used in linear programming problems, and so forth. To state the matter another way, econometrics is concerned with the empirical measurement of economic relations that are simple enough to be expressible in mathematical form. The potential scope of econometrics, thus conceived, is relatively broad. At the present time, it obviously cannot provide answers to all economic questions. It is, however, a potentially promising approach to the study of economic phenomena. This appendix explains the nature of the econometric approach, some of its basic concepts and methods, and its merits and weaknesses.

---

[1]Judge et al., *The Theory and Practice of Econometrics,* New York: Wiley, 1985, p. 1.

THE NATURE OF ECONOMETRICS

A hypothetical example will help clarify the basic features and objectives of econometric study. Suppose that the government plans to initiate a crop-restriction program in order to raise farm prices and increase farm incomes. Historical data on average farm production and average market prices are available on an annual basis for a number of years. An examination of these data indicates that a particular volume of production sometimes sells at one level of price and sometimes at another. This historical knowledge, by itself, gives no indication of the extent to which changes in farm production result in changes in price. For the crop-restriction program to be successful, however, the government must estimate approximately a year in advance the probable level of prices that will be associated with any given level of production. To do this, the government needs accurate quantitative estimates of the demand-and-supply functions of various agricultural commodities.

For example, if the exact nature of the demand curve for wheat is known, it is possible to predict the equilibrium price of wheat with a given level of production, that is, the price that will clear the market. If the size of the wheat crop in a particular year can be estimated on the basis of information about rainfall, prices, acreage planted, and similar factors from previous years, it will then be possible to predict the approximate price of wheat in the given year on the basis of historical knowledge.

The only way to discover the actual demand curve for wheat is to study data of past years on wheat consumption, wheat prices, and similar magnitudes. Economic theory suggests that the demand curve is downward sloping, but it does not provide precise information about the shape of the demand curve or the factors that control its position. In other words, economic theory provides qualitative but not quantitative information about the demand curve. The task of econometrics is to develop this quantitative information.

To obtain some idea of the quantitative properties of the demand curve, it is necessary initially to assume that the quantity of wheat demanded depends on certain measurable data such as the price of corn, the price of beans, national income, population, and so on, as well as the price of wheat. Historical measures of these data may then be used to arrive at a provisional estimate of the extent to which each of the factors influences the demand for wheat. If some of the factors appear not to influence demand at all, they may be eliminated from the relations originally suggested by economic theory. All of the factors studied may not suffice to provide a satisfactory explanation of observed variations in quantity demanded. Certain additional data may then have to be introduced into the relation suggested by economic theory to arrive at a satisfactory quantitative description of the demand curve for wheat.

Econometrics can seldom provide precise knowledge of economic relations by this procedure. While the results are only approximate at best, they may nevertheless provide sufficiently accurate quantitative content to the purely qualitative relationships of economic theory to permit quantitative rather than qualitative predictions. For example, while on the basis of economic theory alone, it is possible only to say that a 10-percent increase in wheat production will lead to a *lower* price of wheat, econometric analysis may make is possible to say that a 10-percent increase in wheat production will lead to a *decline of approximately 20-percent in the price of wheat.* From a practical point of view, there is a vast difference between the two statements.

The first major task of econometrics, therefore, is to provide quantitative supplemental information to the purely qualitative statements suggested by economic theory and by everyday experience. In turn, these quantitative relationships, to the extent they are accurate, permit specific quantitative predictions of future events to be made—the second major task of econometrics.

THE SCOPE OF ECONOMETRICS

Econometrics potentially includes within its scope all work in economics that is concerned with empirical data. As a matter of practice, however, the work is largely confined to certain problems of the type included in partial-equilibrium theory and in national income and employment theory. The first category includes estimating supply-and-demand functions, forecasting price in a single market, and estimating cost curves and production functions. In the national-income-theory field, attention has been given to forecasts of consumer demand at various levels of income and to estimates of the demand for money. However, several large-scale econometric studies (such as the DRI, Wharton, or Chase Econometrics models) have dealt with the overall behavior of the United States economy. Similar attempts have been made to describe the working of the Canadian economy and of many other economic systems. The projects have not been entirely successful from a predictive point of view, but they have yielded much valuable factual knowledge. What is perhaps more important at this stage in the development of econometrics is that they have indicated areas in which further theoretical and empirical research is needed if future projects are to be more fruitful.

CONCEPTS AND GENERAL APPROACH OF ECONOMETRICS

Because econometrics seeks to add quantitative content to relationships of economic analysis, it must concern itself not only with data collection and statements of theoretical analysis but also with interrelationships between them. Specifically, it must select data in terms of relations suggested by economic analysis, and at the same time adapt these relations in a fashion that permits quantification of them with available data and techniques. These problems must be considered in greater detail.

Starting from a given collection of facts about a particular situation, the econometrician's first task is to decide what portion of the information already available is relevant to the task at hand and what further information is required. Neither task is simple.

Suppose that the econometrician is seeking to estimate the demand for a single commodity—corn, for example. For this purpose, it will be desirable to have as much information as possible about past production, consumption, and price, but no collection of statistics on corn alone will permit estimation of the demand for corn unless by remote chance the demand for corn is independent of all other aspects of economic activity. The problem may be clarified by an illustration, as shown in Figure A–1. With quantities of corn consumed measured on the horizontal axis and prices of corn on the vertical axis, a collection of historical quantity-price data may be represented by a *scatter diagram* in which each point corresponds to a single historical observation. If the scatter diagram is like the one in Figure A–1a, curve D might be regarded as a reasonable estimate of the demand curve for corn. If, on the other hand, the scatter diagram is more like the one in Figure A–1b or Figure A–1c, on the other hand, no single estimate of the demand curve would seem more logical than another; on the contrary, it is obvious that some factor other than price is influencing the consumption of corn, and further information must be sought.

Actually, the evidence provided by the scatter diagram of Figure A–1a is just as ambiguous as that in the other two cases. Although the scatter of points appears to show an obvious demand curve, it could represent a *collection* of demand curves, each point being on a different curve, as illustrated in Figure A–2. Indeed, if it were known that hog production had been increasing steadily for a number of years, the second interpretation of the scatter in Figure A-1a might seem more plausible than the first; one would not expect the position of the demand curve to be unchanged year after year if the number of hogs was increasing. Moreover, we have been implicitly assuming that the observed scatter diagram represents price-quantity demanded observations, when in fact those observations are market observations on price and the *intersection* of demand and supply. The supply curve and the demand curve both move over time. It becomes difficult to "identify" the separate curves, as discussed later.

FIGURE A–I
SCATTER DIAGRAMS

Identification of the demand curve requires more information than just past observations on price and quantity. Each observation is an equilibrium point and represents the intersection of the demand-and-supply curves. Because demand and supply shift over time because of changes in the shift parameters, the price-quantity data points do not necessarily map out the demand curve.

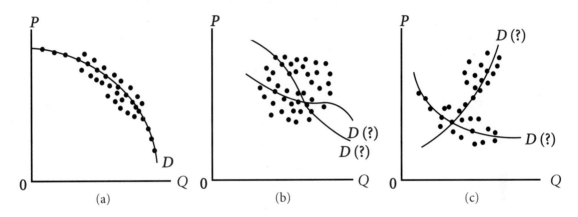

FIGURE A–2
DEMAND-CURVE AMBIGUITY

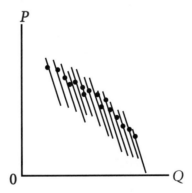

Each observation plotted in Figure A–I(a) may represent a point on a different demand curve.

The implication of this ambiguity is that facts alone never speak for themselves, and no interpretation of factual data can ever be regarded as final unless one knows the precise nature of the process by which the data are generated. In the case of economics, the nature of the data-generation process is seldom known with any precision.

To deal with a problem of the kind illustrated, the econometrician is forced to undertake a kind of "fishing expedition." One starts with certain basic facts and then casts a net as widely as possible to discover whether other facts are available that might have a bearing on the interpretation of the original data. In particular, the researcher must obtain information about factors other than price that may influence the consumption of corn, such as prices in other markets, production and consumption of related commodities, consumer income, government purchasing programs, and so on. The econometrician must also investigate the process by which the price of corn is determined, that is, acquire information about the production and marketing of corn. For example, the amount of corn supplied to the market may come partly from current production and partly from existing stocks. In this case the behavior of the market will depend partly on changes in stocks, making the data required to describe variations in price and consumption more difficult to obtain and more complicated to analyze.

To add to the complications already mentioned, consumption, production, and price reactions observed during one period of time may be the result of events occurring at an earlier period. To take this possibility into account, it may be necessary to attach some references to factual data, that is, to date the various prices on the scatter diagrams. This will almost inevitably increase the range of admissible interpretations of the data and so increase the difficulty of arriving at definite conclusions about the nature of the process by which the data are generated.

THEORETICAL CONSIDERATIONS

The role of economic theory in econometrics is to provide a set of "hooks" upon which facts of particular kinds may be hung. In effect, the econometrician starts with a vast collection of hooks, most of them unencumbered by facts, and then proceeds from one hook to another, asking in each case whether the kinds of facts a particular hook is designed to hold are relevant to the problem at hand. If the hooks are few in number or difficult to discern (that is, if the theory is narrow in scope or ambiguous in meaning), the econometrician may easily overlook relevant facts and arrive at a poor solution to the problem. Alternatively, one may recognize the inadequacy of the theory and be forced to devote as much attention to a search for additional hooks as looking for facts. The ideal situation is one in which the basic theory is relatively comprehensive and reasonably precise, but this is not always the case in practice.

Even if existing theory is adequate, the data actually available to the econometrician are not likely to conform exactly to specifications suggested by theory. Where theory requires daily or weekly data on prices and quantities, for example, the econometrician may have to settle for quarterly or annual figures. Similarly, where theory refers to data involving quantities with adjustments to equilibrium completed, the econometrician is forced to work with actual quantities, and these are not likely to reflect complete attainment of equilibrium. Difficulties of this kind cannot be overcome by ignoring them; the basic theory must be modified so that it can be used to interpret the data that are actually available.

Likewise, in the course of an econometric study, certain calculations often cannot be performed unless relations suggested by existing theory are first simplified. For example, as a practical matter, econometric work is often confined to *linear relations* (represented geometrically by straight lines) rather than *nonlinear relations* (represented geometrically by curves other than straight lines). The precise form of a linear relation is determined simply by its *slope* relative to the axes on which the variables included in the relations are measured. The form of many nonlinear relations, on the other hand, can be specified only if much additional information is provided.

The importance of this consideration can be illustrated by consideration of the usual two-dimensional curve. If the "curve" in question is a straight line, one number (representing the slope of the curve relative to the X axis) suffices to determine the *form* of the relation, and another number (representing, for example, the point at which the line crosses the X axis) suffices to fix the *position* of the line. If the curve contains bends or kinks, however, as would be true if it were part of a circle, knowledge about the slope and position of one section of the curve would not indicate the nature of the curve in other sections. The use of nonlinear relations in econometrics is becoming increasingly common. There is, however, no need to use more complicated relations without first attempting to get along without them, and within a limited range, most curves can be approximated fairly well by straight lines.

Other kinds of simplifications are also used in econometric work, as will be indicated in more detail later. It must be emphasized that these simplifications are introduced to avoid various practical difficulties. However, such simplifications involve the introduction of new and essentially untested hypotheses about the form of relations suggested by economic theory. An important task of econometric research, therefore, is to select simplifications that permit practical work but do not materially alter the character of the original theoretical model.

In current practice, most econometric analyses follow a standard pattern. The data relevant to a given problem are first divided into two classes: data that are to be interpreted by the theory and data that are to be taken as given. The variables of the theory are then divided into two corresponding categories, *endogenous* and *exogenous*, according to the same principle; and a series of theoretical *structural relations* or *structural equations* is established, relating the various endogenous variables to one another and to the exogenous variables. The purpose of this procedure is to arrive at a system of relations (simultaneous equations) that can be used to determine the "unknown" values of the endogenous variables in terms of the "given" values of the exogenous variables.

A theory intended to describe price determination in a single market—say, the market for corn—could be represented by a system of three linear *structural equations*:

$$d_c = a_1 p_c + B_1 h \quad \text{(demand)}$$
$$(1) \quad s_c = a_2 p_c + B_2 r \quad \text{(supply)}$$
$$d_c = s_c \quad \text{(market clearance)}$$

In this system, d_c, s_c, and p_c are *endogenous variables* representing, respectively, the current demand, supply, and price of corn. The symbols h and r represent *exogenous variables* and describe, respectively, the current stock of hogs and annual rainfall. The symbols a_1, a_2, B_1, and B_2 represent given constants called *structural parameters*. The particular values assigned to these structural parameters determine the precise form of the structural relations of the system and so determine indirectly the equilibrium values of the endogenous variables d_c, s_c, and p_c corresponding to given values of the exogenous variables h and r.

A geometric interpretation of system (1) is presented in Figure A–3. The lines d_c^1, d_c^2, and d_c^3 represent three out of an indefinitely large number of possible positions of the demand "curve" corresponding to a *given value* of the structural parameter a_1 (which fixes the slope of each of the demand lines) and *three different values*, h_1, h_2, and h_3, of the exogenous variable h (stock of hogs). The extent to which changes in the value of h alter the position of the demand relation depends on the magnitude of the structural parameter B_1; for example, if B_1 were twice as great, the demand lines illustrated in the figure would be more widely spaced. Similarly, the lines s_c^1, s_c^2, and s_c^3 represent three possible positions of the supply "curve" corresponding to a given value of the structural parameter a_2 (which fixes the slope of each supply relation) and three different values r_1, r_2, and r_3 of the exogenous variable r (rain). The "shift effect" of changes in the variable r will depend, of course, on the magnitude of the structural parameter B_2. The line corresponding to the equation $d_c = s_c$ cannot be drawn explicitly in this graph because the variables d_c and s_c are not measured on separate axes. However, this market clearance condition will be satisfied at the intersection of the supply line and a demand line for given h and r.

Suppose, for example, that h has the particular value h_1 while r has the particular value r_1 and that h_1 and r_1 represent particular numbers such as 3 million hogs and 40 inches of rain. The corresponding demand-and-supply relations are represented by d_c^1 and s_c^1, respectively, and the equilibrium price is given by p_c^1 (a particular number, determined by the market clearance equation, $d_c^1 = d_s^1$). Different values of the exogenous variables r and h would determine different demand and supply lines, and so a different equilibrium price. Moreover, different values of the structural parameters a_1 and a_2 would result in demand-and-supply lines with different *slopes*, and thus a different equilibrium price. Finally, different values of the structural parameters B_1 and B_2 would determine different *positions* of the demand-and-supply lines, and so, once more, different equilibrium prices.

Thus, the implications for price and quantity determination of the system of equations (1) differ depending on the particular values assigned to the exogenous variables h and r and the structural parameters a_1, a_2, B_1, B_2. That is to say, the particular equilibrium values of the endogenous variables d_c, s_c, and p_c that satisfy the three equations in System (1) vary according to the internal structure of the system as determined by the particular values of the structural parameters a_1, a_2, B_1, B_2 and the external factors affecting the system as determined by the particular values of the exogenous variables h and r.

This geometric representation of the system of linear structural equations highlights the three endogenous variables, quantity demanded, quantity supplied, and price, and the two exogenous variables (or shifters), stock of hogs and rainfall. Each demand curve corresponds to a different quantity of hogs and has a slope equal to the structural parameter a_1. The slope of the supply curve is a_2, and different levels of rainfall produce different supply curves.

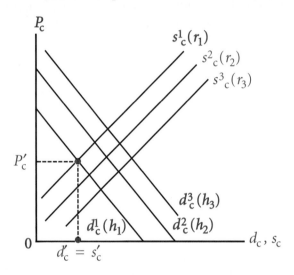

MODELS AND STRUCTURES

A general system of equations such as (1), with the values of the structural parameters not specified exactly, is referred to as a *model*. If *specific* values are assigned to the parameters of the system, the system is known as a *structure* rather than a model. In other words, every model is an infinite class of different possible structures. The model is essentially *qualitative* in character; each structure represents a particular *quantitative* form of the model.

In this terminology, the purpose of econometric study may be restated as follows. First, the study seeks to establish, with the aid of economic theory, a tentatively acceptable model, which is in purely qualitative terms. Next, on the basis of empirical data about past values of the endogenous and exogenous variables, it seeks to determine the particular quantitative structure contained within the model, that is, a set of values for the structural parameters of the model, which produces a set of values of the endogenous variables in accord with actual data of past experience. This structure can then be used to predict the magnitudes of endogenous variables in future periods, on the assumption that the parameters and exogenous variables for these future periods will be the same as in the past or will change in some specified way.

MODELS WITH ERROR TERMS

An obvious difficulty with this procedure is that no structure contained in a linear model (or for that matter, in any theoretical model) is likely to yield predictions that are completely accurate. Even with the most careful work and the most ingenious theories, errors are bound to occur because of imperfections in data, omission of relevant exogenous variables, unanticipated nonlinearities, and unforeseen changes in the behavioral and institutional character of the situation being studied.

To take some of these difficulties into account, and also to avoid working with models that are known in advance to provide a false picture of reality, it is standard econometric practice to introduce certain latent (unobservable) *error terms* into every econometric model. The model described by System (1), for example, would normally be written in the form

$$
\begin{aligned}
d_c &= a_1 p_c + B_1 h + u_1 \\
(2) \quad s_c &= a_2 p_c + B_2 r + u_2 \\
d_c &= s_c + u_3
\end{aligned}
$$

with the additional error variables u_1, u_2, and u_3 in each relation representing various unknown factors not otherwise taken into account in the model.

With a model of this kind, together with certain assumptions about the nature of the error variables u_1, the purpose of econometric study may be modified as that of determining the structure contained in the model that is *most nearly* in accord with known facts—that is, determining values of the structural parameters that lead to predicted values of the endogenous variables d_c, s_c, and p_c, that differ as little as possible from their observed values.

THE COMPLEXITY OF THE MODELS

The preceding discussion gives only a hint of the possible complexity and generality of econometric models. Systems may involved 150 or more equations, consider not only current but also past (lagged) values of both endogenous and exogenous variables, and work with nonlinear as well as linear relations. This does not begin to exhaust the list of possible complications.

PROBLEMS OF ESTIMATION

While collecting data and constructing provisionally satisfactory theoretical models are more than half the battle in most econometric studies, the remaining task is not merely a matter of routine computation. It would be if models that provided perfectly accurate simulation of observed economic phenomena were feasible, for straightforward calculations would suffice to indicate whether a model did or did not provide a precise description of available empirical data.

In actual practice, however, there are major complications. First, available empirical data do not always provide enough information to permit the econometrician to say whether a chosen model is satisfactory; in order to carry out an analysis, it may be necessary to reformulate the model or to search out additional data. Second, even if available data appear to provide some information about the adequacy of a given theoretical model, the information provided may not be detailed or exact enough to permit the econometrician to choose a single "best" structure from the set of structures contained within a given model. Third, there are various alternative methods of calculating numerical estimates of the structural parameters in any given model, and different methods do not always lead to the same results. The advantages and disadvantages of different methods of calculation are difficult to determine on logical grounds. Each of these three problems merits brief discussion.

THE IDENTIFICATION PROBLEM

A simplified example will illustrate the first of the problems of estimation mentioned above, that is, situations in which available empirical data do not permit the econometrician to decide whether a chosen model is or is not worthwhile. Suppose that price in a given market is known to be determined by current supply-and-demand forces, in the sense that the market price always adjusts immediately to the level that is required to make quantity supplied equal to quantity demanded. With available data on prices and quantities exchanged, however, it may not be possible to distinguish between supply-and-demand relations because the data on quantity exchanged represent both quantity supplied and quantity demanded at the equilibrium. This problem is called the *identification problem* because of the impossibility in such cases of separating the data for the various structural relations in the theoretical models, that is, of identifying which data applies to a particular relationship. The difficulty is most easily appreciated by considering the price-quantity data that relate to various demand-and-supply curves. Suppose, for example, that a shifting demand curve is combined with a fixed supply curve, as in Figure A–4. This will yield a series of "observable" equilibrium points on the supply curve. However, the *same* series of "observable" points could just as well have been generated by a shifting demand curve combined with a *shifting* supply curve, as illustrated in Figure A–5.

From a given set of structural relations and given information about shifts in these relations, it is possible to obtain precisely one set of "observable" points; but the *reverse* operation—that of obtaining a given set of structural relations and shifts from a given set of "observable" points—cannot be carried out in the absence of additional information. If it is known, for example, that the supply curve shifts from year to year according to the amount of rainfall, whereas the demand curve does not shift at all, it may be possible to identify the demand curve from observable price-quantity data.

FIGURE A–4
INCREASING DEMAND WITH A FIXED SUPPLY

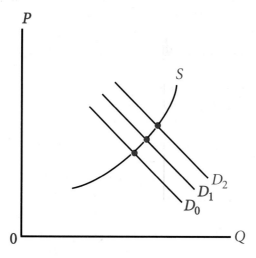

The price-quantity observations may be the equilibrium points of a stable supply curve with shifting demand curves over time.

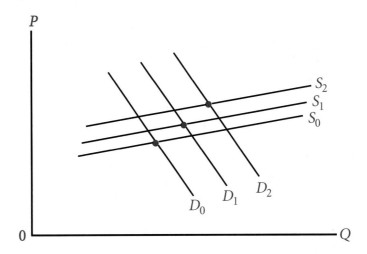

The price-quantity observations in Figure A–4 may be equilibrium points of shifting supply-and-demand curves over time. Connecting the three equilibrium points might give a misleading impression of supply.

Similarly, if the demand curve shifts only in response to changes in income and the supply curve shifts, as before, only in response to changes in rainfall, both the supply and the demand curves may be empirically identifiable.

There are various ways to lessen identification problems by adding extra information to a theoretical model. The structural parameters may be assumed to have positive signs and others to have negative signs. Still other parameters may be assumed to have the value zero; that is, they may be assumed to be absent from some equations. Assumptions can also be made about the values of the error terms in various structural equations. For example, it may be assumed that the average value of the error is zero (implying that "errors" in one direction are approximately offset by "errors" in the opposite direction, at least in any long series of observations).

Whatever procedure is followed to make the structural relations of an econometric model theoretically identifiable, the relations of the model still may not be identifiable in practice. This will happen, for example, if the factors that *might* lead to shifts in structural relations *in fact* do not happen to vary significantly during the period for which empirical data are available. As an illustration, consider an attempt to analyze the effect of income changes on demand. Even if the supply curve is absolutely fixed, empirical data on price, quantity exchanged, and income will not indicate the nature of the supply curve if, during the period of observation, income does not happen to vary. All observable price-quantity points will be the same and will simply indicate the intersection of the given demand-and-supply curves.

The second type of problem described earlier—namely, that because empirical data are not exact or detailed enough to indicate whether a particular theoretical model provides a good explanation of observed events—may be described as the problem of "goodness of fit."

This class of problem may be illustrated with a supply-demand model in which the demand equation is identifiable. With a scatter diagram of the sort illustrated in Figure A–6, there would be no difficulty about estimating the form of the demand relation. The data would indicate very clearly that a straight-line estimate of the demand curve is entirely appropriate. Matters would be very different, however, if on the same assumptions the scatter diagram were of the type shown in Figure A–7. An embarrassingly large number of different demand relations would all seem to fit the data about equally well.

Unfortunately for econometrics, the latter situation is common. The typical econometric model is too complicated, and the data available for estimating the relations of the model are too varied, to permit the investigator to discover by simple inspection whether a provisionally satisfactory model is likely to provide a "good" or a "bad" fit to the data. If it were possible to say, on the basis of casual inspection of empirical data, that a given structure did or did not provide a reasonable explanation of the data, such knowledge could be used to provide a check on the efficiency and validity of various techniques for calculating numerical estimates of structural parameters. In practice, however, the contrary situation is more common: No clear indication of the empirical validity of a theoretical model can be obtained until after the structural parameters in the model have been estimated; and even then, there may be considerable room for doubt unless the particular estimation technique that is used (that is, the particular method for calculating numerical estimates of the structural parameters) is somehow known in advance to yield reliable results. In any event, the net result is a great increase in the amount of work required compared to what would be necessary if the usefulness of the model could be ascertained by simple inspections at an early stage in the process.

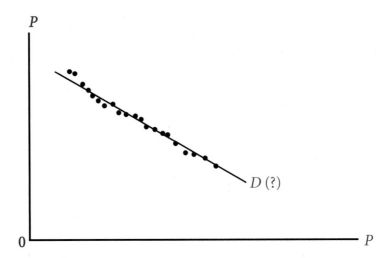

The estimated demand curve fits the data well and generates confidence in the model estimates. Actual observations are close to the estimated model.

FIGURE A–7
A POOR FIT

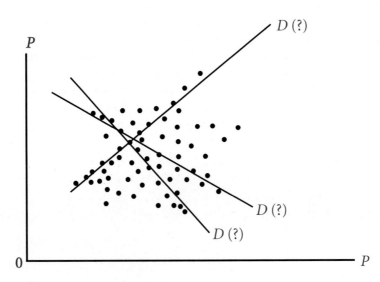

The data do not fit any of the potential demand curves well. Confidence in the estimated model is limited in this case.

CHOICE OF ESTIMATION TECHNIQUES

In many situations, the econometrician faces a serious dilemma. Simple inspection of empirical data does not indicate whether a given model can be used to provide a satisfactory explanation of the data. To make any progress at all, the data must be processed by one of several possible methods so as to yield numerical estimates of the structural parameters in the given model. The values of the endogenous variables, calculated on the assumption that the structural parameters of the model are as estimated, may then be compared with observed values of the same variables to determine whether the theoretical predictions of the model are satisfactory.

If the results of this comparison are unsatisfactory, however, the econometrician may have difficulty deciding what factors are responsible for the failure. Are the data inaccurate? Is the model unsatisfactory? Or is the technique used to calculate estimates of the structural parameters in the model a poor one? The complexity of economic phenomena is such that reliable techniques of estimation are essential if econometric studies are to be fruitful; but reliable techniques of estimation are extremely difficult to establish because of the complexity of the models that must be used to describe economic phenomena.

Much of the difficulty springs from the fact that all of the estimation techniques currently used in econometrics are basically designed to apply to experimental data of the kind studied in physics, chemistry, and the biological sciences. In these sciences, it is possible to maintain some degree of control over sources of error in the construction of models and the measurement of phenomena. Most of the data of economics, however, are nonexperimental in character. Economists have to take whatever factual information is provided by the everyday working of the economic system; they cannot ordinarily arrange experiments in which individuals, communities, or countries are subjected to controlled changes in external conditions and studied like bugs in a laboratory.

The problem would not be serious if different techniques of estimating structural parameters applied to the given data always yielded similar answers; but this is not the case. Neither would it be a serious problem if the theoretical models used in econometrics were known to be capable of simulating observed phenomena with a high degree of accuracy; but this is not true, either. As matters stand, the derivation of empirically significant estimates of structural parameters remains a major unsettled problem of contemporary econometrics. Future progress depends as much upon the solution of this issue as upon the collection of better data and the construction of improved theoretical models.

CONCLUSION

Some of the more important limitations of contemporary econometric research have been indicated in the preceding discussion. Some of these limitations will become relatively more important over time, while others will become less important.[2]

On the other hand, it is essential to recognize that econometric research is a unified activity in the sense that every aspect of such research has a direct bearing on every other aspect. Thus, improved data may lead to improvement in estimation techniques, and improved estimation techniques may lead to the construction of theoretical models that can be used satisfactorily to describe nonexperimental data. While econometric research faces many serious and unsettled problems, it is important to note that the *problems of econometric research are essentially the same as the problems of empirical research in general.* Every science has problems of this kind, many of them far from being completely resolved. In this regard, there is no reason to suppose that the problems of economics are any more serious than the problems of, say, nuclear physics or psychology or political science.

Scientific progress is a gradual phenomenon even in the best of circumstances. Economics in general, and econometrics in particular, have not displayed especially rapid rates of progress in the past; but neither has progress been slow. The fact that more and more professional economists are becoming interested in econometrics research indicates that the present limitations of econometric work are not considered to be permanent. The same fact gives us reason to hope that the results of future econometric research will greatly expand our knowledge about quantitative characteristics of the economic system. Perfectly accurate measurement of econometric relations is an impossibility in any case, but even rather inaccurate measurement is far better than no measurement at all.

---

[2]For an engaging, accessible discussion of econometric difficulties, see E. Leamer, "Let's Take the Con Out of Econometrics," *American Economic Review* 73, (March 1983), 31–43.

APPENDIX B

LINEAR PROGRAMMING

INTRODUCTION

Few economic problems have simple or precise solutions. In the first place, much research effort in economics has traditionally been devoted, not to describing the world as it is, but rather to prescribing how the world ought to be. Second, economic phenomena are inherently complicated, partly because of the great variety of goods and services in a modern economy and the difficulty of describing the processes by which they are produced and distributed. That these processes are largely social rather than physical makes an already arduous task even harder. To make matters worse, the technical and institutional framework of economic activity is subject to constant change. In these circumstances, it is not always possible to formulate economic problems in a clear and meaningful way, and it is hardly surprising that specific solutions can seldom be provided for those problems that can be so formulated.

It is an open question whether economic problems will always be this difficult to manage. In recent years, economists have become increasingly aware of the inadequacy of their discipline, and considerable effort has been spent devising ways to diminish the gap between "theory" and "practice."[1] This effort has included the development, largely since 1930, of *econometrics*, a branch of economics that is concerned with the empirical measurement of relations described in general economic theory. (See Appendix A.)

Even more recently, the formulation of simplified techniques of analysis, commonly referred to as *linear programming*, have made possible the specific numerical solution of problems that have previously been solvable only in vague qualitative terms. Both these developments have enabled economists to use complex computers in their research and so to solve problems that not long ago would have been unmanageable from a computational point of view.

---

[1]See R. Kuttner, "The Poverty of Economics," *The Atlantic Monthly*, February 1985, 74–84.

LINEAR PROGRAMMING AND ECONOMIC ANALYSIS

To appreciate the relation between linear programming and economic analysis, it is helpful to think of the term *programming* as being roughly synonymous with the term *planning*. Almost the whole of microeconomic price theory is concerned with programming in this sense—that is, with the planning behavior of individual consumers and business firms. Typical examples include the consumer's choosing among alternative combinations of goods to maximize total satisfaction, the firm's choosing among alternative combinations of factor inputs to minimize the total cost of any given level of output, and the firm's choosing among alternative levels of output in an attempt to maximize total profit.

In each of these cases, note that nothing is said about the execution of plans. As a general rule, it is simply assumed that once decided on, an optimal plan (that is, a plan that maximizes satisfaction, minimizes cost, maximizes profit, and so on) can be and is carried out. Note also that the relations in terms of which optimal plans are defined are normally represented geometrically by curves (indifference curves, isoquants, total-profit curves, and so on), many of which are not straight lines—that is, by *relations that are nonlinear*. Therefore, the planning aspects of the microeconomic theory consist primarily of techniques that may be called *nonlinear programming*. The only formal difference between this kind of programming and what is now called linear programming is that the latter discipline substitutes various kinds of *linear* relations are substituted for the usually nonlinear relations of traditional theory. This procedure makes it easier to develop quantitative solutions to various problems.

ESTABLISHMENT OF LINEAR RELATIONS

The way in which linear relations are established varies from case to case and is therefore difficult to describe in general terms. The basic idea is simple, however, and is illustrated in Figure B–1. If we start with a curve (say, an isoquant) such as QQ', we may regard the straight line LL' as a rough approximation to QQ'. A better approximation is provided by the broken line MM', and an even better approximation by the dotted line NN'. Indeed, if with an unlimited number of line segments, the original isoquant QQ' might be approximated to any desired degree of accuracy by means of a "line" with an appropriately large number of "breaks."

The curve *QQ'* can be approximated by the straight line *LL'*, but is better approximated by two line segments such as *MM'*, and still better by three line segments such as *NN'*. The greater the number of line segments, the more accurately the piecewise relations estimate the curve.

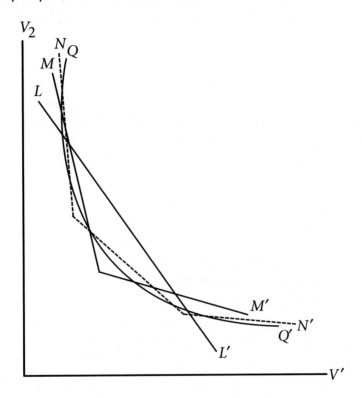

Or to use a more technical expression, the isoquant might be approximated by a *piecewise linear relation*. Thus, the difference between traditional programming problems and those considered in the modern linear-programming literature is a result of substituting piecewise linear relations for the nonlinear relations of traditional theory. This is not the whole story, but it does explain a significant part of the outward differences between linear programming and programming of the kind described in traditional price theory.

SCOPE OF LINEAR PROGRAMMING

Broadly speaking, linear programming is concerned with the solution of practical and theoretical problems in which some quantity (profit, income, the value of national product, aggregate transportation cost, travel time, and so on) is to be maximized or minimized subject to the condition that various technical, institutional, and financial restraints are also satisfied. The subject thus includes the types of problems that in traditional theory involve rational choice among a set of alternative possible plans. Linear programming, though, includes much more than this; many problems that at first do not look like planning problems at all can be treated *as if* they were planning problems and thus be formulated and solved with the same kinds of techniques used to solve the planning problems of individual households or firms. For example, linear programming has been applied with considerable success to broad questions of economic development, interregional trade, general equilibrium analysis, and welfare economics.

LINEAR PROGRAMMING: SOME EXAMPLES

Some specific examples of linear programming problems will help clarify the nature of the methods used and their relations to the methods of general economic analysis. For the sake of simplicity, the examples presented below are drawn mainly from the realm of business practice, but it should be emphasized that the range of problems that can be handled with these and closely related techniques is much wider than the examples might suggest.

THE SELECTION OF AN OPTIMAL DIET

A cattle producer seeks to fatten steers for market in the most economical way while meeting various nutritional requirements to ensure high quality of the final product. The rancher has a choice among various mixtures of two foods; hay and cottonseed cake. Both foods contain a certain quantity of one or more of four nutrients (protein, minerals, vitamins, and calories), so using enough of one or both foods will guarantee the satisfaction of any given set of nutritional requirements. Confronted with fixed prices for each of the two foods, the rancher's problem is to choose a diet that satisfies certain minimal nutritional requirements while minimizing the total cost of feeding a steer.

FIGURE B–2
THE OPTIMAL-DIET PROBLEM

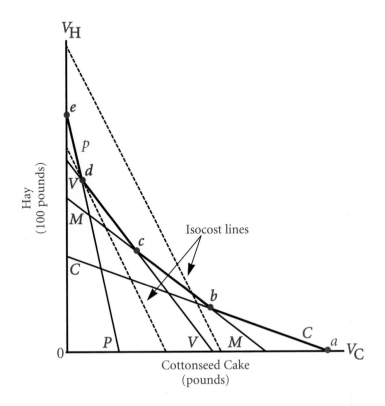

The cattle producer, wanting to minimize the cost of providing a sufficiently nutritious diet for steers, faces the prices of hay and cottonseed cake reflected in the dotted isocost lines. The combinations of the two foods meeting the minimum daily requirements of protein are charted along *PP*, of vitamins along *VV* of minerals along *MM*, and of calories along *CC*. Minimum quantities of all four nutrients are contained in the food combinations along *abcde*, the boundary of feasible diets. The optimal diet is *d*, the cheapest diet that provides the necessary nutrition.

The essentials of the problem are illustrated in Figure B–2. Any combination of hay and cottonseed cake represented by a point on or to the right of the line P is assumed to satisfy the *minimum* protein requirement (the slope of the line reflects the relative proportions of protein in the two foods); all other points represent food combinations that fail to satisfy this requirement. Similarly, the minimum mineral requirement is satisfied by diets corresponding to points on or to the right of line M, the minimum vitamin requirement is satisfied by points on or to the right of line V, and the minimum calorie requirement is satisfied by points on or to the right of line C. These requirements are not satisfied by points that lie to the left of lines M, V, and C. All points on or to the right of the heavy line *abcde* thus represent combinations of cottonseed cake and hay that satisfy all four of the minimum nutrition requirements simultaneously. Any point to the left of the heavy line, however, clearly represents a combination of foods that fails to satisfy one or more of these same minimum requirements. The heavy line thus represents what might be called the lower boundary of *feasible diets*. This boundary is, indeed, a piecewise linear relation of the sort described earlier; it represents a kind of production isoquant in which "nutrition" is the "output" produced. Diets represented by points to the right of this boundary in a sense waste nutrients; more food is contained in such diets than is strictly necessary for fattening purposes. Diets represented by points on the boundary are just enough, in the nutrient-producing sense, to ensure that cattle are fattened in an appropriate way.

Now, suppose that the unit cost of cottonseed cake and the unit cost of hay are known and constant, regardless of quantity purchased. The various diets that can be purchased for any given level of total cost can be presented graphically by points on an isocost line of the kind shown in Figure B–2. The cattle producer's problem is to choose a combination of foods on the boundary of feasible diet combinations, line *abcde*, for which total cost is as small as possible. In the present example, such a combination is represented by point d in Figure B–2 because any other point on the boundary *abcde* will lie on a higher isocost line.

There is a clear analogy between this problem and that of a firm choosing a combination of factor inputs that minimizes total cost for a given level of output; indeed, the main difference is that the present boundary of feasible diets is kinked, whereas the boundary of feasible input combinations in ordinary theory is represented by a smooth isoquant. A considerable gap, however, separates principle and practice in the two problems. Whereas existing computational techniques can be used to obtain an explicit numerical answer to the linear-programming problem even in cases involving hundreds, perhaps thousands, of foods and nutrients, the analogous problem as posed in ordinary economic theory is normally solvable only in principle. The difference between the two cases lies in the more specialized character of the assumptions underlying the linear-programming problem. These assumptions would be of no practical advantage if they were flatly inconsistent with practical experience, but the truth is that in a surprising number of instances they are in fair accord with factual knowledge.

CHOOSING AN EFFICIENT PRODUCTION PROCESS

The manager of a grain warehouse must arrange for the loading and unloading of a certain number of boxcars each month. Two technically efficient processes are available for this purpose—one involving the use of a motor-driven conveyer belt, the other involving the use of motor-driven grain shovels. The major expenses of both processes are fuel and labor costs. Fifty tons of grain per hour can be loaded or unloaded by the conveyer process using 3 gallons of fuel and 1 hour of labor, whereas 2 hours of labor and 1 gallon of fuel are needed to perform the same task with the shovel process.

The essential characteristics of the two processes are illustrated in Figure B–3 by the lines *OC* and *OS* and the related production isoquants. These isoquants show, for each process taken separately, the various combinations of fuel and labor required to move either 50 or 100 tons of wheat per hour. If both processes can be used simultaneously, however, certain fuel/labor combinations other than those illustrated can be used to move a given amount of grain. If the conveyer process is used to move 25 of a required 50 tons an hour, for example, the remaining 25 tons must be moved by the shovel process. The total fuel requirement would then be 2 gallons (1.5 gallons for the conveyer process and one-half gallon for the shovel process), and the total labor requirement

FIGURE B–3
THE OPTIMAL PRODUCTION PROCESS

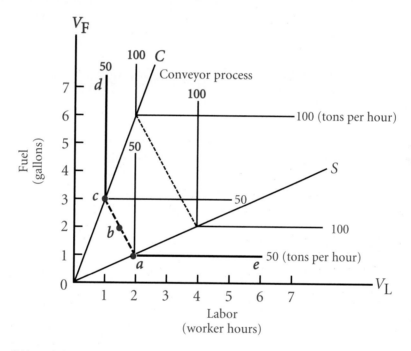

With two available grain-loading processes, the manager can choose only the conveyor process along the expansion path *OC*, only the shovel process along *OS*, or some combination of the two. If the desired output level is 50, the appropriate isoquant is *eabcd*.

would be 1.5 worker-hours (half a worker-hour for the conveyer process and one worker hour for the shovel process). This combination is represented in Figure B–3 by the point *b* on the dotted line joining points *a* and *c*. All mixtures of the two processes that would result in the movement of 50 tons of grain per hour are represented by points on this dotted line. Where a mixture of processes is possible, therefore, the production "isoquant" for grain movements of 50 tons per hour is represented by the broken line *eabcd*; and fuel/labor combinations that permit loading of other quantities of grain can of course be represented by isoquants of the same form. The curve for 100 tons per hour is illustrated on the same figure.

If the warehouse manager is interested in minimizing the total cost of any required grain-moving operation, it is clear that the choice between the two processes (or a combination of the two) depends on the relative costs of fuel and labor. The present problem is precisely the same as that faced by the cost-minimizing firm, except that the number of available "processes" is limited to two (or, as at b, linear combinations of two). The production isoquants of the warehouse problem would have three "kinks" rather than two if three different processes were available, 10 "kinks" if 10 processes were available, and so forth. The merit of the linear programming statement of the problem is that it permits extremely complicated practical problems to be formulated and solved in situations where the more general approach of traditional economic theory could not provide specific answers.

THE TECHNIQUE OF LINEAR PROGRAMMING

The general principles of linear programming are best described by restating one of the preceding examples in mathematical form. The diet problem is particularly appropriate for this purpose. We may begin by representing quantities of cottonseed cake and hay, respectively, by the symbols x_1 and x_2, and the corresponding dollar prices of these goods by p_1 and p_2. The total dollar cost of any given combination of the two goods is then given by the expression

$$(1) \quad C = p_1 x_1 + p_2 x_2$$

where C represents the number of dollars spent. This is called a linear equation in the variables x_1 and x_2 because, for any constant value of the variable C, the expression $C = p_1 x_1 + p_2 x_2$ is represented geometrically by a straight line, as illustrated by the isocost lines in Figure B-2.

The cattle producer's problem is not simply to choose values of x_1 and x_2 (that is, quantities of cottonseed cake and hay) that make C as small as possible. In the first place, the rancher's range of choice is limited by the requirement that purchases of cottonseed cake and hay be nonnegative because negative purchases are impossible. This condition is expressed mathematically by writing the expressions

$$(2) \quad x_1 \geq 0, \ x_2 \geq 0$$

That is, x_1 and x_2 must be equal to or in excess of zero. Geometrically, these conditions require that points representing feasible diets lie to the right of the "hay axis" and above the "cottonseed cake axis" in Figure B–2. The conditions are called *inequalities* (in this case, linear inequalities) because they require that certain numbers (namely, x_1 and x_2) be *different from* or *equal to* a certain given constant (namely, zero).

In the second place, the producer's range of choice is limited by certain nutritional requirements as well as by the requirement that total cost be minimized. Specifically, we may suppose that the minimum quantity of protein required is represented by a number b_1, the minimum quantity of minerals by a number b_2, the minimum quantity of vitamins by b_3, and the minimum quantity of calories by b_4. Similarly, we may suppose that the quantity of protein contained in a unit quantity of cottonseed cake is represented by a given number a_{11}, the quantity of protein contained in a unit quantity of hay by a number a_{12}, the quantity of minerals contained in a unit of cottonseed cake by a number a_{21}, and so on (there are eight of these numbers in total because there are two foods and each food contains some quantity, perhaps zero, of each of the four nutrients). The various nutrition requirements may then be expressed mathematically by writing the four linear inequalities.

$$(3) \quad \begin{aligned} a_{11}x_1 + a_{12}x_2 &\geq b_1 \quad \text{(protein requirement)} \\ a_{21}x_1 + a_{22}x_2 &\geq b_2 \quad \text{(mineral requirement)} \\ a_{31}x_1 + a_{32}x_2 &\geq b_3 \quad \text{(vitamin requirement)} \\ a_{41}x_1 + a_{42}x_2 &\geq b_4 \quad \text{(calorie requirement)} \end{aligned}$$

Taken in combination, the inequalities in (3) define the lower boundary of feasible diets described by the heavy line *abcde* in Figure B–2 (relevant portions of this figure are reproduced below as Figure B–4). More specifically, each separate inequality in (3) *directly* represents an area on or to the right of one of the dashed lines in Figure B–4. Taken as a group, therefore, the four inequalities in (3) *indirectly* describe an area of Figure B–4 within which points representing feasible diets *do not lie*: the area to the *left* of the heavy line *abcde* in Figure B–4. The upper boundary of this area of nonfeasible diets, that is, the line *abcde* itself, is therefore the *lower* boundary of *feasible* diets.

The term *linear inequality* is used to describe each of the relations in (3) because in the special case in which x_1 and x_2 have values for which the requirements are barely satisfied—that is, values such that the four equations

$$a_{11}x_1 + a_{i2}x_2 = b_i \quad (i = 1, 2, 3, 4)$$

are satisfied; the equations describing this situation are presented geometrically by straight lines. Each of the inequalities in (3) describes an area in Figure B–4 that lies on or to the right of one of the dashed lines; the inequalities are referred to as linear inequalities because the area described by any single inequality is bounded on the left by a straight line.

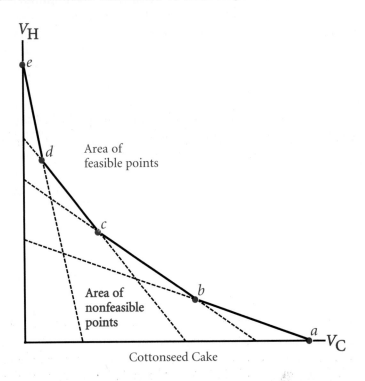

The system of inequalities (3) describes the combinations of the two foods that provide enough nutrition. For example, the protein requirement inequality corresponds to the area on or to the right of line e and defines the diets that contain the minimum amounts of protein necessary. All of four inequalities, and thus all four nutrient requirements, are met by the diets on or to the right of $abcde$. Diets inside the boundary do not provide enough nutrition.

The diet problem may now be stated as that of choosing a pair of numbers $(x1, x2)$ that minimizes that value of the linear equation

$$C = p_1x_1 + 0,\ p_2x_2$$

subject to the condition that the same numbers (x_1, x_2) also satisfy the set of six linear inequalities (2) and (3).

The solution of the problem (already presented graphically in Figure B-2) clearly depends on the values of the constants that appear in the statement of the problem, that is, on the values of the numbers $a_{11}, a_{12}, \ldots, a_{41}, a_{42}, b_1, b_2, b_3, b_4, p_1,$ and p_2. Thus, the numbers $\overline{x}_1, \overline{x}_2$, representing an *optimal diet*, depend on the form and position of the boundary of feasible diets and on the slope of the isocost line, which is to say that $\overline{x}_1$ and $\overline{x}_2$ depend on the nutritional content of the two foods, minimal nutrition requirements, and the money prices of the foods purchased. As a general rule, an unlimited number of possible pairs of positive numbers x_1 and x_2 satisfies the nutrition requirements (the linear inequalities [3]), but only one such pair also satisfies the requirement that total cost be minimized. It is this *particular* pair of numbers that is denoted by $\overline{x}_1, \overline{x}_2$ and referred to as an *optimal diet*. Other diets that satisfy (2) and (3) are also *feasible* (nonfeasible diets are simply excluded from consideration by the inequality constraints); but the *optimal diet* is that particular feasible diet that makes the value of C in an Equation (1) smaller than any alternative feasible diet.[2]

MORE COMPLEX PROBLEMS

The simple-diet problem is probably easier to solve graphically than by using computer techniques. Suppose, however, that we wished to consider a similar problem involving, say, 10 foods and 15 nutritional elements; that is, suppose that the problem required choosing positive or zero values of the 10 variables $x_1, x_2, \ldots, x_{10}$ so as to minimize the value of a linear equation

$$C = p_1 x_1 + p_2 x_2 + \ldots + p_{10} x_{10}$$

subject to 15 linear inequalities of the same form as those given in (3), above. All of the examples given previously—and, indeed, all other linear-programming problems—can be expressed in essentially this way. A computer would have no more difficulty with this problem than with one involving only two variables and three inequalities; but the same could not be said about a human being armed with pencil and paper! We cannot even visualize geometrically a problem that involves more than three basic variables.

The technique of linear programming involves much more, of course, than merely feeding information into hungry computers. The most interesting and important problems of linear programming are not mathematical or computational but are concerned instead with the task of interpreting concrete situations in a way that makes them amenable to linear-programming analysis. As a general rule, problems of planning that arise in actual practice do not lend themselves directly to treatment by linear-programming techniques for several reasons. First, it is seldom an easy matter to define a specific objective. A business firm, for example, may wish to maximize its long-run profit and at the same time maximize short-run payments to stockholders, but these two goals may not be consistent with one another. Similarly, a state government wishing to maximize the "welfare" of its citizens must choose among a wide array of alternative indicators of "welfare" (aggregate income, per-capita income, leisure, property values, and so forth). Second, even if a specific objective is defined, it may be difficult to discover the restraints that are operative in a particular situation—that is, which the legal, social, financial, and other conditions should be taken into account in pursuing the given

---

[2]If the slope of the isocost line is the same as the slope of one of the lines in terms of which the boundary of feasible diets is defined, an infinite number of different diets will minimize total cost. But this is a special case.

objective. Third, even if a specific objective is defined and a given set of restraints is known to apply, the restraints may not be directly expressible as linear inequalities. In actual practice, *precise* linearity of relevant restraints is more likely to be the exception than the rule. Finally, if linearity assumptions appear reasonable, it is always a major task to estimate relevant values of the various constant coefficients that enter into a linear-programming problem (prices, nutrition requirements, capacity limitations, final demands, and so on). Once a problem is formulated, the task of finding an answer or discovering whether an answer is possible is largely a matter of routine computation which may be done with any one of several standard techniques (the so-called *simplex method* is perhaps the one most frequently used at the present time). The task of formulations is another matter altogether, however. Vast ingenuity and intellectual boldness are prime characteristics of the successful linear-programming expert.

INDEX

C

E

Earnings, reinvestment of, 458–459

Econometric models
- complexity of, 605
- with error terms, 605
- estimation problems in, 606–612
- formulation of, 602
- structures of, 604
- typical, 602–603

Econometrics, 14, 613
- concepts and general approach of, 597
- definition of, 595
- nature of, 596–597
- necessary modifications in theoretical analysis, 601
- preliminary research and data collection, 598–599
- scope of, 597

Economic analysis, 3
- comparative, 15, 16
- definition of cost in, 198
- divisions of, 8
- dynamic, 15–16
- linear programming and, 614
- literary, 16
- macroeconomics, 10
- mathematical, 16–17
- microeconomic, 8–9, 14–15
- normative, 9–10
- positive, 9
- static, 15, 16
- traditional assumption of, 27

Economic assumptions, 12–13

Economic growth, attainment of an optimum rate of, 533–535

Economic losses
- causes of, 493
- types of, 492–493

Economic profits, 485–490
- versus accounting profits, 483–485
- definition of, 31

Economics
- of information, 581–582
- normative, 9–10
- positive, 9, 10
- and science, 10–11

Economic system
- functions of, 7–8
- social goals and the, 520–521

Economic theories, 11–14

Economists
- public-choice, 590, 591
- reasons for differences in, 17–18

Economy, role of profits in, 490–491

Edgeworth box, 504

Edgeworth-exchange diagram, 578n

Education, 552–553

Elastic demand segments, 66–67, 68

Elasticity of factor demand, 411

Engel curves, 168–171

Entrepreneurial activity, distinguishing between labor activity, 7

Entry restrictions, 392–394

Equilibrium
- full-employment rate of growth, maintenance of, 533–534
- market, 97–98
- short-run, 260

Equilibrium analysis
- general, 14
- partial, 15

Equilibrium interest rate, 443–445

Equilibrium output, 261

Equilibrium price, 56
- changes in, 58–64

Equilibrium quantity, 56
- changes in, 58–64

Estimation
- choice of techniques for, 611
- problems of, 606–612

Ethical criteria, 520

Excess capacity, 349

Excess inventories, 101

Excessive entry of new firms, 350–351

Excess profits, 486
- tendencies toward the elimination of, 390–392

Exchange box, 504

Excludability, 569

Expansion path, 227–228

Expectations, 53–54

Expected returns, 490

Explicit costs, 199, 200, 485

External diseconomies, 275

External economies, 278

Externalities, 565–569, 576n
- negative, 566–569
- positive, 566–569

Extractive industries, 275